THE MONUMENTS OF SĀÑCHĪ

THE MONUMENTS OF SĀÑCHĪ

BY

SIR JOHN MARSHALL, C.I.E., Litt.D., F.S.A.

Fellow of the British Academy ; Correspondant de l'Institut de France ;
Hon. Fellow of King's College, Cambridge ; Sometime Director General
of the Archæological Survey of India

AND

ALFRED FOUCHER

Membre de l'Institut de France ;
Professeur à l'Université de Paris

With the texts of inscriptions edited, translated and annotated

BY

N. G. MAJUMDAR, M.A., F.R.A.S.B.

Superintendent of the Archæological
Survey of India

Volume one

Swati Publications
DELHI

First Reprinted 1982

Reprinted 1983

Published by : SWATI PUBLICATIONS, 34, Central Market,
Ashok Vihar, Phase-I, Delhi-110052

PRINTED BY MEHRA OFFSET PRESS, CHANDNI MAHAL, DARYA GANJ, NEW DELHI 110002.

To the Memory

of

Her Highness

Nawab Sultan Jehan Begam Sahiba

Late Ruler of Bhopal

PREFACE

FEW words are needed by way of preface to these volumes. Their purpose is to supply a complete and fully illustrated description of the famous group of Buddhist monuments at Sāñchī, which have now been known to the world for more than a century, but of which only brief and inadequate accounts have, as yet, been published. The need of such a description has long been felt and often voiced ; for, leaving aside other remains included in this group, the stūpas of Sāñchī, with their wealth of figural and decorative carvings, are by common consent the most valuable and instructive, as they are also the most imposing and best preserved, of all the monuments that early Buddhism has bequeathed to India.

The idea of publishing these carvings in their entirety was first taken up by the Government of India nearly forty years ago and an admirable series of photographs was prepared for the purpose by the late Mr. Henry Cousens of the Archæological Survey, nearly all of which have been utilized in the present volumes. There, however, for lack of funds, the project was allowed to rest, and no further action was taken until I visited Sāñchī in 1912. An examination of the site which I then made satisfied me that many structures and antiquities might still be lying buried beneath the heaps of accumulated debris to the south and east of the Great Stūpa, and that these areas ought to be thoroughly excavated before attempting to publish the already known remains. With the ready approval and active help of the Bhopal Darbar, to whom Sāñchī and all its treasures belong, this excavation was carried out by me in the course of the next eight years and resulted in discoveries even more fruitful than I had anticipated, many fresh and interesting buildings being brought to light and a large array of sculptures added to the already existing collection. At the same time I was able to take radical and comprehensive measures for the preservation of the whole of this remarkable group of monuments, and to erect a museum on the spot, in which all the moveable sculptures and other objects are now housed.

Consequent on these new discoveries the scope of the projected publication had to be much enlarged. As now designed, it comprises four parts. In the first of these I have sketched the history of Sāñchī and described the site and its remains ; in the second I have discussed the art of the early sculptures and the place they occupy in the Early Indian School : in the third part Mons. Foucher has dealt with the interpretation of the sculptures and the many complex questions of iconography arising out of them ; in the fourth Mr. Majumdar has edited, translated and annotated the inscriptions. Besides these four parts, the book also contains detailed descriptions of the Plates, which for the convenience of the reader are printed opposite to them. The majority of these descriptions, namely, those of Plates X-LXVI, LXXIV-XC and XCV-CIII have been written by M. Foucher ; the remainder by myself.

From the size and weight of these volumes, it might perhaps be thought that the authors had aimed at an exhaustive treatment of their subject. This is far from being the case. The task which they set themselves was to furnish students with such essential data and explanations of these monuments as would prepare the way for their further study. Apart from their artistic, religious and iconographic interest, the early sculptures of Sāñchī are an almost inexhaustible mine of information in regard to contemporary Indian civilization. To attempt even a provisional discussion of them in all their aspects would require many more chapters than this work contains and would call for special theses on a multiplicity of subjects: on the racial types, for example, of which the sculptures afford so many instructive examples; on popular beliefs and superstitions; on arms and accoutrements; on dress and personal ornaments; on musical instruments; and on a score of other subjects for which they furnish invaluable materials. However great the temptation to follow up such studies, it seemed to us that the first thing we had to do was to describe the monuments, explain as far as possible their meaning, and analyze the character of their art. With the ground thus cleared, we felt that the further study of these sculptures could be left to other investigators.

I have said that my distinguished collaborator, M. Foucher, was responsible for Part III of this work and for the bulk of the Plate descriptions. His share of it, however, has gone far beyond these contributions; for not only has he given me at every stage the advantage of his own unrivalled knowledge of Buddhist antiquities, but in manifold other ways he has helped both in planning the work and in seeing it through the press. Two others to whom my grateful acknowledgments are due, are my long-time friend and successor in India, Mr. Harold Hargreaves, who has put us under a special obligation by the scholarly precision with which he has prepared the Index, and Mr. E. G. Aylmer, Manager of the Government of India Press, Calcutta, who from start to finish has given his unremitting care and attention to the printing of these volumes.

Here, too, I would fain pay a tribute to the memory of my former Excavation-Assistant, Munshi Ghulam Qadir, who for ten years was my right-hand man at Sāñchī and did yeoman's service in the task of excavating and restoring its monuments. Officially, I knew him as a man of quick intelligence and indefatigable industry, who never failed in any task allotted to him; but I knew him also as a man of rare integrity and purpose, loyal, fearless and true, with whom to work was a real pleasure.

Finally, I have to thank His Highness the Ruler of Bhopal for the generous and sympathetic interest which he has extended to my labours at Sāñchī as well as to the publication of this book, and for the many kindnesses that he has shown to me when I have revisited his State.

JOHN MARSHALL

TABLE OF CONTENTS

PART I

THE MONUMENTS

By Sir John Marshall

CHAPTER I

HISTORY, ANCIENT AND MODERN

CHAPTER II

THE HILL OF SĀÑCHĪ AND ITS MONUMENTS

CHAPTER III

THE GREAT STŪPA AND PILLAR OF ASOKA

CHAPTER III—*contd.*

THE GREAT STŪPA AND PILLAR OF AŚOKA—contd.

CHAPTER IV

OTHER STŪPAS, PILLARS AND SHRINES ON THE MAIN TERRACE

CHAPTER V

THE SOUTHERN AREA

CHAPTER VI

EASTERN AREA

CHAPTER VII

THE SECOND STŪPA AND NEIGHBOURING REMAINS

PART II

THE ART OF SĀÑCHĪ

By Sir John Marshall

CHAPTER VIII

PRE-HISTORIC AND MAURYAN ART

CHAPTER IX

SCULPTURES OF THE SECOND STŪPA AT SĀÑCHĪ, OF BHARHUT AND BODH-GAYĀ

CHAPTER X

SCULPTURES ON THE GATEWAYS OF THE GREAT STŪPA

CHAPTER X—*contd.*

SCULPTURES ON THE GATEWAYS OF THE GREAT STŪPA—contd.

CHAPTER XI

GATEWAY SCULPTURES—contd.

CHAPTER XII

SOME FURTHER CHARACTERISTICS OF THE GATEWAY SCULPTURES AND THE PROBLEM OF FOREIGN INFLUENCE

CHAPTER XIII

TOOLS AND PROCESSES EMPLOYED BY THE SCULPTORS OF SĀÑCHĪ

PART III

THE MEANING OF THE SCULPTURES

By Prof. A. Foucher

CHAPTER XIV

INTERPRETATION OF THE BAS-RELIEFS OF THE OLDER BALUSTRADES

CHAPTER XV

INTERPRETATION OF THE GATEWAY SCULPTURES

CHAPTER XV—*contd.*

INTERPRETATION OF THE GATEWAY SCULPTURES—contd.

CHAPTER XVI

INTERPRETATION OF THE GATEWAY SCULPTURES—concld.

CHAPTER XVII

STATUES AND STELÆ

PART IV

INSCRIPTIONS

By N. G. Majumdar

CHAPTER XVIII

CLASSIFICATION, AGE, PALÆOGRAPHY AND LANGUAGE

CHAPTER XIX

INSCRIPTION ON THE ASOKA PILLAR

CHAPTER XX

INSCRIPTIONS ON THE RELIC-BOXES AND CASKETS

CHAPTER XXI

VOTIVE INSCRIPTIONS OF STŪPAS 1, 2 AND 3, TEMPLE 40 AND OTHER MONUMENTS

CHAPTER XXII

INSCRIPTIONS OF THE KUSHĀN, GUPTA AND LATER PERIODS

LIST OF PLATES

BOOKS CITED

Acharya, P. K. . *Dictionary of Hindu Architecture. A summary of the Mānasāra.* Leiden, 1918.

Allan, J. . . *Catalogue of the Coins of the Gupta Dynasties.* Brit. Mus. London, 1914.

Annals of the Bhandarkar Institute, Poona.

Annual Reports of the Archæological Survey of India, ed. Sir John Marshall. Calcutta, 1902-27.

Archæological Survey of India Reports, ed. Sir A. Cunningham. Calcutta, 1862-84.

Archæological Survey of Western India Reports.

Arthaśāstra . . See Kauṭilya.

Bachhofer, L. . *Early Indian Sculpture.* Paris, 1929.

Barua, B. M. . *Barhut Inscriptions.* Calcutta, 1926.

Beal, S. . *Si-yu-ki : Buddhist Records of the Western World.* Trübner's Oriental Series. London, 1885.

Beloch, K. J. . *Griechische Geschichte.* 2nd ed. Strassburg, 1912.

Bhandarkar, D. R. *Carmichael Lectures.* Calcutta, 1918.

Bhavabhūti . *Mālatīmādhava*, ed. R. G. Bhandarkar. Bombay, 1905.

Buckingham's Calcutta Journal.

Bühler, G. . . *Indische Palæographie (Grund. d. Indo-ar. Phil.).* 1896.

English Version. *Indian Palæography*, ed. J. F. Fleet. Ind. Ant., 1904.

Burgess, J. . . *Ancient Monuments, Temples and Sculptures of India.* London, 1897.

The Great Stūpa at Sāñchī Kānākheḍā. (J. R. A. S. Jany. 1902.)

Cambridge History of India. Vol. I. Ed. E. J. Rapson. Cambridge, 1922.

Childers, R. . . *Dictionary of the Pali Language.* Pali Text Society, London, 1875.

Cole, H. H. . . *Third Report of the Curator of Ancient Monuments in India.* Calcutta, 1884.

Preservation of National Monuments, India : Great Buddhist Tope at Sanchi. Calcutta, 1885.

Conférences au Musée Guimet. Annales du Musée Guimet, Bibl. de Vulgarisation. Paris, 1910.

Coomaraswamy, A. *Buddha and the Gospel of Buddhism*, 1916.

The Origin of the Buddha Image. (The Art Bulletin, New York, Vol. IX.)

History of Indian and Indonesian Art. London, 1927.

Yakṣas. Smithsonian Miscellaneous Collections, Vol. LXXX, No. 6.

Corpus Inscriptionum Indicarum. Vol. I, 1877 ; new edition by E. Hultzsch, Calcutta, 1925. Vol. III, ed. J. F. Fleet. 1888.

Cowell, E. B. . See *Jātaka.*

Cowell, E. B. and Neil, R. A. . *Divyāvadāna.* Cambridge, 1886.

Cullavagga . . Trans. by T. W. Rhys Davids and H. Oldenberg. Sacred Books of the East. Vols. XVII and XX.

Cunningham, A. . See *Archæological Survey of India Reports.*

The Bhilsa Topes or Buddhist Monuments of Central India. London, 1854.

Coins of Ancient India. London, 1891.

Mahābodhi or the Great Buddhist Temple at Buddhagaya. London, 1892.

The Stūpa of Bharhut. London, 1879.

Dīpavaṃsa . . Ed. and trans. by H. Oldenberg. London, 1879.

Divyāvadāna . Ed. E. B. Cowell and R. A. Neil. Cambridge, 1886.

Dutt, S. . . *Early Buddhist Monachism*. Calcutta, 1924.

Epigraphia Indica.

Fa-Hien . . See Legge, J.

Fergusson, J. . *History of Indian and Eastern Architecture*. 2nd ed. Vols. I-II. London, 1910.

Tree and Serpent Worship. 2nd ed. London, 1873.

Fergusson, J. and Burgess, J. . *The Cave Temples of India*. London, 1880.

Foucher, Alfred *L'art Gréco-bouddhique du Gandhāra*. Paris, 1900, 1918 and 1923.

Beginnings of Buddhist Art and other Essays. Trans. by L. A. Thomas and F. W. Thomas. Paris and London, 1917.

Franke, R. Otto . *Pāli und Sanskrit*. Strassburg, 1902.

Grünwedel, A. . *Buddhist Art in India*. English edition, London, 1901.

Hardy, R. S. . *A Manual of Buddhism, in its Modern Development*. London, 1853.

Havell, E. B. . *Indian Sculpture and Painting*. London, 1908.

Huber, E. . . *Sūtrālaṃkāra of Aśvaghosha*. Paris, 1908.

Indian Antiquary.

Indian Historical Quarterly.

I-tsing . . . . See Takakusu, J.

Jātaka, or Stories of the Buddha's Former Births . Ed. V. Fausböll. London, 1877-97. Trans. under editorship of E. B. Cowell. Cambridge, 1895-1913.

Journal of the Asiatic Society of Bengal.

Journal Asiatique.

Journal of the Bihar and Orissa Research Society.

Journal of the Royal Society of Arts.

Kathāsarit-sāgara See Tawney, C. H.

Kauṭilya . . *Arthaśāstra*. Ed. R. Shama Sastri. Mysore, 1909. Trans. by the same: Books I-IV, Mysore, 1908, etc. Books V-XV., Ind. Ant. 1909-10. 3rd ed., Bangalore, 1929.

Kern, H. . . *Manual of Indian Buddhism* (Grundriss der Indo-Arischen, Philologie, ed. by G. Bühler). Strassburg, 1896.

Law, B. C. . . *Geography of Early Buddhism*. London, 1932.

Lefmann, S. . *Lalita-vistara*. Halle, 1902 and 1908.

Legge, J. . . *Fa-Hien. A Record of Buddhistic Kingdoms*. Oxford, 1886.

Lüders, H. . . *List of Brāhmī Inscriptions from the Earliest Times to about 400 A.D.* (Ep. Ind., Vol. X.) Calcutta, 1910.

MacGovern, W. . *A Manual of Buddhist Philosophy*. Hertford, 1923.

Mahāparinibbāna-sutta . . Trans. by T. W. Rhys Davids. Sacred Books of the East. Vol. XI.

Mahāvagga . . Vinaya Texts trans. by T. W. Rhys Davids and H. Oldenberg. Sacred Books of the East, Vols. XIII and XVII.

Mahāvaṃsa . . Ed. W. Geiger. P. T. S. London, 1908.

Trans. W. Geiger. P. T. S. London, 1912.

Mahāvastu . . Ed. E. Senart. Paris, 1882-1897.

Maisey, F. C. . *Sánchi and its Remains*. London, 1892.

Marshall, Sir John See *Annual Reports, Arch. Survey of India*.

The Monuments of Sāñchī. A. S. R. 1913-14.

Marshall, Sir John — *Mohenjodaro and the Indus Civilization*, 3 vols. London, 1931.
The Monuments of Ancient India (*Cambridge History of India*, Vol. I. 1922).

Memoirs of the Archæological Survey of India.

Mémoires concernant L'Asie orientale. Publiés par l'Académie des Inscriptions et Belles Lettres. Tome III, Paris, 1919.

Oldenberg, H. . *Buddha : His Life, His Doctrine, His Order.* London, 1882.
The Dīpavaṃsa. London, 1879.
See also *Vinaya Texts.*

Pargiter, F. E. . *The Purāṇa Text of the Dynasties of the Kali Age.* Oxford, 1913.

Pischel, R. . . *Grammatik der Prākṛit-Sprachen.* Strassburg, 1900.

Przyluski, J. . *Le Concile de Rājagṛha.* 1926.
La légende de l'Empereur Aśoka (Annales du Musée Guimet). Paris, 1923.

Raychaudhuri, H. *Early History of the Vaishṇava Sect.* Univ. of Calcutta, 1920.

Rapson, E. J. . *Catalogue of the Coins of the Andhra Dynasty, the Western Kṣatrapas, etc.*, Brit. Mus. London, 1908.
Cambridge History of India. Vol. I. Cambridge, 1922.

Revue des Arts Asiatiques . Annales du Musée Guimet. Paris.

Sacred Books of the East . . Ed. by F. Max Müller. Oxford.

Sahni, D. R. . *Catalogue of the Museum of Archæology at Sārnāth.* Calcutta, 1914.

Sāñchī, Catalogue of the Museum of Archæology at —; ed. Sir John Marshall.

Sārnāth, Catalogue of the Museum of Archæology at —; see Sahni, D. R.

Śatapatha-Brāhmaṇa . . Ed. by A. Weber. London, 1855.

Satapatha-Brāhmaṇa — Trans. by J. Eggeling, *Sacrea Books of the East*, XII, XXVI, XLI, XLIII, XLIV. Oxford, 1882-1900.

Senart, E. . . *Les inscriptions de Piyadasi.* Paris, 1881 and 1886.
Le Mahāvastu. Paris, 1882-1897.

Smith, V. A. . *Catalogue of the Coins in the Indian Museum, Calcutta.* Vol. I. London, 1906.
A History of Fine Art in India and Ceylon. Oxford, 1930.

Strong, Mrs. A. . *Roman Sculpture from Augustus to Constantine.* 1907.

Sūtrālaṃkāra of Aśvaghoṣa . See Huber, E.

Sutta Nipāta . Ed. by D. Andersen and H. Smith. P. T. S. London, 1913.
Trans. V. Fausböll. S. B. E—X. Oxford, 1898.

Takakusu, J. . *A Record of the Buddhist Religion as practised in India and the Malay Peninsula*, by I-Tsing. Oxford, 1896.

Tawney, C. H. . *The Kathāsarit-sāgara* Calcutta, 1880-84.

Vinaya Texts . Trans. Rhys Davids and H. Oldenberg. S. B. E.—xiii, xvii, xx. Oxford, 1881-5.

Vogel, J. Ph. . *Indian Serpent Lore.* London, 1926.
Catalogue of the Archæological Museum at Mathurā. Allahabad, 1910.

Waddell, L. A. . *Report on the Excavations at Pāṭalīputra.* Calcutta, 1903.

Wassiliew, W. . *Der Buddhismus, seine Dogmen, Geschichte und Literatur.* St. Petersburg, 1860.

Watters, T. . *On Yuan Chwang's Travels in India.* London, 1904-5.

Whitehead, R. B. *Catalogue of Coins in the Punjab Museum, Lahore.* Oxford, 1911.

Zeitschrift der Deutschen Morgenländischen Gesellschaft.

ABBREVIATIONS

Ann. Bhand. Inst.	Annals of the Bhandarkar Institute, Poona.
A. S. I.	Archæological Survey of India.
Mem. A. S. I.	Memoirs of the Archæological Survey of India.
A. S. R.	Reports of the Archæological Survey of India ed. by Sir John Marshall.
A. S. W. I.	Reports of the Archæological Survey of Western India.
B. M. Cat.	British Museum Catalogue.
C. H. I.	Cambridge History of India.
C. I. I.	Corpus Inscriptionum Indicarum.
C. S. R.	Reports of the Archæological Survey of India ed. by Sir A. Cunningham.
Cull.	Cullavagga.
E. I. or Ep. Ind.	Epigraphia Indica.
Grund. d. indo-ar Phil.	Grundriss der indo-arischen Philologie und Altertumskunde.
I. A. or Ind. Antiq.	Indian Antiquary.
Ind. Hist. Quart.	Indian Historical Quarterly.
Ind. Pal.	Indische Palæographie (Grund. d. Indo-ar Phil.).
J. A.	Journal Asiatique.
J. A. S. B.	Journal of the Asiatic Society of Bengal.
J. B. O. R. S.	Journal of the Bihar and Orissa Research Society.
J. R. A. S.	Journal of the Royal Asiatic Society.
Mah.	Mahāvagga.
P. T. S.	Pali Text Society.
Rv.	Rigveda.
S. B. E.	Sacred Books of the East.
San. Mus. Cat.	Sanchi Museum Catalogue.
Z. D. M. G.	Zeitschrift der Deutschen Morgenländischen Gesellschaft.

PART ONE

THE MONUMENTS

CHAPTER I

HISTORY, ANCIENT AND MODERN

The Early Saṅghārāma

IT is related in the Mahāvagga that when Bimbisāra, King of Magadha, was entertaining the Buddha, he cast round for some spot that would make an agreeable retreat for the Blessed One and his followers—a spot, as he reflected, "not too far from the town and not too near, suitable for going and coming, easily accessible for all people, by day not too crowded, by night not exposed to noise and alarm, clean of the smell of people, hidden from men, well fitted for a retired life."[1] And the king bethought him that there was just such a spot to be found in his own pleasure garden, the *Veṇuvana*, on the outskirts of the city, and therewith he took a golden vessel of water and dedicated his garden as an *ārāma*, or retreat; to "the fraternity of bhikshus with the Buddha at its head." Identically the same words are used in the Cullavagga to describe the well-known Jetavana, the garden of Jeta, near Śrāvastī, which the rich lay-supporter, Anāthapiṇḍika, presented to the Saṅgha;[2] and they might equally well have been applied to most, if not all, of the principal retreats or saṅghārāmas, where the early Buddhists established themselves. Indeed, it could hardly be otherwise; for the requirements that Bimbisāra put before himself, namely, peace and quietude on the one hand, and propinquity to the haunts of men on the other, were in effect indispensable for all such establishments, whose inmates spent half their days begging alms and sustenance among the townsfolk and the other half at their religious devotions. We can readily understand, therefore, how all the more important saṅghārāmas known to us in India are situate near the outskirts of some great city, and how, the greater and wealthier the city, the more imposing the monasteries dependent on it were likely to be. Thus it is that outside the City of Kāśī (Benares) and at no great distance from its suburbs, we find the far-famed Mṛigadāva (Deer Park) with its ever-growing array of buildings, immortalised as the spot where the Teacher preached his first sermon. It is thus, too, that outside Takshaśilā (Taxila), once the foremost city of the Panjāb, we find the great Dharmarājikā Stūpa and Monastery, besides a host of lesser establishments, crowning the hill-tops or hidden in the seclusion of glens and valleys round about the old capital. And it is thus that, near the rich and populous city of Vidiśā in Central India, there grew up the saṅghārāma of Sāñchī, whose magnificent monuments—stūpas, temples, monasteries and memorial pillars—form the subject of this book.

[1] *Mahāvagga*, I, 22, 16, trans. by T. W. Rhys Davids and H. Oldenberg. *S. B. E.*, Vol. XIII, p. 143.
[2] *Cullavagga*, VI, 4, 8. *S. B. E.*, Vol. XX, p. 187.

Sāñchī, Vidiśā and Ujjayinī

The history of these world-famed monuments, the most precious and perfect of all that Buddhism has bequeathed to us, was a long one. It began in, or perhaps even before, the reign of Aśoka in the third century B.C. and lasted for fully twelve hundred years, thus all but synchronising with the rise and fall of Buddhism in India. From first to last, the story of Sāñchī was intimately bound up with the fortunes of the great city in whose shadow its saṅghārāma grew and flourished and on whose wealth it was mainly dependent for its support. That the foundation of Vidiśā went back to a very remote age and that its population was a large one in the early centuries of Buddhism, is abundantly clear from the extent of its well-defined site[1] as well as from the great depth of debris that had accumulated there before the second century B.C. Its importance it owed in part to its commanding position at the junction of the Beś and Betwā rivers, the latter of which afforded valuable water transport during the rainy season, but still more to its position on two great trade routes, one of which ran west to east from the busy seaports of the western littoral through Ujjayinī, Kauśāmbī and Kāśī to Pāṭaliputra, the other south-west to north-east from the Andhra capital at Pratishṭhāna to Śrāvastī,[2] as well as to other cities in Kośala and Pañchāla. With Ujjayinī, the Capital of Avanti, from which it was distant not more than 140 miles, Vidiśā must always have had close commercial and other ties, and there were long periods when it was subordinate to that city, but at other times the two kingdoms of Eastern and Western Mālwā, that is, of Ākara and Avanti, as they were respectively known, were independent of each other and ruled by rival dynasties. That even during the lifetime of its founder Buddhism took root in both areas, may be regarded as virtually certain; for several of his most zealous followers were born at Ujjayinī, notably Abhaya Kumāra, Isidāsī, Isidatta, Dhammapāla, Soṇa Kuṭikaṇṇa and, last but not least, Mahā-Kaccāna;[3] and there can be little room for doubt that, if the new faith found favour in Avanti, it also found favour in the neighbouring district of Ākara.[4]

History under the Mauryas and Śuṅgas

Under the Mauryas, Vidiśā, with the rest of Ākara, was presumably included in the Viceroyalty of Avanti, with the capital at Ujjayinī, though the local administration was probably in the hands of feudatory Śuṅga princes.[5] With the break-up, however, of the Maurya Empire and the transference of the central power to the Śuṅgas, Vidiśā became the premier city in Central India, and before long seems to have superseded Pāṭaliputra itself. For though Pushyamitra, the founder of the Śuṅga dynasty, established himself as the successor of the Mauryas at their own capital in Magadha, his son Agnimitra, who had been Viceroy at Vidiśā, seems to have shifted the seat of government from Pāṭaliputra to that city.

---

[1] *Cf. C. S. R.*, Vol. X, Pl. XII. The city was not confined to the fork between the two rivers but extended at least two-thirds of a mile north of the river Beś. *A. S. R.*, 1913-14, p. 186.

[2] The modern Saheṭh-Maheṭh. *Cf. C. H. I.*, I, p. 523.

[3] For references to these disciples, see *C. H. I.*, I, p. 186, notes 2 to 7.

[4] On historical and philological grounds it has been contended that the particular language in which the Pāli Canon was composed was that current in Avanti and the neighbourhood. See T. W. Rhys Davids, in *Trans. Phil. Soc.*, 1875, and *C. H. I.*, I, p. 187; R. Otto Franke, *Pali und Sanskrit*, 1902.

[5] For the story of Aśoka's halt at Vidiśā, when Viceroy of Ujjayinī, and his marriage to the beautiful Devī, see below, p. 14.

In Pāli literature, Pushyamitra figures as a persecutor of the Buddhists and destroyer of their monasteries, and there is no reason to question the truth of this tradition. After the downfall of the Mauryas it was only to be expected that a strong Brāhmanical reaction should set in against the religion to which Aśoka had shown such marked partiality, and it was natural, too, that, in order to consolidate his own position, the new monarch should take advantage of this reaction by posing as the champion of Brāhmanism. It is evident, however, from the many monuments erected by the Buddhists under Śuṅga rule, not only at Sāñchī but in other parts of the kingdom also, that Pushyamitra's animosity against Buddhism could not have been shared by his successors. Most famous of such monuments is the Stūpa of Bharhut in the Nāgod State of Central India, less than 200 miles from Vidiśā, the ground balustrade of which dates probably from the last quarter of the second century B.C. and the gateways from a generation later.[1] Inscriptions on the latter record that one was erected during the sovereignty of the Śuṅgas by a certain Rājā Dhanabhūti, the other by a member of the same house,[2] which, though feudatory to the Śuṅgas, was evidently the ruling house at Bharhut. Parenthetically, it may be observed that the family of this Rājā Dhanabhūti appears to have been related to the royal families of both Mathurā and Kauśāmbī, which were themselves inter-related, and it is significant that the reliefs on the gateways and railings of the Bharhut Stūpa also exhibit an unmistakable affinity with contemporary work at Mathurā,[3] which from an early date was one of the most active and important centres of stone carving.

Hostility of Pushyamitra to Buddhism not shared by his successors

With the Bactrian-Greek invaders to the north—the Yavanas, as they were commonly known in India—and with the Andhras to the south, the Śuṅgas must have been in close contact and not infrequent conflict. Each of these three powers (as well as the Kaliṅgas on the east coast, with whom we are not here concerned) was bent on carving out for itself new territories from the dismembered Mauryan Empire, and clashes between them were, therefore, inevitable. As the immediate successors of the Mauryas in Magadha and the Midland Country, the Śuṅgas claimed to exercise the same suzerainty over neighbouring states as their predecessors had done, and it was in support of this claim that Pushyamitra celebrated an *aśvamedha* or horse sacrifice—an ancient Vedic rite by which Indian kings were accustomed to assert their title to imperial sway. But, though on that occasion a troop of Yavana cavalry is said to have been defeated by the Śuṅgas while endeavouring to capture the wandering horse, Pushyamitra's claim to be regarded as a *cakravartin*, or paramount sovereign, could have been little justified, seeing that the Greeks not only deprived him of the Eastern Panjāb, including the all-important city of Śākala (Sialkot), but invaded the Midland Country as well, reducing Sāketa and Mathurā, and carrying their arms as far as Pāṭaliputra itself. That they failed to consolidate their

Yavana neighbours of Śuṅgas

[1] *Cf.* below, p. 272. [2] *Cf.* Rapson in *C. H. I.*, I, p. 523. [3] See below, p. 105.

conquests in the Midland Country, was due, we are told, to an internecine war that broke out among themselves in the Panjāb—the war in question probably being, as Rapson has divined, between the rival houses of Eukratides and Euthydemus, the one with its capital at Takshaśilā, the other at Śākala. Possibly it was the same long continued rivalry between the two houses that, a generation later, induced Antialcidas, King of Taxila, to send an embassy under Heliodorus, son of Dion, to Bhāgabhadra, the Śuṅga king of Vidiśā.[1] The inscription referring to this embassy, which is engraved on a column set up by Heliodorus in Vidiśā itself and dedicated by him to Vāsudeva (Kṛishṇa), says nothing of the object for which he was sent there, but seeing that the two states were so remote from one another, with the Greek kingdom of Śākala lying between, it seems more than likely that the purpose of this embassy was to make common cause against that kingdom, which was a menace both to Antialcidas from the south-east and to Bhāgabhadra from the north-west.

The Andhras The other rivals of the Śuṅgas, namely, the Andhras of the Dekhan, were less aggressive perhaps than the Greeks, but none the less dangerous for that. Starting from the Telugu country on the East coast between the deltas of the Kistna and Godāvarī rivers (the modern Telingāna) they had extended their dominion westward and northward along the line of the Godāvarī, and by the beginning of the second century B.C. were in possession of most of the modern Hyderabad, the Central Provinces and Berār (Vidarbha), as well probably as the Northern Konkan (Aparānta), their western capital being at Pratishṭhāna (Paithān) on the north bank of the Godāvarī. From there they pushed north across the Tāptī and Narbadā rivers and took possession of Western Mālwā, with its well-known capital, Ujjayinī, thus gaining control of the great trade routes from Bhṛigukaccha (Broach) and other western seaports to Rajputāna, Central India and the Jumna-Ganges basin, and effectually cutting off the Śuṅgas from an outlet on the Western coast. From numismatic evidence[2] it has been inferred that this occupation of Western Mālwā took place early in the second century B.C. during the reign of the Andhra king, Śātakarṇi I, who seems to have been a contemporary of the Śuṅga Pushyamitra, and like him to have asserted his title to suzerainty over his neighbours by the performance of the *aśvamedha*. Whether or not the Śuṅgas had occupied Western Mālwā before the Andhras, we do not know, but it seems clear[3] that, once the Andhras had taken possession of the province, Pushyamitra and his successors failed to dislodge them from it. On the other hand, the Andhras themselves also failed to annex Eastern Mālwā until after the final overthrow of the Śuṅgas, which, according to tradition, happened about 72 B.C. In the long list of Andhra kings—30 in all—given in the Matsya and other Purāṇas—not less than ten bear the name of Śātakarṇi. One of these ten is mentioned in a donative inscription on the Southern Gateway of the Great Stūpa at Sāñchī, which records the gift

[1] For the date of Antialcidas and Bhāgabhadra, see below, p. 268.
[2] Rapson, *B. M. Cat., Coins of the Andhras*, etc., p. XCII.
[3] This may be inferred from the totally different coinages of Eastern and Western Mālwā during this period.

of one of its architraves by a certain Ānaṁda, described as foreman of artisans of the king in question ; but which particular Śātakarṇi is here designated, can only be surmised. That he was not, as Bühler and other scholars formerly supposed, the famous Śrī Śātakarṇi, who was reigning about the middle of the second century B.C. and who is mentioned in the Nānāghāṭ and Hāthigumphā inscriptions, is evident not only from what we know of the history of Vidiśā, which at that time was in possession of the Śuṅgas, but from the style of the carvings on the gateway, which can hardly be assigned to an earlier date than the middle of the first century B.C. and may be a generation later. Evidently, therefore, the ruler in question was one of the Śātakarṇis who appear later in the Purāṇic lists, and is to be identified either with Śātakarṇi II, whose reign of 56 years fell mainly in the first half of the first century B.C., or less probably with Mahendra Śātakarṇi III, or his successor Kuntala Śātakarṇi, the twelfth and thirteenth kings respectively, who were reigning in the last quarter of the first century B.C.[1] Of these two kings nothing is known beyond their bare names and the fact that the earlier is credited in the Purāṇas with a reign of three years and the later with a reign of eight years. Unfortunately, during the long rule of the Andhras, the history of Mālwā is enveloped in obscurity, and it is not until the reign of the famous Gautamīputra Śrī Śātakarṇi in the second century A.D., that even the scanty light afforded by inscriptions and coins again begins to break. We hear, however, of two interruptions in their rule : the first between the years 61 and 57 B.C., when, according to the Jaina *Kālakācārya-kathānaka*, Ujjayinī was in the hands of the Śakas for four years ; the second towards the end of the first century A.D., when both Western and Eastern Mālwā passed for a few decades into the possession of the Kshaharātas, to be reconquered about 125 A.D. by Gautamīputra Śrī Śātakarṇi and finally lost about 130 A.D. to the Great Satrap Rudradāman. From that time onward the two provinces seem to have remained in the hands of the Western Kshatrapas[2] until the close of the fourth century, when along with Gujarāt and the Peninsula of Surāshṭra they were annexed to the Gupta Empire. This annexation was accomplished by Candragupta II, an echo of whose conquest occurs in an inscription carved on the balustrade of the Great Stūpa, dated in the year 93 of the Gupta era (A.D. 412-13). This inscription[3] records the gift by one of Candragupta's officers named Āmrakārddava, seemingly a man of high rank, of a village called Īśvaravāsaka, and of a sum of money to the Ārya-Saṅgha or Order of the Faithful at the great *vihāra* or monastery of "Kākanāda-boṭa,"[4] for the purpose of feeding monks and maintaining lamps. The Gupta occupation of Vidiśā is also attested by two epigraphs in the caves of the Udayagiri hill, four miles from Sāñchī, one of which records a dedication made by a feudatory Mahārāja during the reign of Candragupta II in 401 A.D. ;[5] the other commemorates the excavation of a cave by a minister of Candragupta II, who came here in company with the king, who was "seeking to conquer the whole world."[6]

Śakas, Kshaharātas and Western Kshatrapas

Imperial Guptas

[1] *Cf.* pp. 275-7 *infra.*

[2] The Western Kshatrapas, including the Kshaharātas, were of Śaka, that is, Scythian, origin and, as their name signifies, were in the position of feudatories to a supreme power, that power being first the Śaka and later on the Kushān.

[3] *Cf.* Inscr. 833 *infra.*

[4] *I.e.*, of Sāñchī.

[5] Fleet, *C. I. I.*, III, p. 25

[6] Fleet, *ibid.*, p. 36 ; Rapson, *Cat. of the Coins of the Andhra Dynasty*, etc., pp. CL ff.

In A.D. 413 Kumāragupta succeeded Candragupta II, and was himself succeeded by Skandagupta in 455. It was towards the close of the reign of the latter emperor (480 A.D.) that the Gupta Empire was overrun by invading hosts of White Huns (Ephthalites), and shorn of the greater part of its western territories. Eastern Mālwā, however, was still unconquered in the reign of Skandagupta's successor, Budhagupta,[1] and it was not until about 500 A.D. that it passed into the hands of a local chief named Bhānugupta, and not until a decade later that it was annexed by the Hun king, Toramāna.

Bhānugupta and the White Huns

In 528 A.D. the power of the Huns was shattered by the victories of Bālāditya and Yaśodharman over Mihiragula, the bloodthirsty successor of Toramāṇa, who well earned for himself the title of the "Attila of India." Then followed a period of quiescence while the country was recovering from the savagery of the invaders. During this period, which lasted until the beginning of the seventh century, there was no paramount authority in the north capable of welding together the petty states, and the latter were probably too weak and exhausted by their sufferings to make a bid for imperial power. Moreover, for five centuries after the defeat of the Huns, that is from 528 until 1023, when the Panjāb was occupied by Maḥmūd of Ghazna, Northern India was virtually immune from foreign aggression and free, therefore, to work out her own destinies. During these five centuries no need was felt of a central power to oppose the common foe; there was little voluntary cohesion among the many petty states, and, with two exceptions, no sovereign arose vigorous enough to impose his will upon his neighbours. The first of these exceptions was Harsha of Thāṇesar (606-647), who within five and a half years of his accession established an empire almost coterminous with that of the Guptas, and for thirty-five years more governed it with all the energy and brilliancy that had distinguished their rule. At the time of his accession, Eastern Mālwā, which in the middle of the sixth century seems for a short time to have been incorporated in the kingdom of the Kalacuris, was again in the hands of the Guptas of Magadha, and it was the seventh of this line, Mādhavagupta, who became feudatory to Harsha. The other exception was Mihira Bhoja of Kanauj, who between the years 840-890 made himself master of an empire which extended from the Sutlej to Bihar and which was maintained intact by his successors Mahendrapāla and Bhoja II. In this empire Eastern Mālwā, which was then ruled by the Paramāra dynasty is known to have been included at the close of the ninth century, but the power of the Pratihāras of Kanauj rapidly declined during the early decades of the following century, and by the time that Rājā Muñja (974-95) came to the throne Eastern Mālwā had seemingly asserted its independence and become the predominant state in Central India. Both Muñja and his nephew, the celebrated Bhoja, who reigned over Mālwā for more than forty years (1018-60), were liberal patrons of literature and art, and themselves writers of no

Harsha of Thāṇesar

Mihira Bhoja of Kanauj

Paramāras of Mālwā

[1] Budhagupta issued coins imitating the types of the earlier Gupta silver coinage. Of Bhānugupta no coins are known, but he is mentioned in an inscription of A.D. 510-11, commemorating a chief named Goparāja, who fell in a "famous battle," while fighting by the side of Bhānugupta—possibly the battle in which Bhānugupta was defeated by Toramāṇa.

mean ability. With the death of Bhoja, about 1060, the power of the Paramāras declined, and during the twelfth century Mālwā passed for a time into the possession of the Cālukya kings of Anhilwāra, but in the following century was again in the possession of Devapāla of Dhār (1217-1240). With the subsequent history of the district we need not here concern ourselves, since there are no Buddhist edifices at Sāñchī after the twelfth century A.D.; and it is probable that the Buddhist religion, which had already been much contaminated by Hinduism, died out altogether about this time in Central India.

Cālukya kings of Anhilwāra

Sāñchī in Modern Times

From the thirteenth century onwards Sāñchī appears to have been left deserted and desolate. The City of Vidiśā had fallen to ruins during the Gupta period and had been superseded by Bhilsa (Bhailasvāmin); but, though the latter town played an important part in local history during Muhammadan times, and though it was thrice sacked by Moslem conquerors and its temples destroyed for a fourth time in the reign of Aurangzeb, yet amid all this devastation the monuments of Sāñchī, in spite of their prominent position on a hill less than five miles away, were left unscathed, and when rediscovered by Gen. Taylor in 1818, proved to be in a remarkably good state of preservation. At that time three of the gateways of the Great Stūpa were still standing erect, and the southern one was lying where it had fallen; the great dome was intact; and a portion of the balustrade on the summit was still *in situ*.[1] The Second and Third Stūpas were also well preserved, and there were remains of eight minor stūpas, besides other buildings, in the vicinity of the Second Stūpa, but no record of their condition is preserved. The beauty and unique character of these monuments was quickly recognised, and from 1819 onwards there appeared various notes, illustrations and monographs descriptive of their architecture and sculpture, though too often marred by the fanciful ideas or inaccuracies of the authors. Most notable among these works were Cunningham's *Bhilsa Topes* (1854), Fergusson's *Tree and Serpent Worship* (1868) and Gen. Maisey's *Sánchi and its Remains* (1892).[2] But the widespread interest which the discovery and successive accounts of the stūpas excited, proved lamentably disastrous to the monuments themselves; for the site quickly became a hunting-ground for treasure-seekers and amateur archæologists, who, in their efforts to probe its hidden secrets or to enrich themselves from the spoils supposed to be hidden there, succeeded in half demolishing and doing irreparable harm to most of the structures. Thus, in 1822, Capt. Johnson, the Assistant Political Agent in Bhopal, opened the Great Stūpa from top to bottom on one side, and left a vast breach in it, which was the cause of much subsequent damage to the body of the structure and of the collapse of the Western Gateway and portions of the enclosing

Rediscovery in 1818, and subsequent spoliation

[1] See J. Burgess, *The Great Stūpa at Sāñchī Kānākheḍā*. *J. R. A. S.*, Jan. 1902, pp. 29-45, where a succinct account is given of the history of the site since 1818.

[2] The earliest account of Sāñchī, by Capt. E. Fell, was published in Buckingham's *Calcutta Journal* for July 1819 and reprinted by Prinsep in *J. A. S. B.*, Vol. III, 490-94. Other notices will be found in the *J. A. S. B.*, Vol. III, 411 ff., 481 ff.; Vol. IV, 712 ff.; Vol. VI, 451 ff.; Vol. XVI, 739 ff.; Vol. XVII, 171 ff. For later accounts, see the *List of Books Cited* in this work.

balustrade.[1] The same blundering excavator was probably responsible, also, for the partial destruction of the Second and Third Stūpas, which until then had been in perfect repair. Then, in 1851, Major (afterwards Gen. Sir) Alexander Cunningham and Capt. F. C. Maisey together contributed to the general spoliation of the site by hasty excavations in several of the monuments, and, though they succeeded in recovering a most valuable series of relic-caskets[2] from the Second and Third Stūpas, their discoveries hardly compensated for the damage entailed in their operations. It is fair, however, to add that we owe to Maisey a very excellent series of drawings which were used by Fergusson to illustrate his *Tree and Serpent Worship*, and later on by Maisey himself to illustrate *Sánchi and its Remains*; and that we owe to Major Cunningham the valuable account of Sāñchī and other Buddhist sites in its vicinity contained in his *Bhilsa Topes*—a book which, but for their excavations, would probably never have been written. During all these years the idea of repairing and preserving these incomparable structures for the sake of future generations seems never to have entered anyone's head, and though in 1869 (as an indirect result of a request by Napoleon III for one of the richly carved gates) casts of the East Gate were prepared and presented to some of the principal national museums of Europe,[3] it was not until 1881, when still more havoc had been wrought by the neighbouring villagers or by the ravages of the ever-encroaching jungles, that the Government bethought itself of safeguarding the original structures. In that year Major Cole, then Curator of Ancient Monuments, cleared the hill-top of vegetation and filled the great breach in the Main Stūpa made by Capt. Johnson nearly sixty years before, and during the two following years he re-erected at the expense of the Imperial Government the fallen gateways on the south and west, as well as the smaller gateway in front of the Third Stūpa. No attempt, however, was made by him to preserve the other monuments which were crumbling to ruin, to exhume from their debris the monasteries, temples and other edifices which cover the plateau around the Great Stūpa, or to protect the hundreds of loose sculptures and inscriptions lying on the site. These tasks, which involved operations far more extensive than any previously undertaken, were left for the writer to carry out between the years 1912 and 1919. The buildings which were at that time visible on the hill-top were the Great Stūpa and the few other remains which the reader will find indicated in the site plan (Pl. 2) by hatched lines.[4] For the rest, the whole site was buried beneath such deep accumulations of debris and was so overgrown with jungle, that the very existence of the majority of the monuments had not even been suspected. The first step, therefore, was to clear the whole enclave of the thick jungle growth in which it was enveloped. Then followed the excavations of the areas to the south and east of the Great Stūpa, where it was evident that a considerable depth of debris lay over the natural rock, and where, accordingly, there was reason to hope (a hope which proved

History of conservation

[1] *Cf. J. A. S. B.*, Vol. IV, p. 712.
[2] See pp. 44, 45 and 81 *infra*.
[3] Among others to South Kensington, Edinburgh, Dublin, Paris and Berlin. See Major H. H. Cole, *Third Report*, App., p. XCIV.
[4] In contradistinction to the recently excavated monuments, which are shown on the plan in black.

to be abundantly justified) that substantial remains might be found. The buildings which were exposed to view in the southern part of the site are for the most part founded on the living rock; but those in the eastern area constitute only the uppermost stratum, beneath which there still lie buried the remains of various earlier structures. These have been left to the spade of some future explorer, as it was clear from trial diggings at different points that they were mainly monastic dwellings similar in character to those already brought to light in other parts of the enclave and unlikely, therefore, to add much to our present knowledge of the monuments.

The third task to be done was to put one and all the monuments into as thorough and lasting a state of repair as was practicable. Most important and most difficult of achievement among the many measures which this task entailed were: first, the dismantling and reconstruction of the whole south-west quadrant of the Great Stūpa, which was threatening to collapse and to bring down with it the South and West Gateways, as well as the balustrade between them; secondly, the preservation of Temple 18, the ponderous columns of which were leaning at perilous angles, and had to be reset in the perpendicular and established on secure foundations; and thirdly, the repair of Temple 45, which had reached the last stage of decay and was a menace to any one entering its shrine. Other measures that are also deserving of particular mention, are the rebuilding of the long retaining wall between the Central and Eastern Terraces; the reconstruction of the dome, balustrades and crowning umbrella of the Third Stūpa; the re-roofing and general repair of Temples 17, 31 and 32; the effective drainage (involving the relaying of the old fragmentary pavement) of the area around the Great Stūpa; and the improvement and beautifying of the site generally by roughly levelling and turfing it and by the planting of trees and flowering creepers.

Finally, there remained the question of protecting the numerous movable antiquities which lay scattered about the site. For this purpose a small but adequate museum was erected, where sculptures, inscriptions and architectural fragments have been duly arranged and catalogued, and where plans, photographs and other materials have been set out to assist the visitor in the study of these unique monuments.

CHAPTER II

THE HILL OF SĀÑCHĪ AND ITS MONUMENTS

The hill described

WITH this brief historical retrospect, we may now turn to Sāñchī itself and its monuments. The hill on which these monuments are clustered is in the Dīwānganj Sub-division of the Bhopāl State, about 5½ miles from Bhilsā on the Great Indian Peninsula Railway, its precise position being Lat. 23° 28′ N. and Long. 77° 48′ E. The hill is not in any way remarkable, nor is there anything in its general aspect to distinguish it from many other eminences that girdle it close on the west and south. It is less than 300 feet in height, of a whale-back shape, with a saddle near the middle, in which nestles the modern village of Sāñchī. As with all the neighbouring off-shoots of the Vindhya range, which here dies down into the plateau of Central India, its formation is of sandstone, which slopes layer upon layer in shelving masses down its sides, wherein the Buddhist builders of old found a quarry for their stone ready to hand and easily worked. On all the steeper slopes around the hill, vegetation still grows free and dense, but most luxuriantly on the southern half, in places where high and shady cliffs afford shelter against the sun. Here, the ever-green *khirṇi* tree (*mimusops kauki*), with its sombre foliage, is especially abundant, and here in the early spring the *dhāk* or "flame of the forest", as it has been so happily named, sets the hill-side ablaze with its clusters of gorgeous blossoms. Twenty years ago, when the writer first started his excavations, the jungle extended over the whole hill-top, and had to be completely cleared from within the enclosure of the ancient saṅghārāma. When the digging had been finished and the buried buildings laid bare, the ground about them was levelled and smoothed and replanted with grass and shrubs and trees, wherever they seemed likely to add to the beauty of the spot.

Varieties of local stone

The Vindhya sandstone of which the Sāñchī and neighbouring hills are formed, varies much in texture and colour. Most of it was quarried in the hill of Sāñchī itself. This local variety is of greyish-purple or greyish-brown colour, very brittle and difficult to chisel, but easy to hammer-dress. It was employed by the builders of all periods for the rougher sorts of masonry, notably for the bodies and berms of stūpas as well as for the foundations, plinths, paving slabs and walls of most of the monasteries and chapels; but in mediæval times it was also used for statues and other sculptures, which notwithstanding its brittleness were carved with exquisite precision and brought to a beautiful finish. A second variety, which was quarried in the neighbouring hill of Nāgourī, is of softer texture and of grey-white, slightly buff or pinkish hue. It was used for the balustrades of the three major stūpas, for the pillars of Temple 40, for the superstructure (but not for the paving slabs) of Temple 17, for the pillars of the Apsidal Temple 18, and for many other structures that need not be specified. A third and still finer variety of white or grey-white sandstone came from the Udayagiri hill some four miles from Sāñchī and was used in the early period for the gateways of Stūpas 1 and 3 and, later on, for many free-standing statues, the advantages which this Udayagiri stone had over the Nāgourī variety being that it was freer from faults and blemishes, could be quarried in larger blocks, and, thanks to its finer texture, lent itself to the most delicate kinds of carving.

Ancient names of Sāñchī

Besides the village of Sāñchī, which, as may be seen from the plan on Pl. 1, lies on the eastern side of the saddle, there is a second village, called Kānākheḍā, at the north-western foot of the hill. Both are poor, squalid little hamlets, and their names, like their habitations, appear to be quite modern; at any rate, there is no mention of either among the many place-names recorded in the old *ex-voto* inscriptions. In the early Brāhmī records the ancient name of Sāñchī is given as Kākaṇāva or Kākaṇāya (*cf.* Inscrs. 7, 17*b*, 394, 396 and 404), but in the reign of Candragupta II it appears as Kākanādaboṭa (*cf.* Inscrs. 833 and 834) and still later, towards the end of the seventh century A.D., as Boṭa-Śrīparvvata (Inscr. 842)—a name which, as Mr. Majumdar points out below, is probably to be identified with the Śrī-parvvata mentioned in Bhavabhūti's *Mālatīmādhava*.[1]

Ancient and modern roads

The main road by which the hill is now ascended leads straight from the little railway station, passes up the rocky slope in the direction of the village of Sāñchī, and bends sharply to the right near a small pond, the embankment of which is of ancient date. From this point the road is paved and stepped with heavy stone slabs up to the brow of the hill, after which it runs south for a distance of about 80 yards and enters the enclave at its north-west corner. Despite its age-old appearance, most of this road is a recent construction. In early days there was doubtless a pathway of some sort descending from the northern entrance of the saṅghārāma as far at least as the small tank at the bend of the ascending road to which reference is made below, but the road as it now exists was made to a large extent by Major Cole, R.E., in 1883, and subsequently remade and paved throughout by the writer in 1915, when the new road leading from the small western entrance of the enclave to the Second Stūpa and thence to the bottom of the hill was also made. At the time when Vidiśā was a flourishing city, the chief approach to the hill-top came direct from the north-east, ascended the hill-side near the north-western corner of the Purainiā Tank (see plan, Pl. 1), crossed the Chiknī Ghāṭī and wound round to the north of the plateau, which it reached about 50 yards to the east of the modern entrance; while a side-path also branched off from it to the middle of the eastern side. Of the latter, a short section still exists outside the circuit wall, and of the old main road two longer sections are preserved at the Chiknī Ghāṭī and just below the northern wall of the enclave.

[1] See p. 300 *infra*.

In each of these sections the roadway is constructed of long, narrow slabs of stone laid transversely across the track on the rock foundation. Most of the slabs are now broken in pieces, but those which are intact measure as much as twelve feet in length, and call to mind the slabs used in the long steep ascents to some of the early Buddhist temples in Ceylon.

A second road, constructed in the same fashion and no doubt contemporary with the first one, started at the foot of the hill not far from the back of the modern Rest-house, followed the same line as the modern road as far as Stūpa 2, and thence swept round in a curve in a south-easterly direction, passed a disused quarry on the left which was subsequently converted into a tank, and so ascended on to the plateau a little to the south of the modern flight of steps.

Water Supply and Irrigation

Standing on the brow of the hill at this point one sees spread out below to the south-west (*cf*. Pl. 1), the smaller isolated hill of Nāgourī, and, connecting it with the Sāñchī hill, a broad artificial embankment or *pār*, as it is locally known, with a second and longer embankment on the west side of the Nāgourī hill, linking it with the line of low hills to the west (not shown on the plan). Both embankments are massive constructions of black earth, revetted with heavy stone masonry on their inner faces. In height they average some 12 to 15 feet, and in thickness about 35 yards. Evidently their purpose was to hold up the drainage of the surrounding hills and so form an extensive lake between them, from which the lower lands on the further side of the embankments could be irrigated. When these embankments were built is not known, but the character of their construction suggests that it was at some time prior to the Christian era, possibly during the Śuṅga period, when Vidiśā was at the height of its power and much building was being done in the saṅghārāma at Sāñchī.[1] Agriculture was not of course an occupation in which the monks themselves were allowed to take part, but irrigation meant increased wealth to the proletariat and this was an indirect advantage to the church no less than to the state.

Besides this large irrigation lake there were three small reservoirs from which the saṅghārāma obtained its water supply. The largest of these is the Purainiā talāb against the east side of the hill, not far from its N.E. corner—a sheet of water over 400 yards long by 130 to 140 yards broad, which is held up by an artificial embankment on three sides. Lying as it does at the foot of the hill, at the point where the main road from Vidiśā started its ascent, this reservoir probably furnished the main water supply for the monastery. A smaller reservoir divided by a causeway into two halves, which are known respectively as Dahorī and Madāgan, is situated below the saddle of the hill on its west side, where the villagers of Kānākheḍā and Sāñchī now do their bathing and their washing;

[1] In the embankment uniting the Nāgourī and Sāñchī hills there is a breach (*jhorā*) made at some unknown date, in order to drain the lake.

but it seems probable that, like the group of *satī* stones[1] to the south of it, this reservoir dates from the late Mediæval period. The third and smallest of the three reservoirs is on the hill-side less than half-way up the modern ascent. At this point there is a ledge of rock which, like the Purainiā talāb, was enclosed on three sides by a solid embankment formed of rude blocks of stone laid in *murum* (small shale) and clay. Notwithstanding its unpromising situation, this tank still holds water and serves the villagers of Sāñchī for watering their cattle. That it goes back to an early age—earlier perhaps than the Purainiā reservoir—and that it was designed for the use of the monks, is clear from its position nearly half-way up to the monasteries.

Date of foundation of the saṅghārāma

When did the Buddhists first establish themselves on the hill of Sāñchī? Was it during the reign of the Emperor Aśoka, or was it at some more remote age, may be during the lifetime of the Great Teacher himself? To this question no positive answer can be given. In the *Mahāvaṁśa*—the Buddhist chronicle of Ceylon—is a story which has been taken to imply that there were Buddhist monuments here before the time of Aśoka, but there are no real grounds for this inference. The story goes that Aśoka, then Viceroy of Ujjayinī (Ujjain), halted at Vidiśā on his way from Pāṭaliputra to his new Province, and there married the beautiful daughter of a local banker, one Devī by name, by whom he had two sons, Ujjeniya and Mahendra, and a daughter, Saṅghamitrā. It is also related that, after Aśoka's accession, Mahendra headed the Buddhist mission sent under the auspices of the emperor to Ceylon, and that before setting out he visited his mother at Vidiśā and was taken by her to a beautiful *vihāra* or monastery at a spot called Cetiyagiri.

Possible identity of Sāñchī with Cetiyagiri

Now, the name Cetiyagiri implies a hill with a *caitya* and, assuming the story of Mahendra as told in the Ceylonese Chronicle to be correct—and there seems no sufficient reason for discrediting it—it has been suggested that the hill in question is to be identified with Sāñchī, where Aśoka himself set up a stūpa and a pillar and where alone in this neighbourhood there are any remains of his age to be found. Unfortunately, we have no proof of when the name "Cetiyagiri" came into use. If it was before Aśoka's time, the *caitya* in question is not likely to have been a stūpa or stūpa-chapel, since, as we shall presently see, stūpa-worship was virtually started by Aśoka; but it might conceivably have been some other form of religious edifice or object of cult-worship. On the whole, however, it seems more likely that the name Cetiyagiri was given to the hill after the erection of Aśoka's own stūpa there. In what precise year that stūpa was erected we do not know.[2] It may well have been fifteen or twenty years before the Mahendra mission started to Ceylon, which was not until the Third Council had been held at Pāṭaliputra—21 years after Aśoka's coronation. Even if it had been erected only five or ten years before, there was ample time for the hill to have become known as Cetiyagiri.

[1] One of these *satī* stones is dated in the year 1264-5 A.D.

[2] The date of the Edict on the pillar beside the stūpa is no evidence of the date of the pillar itself, still less of the stūpa, which unquestionably antedated the pillar. In certain of his Edicts (*e.g.*, No. VII) Aśoka himself gave orders that they were to be engraved on already existing pillars or slabs, *i.e.*, on pillars that he himself had set up in earlier years (see p. 45 below). Although, therefore, the Edict at Sāñchī, like the other Minor Edicts at Sārnāth and Kauśāmbī, was probably not issued until after the Third Council at Pāṭaliputra, the pillar may have been erected some years before, and the stūpa, again, some years before that.

A third possibility is that the name Cetiyagiri had come into use at some time anterior to the fifth century A.D., when the Ceylonese chronicler wrote, but not as early as Aśoka's reign. In this connexion it is noteworthy that even in the author's day some doubt seems to have existed regarding the name of the hill, which in some versions of the *Mahāvaṁśa* appears as Vedisagiri instead of Cetiyagiri.[1] Whatever the actual name of the hill, however, may have been, the question of its identity with Sāñchī is not thereby affected.

As to the date, then, when the saṅghārāma of Sāñchī was first founded, it is evident that nothing certain can be deduced from the Ceylon Chronicle. It is quite possible that a Buddhist settlement of some sort existed here before the time of Aśoka and that it was because and for the sake of this settlement that the Emperor chose this site for his stūpa and pillar. This, however, is merely a surmise. It is equally likely that Aśoka himself founded the saṅghārāma and built his stūpa here, not only because Vidiśā was one of the greatest cities of his empire, but because he wished to honour it as the birthplace of the beautiful Devī, and a spot invested with specially happy memories for himself.

Otherwise unknown in ancient literature

In the case of other famous monuments, such as those of Bodh-Gayā, Sārnāth and Kasiā, the sites chosen for their erection were those which had been hallowed by the presence of Buddha himself, and the monuments were designed to commemorate some act in his life, as, for example, his Enlightenment at Bodh-Gayā, his First Sermon at Sārnāth, his passing-away at Kasiā. Sāñchī has no such association with the life or acts of the Master. Apart from the uncertain reference, alluded to above, in the *Mahāvaṁśa*, it is not mentioned anywhere in Pāli literature, as it certainly must have been, had it had any direct connexion with the Buddha's life. And even the Chinese pilgrims, Fa Hien and Hiuen Thsang, who visited India between the fourth and seventh centuries, when Sāñchī was still in its prime, and who have so much to say about countless other saṅghārāmas, have nothing to tell us about this one. Such a conspiracy of silence would have been surprising enough, if Sāñchī had had but a tithe of the claim to distinction to which her monuments entitle her; it is little short of a miracle, when we reflect that of all the Buddhist remains that have survived in India, these are at once the most magnificent and the most instructive.

Groups of monuments on the hill-top

Most of the monuments are grouped together on the top of the hill in an enclosure which is roughly oblong but irregular in shape, measuring some 420 yards from north to south by 220 from east to west. Within this enclave the rocky surface of the hill originally sloped upward in a gentle gradient from west to east, reaching its highest point beneath the foundation of Temple 45, whence there is a steep drop of nearly 300 feet to the plain

[1] *Cf.* W. Geiger, *The Mahāvaṁśa* (P. T. S.), p. 88.

below But in the reign of Aśoka, when the Great Stūpa was built, a level area was provided near the middle of the western half of the enclave partly by cutting away the uneven surface, partly by filling it up with debris and then flooring it over; and on the terrace thus formed were erected, first, the Great Stūpa and Pillar of Aśoka, and subsequently a large number of smaller stūpas, shrines and memorial pillars, among which the most important were the Stūpas 3 and 5 (Pl. 2), the Shrines 17, 18 and 31 and the Pillars 25, 26 and 35. The level terrace on which these monuments stand once extended further towards the east, and doubtless there were other structures of the same class and age in that direction, but later on they fell to decay, their remains were levelled up to form a foundation for new ones, and so the process of rebuilding and accumulation went on century by century, until by the Late Mediæval Period a lofty terrace had been formed in this part of the site, some 14 feet above the Main Area on the west and divided from it by a high retaining wall. Thus, the buildings to the east of this retaining wall now constitute, as it were, a separate group, being on a higher terrace, which may conveniently be called the "Eastern Area", and belonging for the most part to a later age than those in the Main Area. This group comprises the mediæval monasteries 44, 45, 46 and 47, the small three-chambered shrine 32, and the cruciform structure 43 with round turrets at its corners, which is perhaps the latest monument on the site. A third group of buildings, more or less distinct from both of the above, occupies the uneven ground to the south of the enclave (Southern Area) and comprises, besides other structures, the three small mediæval monasteries 36, 37 and 38, the large pillared hall 40, which is one of the oldest buildings at Sāñchī, and the square basement No. 8.

Circuit wall

The solid stone circuit wall which encircles the plateau, appears to have been first constructed in the eleventh or twelfth century A.D., but was extensively rebuilt in 1883 and again by the writer in 1914-15. For the greater part of its length it is founded on the living rock, but a section of it on the eastern side is carried over the ruins of some of the later mediæval buildings. The existing entrance at the north-west corner of this wall is a modern innovation due to Major Cole, the old entrance having apparently been located at a little distance towards the east, at a point where the ancient road had passed prior to the construction of the circuit wall.

The Second Stūpa

Besides these monuments within the saṅghārāma proper on the hill-top, there is an important stūpa (No. 2), second only in interest to the Great Stūpa itself, which is situated on an artificial terrace half-way down the hill on its western side (Pl. 1); and there are a number of other ruins also of less importance, scattered here and there on the same side of the hill. In the account that follows of these remains it would be an advantage in many respects to describe them chronologically, according as they were erected or added to in the Maurya, Śuṅga, Andhra or later periods. To do so, however, would mean describing many of the buildings piecemeal, part in one place, part in another;

and such descriptions would probably be too complex in detail for the reader to follow We shall, therefore, adopt the simpler plan of dealing with them group by group, and describing each one of them entire before passing on to the next.[1] At the same time the schedule of dates appended below will assist the reader in following the successive additions and changes that were made in the course of the centuries.

[1] The numbers by which the various monuments are designated in the plan on Pl. 2 are not, it will be observed, arranged in regular sequence, the reason being that the numeration of the stūpas adopted by Sir Alexander Cunningham in the plan which he published in 1854 has been generally followed by subsequent writers, and it seemed likely to lead to inconvenience and confusion if it were now abandoned. Accordingly I have, with one exception, retained Gen. Cunningham's numbers and added others to distinguish those monuments which I myself have discovered, arranging them in such systematic sequence as has been practicable. The exception referred to is the early structure numbered 8 on my plan. In Gen. Cunningham's sketch a stūpa numbered 8 is shown to the north of Stūpa 3, but on the spot in question there is no vestige of any such structure; nor is any indication of its existence given in either of the plans prepared by Gen. Maisey and Mr. Thompson. On the other hand, Gen. Maisey, who was associated with Gen. Cunningham at Sāñchī in 1851 and in other respects follows his numeration, places No. 8 south, instead of north, of the Great Stūpa, at a spot where nothing appears on Gen. Cunningham's plan, but where I unearthed a stone basement of an early shrine. Accordingly, I conclude that Gen. Cunningham, whose plan in other respects is far from accurate, made the mistake of placing this monument to the north instead of the south of the central group. *Cf.* pp. 45, note 1, and 68, note 1, *infra*.

TABLE SHOWING DATES OF MONUMENTS

MAURYAN	*ŚUṄGA*	*ANDHRA*	*GUPTA* (*4th to 6th cent. A.D.*)	*MEDIÆVAL* (*7th to 9th cent. A.D.*)	*LATE MEDIÆVAL* (*10th to 11th cent. A.D.*)
			MAIN TERRACE		
Stupa 1: Original structure of brick; umbrellas of polished Chunar sandstone.	Stūpa 1: Stone envelope; ground, stairway, berm and harmikā balustrades; lid of harmikā relic-box; pavement of procession path and main terrace.	Stūpa 1: Four gateways and extensions of ground balustrade.	Stūpa 1: Four image shrines in procession path.		
	Stūpa 3: Body and berm of stūpa; stairway, berm and harmikā balustrades; relic-boxes.	Stūpa 3: Ground balustrade and gateway. ? Corner pillar of landing balustrade.			
	Stūpa 4.				
	Stūpa 6	....	....	Stūpa 6: facing	
			——Stūpas 5, 7, 12, 13, 14, 15, 16.——	——	
			Stūpas 28 and 29.		
Pillar of Aśoka . .	Pillar 25	....	Pillars 26, 34 and 35.		
——Temple 18: Lowest floor	——	Temple 18: Third floor (counting from top).	Temple 18: Second floor .	Temple 18: Stone pillars and walls; terra-cotta tablets.	Temple 18: Stone filling in apse; carved jambs of inner doorway.
			Temple 17.		
			Shrine 9.		
			Temple 31: Plinth and pedestal beneath lotus throne of image; two pillars; Nāgī statue.	Temple 31: Reconstructed walls; pillars, lotus throne and image.	
				Structures 19, 20, 21, 23 and Road 29.	
			SOUTHERN AREA		
Building 40: Apsidal Hall foundations.	Building 40: Pillared Maṇḍapa built on ruins of Apsidal Hall.	....	....	Building 40: Shrine and portico on east side of Maṇḍapa plinth.	
	Building 8 . . .	....	....	Building 8: Enclosure wall south of stairway ramp.	
			Monastery 36 . . .	Monasteries 37 and 38.	
Pavement W. and S.-W. of Temple 18 (or possibly pre-Mauryan).	South retaining-wall of Main Terrace; foundation walls over pavement W. and S.-W. of Temple 18.	....	....	Building 42.	
			EASTERN AREA		
				Temple 45: Plinth of earlier shrine; cells on N., S. and W. sides of court; stone kerb and plinths of 3 stūpas in court; corner pilasters in later sanctum and 2 pilasters in ante-chamber of same.	Temple 45: Existing shrine and statue in sanctum; platform in front of same, and cells and verandahs to north and south.
				Building 44.	
			Monasteries 46 and 47: Remains in lower stratum beneath pavement of court 47.	Monasteries 46 and 47: Remains in upper stratum beneath pavement of court 47.	Monasteries 46 and 47: Existing superstructures.
					Buildings 49 and 50, with boundary wall adjoining.
					Building 32.
				Building 43: Earlier remains beneath courtyard.	Building 43.
		WESTERN SIDE OF HILL			
	Stūpa 2: Body and berm of structure; ground, stairway, berm and harmikā balustrades; relic-caskets.	Stūpa 2: Later sculptures on Pillars 22 and 27 of ground balustrade.			
	Platform and broken pillar N.-N.-W. of Stūpa 2.				
	? Remains of Apsidal Temple on west slope of hill.				

CHAPTER III

THE GREAT STŪPA AND PILLAR OF AŚOKA

Description of Great Stūpa

AS it now stands, the Great Stūpa (Pls. 3-6) consists of an almost hemispherical dome (*aṇḍa*) truncated near the top and surrounded at its base by a lofty terrace (*medhī*), the berm of which served in ancient days as a processional path (*pradakshiṇa-patha*), access to it being provided by a double flight of steps (*sopāna*) built against it on the southern side. Encircling the monument on the ground level is a second procession path enclosed within a massive balustrade of stone (*vedikā*). This balustrade, which is of plain design unrelieved by carvings of any kind, is divided into four quadrants by entrances set approximately at the cardinal points, each one of which is adorned with a gateway (*toraṇa*) lavishly enriched with reliefs on the inner and outer sides. It used to be supposed that the Great Stūpa was built, just as it stands, at the same time as the inscribed pillar near its Southern Gateway—that is, in the reign of the Emperor Aśoka—, that the balustrade around its base was approximately contemporary with the body of the building, and that the gateways were added in the course of the second century B.C. All these suppositions were incorrect. In his description of the opening of the Great Stūpa by Capt. Johnson in 1882, Dr. Spilsbury states[1] that the core of the structure was composed of bricks (burnt) laid in mud; and in the sectional drawing which accompanies Capt. J. D. Cunningham's account[2] the diameter of this brick core is shown as about half that of the entire edifice. Furthermore, Capt. Maisey, who helped Sir Alexander Cunningham to sink a vertical shaft down the centre of the stūpa, notes that the bricks of which the core was composed measured 16×10×3 inches. The details as to the brick core given by these writers were fully confirmed in the course of the extensive rebuilding of the stūpa which the writer carried out in 1916-17, when, owing to the dangerous subsidence of the south-western quadrant, it became necessary to dismantle more than a third of the whole body of the structure down to its foundations, thus exposing to view the brick core[3] as well as the surrounding envelope of stone. Knowing the details that he did, it is a matter of surprise that Gen. Cunningham should have taken it for granted that the brick core was of the same age as the outer envelope; for seeing that the outer envelope was of stone, there would manifestly have been no purpose in the builders going to the trouble and expense of making bricks for the core, when stone would have served equally well, and might have been quarried far more cheaply, on the spot. The truth of the matter is that this is but one among countless examples in India and

The original brick stūpa

[1] *J. A. S. B.*, Vol. IV, p. 712.
[2] *J. A. S. B.*, Vol. XVI, p. 746 and Pl. XXVII.
[3] In V. Smith's *History of Fine Art in India and Ceylon* (2nd Ed.), p. 20, it is stated that the earliest stūpas at Sāñchī, Bharhut, etc., were of *unburnt* brick. This is incorrect.

Practice of enlarging stūpas by addition of successive envelopes

Burma of the practice, common in all ages among the Buddhists, of adding envelope after envelope to their stūpas, each more imposing and ornamental than its predecessor. The more famous the stūpa, the more likely was it to be enlarged in this way. In the case of the stūpa built by Aśoka in the Deer Park at Sārnāth there were not less than four such successive envelopes [1], and in the case of the Great Stūpa at Nālandā, not less than five.[2] That, in the Sāñchī Stūpa, the brick core represents the original structure and the stone casing a subsequent addition, can no longer be questioned. The only queries to be answered concern the respective dates of the original structure and of the later casing. As

Authorship of original stūpa

to the former, I have already anticipated the answer by referring to Aśoka as the author of the stūpa. My reasons for so doing are, first, that the brick stūpa springs from the same floor level as the Lion Pillar near the South Gateway, which, as I shall presently show, is also attributable to the same emperor ; secondly, that the bricks themselves closely resemble in fabric and size the bricks used in other structures of Aśoka's reign ; thirdly, that every other known stūpa of his time was constructed of brick ; fourthly, that the existence of a stūpa built by this emperor at or near this spot is suggested by the discovery in the debris near the Great Stūpa of several pieces of an umbrella made of fine Chunar sandstone—the stone commonly used in his monuments—and cut, ribbed and polished in the manner peculiarly characteristic of his reign.[3]

Taken together, these several pieces of evidence leave no room for doubt as to the authorship of the monument, but even without them we should have been quite safe in assigning it to Aśoka. For it may be taken for granted that the original stūpa was erected before, not after, the Lion Pillar alongside it, and inasmuch as the latter bears an inscription of Aśoka, it follows that the stūpa must have been built either by that emperor or by one of his predecessors. Now, we know that the stūpa was a very old form of

Antiquity of the stūpa in India

memorial in India. In its origin it was a tumulus or funeral mound, and went back to the most ancient days in India, as it did in other countries. The Buddha's own body-relics, it will be remembered, were divided among the neighbouring princes and cities, and over them eight stūpas were raised : at Rājagṛiha, Vaiśālī, Kapilavastu, Allakappa, Rāmagrāma, Veṭhadīpa, Pāvā and Kuśinagara.[4] We read, too, in the Chinese pilgrims, Fa Hien and Hiuen Thsang, of similar memorials having been raised over the remains of the former Buddhas—over those of Kāśyapa near a town in the Śrāvastī district ; over those of Krakucchanda and Kanakamuni in the district of Kapilavastu.[5] From these and other

[1] *Cf. A. S. R.*, 1907-08, Pl. XVIII *b.*

[2] *Cf. A. S. R.*, 1927-28, Pl. XLI.

[3] See below, p. 24. Pieces of a similar umbrella, ribbed on the underside and polished in precisely the same way, were found near Aśoka's stūpa in the Deer Park at Sārnāth.

[4] The passage in the *Mahāparinibbāna-sutta* (Ch. V, § 26) which describes the cremation of Buddha and the erection of a stūpa over his relics, is of little value, but it is well worth repeating. The Buddha, it is there related, was asked by Ānanda what should be done with his remains after death. He answered that they were to be treated as men treat the remains of a King of Kings ; and after explaining how the body of a King of Kings was wrapped in successive layers of carded cotton wool and new cloth and placed in a vessel of iron and burnt on the funeral pyre, he said 'And as they treat the remains of a King of Kings, so, Ānanda, should they treat the remains of the Tathāgata. At the four cross-roads a *dāgaba* (stūpa) should be erected to the Tathāgata. And whosoever shall there place garlands or perfumes or paint, or make salutation there, or become in its presence calm in heart—that shall long be to them for a profit and a joy.' And this, we are told, was afterwards the mode of the Buddha's cremation. (*S. B. E.*, Vol. XI, p. 93. *Cf.* also Ch. VI, § 33.)

[5] *Cf.* T. Watters, *On Yuan Chwang*, Vol. I, p. 400, and Vol. II, p. 5. Hiuen Thsang ascribes the first of these three stūpas, as he ascribes most of the very old monuments, to Aśoka, but the earlier pilgrim Fa Hien says nothing of Aśoka. Whatever the actual age of these monuments seen by the Chinese pilgrims, the fact that they were ascribed to the former Buddhas points to the erection of such monuments having been regarded as an age-old custom.

passages it is evident that the erection of stūpas must have been a familiar institution in India, even in the time of the Buddha. Nevertheless, among the Buddhists themselves the stūpa did not become an object of marked veneration until the time of Aśoka. Early Buddhist literature is replete with information about the buildings within the saṅghārāmas, and furnishes meticulous details, often too meticulous, about the daily life of the brethren and sisters, but in none of the books prior to the time of Aśoka is there a word about the veneration of stūpas. Such an omission would be unimaginable, if these memorials had been venerated by the early church, as they afterwards came to be by the later. No doubt the eight stūpas in which the Buddha's own body-relics reposed were objects of reverence from the time of his death onwards, but there is nothing to indicate that the stūpa was adopted as a recognised emblem of the Buddhist Faith before the time of Aśoka. The evidence of the monuments, no less than of literature, is clear on this point. Among the myriads of Buddhist stūpas that have come down from ancient times there is not one that can be ascribed to the pre-Aśokan age. The truth is that, so far as Buddhism is concerned, the cult of the relic-stūpa was virtually initiated by Aśoka. That, when he broadcast this cult, Aśoka himself foresaw the remarkable effect which it was destined to have on the Buddhist Church, is clearly impossible, but that he used the cult with the definite purpose of unifying and consolidating the State religion, can hardly be doubted ; and his reasons for doing this are manifest, if we consider the state of the church at this time. By the middle of the third century B.C. manifold heresies and schisms had made their appearance. New religions and social ideals were taking the place of the old. The early church, with its restricted outlook, its puritanism, its cold reasoning and its individualism, no longer sufficed. It was too monastic in its outlook, too detached from the life of the world. The way of knowledge that it taught was over-academic. There was another way that was rapidly gaining ground in the thoughts of men—the way of love, of the heart, of action : the way that leads to the saving of others as well as of self. And with these changing ideals, the position of the Buddha himself was also changing. He was no longer merely the Teacher who had disclosed the path of liberation ; he had become, or at least was rapidly becoming, the divine saviour and consoler of mankind. He might be dead ; he might, according to his own doctrine, have attained a vague, incomprehensible state ; yet, for all that, to hosts of those who believed in him, he was still a living, immanent reality, to be prayed to and worshipped. If, then, the Church was to be unified and strengthened, if it was to make a more effective appeal to its own adherents and to the world at large, it was indispensable that it should adapt itself to the new ideals and endeavour to reconcile them with the old ; nay more, if it was to be established, as Aśoka himself purposed, on a broad national basis, it must show a far more catholic spirit than it had shown in the past, must cast its net wider among all races and all classes of society, and be prepared to admit and develop, as part and parcel of its own organism, doctrines and superstitions undreamt of by the Founder. This much, we may well believe, was clear to Aśoka, who set to work to adapt Buddhism by every means in his power to the needs of

Stūpa-worship among the Buddhists virtually initiated by Aśoka

State of the Buddhist Church in third century B.C.

Aśoka's efforts to establish Buddhism as a State religion

his empire. He himself was a member of the Saṅgha, and a very devout one, but he was also a broad-minded and practical man. He held a Council at Pāṭaliputra to settle authoritatively the canon of the scriptures and rid the Church of dissensions, but his concern was more for the unity of the State-established Church than for any metaphysical or theological doctrines. The latter might be of primary importance to the fraternity and perhaps to many of its educated lay-members, but they were above the heads of the majority of his subjects. And so in his Edicts the emperor says nothing of the fundamental tenets of the Faith—of the Four sacred Truths, of the Chain of Causality, of the Noble Eight-fold Path, of Nirvāṇa and the like. In the Bhabra Edict he proclaims his respect for the Buddhist Triad : the Buddha, the Law and the Order, and he commends for meditation certain sayings in the scriptures of the Buddha himself, but the *dharma* on which he constantly lays stress is not the *dharma* peculiar to Buddhism ; it is a Law of Piety promulgated by himself, and, though wholly consistent with the tenets of Buddhism, is hardly more distinctive of it than of Jainism or Brāhmanism or other Indian creeds. Its main principles were purely ethical :—truth and purity ; moderation and restraint ; respect for the sanctity of life ; obedience to parents and elders ; honour to teachers ; liberality to relatives and friends, Brāhmans and ascetics ; kindness and consideration for servants and slaves ; and, last but not least, religious toleration. In proclaiming these simple sound principles of behaviour, ethic and morality, Aśoka hoped to make Buddhism a more vital force in society, to provide a common ground on which its warring sects could meet and be reconciled, and to attract within its fold men of alien races and creeds. And it was in pursuance of these hopes that he set about the active propagation of his *dharma*, not only within his empire, but beyond its borders. Nothing, however, that he did in this direction—neither his ordinances nor his precepts, nor his lavish benefactions and foundations, nor his missionary activities, nor his own indefatigable zeal and example—was destined to have such a revolutionary effect upon Buddhism as the one act by which he gave a portion of the body-relics of the Buddha to every town of importance in his realm, and ordered the erection of stūpas fit for their reception. According to the Avadāna, the number of these stūpas was 84,000. This no doubt is an exaggeration ; but it involves no exaggeration of the prodigious effect on the Saṅgha and its doctrines produced by Aśoka's royal gifts. Relic-worship is an age-old, world-wide superstition, but among the Buddhists of India it forthwith acquired a significance and importance unparalleled in any other sect or country. In the third century B.C. the day of the icon had not arrived ; the Buddha was, to all intents and purposes, a divinity, but there were as yet no images or pictures of him to which the prayers and devotions of the faithful could be directed. They were offered, therefore, to the newly-gifted relics, which became the centre and focus of liturgical worship. Like all such relics, they were believed to be invested with miraculous properties, but their virtue went deeper than this ; as part of the body of the Blessed One, they helped to bring him from the unimaginable back to earth, strengthened the belief of the faithful in him as a very-present power in their lives, and awakened in them a spirit of

His distribution of Buddha's body-relics, and the effect produced on Buddhism

personal allegiance and love that few of them, probably, had experienced before. This was the first and immediate result of Aśoka's precious gifts. A second followed when worship was extended to the relics of the lesser lights of the Buddhist Church : to those of the Buddha's companions, Śāriputra and Mahāmogalāna, and even to teachers and missionaries of much later times like Kāśyapagotra, Madhyama and the others whose remains, as we shall presently see, were enshrined in Stūpa 2 at Sāñchī. A still further stage was reached when stūpas were erected, not for the enshrining of relics, but simply as memorials to commemorate some specially holy spot. The last stage—and this was perhaps the most wide-reaching development of all—was when worship was transferred from the relics to the stūpa itself, which henceforth became the most outstanding and ubiquitous emblem of the Faith. To build or create a stūpa of any shape or form or size came to be regarded as a work of religious merit, which brought its author a step nearer his goal of salvation. Hence arose on every hand myriads of these monuments. Some were imposing edifices of brick or stone standing in the open, like the Great Stūpa at Sāñchī, with a crowd of smaller stūpas of varying heights set round about them ; others were placed in the apses of chapels, where they could be worshipped under cover. But stūpa-worship went further than this. Stūpas, big and small, in endless repetition, were chiselled in relief or painted in colours on gateways, railings and the walls of chapels ; and later on—but this was not until mediæval times—miniature effigies of them were stamped on clay or plaster, and buried by scores and hundreds in the cores of larger structures. Before the beginning of the Christian era the stūpa had become the nucleus of every saṅghārāma in the land, and was regarded as the outward and visible manifestation of Buddhism.

Growth of stūpa-worship

It would be interesting to follow up the history of the stūpa-cult still further and show how it inevitably led to image-worship, but I have already digressed long enough What I wished to point out and what I hope will now be clear to the reader, is that the whole remarkable development of the stūpa-cult, which produced such wide-reaching and revolutionary changes in the Church, is to be traced back directly to the relic-stūpas erected by Aśoka, that before his time there was no cult-worship among the Buddhists either of relics or of stūpas, and that the Great Stūpa at Sāñchī cannot, therefore, be referred back to an earlier date. Let it be added here, in parenthesis, that not only the stūpas of Aśoka, but his memorial and edict pillars also came to be invested with a peculiar sanctity of their own and to serve, in a lesser degree, as accepted emblems of the Faith. They were the prototypes for the later pillars 25, 26, 34 and 35 at Sāñchī itself, and for innumerable other pillars of a like kind erected on other sites ; and, as we shall presently see, they are a conspicuous feature among the reliefs of the railings and gateways.

The original brick stūpa mutilated probably by Pushyamitra

To return, however, to the Great Stūpa. From my examination of its core it was evident that the original structure of burnt brick had suffered great damage before the outer casing was added to it, and, moreover, that this damage could not have been due to mere weathering, but must have been wantonly inflicted. Who the author of it was, is not known for certain, but it may safely be inferred that it took place sometime after the downfall of the Mauryas, though necessarily before the addition of the outer envelope; it is a plausible conjecture, therefore, that it was done by the order of Pushyamitra, the first of the Śuṅga kings, who was notorious for his hostility to the Buddhists and his vindictive acts of vandalism in destroying their sacred monuments.[1] Unfortunately, the wrecking of the stūpa was so thorough, that it is impossible now to determine precisely

Its dimensions and form

its original design. There can be little doubt, however, that it was of about the same size as the Stūpa of Aśoka at Sārnāth,[2] *i.e.*, about 60 feet in diameter at the base including the raised terrace, and, like that stūpa, approximately hemispherical in shape, with a raised terrace surrounding its base and a crowning pinnacle (*harmikā*)[3], surmounted by one or more umbrellas (*chattrāvalī*), within a small square railing, similar to the monolithic one on the Sārnāth Stūpa.[4] There is also little doubt that it would be encompassed by a processional path (*pradakshiṇa-patha*) and circular railing on the ground level, and by another smaller railing on the berm of the terrace. Several pieces of an umbrella of Mauryan date were found by me in the debris near the stūpa, and may be presumed to have belonged to the crowning pinnacle (Pl. 104 *a*)[5]. Like the fragmentary umbrella of the same age found at Aśoka's Stūpa at Sārnāth, they are made of sandstone from the quarries of Chunar[6] near Benares, of which the Edict Pillar is also made, and, like that umbrella, are plain and highly polished on the outside but relieved on the inside by four concentric bands of most delicately defined ribs, the cutting of which displays the same exquisite precision that characterises all the known stonework of Aśoka's reign, and which has

Its balustrades presumably of wood

probably never been surpassed in the stone carving of any country. The balustrades about the base and raised terrace were presumably of wood, since all vestiges of them have perished. In Aśoka's time the use of stone for any purpose other than rough hammer-dressed masonry was rare, and, so far as railings are concerned, the only specimen of that age in stone that we possess is the small monolithic rail alluded to above, which crowned Aśoka's Stūpa at Sārnāth. Ordinarily, the railings around his monuments were no doubt of wood, and we shall see presently how the technique of the older wooden railings was copied with scrupulous but mistaken fidelity in the later railings of stone. Stone, be it remarked, came into more general use in the second century B.C.—perhaps as a result of the conquest of the Panjāb by the Bactrian Greeks and the extension of their influence to Hindustān and Central India. Let it be added here that railings were the unvarying concomitants of all early stūpas, but they were by no means restricted to this class of cult object. They were erected around trees, pillars, shrines and other objects of a sacred character and served at once to protect them and proclaim their sanctity. The

[1] Pushyamitra is said to have offered a hundred *dīnāras* for the head of every Buddhist monk. *Cf. Divyāvadāna*, pp. 433-4. *C. H. I.*, I, p. 519.

[2] *Cf. A. S. R.*, 1907-8, Pl. XVIII *b*, the sectional drawing on which well illustrates how these monuments were enlarged from time to time.

[3] In order to avoid the multiplication of technical terms, the word *harmikā* is used here and elsewhere to signify the small pinnacle on the summit of the dome which served as a base for the crowning umbrella, whether the railing around it was free-standing or, as in later times, engaged in its sides. As reconstructed in Śuṅga times, the *harmikā* of the Great Stūpa took the form of a relic-coffer (*cf.* p. 32 *infra*).

[4] The railing referred to, which originally surmounted the dome of Aśoka's Stūpa, was subsequently thrown down and broken and then installed in the nearby chapel of the Main Shrine.

[5] *Cf.* also *A. S. R.*, Pt. I, 1912-13, Pl. VIII *a*.

[6] On the right bank of the Ganges between Mirzapur and Benares.

significance of the railing in such cases followed as a natural sequence on their use for utilitarian purposes and derived no doubt from times long before the Buddha. But, though they were often employed in this way (and sometimes, indeed, without any practical *raison d' être* whatever) to distinguish sacred objects, they continued nevertheless in common use for secular purposes, as the reliefs on the gateways abundantly show, and hence their presence can never be taken as necessarily indicative of an object's sanctity.

Built, like all other stūpas of Aśoka, to enshrine relics of the Buddha

From the fact that he failed to find any relics in the stūpa, Gen. Cunningham concluded that it had been dedicated, not to Gautama Buddha, but to Ādi-Buddha—the primeval Buddha from whom all other Buddhas emanated. Incidentally, also, he was led to advance the theory that the stūpa was in existence "not long after the period of the Second Synod", and that the existing massive stone balustrade was erected in the reign of Aśoka. These theories have no foundation in fact. We have seen that the original stūpa dates from the reign of Aśoka, and that at that time stūpas were erected for the purpose only of enshrining corporeal relics, not as cenotaphs or memorials. It is natural, therefore, to conclude that this was one of the numerous relic stūpas of which Aśoka was the author. If my surmise is correct that Pushyamitra, the Śuṅga, wrecked this stūpa and the saṅghārāma, the one thing above all others that he would have been most likely to do, was to destroy the relics. In early stūpas, the relic-chamber was generally set either in the foundations or in the heart of the dome. This was not, however, an invariable rule, and it may well have been that the relic-chamber in this example was at the top of the dome, where also it seems to have been placed after the stone envelope had been added.[1] But, wherever it may have been, the wreckers would have experienced little difficulty in breaking through the brickwork, which was laid only in mud, and getting at the relics.

Pillar of Aśoka

At a distance of about 50 feet from the South Gateway of his stūpa the Emperor Aśoka set up one of his magnificent pillars or *lāṭs*. It is said that many years ago this pillar was broken into pieces by a local landowner, who was endeavouring to cut up its shaft and utilize it in a sugar press. The stump, however, still remains *in situ* (Pls. 7, 106 and 107), and some broken lengths of the shaft lie alongside ; the capital and crowning lions are in the local museum. When intact, the pillar was about 42 feet in height and consisted of a round and slightly tapering monolithic shaft with bell-shaped foliate capital surmounted by a cable necking, above which was an abacus supporting the forefronts of four magnificent lions, possibly intended to typify Śākyasiṁha, the Lion of the Śākya race. The bell-shaped capital and crowning lions were a single block of stone. The abacus was adorned with four "honeysuckle" motifs, separated one from the other by pairs of geese, symbolical perhaps of the flock of the Buddha's disciples (Pl. 107 *a*). The art revealed in this remarkable piece of sculpture will be discussed in a subsequent chapter ; here we

[1] See p. 32 *infra*.

need remark only that in point of both style and technique the four lions exhibit a very close affinity to those on the Aśoka pillar at Sārnāth, though their modelling is not up to the same high standard, but the design of the crowning ornament differs from that of the Sārnāth example in that the latter supported a "Wheel of the Law" (*dharmacakra*) rising above the heads of the four lions, whereas at Sāñchī there was no such emblem.[1] Lions, capital and shaft are finished and polished to the same glass-like lustre that distinguished all the carved stonework of Aśoka's time.

The fine, hard-grained, buff-grey sandstone of which this pillar is made, came from the same Chunar quarry that produced the umbrella described above, and it says not a little for the skill of Aśoka's engineers that they were capable of transporting a block of stone over forty feet in length and weighing almost as many tons a distance of some five hundred miles. No doubt, they availed themselves of water transport, using rafts during the rainy season up the Ganges and Jumna and Betwā rivers, the last of which flows but a mile away from Sāñchī, but, even so, the task of quarrying so ponderous a mass, of shifting it on and off the rafts, and of hoisting it up the steep hill-side at Sāñchī was one which any engineer to-day might well be proud to accomplish.

Foundations of the pillar, and succession of later floors

At the time when this pillar and stūpa were set up by Aśoka, the floor of the levelled area on which they stand was substantially lower than it now is, or than it was when the existing stone railing was erected around the Great Stūpa. This was made evident when the base of the pillar was opened up by the writer, and was confirmed further by the disclosures of certain trial trenches and pits sunk at various points in this area. The bottom of the pillar, it was found, rested directly on the bed-rock and, like other pillars of Aśoka, was circular and hammer-dressed to a height of eight feet, above which it was chiselled and polished. The rough base was imbedded in a packing of heavy stones retained in position by massive walls, and on the top of these retaining walls and packing was spread a layer of earth and small debris, and over it a floor of *bajrī* (broken brick) six inches in thickness, which met the pillar at the dividing line between the rough-dressed base and polished section of the shaft above. Thus, there could be no question that this *bajrī* floor was laid very soon, perhaps immediately, after the erection of the pillar—at the time, that is to say, when the floor level corresponded with this line of demarcation between the rough and polished sections of the shaft. It was also found that the *bajrī* floor extended over the whole of the area round about the stūpa; and, furthermore, that it was the earliest floor of which any traces existed. Beneath it there was nothing but a layer of earth and vast numbers of heavy rubble stones, which had been used by the Maurya builders to fill the depressions and cavities in the irregular surface of the rock, and thus bring it up to a uniform level.

[1] It has often been asserted that the Sāñchī capital, like the Sārnāth one, supported a *dharmacakra*. That it did not do so is conclusively proved by the careful finish of the small block of stone in the centre between the four lions.

Above the *bajrī* floor, on the other hand, there was a succession of later floors separated by layers of debris, which furnished clear testimony to the continued occupation of the site during the period following Aśoka. The relative positions of these floors with reference to the early *bajrī* floor and the Aśoka pillar will be clear to the reader from the section reproduced in Pl. 7 *a*. First came a layer of debris, 4 to 5 inches in thickness, covered with a thin floor of *bajrī* in clay;[1] then, about 13 inches more of debris and another floor of pounded brick in lime; above this, another layer of debris, 14 to 15 inches in thickness, followed by yet another floor of *bajrī* overlaid with lime plaster; then more debris consisting of small stones in mud; and, last of all, a stone pavement of large thin slabs, which seems to have extended over the whole of this area around the Great Stūpa. Now, there is no gainsaying the fact that the earliest of these floors was laid on a very poor foundation of earth and debris, and it is highly probable that it soon became necessary to level up subsidences in it and lay the next floor, but no such subsidences will explain the steady accumulation of debris that subsequently took place between the laying of the several later floors. Any one familiar with the excavation of Buddhist sites in India will not need to be told that such accumulations came about very slowly and gradually. In this case, it is hardly possible that they could have been formed, and the several floors laid, in less than a century. The process, indeed, may have lasted longer than that; but, assuming that the pillar was erected about 254 B.C., it becomes evident from this stratigraphical evidence that the laying of the last stone pavement and the erection of the great stone railing, which is contemporary with it, can hardly be referred to an earlier date than the middle of the second century B.C.

The Edict later than the pillar

Before leaving the Aśoka pillar it remains to add a few words about the Edict engraved on its face. The contents of this Edict and the palæography of the writing are discussed by Mr. N. G. Majumdar in a later chapter.[2] Here I wish only to remark on the slovenly character of the engraving. Not only is the lettering singularly poor, but the lines are not even horizontal. Had the pillar been erected for the purpose of engraving this Edict upon it, we may be sure that the sculptor responsible for the pillar itself and its superb capital would have seen to it that the lettering of the inscription was more worthy. What evidently happened in this, as in some other cases, was that the pillar was erected by Aśoka either as a memorial to mark some holy spot of which nothing is now known, or perhaps as a memorial to the Lion of the Śākyas. Then, some time afterwards, the Edict concerning schism in the Saṅgha was issued, and orders were given for it to be engraved on the pillars at Sāñchī, Sārnāth and Kauśāmbī (where there are copies of the same Edict) and possibly on other pillars or rocks which have not survived. At the end of the Sahasrām Rock-Edict and of the seventh Pillar Edict it is expressly ordered that the Edicts are to be engraved "on rocks or on stone pillars, wherever such exist," and these passages have been interpreted as implying that the pillars referred to had been set up before Aśoka's time.[3]

[1] In the section on Pl. 7 *a*, the *bajrī* is, by a slight error, described as red concrete.

[2] *Cf.* pp. 283-7 *infra*.

[3] *E.g.*, *C. H. I.*, I, p. 501.

This interpretation does not seem to be warranted. In his Seventh Edict the emperor speaks of the *dharma-stambhas* that he had himself erected, evidently alluding to the pillars bearing the six previous *dharma*-Edicts.[1] Of these pillars, six still exist, namely, the Delhi-Toprā and Delhi-Mirāth pillars, the Lauriyā-Ararāj and Lauriyā-Nandangarh pillars, the Rāmpurvā pillar and the Allāhābād-Kosam pillar. We are safe, therefore, in assigning these six pillars to Aśoka, and to these may be added the Rummindei and Nigālī Sāgar pillars, both of which bear inscriptions stating that they were erected by Aśoka (*Devānāṁpriya Priyadarśin*)—the one to commemorate the birthplace of the Buddha Śākyamuni, the other in honour of the former Buddha Kanakamuni (Konākamana). Apart, therefore, from the testimony of the Chinese pilgrims, Fa Hien and Hiuen Thsang, both of whom tell us that Aśoka set up the still existing pillar at Sāṅkāśya (Sankissa) besides numerous other pillars of a like kind that have since perished, we can definitely assign to Aśoka eight out of the thirteen pillars which have survived. But all these thirteen, including the one we are discussing at Sāñchī, are so remarkably alike that we could not know the author of one without knowing the author of them all. It is not merely that they bear a superficial resemblance to one another; that their shafts are all circular and monolithic, and approximately of the same height and diameter; and that they all have the same bell-capital and cable-necking. The likeness goes further than this. All that have been exposed to view have the same length (about 8 feet) of rough circular base; the shafts have the same slight taper; the dressing and polishing of the surface are identical; and the details of the bell-capitals and neckings are all to one pattern. Naturally, the crowning ornaments are varied, and there is considerable disparity in their style, but the latter was inevitable, where so many hands—some Yavana and some Indian—were employed, and it does not affect the question of the homogeneity and common authorship of these pillars.

Date of pillar and Edict

So far, then, as the Sāñchī pillar is concerned, the only possible conclusion to be drawn is that it was erected by Aśoka some years before the Edict was engraved upon it. Precisely how long before, can only be surmised, but, for reasons that will appear later, it seems probable that this and the Sārnāth pillar were the two earliest monuments of their kind to be erected, and since we know that the inscribed Rummindei and Nigālī Sāgar pillars date from the 20th year after Aśoka's coronation (*abhisheka*), it follows that the Sāñchī pillar must be ascribed to some time prior to that date. On the other hand, the Edict engraved on it was probably issued some time after the Third Council at Pāṭaliputra, when questions of schism in the Church, with which the Edict deals, were discussed.[2] Assuming, then, that the year of Aśoka's coronation was 270 B.C.[3]—the date commonly accepted for it—we shall probably not be far wrong, if we conclude that the

[1] *Cf. C. I. I.*, I, p. 134, note 11, and Bühler, *Z. D. M. G.*, 46, 90.

[2] *Cf.* pp. 286-7 *infra.*

[3] The date of the coronation is closely connected with the identity of the Alikasudara or Alikyashudala of the Thirteenth Rock-Edict. If the king referred to was Alexander of Epirus (272-258 B.C.), then the coronation could not have been later than B.C. 270; on the other hand, if Alexander of Corinth (B.C. 252-244) is meant, then the coronation may have been as late as 264 B.C. *Cf. C. I. I.*, I, XXX-XXXI; Beloch, *Griechische Geschichte*, Vol. 3, part 2, p. 105; *C. H. I.*, I, p. 502. The view of the writer is that Alexander of Epirus was referred to.

stūpa was erected about 255 B.C., and the pillar, say, in the following year; and that the Edict was engraved on the latter some ten years later.

Reconstruction of Great Stūpa during the Śuṅga period

To return, however, to the Great Stūpa. The additions next made to it were tantamount almost to a complete reconstruction. These were effected under one of the Śuṅga kings, about the middle of the second century B.C. They comprised the existing envelope of stone, in which the whole body of the original brick stūpa was encased; the lofty stone terrace and two flights of stairs at its base; the stone flagging of the procession path; the three stone balustrades—in place of the older-fashioned ones of wood—one around the ground-level procession path, a second around the terrace berm, and a third on the top of the dome; and, lastly, the *harmikā* and umbrellas (*chattrāvalī*) which crowned the whole. Under which particular king this transformation took place, we do not know. All that can be said, is that it could not have been during the reign of the anti-Buddhist Pushyamitra (*circ.* 184-148 B.C.); nor, for palæographic reasons, can it be brought down much later than the middle of the second century. It seems probable, therefore, that it took place during the reign of Pushyamitra's son, Agnimitra, or of the latter's immediate successor, Vasujyeshṭha.

The dome and terrace

By the enlargement of the dome (*aṇḍa*) the diameter of the structure was increased to over 120 ft. and its height to about 54 ft., exclusive of the crowning rail and umbrella. This enlargement was carried out by the simple and natural method of building a thick encircling wall of stone at a given distance from the original edifice and, as the wall rose course by course, filling in the interval between the two with heavy rubble stone. Precisely the same process was adopted, as we shall presently see, in the case of the Pillared Hall 40. The stone used for the new dome was the dark purple-grey local sandstone. The masonry courses, which are of uneven width and thickness, were roughly hammer-dressed, not chiselled, and were laid horizontally—not, as Capt. J. D. Cunningham[1] and Fergusson[2] have shown them, sloping down towards the centre of the dome. The lofty plinth around the base of this enlarged dome, which served as a second procession path as well as a buttress to withstand the outward pressure of the dome, has an average height of 15 ft. 6 in., with an average projection of 5 ft. 9 in. at the foot of the dome, and a batter of 1 in 5 on its outer side. Some writers[3] have described the Great Stūpa as a dome resting on a lofty plinth, as if the plinth had been constructed before the dome was raised above it. This description is misleading. The dome was first built in its entirety, with its foundations carried down to bed-rock, and the terrace was then added to it; but there was no masonry bond between the two, and the foundations of the terrace were carried down only a few feet below the surface, not to bed-rock. The terrace, however, was not an afterthought, as might seem to be implied by the peculiarity of the construction. This is clear from the fact that the plinths around the Second and Third Stūpas are built in

[1] *J. A. S. B.*, 1847 (XVI), Pl. XXVII.

[2] *History of Indian and Eastern Architecture* (1910), I, p. 69, fig. 14.

[3] *E.g.*, Fergusson, *op. cit.*, p. 70.

identically the same fashion, and from the fact also, which I ascertained by practical examination, that the concrete facing, from 2 to 5 in. in thickness, with which the dome and terrace were finished off, does not extend over the lower part of the dome behind the encompassing berm. Accordingly, we must conclude that the terrace was designed at the same time as the envelope to the dome, and that it was built on structurally unsound principles for the simple reason that the architects knew no better.

Stairway

The stairway (*sopāna*) by which the berm is ascended is on the south side of the stūpa and is constructed of the same rough masonry as the rest of the terrace. It comprises two flights of steps, ascending from the south-east and south-west quadrants, respectively, and meeting in a small landing at the top. In each flight there are 25[1] steps, with treads about 17 in. broad at the middle and risers about 7 in. high. On the outer face of the landing is a shallow projection directly opposite the main entrance to the stūpa, which was invariably on the south. It will be observed, however, from Pl. 4 that this entrance did not face due south, but about 15 degrees west of south. Probably this aberration was due to the position of the Aśoka pillar—a fixture of a kind that could not easily be shifted. As we have seen, this pillar stood about 50 ft. in front of the south entrance of the original brick stūpa of Aśoka, and, had the enlarged stūpa been built on the same axis as the original one, the pillar would have stood right in the middle of the south entrance-way, where it must inevitably have caused inconvenience to the worshippers passing in and out. To avoid this difficulty, the axis of the restored stūpa seems to have been shifted round about 15 degrees, thus leaving the pillar to stand clear of the new constructions in the angle of the balustrade. If, as I suppose, this alteration of the axis was due to the awkward position of the pillar, it seems to indicate that the extensions to the gateways, as they now exist, though admittedly later than the ground balustrade, were nevertheless part and parcel of the same design ; for, unless this had been so, it would not have been necessary to deviate so far from the true south.

Orientation of south entrance

Finishing plaster

The thick layer of concrete alluded to above, which was laid over the masonry of both dome and terrace, was doubtless finished off with a coating of finer plaster, which has since perished, and—if we may use the sculptures on the gateways to fill in the details of our picture—was probably embellished by swags or garlands in relief. Extensive patches of this concrete still adhere to the face of the stonework on three sides of the dome, but on the fourth side it was broken away when the stūpa was opened by Capt. Johnson in 1822. The concrete is made of a coarsish, ungraded aggregate of broken stone and brick mixed with lime.

Harmikā balustrade and crowning umbrella

When the body of the stūpa was complete, the first adjunct to be added to it was the indispensable umbrella (*chattra*) and surrounding balustrade (*vedikā*) on the summit.

[1] The plan on Pl. 4 erroneously shows 36 steps in each flight.

Regarding both these features a notable mistake was made by Cunningham[1] and perpetuated by later investigators, including Maisey[2] and Fergusson. According to Cunningham, the *harmikā* in the centre was a square pedestal adorned with a balustrade engaged in its sides, and surmounted by a heavy corbelled cornice and toothed battlement. In restoring the *harmikā* thus, Cunningham appears to have been led astray by the representations of stūpas of a later age figured among the gateway reliefs, and to have failed to give due consideration to the actual remains on the spot or to the evidence of the sculptures more nearly contemporary with the Great Stūpa. One of the latter is a small railing pillar belonging to the Third Stūpa, on which is carved in low relief a small but well-delineated stūpa surmounted by nothing more than a square railing standing free and detached, with an umbrella in its centre and a staff to either side from which garlands are suspended.[3] That such square, detached railings were the crowning feature of the early stūpas at Sāñchī, is now conclusively demonstrated by the remains I recovered at each of the three principal monuments. In the case of the Great Stūpa, the actual pieces of the *harmikā* balustrade that I was able to assemble numbered over seventy,[4] and were amply sufficient to enable me to restore it with confidence. The stone of which it was made was the fine, grey-white sandstone of Nāgourī,[5] which was chisel-dressed and fitted with more than usual accuracy. In design and construction it resembled other balustrades of the same period. It consisted, that is to say, of a series of upright posts (*stambha*) spaced at even intervals, with horizontal cross-bars (*sūci*) between them, and a coping (*ushṇīsha*) over the tops of the posts, to hold the whole together (Pl. 7 *d*). The posts are 9 ft. 11 in. in height, including about 2 ft. 6 in. of hammer-dressed base, which was imbedded in the masonry of the stūpa top ; the coping stones are rounded above and provided with sloping instead of vertical joints—a relic of the times when these balustrades were made of wood. From the plan of the Great Stūpa on Pl. 4 and from Pl. 7 *d*, where details of its plan and elevation are given, it will be seen that this *harmikā* balustrade was arranged in a square, measuring 21 ft. 6 in. on each side and 30 ft. 1 in. on the diagonal. The size of the square can be precisely determined by the coping stones, of which there were not less than three on each side, *viz.*, a centre one extending over three intercolumniations, and a corner one on each side of it extending over two, thus providing for seven intercolumniations and eight posts on each side. Had there been more than one length of coping stone between the two corner coping stones, it would have meant adding three more intercolumniations on each side, and, seeing that the flat top of the stūpa has a diameter of only about 38 ft., this would have brought the corners of the square too close to its edge and made the railing out of proportion to the rest of the structure.

From Pl. 7 *d* it will be observed that this balustrade is unrelieved by any carving and that even the arrises of the posts are not bevelled, as they are in the ground

[1] *The Bhilsa Topes*, p. 185 and Pl. VIII ; *C. S. R.*, Vol. X, pp. 56-57.

[2] *Sánchi and its Remains*, Pl. II.

[3] *Cf.* p. 42 *infra* and Pl. 93 *i* ; *A. S. R.*, 1912-13, Pt. I, Pl. IX *b*.

[4] *Cf. A. S. R.*, 1913-14, p. 14, and Marshall, *A Guide to Sāñchī*, p. 33, note 1.

[5] *Cf.* p. 11 above.

balustrade. This severe plainness calls to mind the monolithic balustrade which crowned the stūpa of Aśoka at Sārnāth. There may, indeed, have been a connexion between the two ; for nothing is more likely than that the original balustrade on Aśoka's Stūpa at Sāñchī was of the same pattern as the one at Sārnāth, though executed perhaps in wood instead of stone, and it is equally likely that this older pattern was copied by the restorer. It remains to add that four donative inscriptions in the early Brāhmī character (Nos. 607-610) are engraved on this balustrade, showing that, as in the case of other balustrades, its various members, posts, cross-bars and coping stones were the gifts of different donors.

Relic-coffer on summit of dome, and nature of relics

As to the umbrella (*chattra*) which stood within this square railing, two pieces of it are alleged to have been seen by Cunningham and Maisey, one near the top of the dome, the other at the foot of the breach which then existed in the south-west side of the stūpa. Fortunately, both these pieces are still preserved and prove to be parts, not of an umbrella at all, but of the lid of a massive stone relic-coffer which stood, crowned by an umbrella, on the summit of the dome. It was this relic-coffer, no doubt, which Capt. Fell saw in 1819 and which he described as then being split in pieces. The lid is illustrated on Pl. 4. It is of local Sāñchī stone, 5 ft. 7 in. in diameter and 1 ft. 8 in. high, concave on the underside and provided with a rim around its under edge and with a square mortise hole on the top, into which the umbrella shaft (*yashṭi*) was presumably inserted. Such a ponderous stone lid, fitted securely on to a still more ponderous box, was well calculated to support an umbrella, even though the latter was of stone. This relic-coffer, which is not of Maurya workmanship, was no doubt contemporary with the outer stone envelope. What relics it contained can only be surmised, but *prima facie* it seems hardly likely that any relics other than those of the Buddha himself would have been preserved in so important a monument. The Sāñchī Stūpa, be it remembered, was *facile princeps* among all the stūpas in the neighbourhood of Vidiśā, and Vidiśā itself was the family home of the Śuṅga dynasty and for long the capital of their kingdom. Whichever Śuṅga king, therefore, it may have been who rebuilt and enlarged this stūpa, we may be sure that he would have done his best to secure for it the most treasured relics he could find ; and from among all the relic stūpas of Aśoka which were accessible to the Śuṅga kings, it could not have been difficult to obtain some relics of the Blessed One.

The ground balustrade

Following the crowning pinnacle and its balustrade, the next additions to be made to the stūpa were the massive balustrade on the ground level (Pl. 7 *a* and *e*), the pavement of the procession path which this balustrade enclosed, and a smaller balustrade on the outer edge of the double stairway and of the terrace berm. The ground balustrade is the biggest and most massively built of all the stūpa balustrades known to us, and it looks all the more massive because it is destitute of any kind of ornamentation. In this respect it resembles the smaller *harmikā* balustrade on the summit, but it differs from the latter in that both uprights and cross-bars are wider in proportion to their length and that the arrises of the uprights are bevelled off. The stone of which it is built comes from the neighbouring quarries of Nāgourī, and is buff to pinkish in colour, sometimes running to grey or light purple. The height of the balustrade above ground averages 10 ft. 7 in., the uprights 8 ft. 4 in. and the coping 2 ft. 3 in.[1] It is necessary to give these measurements in averages, because they are far from being strictly uniform. Indeed, the variation is sometimes so great as to be noticeable to the eye.

In spite of its great weight, the foundations for this ground balustrade were very poor. They consisted of nothing more than three small slabs of stone—in some cases reduced to two or even to one—laid either in the debris or on one of the old floors underneath the base of the uprights (see Pl. 7 *a* and *e*); of boulders or metalling under these slabs, or of packing at their sides, there was none. With such defective foundations, one cannot be surprised that this and other balustrades built on the same principles subsided here and there and eventually collapsed. The wonder is that any part of them managed to survive the centuries *in situ*.

In the drawing of this balustrade published by Maisey and Cunningham[2] the joints of the coping are wrongly shown as vertical instead of slanting. The mistake is a small one, but not altogether unimportant, since the slanting joint indicates, not only that the balustrades were imitated from older prototypes of wood, but that the masons engaged on them were still unused to the new material in which they were working, and it thus supports the inference, which we drew on other grounds, that the balustrades around the original stūpa erected by Aśoka in the preceding century were of wood.[3]

If the reader will turn to Pl. 4 he will observe that there are four entrances dividing the ground balustrade into four quadrants. These four entrances follow the plan of the ordinary city gateways of the period, with a sort of barbican in front provided with a second gateway at right angles to the inner one. Later on, as we shall presently see, an ornamental arch or *toraṇa*, such as was also found at city gates, was added parallel to the inner entrance and with it an extra length of balustrade, thus forming a second barbican, as it were, outside the first. In each quadrant, excluding the later additions at the approaches, there are 30 uprights or pillars, making 120 in all. Of these, 106 are original and 14 restored, the latter being differentiated in the plan from the former by being shown in outline only. Around the northern half of the stūpa, the balustrade is set at a distance of about 9 ft. 6 in. from the base of the terrace, and in correspondence with it follows a semi-circular plan; around the southern half, owing to the presence of the double flight of steps, its plan is elliptical, the deviation from the circle at the south entrance being approximately 5 ft., with the result that the width of the procession path between the balustrade and the foot of the stairs is only about 2 ft. 6 in. less than in the northern quadrants.

[1] The full length of the uprights averages about 10 ft. 4 in., but 2 ft. of this at the base is hammer-dressed and buried in the ground; their width is 2 ft. ¾ in., which is the same as that of the cross-bars, and their thickness 1 ft. 10 in. The thickness of the coping is about 2 in. more than that of the uprights; of the cross-bars it averages 9 in. at the middle.

[2] *Sánchi and its Remains*, Pls. II and III; *The Bhilsa Topes*, Pls. VIII and IX.

[3] Vertical joints in copings were to be introduced at no very distant date. As far as I am aware, they are found in all railings of Kushān date.

Inscriptions on Ground Balustrade

Most of the pillars, cross-bars and coping stones of this balustrade bear votive inscriptions recording the names of the donors who presented them, mostly mendicant monks or nuns (*bhikshu* or *bhikshuṇī*) but many also laymen. To those not familiar with the practices of Buddhism it may seem strange that monks and nuns should have been able to make these gifts, seeing that by the rules of the Order they were precluded from possessing money or property of any kind other than a few simple articles of apparel and furniture, such as an alms-bowl, razor, needle and water strainer. We must remember, however, that monks and nuns could at any time give up the monastic life and return to the world, if they wished, and, though on entering the Order they nominally relinquished all rights over their property, which was regarded as "given away", in practice their families might look after it during their absence and restore it on their return. And in such cases they could, under the rules of the Order, have certain things which it was lawful for them to possess, made and paid for out of their own estate.[1] This being so, it may be presumed that a monk or nun might pay from the same source for a gift meant for the common good of the Saṅgha, though he or she might have to avoid actually handling the money.[2]

Time required for erection of balustrade

From the multiplicity of these *ex-voto* gifts Fergusson computed that the balustrade must have taken at least a century to complete. This computation is wholly excessive and at variance with the palæographic evidence of the *ex-voto* inscriptions themselves. At the time when the balustrade was erected in the second century B.C., there must have been multitudes of good Buddhists anxious to help on the work—lay-worshippers and other townsfolk from Vidiśā, monks and nuns from Sāñchī and the neighbouring monasteries of Ākara, pilgrims from further afield—most of whom would be eager to contribute what they could to the restoration of the Great Stūpa. We need not, therefore, presume any difficulty or delay over the getting together of donations for this enterprise; nor need we presume that there would be any shortage of skilled masons; for, though the cutting of stone on a large scale was a new craft at Sāñchī in the second century B.C., the reconstruction of the body of the Great Stūpa, by whomsoever it was done, must have involved the bringing together or training of a large number of masons, and, when the body of the stūpa was finished, these would have been available for work upon the balustrade. All things considered, therefore, and in the light of my own personal experience in quarrying and restoring a vast amount of stonework at this site, I see no reason to suppose that the construction of this balustrade need have taken more than five or six years, notwithstanding that the Buddhists were notoriously slow builders. Under modern conditions, it could be done in a quarter of that time.

---

[1] *Cf.* Oldenberg, *Buddha*, trans. by W. Hoey, p. 355. Similarly, though a wife was only a "sister" to a monk, so long as he was in the homeless state, she might become his wife again on his return to the world. *Suttavibhaṅga*, Pār. I, 5 and 8; *Mahāvagga*, I, 8, 78.

[2] In spite of the strictest prohibitions against monks or nuns possessing or handling money, many finds of coins—sometimes in large numbers—have been made beneath the floors of monastic cells and in other convenient hiding places in ancient Buddhist monasteries in India.

Procession Path

Simultaneously with the erection of this balustrade, or very soon after its completion, the paving of the procession path (*pradakshiṇa-patha*) inside it was also laid. Over the greater part of its circuit the width of this path was, as already stated, approximately 9 ft. 6 in., increasing to about 12 ft. 9 in. at the foot of the stairways and thence narrowing again towards the southern entrance. This space was spanned throughout by single slabs of stone stretching from side to side of the passage, most of which appear from the inscriptions engraved on them[1] to have been the gifts of separate donors. The slabs are wedge-shaped and average about 3 in. in thickness by about 3 ft. 7 in. in width on the inner side and 3 ft. 9 in. on the outer side. In the north-east quadrant this pavement is almost intact; in the other three quadrants it has survived in patches only, and in the south-west quadrant not a little of it was destroyed when a modern buttress was erected in the nineties of last century to support the bulging wall of the terrace.

Terrace and stairway balustrades

The berm and stairway balustrades (Pls. 7 *b* and *c* and 8) are relatively small and distinguished from the other balustrades by the medallions and other reliefs which adorn their upright pillars, as well as by their more refined treatment in general. In the case of the *harmikā* and ground balustrades, the bases of the uprights were imbedded in the masonry of the stūpa or in the ground, but as this method could not be applied to the uprights of the balustrades at the outer edge of the stairs and terrace, the latter were provided with heavy kerbstones, into which the uprights were fitted by means of a mortise-and-tenon joint. Seen from the outside, these kerbstones on the stairways have the appearance of "strings", but in reality they are unconnected with the treads, being built independently into the masonry wall at their side in the manner shown in Pl. 8 *c*. Each of the kerbstones is between 9 and 10 in. in thickness and from 5 ft. 3 in. to 7 ft. 7 in. in length.[2] The newel-posts at the foot of the stairs are 3 ft. 10 in. high by 8 in. wide and 9¼ in. across the face; the other balusters are of the same width but 2 ft. 5 in. high; and the copings 10½ in. high by 7¾ in. thick. The newel-posts, which were imbedded in the ground and at the same time mortised to the end of the lowest kerbstones, are distinguished from the other balusters by the more elaborate carvings on three of their faces (Pl. 8 *d* and *e*). The rest of the stairway balusters are adorned, on their outer face only, with one complete and two half discs having lotus or other floral or animal designs sculptured in relief (Pl. 8 *c*); the plainness of their inner face is relieved at the top and bottom only by two half discs, the upper one of which frequently has an inscription engraved upon it, but, except in a single instance, is otherwise devoid of carving.

Whereas in the raking balustrades of the stairways described above there are only two cross-bars between each pair of uprights, in the horizontal balustrade on the small landing at the top of the stairs the cross-bars are three. It is the same with the

[1] *Cf.* pp. 343 *sqq. infra.*

[2] Turned upside down these raking kerbstones, which are stepped on their underside, have the appearance of toothed battlements, and for such they seem to have been mistaken by Cunningham, who restored them round the top of the *harmikā*, notwithstanding that the donative inscriptions carved upon them were thus upside down!

balustrades of the Second and Third Stūpas, and in each of these cases the transition from two to three cross-bars appears to have been effected in the manner shown in Pl. 94 *c*, an irregular and somewhat awkward space being left near the base of the juncture.

The kerbstones of the berm balustrade were not, like those of the stairways, built into the masonry, but were merely laid on its surface, the balustrade depending for its stability upon its circular shape and weight, and upon the mortise-and-tenon joints which connected its members together. All the uprights of this balustrade, except the two newel-posts at the stairway entrance, are of the same size and decorated in the same fashion as those on the landing, though, naturally, with different designs (Pls. 7 *c* and 8 *a*, *b* and *f*). The newel-posts have their outer arrises chamfered like the stairway newels, but, unlike the latter, they are sculptured on the front and outer faces only, while the back is left plain. There are no half discs at the back of the newel-posts, as there are on all the other berm uprights. The berm and stairway balustrades, let it be added, are of Nāgourī stone.

Appearance of Great Stūpa, as enlarged under the Suṅgas

Such was the Great Stūpa as restored and enlarged under one of the Śuṅga dynasts. To picture it as it then stood—in the second century before our era—is not difficult, now that it has been so extensively repaired. If we eliminate the four imposing gateways, which were to be added by the Andhras a century later, its form was the same as it is to-day. Only its colouring was different, and how different! Instead of the present sombre greys and blacks, the dome was probably glaringly white, with the swags around it perhaps picked out in colours, while the balustrades, and, later on, the gateways, were red.[1] The umbrellas on the summit may have been red or possibly gilded, as they often were in later times, but whatever touches of gilding there may have been here or there, it is certain that they could have done little to redeem the red-and-white garishness of the whole. Age, indeed, has been as kind to this stūpa as it has been to the fabrics of our own great Gothic cathedrals, now all grey and discoloured, but once covered from plinth to pinnacle in whitewash, which few probably would now care to see restored.

The four gateways: their sequence

The last of the additions to this remarkable stūpa, and its crowning glory, are the elaborate and richly carved gateways or *toraṇas*, as they are called, which front the entrances between the four quadrants of the balustrade, and constitute a most striking contrast with the massive simplicity of the structure behind them. The first of the four to be erected was the one at the south entrance, in front of the steps by which the stūpa berm was ascended, and this was followed, in chronological order, by those at the northern, eastern and western entrances. When these *toraṇas* were erected, they obviously could not be set sideways like the then existing entrances, and accordingly a short length of balustrade, of three pillars only, was added and another entrance formed at right angles to the former one. Now, an examination of these four short extensions reveals the

[1] See below, pp. 162-3.

significant fact that the two at the southern and northern entrances are in all respects similar to the original balustrade, the pillars being of the same height and cut, dressed and chamfered in the same way to a flat surface, while the two at the eastern and western entrances are not only less carefully adjusted and dressed, but their pillars are shorter and have a shallow, concave chamfer. Notwithstanding these and other differences, however, it is probable that not more than two or three decades intervened between the building of the four gateways; for the inscriptions engraved on them show that the right pillar of the Western Gateway was donated by the same person as the middle architrave of the Southern Gateway, *viz.*, "by Balamitra, the pupil of Aya-cuḍa," and the south pillar of the Eastern Gateway and the north pillar of the Western Gateway were also the gifts of the same donor, *viz.*, Nāgapiya, a banker of Achāvaḍa and native of Kurara.[1]

Description of gateways

All four gateways were of similar design—the work of carpenters rather than of stone masons, and the marvel is that erections of this kind, constructed on principles so unsuited to work in stone, should have survived in such remarkable preservation for nearly two thousand years. The best preserved of the four is the Northern (Pls. 20, 21 *sqq.*), which still retains intact most of its ornamental figures and enables us to visualize the original appearance of them all. Each gateway was composed of two square pillars surmounted by capitals, which in their turn supported a superstructure of three architraves with volute ends. Separating the architraves from one another were four square blocks, or "dies," set in pairs vertically above the capitals, and between each pair of blocks were three short uprights, with the open spaces between them occupied by a variety of figures in the round. The capitals were adorned with the forefronts of lions set back to back, or with standing elephants or dwarfs; and springing from the same abacus as these capitals and acting as supports to the projecting ends of the lowest architraves were Tree-nymphs (*Yakshī*, *Vṛiksha-devatā* or *Śālabhañjikā*[2]) of graceful and pleasing outline, though ill-designed to fulfil the functional purpose for which they are intended. Similar Tree-fairies of smaller proportions stood on the architraves immediately above them, with lions or elephants set on the volutes at their sides, and in the other open spaces between the architraves were figures of horses or elephants with their riders. A curious feature of the horses and their riders, as well as of one of the small Yakshīs mentioned above,[3] is that they were provided with two faces, so that they might look, Janus-like, in both directions. Emerging from the ends of the three architraves of the Southern Gateway (Pls. 26 and 30 *a*) are winged Gandharvas, but on the Northern Gateway these are found at the ends of the bottom architrave alone, and not at all on the two other gateways. Finally, on the summit of the gateways, crowning and dominating all, stood the emblems so peculiarly distinctive of Buddhism: in the centre, the "Wheel of the Law" (*dharmacakra*) supported on elephants or lions and flanked on either side by a guardian Yaksha holding a

---

[1] *Cf.* Inscrs. 397, 399, 402 and 403 *infra*.
[2] *Cf.* p. 232, note 1.
[3] *Viz.*, the Yakshī between the top and middle architraves on the west side of the Northern Gateway (Pls. 26 and 30 *a*).

fly-whisk (*caurī*) in his hand; and, to right and left of the Yakshas, the *triratna*, symbolising the Trinity of Buddhism: the Buddha, the Dharma (Law) and the Saṅgha (Religious Order). For the rest, both pillars and superstructure were elaborately enriched with bas-reliefs illustrative of the Jātaka legends or of scenes from the life of the Buddha or of events in the history of the Church. Besides which, there are representations of the sacred trees and stūpas symbolical of Gautama Buddha and of the other Mānushi Buddhas who preceded him, of real or fabulous beasts and birds, and of flying Gandharvas, as well as many sacred or decorative devices of a rich and varied conception. The interpretation of all these sculptures is discussed by M. Foucher in Part III, and his detailed descriptions of the many scenes are given opposite to the Plates themselves. For the inscriptions, which are carved here and there on the gateways and which record the names of the pious donors or call down imprecations on the head of any one who should dare to remove them, the reader should turn to Mr. Majumdar's notes, transcriptions and translations in Part IV.

Images on the Procession Path

In the Gupta age, when the worship of cult-images had long been fashionable, four small canopied shrines were set up in the procession path against the terrace wall facing the entrances of the Great Stūpa, and in them were installed four images of the Buddha in alto-relievo. These are the four images referred to in the Gupta Inscription No. 834, of the year 131 (A.D. 450-51). Each of the four represents Buddha in the attitude of meditation (*dhyāna-mudrā*) with an attendant standing on either side, and behind his head an elaborate halo, across which two Gandharvas are flying. The statement made by Sir A. Cunningham and repeated by Dr. J. Burgess[1] that the statue facing the southern entrance was a standing figure, is incorrect. The sculpture referred to by these writers,[2] which represents Buddha taming the elephant at Rājagṛiha, was found near the Southern Gateway, but is a work of about the seventh century A.D. and had nothing to do with the pedestal opposite.[3] The four statues in the procession path are figured on Pl. 70 *a-d*. In the treatment of the four images and particularly in the attitudes of the attendants there are various minor differences, and the northern image is distinguished from the rest by the presence of three miniature figures sculptured in relief on the face of its pedestal; but these differences are not such as to enable us to determine whether these images were intended to represent particular Dhyāni Buddhas or not. In mediæval times it was a common practice to place figures of the Dhyāni Buddhas in niches round the base of a stūpa facing the cardinal points, and it was usual to place Akshobhya on the east, Ratnasambhava on the south, Amitābha on the west, and Amoghasiddha on the north. Possibly these are the four Dhyāni Buddhas intended to be represented here, but their identity cannot be established either from their attitudes or their attributes.[4] From an artistic point of view, the image at the Southern Gateway is the best of the four,

[1] Cunningham, *Bhilsa Topes*, p. 192; Burgess, *J. R. A. S.*, 1902, p. 31. [2] *Sāñchī Mus. Cat.*, No. 9. [3] Pl. 126 *b infra*.
[4] *Cf.* M. Foucher's remarks on p. 252 *infra*. The head wearing a high *mukuṭa* or crown with a seated Buddha in front, which is figured in Maisey's *Sánchi*, Pl. XV, 10, does not, as he imagined, belong to the northern statue.

the modelling of the attendant figures being especially graceful and pleasing. The south being the most important of the four entrances and the one where the first of the four gateways had been set up, we may assume that the execution of the image at this entrance was entrusted to the most skilful of the sculptors. In style and workmanship it calls to mind some of the reliefs at the Udayagiri Caves, four miles distant from Sāñchī, and may have been executed about the same time [1], and perhaps even by the same hand—a possibility rendered the more likely by the fact that the statue is carved out of Udayagiri stone. This statue is somewhat smaller than its fellows, its height being 3 ft. 8 in., while that of the others is between 5 ft. 5 in. and 6 ft. 3 in. [2] The canopies in which the images were placed stood on small rectangular plinths, with two pillars in front to support the roof and two pilasters, corresponding to them, in the rear. The mouldings round the plinths at the south, north and west entrances resemble that around the base of Temple 17 (Pl. 114), only that, in the canopies, there are two similar mouldings one above the other, divided by a flat and deeply recessed band. [3] The plinth mouldings at the east entrance are more nondescript. The pillars and pilasters were of the same pattern as the one at F in Temple 31 (Pl. 114 *g*), and the roofs which have disappeared were no doubt similar to that over the porch of Temple 17 (Pl. 114 *a*).

Conservation of the Great Stūpa

Considering the exposed position it occupies on the bare hill-top, it is remarkable how well this stūpa and its gateways have withstood for two thousand years the ravages of time and the elements. Many of the sculptured reliefs, particularly those on the Western Gateway, seem almost as fresh to-day as when they left the chisel of the sculptor, and such harm as the others have suffered has been chiefly wrought in modern days by Moslem iconoclasts, many of whom until a few years ago used to take a delight in defacing the figures Other causes which have contributed to the decay of the fabric of the stūpa are the ponding of water round its base and the reckless damage done by the amateur excavators in 1822, when a vast breach was made in the south-western portion of the dome. The former mischief was due, not so much to the sinkage of the foundations, which for the most part rest on the living rock, as to the steady deposit of debris which was going on century by century from the early mediæval period, and which accumulated to a height of several feet round about the monument, with the result that each monsoon saw the latter submerged in a sheet of water. Small wonder, in these conditions, that the two gateways, together with considerable sections of the ground balustrade, should have subsided and collapsed. The wonder is that any gateway designed on such fragile principles could have survived at all. In order to provide for the effective drainage of the monument, the whole area around it down to the level of the stone pavement referred

[1] From Inscr. 834 *infra* it is clear that the four statues had been erected in the *pradakshiṇa-patha* sometime previous to the Gupta year 131=A.D. 450-51. The caves at Udayagiri appear to have been excavated in the reign of Candragupta II about the beginning of that century or a little earlier. *Cf.* J. Allan, *Brit. Mus. Cat. of the Coins of the Gupta Dynasties*, pp. XXXV-XXXIX.

[2] The eastern statue is 5 ft. 5 in., the western 5 ft. 8 in., and the northern 6 ft. 3 in. high.

[3] The canopy plinth at the North Entrance is 7 ft. 1½ in. wide × 5 ft. 0 in. deep × 2 ft. 10 in. high; the pillars and pilasters (of which only one has survived) were 5 ft. 2 in. high × 9 in. wide. At the other three entrances the canopies were smaller, the one at the south being only 4 ft. deep and the one on the east only 4 ft. 3 in.

to above, was cleared by the writer, and what remained of the pavement—most of it very fragmentary and broken—was taken up and relaid at a slope away from the stūpa, while on the eastern side, where there is a considerable rush of water from the upper plateau, an open drain was constructed, discharging into the rocky slope behind the Gupta Temple 17.

As to the breach in the side of the dome, we have seen above how the original stūpa of Maurya date was constructed of solid brick, and the later envelope of dry-stone masonry, so firm and substantial, that, on the side where it has not been interfered with, its contour is still practically perfect. Unfortunately, when the breach was repaired in 1881, it was merely filled with random rubble and earth, which was not apparently allowed to settle before being faced with masonry. The disastrous effect of this unworkmanlike proceeding was a settlement in the core of the fabric, which caused the upper part of the dome to cave inwards and the lower part, together with the terrace in the south-west quadrant, to bulge outwards, thus seriously imperilling the safety of the balustrade and gateway below it. In order to remedy this mischief, the whole south-west section of the structure had to be dismantled and rebuilt, and the further percolation of rain-water into the core prevented by laying the facing stones in lime concrete. The task was necessarily an arduous and costly one, but, when the safety of so priceless a monument was at stake, neither trouble nor expense could be allowed to stand in the way. When it had been accomplished and the fabric of the stūpa once more made secure, the balustrades that had fallen from the stairway, terrace and summit, were replaced and restored, so that this unique edifice now stands virtually complete in all its essential features.

Stone paving around the Great Stūpa

The stone paving alluded to above as covering the open area round the Great Stūpa, was composed of large rectangular slabs, which seem to have averaged between 6 and 8 ft. in length by 3 to 4 ft. in width and 3 in. in thickness. The pavement was laid, not only over the whole of the central plateau up to the limits of its present boundaries, but for a considerable distance beyond the long retaining wall on the east, which runs from the back of Temple 31 almost as far as Building 42. This wall, as we shall see anon, was constructed for the purpose of holding up the debris of ruined stūpas and other structures which had accumulated here during the mediæval period. But at the time when the pavement was laid—probably as soon as the Great Stūpa had been enlarged and its ground balustrade completed—the level around the Great Stūpa extended for at least another 30 yards in this direction, terminating at a point where the hill-slope, rising rather rapidly towards the east, protruded its rocky surface, and where, in aftertimes, a series of monastic buildings came to be erected. A section of this pavement, in a perfect state of preservation, was unearthed at a depth of some 14 ft. beneath the north-west bastion of Building 43; while a little further on, in the centre of the same building, there came to light the living rock itself, and on it the ruins of some monasteries of the Gupta and earlier epochs, which will be described later.

CHAPTER IV

OTHER STŪPAS, PILLARS AND SHRINES ON THE MAIN TERRACE

(a) *Stūpas*

BESIDES the Great Stūpa, there are at Sāñchī four other monuments of the same character but of smaller dimensions, which belonged to the time of the Śuṅga kings, *viz.*, the stūpas numbered 2, 3, 4 and 6 on the plan (Pls. 1 and 2). Of these, the Third, Fourth and Sixth Stūpas are situated on the Main Terrace; the Third near its north-east corner, about 50 yards from the Great Stūpa; the Fourth a few yards behind the last-mentioned; and the Sixth near the south-east corner. Apart from its size, the only essential points in which Stūpa 3 differed from the Great Stūpa were the possession of one instead of four gateways, the decoration of its ground balustrade and the more hemispherical contour of its dome, which was of a slightly later and more developed type. The diameter of this stūpa, including the raised terrace but not the ground balustrade, is 49 ft. 6 in.; its height is 27 ft. or, including the *harmikā* and umbrella, 35 ft. 4 in. The core is homogeneous throughout and composed of heavy unwrought blocks of local stone mixed with spalls. As in the case of the Great Stūpa, the body of the structure was first completed and the raised terrace added afterwards, the latter being composed of somewhat small rubble, faced with a single course of cut stone.[1] Standing, as this stūpa does, on the gently shelving hill-side, and its foundations being carried down to bed-rock, the terrace or plinth was necessarily higher on the one side than on the other; but a level space around its base was provided for the procession path and ground balustrade by banking up the ground on its western side. At a later date this bank was strengthened by a retaining wall, 3 ft. in height, on the north-west side, which was built of roughly dressed stones with a core of spalls and broken brickbats, the latter taken no doubt from some older Maurya ruin. Immediately inside it stood the ground balustrade, of which four pillar bases were found *in situ* in the south-west, and one in the south-east, quadrant, while some of the broken shafts were also unearthed in the debris on the procession path, as well as in front of Temple 45, where they had been used for paving the raised plinth.

Stūpa 3

Of the stairway balustrade, the two newel-posts, broken off near their base, were found in position at the foot of the steps, and other uprights, along with kerbstones, cross-bars and copings, were unearthed where they had fallen, immediately below the

Stairway Balustrade

[1] There was no bond between the body of the structure and the terrace.

steps. This balustrade was of the same pattern and almost of the same dimensions[1] as the stairway balustrade of the Great Stūpa, and, with the exception of one upright, is virtually indistinguishable in style from it. The exception in question is a single upright that had survived from the landing at the top of the stairs. On its southern face (Pl. 93 *i*) is depicted, at the top, a small but instructive representation of a stūpa of the period, with banners and garlands borne on two staffs, which project from the *harmikā* rail. Below this is a makara spouting forth a lotus on which two birds are perched; and below the makara, again, one of those conventional leaf designs that are peculiarly characteristic of the Early School in Central India. The east face of this pillar is divided into two panels (Pl. 93 *g*). In the lower of these are two lines of rosettes separated by a line of upright lotus blooms. In the upper appears, in the foreground, a typical hall with arched entrance, pinnacled roof and small window; behind it, two umbrellas supported on tall staffs, and between them an octagonal pillar with bell-shaped lotus capital surmounted by a group of three animals: in the middle, an elephant *en face*, and to either side, a lion with a garland suspended from its jaws. Both pillar and caitya hall are interesting; the former, because it is unusual at this period to find different species of animals grouped together on the same capital; the latter, because it depicts a form of building of which no structural examples have survived from quite so early an age.[2] This landing upright exhibits a more mature and elaborated kind of relief than the other uprights of the stairway or berm balustrades, and it may be inferred, therefore, that, while the rest of the stairway and terrace balustrades were constructed soon after the body of the stūpa, this particular pillar was inserted on the occasion of some later repair.

Terrace and Harmikā Balustrades

Of the terrace and *harmikā* balustrades (Pls. 93 *h* and 94) numerous *disjecta membra* were retrieved from amid the debris round the base of the structure, and have been replaced in their appropriate positions.[3] To judge by the style of the carvings on their pillars and coping, they also are of the same date as the stairway balustrade, and we may, therefore, conclude that the whole stūpa was designed and completed in its entirety and with all its balustrades, except the ground one, not long after the Great Stūpa, the only subsequent additions being the single upright of the landing balustrade described above, the ground balustrade and the *toraṇa* of the South Gateway.

Umbrella and Harmikā

The stone umbrella which rose from the summit of this stūpa had fallen down on the north-eastern side, and was found lying near Stūpa 4. It measures 4 ft. 4 in. in diameter, and is hollowed out on the underside in the manner shown in the section on Pl. 94 *e*, with a square mortise sunk in the centre for the reception of the tenon of the shaft. In his description of this monument in *The Bhilsa Topes*,[4] Gen. Cunningham speaks of the dome being crowned by a pedestal 4½ ft. square. It is quite likely that the

[1] The dimensions of the stairway balustrade are as follows:—*pillars*, 2 ft. 4 in. high × 8 in. broad × 5¾ in. thick; *cross-bars*, 7½ in. long × 9 in. broad; *coping*, 8¾ in. high × 7¼ in. thick.

[2] The earliest structural example known is the Apsidal Temple in Sirkap at Taxila, which dates from the middle of the first century A.D.

[3] Dimensions of terrace uprights = 36 in. high × 7¾ in. broad × 5½ in. thick.

[4] P. 295.

harmikā was of the dimensions stated, but, seeing that the upper part of the dome had fallen long before Gen. Cunningham started his explorations, it is not clear how he could have seen the pedestal referred to.

Age of Stūpa 3 and subsequent additions

On palæographical grounds Mr. Majumdar concludes that the inscriptions on the relic-boxes, stairway and berm balustrades of this stūpa belong to the same period as those on the ground, berm and stairway balustrades of Stūpa 1, namely, to about the middle of the second century B.C., and this conclusion is confirmed by three inscriptions (Nos. 618, 620 and 722) on the stairways of Stūpa 1 and Stūpa 3, which record that parts of them were donated by one and the same person—a certain Arahaguta from Kurara.[1] On the other hand, it is evident from its inscriptions that the ground balustrade of Stūpa 3 was not added until about a century or more later, when the *toraṇas* of Stūpa 1 were also erected.[2] This balustrade (Pl. 94 *d*) stood nearly 8 ft. high, the coping being 1 ft. 8 in. and the uprights 6 ft. 3 in., exclusive of their rough-dressed bases. Like the uprights of the stairway, terrace and *harmikā* balustrades, the latter have their arrises chamfered to a slightly concave section, and are adorned with conventionalised, but boldly executed, lotus patterns, varied on each upright according to the fancy of the sculptor[3] (Pl. 93 *c-f*). From the position of the later *toraṇa* on the south side, coupled with the alignment of the pillars still *in situ*, it is evident that the balustrade must have had an entrance on this side similar to those of the Great Stūpa and of the Second Stūpa ; and, on the analogy of those stūpas, it may be safely inferred that there were entrances of a like kind at the other cardinal points. The balustrade would thus have comprised 22 uprights in each quadrant, including the gateways, or 88 uprights in all.

Carved Toraṇa

Following this ground balustrade came the erection of the richly carved *toraṇa* on the south, which is the latest of all the five *toraṇas* at Sāñchī, and was added probably in the early part of the first century A.D. (Pls. 93 and 95-103). By the time it was erected, some debris had collected in and around the procession path, and the ground level had risen between one and two feet, thus concealing the original surface of the path and hiding from view the lowest steps of the ascending stairways. In order to expose the latter, it was necessary to remove the ancient accumulation ; but the digging was stopped short near the foot of the steps, so as to avoid endangering in any way the foundation of the *toraṇa*.

This *toraṇa* stands 17 ft. high and is enriched with reliefs in the same style as those on the four gateways of the Great Stūpa. No doubt, too, it was adorned with precisely the same class of figures in the round, including Yakshas, Yakshīs and horsemen, and the same characteristic emblems of the Faith : the *triratna* and *dharmacakra*. For the

[1] *Cf.* p. 269 *infra*.

[2] *Cf.* pp. 274-5 *infra*.

[3] The pillars were set at equal distances of about 3 ft. 2 in. apart, measured from centre to centre, the uprights being about 1 ft. 6 in. broad by 10¼ in. to 13¼ in. thick ; the cross-bars between them are 1 ft. 8 in. long.

interpretation of these sculptures, the reader is referred to the descriptions opposite Pls. 95 to 105 and to M. Foucher's further account of them in Part III. The style of the reliefs is discussed by the writer in Part II.

The relic-chamber and its contents

The relic-chamber, in which the relics were found intact by Gen. Cunningham, was set in the centre of the dome, on a level with the terrace berm. Covering it was a large slab upward of five feet in length, and inside were two stone boxes, each with a single name inscribed in early Brāhmī characters upon the lid. On the one to the south was *Sāriputasa*; on the one to the north, *Mahāmogalānasa*. The lids of the boxes, which I found buried in the debris near the stūpa, are of Nāgourī stone and measure 2 ft. 1 in. square, not 1½ ft., as stated by Gen. Cunningham.[1] In Śāriputra's box was a flat casket of white steatite, 6 in. broad by 3 in. high, covered by a thin saucer of black lustrous earthenware (broken), and, by its side, two small pieces of sandalwood, which Gen. Cunningham imagined to have been taken from the funeral pyre. Within the casket was a small fragment of bone and several beads of pearl, garnet, lapis lazuli, crystal and amethyst; and written in ink inside the lid was the letter "*Sa*", no doubt the initial of "Sāriputa". In Mahāmogalāna's box was a second casket of steatite, somewhat smaller than Sāriputa's, which was initialled in the same way with the letter *Ma*; it contained two small fragments of bone only.

Sāriputa and Mahāmogalāna

The two people whose body-relics were enshrined in these caskets, were the two well-known disciples of the Buddha. Both Brāhmans and both close friends from boyhood and fellow-pupils of Sañjaya, they left their early teacher to throw in their lot with Gautama and followed him faithfully for the rest of their lives. In the Buddhist Church they were known as the Right and Left hand *sthaviras*, and took rank immediately after their Master. They died only a few years before the Buddha himself. This is not the only monument erected in honour of the two disciples. The Second Stūpa at Satdhārā, between six and seven miles from Sāñchī, also contained a portion of their relics[2]; and, according to both Fa Hien and Hiuen Thsang, there was another stūpa at Mathurā containing their relics, along with those of Pūrṇamaitrāyaṇīputra, Upāli, Ānanda and Rāhula.[3]

Distribution of their relics

Śāriputra, the more famous of the two, died at Rājagṛiha, where a stūpa is said to have been raised over his remains.[4] It may be from this stūpa that the relics at Sāñchī, Satdhārā and Mathurā were obtained, but when and by whom, can only be guessed. Gen. Cunningham suggests that they were probably distributed by Aśoka at the same time as the relics of Gautama Buddha, but Gen. Cunningham was under the illusion that the Third Stūpa at Sāñchī was built, along with the ground balustrade of the Great Stūpa, in the reign of

[1] *The Bhilsa Topes*, p. 297. The drawing of the box on Pl. 94 *f* is questionable. The lower parts of the boxes, which have disappeared, were probably about one foot deep, not as shown by the draftsman.

[2] Cunningham, *op. cit.*, p. 324.

[3] T. Watters, *On Yuan Chwang*, I, p. 302; *Fa Hien*, Ch. XXVIII. Watters throws doubt on Hiuen Thsang's statement, because, he says, none of the disciples named was buried at Mathurā, and there is no authority for stating that the relics of any of them were conveyed to the Mathurā district. Seemingly, he was ignorant of the relics of these disciples found at Sāñchī, Satdhārā, etc., else he could hardly have raised this objection.

[4] Legge, *Travels of Fa-Hien*, p. 81.

Aśoka. Now that we know that neither the Third nor any other of the subsidiary stūpas is referable to an earlier period than that of the Śuṅgas, the grounds for Gen. Cunningham's inference no longer exist. Indeed, it seems hardly possible that Aśoka could have had anything to do with the division of these relics of the disciples. That emperor, as we have seen, was undoubtedly the first to promote the worship of the Buddha's relics throughout his dominions, but, so far as we are aware, the cult encouraged by him was limited to the relics of the Buddha himself; there is no evidence of its having extended to the relics of the disciples or of any other lesser lights of the Church until a later date. Moreover, when discussing the history of these Mālwā stūpas, we must always bear in mind that Vidiśā was the home and capital of the Śuṅga kings, Pāṭaliputra the capital of the Mauryas; and *prima facie*, therefore, it is much more likely that these remarkable monuments, the like of which are unknown elsewhere in India, were erected under one of the Śuṅga kings than under Aśoka, notwithstanding any romantic attachment that the latter may have had for this city. It remains to add that, following Gen. Cunningham's exploration, the remains of this stūpa became a complete ruin (see Pl. 95) and had to be almost entirely rebuilt by the writer out of the fallen debris. Its carved gateway had already been reconstructed by Col. Cole in 1882.

Immediately behind and to the north-east of the Third Stūpa is another stūpa of slightly smaller dimensions, which is now reduced completely to ruin. What remains of it is constructed after precisely the same fashion as the Third Stūpa, and there can be no doubt that it was approximately contemporary with the latter. Remnants of the slabs with which the lower procession path was flagged, still survive, but no trace was found of any ground, stairway or berm balustrades, and it seems unlikely, therefore, that any of these balustrades ever existed. On the other hand, an admirably carved coping stone, forming part of a *harmikā* balustrade, was found not far to the south of this stūpa, and may well have belonged to it. This coping stone (Pl. 104 *j*) is 5 ft. 7 in in. length, but broken at one end; it is embellished on the outer face with an undulating garland of lotus blooms and leaves, with birds perched among them.[1] Stūpa 4

The other stūpa on the hill-top referable to the Śuṅga period is No. 6, which stands a little to the east of Temple 18 at the south end of the Main Terrace. The core of this stūpa, like that of the Third and Fourth Stūpas, is composed of heavy blocks of local stone interspersed with chippings, and is evidently contemporary or approximately contemporary with them. The existing face masonry, however, is much more modern, having been added probably in the seventh or eighth century A.D., by which time the original Stūpa 6

[1] In his plan of the hill-top of Sāñchī (*op. cit.*, Pl. IV and pp. 296-7) Cunningham shows the two stūpas described above as standing within an enclosure, which he further describes as being "90 ft. square" and "surrounded by a very thick wall." Of this enclosure there is now no trace, and it is virtually certain that it never existed. In Cunningham's plan, Temple 31 is shown standing at the S. E. corner of the enclosure, the east wall of which coincides with a wall which still runs north from the N. E. corner of the Temple. Now, measuring 90 ft. from this wall (the width of the square given by Cunningham), we find ourselves opposite the south entrance of the Third Stūpa, through which it is manifestly impossible for the western wall of the enclosure to have run. Cunningham's plans and description seem to have been compiled from over-hasty notes. In this case, the three enclosing walls referred to by Cunningham were probably those to the east of Temple 31, which are just 90 ft. apart. Elsewhere (p. 17, note 1) we have seen that Cunningham's plan shows structure 8 as being north instead of south of the Great Stūpa. *Cf.*, also, p. 68, note 1.

facing had presumably collapsed. The later masonry is laid in small, even and well-dressed courses, varying from 2 in. to 6 in. in thickness, with narrower courses inserted at intervals, additional stability being secured by the provision of footings (which are never found in earlier structures) at the base both of the superstructure and of the plinth. Like the plinths of most of the mediæval stūpas on this site, the latter is square in plan and of no great height. Its measurement along each side is about 39 ft. 6 in.; its elevation, about 5 ft. 4 in. As evidence of the early date of the core of this structure, it is noteworthy that the lower parts of the old walls around the court in which it stands, are composed of the same massive kind of masonry as the core itself, and that the floor level of the original court was several feet lower than it is at present. At a later age the upper parts of these walls were repaired, like the stūpa itself, in smaller and neater masonry.

Stūpas 5, 7, etc.

The rest of the stūpas on the plateau belong to mediæval times. Most conspicuous among them is No. 5 (Pl. 115 *a*), which was erected probably about the sixth century A.D. Like all the stūpas of the mediæval period, its core is composed mainly of small rubble and earth, and its face masonry is laid in neat narrow courses, with footings at the base similar to those of Stūpa 6. In this case, however, the plinth is circular instead of square, having a diameter of 39 ft. Projecting from its south side is a statue plinth of Nāgourī stone, the design and construction of which indicate that it was set up about the seventh century A.D. This possibly was the base to which originally belonged a seated Buddha statue that was wrongly set up some years ago in the procession path of the Great Stūpa, opposite the South Gateway (Pl. 125 *e*). The plinth itself shows more developed forms of mouldings than the statue plinths in the procession path of the Great Stūpa

Stūpa 7

To about the same period as Stūpa 5 are to be referred also Stūpa 7 at the south-west corner of the plateau, and the group of Stūpas 12, 13, 14, 15 and 16, which are ranged in two lines near Temple 17 (Pl. 105 *a*). All these stūpas are alike in shape and construction. Their plinths are square and constructed of rubble and earth faced with neatly dressed masonry and strengthened by footings round the outside. Some of them have a small square relic-chamber in the centre; the others are solid throughout. No. 7, which was opened by Cunningham but proved to contain no relics, is standing to a height of about 7 ft. On all four sides of it are the remains of what appears to have been a later terrace, which increased the dimensions of the base from 28 ft. 6 in. to 38 ft. square. That this terrace is more modern than the body of the stūpa, is proved both by its rougher construction and the fact that its foundations rest on a layer of debris, which had accumulated round about the original structure. Projecting out, again, from this terrace on the northern side, and probably contemporary with it, are the remains of what may be assumed to have been a *caṅkama* or promenade, at the western end of which were built two small circular stūpas of the ordinary type.

Of Stūpa 12 the relic-chamber had been almost completely destroyed, but amid the fallen masonry of the walls was discovered a statue pedestal of the Kushān period executed in Mathurā sandstone (Pl. 124 *d*). The pedestal, which is 8¼ in. in width, is unfortunately broken and nearly half of the relief which adorned its face, as well as part of the inscription engraved upon it, are gone.[1] What is left of the carving consists of a seated figure of the Bodhisattva flanked on his proper left by two female devotees bearing garlands in their right hands. The inscription (No. 830 *infra*) records the dedication of an image of Bodhisattva Maitreya by the daughter of one Vishakula. **Stūpa 12**

In Stūpa 14 was brought to light another statue [2], not lying in the debris, as in the case of the last-mentioned, but set up against the western wall of the relic-chamber, with a second wall immediately in front of its face to protect it from damage (Pl. 105 *b*). This statue represents Buddha seated cross-legged in the *dhyāna-mudrā*, the familiar attitude of meditation. Like the pedestal described above, it, too, is of Mathurā sandstone and a product of the Mathurā School, but the features of the face, particularly the lips and eyes, the highly conventionalised treatment of the hair and the no less highly stylised disposition of the drapery, proclaim it to be of the early Gupta, not of the Kushān, period. As this statue had already suffered much from wear and tear before it was enshrined in this stūpa, it affords additional evidence of the relatively late date of the building, which on other grounds is to be assigned to about the seventh century A.D. Probably the statue was taken from one of the many shrines of the early Gupta age, which were then falling to decay, and entombed here as an object of special veneration. The burial of older cult statues, whole or fragmentary, in Buddhist stūpas is a practice which appears to have been common during the mediæval age; for I have found instances of it, not only at Sāñchī, but at Sārnāth, Saheṭh-Maheṭh and other sites. **Stūpa 14**

Time was when the Great Stūpa was surrounded, like all the more famous shrines of Buddhism, by a multitude of stūpas of varying sizes crowded together on the face of the plateau. The majority of these appear to have been swept away during the operations of 1881-83, when the area about the stūpa was cleared for a distance of some 60 ft. around the ground balustrade. Apart from those described above, the only remains of this class that have survived are a few clustered together near Stūpa 7 and on the east side of the Main Terrace (see plan, Pl. 2), where a deep accumulation of debris served to protect them from harm, and a considerable number of small solid stone stūpas, such as have been found in crowds at Bodh-Gayā and Sārnāth. Among the structural examples, two especially are deserving of mention, namely, those numbered 28 and 29 on my plan, **Stūpas 28 and 29** which are situated to the right and left of the steps by which Temple 31 is approached. Each of these small stūpas is provided with a high square base, cornice and footings characteristic of the early Gupta age, to which they belong, and each has the same outward

[1] Inscr. 830 *infra* and pp. 253-4. *Cf. A. S. R.*, 1913-14, p. 16; *Guide to Sāñchī*, p. 86; *Sāñchī Museum Cat.*, p. 31, A84.
[2] See *Mus. Cat.*, No. 19.

appearance. Their interior construction, however, is not identical. The one to the west of the steps is built throughout of stone; but the one to the east (29), which measures about 8 ft. square at the base, has a core of large-sized bricks, taken no doubt from some much more ancient structure.[1] In the centre of this core and at a height of 3 ft. from the ground level, was found a tiny relic-chamber, and in it a casket consisting of a small cup of coarse earthenware, with a second cup of similar fabric inverted over it as a lid. Inside this rough and ready receptacle was a small bone relic and the remains of a broken vase of fine terra-cotta with polished surface, such as was manufactured during the Maurya and Śuṅga ages. The presence of this early and fragmentary vase inside a casket which was itself quite intact, coupled with the antiquity of the bricks forming the core of the edifice, leaves no room for doubt that the relic had originally been enshrined in another and older stūpa, and that in the early Gupta period, when this stūpa had presumably fallen to decay, it was transferred to the small structure in which it was found, together with the fragments of the casket in which it had previously reposed. From the upper part of this same stūpa (about 1 ft. 3 in. below the surface) came the pedestal of a statue of Mathurā sandstone figured in Pl. 105 *c*, the inscription on which (No. 829) records that the statue was one of the Bhagavat Śākyamuni and that it was set up by one, Vidyāmatī, in the reign of King Vaskushāṇa, in the year 22. The carving is typical of the Mathurā School of the time of Huvishka and Vāsudeva.[2]

(*b*) *Pillars*

Seeing how quickly the fashion of erecting stūpas spread after the time of Aśoka, and how religiously the form of the stūpas established by him was copied in succeeding generations, it is not surprising to find that the magnificent pillars which he set up, not infrequently by the side of one of his stūpas, also came to be accepted in the Church as the consecrated type for all such memorials, and that they were invested for a while with a sanctity only second to that of the stūpas themselves. So manifold are the copies and representations[3] of these pillars, that they have been taken by some as evidence of a primitive pillar cult which went back to a time long anterior to the Buddha. For this view, however, there are no real grounds. Pillars of one kind or another were no doubt common in India from time immemorial. There were, for example, the well-known Yūpa posts used on the occasion of sacrifices as far back as the Vedic period;[4] and, though normally of wood, such posts were sometimes copied in stone.[5] It is likely, too, that the idea of the memorial pillar was already familiar before the age of the Mauryas. But so far as Buddhism was concerned, it was Aśoka who first set the fashion of erecting such pillars, and once the fashion had been set, his pillars became sacrosanct in the eyes of

[1] The brick core is square, 3 ft. 5 in. along each side; some of the bricks in it measure 19 in. × 7½ in. × 4 in.

[2] *Cf.* Inscr. 829 *infra*; *Sāñchī Mus. Cat.*, A83.

[3] For representations of these pillars among the Sāñchī reliefs themselves, see, for example, Pl. 74, 3*a* and 5*a*, and Pl. 95.

[4] The making of the sacrificial Yūpa post is described at length in the *Śatapatha-brāhmaṇa* (Trans. Eggeling, *S. B. E.*, Vol. XXVI, pp. 162 ff.).

[5] *E.g.*, the two stone Yūpa posts from Isāpur, near Mathurā, of the second century A.D. *Cf.* Vogel, *A. S. R.*, 1910-11, pp. 40-48.

the faithful, and it soon came to be regarded as a work of religious merit to set up others in imitation of them.[1] The later examples were not necessarily meant to be exact replicas of the earlier. Variety was introduced by making the shaft octagonal or sixteen-sided, or by substituting a square block simulating a balustrade in place of the round abacus, or by the modification of other minor details; but as a rule the plain round shaft was preserved and the capital was almost invariably of the characteristic bell-shaped type; so that, in spite of variations, there is no mistaking the family likeness.

Of the several pillars that stood on the Main Terrace near the Great Stūpa,[2] the one erected by Aśoka has already been described in full (pp. 25-28). A second, figured in Pl. 106 *b* and numbered 25 on the plan (Pl. 2), was set up about the same time as the Khām Bābā pillar in Vidiśā, that is, during the sovereignty of the Śuṅgas in the second century B.C., not as Maisey and others supposed, during the sovereignty of the Guptas. At a height of about six feet from the ground on its south side are a few letters of a mediæval inscription (No. 836)[3] and near the base on its south-west side are some defaced characters, apparently of the shell class; but both of these records were engraved on the pillar long after its erection, and they afford, therefore, no clue to its date. That it belongs, however, to the period of the Śuṅgas, is clear alike from its design and from its surface-dressing. The height of the pillar, including the capital, is 15 ft. 1 in., measured from the old ground level; its diameter at the base is 1 ft. 8½ in. Up to a height of 4 ft. 7 in., the shaft is octagonal; above that, sixteen-sided. In the octagonal portion, six of the facets are flat and two only (facing N.-W and S.-W., respectively) are fluted; in the upper section, the alternate facets are fluted, the eight fluted facets being produced by a concave chamfering of the arrises of the octagon. This and a very effective method of finishing off the arris at the point of transition between the two sections, are features especially characteristic of the second and first centuries B.C., but are not, so far as we are aware, found in later work. The west side of the shaft is split off, but the tenon at the top, to which the capital was mortised, is still preserved. The capital is of the customary bell-shaped lotus type, with leaves falling over its shoulder; above this is a circular cable necking; then a larger circular necking relieved by a bead-and-lozenge pattern; and, finally, a deep square abacus adorned with a balustrade in relief. The crowning feature—probably a lion—has disappeared. Pillar 25

A third pillar, numbered 26,[4] stands a little to the north of the one just described and belongs to the early Gupta age. Apart from its design, it is distinguished from the other pillars on the site by the unusual quality and colour of its stone, which comes from the Nāgourī quarries and is of a buff variety, splashed and streaked with purplish-brown. This pillar was composed of two pieces only—one comprising the circular shaft and square Pillar 26

[1] From the Buddhists the practice spread to the Jains and Hindus. For the Khām Bābā pillar at Vidiśā erected by Heliodorus in the second century B.C., in honour of Kṛishṇa (Vāsudeva), see above, p. 4.

[2] Numbered 10, 25, 26, 34 and 35 in the plan (Pl. 2). As regards the Pillar 34, see the description of its lion-capital (which is all that now remains of it) opposite Pl. 108 *c*.

[3] *Cf.* p. 391 *infra*. The inscription, which refers to the dedication of a pavilion and gateway, is of the fifth century A.D.

[4] P in Maisey's plan.

base (characteristic of the Gupta period), the other the bell-capital, necking, lions and crowning *cakra* (Pls. 106 *d* and 108 *a*). Unfortunately, the shaft is now broken into three sections, which owing to the splitting of the stone cannot be fitted together again. The height of the whole pillar was approximately 22 ft. 6 in., that of the broken section, which is still *in situ*, is 5 ft. 11 in., measured from the top of the square base.[1] On the north-west side of this section is a mutilated inscription in Gupta characters (No. 835 *infra*) recording the gift of a Vajrapāṇi pillar (No. 35), two pillars of a gateway, the maṇḍapa of a monastery and a gateway, by one Rudrasena or Rudrasiṁha, son of Gośūra-siṁhabala, the Superintendent of a monastery.[2] As was usual with pillars of the Gupta age, the square base projected above the ground level, the projection in this case being 1 ft. 2 in., and was enclosed by a small platform, 4 ft. 2 in. square. The lion-capital of this pillar is a feeble and clumsy imitation of the one which surmounted the pillar of Aśoka, with the addition of a wheel at the summit and with certain other variations of detail (Pl. 108 *a*).[3] The variations in question occur in the cable-necking above the bell-capital, which is composed of a series of strands bound together with a riband, and in the reliefs on the circular abacus, which consist of birds and lotuses of unequal sizes disposed in irregular fashion, not with the symmetrical precision of earlier Indian art. Like the grotesque lions on the Southern Gateway, the lions here also are provided with five claws on each foot, and in other respects their modelling exhibits little regard for truth and little artistic feeling. It should be added that on the four faces of the square block which supports the wheel, are fanciful birds and floral designs in relief.[4]

Pillar 35

It was in the Gupta age, also, that the massive pillar near the North Gateway, numbered 35[5] in the plan, was erected. This pillar has repeatedly been described as the counterpart of and contemporary with the pillar of Aśoka near the Southern Gateway,[6] but a very perfunctory examination is sufficient to show that there is no justification for its ascription to the Maurya epoch. Every feature, whether structural, stylistic or technical, is typical of Gupta workmanship Most of the shaft has been destroyed, but the stump still remains *in situ*, and the foundations are intact (Pls. 106 *c* and 108 *b* and *d*). The capital, too, and the statue which surmounted it are both relatively well-preserved. What remains of the shaft is 9 ft. in length, 3 ft. 10 in. of which, measured from the top, are circular and smooth, and the remainder, constituting the base, square and rough-dressed. Its diameter at the dividing line between the square and circular sections is 2 ft. 7 in. and, immediately beneath the capital, 2 ft. 3 in. The material of both shaft and capital is the local stone of Nāgourī. In the Gupta age, it was the common practice to keep the bases of such monolithic columns square, whereas those of the Maurya age were, so far as I am aware, invariably circular. Again, every known column of Maurya

---

[1] The pillar has a diameter of 15½ in. at the base; the base measures 18×20½ in.

[2] See p. 391.

[3] *Cf.* *C. S. R.*, X, Pl. XXI and pp. 62-3.

[4] The torso (now in the South Kensington Museum) figured in Cunningham's Report (X, Pl. XXI) as leaning against this pillar, had nothing whatever to do with it, and there is no evidence, as Vincent Smith supposes, that it stood at the base of a column. *Cf.* Smith, *op. cit.*, p. 84.

[5] Distinguished by the letter M in Maisey's plan.

[6] *Cf.* Burgess in *J. R. A. S.*, 1902, p. 30.

date is distinguished by its exquisitely accurate chisel-dressed and highly polished surface. In this case the dressing of the capital was done with a small pick tool instead of a chisel; and, though much care was evidently expended over the smoothing of the shaft, the secret of the Maurya polish had been lost, and the brilliant lustre of the older pillars is lacking. As to the foundations, which consist of heavy stone boulders retained by stout walls, we have not yet accumulated sufficient data from other sites to use them as wholly reliable criteria of age, but it is noteworthy that they are constructed on a more uniform and regular plan than the foundations of the Aśoka column near the South Gateway. On the other hand, the stone platform which enclosed the base of Pillar 35 is both designed and constructed in the characteristic manner of the Gupta period, and the iron chisels which were discovered wedged beneath the bottom of the shaft where they had been used to maintain it in the perpendicular, have yielded on analysis almost identically the same results as other implements of that epoch. This analysis, for which I am indebted to the kindness of Sir Robert Hadfield, F.R.S., is as follows :—

C	Si	S	P	Mn
·05	·09	·009	·303	·09

With this it is interesting to compare the analysis of the Iron pillar of Candra at the Quṭb, near Delhi, namely :—

C	Si	S	P	Mn
·08	·046	·006	·114	*Nil*

The Persepolitan bell-capital and square abacus ornamented with a balustrade in relief measure 6 ft. 1 in. in height, and are cut entire from a single block of stone.[1] So, too, is the statue which Cunningham and Maisey found lying alongside the capital, and which they rightly inferred had fallen from the top of this pillar. This statue (Pl. 108 *b*), which, like the shaft and capital, is of Nāgourī stone, represents the Bodhisattva Vajrapāṇi in a standing attitude.[2] The figure is clad in a *dhotī* and adorned with bracelets, earrings, bejewelled necklace and head-dress of *kīrtimukha* heads, swags and jewels. The hair falls in curls over the shoulders and back, and beneath it, at the back, fall the ends of two ribands. The right hand held a *vajra*, one end of which is still traceable on the right hip ; the left hand held the end of a scarf. A specially interesting feature of this statue is the halo, which is pierced with twelve small holes evenly disposed around its edge. Manifestly this halo, as we now see it, is too small in proportion to the size of the statue, and these holes were no doubt intended for the attachment of the outer rays, which were probably fashioned out of copper gilt, the rest of the statue itself being possibly painted or gilded. That this statue stood, as Cunningham and Maisey say, on the summit of the pillar, there is no reason to doubt, and that it is a work of the Gupta period, needs no demonstration to any one familiar with the history of Indian

[1] *Cf.* Maisey, *Sánchi and its Remains*, Pl. XXXII, fig. 2.
[2] *Cf.* p. 254 and Inscr. 835, in which reference is made to this Vajrapāṇi pillar ; also *Sāñchī Mus. Cat.* A99.

sculpture. The plinth of the pillar, which may have been added slightly later, is 9 ft. 2 in. square and 2 ft. 4 in. high. Its mouldings are now very weather-worn, but seem to be of about the same date as the pillar itself (fifth century A.D.).

Pillar 34

The fifth and last pillar to be noticed is No. 34, which used to stand in the recess on the south side of the East Gateway of the Great Stūpa.[1] Nothing of this pillar is now left *in situ*, but a drawing of it, as it stood intact in 1851, is reproduced in Gen. Maisey's work,[2] and two pieces of it were found by the writer lying among the debris round the stūpa. One of these comprises the bell-capital with its cable necking and 8½ in. of the shaft beneath; the other, the crowning lion and circular abacus on which it stood (Pl. 108 *c*). These carvings clearly belong to the Gupta School,[3] but, compared with other contemporary works, their execution is rough and clumsy, and the design of the double capital is singularly bizarre and degenerate. The stone comes from the quarries of Udayagiri.

(*c*) *Temples*

Temple 18

Of the several temples on the Main Terrace, the most important in point of size and interest is the one numbered 18 on the plan, which stands on a raised platform directly opposite the South Gateway of the Great Stūpa (Pl. 112 *a* and *b*). As revealed by recent excavation, the plan of this temple (Pl. 111) turns out to be similar to that of the rock-cut caitya-halls at Kārlī and elsewhere, with this noteworthy difference—that in this case the apse is enclosed, not by columns, as in the Cave Temples, but by a solid wall, the difference being due, of course, to the fact that in a free-standing building light could be admitted to the aisles through windows in the outer wall. How these windows were arranged and what were their dimensions and number, there is now no means of determining, since the outer wall is standing to a height of less than two feet above the interior floor level, but we shall probably not be far wrong, if we assume that they followed approximately the same disposition as the windows in the great Jaṇḍiāl temple at Taxila, which are spaced at even intervals to the number of 8 in each side and 4 in the back wall. The inner wall around the apse is 3 ft. thick and constructed of dry-stone masonry, similar to that employed in the mediæval stūpas described above. Its foundations, which descend only a few inches below the floor level, rest on a layer of debris about a foot thick, but beneath this layer is another earlier wall, which follows the same alignment as the latter and rests on a solid foundation of boulders. The outer wall is of the same construction and, in the forepart of the temple, is also founded on loose debris, but, at the back of the aisle, rests on the remains of an earlier wall. The pillars and pilasters of the nave are monoliths of buff or purple-grey Nāgourī stone, approximately square in section, 17 ft. in height and tapering slightly towards the top. At the base, they measure

[1] At the spot indicated by the letter N in Gen Maisey's plan (Pl. I).
[2] Pl. XXXIII, fig. 2.
[3] For other well-known pillars of the Gupta age, see Vincent Smith, *A History of Fine Art in India and Ceylon*, 2nd Ed., pp. 83-4.

from 21 to 23 in. along the sides. They are not sunk in the ground but rest on foundations of stone, which in themselves are not very strong or secure, the architect having relied upon the wooden timbers of the roof to tie the pillars together and thus maintain them in position. This, no doubt, they succeeded in doing, so long as the timbers were intact, but since their collapse three of the pillars at the north-west corner and the pilaster on the western side had fallen, and the others were leaning at parlous angles, being saved from falling only by the heavy architraves above them. The curious and interesting design carved on the four faces of these pillars (Pl. 111 *a*), which has the appearance of having been left in an unfinished state, was a favourite one at Sāñchī in the seventh century A.D., and is found in buildings of the same age in places as far remote as Ellorā in the Dekhan and Aihole in the Dhārwār district of the Bombay Presidency, but is not, so far as I am aware, found in any architecture of a later period. These pillars indicate 650 A.D. as approximately the date when this temple was erected, and this date is confirmed by other considerations, notably by the structural character of the walls, by the subsequent additions which were made to the temple, and by the succession of earlier structures which had stood here before it was erected. Of the later additions referred to, one is the stone filling in the apse, by which its level was raised about 13 in., and another the stone jambs of the inner doorway, of which the eastern one was still standing a few years ago (Pl. 113 *c*). This jamb, which is of the same Nāgourī stone as the pillars of the interior but greyer in colour than the latter, is 10 ft. 8 in. long by 2 ft. broad and 1 ft. 4 in. thick, and is adorned with sculptures in relief, the style of which proclaims them to be a work of the same period as Temple 45 on the Eastern Terrace, that is, of the 10th-11th century A.D. At the base are a male and female figure, side by side, the latter standing on a *makara*. At their feet are three small chubby figures, one on each side and one between. The middle and left hand ones are standing ; the other is kneeling. Above are four vertical bands, the inside one enriched with scroll devices in relief, the next with a series of eight dwarfs, one above another, the third with six pairs of quasi-erotic male and female figures, and the fourth with an architectural pilaster.

Within the apse of the temple there once stood a mediæval stūpa, the remains of which were found by Gen. Maisey in 1851, and among them a broken steatite vase,[1] which may be assumed to have contained relics. The stūpa appears to have stood well back in the apse, and, like the walls of the temple, to have been built on very shallow foundations, since all trace of it has now vanished. The floor of the temple was paved with stone flags, and stone flags also were used for paving the small court in which the temple stands. From the ground plan on Pl. 111 it will be seen that this court was not of sufficiently large dimensions to comprise the whole side of the temple, the ante-chamber of which projects beyond its northern wall, and that no direct communication, therefore, existed between the temple and the court, the only entrances to the latter having

[1] *Cf.* Maisey, *op. cit.*, p. 74.

apparently been in the short lengths of wall to the east and west of the temple, where the remains still exist of two moon-stone slabs.

Minor antiquities in Temple 18

Of the minor antiquities found in this temple, the only ones that need be mentioned are a number of terra-cotta tablets---56 in all---of the seventh or eighth century A.D., which were found in a heap on the floor of the aisle on the eastern side of the apse.[1] They are of varying sizes but of an almost uniform pattern, each being stamped with two separate impressions and roughly adorned around its edge with a scalloped border (Pl. 113 *a* and *b*). In the lower impression, which is the larger of the two and shaped like a *pīpal* leaf, is the figure of Buddha seated on a lotus throne in the earth-touching attitude (*bhūmisparśa-mudrā*) with miniature stūpas to the right and left of his head, and the Buddhist creed in characters of the seventh or eighth century A.D. to the right and left of his body. In the upper impression, which is oval or round in shape, the Buddhist creed is repeated.

Earlier structures on the same site

In speaking of the age of this temple, we have alluded to the existence of earlier structures on the same site. The remains of these structures consist of a series of floors separated by layers of debris beneath the floor of the apse, of stone foundations beneath the walls at the back of the apse and aisle, and of stout retaining walls around the temple enclosure, which date back to an early period. The earlier floors are three in number, and, to judge by the remains in other parts of the site, the uppermost of the three, which is composed of lime concrete, is to be assigned to the fifth or perhaps sixth century A.D.; the next to about the first century B.C., and the lowest to the Maurya or, more probably, Śuṅga period. Like the original *bajrī* floor around the pillar of Aśoka, this last floor is laid on a foundation of stone boulders extending down to the natural rock, but, inasmuch as it was intended for the interior of a covered building, it was composed, not of coarse *bajrī*, like the floor around the Great Stūpa, but of lime plaster over a layer of pounded clay. To the same age as this early floor belong also the early retaining walls on the east, south and west of the temple compound, and along the edge of the central terrace to the west of it. On this side of the hill-top the natural rock shelves rapidly away towards the south, and, in order to provide a level area for their structures, the architects had to erect massive retaining walls and then level up the enclosed space with a filling of heavy stone boulders and earth. These retaining walls are constructed of hammer-dressed blocks similar to those used at a later period for the enlargement of the Great Stūpa, and are between 12 and 13 feet in height. Seemingly, the retaining wall on the south side of the temple must have proved inadequate to meet the strain imposed on it; for a second wall was subsequently constructed on the outside of it and the space between the two filled in with stone boulders. This second wall, which appears to have been built very soon after the first and is also founded on the natural rock, has a thickness of over 4 ft. at the

[1] *Cf. Mus. Cat.* C752-808.

base, with several footings on its outer side. Whether it was as high as the first wall, cannot be determined, as the upper part of it has fallen.

Terra-cotta roof-tiles and standard bowl

In the angle formed by the retaining wall on the west side of the temple and the wall at right angles to it along the south face of the main terrace, a deep accumulation of debris had formed, much of which must have fallen from the temple above. Near the bottom of this debris were large numbers of terra-cotta roof-tiles of the pattern illustrated in Pl. 111 *d*, and along with them a standard stone bowl of fine Maurya workmanship. The tiles, which are rather crudely baked, measure 9×6 in. and are 1 in. thick at the lower end, ½ in. at the upper. No doubt they came from the roof of the early building, the superstructure of which, on the analogy of other edifices of that age, may be assumed to have been mainly of wood. The standard bowl is made of the same polished Chunar sandstone as the Aśoka pillar and broken umbrellas from the Great Stūpa. The sides of the bowl and much of the base are unfortunately missing, but what remains shows it to have been an excellent example of the stonecutter's craft. It consists of a square moulded base and octagonal tapering shaft, with delicately fluted sides, surmounted by a cup-shaped capital on which rested the bowl.[1] The height of this relic, without the missing bowl, is 2 ft. 5 in.; with the bowl, it was approximately 3 ft. 5 in. (Pl. 104 *b*). On another bowl of local manufacture and perhaps of slightly later date, there is an inscription in archaic Brāhmī lettering, reading *Bhāgāya pasādo*, from which it is evident that the bowl was intended for the distribution of food offered to the saṅghārāma.[2] It may be surmised, therefore, that the Mauryan standard bowl was for the same purpose; and there can be little doubt that this was the purpose also of the giant bowl, to be described later, which stands on the hill-side above the Second Stūpa.

Early pavement and walling west and south-west of Temple 18

Beneath this debris the whole area at the foot of the south retaining wall[3] of the main terrace is paved with large slabs of local Sāñchī stone, noticeably rougher and more irregular than those belonging to the Śuṅga pavement of the main terrace. Over this pavement was built a considerable length of later walling, of which only one or two foundation courses remain. Starting from the south retaining wall of the main terrace, at a point 32 ft. 6 in. from its western end, it runs south for a distance of 135 ft. 6 in., and then turns east for a few yards over the rocky surface. This walling appears to be contemporary with the original parts of the retaining wall of the main terrace. If, therefore, the latter is Mauryan, it is probable that the pavement to the south of it, which is older than the walling, is pre-Mauryan; if, as seems more likely, the retaining wall is of Śuṅga date, the pavement is probably Mauryan.

Character of Temple 18

As to the character and design of this early building, it appears to have been intended as an apsidal caitya-hall, similar to the earliest edifice on the site of Temple 40;

[1] The restoration of the base is not quite certain. It might have been slightly larger or slightly smaller. *Cf. Mus. Cat.* A10, p. 20 and Pl. VI.
[2] *Cf. Mus. Cat.* B1, p. 37 and Pl. XIV; Inscr. 805 *infra*.
[3] This early pavement extends from east to west along the whole length of the retaining wall; how far it extends to the south, has not yet been determined.

it was not until a much later date that a stūpa was erected in the apse. That the earlier wall at the back of the apse, or the earlier outer wall at the back of the aisle, was of Mauryan date, seems unlikely; for, had their foundations been laid at that time, they would probably have been carried down to the bed-rock, instead of being allowed to rest on the surface of the rubble filling. We may infer, therefore, that these foundations were of the Śuṅga rather than of the Mauryan age. Resting on the early stone foundations beneath the forepart of the apse was a heavy block of stone, nearly 4 feet square and hollow in the centre (Pl. 111 *c*); probably it was left there last century by one of the earlier explorers, but, however this may be, there seems little doubt that it was made in mediæval times as a base collar for the support of one of the pillars of Temple 18, the dimensions of which correspond precisely with the hollow square in the middle of this block.

Conservation measures

The preservation of this interesting fabric was a matter of much difficulty and labour, which increased owing to the impossibility of procuring adequate appliances on the spot. Several of the pillars of the nave were leaning at dangerous angles,[1] and the first thing that had to be done, after clearing away the debris and jungle, was to reset them in the perpendicular. To achieve this without running the risk of bringing them down altogether, it was essential to have an exceptionally strong scaffolding, and, as timbers were not obtainable, recourse was had to walls of rough rubble in lime, strengthened with hoop iron. The walls were erected in two lines, parallel with one another, inside and outside the colonnade, with short cross-walls between the columns; and in order to provide access to the base of the latter, low semi-circular arches were constructed opposite to each, in both the inner and outer walls. With this secure and solid scaffolding forming a well, as it were, around each of the columns, the remainder of the task was simplified. First of all the architraves were raised with screw-jacks and held up on balk-timbers, then the capitals were lifted, and the columns jacked back into the perpendicular. The foundations of the columns were next grouted with Portland cement, steel chisels were driven in under their bases, and grout forced under pressure into the open crevices. Capitals and architraves were afterwards lowered and reset in their correct positions and securely clamped together with copper clamps of 1 in. section, imbedded in lead. Besides resetting these pillars in the perpendicular, it was also necessary to dismantle and rebuild a large part of the early retaining walls on the south and west of the temple-court, which were bulging outwards, and to repair in places the low walls of the temple itself (*cf.* Pl. 112 *a* and *b*).

Temple 17

The little Gupta shrine, No. 17, which stands near the north-east corner of the temple just described, is a very unpretentious building, but one of the most attractive of its kind to be found in India (Pl. 113 *d*). Its plan (Pl. 114 *b*) is that of a "prostyle" temple of Greece. It consists, that is to say, of a single square chamber with a portico

[1] See *A. S. R.*, 1913-14, Pl. XV *a*.

in front supported on four pillars, and an *anta* on either side of the entrance corresponding to the corner pillars. Excluding its base mouldings, the chamber measures 12 ft. 5 in.× 12 ft. 9 in. externally, and is 13 ft. high. Its walls, which are built of Nāgourī stone, are unusually thick and faced inside and outside with ashlar masonry, some blocks of which run to as much as 5 ft. 3 in. in length, but, though seemingly very strong, the core of the walls is composed of loose rubble, and there are few headers in the face masonry to bond together the inner and outer faces. Moreover, the plinth is destitute of foundations (a fault common to most structures of this age), and it is not surprising, therefore, that the percolation of water into the walls has resulted in the buckling of the ashlar facing, followed by the partial collapse of the roof. Fortunately, the damage was not such as to necessitate any excessive dismantling of the walls. With the help of screw jacks, it was found possible to work the displaced masonry back almost into its original bed, and by underpinning the walls—particularly at the back of the temple—and grouting the open crevices, to render it thoroughly secure and waterproof. The roof of the shrine was originally composed of very massive slabs of stone, 8 to 10 inches thick, stretching from side to side across the porch and sanctum. The porch had been covered by two such slabs and the sanctum by three, of which two were broken and useless. Adorning the jambs of the doorway, on its outer side, are the vertical bands of foliate and rosette designs illustrated in Pl. 114 *c* and *d*, and, next to them, small pilasters with bell-capitals and four-, eight- and sixteen-sided shafts. The portico pillars and two *antas*, also, have similar shafts with bell-capitals, cable-filleted necking and block abacus surmounted by a second squared lion cap, the animals on which have double bodies meeting in a single head at each corner, with a palm tree in the middle of each face, obviously copied from the neighbouring gateway sculptures.[1]

The limits which we have set ourselves in these volumes do not allow of our discussing either the architecture or sculpture of the Gupta age, but it is worth remarking, *en passant*, that there are few monuments of this period that exhibit so clearly as this small shrine the quality of intellectualism and logical beauty which were the keynotes of Gupta art and literature. Compare it, for example, with the neighbouring gateways of the Great Stūpa, and mark how the irrational and almost fantastic wooden forms of the Andhra period have now given place to rational lithic ones ; how each member of the architecture, whether plinth or column, capital or cornice, now fulfils a clear and logical function, well suited to the need of the material ; and how relatively restrained and simple the decoration has become. In these respects there undoubtedly exists a close kinship between this Gupta architecture of mediæval India and the classical architecture of ancient Greece—a kinship which, taken in conjunction with the general resemblance in design between this shrine at Sāñchī and the prostyle temples of Greece, cannot but suggest that it is inspired by

[1] For similar flat-roofed shrines of the Gupta age at Tigowā, Erān, Gaṛhwā, Udayagiri and other places, *cf.* Coomaraswamy, *History of Indian and Indonesian Art*, pp. 78-9 and V. Smith, *A History of Fine Art in India and Ceylon*, p. 79.

western prototypes. And it is quite possible, indeed, that this was so; for in the Gupta epoch Indian art was manifestly indebted to the Western world for many of its motifs and ideas. We should be quite wrong, however, if we attributed the characteristic classicism of the Gupta age, which manifests itself in all spheres of art and literature, to a mere superficial imitation of foreign models. The source of this classicism lies much deeper and is to be found in the fact that, for reasons which I have elsewhere explained,[1] the mentality and genius of the people of Central India and Hindustān had been undergoing much the same striking development as the genius of Greece had undergone in the period preceding the fifth century B.C.; and it need not, therefore, surprise us, if her art, like her thought, found expression in the same intellectuality, in the same humanism and in the same logical qualities as the art of Greece. This little shrine, in fact, reflects in its every stone the temperament of the people and of the epoch which produced it—an epoch which was primarily creative, not imitative; and if we take the trouble to compare it with the creations of the Andhra period, we shall find in it an eloquent index to the change which had come over Indian culture during the first four centuries of the Christian era.

Shrine 9

On the opposite side of the entrance to Temple 18 there once stood another shrine of about the same age but of slightly larger dimensions than the one last described. All that is left of it *in situ* consists of the stone base of the plinth and of the porch in front facing the east; but, lying in the debris above its plinth, were two large and two small stone pilasters, besides various other architectural members, the style of which indicates that the structure belongs to the early Gupta age. The larger pilasters are 6 ft. 10 in. in height, with fluted vase capitals, cable necking and shafts that pass from the square to the octagon and sixteen-sided above. The smaller pilasters are of the same design and 4 ft. 7 in. high, the jamb on which they are carved measuring 6 ft. 7½ in. over all.

Temple 31

A fourth temple on the main terrace is situated at its north-east corner, immediately behind Stūpa 5 (Pls. 114 *e* and *f*, and 115 *a*). It consists of a plain pillared chamber with a flat roof, standing on a broad plinth, and contains an image of the Buddha seated on a lotus throne opposite the entrance (Pl. 115 *c*). The plinth was constructed for an earlier temple which stood on the same site, and to this earlier temple also belonged the pedestal beneath the lotus throne of the cult-statue, which is still in its original position at a slightly lower level than the floor of the present temple. This earlier shrine must have been built in the sixth or seventh century A.D., and it is not improbable, therefore, that two of the pilasters now standing in the later building, which are similar in design to the pillars of Temple 18, and which no doubt date from the same period, had originally belonged to it. On the other hand, two of the other pillars are of the early Gupta age (Pl. 114 *g*) and must, therefore, have been taken from some other structure—possibly one of those of which the plinths have been exposed beneath the long retaining wall on the

[1] In "Racial Influence on Indian Art", Birdwood Memorial Lecture, *Jour. Roy. Soc. of Arts*, 1923.

east of this area. The cult-statue inside this shrine is of the purplish-brown sandstone of Sāñchī, and represents the Buddha seated on a lotus. The hands and forearms, unfortunately, are missing, but to judge from the two marks of breakage on the breast, which indicate that both hands were raised, he must have been portrayed in the attitude of teaching (*dharmacakra-mudrā*). Although referable to the same epoch as the pedestal on which it stands, *i.e.*, to the sixth or seventh century A.D., it does not fit the base, and we must, therefore, presume that, like some of the columns, it also was brought here from another shrine. The halo of this statue is in almost perfect preservation, and a splendid specimen of rich foliate design. It is in one piece with the statue, and the decoration on it is divided into four concentric bands : in the two inner ones it consists of lotus leaves, in the next of rosettes, and in the outermost of an undulating foliate motif ; the outer edge of the halo is beaded.

Conservation measures

The preservation of this building involved extensive measures. The high platform on which it stands had given way on the western and northern sides ; the walls of the temple, built of the small loose masonry in vogue in the later mediæval period, had buckled outwards in several places ; the columns had sunk or inclined from the perpendicular, and the roof was much broken up.[1] It was necessary, therefore, to jack up the roof and reset the columns which supported it ; to dismantle and rebuild large sections of the walls, using mortar instead of mud as a binding material ; to renew the concrete on the roof top, floating it in cement, and to repair and repave the platform, as well as the steps which give access to it. The two stone door-jambs at the entrance had entirely vanished, and as new ones were not required for supporting the lintel, the dry-stone masonry at the back of the jambs was relaid in mortar, in order to prevent any further disintegration.

Nāgī statue

A monument of interest which came to light during the excavations of this temple platform was a Nāgī statue, 7 ft. 6 in. in height (including the tenon at the base), which used to stand in the angle formed by the approaching flight of steps and the face of the platform on its west (Pl. 115 *a* and *b*). This statue, which is of Nāgourī stone, was executed in the fourth or fifth century A.D., and must once have stood free on a spot where it could be seen from all sides. Beneath its base is a tenon, which was, no doubt, originally mortised into a stone plinth, but in late mediæval days, when it was set up in its present position, the plinth was discarded and the base of the statue imbedded in dry-stone masonry. Subsequently the image was broken into two, at a point a little above the ankles. The lower part was found still *in situ* ; the upper was lying a little distance away. From the indications afforded by the masonry, it appears likely that there was a second Nāga or Nāgī statue in the corresponding position to the east of the steps.

[1] *Cf. A. S. R.*, 1913-14, Pl. XVI *b*.

Retaining wall between the Central and Eastern areas

Before leaving the main terrace, it remains to say a few words about the retaining wall along its eastern side and the remains of the several structures visible beneath its foundations. When speaking of the open paved area around the Great Stūpa, we remarked that it had once extended on the same level for a considerable distance east of this retaining wall. That was in the first century B.C., and it is probable that for the next three hundred years, or even longer, the pavement was kept clear of debris. Then, as the buildings in this part of the site began to fall to decay, their ruins gradually encroached more and more upon the paved area, other buildings rose over their remains, and so the process of accumulation went on, until, by the seventh century, an artificial terrace had been formed five or more feet in height and extending almost to the limits of the retaining wall. It is to this period that the structures 19, 21 and 23, as well as the road (No. 20) to the north of the first mentioned, probably belonged (Pl. 2). The road in question, which, to judge by the worn condition of its cobble stones, must long have been in use, is 9 ft. wide and rises eastward by a gradient of about 1 in 6. Of Building 23, only the entrance steps, with a 'moon-stone' threshold of local sandstone, has been exposed. Of Building 19, the walls are standing to a height of between 1 to 2 ft. only, and are composed of the ordinary dry-stone masonry. Building 21, on the other hand, is constructed of massive blocks of Nāgourī stone with a torus moulding at its base, from which it may be judged to belong to the Gupta age. The retaining wall over the ruins of these edifices, erected when the terrace to the east had risen as high as 14 feet, can hardly be earlier than the tenth or eleventh century A.D.; probably it was contemporary with the later Temple 45. At the time it was built, there must have been some accumulation of debris also on its western side; for its foundations did not descend more than nine feet from the top of the terrace. In repairing this wall, it was found possible to underpin and bank up that section of it which is north of the modern flight of steps leading to the upper terrace. The rest had to be dismantled and rebuilt completely, the foundations being carried another seven feet lower down.

CHAPTER V

THE SOUTHERN AREA

BEFORE discussing the remains of the Southern and Eastern Areas, where the living quarters of the monks were situate, it is well to say something about the various buildings which in pre-Mauryan times constituted the Buddhist saṅghārāma. According to the Vinaya Texts, these buildings comprised the following: living and sleeping quarters for the bhikshus; a refectory or service-hall (*upaṭṭhāna-sālā*); a fire-hall (*aggi-sālā*), frequently translated as "kitchen"; an open pillared pavilion (*maṇḍapa*); a promenade and cloister for walking exercise (*caṅkamana-sālā*); a bath-room for hot baths (*jantāghara*); a *kaṭhina*-hall for tailoring; a privy; a well and well-house (*udapāna-sālā*); a store-room (*koṭṭhaka*); and a provision and drug store (*kappiya-kuṭi*).[1] These various parts of a monastery seem to have been, for the most part, detached structures; at any rate it is quite clear that, when the Vinaya Texts were composed, the saṅghārāma did not consist of one single and comprehensive building, as it frequently came to do in later times. The residences permissible for the monks and nuns might be of five different kinds (*pañca-lenāni*), *viz.*: *pāsādas*, *vihāras*, *aḍḍhayogas*, *hammiyas* and *guhās*.[2] The *pāsāda* was a storeyed mansion, a common form of which seems to have been pyramidal, each succeeding storey being smaller than the one below it, and in some cases provided with a pillared verandah (*ālinda*).[3] The *vihāra* of those days was not the standardised type of building that we have come to associate with the Buddhist monastery of later times, that is, a large and usually two-storeyed structure, with one or more open rectangular courtyards enclosed by lines of cells and other chambers. Some early *vihāras* undoubtedly contained living and sleeping cells (*pariveṇa*) for a large number of inmates, but in others there was accommodation only for two or three persons, or sometimes for a single one. That even the larger *vihāras* were not at this time built on the same plan as the later ones, *i.e.*, with the cells all facing inwards into the closed court, is clear from the many precautions taken to screen the inmates from the public gaze.[4] What form the *aḍḍhayoga* and *hammiya* took, and how they differed from the

The saṅghārāma in pre-Mauryan times

[1] The statement made by V. Smith (*op. cit.*, p. 26) that "the central and all-important building of the early monasteries seems to have been the *Sabhā* or hall of meeting of the community" is not borne out by the Vinaya Texts, which make it abundantly clear that among the ordinary saṅghārāma buildings there was no such hall for the holding of the Uposatha ceremonies. See, for example, *Mahāvagga*, II, 8, where the Bhikkhus are enjoined to appoint a specific place for the recitation of the Pātimokkha, either a *vihāra* or any other of the *pañca-lenāni* buildings. Smith's observation is probably true of post-Mauryan, but not of pre-Mauryan times.

[2] *Cf. Mahāvagga*, I, 30, 4; *Cullavagga*, VI, 1, 2.

[3] *Cull.*, VI, 14, 1. In this instance the pillars of the verandah had elephant-head capitals, like those, for example, of the North Gateway at Sāñchī (Pl. 27) The word *pāsāda* was also applied to a storeyed shrine, such as the Gandhakuṭi at Bodh-gayā. For the description of the famous nine-storeyed Lohapāsāda in Ceylon, see *Mahāvaṁsa*, Ch. XXVII (Geiger); and for the Sat-Mahal Pāsāda at Polonnāruva, *cf.* Coomaraswamy, *Hist. of Indian and Indonesian Art*, p. 165 and fig. 287

[4] *Cull.*, VI, 3, 3. The precautions taken comprised the use of curtains, the erection of screen walls half the height of the *vihāra*, and the const.uction of cells (on the ground floor) of such a form that they could not be looked into.

pāsāda and *vihāra*, is not apparent,[1] but that the former was a fairly large and elaborate structure is implied by the fact that the time estimated in the *Cullavagga* for its building was seven or eight years, while for a *pāsāda* or large *vihāra* it was ten or twelve years, and for a smaller *vihāra* five or six years.[2] By *guhā* was meant a cave or small hut.

Of the other structures enumerated in the Vinaya Texts, the *maṇḍapa* was an open pavilion supported by pillars, of the type familiar in India throughout the ages, but at this time it seems to have been more in the nature of an arbour, with wooden pillars and thatched roof, in which the bhikshus could recline and converse, or in which temporary accommodation might, on occasion, be provided for pilgrims and others, as it is still provided in the temple *maṇḍapas* to-day.[3] The *caṅkama* or promenade[4] was at first simply a narrow strip of level ground, where the monks could walk up and down and meditate; later, it was raised on to a high plinth, furnished with steps, balustrade and railing, and completely roofed in, thus constituting a *caṅkamana-sālā*. The simple, unroofed type of *caṅkama* is figured several times among the gateway reliefs at Sāñchī (*e.g.*, Pls. 50 *a* 1 and 51 *b* 1). Subsequently, when the stūpa-cult had come into vogue, the procession path around the base or on the berm of the stūpa to a large extent took the place of the *caṅkama*, but the associations of the latter with the Blessed One were never wholly forgotten, and as late as the second half of the sixth century A.D. the Chinese pilgrim I-tsing describes a stone promenade which he saw at the monastery of Nālandā.[5] The bath-room (*jantāghara*) was for hot vapour baths. It was equipped with a fire-place, a hot water bath and seats for the bathers, whose faces were smeared over with clay in order to protect them from the excessive heat.[6] Attached to it were a cooling room, an ante-chamber for keeping the water in (*udaka-koṭṭhaka*) and a hall. The *kaṭhina*-hall took its name from the *kaṭhina*, which was seemingly a sort of framework for the tailors to lay out their work on; it was where cloth was sewn and made up into robes for the bhikshus.[7] The store-room (*koṭṭhaka*), which may have been located in the gateway (also called *koṭṭhaka*), was used for the storage of miscellaneous articles other than provisions and drugs. The latter were kept in the provision store (*kappiya-kuṭi*), which might be located in any building—*vihāra*, *aḍḍhayoga*, *pāsāda*, *hammiya*, *guhā* or *goṇisādika* (ox-stall) or even in a layman's premises, provided that such building was outside the actual dwellings and had been duly proclaimed as a *kappiya-bhūmi*.[8]

---

[1] *Cf. Mah.*, I, 30, 4, and *Cull.*, VI, 1, 2. Buddhaghosha's note on the latter, in which *aḍḍhayoga* is explained as a "gold-coloured Bengal House", is not enlightening; neither is the explanation given by the editors that the *hammiya* is a *pāsāda* with an upper chamber on the topmost storey (*S. B. E.*, XIII, p. 173, note 1). It was a relatively small building and may have been in the form of such a chamber.

[2] *Cull.*, VI, 17, 2.

[3] The *maṇḍapa* at this time does not seem to have been a suitable building for the holding of the Uposatha and other ceremonies. At any rate, it is not mentioned among the buildings where the Uposatha might conveniently be held. (*Mah.*, II, 8, 1.)

[4] *Cull.*, V, 14, 1; *Mah.*, V, 1, 14.

[5] *S. B. E.*, Vol. XVII, p. 7, note 2; *I. A.*, X, 192.

[6] *Mah.*, I, 25, 12; *Cull.*, VIII, 8, 2; *Cull.*, V, 14, 3 ff.

[7] *Cull.*, V, 13, 3; *S. B. E.*, Vol. XX, p. 92, note 8. The *kaṭhina* ceremonies were so called because the garments distributed on that occasion were made on the *kaṭhina*.

[8] *Cf. Mah.*, VI, 33, and S. Dutt, *Early Buddhist Monachism*, p. 184. The appointment of a building for provisions apart from the actual residences was a fiction to circumvent the rule of the Order which forbade the storage of provisions (Pācittiya Rule 35).

Decoration and construction of buildings

For finishing off the interiors of these buildings, whitewash was allowable, with which black or red colouring matter might be mixed, the red (*gerika*) being commonly used for the walls and the black for the floors. Additional decoration was restricted to paintings or incised or relief work of swags, floral patterns and bone or horn pegs, such as are frequently met with in later art. Another device called *pañca-patikam* was also permissible, but the meaning of it is uncertain.[1]

The fact that even on such important sites as Sārnāth, Bodh-gayā, Rājagṛiha and Kasiā, which were some of the earliest to be occupied by the Buddhists, no remains of any of these structures have been found which can be referred to pre-Mauryan times, would have gone far to prove that they were built of perishable materials; but any doubt that might have existed on this point is set at rest by the particulars of them given in the Vinaya Texts. The rules there laid down permit of these buildings, including even the promenade, the hot-bath, the well-house, and the store-room, being raised above flood level on a high plinth (*caya*), which might be faced with stone, brick or wood, and provided with steps of the same material, but it is evident that the superstructures were to be of mud plaster or wattle-and-daub (*kuḍḍa*)[2] or timber, even when the building was a large one, as, for example, the residence referred to in the Pācittiya Rule 19. From the *Cullavagga* we learn that the *vihāra* walls, being of mud plaster, sometimes decayed, with the result that rain water percolated through, and that permission was, therefore, given for them to be strengthened by supports or dados of timber and provided with a further protection of some sort (perhaps a *chajja*=eaves) covered with cement.[3] From the same source we also learn that the roofs were thatched and that ceiling cloths were stretched inside, just as they are in many bungalows to-day, to prevent snakes or other vermin falling from above.[4] In other buildings, such as the *kaṭhina*-hall, the promenade-hall, the hot-bath house and well-house, the roofs were covered with skins and plastered.[5] The mud or wattle-and-daub walls of the fire-hall and bath-house were faced inside with a dado of brick.[6]

Self-contained monasteries not yet evolved

From the descriptions of these monastic buildings in the Vinaya Texts it is abundantly clear that, at the time those texts were written, the monastery, as we know it in later times, had not yet been evolved, and a further inference which, I think, can safely be drawn from these texts, is that the principle of monasticism itself was still in its infancy, and had not been borrowed by the Buddhists from any older sect. These are points that need to be stressed, because it has often been taken for granted that monasticism came down from an immemorial age in India, and that the standard type of monastery had been developed as early as the days of Aśoka. As a fact, it was not until the Kushān period that the self-contained monastery, which we are wont particularly to associate with the

[1] *Cf. Cull.*, V, 11, 6; VI, 3, 1; VI, 17, 1; VI, 20, 1; VI, 27; VIII, 3, 1; *Mah.*, I, 25, 15; *S. B. E.*, XX, p. 218, note 5. Swags, floral designs and garlands suspended on bone pegs are abundantly illustrated among the Sāñchī reliefs and Ajaṇṭā paintings.

[2] *S. B. E.*, XIII, p. 35, note 1, and XI, 99, note 2 (*Mahāparinibbāna Sutta*, V, 41). In many of the monasteries at Taxila of early and late Kushān times the walls are of mud or of stone and mud combined, on a stone plinth two or three feet high.

[3] *Cull.*, VI, 3, 4.

[4] *Cull.*, VI, 3, 4.

[5] Roofs might be of this type or constructed of brick, stone or cement, straw or leaves (*Cull.*, VI, 3, 10).

[6] *Cull.*, V, 14, 3.

Buddhist saṅghārāma, made its appearance in the North-West of India, and not until the early Gupta age that it found its way into Hindustān and Central India. It is a moot question, therefore, whether this type of monastery was evolved in India or introduced from abroad. In any case, we must obviously be careful not to draw any hasty inferences from these later foundations as to the character of the older saṅghārāmas.

Pillared Hall No. 40

With these prefatory remarks, we may now proceed to consider the individual buildings in the Southern and Eastern Areas. Earliest and most important of the remains in the former is the structure numbered 40 in the plan (Pl. 2), which, like all the other structures in this part of the site, was only recently unearthed. In its original form this temple was an apsidal caitya-hall, and is probably the earliest structure of this type of which any remains have been preserved to us. The plan and section of the original building, as well as of the additions subsequently made to it, will be readily understood from the drawings and photos on Pls. 109 and 110. What is left of the original structure consists of a rectangular stone plinth, 11 ft. high and 87 ft. long by 46 ft. wide, approached by a flight of steps on its eastern and western sides. In the outward aspect of this plinth there was nothing to indicate that its superstructure had taken an apsidal form, but, when the core of the apparently solid masonry came to be examined, it was found to be composed in reality of two distinct walls with a filling of debris between. Of the outer wall, the exterior face is rectangular, but the inner face at the south end is curved in the form of an apse, and the inner wall corresponds to it in shape. Of both walls the masonry is strikingly rough, and it is clear that they were intended to do duty only as foundations; but the plan of these foundations leaves little or no doubt that the superstructure was apsidal in shape, resembling in this respect the great caitya-halls at Taxila, Ter, Chezārla and among the Cave Temples of Western India, though with this noticeable difference, that, whereas the latter are provided with one or more entrances directly opposite the apse, this structural hall at Sāñchī had entrances in its two longer sides—a feature in which it resembles the Sudāma and other Maurya cave-shrines in the Barābar hills.

Original structure apsidal in plan

That the superstructure was mainly of wood and was burnt down at a relatively early age, is evident from the fact that no vestige of it had survived except some charred remains of timber, which were found on the original pounded clay floor of the building. Of the approximate date at which this conflagration took place, an indication is afforded by the stone pillars which were subsequently set up on the same plinth. These pillars are ranged in five rows of ten each, partly on new foundations, partly on the foundations of the original structure. Seeing that the pillars in question bear records carved upon them in Brāhmī characters of the Śuṅga period (second century B.C.),[1] it may fairly be concluded that the original structure was erected in the preceding

[1] *Cf.* Inscrs. 776-790, 793-798, 800, 826 and 827 *infra*. The script of these records is identical with that used on the ground balustrade of the Great Stūpa.

Maurya period—and probably burnt down when Aśoka's stūpa was destroyed by Pushyamitra; and that its reconstruction dates from the same time as the reconstruction of that stūpa after the middle of the second century B.C.

Date of erection and reconstruction

At the time when this reconstruction took place, the original plinth (*caya*) was much enlarged by erecting a thick retaining wall on all four sides but at some distance away from it, and filling in the space between with heavy boulders and worked stones, probably taken from the earlier building. The effect of these measures was to increase the length of the plinth to 137 ft. and its width to 91 ft. At the same time, the height of the floor was raised by about 1 ft. 4 in. and a new pavement was laid, constructed of large slabs similar to those with which the main terrace round the Great Stūpa was paved. On three sides of the enlarged plinth—that is, on the north, south and west—are projections of varying dimensions, and it may be surmised that there was a similar projection also on the eastern side, which has not been excavated. All of these projections appear to be contemporary with the retaining wall.

Description of later building

By this enlargement of the older plinth the two stairways that led up to it on its eastern and western sides were buried from view, and their place was taken by two new flights constructed in the thickness of the northern retaining wall, which was more than doubled for the purpose. Similar stairways are also found built into the end wall of the temple at Sonāri, which is to be ascribed to about the same age as this reconstruction.

We have said that the octagonal stone columns of this hall were disposed in five rows of ten each, and this is the disposition shown in the plan (Pl. 109). So far as these fifty columns are concerned, their arrangement is not open to question, since many of the broken shafts of the columns were found *in situ*. But it seems probable that the number of columns in the hall was considerably over fifty, the extra ones having formed one or more rows at the sides or ends of the existing group. Indeed, at first sight it looked as if this must have been the case; for in the debris round about the building were found a number of other broken pillars of precisely similar pattern to those *in situ*, which it was natural to infer had stood on the enlarged plinth and been thrown down, when the upper part of the later retaining wall collapsed, bringing down with it some six or more feet of the boulder filling behind it. This inference, however, is not beyond question, since every shaft without exception is broken, and most of the pieces are only three or four feet in length. Those which were found lying in the debris, therefore, may in reality have been the upper sections of pillars which are still *in situ*, and what appear to be rough bases may in reality have been nothing more than the unfinished tops of the shafts. All things considered, however, it seems more likely that the first inference is the correct one, *viz.*, that there were some additional rows of pillars besides those shown on the plan.[1] It is

Disposition of larger pillars

[1] This inference is confirmed by the discovery of three pillar-tops furnished with square tenons or mortise-holes for the fixing of the wooden capitals or architraves.

only because the evidence on the point cannot be regarded as absolutely conclusive, that the alternative hypothesis has been suggested, and that only those pillars which were actually *in situ* have been indicated on the plan.

From this plan the reader will observe that the majority of the pillars are set on the foundation walls of the original plinth, but in every case, whether they stood on the older foundations or not, special foundations were laid for them consisting of stone slabs of varying thickness, laid one above the other with earth and small stones between. The top of these foundations, which are similar in character to the foundations of the ground balustrade of the Great Stūpa, coincided roughly with the floor level of the older apsidal hall, but, by the time the stone pillars were erected, the floor level had risen by about 1 ft. 4 in., and the bases of the pillars were buried to that depth in the debris between the two floors.

Smaller pillars

Besides the large octagonal pillars, there were also found a number of smaller ones of about the same age : square below and octagonal above, with donative inscriptions in early Brāhmī engraved on some of the shafts. These pillars, which, like the pavement slabs and masonry of the plinth, are of local purplish-brown or grey stone from the Sāñchī hill, are 9 ft. 7 in. high, excluding the rough base (1 ft. 7 in.). Some of them were ranged in a row alongside the eastern edge of the old plinth, but this position could not have been the one which they originally occupied ; for the dressed faces of their shafts proved, on excavation, to extend some distance below the level of the earliest clay floor, and—which is more significant—broken pieces of the larger octagonal pillars were found built into their foundations, thus demonstrating that they had not been set up here until after the bigger columns had fallen. What their original position was, can only be surmised. Possibly they were intended to support an open verandah around the main body of the hall, or possibly they had been employed in a subsidiary structure on the south side. Wherever they may have stood, it is clear from their rough bases that it was on the ground floor and not in an upper storey.

Was the maṇḍapa ever completed?

Whether or not this pillared hall was ever brought to completion, is questionable. To judge by the distance (about seven feet) between the octagonal pillars, it seems probable that architraves of stone rather than of wood may have been originally intended ; but, if this was so, they were certainly never constructed ; for there was not a trace in the debris of architraves or capitals or of any other architectural features except the columns. If, therefore, the building was ever completed, the whole superstructure with the exception of the pillars must have been of timber, as it was in many of the early edifices of Ceylon. At a much later date, *i.e.*, about the seventh or eighth century A.D., a shrine with a portico and entrance facing the west was constructed on the eastern side of the plinth, and it was probably at this time that the smaller square columns were set up in the position described above. The three steps which gave access to the portico of this shrine will be seen on the ground plan directly over the eastern aisle of the original apsidal hall, the bases of the stone pillars in front of them having been cut off short at the floor level, so as not to interfere with the entrance. The portico itself has an inner measurement of 24 ft. from the north to south by about 9 ft. from east to west. Behind it were a few remnants of the wall of the shrine.

Another question of interest that presents itself is how this pillared hall came to be so ruthlessly destroyed. It could hardly have been through wanton vandalism; for between the reign of Pushyamitra, to which this hall is undoubtedly posterior and the later mediæval period—long after the hall had been destroyed—there is no evidence of any of the monuments of Sāñchī having been wantonly maltreated, and it is incredible that this structure alone should have been selected for destruction. Possibly fire may have been the cause. And if the superstructure was mainly of wood, the intense heat of the conflagration would have been quite enough to split the pillars into pieces, but in that case we should have expected to find clearer evidence of the burning on the calcined surface of the stones. The enigma is one that for the time being must be left unsolved.

And how was it destroyed?

As to the purpose of this edifice, there can be no question that, when converted into a pillared hall, it was designed to serve as a *maṇḍapa*—a class of structure which, as we have already seen, was intended in pre-Mauryan days as a reclining place for the monks or for the accommodation of visitors. In those days, however, the *maṇḍapa* seems to have been little more than a wooden arbour with a thatched roof. By the time of the Śuṅgas it had evidently developed into something more pretentious, and was possibly being used for ceremonies such as the Uposatha, though of this there is no positive evidence. The purpose of the original apsidal building is far more problematical. It dates, as we have shown, from the Maurya period, when many large stūpas containing relics of the Blessed One were erected by the Emperor Aśoka, but when the stūpa-chapel had not yet been evolved. It is clear, therefore, that this structure could not have owed its rounded apse to the presence in it of a circular stūpa, though it may conceivably have owed it to some other cult object of the Buddhists, at the nature of which we can only guess. On the other hand, it is equally, if not more, likely, that these apsidal halls of the Buddhists had been copied from Brāhmanical or other sectarian shrines in which the presence of a *liṅga* or some such other object of worship had led to the rounding of the apse, and that this *raison d'être* had been lost sight of in the copies, though the apsidal form itself had been retained. But, whatever the origin of the apse may have been, it is obvious that the idea of its having been due to the shape of the stūpa must now definitely be abandoned.[1]

Purpose of the maṇḍapa and earlier Apsidal Hall

[1] The plan of the apsidal hall may well have been derived from a combination of the circular shrine with a rectangular hall in front, as they appear in the Devadhamma Sabhā on one of the Bharhut reliefs, the intervening wall between the two being at first retained, as in the Lomas Rishi and Sudāma Caves in Bihar, and later on eliminated. *Cf.* Coomaraswamy, *op. cit.*, p. 19 and fig. 43.

Among the debris packed between the older apsidal building and the later pillared *maṇḍapa*, and earlier, therefore, than the latter building, was found the mutilated stone elephant figured in Pl. 104 *i*. No doubt, it was thrown down and damaged when Aśoka's Stūpa was destroyed, and it may safely be assigned, therefore, either to the Mauryan or pre-Mauryan epoch. As a work of art, it is of no particular distinction, but it is interesting, nevertheless, owing to its age and the fact that it is unlike other sculptures of that period.

Building 8

Another early building in the Southern Area is that numbered 8 on the plan.[1] It consists of a solid square plinth (*caya*) standing, on the north side, about 12 ft. above the bed-rock ; in front of it, in the middle of the east side, is a projecting ramp with a few steps at its base, the remaining steps, together with a portion of their substructure, having been destroyed. The lofty plinth was constructed of masonry similar to that used in Building 40 described above, but in this case the whole core of the plinth is filled in solid with rough boulders, and there are no interior foundation walls. In the centre of its core Cunningham sank a deep pit, and, finding only a filling of rough boulders, assumed, without discovering the plan of the building, that it was another early stūpa. In the period to which this building belongs, stūpas were never built with square bases, and there is no reason to suppose that an exception to the rule was made in this case. The plinth is just such a *caya* as is described in early Buddhist literature. What form the timber superstructure took or for what purpose it was used, we do not know. All that can be said is that, with such a lofty and imposing plinth, the building must have been an important one and hardly likely to have been used at this time for residential, cooking or other such purpose. In the angle formed by the south side of the stairway ramp and the east side of the plinth, a rectangular space was enclosed in after-times by a wall, which to judge from the style of its masonry dates from mediæval times.

Monasteries 36, 37 and 38

The remaining structures excavated in the Southern Area are the three monasteries 36, 37 and 38 (Pl. 2). All three are built approximately on the same plan and are small —almost miniature—editions of the self-contained monasteries alluded to above, which came into fashion in the North-West of India in the Kushān period. They consist of a square courtyard surrounded by cells on the four sides, with a verandah supported on pillars around the court, a raised platform in the centre of it, and, in two cases, with an additional chamber outside. The entrance passed through the middle chamber in one of the sides and was flanked outside by projecting pylons. The upper storey was probably constructed largely of timber or mud, the lower storey being of dry-stone masonry. All three monasteries belong to the mediæval age, No. 36, which is nearer to the centre of the site, being the earliest of the three, No 38 coming next, and No. 37 last.

[1] Erroneously shown in Cunningham's plan as being north, instead of south, of the Great Stūpa. *Cf.* p. 17, note 1, and p. 45, note 1, *supra*.

In Monastery 36, the masonry is rough and carelessly laid (Pls. 122 *b* and 123 *a*). The square platform in the centre of the courtyard is covered with a layer of brick-and-lime concrete, about 3 in. thick. Round the outer edge of the platform was a low wall, in which were engaged the columns of the verandah. The staircase, which gave access to the upper floor, was in the north-west corner, but only one step, worn by the passage of many feet, has been preserved. Water from the court was discharged through an underground drain covered with stone flags, which passed beneath the passage at the south-west corner. The entrance to this monastery was on its eastern side, and in front of it was an irregularly shaped compound, most of the walls of which are still traceable. **Monastery 36**

The plan of Monastery 37 (Pl. 123 *b*) is more spacious and developed than that of 36, and the masonry is neater and better laid than in the latter. It is assignable to about the seventh century A.D. Like the square stūpas of the same age, its walls are provided with footings on the outside. At the entrance between the pylons is a square slab of stone, the purpose of which is not obvious. Built into the corners of the platform inside the courtyard are four square stone blocks which served to strengthen the masonry and support the pillars of the verandah. The chambers at the back of the cells on the south and west sides are unusual, and the specific use to which they were put is uncertain. **Monastery 37**

Monastery 38 (Pl. 121 *b*) is not much later than Monastery 36, and like it is built of singularly rough and uneven masonry. Apparently there was an earlier building on this site, of which some of the foundation stones still survive, and in the central chamber on the north side there is also a brick wall—subsequently added—the bricks of which it was constructed having been taken from some older building. Instead of the usual raised platform in the middle of the courtyard there is, in this monastery, a square depression, like that in a Roman atrium, with a raised verandah round it. The stairway leading to the upper storey is in the south-west corner. The ground about this building has not been excavated, but it may be assumed that, like Monasteries 36 and 37, it also had a compound, and that the latter probably occupied the ground on its western side, since the entrance of the monastery is in that quarter. **Monastery 38**

The last building to be noticed in this area is that numbered 42 on the plan, which is situated north of No. 40. It is standing to a height of about 6 ft. and, so far as it has been excavated, appears to be a shrine somewhat similar, perhaps, to No. 44. **Building 42**

CHAPTER VI

EASTERN AREA

WE now pass from the Southern Area to the higher terrace on the east, the summit of which is crowned by the Temple and Monastery No. 45 (Pls. 116-120). As it stands, this temple dates from the tenth or eleventh century of our era, and it is, therefore, one of the latest buildings on the site. Several centuries before this, however, another temple had been erected on the same spot with an open quadrangle in front, containing three small shrines and surrounded by ranges of cells for the monks. These earlier remains are at a lower level than the later, and readily distinguishable from them (Pl. 119 *a*). To the later period belong the temple on the east side of the quadrangle, together with the platform in front of it, and the cells and verandahs flanking it on the north and south ; to the earlier belong the ranges of cells on the north, south and west sides of the quadrangle, the plinths of the three detached stūpas in the courtyard, and the low stone kerb which served to demarcate the edge of the verandah in front of the cells.

Temple and Monastery 45

The cells of the earlier monastery are built of dry-stone masonry of the small neat variety in vogue at the period, the foundations being carried down as much as nine feet to the bed-rock. Access to the corner cells was provided not, as was often the case, through the cell adjoining, but by an open passage between the two cells, while another open passage also led from the entrance into the quadrangle. The verandah in front of the cells was a little over 8 ft. broad, raised about 8 in. above the rest of the court, and separated from it by a stone kerb. This kerb is divided at regular intervals by square blocks which served as bases for the pillars of the verandah. A specimen of the latter has been re-erected in its original position at the south-east corner of the quadrangle (Pl. 117 *b*).[1] It is 6 ft. 9 in. in height, with its corners partly chamfered to the form of an octagon, leaving short sections of it square. The stone pavement of this earlier court, which is about 2 ft. 6 in. below the pavement of the later court, is made of heavy stone slabs of irregular shapes and varying sizes. Of the three small stūpas which stood on it, two had apparently perished down to their plinths before the later building was started ; the third, at the south-west corner of the steps, looks as if it had been intentionally dismantled in part, in order to make way for the pavement of the later temple. It is now standing to a height of 2 ft. 1 in. and is of the familiar cruciform type, with niches in the face of each of the four projections, in which no doubt statues were aforetime placed. The remains of the early temple itself, as well as of the cells adjoining it on the eastern side of the

Earlier structures on same site

[1] *Cf.* also *A. S. R.*, 1913-14, Pl. XXII *a*. The pillars are from 1 ft. 2 in. to 1 ft. 4 in. square.

court, are completely buried beneath the later structures, but parts of the platform in front of the former have been exposed by removing the filling beneath the corresponding platform of the later edifice. Apparently, this earlier platform, though slightly smaller than the later one, was designed on much the same lines and it may safely be inferred that the plan of the sanctum itself was also generally similar.

Like so many other buildings on the site, this earlier temple appears to have been burnt down and left for a long space of time in a ruined condition. This is evident from the quantity of charred remains that were found on the floor of the courtyard and from the accumulation of earth that had formed above them. It might have been expected that, when the Buddhists set about rebuilding it, their first step would have been to clear away all this debris and restore, as far as possible, the old structures; but, whether from religious or other motives, they preferred to level up the old remains, lay a new pavement about 2 ft. 6 in. above the old one, and completely rebuild the shrine and cells adjoining it on the east side of the court. At the same time they repaired and renovated the cells on the other three sides of the quadrangle, raised their walls and roofs between five and six feet, and constructed a verandah of the same altitude in front of them, which was thus elevated about three feet above the new courtyard (Pl. 118 *a*).

Later structures: Temple

The design of the later temple will be clear from Pls. 116, 117 *b* and 118. It consists of a square sanctum (*garbha-gṛiha*) approached through a small ante-chamber and crowned by a hollow spire or *śikhara*, the upper part of which has fallen. The temple stands at the back of a raised terrace ascended by steps from the west, and round three sides of it runs a procession path (*pradakshiṇa-patha*) enclosed by a high wall. Like most of the temples of this date, it is constructed of massive blocks, well dressed on their outer faces but otherwise very rough and loosely fitting together. Much of the material of which it is composed was taken, no doubt, from the earlier edifice on the same spot, as well as from other structures, but the majority of the decorative carvings are in the later mediæval style and were manifestly executed expressly for this temple. Such are the sculptured threshold door-jambs, the ceiling of the sanctum, the statues in the niches in the outside walls, and the ornamental work on the spire and round the face of the terrace. To an earlier age, on the other hand, belong the corner pilasters in the sanctum. This

Temple sanctum

sanctum is all but square in plan, measuring 11 ft. from east to west by 11 ft. 5 in. from north to south and 16 ft. 8 in. in height. The pilasters in its corners have their upper halves richly decorated on both faces with the pot and foliage design set over a *kīrtimukha* head, and surmounted by a band of floral ornament with a border of palmettes above (Pl. 116 *d*). The capitals are moulded and fluted and provided with a narrow necking adorned with a conventional garland design. Above them are Hindu corbel brackets of a simple pattern. The style of the carving on the pilasters, which is strikingly like some of the earlier carvings at the temple of Bāro in Gwalior State, proclaims them to be work of the eighth-ninth century A.D., and it is evident, therefore, that they were not originally designed for this temple. This conclusion is also borne out by the rough drafts at their inner edges, which prove that in their original position they must have been partly engaged in the wall masonry. The ceiling of the sanctum (Pl. 116 *c*) is constructed on the usual principle of diminishing squares, and is carried on architraves resting on the Hindu brackets above the pilasters, and further supported by corresponding brackets in the middle of each wall. Of these brackets, it is noticeable that the one in the back wall has been left in an unfinished state, and it is also noticeable that the architrave above it has been partly cut away for a space of about 2 ft., apparently to make room for some object in front of it. That this object was the halo of a cult image of the Buddha, may safely be inferred, though whether it was the image which is now in the shrine and which may once have been elevated on a higher plinth, or whether it was a taller image for which the present one was afterwards substituted, is open to question. Clearly the existing image (Pl. 120 *c*) does not fit and was not designed for the plinth on which it rests, nor could it have been intended that the wall behind and the decorative pilasters should be half hidden by the masonry which it has been found necessary to insert for its support. This image represents the Buddha in the 'earth-touching' attitude (*bhūmisparśa-mudrā*) on a lotus throne, with a second lion throne beneath, which, however, belonged to an older statue. Across the lower row of lotus leaves is inscribed the Buddhist creed in letters of the ninth-tenth century A.D.[1] On a projection in the centre of the lion throne are two much mutilated figures, one lying prostrate on its back, the other standing apparently in a posture of victory over it. Similar figures are found in front of the throne of a Buddha statue in Cave XI at Ellorā, which dates from the seventh century A.D. We suggest that they are symbolical of the victory which Buddha won beneath the Bodhi tree over the armies of Māra. The statue, which has a height of 10 ft. ½ in. including the pedestal, is composed of a fine-grained purplish-brown local sandstone of the variety frequently employed for sculpture in the later mediæval period; its surface is half polished and covered with an artificial red paint, as is also the earlier plinth of Nāgourī stone below.

Cult image

Unlike the pilasters of the sanctum, the two pilasters of the ante-chamber are roughly decorated with unfinished designs, one of which (on the north side) was cut through, when the pilaster was adapted to its present position, and accordingly it may be concluded that the building from which they were taken had never been finished. The sculptures on the entrance doorway are strikingly rich and elaborate (Pl. 118 *b*). Projecting from the middle of the threshold is a branching lotus with birds seated on the flowers, and on each side of it a half *kīrtimukha* head; then come little figures holding vases, conventionalised lions, and, in the corners, a seated figure of Pāñcika[2] and (?) Maṇibhadra. Much of the left jamb, as well as the lintel above, has fallen, but the right jamb is almost intact. On the outer band is a stylised female figure standing beneath a tree with a flowing arabesque above. Framed within this border are four vertical bands, with a group

Ante-chamber and portal

[1] *Cf.* p. 252 *infra*.

[2] *Cf.* pp. 245-6 *infra*.

of four figures at their base. Of these, the principal one is Yamunā (the River Jumna), with her vehicle, the tortoise, at her feet. Behind her is a female attendant holding a parasol above her head, and between these two is a smaller figure, perhaps of a child, while a still smaller figure sits in the corner of the slab near Yamunā's right foot. Above Yamunā's head is the bust of a Nāga, and above her attendant's head, a lotus supporting a tiny figure of the Buddha in the *bhūmisparśa-mudrā*. Of the vertical bands above, the innermost is covered with a scroll device; the next, which is supported by a demon dwarf (*kumbhāṇḍa*), with leogryphs and riders standing on elephants; the third, also supported by a dwarf, is divided into three panels, each with an erotic scene comprising a male and two female figures; the fourth is in the form of an ornamental pilaster. The decoration of the left jamb, so far as it is preserved, is an exact counterpart of the right one, with the single difference that the Gaṅgā (the River Ganges), with her vehicle, the crocodile, is substituted for Yamunā.

Images in exterior walls

The plainness of the exterior walls is relieved only by three niches sunk in the middle of their southern, eastern and northern faces. In the southern one of these niches is the image of a god, perhaps Mayūravidhyārāja, seated on a lotus throne and holding a lotus stalk in his left hand, with his *vāhana*, the peacock, beneath and a female attendant on either side. In the eastern niche is an image of Buddha seated in the attitude of meditation (*dhyāna-mudrā*) on a lotus throne supported by two lions and accompanied on either side by an attendant, who holds a lotus stalk in the left hand and a fly-whisk in the right. These figures are of the same purplish-brown stone and in the same style as the statue in the *garbha-gṛiha*. The other niche on the north is empty. Carved on some of the stone blocks of the temple walls are several names (perhaps of the masons who cut them), some of which are now upside down, thus proving that the writing, which is in characters of the tenth century, was engraved on them before the building was constructed.

Spire

The spire (*śikhara*) with which this temple was roofed, was of the usual curvilinear type which distinguishes Hindu temple architecture of the northern style. Its summit was crowned with a massive *āmalaka* and *kalaśa* of orthodox form, dismembered fragments of which were lying immediately to the north-west of the temple (Pl. 119 *e*); and from the multitude of other members which were discovered in the debris it is clear that the exterior was relieved on its four faces by repetitions of the same *āmalaka* motif alternating with stylised *caitya* designs (Pl. 119 *f*); but out of the confused mass of fragments it is impossible to restore the original elevation with any degree of certainty. All of the *śikhara* that is still actually standing, is a hollow chamber immediately above the roof of the sanctum, and the vestiges of a small porch in front of it, which extended partly over the roof of the ante-chamber (Pl. 117 *b*). No access to this chamber was provided either inside or outside the temple, and it might appear, therefore, that both chamber and porch were devoid of purpose. As a fact, however, the chamber serves a distinct purpose, in that it lightens the body of the spire, while the porch had a useful decorative effect.

Pradakshiṇa windows

In the outer wall which surrounds the *pradakshiṇa-patha* are two windows of pleasing proportions, provided with heavy pierced stone screens, which are nearly 3 ft. thick and of the usual cross-batten type. Both the outer and inner faces of these screens are decorated with rosettes and floral medallions and enclosed in a frame of conventional lotus leaves.

Raised platform

The raised platform in front of the temple (Pl. 119 *a*) was paved with architectural members taken from several earlier structures, among which were a number of broken pillars and cross-rails belonging to Stūpa 3. These pavestones were clamped together with iron clamps. The vertical faces of the platform are adorned with niches and further relieved by salients and recesses, as well as by deep horizontal mouldings, which produce an effect of criss-cross light and shade almost as indeterminate as it is in Chalukyan architecture. In the niches are one or more figures—sometimes erotic—in the stiff conventional style of the period (Pl. 119 *b* and *c*). Equally conventional are the decorative devices, simulating roofs, over the niches, and the lotus and other floral patterns on the horizontal mouldings.

Temple wings

To the north and south of the temple are two wings, each containing three cells, with a verandah in front. The door-jambs of the two cells nearest the temple are enriched with carvings closely resembling those on the doorway of the temple itself, but are spanned by lintels of a later and totally different style (Pl. 120 *a* and *b*). Seemingly, the building both of the temple and of the wings must have been suddenly interrupted—for what reason, is not known—and not resumed again until many years later.

In constructing the verandah of these wings, some of the pillars belonging to the earlier monastery on the same site were employed, and it is interesting to observe that the carvings on one of these pillars had also been left unfinished and subsequently cut away at the top, in order to adapt the pillar to its new position. These carvings consist of a pot-and-foliage base and capital and three *kīrtimukha* heads on the square band between. They are in the same style as those on the pilasters in the corners of the sanctum, which were also, no doubt, taken from the earlier monastery located on this site. In the south verandah is a seated Buddha in the *bhūmisparśa-mudrā*, evidently of the same age as the statue in the sanctum, and made of the same stone (Pl. 120 *d*). Where this statue originally stood, is not known.

Building 44

South of the temple described above is the structure No. 44, which was erected probably about the same time as Temple 45 and which appears from the disposition of its foundations to have been a small shrine of somewhat unusual type. Its masonry is of the typical late mediæval kind. The eastern wall, unfortunately, is buried beneath the circuit wall of the enclave, but there is no doubt as to the plan. It consisted of an ante-chamber stretching across the whole width of the building, and of a rectangular hall behind it containing the remnants of a pavement, with what appears to have been a stūpa in its centre. On either side of the hall are foundations which seem to indicate that a row of small chambers was built above them; but the chambers must manifestly have been too small for habitation by monks, and, if the foundations correctly represent the plan of the superstructure, we must infer that the cells were intended for the reception of images, as in some of the Gandhāra chapels and in many temples of the Jains. The building stands on a stone plinth, 4 ft. high and ascended by a flight of steps in the middle of its western side. Its walls are constructed of rough rubble faced on both sides with well-cut, small ashlar of the local purplish stone, and provided on the outside with footings, which start immediately above the plinth referred to. In the rectangular hall stand three images of the same purplish-brown stone—two of the Buddha in the *dhyāna-mudrā*, the third of Maitreya seated in western fashion.[1] That they stood here in ancient times seems not improbable.

Monasteries 46 and 47

Another building on a more elaborate plan abuts on to the northern and western sides of the court in front of Temple 45. This was not erected until after Temple 45 had been reconstructed, and it can hardly be assigned to an earlier date than the eleventh century A.D. As will be seen from the plan (Pl. 121 *a*), it comprises two monastic courts, numbered respectively 46 and 47, the larger of which, including the verandahs and chambers ranged about three of its sides, measures 103 ft. from north to south by 78 ft. from east to west. On the south side of this court is a pillared verandah, with a small cell and a long narrow chamber at the back; on the west is a closed colonnade, and on the north a pillared verandah (Pls. 117 *a* and 122 *a*), with a shrine containing a small ante-chamber and sanctum at its western end, and, behind it, a corridor and five cells. In the sanctum of this shrine is a statue-base measuring 4 ft. 9 in. long by 2 ft. 2 in. wide and 7 in. high. The main entrance to this court is at the northern end of the western colonnade, and a second doorway leads by two steps from the eastern end of the northern verandah into the smaller court 46, which is on a somewhat higher level and, like the larger court, provided with chambers on three sides. This monastery is still in a relatively good state of preservation, portions of the roof as well as many of the pillars being still intact. For the most part the walls are built of neat regular masonry, but the construction of the verandah and chambers on the southern side, as well as of some of the interior walls of the smaller court, is noticeably inferior, and it seems probable that these were later additions. The pillars and pilasters in the verandah and cells are roughly dressed and relieved only by chamfering of the edges. They were set on simple squared bases and surmounted by capitals of the common Hindu bracket type. The roof, which was flat, was composed of thick stone slabs, 4 to 7 in. thick, resting on plain solid architraves, and once, no doubt, covered with a thick layer of earth or lime plaster. Throughout the monastery the stonework is coarsely and plainly treated, the only effort

[1] The two images of Dhyāni Buddha are headless; they measure 3 ft. 10 in. and 3 ft. 8 in., respectively, in height. The Maitreya Buddha, which is broken in the middle and much defaced, is 4 ft. 3½ in. high.

towards decorative carving being on the bracket capitals, the faces of which are relieved with simple roll mouldings, and on the jambs of the doorway leading into the corridor on the north side, which are adorned with a lotus-leaf border. Probably both pillars and walls were intended to be covered with plaster, though, in the absence of any trace of it, it seems unlikely that the intention was ever carried into effect.

The quadrangles of both the larger and smaller courts were paved with massive stone slabs between 4 and 8 in. in thickness and considerably heavier, therefore, than those employed in and around the earliest stūpas and in Temple 40. Beneath the pavement in the larger court were found numerous architectural members of an earlier age, including a column in the Gupta style. Still lower down—at a depth, that is to say, of about 3 ft. below the pavement—was brought to light a stone floor of an earlier building ; then, a second *kachcha* floor, 9 in. lower ; and, again, a third floor of concrete, 2 ft. 3 in. below the second. These floors belonged to earlier monasteries, but, inasmuch as the lowest of them was not more ancient than the Gupta times, it was not deemed worth while to continue the excavation. Let it be added that all the walls, most of the roof slabs and some of the pavement slabs are of local purplish-brown stone, while the pillars, architraves, kerbstones and others of the pavement slabs are of grey Nāgourī stone.

Buildings 49, 50 and 32

The long boundary wall, about 7 ft. high, at the back of the structures 49 and 50, which abuts on to the north-west corner of Monastery 47, appears to be older than the latter, since the western wall of the monastery is built on to it. It stands about 7 ft. high, and is built of somewhat loose masonry. Near its southern end, on its west side, was subsequently erected a small building, of which only the raised plinth (No. 49) survives. Another building, also subsequently erected, is that numbered 50 on the plan (Pl. 2), the construction of which necessitated the demolition of part of the boundary wall. All that now remains of this building, consists of some stone pavements, walls and column bases, but these are sufficient to indicate that it was a monastery and, moreover, that it dates from approximately the same age as Monastery 47. Included within its precincts and situated apparently in the middle of one of its courts, is the small structure 32. This structure, which dates from the late mediæval period, is standing to a height of about eight feet above the ground level and consists of three small rooms, with an ante-chamber in front and an underground cellar beneath the central room. It is entered by a doorway in the eastern side of the ante-chamber, and there is another doorway opposite, leading into the central chamber, but the side chambers, curiously enough, are provided only with windows, through which any one wishing to enter would have to crawl. The structure measures 39 ft. 6 in. from north to south by 19 ft. 10 in. from east to west. Like the outer walls and verandahs of the later Temple 45, it is constructed of large blocks of Nāgourī stone well dressed on their outer faces, the roof being composed of thick stone slabs carried on solid architraves, which are supported in turn by corbel brackets projecting from the walls. In the central chamber there are six such brackets—four at the corners and two in the side walls—but in the side chambers there are four only at the corners, and these four are supported on pilasters surmounted by square capitals.

Building 43

One of the last of the monuments to be erected on the site of Sāñchī is the Building 43, which stands partly on the high ground of the eastern terrace, partly on the lower ground to the south of it (Pl. 122 *b*, background). In plan, this structure resembles the famous Stūpa of Kanishka at Peshawar, being cruciform in shape, with a round bastion at each of its four corners ; but, in the absence of any remains of a superstructure, it must remain doubtful whether it ever served as the base of a stūpa. As it stands, it is nothing more than an elevated court surrounded by low parapet walls, with traces here and there of a few interior walls, which appear to have been later additions and have, accordingly, been omitted from the plan. The surrounding walls of this court, as well as of the bastions, are rather less than 4 ft. 6 in. in thickness and are constructed of massive blocks of stone of varying sizes, among which are many that have been taken from dismantled buildings of the tenth or eleventh century A.D., but, as these particular blocks were built only into the top of the wall, it is possible that they belonged to a relatively late repair. On the south side, the wall has an altitude of eight to ten feet outside, and here the foundations descend another four or five feet ; but on the north, where the ground is higher, the foundations are quite shallow and the wall itself has a height of not more than three feet.

In the plan on Pl. 2 there are shown, almost in the centre of this edifice, the remains of some cells with a courtyard on their northern side. These remains were exposed in a trench sunk beneath the floor of the courtyard and belong to a monastery which was erected on this site, probably in the seventh or eighth century A.D.[1] The floor of this monastery is 12 ft. below the present level of the court, and its walls, which are built of ordinary dry-stone masonry, are standing to a height of between six and seven feet ; so that their tops come within five or six feet of the present surface. Besides this excavation in the middle of the courtyard, shafts were also sunk in the south-western and north-western bastions. Beneath the former was found, as already observed, a section of the old stone pavement laid around the Great Stūpa in the Śuṅga period. At the base of the latter and at a depth of 14 ft. from the surface, was brought to light a large earthenware jar inverted over a stone slab, but whether this jar had any connexion or not with the building of the bastion, was not evident.

[1] For an inscription of about this period found on this site, *cf.* p. 398, Inscr. 842.

Chapter VII

THE SECOND STŪPA AND NEIGHBOURING REMAINS

THE Second Stūpa, which, after the Great Stūpa, is in many ways the most important monument at Sāñchī, stands on a small terrace projecting out from the hill-side some 350 yards down its western slope. The terrace is of artificial construction, the retaining walls which support it having a length of some 37 yards with a height of 11 ft. on the west side, of 38 yards on the south side, and of 20 yards on the north. The location of the stūpa on this terrace is significant, since at the time when it was built there must still have been a considerable area unoccupied on the hill-top above, and it is not at first sight clear why so much trouble was taken to build up this small terrace apart from, and below, the other stūpas. The reason, I think, is to be found in the character of the body-relics enshrined in the Second Stūpa. The Great Stūpa, as we have seen, was built for the relics of Gautama Buddha himself ; and it was fitting that the relics of his two chief disciples, Śāriputra and Maudgalyāyana, should be buried nearly on the same level though in a less pretentious monument. In like manner in the Tāj Mahal at Agra, the tombs of the faithful maids-of-honour of the Mughal empress were placed round about the mausoleum of their mistress, that they might wait on her in death as they had waited on her in life. And there can be little doubt that the relics in the other two stūpas of this age on the same terrace, *viz.*, the Fourth and the Sixth, were those of other companions of the Buddha. But the Second Stūpa was designed, as we shall presently see, to hold the relics of ten of the church dignitaries who were living in the time of Aśoka—less than a century before the stūpa was erected ; and, whatever the achievements and fame of the dead may have been, there must manifestly have been an objection to burying their remains side by side with those of the Buddha and his personal disciples.[1]

Location of Stūpa 2

In point of size, as well as of construction and design, the Second Stūpa (Pls. 71-73) was almost a replica of the Third, the main difference between them being in the decoration of the ground balustrade. Its diameter, exclusive of the procession path and enclosing balustrade, was 47 ft.; its height, to the top of the dome, 29 ft., and to the top of the crowning umbrella, 37 ft.[2] In the four quadrants of the ground balustrade there are 88 pillars in all, of which 3 are modern restorations.[3] A drawing of the balustrade in elevation and section is given on Pl. 72 *a*, and photos of the whole repertoire of reliefs

Form and construction

Decoration of balustrade

[1] The line thus drawn in regard to these relics in the second century B.C. is significant in connexion with what has been said above about the development of relic and stūpa cults.

[2] The dome of the Second Stūpa was wrongly restored by a former political officer in the shape of a Muhammadan dome. This faulty restoration has now been corrected, as far as was possible without rebuilding the whole ; but its shape is still a little misleading.

[3] The height of the pillars varies from 5 ft. 10 in. to 6 ft. 4 in., a few inches less than the corresponding pillars of the Third Stūpa ; of the coping it is 1 ft. 5 in., making 7 ft. 3 in. to 7 ft. 9 in. over all. The coping is 13¾ in. thick, and the cross-bars 17½ in. long by 18 in. broad.

which adorn them, in Pls. 74 to 91. It is these reliefs that give the balustrade its unique value and make it an outstanding landmark in the history of Indian art no less than of Buddhism. The subjects portrayed are generally similar to those on the gateways of the Great Stūpa. Among them, the four chief events of the Buddha's life are conspicuous: his Birth, his Enlightenment, his First Sermon, and his Death—each represented by its own peculiar symbol: the lotus, the *pīpal* tree, the wheel and the stūpa. Then, there are the familiar figures of Yakshas and Yakshīs, many-hooded Nāgas, and a host of real and fabulous animals, sometimes with riders, sometimes without, like those which adorn the false capitals on the gateways of the Great Stūpa: elephants, bulls, horses, deer, winged lions, *makaras* and griffins, and other creatures of the fancy, also, that do not occur on the gateways, such as horse-headed and fish-tailed men or centaurs with women on their backs—forms which seem to have had their origin in Western Asia rather than in India. Among plants, the favourite one is the lotus—magic symbol of birth and life and giver of bounteous gifts to mortals—sometimes quite simply treated, sometimes in rich and elaborate devices; among birds, the peacock, the goose and the *sāras* are prominent; and among characteristic Buddhist emblems other than those already mentioned, the *triratna, nandipada,* and *śrīvatsa,* and pillars crowned by lions or elephants. The iconography and symbolism of these remarkable reliefs is discussed in full by Mons. Foucher in Part III, and the place which they occupy in early Indian art is dealt with in Part II. Meanwhile, all that need be said as to their style, is that they exhibit the true indigenous character of archaic Indian art, the keynote of which is a strikingly crude treatment of the living figure, combined with a no less striking power of decorative design. The age of these reliefs, as indicated by their style as well as by the palæography of the inscriptions which accompany them, may be fixed in the last quarter of the second century B.C. A century or more later, a few reliefs, in a much more mature style of art, were superimposed on the earlier ones, and afford a most instructive demonstration of the rapid and remarkable development which the sculpture of Central India underwent in the first century B.C. (Pls. 78 and 79—Pillars 22 *a* and 27 *a* and *b*).

Stairway, berm and harmikā balustrades

The smaller balustrades belonging to the stairway, berm and *harmikā* so closely resemble the corresponding features of the Third Stūpa, that neither their form nor their construction call for further remark. But the following minor points connected with their surface decoration are deserving of notice. With the exception of the newel-posts, which are more elaborately adorned, the uprights of the stairway balustrade are relieved on both their inner and outer faces with one complete and two half discs of varying pattern (Pl. 72 *b*). Similar rosettes are found also on the inner face of the landing balustrade, but the outer face of this balustrade is further embellished with narrow perpendicular bands of carving between the discs, or, in the case of the corner posts, with still more elaborate designs. The berm balustrade, on the other hand, has merely plain discs on its inner face, of which the centre one is sometimes omitted. The discs on the outer face are relieved with lotus designs and other floral or animal devices, *e.g.*, a lion, a bull or an elephant (Pl. 72 *c*). The coping of the *harmikā* balustrade is enriched, on its inner face only, with a row of full-blown lotuses. The corresponding coping of the Third Stūpa is decorated on its outer, not on its inner, face.

Relic-chamber and relics of well-known teachers

This stūpa was first opened and half destroyed by Capt. Johnson in 1822, but it was reserved for Gen. Cunningham, who continued the digging in 1851, to discover the relics, and, unfortunately, also to complete the destruction of the dome. The chamber in which the relics were deposited was not in the centre of the structure, but two feet to the west of it, and at a height of seven feet above the raised terrace. The relic-box was of grey-white sandstone, 11 in. long by 9½ in. broad, and the same in height, including the lid. It contained four small caskets of steatite, in each of which were some fragments of human bone.[1] On the side of the relic-box was an inscription in early Brāhmī characters, to the effect that it contained the relics "of all teachers including Kāsapagota and Vāchi-Suvijayita".[2] On the four steatite caskets were other inscriptions giving the names of the ten saints whose relics were enclosed within, some of whom are said to have taken part in the Third Convocation held under the emperor Aśoka, while others were sent out on missions to the Himālayas, to preach the doctrines then settled. These ten saints are as follows:—Kāsapagota, the teacher of all the Hemavatas;[3] Majjhima; Hāritīputa; Vāchi-Suvijayita, pupil of Gota; Mahavanāya; Āpagira Koḍiniputa; Kosikiputa; Gotiputa; and Mogaliputa. The last of these was identified by Cunningham and Geiger with Mogaliputa Tissa or Upagupta, as he was otherwise known, the president of the Third Council at Pāṭaliputra, and author of the *Kathāvatthu*, in which are set forth the differences that led to the holding of the Council, but Mr. Majumdar rightly points out that this identification is hardly tenable, since Mogaliputa was the pupil of Gotiputa, who in turn was the heir of Dudhubhisara, and the latter is to be identified with the Dandubhissara mentioned in the Dīpavaṁsa as one of the five missionaries sent by Upagupta to the Himālayas after the close of the Third Council, the other four being Kāsapagota, Majjhima, Sahadeva and Mulakadeva. Of these, the relics of Kāsapagota himself and of Majjhima have been found in this Second Stūpa at Sāñchī, and of Kāsapagota, Majjhima and Dudhubhisara in the same stūpa at Sonāri.[4] Another portion of the relics of Kosikiputa were also found in the same stūpa at Sonāri.

Age of Stūpa 2

Because Sāriputa and Mahāmogalāna, whose relics were enshrined in the Third Stūpa, were companions of the Buddha, it does not of course follow that that stūpa goes back to the time of the Buddha; nor, because some or possibly all of the teachers whose relics were deposited in the Second Stūpa, were contemporaries of Aśoka, is it to be concluded that this stūpa was erected during the Maurya epoch. On the contrary, as these

---

[1] *The Bhilsa Topes*, pp. 286-7.

[2] *Cf.* below, pp. 289-91; Cunningham, *loc. cit.*, and Lüders, *List of Brāhmī Inscriptions* (*Ep. Ind.*, Vol. X), No. 654.

[3] The term 'Hemavata' used here has usually been thought to have reference to the missions despatched to the Himālayas. But the Haimavatas were a branch of the Theravāda School, and Mr. Majumdar is probably right in translating 'Hemavata' as a member of the Haimavata Order. See p. 292 *infra*.

[4] Geiger, *Mahāvaṁsa*, Introd., p. XIX; *J. R. A. S.*, 1905, pp. 683 ff.

teachers could not have died at one and the same time, it is evident that their relics must have had some other resting places before portions of them were brought to Sāñchī, and it is natural to conclude that this transference did not take place until the Śuṅga period, when there are other grounds for believing that this stūpa was erected. Cunningham[1] opined that the stūpa was at first intended only for the relics of Kāsapagota and of Vāchi-Suvijayita, whose names alone are found on the outside of the stone box. This view is questioned by Mr. Majumdar,[2] but in any case there is no implication that the building of the stūpa followed immediately after the death of either of these divines. Its date may be fixed with virtual certainty in the last quarter of the second century B.C., and to this period also belong its ground balustrade and the bulk of the reliefs which embellish it[3].

Other remains in the vicinity of Stūpa 2

Alongside the old road[4] which descended from the main terrace to Stūpa 2 can still be traced the foundations of several monuments that once stood on this side of the hill. Noteworthy among them is the ruined base of an apsidal shrine about 61 ft. long by 32 ft. 6 in wide, facing towards the east (Pl. 1). The other remains are nothing but ruined platforms of rough stone masonry, from which the superstructures have disappeared. Three of these are situate to the west and north-west of the apsidal shrine, and a fourth to the east of it; then there is a fifth, about 70 yards north of the last-mentioned, on the opposite side of the old road; and two more, close together, on the north side of the road, some 80 yards higher up. North of them, again, and partly cut through by the modern road, is an extensive mound of stone rubble and brick, which marks the site of a mediæval monastery; and near by, to the west, a smaller mound with a stone bowl on its summit. The bowl is of immense size, having a diameter at the top of 8 ft. 8 in., and Cunningham conjectured that it once held a nettle which Buddha himself was reputed to have bitten off and planted. For this conjecture, however, there are no grounds, since it depends in the first instance on the false identification of Sāñchī with Sha-chi of Fa Hien. Probably the gigantic bowl was intended for the distribution of food offered at the shrine, like the bowl inscribed *Bhāgāya pasādo*, to which allusion has already been made.[5]

On the other side of Stūpa 2, and a little below it to the N.-N.-W., is another rectangular platform, 7 by 9 yards, which juts out from the hill-side towards the west. On it once stood a stone pillar, several pieces of which, together with what were probably parts of the lion-capital (Pl. 104 *g*), were found by its side. From these it appears that the shaft of the pillar, like that of Pillar 25 on the main terrace,[6] was octagonal below and sixteen-sided above, with a gentle upward taper, and that, just as on that pillar, some of the facets were fluted, others flat, but that the former did not alternate with the latter. Pillar and platform are referable to the Śuṅga period, and are, therefore, contemporary or thereabouts with Stūpa 2.

[1] *Op. cit.*, p. 291. [2] *Cf.* p. 289. [3] *Cf.* pp. 95 and 270 *infra*. [4] *Cf.* p. 13 *supra*. [5] *Cf.* p. 55 *supra*. [6] *Cf.* p. 49 *supra*.

PART TWO

THE ART OF SAÑCHĪ

CHAPTER VIII

PREHISTORIC AND MAURYAN ART

UNTIL quite recently it was commonly assumed that the history of Indian art virtually began during the Mauryan rule under the influence of foreign—mainly Yavana—teaching; and that, whatever art there may have been before then, was, at the best, of a crude, primitive kind, executed in materials, such as wood, clay or paint, which have long since perished. This assumption was not an unnatural one. Sanskritists had been unanimous in attributing everything of merit in Indian culture to the invading Indo-Āryans, and in the literature of these Indo-Āryans there was nothing to indicate that they possessed any marked degree of skill, either in building or in the formative arts. Hence it was inferred that there was little in the way of architecture or art to be looked for until the coming of the Greeks; and this inference seemed to be confirmed by the monuments themselves, since the earliest remains that had any pretensions to artistic merit were the pillars set up by the emperor Aśoka in the third century B.C., which were demonstrably the outcome of foreign inspiration, while the more truly Indian monuments that succeeded them were not only more primitive in style, but were also palpably copied from wooden prototypes, so that there could be no question but that up to the time of the Mauryas wood had been the principal material employed by Indian builders. Had this long-established view represented the whole truth as to the beginnings of Indian art, we should hardly have to go beyond Sāñchī itself in order to follow its evolution from the start; for, as we have already seen, one of the finest pillars of Aśoka stands on this very site, and from the time of its erection onwards down to the Christian era—the period that here chiefly concerns us—the remains of Sāñchī comprise the most complete and instructive series of sculptures that we possess. Far from starting in the third century B.C., however, it is now evident that Indian art had its roots extending far back into the Copper and Stone ages. One chapter in the long story of this art has recently been revealed by the revolutionary discoveries at Harappā and Mohenjo-daro, and we can already see how, long anterior to the coming of the Vedic Āryans, India possessed a brilliant civilization of her own, comparable to the contemporary civilizations of Sumer, Babylonia and Egypt. And though the remains of this civilization are for the most part of a severely utilitarian rather than artistic character, there are nevertheless many examples of creative art of a very high order, including statuettes and engraved seals unsurpassed even by the finest products of Minoan Crete. Any attempt, therefore, that may be made to unravel the tangled origins of Indian art in the historic period, is bound to take account of these earlier achievements; and, indeed, this is true not

The beginnings of art in India

The Indus civilization and the debt which historic India owes to it

only of India's art, but of almost every aspect of her ancient culture, since, however remote in time the Indus civilization may have been, it can hardly be doubted that its authors were closely related to the peoples of non-Āryan India, who have continued down to the present day to form the bulk of her population ; nor can it be doubted that later India owed many of her institutions and beliefs, as well as much of her material culture, to this older civilization. The extent of this debt in the sphere of religion has already been abundantly proved. So far as popular Hinduism is concerned, it is not too much to say that its fabric was largely woven out of cults and practices that can be traced back to the Indus age—out of the cults of stones and of water, of trees and of animals, of the *liṅga* and *yonī*, of Siva and of the Earth and of the Mother Goddesses. And if these age-old cults did less for the fashioning of Buddhism than of Hinduism, nevertheless the sculptures of Sāñchī and Bharhut afford manifold illustrations of sacred objects and divinities drawn from the ancient religion of the people : of symbols and amulets, of tree and animal cults, of the Yakshas and Yakshīs, Nāgas and Nāgarājas. For all that the *pīpal* might be camouflaged as the Bo-Tree of the Buddha, it still remained the Indian Tree of Life and Knowledge, as it had been from time immemorial; and though Lakshmī might figure as the mother of the Buddha, the Goddess of Prosperity was too time-honoured and familiar a type to be mistaken. The names might be transformed, but the cults continued immutable.

in the sphere of religion

Such cults were not, of course, the only elements taken over by Buddhism from the popular religion. There must have been other more abstract and intangible features also ; the doctrines, for example, of *karma* and *saṁsāra*, and the idea of *bhakti*, which Buddhism no less than Hinduism inherited from non-Āryan sources, but which in the nature of things did not lend themselves to portrayal in figurative art. We need not, however, pursue this subject of religion further. Our only purpose in referring to it at all is to make it clear that in this particular domain we have to reckon with an abundance of survivals from the prehistoric past, and that it would be surprising if similar survivals were not found in the domain of art. Let it be said at once, however, that Indian art was by no means so conservative as Indian religion. The arts of the prehistoric and early historic ages undoubtedly have much in common. Their underlying spirit betrays a kinship which is specially observable in their intuitive feeling for animal forms—a feeling that is as characteristic of the engraved seals of Mohenjo-daro and Harappā as it is of the bas-reliefs of Sāñchī, though at two such distant ages it does not of course manifest itself in identically the same way. At Sāñchī, the most striking of all the animals represented is the elephant ; and it is not too much to say that for simple truthfulness to nature the varied poses in which this beast is depicted are unsurpassed ; indeed, it is the convincing and unpremeditated naturalness of the figures, both animal and human. at Sāñchī, that constitutes one of the greatest merits of these sculptures. At Mohenjo-daro, on the other hand, the elephants, though well enough engraved, are less

and of art

successful than some of the humped bulls and bison; and the latter, moreover, while exhibiting a keen observation of nature, appeal to us less for this quality than for their subtle stylishness, though by this I do not mean to imply that the reliefs of Sāñchī are lacking in stylishness; for the elephants on the South Gateway (Pl. 15) have a decided stylishness of their own, which gives them an attraction unshared by any other group of these animals on the gateways. Nevertheless, speaking generally, it must be admitted that this particular trait is definitely more distinctive of the Indus engravings, and that unaffected naïveté is the hall-mark of the Sāñchī reliefs.

But, whatever the minor differences of style—and, considering the long interval that elapsed between the two periods, it would be surprising if these had been less marked than they are—it still remains true that the sculptures of Sāñchī betray the same instinctive understanding of animal forms and the same aptitude in portraying them as their predecessors of two or three thousand years before. On the other hand, it is a significant fact that, among all the remains unearthed at Mohenjo-daro and Harappā, not a trace is to be found of any of the traditional decorative motifs, such as the full-blown and half-blown lotus, the suspended garland or the sinuous creeper pattern, that have characterised Indian art during the last two thousand years, and which constitute the most easily recognisable links between its many different Schools and Periods. We are not speaking here of religious symbols and forms, some of which, as we have already seen, can be traced back to the Chalcolithic age, but only of those purely ornamental and highly stylised devices which form the groundwork, as it were, of so much Indian sculpture and painting, and which could only have been perpetuated by a continuity of artistic, as distinct from religious, tradition. In respect of such devices the art of Sāñchī bears a closer affinity to that of Assyria or Achæmenid Persia than of Mohenjo-daro and Harappā.

Break in traditions governing decorative art between prehistoric and historic ages

How and when these and other motifs that characterise the Sāñchī reliefs were introduced into India, will be discussed a little later, when we come to deal with the official art of Aśoka's reign. The point that has to be stressed here, is that, up to the present, no grounds have been found for associating these motifs with the Indus or other contemporary civilization of the Chalcolithic age. So far as they are concerned, there seems to have been an almost complete break in continuity between the prehistoric and historic ages. And this is equally true of the technique of sculpture. For, whereas the sculptor of the Indus period had effectually emancipated his art from the bonds of the "memory image" and the law of "frontality", and had learnt to model his figures completely in the round, without a trace of archaic stiffness, it is evident from the crude efforts of his successors in the historic period, that the old-time skill in the modelling and carving of figures out of stone had been entirely forgotten, and that the lessons by which it had been acquired had to be learnt afresh.

Parallel furnished by Early Greece

Thus, the relation of historic to prehistoric art in India was closely parallel to what it was in Early Greece. In both countries, figurative art had attained an astonishing degree of excellence during the Copper and Bronze ages; in both countries, its progress was summarily interrupted by the Āryan invasions; and its memory was forgotten during the Dark ages that followed. All that survived the wreck of those invasions was the inborn artistry that ran in the blood of the people, and those elements of language and religion which nothing short of extinction could efface. Before art could blossom again, its technique had to be rediscovered almost from the start. In Greece, this was achieved between the sixth and fifth centuries B.C.; in India, not until three centuries later. In Greece, the artist was helped to some extent along his way by the teachings of Egyptian, Assyrian and Persian art; in India, he had the added experience of Hellenic art to assist him.

Mauryan sculptures at Sāñchī

To turn now to the surviving sculptures of Sāñchī—the earliest of these are the Lion Capital of the Aśoka pillar described on pp. 25-6 above, and the standard bowl and broken umbrellas described on pp. 24 and 55. As already remarked, these objects have three features in common—features which are also shared by all other known specimens of the official art of this period: their material is the hard buff-grey sandstone from the quarries of Chunar, their chiselling is exquisitely sharp and accurate, and their surface is polished to a brilliance almost resembling that of glass. The process by which this polish was imparted to the stone, is not known, and efforts made by experts to imitate it have not been successful, though it seems clear from microscopic examination that it was produced with the help of abrasives only, and without artificial glaze of any kind. The polishing of stone has been practised (need it be said?) at all ages in India, and we shall see presently that the reliefs on the gateways of the Great Stūpa were originally both polished and coloured, as, also, were many mediæval statues. We must be careful, therefore, not to jump to the conclusion that, because a sandstone object is polished, therefore it must be of Mauryan date. Later craftsmen, it is true, were not able to get quite the same degree of lustrous sheen as their Mauryan predecessors had done, but that may have been partly because other sandstones were not so exceptionally fine-grained as the Chunar variety, and not capable, therefore, of taking such a high degree of polish. Be this, however, as it may, it needs a very practised eye and sometimes microscopic examination of the stone to distinguish the polish of different periods.

Lion Capitals at Sāñchī and Sārnāth compared

Of all the sculptures of Aśoka's reign, the Lion Capitals of his two pillars at Sāñchī and Sārnāth are immeasurably the finest. Though not themselves of equal merit, they stand in a class by themselves, and for this reason have been reproduced, side by side, on Pl. 107. The resemblance between the two is obvious: a bell-shaped foliate capital supporting a circular abacus, on which stand four lions addorsed—that is the design of both, and their style, too, is in correspondingly close accord. On the other hand, there are notable differences of detail. In the Sāñchī example, the bell-capital is not so squat as it is at Sārnāth, and it is better adapted, therefore, to its position on the top of a lofty pillar, where it was necessarily foreshortened. In the Sāñchī example, again, the necking takes the form of a cable moulding; in the Sārnāth one, it is plain. In the former, the abacus is noticeably thinner than in the latter, and is adorned with four pairs of geese—symbolical, perhaps, of the Buddha's followers—alternating with conventional honeysuckle patterns; in the latter, it is adorned with four "Wheels-of-the-Law" (*dharmacakra*) alternating with the four animals that guard the Four Quarters:[1] the horse, the elephant, the lion and the humped bull. In the former, the crowning feature was the group of four lions which stood alone on the abacus; in the latter, the lions supported a Wheel-of-the-Law, which rose between them in the manner depicted in Pl. 106 *d*. Nor are these the only differences. Although the pillars are identical in material and technique, and correspond closely in style, the Sāñchī capital misses the subtle artistry, the finer feeling for form of the other. Both groups of lions exhibit the same tense muscular development, the same spirited realism combined with the same formal tectonic qualities, which the artist rightly introduced in order to harmonise them with the architectural character of the monument; but we cannot help remarking how much less true to nature and, therefore, less vital and convincing is the modelling of the Sāñchī beasts, how disproportionately broad and swelling their chests, how widely spaced their legs, how much more mechanical the treatment of their manes. That the original designs of the two capitals were the work of one and the same artist can hardly be disputed, but the difference in workmanship makes it virtually certain that the actual carving of the Sāñchī capital was done by some less gifted assistant.

Their author not Indian

Now, the question before us is, whence came the artist who designed these capitals, and what traditions had he behind him? Was he an Indian or a foreigner? Certainly he was not an Indian. In the third century B.C., when these monuments were erected, indigenous art in India was in a quite immature state. Sculpture, especially decorative sculpture, both in relief and in the round, was probably common enough, but it was executed in wood or other impermanent materials, and no specimens of it have survived. The state of its development, however, can be fairly gauged from the sculptures of the following century at Sāñchī and other places, and it is safe to say that it was wholly incapable of producing works of this calibre, which represent the most developed art of which the world was then cognisant—as incapable as the archaic age of Greece would have been of producing, let us say, the Altar of Pergamum. Indeed, even more so; for these two capitals are wholly alien to the spirit of Indian Art, and there was no subsequent school or epoch in the history of that art which might conceivably have produced them.

[1] The horse is guardian of the South, the bull of the West, the lion of the North, and the elephant of the East. *Cf.* V. Smith, *The Monolithic Pillars of Aśoka*, *Z. D. M. G.*, 1911, pp. 237 ff., and Bachhofer, *Early Indian Sculpture*, Vol. I, p. 5 and note 17.

but Asiatic Greek

If, however, the artist was not Indian, whence came he? Twenty years ago I pointed out that it was only an Asiatic Greek sculptor with generations of artistic effort and experience behind him who could have created the Sāñchī capital, and I opined that Aśoka had probably brought this sculptor and doubtless others with him from Bactria. I suggested Bactria, because it was evident that the author of this capital was not only steeped in Greek tradition but had come under Iranian influence also, and for many reasons Bactria seemed the most probable source from which he had drawn his inspiration. Bactria, as I pointed out, had once been a satrapy of Achæmenid Persia, and had been planted less than three generations before with a powerful colony of Greeks, who, living as they did on the very threshold of the Maurya dominions, must have played a dominant part in the transmission of Hellenistic or Perso-Hellenistic ideas into India. Be it remembered, too, that the smooth, unfluted shafts which characterise these *lāṭs* of Aśoka, their bell-shaped capitals and the lustrous polish with which their surfaces were finished, are all traceable to a Persian origin, and, moreover, that a strong Persian influence is observable in the Edicts which are engraved on Aśoka's pillars. For all these reasons there seemed to me a strong presumption in favour of Bactria. But whether the artist was a Bactrian or not, there can be no reasonable doubt as to his having been trained in the Hellenistic School or to his being familiar with Iranian models. It was not, of course, for a moment presumed that a single sculptor was responsible for all the monuments of Aśoka, which were certainly very numerous, nor yet that all the sculptors employed were of equal ability. I took the view that many Indians were employed to assist the foreign artists in the mechanical part of their work, and that these assistants may have been responsible for many of the less successful sculptures. I maintained, however, and still maintain, that no Indian hand at that period could either have modelled in clay or chiselled from the stone such perfected forms as those of the Sārnāth capital. Moreover, notwithstanding the relative inferiority of the Sāñchī capital, I still deem it highly improbable that it could have been the work of an Indian apprentice, with little or no previous knowledge of stone carving.

Confirmation afforded by discoveries at Sārnāth

These views of mine on the authorship of these sculptures have since been generally accepted, and have received fresh confirmation from a number of Mauryan heads and other fragments unexpectedly unearthed by Mr. Hargreaves at Sārnāth itself,[1] which though evidently of local workmanship, nevertheless prove by various details, notably by the wreaths and mural crowns with which some of the heads are crowned, how strong Western Asiatic influence must have been at this time. Further corroboration, too, of these views has been furnished by Dr. Ludwig Bachhofer in his valuable book *Early Indian Sculpture*[2], where he points out certain specific features in which the lions of the Sāñchī and Sārnāth capitals resemble Greek works of the same class, but differ radically from Indian, *viz.*, the distinctive treatment of the "cheek-bones and moustache and the deep

[1] *A. S. R.*, 1914-15, p. 111.

[2] Vol. I, p. 7.

sinking of the eyes, which he contrasts with the protruding eyes of Indian lions. While endorsing my opinion, however, as to the sculptor of these capitals having been steeped in the tradition of Græco-Asiatic Art, Dr. Bachhofer believes, nevertheless, that he was a Hindu, though how or where he managed to acquire so consummate a mastery of that art, he does not attempt to explain. Many instances might be quoted of oriental potentates sending for skilled craftsmen from foreign lands, but I do not recall a single instance of their sending their own craftsmen to study abroad. In his Edict relating to the palace at Susa, Darius tells us how, for the building and adorning of it, craftsmen of many nations were brought together. "The artisans who wrought the stone, they were Ionian Greeks and Sardians; the goldsmiths who wrought the gold, they were Medes and Egyptians; the men who wrought the *išmalu*, they were Sardians and Egyptians; the men who worked on the baked brick, they were Babylonians; the men who adorned the walls, they were Medes and Egyptians."[1] If, then, Aśoka imported Yavanas from Bactria or elsewhere, to help in the building of his palace at Pāṭaliputra and the carving of his edict-pillars, he was only following the precedent of the great king whose edicts he was using as models for his own—a precedent that was followed by many an Indian monarch down to the Mughal emperors of Delhi.[2] It may be, however, that Dr. Bachhofer credits his Hindu sculptors with having learnt their art from Greek models in India. If so, then we have to conclude that Greek sculptors had already found their way to India before these pillars were designed, since it is manifestly unlikely that heavy pieces of stone carving would have been imported there by way of trade, and equally unlikely that, from mere observation of them, Indian craftsmen could have mastered so succesfully all the secrets of the sculptor's art. And if we are to postulate the presence of Yavana sculptors in India at all, why should we not attribute to them these particular capitals, which are entirely foreign to Indian genius? But there is another insuperable objection to Dr. Bachhofer's theory; for, if in the third century B.C. Hindus were capable of designing and carving such capitals, how comes it that a century later, when the Yavanas had settled in large numbers in the Panjāb and when there must have been far more numerous models of Hellenistic or Perso-Hellenistic art to inspire the Indian, he could achieve nothing more advanced than the reliefs on the railings of Stūpa 2 at Sāñchī or of the Stūpa of Bharhut? If Dr. Bachhofer is right, we have no alternative but to conclude that early Indian sculpture had a history unparalleled in the art of any other country: that it achieved its most mature results almost at its birth, then returned to a primitive state, and passed through all the usual stages of archaism before it finally arrived at maturity. That is a proposition to which few familiar with the history of art are likely to assent. A somewhat similar view to Dr. Bachhofer's is taken in Smith's *History of Fine Art in India and Ceylon*, and the curious argument is there put forward

Custom among oriental potentates of employing foreign artists and craftsmen

Views of Bachhofer and V. Smith

---

[1] *Cf.* R. C. Kent in *J. A. O. S.*, 1933, No. I, p. 9.

[2] *E.g.*, Bindusāra, father of Aśoka, who wrote to Antiochus I, asking him to send, among other things, a sophist to teach him how to argue (Athenæus XIV, 67, 652 *f* and 653 *a*; *C. H. I.*, I, 432-3); Gondophares, who brought St. Thomas from Palestine or thereabouts as a carpenter; and Shāh Jahān, who recruited numbers of foreign artists and craftsmen for the building of the Tāj Mahal.

that no foreigner would have been capable of modelling the distinctively Indian animals on the abacus of the Sārnāth capital!—an argument that is all the more curious, because the only Indian animals on the abacus are the elephant and the humped bull, and as it happens, neither of these are specially well modelled. The elephant's eye is much too large, and in other respects it is well below the standard of many of the elephants carved on the Sāñchī gateways, while the humped bull bears no comparison to some of the magnificent animals carved on the Indus seals. On the other hand, the horse, which is the only really spirited animal among the four, is portrayed in a manner typical of Greek art but never, so far as I am aware, adopted into Indian. The shallowness of Smith's argument is patent; for a Greek artist would have had no more difficulty in portraying the elephant or humped bull than European artists have to-day; and countless instances might be cited of the latter having achieved the task with signal success.[1]

Royal and demotic art under Aśoka

The sculptures discussed above and most of the surviving monuments of Asoka represent only the royal or official art of this period, just as the palaces of Susa and Persepolis represent only the royal art of the Achæmenids. Side by side with this royal art, however, there was undoubtedly a popular demotic art which, within the next two centuries, was destined to undergo a remarkable development. In the reign of Aśoka this popular art was still in an archaic state. What had been its history before the advent of the Mauryas, we have as yet no means of knowing; all we can conjecture is that, with the eclipse of the Indus civilization, its art, too, had virtually perished, but that it had lifted its head again in a new and humbler guise, when the storm and stress caused by the Indo-Āryan invasions had subsided, just as the art of Greece did in the sixth century B.C., and that it remained in a more or less static and undeveloped condition until its growth was stimulated by contact with other and artistically more advanced peoples. In the Mauryan period this popular art must have been still finding expression mainly in wood and other perishable materials, since, save for the royal monuments, stone had not yet come into fashion, and the only certain specimens of it we now possess are a few small terra-cottas.[2] Nevertheless, from these as well as from the stone statues and reliefs of the succeeding centuries, it can safely be inferred that in the third century B.C. Indian art was still in much the same rudimentary state as Greek art had been in the sixth century B.C. Statuary in the round had not yet passed the stage represented by the unifacial image from Parkham, and relief-work could hardly have reached the stage represented by the archaic carvings on the balustrade of the Second Stūpa at Sāñchī.

The caurī-bearer of Dīdargañj

Parenthetically, it may be noticed that some confusion regarding the character of this indigenous Mauryan art has been occasioned by the attribution to this period of the statue of a female *caurī*-bearer in the round, discovered in 1917 at Dīdargañj near

[1] I need quote only the admirable statues of elephants which stand in front of the Delhi Gate of the Delhi Fort, modelled by Mr. R. Mackenzie, and Vereshchagin's famous picture at Calcutta. Elephants, it may be noted, were a common sight in the armies of the Seleucid and Bactrian kings; and humped cattle had a range far beyond the borders of India.

[2] Whether the broken elephant from the debris of Building 40 (Pl. 104 *f*) represents this popular art or not, it is difficult in its present mutilated state to say.

Pātna.[1] The only reason for assigning this statue to the Mauryan period seems to have been that it is made of Chunar stone and boasts a polished surface. But we know that this variety of stone continued to be used by sculptors for centuries after the Mauryas, and we know, too, that the practice of polishing statues and reliefs survived down to modern times, and was common in the first century before our era, when the Sāñchī gateways were erected. This is the age to which the developed style of the Dīdargañj statue and the character of its modelling clearly indicate that it belongs, and this is the age to which it should be assigned, unless much stronger evidence is forthcoming to prove its Mauryan origin.

Influence of Aśoka's monuments on Buddhist art

The influence which Aśoka's monuments exerted on the subsequent history of Buddhist art was as profound as it was widespread. Up to the time of the Mauryas, art in the Buddhist Church had been a negligible factor. By the rules of the Order figural representations of any kind had to be scrupulously avoided, and the decorations that were permissible were restricted to the simplest designs, chiefly of a floral kind, which, though no doubt drawn with characteristically Indian grace and charm, could not have been of a type to make much impression on the Faithful. The field of art, therefore, was virtually clear, and it is not surprising that the monuments erected by Aśoka—the temple at Bodh-Gayā, the many monolithic pillars of glistening stone, and the still more numerous stūpas of brick and plaster which he broadcast throughout his dominions—should have fired the imagination of the Church and revolutionised its incipient art, even as the emperor's institution of the relic-stūpa cult as part of the State religion was revolutionising its spirit. So long as the simple decorations allowable in the Church had been executed in perishable materials and confined to the cells, common rooms and halls of the monks, it was hardly to be expected in any case that much attention would be paid to them, or that they would have any appreciable effect on the course of religious art. But when once Aśoka's sculptors had shown how stone could be substituted for wood, when they had broken with the rules which prohibited figural representations and set up sculptured monuments which future generations were to regard as the works of genii; and when in his relic-stūpas this emperor had provided objects of cult-worship worthy, for their own sake, of being beautified in permanent form—when these things had happened, the whole outlook for art in the Buddhist Church changed; within a little time it came to be recognised as a valuable means of instructing and edifying the Faithful; countless copies were made of Aśoka's monuments—both stūpas and pillars—and infinite pains were taken to embellish the former with reliefs in stone illustrating the last life or the previous births of the Teacher. And thus a new hieratic art came into being, in which the stūpas and pillars erected by the emperor took their place among the most conspicuous and frequently

[1] *Cf.* Spooner, D. B., 'The Dīdargañj Image,' *J. B. O. R. S.*, March 1919, p. 111; Bachhofer, L., *Early Indian Sculpture*, Vol. I, pp. 9 and 10 and Pl. 9; Coomaraswamy, A. K., *History of Indian and Indonesian Art*, p. 17 and fig. 17.

repeated emblems of the Buddhist faith and to which other symbolic and decorative motifs were contributed from the same source.

Western Asiatic features imported mainly during the Mauryan period

The full extent of the influence exerted by the monuments of Aśoka can hardly now be gauged, since only a fraction of them has been preserved, and much that concerns the contents and motifs of this art is now hidden from us. It is impossible, therefore, to be sure whether it was from this or from some other source that many of the Western Asiatic features found in the Early School of sculpture were derived. Everything, however, points to these features having reached India during the Mauryan period (though to some extent during that of the Indo-Creek sovereignty in the Panjāb) rather than earlier. Grünwedel, it may be recalled, conjectured that these Western Asiatic features were traceable to the period when the Panjāb and Gandhāra were provinces of the Achæmenid empire, and at first sight this conjecture appears a very plausible one; for what more likely than that these forms and motifs, which had been absorbed into the cosmopolitan art of Persia, should have followed in the wake of Persian conquest to India? But the fresh light which archæological discoveries have thrown on this problem during the last thirty years does not tend to confirm Grünwedel's view. At Taxila, where, of all places in India, Achæmenid art might have been expected to reveal itself, not a trace of it has been found. Nor is this, in fact, surprising; for it must be remembered that Achæmenid art no more represented the traditional, indigenous art of Persia than the royal art of the Mauryas represented the indigenous art of India; it was a blend made up of the fusion of many foreign and heterogeneous elements, and we cannot conceive of its having been transmitted to other countries until it had had time to become naturalised, as it were, on Persian soil and identified with the art of the country.[1] The effect of these royal edifices on the imagination of the people must, doubtless, have been profound, and we can well believe that they made a lasting impression on the character of Persian art, but the process of imitation and absorption would naturally take time, and before their influence could have spread as far afield as India, the power of the Achæmenids was on the decline, and, notwithstanding that they may have retained their Indian provinces down to the reign of Darius III, it is improbable that from the time of Xerxes onwards (if, indeed, before then) their culture or their art can have had much direct influence in Gandhāra and the Panjāb.

[1] Unless (and this is too remote a contingency to be taken into account) the artists and artificers who created it—the Ionians, Sardians, Medes, Egyptians and others who built the palaces of Susa and Persepolis and Ecbatana—had themselves been responsible for diffusing it further afield.

CHAPTER IX

SCULPTURES OF THE SECOND STŪPA AT SĀÑCHĪ, OF BHARHUT AND BODH-GAYĀ

FROM the monuments of Aśoka we pass to the sculptures of the Second Stūpa at Sāñchī. Between them come the minor carvings on the berm and stairway balustrades of Stūpas 1 and 3, which were executed shortly after the middle of the second century B.C., but the light which the latter throw on the history of local sculpture is a negligible one, and it is unnecessary, therefore, to pause and discuss them. As stated in a previous chapter, the sculptures of Stūpa 2 date from the last quarter of the second century B.C. (probably from about 110 B.C.), and being, as they are, the earliest important examples of indigenous relief-work in stone, they constitute a specially valuable landmark in the evolution of Indian art—the starting point, in fact, from which the whole progress of this indigenous art—as distinct from the foreign, official art of the Mauryas—can be traced down the centuries. To understand aright these first beginnings of sculpture, we must endeavour to visualise the conditions in which they were made and the difficulties that confronted the Buddhist sculptors. The greatest of these difficulties were the technical ones. Stone carving was a relatively new form of craftmanship to the Indian. In wood and ivory carving he was expert enough, for he had been practising them from time immemorial; and he was skilled, too, in painting and in the hammering out of designs in relief from copper and bronze. But to carve figures out of brittle and refractory stone, was a very different proposition. Stone was not ductile, like metal, and capable of being hammered into shape; nor could it be cut easily and sharply like wood, however finely tempered the chisels of steel[1] might be. Hammer blows were needed to chip away the new material, and a blow that was a fraction too sharp might ruin the work. To be sure, there was the marvellous lion-crowned pillar of Aśoka to demonstrate how stone could be carved: none could wish for a more perfect model! But that had been made of old by the *devas*; and there was none now to teach the sculptors how to set about such work. What they had to do, then, was to try and make the best of their own traditional methods; to carve the stone as they were accustomed to carve wood and ivory; and if they could produce in it the same kind of figures in relief, they would be more than satisfied. Of the essential difference in texture between stone and wood and ivory, they knew, of course, nothing; nor had they any idea of how the peculiar texture of stone can be turned to account in the hands of a skilful sculptor.

Importance of carved balustrade of Stūpa 2 in history of Indian art

Technical difficulties

[1] Pieces of virtually pure steel swords were found used as wedges beneath the pillar of Heliodorus at Besnagar, which was contemporary with Stūpa 2 at Sāñchī.

Their one objective was to get the same effects in durable, that they had been wont to get in perishable, materials, and to achieve this, they went to work as nearly as possible in the same way.

Problem of subject matter

Then there was another problem. With what sort of themes were they to decorate the new balustrades? Clearly the decorations must be as distinctive as possible of the Buddhist faith, but how to make them so? The art of the Church was still in its infancy, and its imagery strictly limited. Of course, there were the relic-stūpas and wheel-crowned pillars of Aśoka. These were now the outstanding features of the saṅghārāma; everybody was worshipping them, and countless copies had been made of them; so that they were already familiar motifs for the artist, and had already come to symbolize two great events in the life of the Master, namely, the Great Decease and the First Sermon. Naturally, therefore, they must figure prominently in the new sculptures. So, too, must the effigy of Māyā[1] supported on a lotus, which would remind the Faithful of the Master's miraculous Birth, and the Bodhi Tree, which would equally remind them of his Enlightenment. Then, there were certain emblems which the Church had appropriated to itself and which were now looked upon as peculiarly characteristic of the Buddhist Faith:—the ever-moving Wheel that typified the Master's Law; the three-pointed *Triratna*, mystic symbol of the Three Jewels—Buddha, the Law and the Order; and the "shield" or *Śrīvatsa*, the meaning of which has long since been lost in oblivion. These motifs, also, could find an appropriate place among the sculptures; but after all they were not many and would not go far on a massive railing of 88 pillars. Still, even if there was only a sprinkling of them here and there among the reliefs, they would give a decidedly Buddhist flavour to the whole. For the rest, there was variety enough in the stock-in-trade motifs and designs that made up the ordinary mundane art of the day. At stylised plants and flowers, the artists were marvellously adept; could weave them into countless lovely patterns and suit them to almost any shape of surface. Their special forte was the lotus, which they could draw to perfection in every form of leaf and bud and blossom. Even the boasted art of the Yavanas could show nothing quite to equal it. Trees, too, they were fond of, and could carve not unskilfully, bringing out the salient points of each—the long pointed leaves, for example, of the *pīpal* or the pendent suckers of the banyan; nor did they find any difficulty in hanging woven garlands and necklaces and jewels from the boughs of the enchanted *kalpavṛiksha* or in showing birds perched among its foliage or lions and deer starting in pairs from its stem. Bird-life did not appeal over-much to them, though there was no mistaking such birds as the parrot, the peacock or the goose, when they chose to represent them. What they really loved best of all was

Buddhist emblems

Mundane art: Plants, trees, birds and animals

[1] For representations of Māyādevī and the Nativity, see pp. 183-6 and 197 *infra*. Some of the Māyā figures on the balustrades and gateways are identical with the familiar type of Śrī-Lakshmī, standing or seated on a lotus, which the Buddhists evidently appropriated, along with so many other formulæ and motifs, from the current art of the period, since it can hardly be doubted that the Śrī-Lakshmī type goes back to a more remote age than Buddhism. Dr. Coomaraswamy inclines to the view that in the figures of this type the Buddhists recognised, not Māyā, but Śrī-Lakshmī herself; but an insuperable objection to this view is that the type appears six times on the square dies of the gateways of Stūpa 1, which were reserved exclusively for the Four Great Miracles—the Nativity, Illumination, First Sermon and Decease. *Cf.* Pls. 24, 25, 30, 41, 44, and 56; and A. K. Coomaraswamy in *The Indian Historical Quarterly*, Vol. xi, 2, pp. 357-60.

the four-footed animals, both wild and tame: the deer and the bull, the horse and, most of all, the elephant, which they were never tired of modelling, sometimes with consummate skill, in one or other of its characteristic attitudes. With the camel and lion, on the other hand, they were less at home, for the reason, no doubt, that they seldom, if ever, came into contact with either; nor are their efforts at portraying the rhinoceros, boar, bear and dogs very successful. Then, there was a whole galaxy of fabulous creatures on which to ring the changes: fish-tailed *makaras*, winged human-headed lions, griffins with parrot beaks, centaurs with riders, horses with human heads or women with horses' heads, stags with elephants' heads and fishes' tails, cobra-hooded nāgas with human bodies, and weird monsters of the deep—these and other creatures of the imagination could be used at will to fill some of the empty spaces. Some of them, like the nāgas, were of Indian origin and from time immemorial had been fraught with a religious significance, albeit not Buddhist; others, like the winged lions and griffins and mounted centaurs, had arrived more recently from the West and were still mainly of a decorative order. **Fabulous creatur**

With the figures of men and women, the sculptors had more difficulty than with animals or plants. Their Yakshas and Yakshīs were still stiff and disjointed, with awkward feet, and attitudes never quite natural. And when a group of figures had to be portrayed, the best that could be done was to range them side by side or one above the other, in more or less rigid isolation. In the constricted spaces on the railing, there was of course no room for elaborate groups; otherwise, they might perhaps have attempted to depict other incidents in the Buddha's life or in the Jātaka stories that told of his previous births. That, however, was impracticable. The most they could do was to recall the best known episodes by inserting some allusive figures or emblems. Thus, an elephant with a lotus, or a lotus alone, would, like the figure of Māyā, suggest the Nativity; a deer would call to mind the Deer Park (*Mṛigadāva*) and, no less than the wheel (*dharmacakra*), suggest the First Sermon that the Buddha preached there; and even a single figure, like a horse-headed Yakshī, might stand for one of the Jātaka stories.[1] **Human f** **Allusive emblems**

Such, roughly, was the range of subjects which the artists of the day had at their command, and on which they could draw for the adornment of this railing. Now let us turn to the railing itself, and see how they succeeded in carrying out their task; and first, let it be noted, there is not only a general absence of uniformity in the designs of the carvings; but some measure of disparity also in the quality of their workmanship. This could hardly have been otherwise; for the posts, cross-bars and coping stones were the gifts of many donors—presented, not all at once, but over a period, it may be surmised, of several years; and we should be safe, therefore, in inferring, even if the carvings themselves did not demonstrate it, that many artists were employed in their execution, who doubtless varied the designs according to the amount of money available, or to suit their own taste **Disparity of workmanship**

[1] *E.g.*, No. 432. *Cf.* p. 181 *infra*.

or the wishes of their clients. It is obvious, for example, that such simple patterns as those on Pillars 2 *b*, 4 *a* and 4 *b* of Pl. 74 would have cost less than the more elaborate designs of Pillars 1 *a*, 1 *b*, 1 *c*, or 2 *a* of the same Plate, and we may conjecture, too, that floral or foliate devices, generally, were cheaper than figure work. As to the differences of style and workmanship, they are patent to the eye on every side. Consider, for example, the three purely decorative reliefs figured on Pl. 78, Pillars 23 *a*, *b* and *c*. From the point of view of design, the first of these is as attractive a piece of carving as occurs in the whole realm of Indian art, not even excluding the superb lotus designs of the Gupta age, the modelling being at once sensitive and full of life, and the chiselling of a very high order. The third example (Pillar 23 *c*), which is probably by the same hand, exhibits just as crisp and vigorous a spirit, but the insertion of the two small human figures in the middle register inevitably detracts from the success of the design as a whole. The second example (Pillar 23 *b*) is also an exquisite bit of relief work; indeed, it surpasses the other two in delicacy and precision of finish, but, on the other hand, lacks something of their stylishness; albeit not by the same hand as the other two, it is evidently closely related to them, and may well have been by a sculptor of the same family.

Examples of highest class of carvings

But the generality of carvings on the balustrade are on a noticeably lower level than the foregoing; indeed, there is a sameness and monotony about most of them that might, at first sight, be thought to place them all in one category. In reality, however, there is much inequality in their workmanship, and it is clear to see, on closer inspection, how many different hands have been employed on them. Typical examples are the carvings on Pillars 3, 5, 44, 49, 66 and 71 (Pls. 74, 75, 82, 83, 86 and 87). The first two of these pillars stand at the northern, the second two at the southern, and the last two at the western entrance. These particular pillars are specially instructive, because the principal designs which adorn them are repeated three times over and therefore lend themselves more readily for comparison. The earliest of these carvings are those at the southern entrance, and it is interesting to observe how the sculptors who subsequently copied them at the northern and western entrances endeavoured to improve on them, not always with success. Take, for example, the lotus Tree of Life on the north face of pillar 49.[1] At the best, it is not a very attractive design, being over-formal and rigid in its leading lines, as well as rather weak and nerveless in detail; but, for all its formality, the sculptor has managed to infuse into it a measure of artistry by drawing the main intertwining lotus stems in freehand curves which help to soften the rigidness of their symmetry. Now, compare with it the two copies on Pillars 66 *a* and 71 *b* at the western entrance, and another copy on Pillar 3 *b* at the northern entrance. In the two former, which are both by one and the same hand, the artist has been at pains to copy the original in all its essential features, but he has made his copy harder and more mechanical by substituting compass-drawn circles for the free-hand curves of the main lotus stems,

Varying style among less successful carvings

'Tree of Life' designs compared

[1] For the symbolism of this and other examples of the Tree of Life, see pp. 144-7 *infra*.

and in some other respects also has failed to preserve its pristine charm. In the copy at the north entrance, too, the author has been guilty of the same fault of reducing the pattern to a series of circles, but he has evidently been conscious of a weakness in the minor details of the original and tried to improve on them, though without sufficient imagination. His elephant, however, is much better drawn than the one in the corresponding position on Pillar 66.

Māyā-Lakshmī figures compared

Take, again, another form of the same lotus tree on Pillar 49 *a* at the south entrance crowned by a standing figure of Māyā (Lakshmī). As a composition, it could hardly be feebler, but in execution it is decidedly superior to the copy of it on Pillar 71 *a* at the western entrance. The superiority comes out especially in the treatment of the human figures; for, whereas in the latter they are stiff, flat and sharply silhouetted at the edges, in the former, a real effort has been made to render the roundness of the arms and breasts, and to give a more natural suppleness to the limbs. On Pillar 1, also, all three faces of which are by the same sculptor (Pl. 74, 1*a*, 1*b* and 1*c*), the same incipient appreciation of plastic form is apparent. In this case, the artist seems to have made somewhat of a speciality of figure sculpture, and to have gone further than his contemporaries. The relief on the west face, of the Yakshī standing on a lotus and holding on to the bough of a tree, is particularly striking. It is not, of course, up to the standard of the Yakshī Culakokā on the Bharhut balustrade, but it represents a genuine attempt at more organic modelling by cutting deeper into the surface of the stone and rounding off both contours and interior details. The sculptor, whoever he was, did not possess a high sense of the decorative, though his Yakshī panel is pleasing enough, but he evidently had a more than ordinary appreciation of form, and was not satisfied with the then accepted formulas for expressing it. Thus, in his Māyā on the outer face of the pillar, he has done his best to get away from the conventional "memory image" of the feet by pointing them both to the front instead of turning them sideways and presenting them in their broadest aspect; and if he failed for lack of the necessary knowledge of foreshortening, his effort towards greater truth was at any rate in the right direction. Again, in the relief at the bottom of the same panel, as to which there will be more to say presently, he has obviously had a difficulty in portraying the limbs of the prostrate figure correctly, but it is surprising how well he has succeeded, especially with the legs, and it is surprising, too, how much vigour he has put into his modelling of the elephant. Work such as this affords the best evidence of the vitality and progressiveness of Indian art at this period, as well as the best guarantee for its future.

"Pillar of the Law" combined with 'Tree of Life'

A third motif on this balustrade that offers itself readily for comparison is the pillar surmounted by a "Wheel of the Law" (*dharmacakra*) and itself supported by a Tree of Life. Four repetitions of this motif are found, with variations, on the balustrade, namely: two on Pillars 3 *a* and 5 *a*, one on Pillar 44 *b*, and one on Pillar 66 *b*. The earliest is that on Pillar 44 at the southern entrance. Here, the lion pillar is represented as forming part, as it were, of the Tree of Life, the buds and blossoms and leaves of which are depicted sprouting from its sides.[1] The effect, however, was not a happy one, and the sculptor of Pillar 66, who adopted the same motif, sought to remove the weakness by inserting a suppliant figure on each side of the pillar shaft in place of the lotus leaves and blossoms; at the same time he also improved on the design of the Tree, and especially of the heraldic-looking animals[2] leaping from its sides, and substituted four elephants addorsed in place of the four crowning lions on the capital of the column. For the two other variations of this "Column and Tree" motif on Pillars 3 *a* and 5 *a*, respectively, another sculptor was responsible. In both cases he avoided showing the balustrade at the base of the column in perspective, and carried it across the full width of the panel, thereby dividing the decoration into two registers and disconnecting the column from the tree, of which it was meant really to be part and parcel. He also added a vertical band down the shaft of the column, intended perhaps to represent it as octagonal instead of circular. Like the sculptor of Pillar 66, he, too, seems to have been conscious of the inappropriateness of the lotus buds and blossoms bursting from the sides of the column, and replaced them on Pillar 3 *a* by two suppliants, and on Pillar 5 *a* by formal rows of the full-blown flowers. On the former pillar, he retained the Lion Capital intact, but substituted another form of the Tree of Life, of a clumsier and less attractive pattern; on the latter pillar, he retained the original form of the Tree but replaced the upper pair of deer by lions, and varied the lions on the capital above by substituting an elephant in place of the middle one.

General uniformity of style

Notwithstanding their unequal merits, however, the reliefs on this balustrade (with the exception of a few panels to be noticed anon) form a thoroughly homogeneous group characterised by traits which are common to the archaic sculpture of most countries. These traits are mainly of a technical kind. All the figures in the reliefs are kept strictly in one plane and there is little attempt to obtain tactile depth in the stone cutting, whether for the human and animal figures or for the floral and other decorative devices. The human figures exhibit, as we have seen, considerable variety of technique, but in no instance have they advanced entirely beyond the archaic stage. The laws of "frontality" and of the "memory picture" are still to some extent operative, though the sculptors are obviously endeavouring to emancipate themselves from them. Hence most of the figures are presented front-face in their broadest aspect; but, though the body is to the front, the feet are usually turned sideways, either both outwards, with heel to heel, or both in the same direction;[3] only occasionally are they shown pointing in the same direction as the body (*e.g.*, Pls. 74, 1*b*, 1*c*; 76, 12*b* and 15*a*; 78, 21*b* and 23*c*). Even in the most frontal and rigid of these figures, however, it is rarely that the weight is thrown on both legs or that

[1] Albeit crowned by four lions, the pillar is not a direct copy of the Aśoka pillar which stood near the South Gateway of the Great Stūpa. Ultimately the origin of all such pillars is traceable to the Aśoka *lāṭs*, but in this case the leaves falling over the shoulder of the bell-shaped capital seem to indicate that it was copied from a pillar of Śuṅga date.

[2] For these animals starting out from the sides of the Tree, see p. 146 *infra*.

[3] See also p. 133 *infra*. This unnatural position of the feet may be due as much to the exigencies of low relief as to the memory image.

both arms are held in the same position. The figures in which this happens—in which, if the body were to be bisected vertically, the two halves would correspond more or less exactly—are those of deities such as the Māyā-Lakshmī of Pillars 12 *b*, 15 *a*, and 49 *a*, whose images had doubtless been consecrated in this particular form by long tradition. In other figures, the arms and legs are generally in varying postures, one arm being raised, while the other hangs down or is held horizontally across the waist, and either one knee being bent more than the other, or both knees being in the same direction. In all cases, the figures stand out from the background in well-defined relief, but their contours are softened and moulded to the rounded form of the trunk and limbs, not outlined with the sharp-cut vertical chiselling so characteristic of the earlier phases of archaic art, and still lingering on in some of the later Bharhut reliefs. Frequently, too, the modelling of the breasts and other details shows a lively feeling for plastic form, as in Pillar 1 *a*, but in no case has the artist acquired sufficient mastery over the difficult technique of relief to grade the parts correctly according to their relative depths. Thus, in the figure alluded to on Pillar 1, both legs, though turned sideways, are in one and the same plane, and the features of the face are conspicuously flattened. In the majority of figures, such as those on Pillars 49 *a* and 71 *a*, this flatness is still more pronounced; and the angularity of the limbs, moreover, is more obtrusive, the line of the shoulders being sometimes indicated by a straight incision (as in Pillar 7 *b*, centaur medallion in centre) and the arms and legs presenting a disjointed appearance, as if they had no organic articulation.

But certain exceptions of a more developed style

From the above observations it may be inferred that the bulk of the reliefs on this balustrade represent a stage of art which was struggling to escape from the set rigidity and stiffness of archaism, and there is little room for doubt that this was the general state of indigenous Indian art in the latter part of the second century B.C. This observation, however, is not exclusively true of all of the carvings on the balustrade. Apart from the panels which were added about a century later and which belong to the same phase of art as the gateways of the Great Stūpa,[1] there are a few figures, both human and animal, which seem to betray an acquaintance with relief-work of a relatively high order and well in advance of the prevalent style of the period. One such group of figures has already been noticed, *viz.*, the elephant and riders trampling on a prostrate foe, at the base of Pillar 1 *b* (Pl. 74). In this group, the riders are sitting the beast with relative ease, the elephant itself is portrayed with an unusual degree of freedom and energy, and, despite the distortion of its left arm, the figure on the ground shows little of the stiffness and constraint that characterise the other figures on this pillar. The same ease and freedom of pose is observable in the elephant rider of Pillar 11 *a* and the horse rider of Pillar 63 *b*, both of whom are sitting their animals quite naturally, with their shoulders and heads turned three-quarters to the front, in a manner unknown among

[1]As to these panels, see pp. 148-9 *infra*.

the generality of these sculptures. Another example is the seated figure in the centre medallion of Pillar 14 *a*. Here, the arms are stiff and the modelling in other respects crude and careless, the head being disproportionately big for the body and legs, but there is little of the archaic in the easy pose of this figure, with its right leg half concealed behind the left, nor yet in the grading of the surfaces. Still more mature are the two elephants of Pillars 15 *b* and 41 *b*. Observe, in these, the strikingly realistic attitudes of the beasts, and the delicate but vigorous modelling of their heads; and contrast them, for example, with the elephant on Pillar 72 *b*, where, owing to ignorance of foreshortening, the two flanks of the animal and the two hind legs are shown protruding grotesquely to the right and left. It is not too much to say that these two elephants are surpassed by few of their kind even on the gateways of Stūpa 1. Now, the problem that confronts us is, how these few relatively mature productions are to be reconciled with the typically archaic work about them. It is a problem not easy of solution. There is no question of these particular reliefs being of foreign authorship. They are as essentially and indisputably Indian as the rest of the reliefs. This is amply demonstrated by their character, but should any doubt be felt on the point, it must be dispelled by the reliefs on Pillar 1, where the same sculptor has been responsible for the elephant group at the foot of the outer face, as well as for the characteristically archaic figures on that and the other two faces. Now, in this instance it seems virtually certain that the sculptor must have imitated his elephant group from some well-known prototype of that subject with which he was familiar, and which was much more advanced in style and technique than the local art of Mālwā. It is not suggested that he attempted to copy this model exactly—that, indeed, may have been beyond his capacity—but, with the model before him or with the memory of it to guide him, he was able in his own way to elaborate a far more natural and convincing group than he could have done by his own unaided efforts. This, in the view of the writer, is what probably happened also in regard to the other advanced reliefs. When a stock theme was needed, the artist fell back on some well-known presentment of it, and proceeded to imitate, as far as he was able, both the treatment of the subject and the technique of the model. But this does not solve the whole problem. It pushes the solution only a step further back. There still remains the question whence these superior models were obtained, and how they had come to be evolved. One thing may be regarded as certain, *viz.*, that such widely different grades of workmanship cannot have been due merely to the varying genius of the sculptors employed. Some sculptors may have been, and doubtless were, much cleverer than others, but it is impossible that any could have been so far ahead of their time as to overcome at a stroke, and without external aid, the difficulties of archaic technique with which their fellow artists were struggling. In no other country does archaic art offer a parallel to such a phenomenon, and there are no grounds for regarding India as an exception to the general rule. It is not a question of a single genius, like Masaccio, leaping ahead of his age. These reliefs were the work of several hands and the sculptors who carved them were not great geniuses; they were

Suggested explanation of more mature work

clever craftsmen, who had a fine innate sense for the decorative and, when dealing with certain subjects—but only with certain subjects—could portray them with surprising facility and freedom. The most likely explanation, as it seems to me, is that in the second and first centuries B.C. the dissemination in India of Asiatic Greek art in the form of coins, gems, terra-cottas, small carvings and textiles, acted as a valuable stimulus to indigenous art, not only providing it with many new motifs, but leading in many cases to the adoption of more developed methods of technique. The influence of these foreign *objets d'art* would naturally be strongest in the Panjāb and on the North-West Frontier, where Greek principalities had been established for three generations before this balustrade was erected ; but abundant examples of them have been found in the Midland Country and even as far afield as Bodh-Gayā and Patna. Even at Sāñchī itself, as we have already seen, sculpture of first-rate quality in the Hellenistic style had been executed in the previous century by the foreign artists of Aśoka, and among the carvings of this balustrade concrete testimony to the strength of Western Asiatic influence is to be found in such motifs as the centaurs,[1] human-headed lions and horses,[2] griffins[3] and fish-tailed stags and mermaids[4] that are figured here, and perhaps also in the Yakshī grasping the bough of a tree—that is, if we concur in the view as to the Western origin of this motif.[5]

Dissemination in India of Yavana art

This foreign influence takes different forms and is not in all cases equally apparent. In some sculptures, both subjects and rendering betray their extraneous inspiration, as in the four-horse chariot of the Sun-God on the balustrade at Bodh-Gayā, or, still more conspicuously, in certain terra-cotta heads from Basārh and Sārnāth ; in others, the conception only is exotic, the rendering of it Indian, as in the sinuous garlands supported by little dwarf-like figures on the reliefs of Mathurā and Amarāvatī, or in the "Yakshī and Tree" motif referred to above ; in others, on the contrary, the motif may be Indian, the rendering of it foreign, as in the multitudes of reliefs belonging to the Gandhāra School, where the Hellenistic style and workmanship is beyond dispute, though the content is a medley of Indian and Western ideas.

There are the best of grounds, therefore, for inferring that in certain cases the technique, as well as the motifs, of Hellenistic and Western Asiatic art may have been borrowed by the artists of India. Confirmation of the correctness of this inference is supplied by some of the sculptures on the Bharhut Gateway, which are distinguished from their fellows not only by the superior skill of their technique, but by the un-Indian countenances of the figures portrayed, as well as by the presence of Kharoshṭhī characters engraved as masons' marks in contradistinction to the usual Brāhmī characters which appear on the balustrade, thus clearly indicating the North-West as the direction whence this influence came.[6] The effect of foreign methods of technique, be it added, may not be

Influence of foreign technique as important as influence of foreign motifs

[1] *Cf.* Pl. 75, Pillar 7 *b* ; Pl. 89, Pillar 81 *b* ; Pl. 90, Pillar 82 *a*.
[2] Pl. 75, 8 *a*.
[3] Pl. 75, Pillar 7 *a* ; Pl. 81 *b*, Pillar 35 *b*.
[4] Pl. 87, Pillar 75 *a*.
[5] *Cf.* Vincent Smith, *A History of Fine Art in India and Ceylon*, pp. 71-3.
[6] *Cf.* my remarks in *C. H. I.*, I, p. 625.

so patent in these sculptures as the presence of foreign motifs, but it is none the less real, and is probably, in fact, a more potent factor in the evolution of the Early School ; for without the help of such technique it is more than doubtful if the school could have made the remarkable progress that it did between the second and first centuries B.C. A mistake, as it seems to us, that writers on this subject have commonly made, has been to admit (because they could not deny) the existence of extraneous motifs in the productions of this school, but to ignore the possibly wider-reaching influence of technique.

The carvings of the Second Stūpa described above are by far the most important remains of their kind at Sāñchī that can be ascribed with certainty to the age of the Śuṅgas. The next sculptures that we have to consider are those on the four magnificent gateways of the Great Stūpa, and these were not executed until nearly a century later,, when the ruling dynasty of the Śuṅgas had been replaced in Eastern Mālwā by that of the Andhras. Before, however, we can proceed to the discussion of these gateways, it is necessary to say a few words about two other notable monuments that were erected in the meantime, *viz.*, the balustrade and gateway of the Stūpa of Bharhut and the balustrade at the Temple of Bodh-Gayā. The former of these, like the balustrade of the Second Stūpa at Sāñchī, were erected under the supremacy of the Śuṅgas, but various features of the carvings, as well as the palæography of the inscriptions, indicate that the gateway and certain parts of the balustrade were posterior to the Sāñchī balustrade, though not, probably, by more than two or three decades.[1] In point of style and technique the two series of sculptures necessarily have much in common ; since both are characteristically Indian and both are in the stage of struggling from the trammels of archaism into freedom. It is inevitable, therefore, that both should exhibit somewhat similar traits of awkwardness and stiffness due to the constraint of the "memory image", lack of perspective, and the still effective law of "frontality" Strangely enough, too, the reliefs of Bharhut, like those of Sāñchī, are distinguished by the presence of a small percentage of carvings of unusually free and advanced style, which there are good reasons, as we have already seen, for ascribing to north-western influence. Taken as a whole, however, the reliefs of Bharhut mark a definite advance on those of Stūpa 2 at Sāñchī. In regard to subjects, they are altogether more ambitious ; the sculptors are no longer content with a few sacred symbols to advertise the Buddhist character of the balustrade, nor yet with such simple decorative or figural groups as were deemed adequate at Sāñchī. The decoration is to be as illustrative of the Faith as they can make it, and to this end they set themselves to portray a variety of scenes depicting episodes in the life of the Teacher or in his previous births. Scenes of a kindred kind—scenes of court and city and jungle life—had no doubt been long familiar to the Indian artist, and no great imagination was now needed to adapt

The Bharhut balustrade: its sculptures compared with those of Stūpa 2 at Sāñchī

[1] For the date of Stūpa 2 and its balustrade, see pp. 81-2 and 269-70 ; for the date of the Bharhut balustrade and gateway, pp. 270-2.

them to the needs of Buddhist legend and give them a sacred instead of a mundane label. In the relatively small spaces available on the coping stones and in the circular medallions of the pillars, the stories naturally have to be told in the briefest possible way and with correspondingly few figures, but even in these constricted spaces it is surprising how many figures are sometimes squeezed in, while in the larger rectangular spaces on the jambs of the gateways the figures are almost as crowded as they are in the gateway reliefs at Sāñchī. Between the latter, indeed, and the reliefs of Bharhut there is a remarkably strong family likeness—not only in the methods of narration, in the formal composition of many of the groups, and in the postures of many individual figures, but in a score of other details, both stylistic and technical, into which we cannot enter here; and it is impossible, therefore, to question the debt which the sculptors of the Sāñchī gateways owe to the groups of artists who preceded them at Bharhut and elsewhere.

Differences between Mālwā and Bharhut Schools

But if we recognize the intimate connection between these monuments, we must recognize also the differences that distinguish them sharply from each other. The sculptures of Sāñchi belong to one school, the sculptures of Bharhut to another; and each of these schools has its own traditions and its own methods. At Sāñchī, the art is natural and unconstrained; the poses of the figures as free and easy as the skill of the sculptor can make them; their contours smooth and rounded; their minor features unaccentuated. At Bharhut, on the contrary, the sculptor is striving after conscious definition and truth rather than unaffected simplicity; there is nothing lax in his style; rather is it tense and artificial. His contours are clear-cut and precise; his anatomical details conscientiously and incisively defined; every ornament put in with meticulous accuracy. As a result, there is a certain restrained mannerism, a pleasing affectation and dignified stylishness about these sculptures, such as are found neither on the earlier balustrade of Stūpa 2, nor on the later gateways at Sāñchī. These traits lift the art of Bharhut a measure above the commonplace, everyday world, and make it peculiarly fitted to the needs of the Buddhist Church. One of the weaknesses of early Indian art, and especially of the Mālwā School, is that it is all so provocatively mundane, so lacking in religious tone. Had the school of Bharhut survived for another century, it might have placed at the service of the Church an art that was at once more truly ecclesiastic and more impressive than the art of Sāñchī; for there is, in the sculptures of Bharhut, a promise of beauty and strength to come, which calls to mind the promise inherent in the nascent charms of archaic Attic work. As events proved, it was the mundane and more commonplace school of Mālwā that was destined, for a time at least, to live on; and such hieratic quality as later Buddhist art possessed, came less from it than from the half-Hellenistic School of Gandhāra. How and when the Bharhut School was eclipsed, we know not, but there are good grounds for inferring that it was closely connected with the early school of Mathurā, and may, indeed, have had its principal centre there; and if this inference is correct, its eclipse may well have been due to the Śaka conquest of that city, which took place in the early part of the first century B.C. However this may be, one thing is certain, that, though the school itself perished—and it seems to have done so soon after the erection of the Bharhut rail—nevertheless its influence survived and is discernible not only in the later school of Mathurā, but even in the far-off school of Amarāvatī.

The Bodh-Gayā balustrade

Though the balustrade round the Great Temple at Bodh-Gayā has none of the originality and little of the attractiveness of its predecessor at Bharhut, its carvings have a special interest for us here, first, because they embody two distinct traditions: that of the Bharhut-Mathurā School on the one hand, and that of the Mālwā School on the other; secondly, because they afford examples of workmanship belonging to two different ages, the majority of them dating probably from about the middle of the first century B.C. and a few (and these are the more elaborate compositions) from about the beginning of the Christian era. In neither case, unfortunately, can the date be determined with precision, but the design and construction of the original parts of the balustrade, as well as the style of the original carvings, indicate for them a date between the Bharhut balustrade and the Sāñchī gateways: that is, according to our reckoning, a date somewhere about 60 B.C., and this date is corroborated by the inscriptions on the older part of the balustrade.[1]

Earlier carvings at Bodh-Gayā

The influence on these earlier reliefs of the Bharhut-Mathurā tradition is specially apparent in the lotus-medallions centred with human heads or busts, but the Bodh-Gayā heads lack the breadth of style and the firm, precise modelling of their predecessors; the treatment of their features is insignificant by comparison, and the workmanship relatively poor. At the same time, the influence of the Mālwā tradition is equally apparent in the easy postures and soft rounded contours of some of the figures and in the simplification and orderliness of the compositions. If we compare, for instance, the Jetavana Garden scene as depicted on the balustrade at Bodh-Gayā with the same scene as depicted at Bharhut, we are struck at once by the radical difference between the two: in the latter by the medley of distorted, angular figures mixed up with the equally distorted bullock cart and buildings; in the former by the simplicity of the scene with the three figures in the foreground in relatively natural poses, and the four trees in the background. And yet we must admit that, for all its distortion and worried confusion, there is a vigour and character in the earlier that the later one entirely misses. We need not, however, dwell further on the details of these Bodh-Gayā reliefs. What we wish only to emphasize—for the clearer understanding of our Sāñchī art—is that relatively few and meagre in composition as they are, they show us the Mālwā style in a later and more developed phase than we met it on the balustrade of the Second Stūpa at Sāñchī; and they show us this style steadily and surely gaining strength, while the Bharhut-Mathurā style was already on the wane.

[1] Both palæographically and by the mention of two kings, Indramitra and Brahmamitra, whose coins (assuming that they have been rightly assigned) indicate that they were reigning about this date. For the date of the Bodh-Gayā balustrade, see also p. 271 and n. 2 *infra*.

Later carvings at Bodh-Gayā

The few later carvings on the Bodh-Gayā balustrade are found only on some of the corner and entrance pillars, where they had no doubt been substituted for older ones, just as later carvings were substituted for older ones on some of the entrance pillars of the Stūpa 2 Balustrade at Sāñchī.[1] They, too, illustrate the fusion of the Mālwā and Bharhut traditions, but the fusion in their case is more complete, since they were probably not executed until after the gateways of Sāñchī (*i.e.*, until after the opening of the Christian era), and the two styles had had more time by then for mutual assimilation. A marked feature of the later, as well as of the earlier sculptures, at Bodh-Gayā, is the presence among them of various motifs of Hellenistic or Western Asiatic origin, such as centaurs, winged and fish-tailed monsters, tritons, schematic animal friezes and—most significant of all—the Sun-God in his characteristic four-horse chariot. These motifs show how freely at this period Indian sculptors were borrowing from the hybrid cosmopolitan art of Western Asia, and one of them at least—the Chariot of the Sun-God—gives a clear indication of the debt they may have owed to that art in the matter of technique.

[1] The fine group of a man helping a young girl to climb a tree belongs to a later period, not, as Dr. Bachhofer supposed, to the earlier. See his *Early Indian Sculpture*, I, Pl. 34.

CHAPTER X

SCULPTURES ON THE GATEWAYS OF THE GREAT STŪPA

WHILE discussing the balustrade of the Second Stūpa, we saw that the majority of its carvings were still in a typically archaic stage, but that, for some reason for which it is not easy to account, a few among them exhibited a more advanced knowledge of relief-work, and we noted that the same phenomenon was observable among the carvings of Bharhut. Much disparity in style and technique also confronts us when we come to the sculptures of the four gateways of the Great Stūpa erected a century after the balustrade of the Second Stūpa, but in their case the disparity arises from different causes. In the second century B.C., when the stūpa in question was built, art in Central India and Hindustān was still prevailingly archaic in character; only here and there, and by way of exception, does it flash out unexpectedly into more mature expression. A century later, on the other hand, when the gateways were built, its character has become prevailingly mature; at any rate, it is well past the archaic state; and such spasmodic examples of archaism as still make their appearance are due mainly, if not exclusively, to religious conservatism. Needless to say, there is plenty of inequality in the standards of workmanship, and we shall see presently that, while many of the reliefs of the gateways are of outstanding merit, others are less successful, and a few definitely bad. Meanwhile our immediate concern is with those reliefs which, in contrast with the highly developed work around them, exhibit an archaic and out-of-date character. Typical examples of such reliefs are to be found on Pl. 34 *a* (top panel), Pl. 34 *c*, Pl. 35 *a* (middle panel) and Pl. 65 *b* (bottom panel). If we place them by the side of analogous reliefs on the Bharhut Gateway, *e.g.*, those on the Ajātaśatru pillar (Cunningham, *Stūpa of Bharhut*, Pl. 17), we perceive at a glance how difficult it was for the sculptors to get away from the old-established methods of portrayal; they have gained far more mastery over the material and can draw and model with relative freedom, but in these particular scenes they still persist in adhering to the archaic convention of arranging the figures in formal horizontal tiers and balancing them, one against the other, to right and left of the object they are worshipping. At the same time, there appears to be no conscious endeavour to imitate the archaic poses of the individual figures, as we see them in the Bharhut reliefs. The disposition of the figures in set rows necessarily tends to make them more rigid and formal, but their poses are noticeably more varied than in the earlier reliefs. In the latter, the figures are only occasionally shown three-quarter face; as a rule, they are full-face, side-face or seen from the back; in the archaic reliefs of Sāñchī, on the other hand, most of the figures are

The Gateway sculptures

Disparity of style and technique

Archaistic character of certain reliefs

three-quarter face ; full-face and side-face figures are relatively rare, and the back view still rarer. In the earlier, an effort at depth is made, here and there, by grading the figures in two clearly defined planes, with little or no distinction in the size of the figures of the deeper plane ; in the later, the figures are kept for the most part in one plane, and, if some of them are recessed, the grading is such that the difference in level is hardly noticeable. On the other hand, a suggestion of perspectival depth is given by diminishing the size of the figures, tier by tier, behind the front rows and thus making them appear more distant, as they would on the flat canvas of a picture. In all the sculptures at Sāñchī, the lowest tier of figures is supposed to be nearest to the spectator and the topmost furthest away, and the illusion is helped out by the fact that, though several rows are in the same plane, the heads of the lowest row project in front of the legs of the row above, and so on up to the top. In conformity with this principle, the figures at the bottom, which, in scenes such as we are now discussing, generally have their backs turned to the spectator, are sometimes portrayed on a considerably larger scale than those in the rows above (*e.g.*, Pl. 65 *b*). This, however, is not always done, and it is worth noticing that, in panels such as that in Pl. 35 *a*, the smaller figures appearing behind the lowest row are smaller, not only than the latter, but also than the front figures of the row above, notwithstanding that they are supposedly nearer to the spectator than the latter ; and, similarly, the figures behind the second row are smaller than the front figures of the third row. We have here, therefore, a very good illustration of an attempt to reconcile a simple kind of perspective with the old-fashioned convention, in order to gain depth and distance, not by actual cutting into the stone, but by illusion. We shall see presently how this method is further developed in the more elaborate reliefs.

Another panel treated on much the same formal lines is Pl. 34 *c*, which illustrates the descent of the Buddha from the Trayastriṁśa Heaven. The same subject is depicted on the corner pillar of the western gate at Bharhut (Cunningham, *op. cit.*, Pl. XVII, middle bas-relief), and the student will find it well worth while to compare the two, and observe the points in which they resemble and differ from one another. A feature of particular interest in the Sāñchī relief, is the distinction made between the divine and human beings on either side of the stairway. The latter, in the foreground at the foot of the stairway, are about half the size of the former, who are ranged in tiers above them, and, as a consequence, the perspectival method of showing the larger figures in front is here reversed. The same distinction appears to be made in the paradise scene on the middle panel of Pl. 34 *a*, which is evidently by the same hand as the Trayastriṁśa panel. The other panels we have been discussing are all by different hands.

Their salient features

Before leaving these few sculptures in which the archaizing tendency is unusually pronounced, it is well that we should get their characteristics fixed firmly in our mind, since they constitute, as it were, a half-way house between the old and the new and, thanks to the simplicity of their designing, enable us to appreciate more clearly the remarkable advances made in the latter. In the matter of composition, their imitation of the older work is of course patent in the formal marshalling of the figures in parallel rows and in the isocephalism that necessarily results from it, though no conscious effort is made—as it is sometimes made in later Roman reliefs—to bring the heads of all the figures, whether seated or standing, up to the same level. Of background in these reliefs, there is none, just as there is none in the older reliefs of the previous century ; nor is there any real attempt at tridimensional depth or illusionism. It is true, as we have already seen, that some of the figures are recessed back slightly from the front plane, and at the same time reduced in size in order to produce the illusion of distance, but apart from these expedients, which are certainly not based on any true knowledge of perspective, figures and objects are kept side by side in the one front plane ; or more correctly, I should say, as regards the rear ranks of figures, that their heads and upper parts are kept in this front plane, while their legs recede behind the rank below them. With rare exceptions, we shall find that this is the ordinary method adopted in all the Sāñchī reliefs, however developed in other respects they may be. As to the individual figures, they are no longer under the constraint of the "memory picture", no longer the awkward automata-like figures to which we have grown accustomed in the earlier monuments ; they are now of flesh and blood, organic entities, and able—were it not that the composition enforces strict composure—to move their hands with natural ease and freedom. But one essential quality they still lack ; there is no variety in their faces, no individuality in their expressions, no mutual interplay of feeling between them. To the extent that they are doing the same thing in the same way, that they are all worshipping, that is to say, one and the same object, there is a certain material or physical unity in their action, but it is very different from that deeper psychological unity, wherein each face and figure has its own individuality and each reacts in its own way to a common emotion. That is a kind of unity in which none of the sculptures of Sāñchī, nor any others of the Early School, have any part.

Among the rest of the gateway carvings which we have now to consider—and these constitute more than ninety per cent. of the whole—the tendency to archaize is small. Here and there one can see some old force of habit peeping out, some old stereotyped tradition still lingering on and impeding the freedom of the artist's efforts, but for the most part these sculptures appear to be representative of the most advanced art of which India was then capable. That manifold hands must have been engaged on the execution of such an elaborate series of sculptures, goes without saying. And we shall see presently how this varied authorship constantly comes out in the designs and workmanship, as well as in the unequal merit of many of the sculptures. For the moment, however, we want to concentrate on a few of the finest reliefs, especially on those in which the human element predominates, so that the reader may get at once a clear-cut

Examples of reliefs in finest style

idea of just what the best of this sculpture was able to achieve and of what it fell short. This done, we shall then be in a better position to discuss the remainder of the figural sculptures, including those which do not attain to the same high standard, as well as the animal and decorative designs. The reliefs which I would select as of outstanding interest and merit, are the following :—*Southern Gateway*, Pls. 15 and 17, back of lowest architrave ; Pl. 18 *a* and *b*, bottom panels ; *Northern Gateway*, Pl. 29, back of middle architrave ; *Eastern Gateway*, Pls. 49 *a* and 50 *a*, upper half ; *Western Gateway*, Pls. 61-63, back of middle and lowest architraves. All the sculptures are elaborated to a degree of complexity far transcending anything we have hitherto met with. Consider, for example, the scene on the middle architrave of Pl. 61, which is one of the most typical. To the left is a city, somewhat summarily represented, and sweeping up towards its gateway a vast throng of people, soldiers and civilians, chiefs and their attendants, some on foot, some on horseback, others on elephants or in chariots, all surging onwards to the accompaniment of drum and flute and conch-shell. Among all the sculptures of the ancient world, it would be difficult to point to any in which the concerted movement of such an immense crowd, in all its pageantry and splendour, is more convincingly depicted. How is the effect obtained ? Let us look at the details more closely. In the first place, all the figures are kept religiously in one plane. In some reliefs, as we have already seen, a figure here and there is thrust back into a second deeper plane, or a sense of distance is obtained by purposely diminishing the size of some of the figures. Here, nothing of the sort is attempted. Naturally, there is some variation in the size of the heads, but it is not for the purpose of giving perspectival depth. On the other hand, although the figures are all in one plane, there is not a vestige of flatness about them. They are in every sort of attitude, turned at any angle, overlapping and half hidden one behind another, and yet each stands out perfectly clear—isolated, as it were, in its surrounding shadow. This effect is achieved by cutting deeper into the stone between and around the figures, and dispensing with the background, thus enhancing the sense of atmosphere in relation to the moving figures—of *ambiente*, as the Italians call it. Here, the actors are not passing in front of a stage scene, as they so often are in Hellenistic and Roman reliefs or in the later Indian paintings at Ajaṇṭā ; they are moving in the void, unrelated to anything fixed and static except the city to the left, so that we are hardly conscious even of the flat surface of the stone from which they are cut, or of the fact that they are, one and all, in the same vertical plane. And this sense of unlimited depth and of free unrestrained movement is accentuated by the suppleness of the individual figures, the multiplicity of their poses and the varying directions in which they are turned. Observe, for example, how admirably the three elephants in the centre of the crowd are handled, the biggest one shown almost in profile, the other two turning more to the front ; and how diversified and natural the postures of their riders ; and observe, too, how successful is the foreshortening of the horse and rider shown three-quarter face at the top edge of the relief, immediately behind the last of the three elephants.

Pl. 61, 2: The "War of the Relics"

As to the scheme of composition, it is basically the same as we observed in the archaic panels, though much more elaborate and involved. The figures, that is to say, are disposed in rows one above the other, all except the front row being half hidden behind the next row below it, but the figures here are so varied in size and the rows so admirably broken up and deflected by the horses, elephants and chariots interspersed among the people, that all trace of horizontalism and formality has vanished. Considering, indeed, the narrowness of the architrave, the grouping of the figures could hardly be better balanced or more effective. Note, in particular, how the guiding lines of the composition rise from either side towards the crown of the great elephant's head in the centre of the relief, and how, to obtain this effect, the stature of the foot soldiers in the front row has been increased towards the centre, while the elephants in the row behind slope away towards the chariot on the right. This is not a haphazard piece of composition, but the outcome of careful thought on the part of the artist, whose object has been to secure the maximum degree of diversity without sacrificing either symmetry or balance. Another feature of this composition that deserves our admiration, is its convincing unity. In the expressions on the faces of the people there is nothing, it is true, that by any stretch of imagination can be interpreted as indicative of a common purpose or making for psychological unity. Many of them, especially in the right half of the crowd, have quite charming little countenances and, considering their exceedingly small size (the entire height of the relief is no more than 16 inches), this is perhaps as much as can reasonably be hoped for ; but, be this as it may, there is certainly no emotion visible in their expressions to tell us what the object of their march may be, whether they are advancing into battle or taking part in a pageant of victory. On the other hand, there is an unmistakable unity of purpose and coherency of effort in the forward urge of men and beasts towards the city's gate, and this sense of unity is enhanced by the ordered disposition of all the component figures in one plane, by the unifying effect of the alternating lights and shadows which help to bind the relief together, and by the disciplined correlation and symmetry of the whole.

When we turn to look in detail at the individual forms in this sculpture, what beguiles and delights us most is their unaffected naturalness. The material from which they are cut might almost be clay instead of stone, so soft are their contours, so unconstrained their movements, so plastic their limbs ; nor is there a trace to be seen of the rigid frontality or of the effects of the "memory image", which we encountered in the sculptures of the previous century. Here and there only is a little weakness perceptible in the drawing, notably in the legs of some of the figures, which are seldom handled successfully in any of the reliefs, and in the heads of the two horses drawing the chariot, which are switched round too violently to the front, but on the whole the drawing is astonishingly good and the carving of the more minute details, especially of some of the faces, quite exquisite. One cannot help feeling, as one looks at them, that, like many of the other fine and delicate carvings on these gateways, they must have been executed by artists accustomed to miniature work in ivory or gold or other precious substances rather than to the relatively coarse chiselling of stone.

Whether the design we are discussing was done by one or more artists, is open to question. In all probability the original drawing for the whole design was the work of a single hand, but there is no doubt that the task of actually carving the stone was divided between two. This is patent, if we compare the figures on the right and left of the relief. Those at the right end all have soft, rounded forms, and pleasing girlish faces; those to the left are more virile and muscular, with plain, if not ugly, features. The contrast between them is very marked, and can only be explained on the hypothesis that they are the handiwork of different sculptors. As a fact, we shall see that the common (though not invariable) practice was to divide the carving of the architraves between two or more people, and we shall see also that every artist employed on them as well as on the other panels, has his own favourite forms and his own favourite cast of features, from which he seldom departs to any great extent. In this case, the figures at the right end of the architrave, as far as the head of the smallest of the three elephants, form a homogeneous group, each member of which is distinguished by identically the same charm of expression; the remaining figures on the architrave—constituting about two-thirds of the whole—are quite distinct, and, though not quite so strikingly homogeneous in themselves, are almost certainly by a single hand, including the three figures inside the city wall.

Pl. 61, 3: "The Temptation"

In the lowest architrave on the same plate (Pl. 61, 3) it is equally evident that there has been a division of labour, but in this case, not only in the carving of the stone, but in the initial designing as well. The scene here depicted is the "Temptation of the Buddha". In the centre is the throne of the Blessed One beneath the Bo-Tree; to the right, the routed hosts of Māra fleeing away in disorder; to the left, a throng of deities advancing, with standards and banners and beat of drum, to do homage at the throne. It is a study in contrasts, for which a single artist has certainly not been responsible. Consider, on the one hand, the group of deities, how well-meaning and characterless they all are, like some chorus in a Greek play; how exactly each resembles his neighbour; how prosaic their forms; how fatuous their smiles. There is but one type for the gods—the type of the earthly prince—and the sculptor never varies it, perhaps because it is stereotyped by tradition, and tradition is not to be defied. And note how these deities are disposed in two rows only, instead of three, with the result that the back row is as much in evidence as the front. This, too, may be due to the force of tradition, which demanded that the gods should all be equally prominent, but artistically it is a defect, because it tends to destroy the illusion that the two rows are standing on one and the same level. Now look, on the other hand, at the striking contrast presented by the rout of Māra's armies on the right: the panic-stricken elephants and horsemen trampling one another down in their headlong flight, while a few fearsome-looking demons near the temple make a last effort to overawe the Buddha. The scene is as different from the group of unimaginative devas as can well be conceived, and the difference is not one of subject matter only, which in any case would be likely to afford a sharp contrast, but extends to the whole genius and technique of the work. Note, for example, what a fine sense of composition this sculptor of Māra's host possesses; with what abandon he throws in his figures of men and beasts into the disorderly tumult, and yet unerringly preserves the rythm of the whole; and note, too, with what masterly freedom he models the grotesque features of his demons and adds a humorous touch into the bargain, of one demon spearing his fallen comrade with a pitchfork. The weakest spot in the composition is the pair of horses on the right; they are moving at a leisurely walk, not fleeing for their lives, like the rest of the host. It may be that this is intentional, if the chariot to which they are yoked has been half crushed by the elephant coming up behind; but in any case their slow-paced walk is out of keeping with the rest of the scene, and quite unconvincing. In this, as in many other cases, the sculptor seems to have followed the easy method of taking a familiar standard type and introducing it into his design with little modification, and without considering whether the action of the horses was appropriate or not. The two-horse chariot is a frequent motif among the gateway reliefs (*e.g.*, Pls. 11, 2; 15, 3; 18 *a*, 2; 35 *a*, 1; 35 *b*, 2; 50 *a*, 1; 61, 2; 62, 2, etc.), and shows relatively little variation, though the idiosyncrasies of the different sculptors are patent enough in the drawing and modelling of their horses, no two pairs of which are the work of the same hand.

Comparing this scene of Māra's rout with the 'War of the Relics' on the architrave above it, we are bound to admit its superiority as a work of art. The latter lacks its bold and vigorous composition. One feels that, whoever designed this 'War of the Relics' knew all that could then be learnt about composition and technique, but had little of the natural inborn mastery over design that distinguishes the other relief. For the most part, his figures are conventional, and he arranges them on sound, formal lines; but if he has any imagination, he is afraid of giving rein to it, of letting his hand be guided by instinct rather than by the rules of his art. Hence there is a certain savour of artifice and formality about this relief, which is absent from the rout of Māra's army. All said and done, however, it is an excellent piece of work, and its excellence will be all the more appreciated, if we allow our eyes to range for a moment to the architrave immediately above it (Pl. 61, 1). Here, the scene is closely akin; for it, too, depicts the city of Kuśinagara, with the chief of the Mallas returning home on an elephant with his retinue around him, and bearing on his head the body-relics of the Blessed One. But what a world of difference between the two reliefs! The sculptor of this one is no artist, but a craftsman, and not a skilful craftsman either. The figures are no longer moving freely in space; they are of a piece with the background, which, though not obtrusive, is unmistakably there, and takes the place of the dark *ambiente* of the other relief. Nor have these figures the careless ease and freedom of the latter's; evidently the sculptor (in this case the entire relief is by one hand) has found a difficulty in portraying them at varying

Pl. 61, 1: The chief of the Mallas bringing home the Buddha's relics to Kuśinagara

angles and giving them depth and correct modulation of form. Some of the men, it is true, are shown three-quarter face, but they are indifferent efforts at the best; and, with one exception, the animals appear flattened sideways, like so many mechanical puppets, against the background. The one exception is the full-face elephant at the right end of the relief. In this case, the foreshortening is not unskilful, but the figure makes an awkward contrast as it stands, and the procession would have been better without it. The faults of this relief are due not to any imitation, conscious or unconscious, of archaic methods, but simply and solely to the incompetence of the sculptor, who was as deficient in technical craftsmanship as he was in story-telling.[1]

Pl. 29, 2: Another version of Māra's Repulse

To revert, however, to the relief of Māra's Repulse. The same subject is portrayed on the middle architrave at the back of the Northern Gateway (Pl. 29, 2), but here the demon hosts of Māra are depicted, not as fleeing in discomfiture from the temple, but as making merry with music and dance, while Māra himself and his daughters are essaying to tempt the Blessed One. This relief is a peculiarly striking example of what may happen, if the designing as well as the chiselling is divided between two experts. In conception and in spirit, the two halves of the composition have virtually nothing in common. In the left is the very commonplace, if unexceptionable, group of Māra and his daughters—all conceived in a very human mould, with the throne of the Buddha and the Bo-Tree, beneath which he sat, when Māra came to tempt and terrify him. It is a group made up of familiar stock types, without any particular character or distinction: a group, in fact, that might have been turned out by any reasonably competent sculptor of the time. In the right half, by contrast, is one of the most imaginative and arresting compositions to be found at Sāñchī. The strange and grotesque demons that fill this half of the architrave are treated very differently from those on the Western Gateway. Naturally, they belong to the same class of pot-bellied short-legged creatures, with enormous heads and coarse, fleshy features; that is their traditional form; but the artist is not satisfied with any ordinary kind of demons; he has no great flair for rhythmic design, such as the author of the kindred relief on the Western Gateway had, but he has a very keen sense for the ludicrous and grotesque, and he takes a delight in giving these sprites of evil the drollest grimaces that he can. Like every other sculptor who worked on these gateways, he has but one type of countenance peculiar to himself: a countenance with a large fleshy nose, saggy prominent eyes, elastic mouth and pointed ears, but he makes the most of it. It is a face that he himself has evolved; and he knows it from every angle, in every mood; and it is out of it that he creates his crowd of laughing, weeping, singing and rollicking demons. Most of his sprites are taking part in a characteristic nautch and are boisterously hilarious; but one there is in the background—a sad and tearful face—that seems, like the proverbial skeleton at the feast, to make mock of all their gaiety. It is tempting, indeed, to think

[1] *Cf.* M. Foucher's remarks on this relief, p. 215 *infra*.

that this was the idea at the back of the artist's mind: that he meant by this cartoon to point the evil associations of such wanton pleasures and the sorrow that inevitably lurks behind them. Music and dancing were not inherently wrong in the eyes of the Church; they were forbidden to the Buddhist monk, as they were to the Brahmacārin, but that did not imply that they were a monopoly of the wicked. Among these very sculptures there is ample evidence to show that they were looked upon as pastimes equally becoming to men and gods, and appropriate even to the celebration of sacred rites and festivals. Thus, on the right jamb of the Northern Gateway, we see the Mallas of Kuśinagara dancing to the accompaniment of 'drum and fife' around the resting place of the Blessed One (Pl. 36 *c*, 1); and, on the lowest architrave of the Eastern Gateway, musicians are playing their part in the ceremony of watering and worshipping the Bo-Tree; while on the left jamb of the Southern Gateway (Pl. 18 *b*), the devas of the *Trayastriṁśa* heaven are celebrating with dance and music the festival of Bodhisattva's head-dress. We can hardly believe, therefore, that the sculptor in this particular case regarded these diversions as specially demoniacal, though he may have intended to imply that the wild, unruly abandonment to which his demons are giving way, was inspired by the Evil One. Another item in this relief that deserves notice, is the wreath worn by one of the demons at the top, left-hand corner of the group. It recalls certain wreathed heads of Mauryan date found by Mr. Hargreaves at Sārnāth, and reminds us of the contact that had long been taking place with the Yavanas of the North-West; for the wearing of such wreaths was a Yavana, not an Indian, custom, and we may guess, perhaps, that the inclusion of this wreathed figure among the followers of the Evil One was not prompted by any friendly sentiments towards the Yavanas.

The reliefs we have been discussing on the Western and Northern Gateways, albeit excellent pieces of work, are not, in point of pure original artistry, the finest at Sāñchī. That honour belongs to the sculptures on the back of the middle and lowest architraves of the Southern Gateway (Pl. 15, 2 and 3). In appraising these two pieces, the reader is, unfortunately, handicapped by the poorness of the reproduction on Pl. 15, which is all the more regrettable, because the original photographs taken by Mr. Cousens were as fine as any in the series. So far as the schemes of the two designs and their composition are concerned, the reproductions no doubt give a tolerably good idea of the reliefs, but what they miss altogether is the sensitive modelling and exquisite refinement of the work. Let us see how the 'War of the Relics' on the lowest of the architraves compares with the presentation of the same subject that we have been examining, on the middle architrave of the Western Gateway (Pl. 61, 2). The latter, as we have seen, is an estimable piece of work, so far as it goes, and in point of technique unsurpassed except by one small panel on the Southern Gateway—the panel donated by the ivory-carvers of Vidiśā. The figures freely moving in space, the alternation of light and shade, the rhythm of concerted movement, the focussing of interest in the centre of the picture, the rise and fall of the

Pl. 15, 3: Another version of the War of the Relics

lines of the composition, the full roundness of the individual figures, and the plastic feeling for form—all these are traits showing how well the sculptor understood the essentials of his craft. But with the fullest admiration for these qualities, we cannot disguise from ourselves that the work lacks spontaneity. We feel that the author has relied less upon his own creative genius than upon what he has been taught about the handling of such scenes. His city he puts in the conventional position to one side of the relief ; his houses are stereotyped ; the heads framed in the openings of their balconies, lifeless. And for the rest of the scene, we seem to see him piecing it together on the most approved and orthodox lines, putting in his elephants and chariot just where he has been taught to put them, grouping his figures about them as he has grouped them a score of times before : all with consummate technical skill, but with no real originality. How radically different the handling of the scene on the Southern Gateway ! There is a story to be told, and the artist sets about telling it in his own simple, dramatic way. The moment he selects is when the siege of Kuśinagara is in full swing, not, as in the other relief, when the fighting is done and the townspeople have come to make their submission. The town itself he places boldly, against all precedent, in the centre of the composition. Space demands that his sketch of it shall be but the barest summary ; yet he manages to give us a remarkably clear idea of how an ancient Indian town looked, with its battlemented walls of stone or brick, its storeyed towers and bastions, its plastered gateways, its timbered superstructures, pillared balconies and vaulted roofs. And the siege he depicts is a very real siege : such a one as in after-days Roman sculptors were to carve on the columns of Trajan and Marcus Aurelius. Some of the assailants are struggling across the moat and scaling the wall beyond ; others are hammering away at the gates ; others shooting into the upper storeys ; while the defenders with every sort of weapon, including stones torn from the battlements, seek to repel the attack. This is the centre of the picture—the *pièce de résistance* ; but, to right and left of the town, come the armies of the Seven Chiefs, not moving from side to side as in the other panel, but swinging into the scene of action out of the background, and seemingly closing in on the town. Among the figures, needless to say, are some of the stock-in-trade motifs of contemporary art : the stereotyped chariots, the familiar elephants and their riders ; but the artist is far from being a slave to tradition and precedent. He is a master of his design and handles it with unusual freedom, putting in his figures to suit his own fancy and multiplying with marked effect the directions in which they move. To the technical principle of keeping the figures in one plane, he adheres, but he varies, here and there, the depth of his relief, as well as the intervals between the figures, and so diffuses or intensifies the shadows that the colouristic effect, obtained by the alternation of light and dark, is less accentuated and less monotonously regular than in the other panel.

A point of interest in this relief concerns the artist's method of narrating his story. Although he depicts the siege in progress, nevertheless he gives a clear hint of the victory that is to follow for the Seven Chiefs, by showing their figures repeated—three on the left and four on the right side (including the false caps and architrave ends)—as they ride off with the relics on the heads of their elephants. This method of "continuous narration," in which the past, present and future are shown in one unbroken scene, is a favourite device among the sculptors of ancient India, as it was among the sculptors of ancient Rome, and we shall notice presently several other examples of it, in which the succession of events is even more obvious than here.[1]

The delicate refinement that distinguishes the workmanship of this particular panel, extends also to the projecting false capital adorned with two seated elephants on the east side of the Southern Gateway (Pl. 16 *b*), as well as to the formal lotus design with which the volute at this end is finished off, but not, be it remarked, to the western false capital. The elephants on both these false capitals are evidently meant to be included in the war scene, the one turned inwards towards the city suggesting the advancing hosts, the other turned away from it, with the relic casket on its head, the victory achieved. And no doubt the whole architrave, including the two false capitals, was designed by the same master hand, but in execution the western false capital and the terminal of the architrave beyond it fall far short of the rest of the work. What strikes one forcibly about the elephants on the eastern false capital is their unaffected truth to nature. The modelling of these creatures, if it is to be really convincing, is not such an easy matter as might be supposed. Any reasonably qualified craftsman can turn out stolid conventional beasts like those on the western false capitals; for, given the initial design, the rest is a matter mainly of mechanical skill. But it requires a true artist, and one with a highly practised hand, to create such living forms as those on the eastern false capital, to reproduce the subtly shaded modelling of their skulls, the fleshy softness of their trunks and bodies. And it is only a true artist who would take the trouble to bring out the shape of the beast beneath the body-cloth, to engrave the finely embroidered patterns on the cloth itself, or to put in such an exquisite little leaf pattern alongside the volute. Refinements like these come of sheer love of beauty and of pride in the perfection of workmanship; for it is quite certain that no worshipper could have been expected to see them from below, any more than a worshipper in the Parthenon could have been expected to see the superb details of its famous frieze. The impression that these reliefs leave, is that their author had an exquisitely fine sense for the beautiful and relied mainly on his own instinct to give expression to it, but, like many a gifted artist, could be singularly negligent over details. He has an architrave to decorate with a battle scene, and he makes a first-rate design for the purpose, but is inexplicably careless about accommodating it to the lower edge of the volute, though he inserts such a graceful motif to fill the vacant angle at the top. Such

[1] Another item of interest in this relief is the peculiar dress worn by the archers sitting behind some of the chiefs on the elephants. It consists of a tunic with pleated kilt (perhaps a single garment), a corded girdle or *kamarband* (such as chaprasis still commonly wear), and a pull-over "balaclava" cap tied with ribbons around the neck. The ordinary garment worn in these reliefs is the Indian *dhotī*, but soldiers are girt up with a broad banded or corded *kamarband*. For the dress of the Mallas in Pl. 36 c, 1, see p. 157, note 1, *infra*.

lapses over detail are found in not a few of India's great works of art, but can hardly be said to impair their beauty. This particular architrave was the first of its kind to be carved at Sāñchī, and the sculptor of it was necessarily feeling his way. Those who came after him might imitate his work and correct, as they undoubtedly did, certain of its blemishes, but they never succeeded in equalling its intuitive genius.

Pl. 15, 2: Shaḍdanta Jātaka

Much that has been said above applies also to the relief on the inner face of the middle architrave, depicting the Shaḍdanta Jātaka, which we also have the advantage of being able to compare with two other reliefs of the same subject, one on the back of the Northern Gateway (Pl. 29, 1), and the other on the front of the Western Gateway (Pl. 55, 3). It was not, however, the same artist who carved the middle and the lowest architraves on the back of the Southern Gateway. The author of the former was, in his own way, not less gifted than the author of the latter, but his technique suggests that he was more expert with the pencil or the brush than with the chisel. His work owes almost everything to its design, almost nothing to relief. Indeed, the relief is so low, that the chiselling does little more than bring out the contours and such interior details as might be emphasized in a pencil sketch. And yet, what a masterly piece it is! What unity and breadth of treatment! What fine sense of line and rhythm! We may criticise it for its sketchy, tapestried effect, for its lack of depth and of contrasting light and shadow; we may take the individual elephants and compare them, to their disadvantage, with the splendidly modelled beast on the eastern false capital below, and yet, whatever our criticism, the fact remains that the design is a delightfully satisfying one, and the grouping of the elephants the finest thing of its kind that the Early School can boast. Place it by

Pls. 29, 1 and 55, 3: Two other versions of the Shaḍdanta Jātaka compared

the side of the topmost architrave on the back of the Northern Gateway (Pl. 29, 1), and see what an inferior sculptor, who tried to improve on its technique, could achieve. Greater bathos can hardly be imagined than the two cumbersome, distorted creatures that confront us, or the elephant falling over a crocodile in the water on the extreme right. True, this is one of the worst among all the sculptures of Sāñchī, and the later representation of the same Jātaka on the Western Gateway (Pl. 55, 3) shows a decided advance on it, but even the latter is far behind the relief on the Southern Gateway. Technically, it has almost every merit that the latter misses. The banyan tree in the centre is more convincingly true to nature; the relief deeper, the modelling more expressive, the play of light and shade more telling; yet it fails as a work of art, because it lacks the inspiration and touch of genius; because the detail is too crowded and confusing, the composition too mechanical.

The two architrave reliefs described above are not the only works of real excellence on the Southern Gateway. On the left jamb of this gateway there is the well-known panel which depicts a company of deities in the *Trayastriṁśa* heaven, rejoicing over and worshipping the hair and head-dress (*cūḍā*) of the Bodhisattva (Pl. 18 *b*, 2). It was carved, as the inscription on it tells us,[1] by the ivory workers of Vidiśā, and affords an instructive illustration of how perfectly these craftsmen could adapt their technique to stone. The panel is remarkable for several features: for its highly refined workmanship, for the delicate modelling of the tiny faces, and for the suppleness of the dancer's limbs; but a more important feature than these is the effort to obtain a true perspectival effect by recessing the figures at the top of the group from the sides inwards, and at the same time diminishing their size as they go backwards. In other reliefs, as we have seen, the heads and busts which are supposed to be behind the front row are not infrequently reduced in size so as to give an illusion of perspective; but if they are set back at all in those reliefs, it is only very slightly; here, the recessing is very marked, and we thus get a material or tactile combined with an illusional perspective. The principle is a very sound and natural one, which was developed in many Roman reliefs of the Imperial age,[2] but it is a principle that is obviously more suited to framed panels of restricted size, where a little deeper cutting does not impair the general unity, than to bigger compositions like those on the architraves of these gateways or, still more, on the columns of Trajan and Marcus Aurelius, where the preservation of a uniform surface was imperative. Another series of panels in which the same methods are adopted for obtaining a limited perspective, are those on the right jamb of the Eastern Gateway, depicting the six inferior heavens or *devalokas* of the gods (Pl. 49 *a* and *b*). Here, each of the six heavens is represented by the storey of a palace, the front of which is divided by pillars into three bays, and these small and narrow bays lend themselves peculiarly well to this kind of technique. Here, too, be it noted, the marked refinement and precision of the workmanship suggests that it was done by ivory-carvers, though not by the same hands that executed the unique panel on the Southern Gateway. Adjoining the latter, but on the front face of the pillar, is another admirable relief, which M. Foucher takes to represent the deities hastening on horseback and on elephant to do homage to the Bodhisattva's hair (Pl. 18 *a*, 3). It is likely that, as both panels apparently relate to the same subject and both are framed with the same dainty vine leaf border, they may both have been executed by the ivory-carvers of Vidiśā; but I do not think that they could have been by the same hands. Their styles are so radically and essentially dissimilar. In the one, with all its jewel-like finish, the grouping is tight and compact, the composition academic; in the other, the grouping is joyously free and unconstrained, with that feeling for decorative rhythm, for balance between the component parts, which is all the more telling, because it pays little regard to realities and no regard to symmetry in the ordinary acceptation of the term. What the sculptor aimed at depicting was the joy of the heavenly host, as it sets out to join the throng of worshippers, and, in the small space at his command, he succeeded remarkably well. His feeling for mass and his methods of giving expression to it call to mind in some respects the "Repulse of Māra's Army" on the Western Gateway (Pl. 61, 3), but in the

Pl. 49 *a* and *b*: The six devalokas

[1] *Cf.* Inscr. 400 *infra*.

[2] *E.g.*, in panels on the Arch of Titus, and in the Flavian and Antonine panels on the Arch of Constantine.

panel we are considering there is greater freedom in the handling of the figures, and there is an air of gladness and confidence that has no part in the other composition. Let it be added, too, that there is a quality in the figures themselves and in the manner of chiselling them, which is not paralleled among the other reliefs at Sāñchī.

The background

In the reliefs discussed above, the usual practice, as we have seen, was to portray groups of figures as moving in space, without any background to limit or define the scene. The kind of artificial stage-setting that was characteristic of Alexandrian reliefs and passed later into Roman art, was unknown in the Early Indian School. Backgrounds, it is true, are not entirely wanting among the Sāñchī reliefs ; sometimes they take the form of a park, sometimes of the jungle, sometimes of buildings, but in every case these backgrounds were introduced, not because the need was felt of an artificial setting, but because they were integral parts of the scene, and in some pictures as indispensable as the figures themselves. An instance in point is the glimpse of Indra's Paradise at the top of the left jamb of the Western Gateway (Pl. 64 *c*), where the fruits and blossoms, the clipped and shapely trees, and the river Mandākinī flowing in the foreground, are as necessary to the conception of this scene as are the couples dallying on couches in the shade. Another example is the Viśvantara Jātaka scene on the lowest architrave of the Northern Gateway, where the jungle is not in the nature of a detached background, but is the actual environment in which the actors are living and playing their parts (Pl. 29, 3). Other typical examples, to which the same remarks apply, are the Śyāma Jātaka scene with its hermitage surroundings on the Western Gateway (Pl. 65 *a*, 1), the Jetavana Garden on the east jamb of the Northern Gateway (Pl. 34 *a*, 2), another "Paradise" panel on the same pillar (Pl. 34 *b*, 2), and the long Kapilavastu panel on the right jamb of the Eastern Gateway (Pl. 50 *a*, 1). This last relief merits special attention, not only because of the excellence of its workmanship, but because it affords one of the best illustrations of the difficulties attendant on the setting out of such an ambitious picture without a correct knowledge of perspective. The scene which the sculptor has to portray is the meeting of King Śuddhodana with his son on the latter's return to Kapilavastu, together with the miracle which the Buddha performed on that occasion by walking in the air, and the subsequent gift of a banyan park made by his father. How does he set to work ? The surface to be decorated is a tall and narrow one ; so he cannot deploy the scene in the normal way to right and left, as he might have done on one of the gateway architraves. He therefore decides to show a narrow section only of the city directly fronting the spectator, with its buildings rising tier upon tier in the distance, and the royal cortege wending its way between them. The miracle will then be performed in the foreground in front of the city's gates, and a symbol of the king's gift added below it. Consider, however, the difficulties which confront the sculptor ! He is evidently a gifted artist, with a sound grasp of design and modelling ; his elephant heads are first-class work, and the horse nuzzling at the neck of its companion is one of the most natural and telling

Pl. 64, *c* : Indra's Paradise

Pl. 29, 3 : Viśvantara Jātaka

Pl. 50 *a*, 1 : Meeting of King Śuddhodana with the Buddha at Kapilavastu touches among the sculptures at Sāñchī. But what of his knowledge of perspective and foreshortening—the two things most essential to designing a relief such as this? Let us try and grasp what he did and did not know about these subjects. And first as to perspective: we have seen that, in regard to the grouping of figures, the common convention was to arrange them in rows or tiers one above the other, each succeeding row being supposed to be further away than the one below it. The idea underlying this arrangement is that the spectator is looking down diagonally on the scene from above, and that he actually sees the figures as represented; but obviously it involves a certain convention, since figures seen from such an angle would necessarily have to be foreshortened, not represented, as they are, at full length. Apart from this, however, the principle is not an irrational one, and works quite effectively when applied to throngs of living beings, provided always that the figures in the back rows are partly concealed behind those in front of them; it breaks down at once and the illusion vanishes, if the feet of those behind are visible above the heads of those in front. Turn, for example, to the throng in Pl. 61, 2. There is nothing in this relief obtrusively repugnant to our ideas of perspective, because the figures in the back rows are actually hidden in part behind the front ones, and a certain illusional perspective is maintained, notwithstanding that their heads are all in the same plane. But compare this with the relief we are discussing on Pl. 50, where the chariot horses are seemingly standing on the heads of the figures in front of them—and at once we are conscious of the unnatural strain put on our imagination by the latter, just as we are conscious of it when looking at many Hellenistic and Roman reliefs in which the same fault occurs. And this strain is equally great when we turn to the architectural features, where it is more difficult to gloss over the defects of incorrect perspective. So long as the artists of the Early Indian School could give a passably good impression of architecture, they were content; and in certain classes of pictures they succeeded in doing this sufficiently well. Thus, in the "War of the Relics" scene in Pl. 15, 3, the picture of Kuśinagara is quite adequate for its purpose. We are given a view of one side of the city, and we have no difficulty in discerning how the square bastions with their open balconies and vaulted roofs project out from either side of the gateway, nor yet how the half-concealed houses behind the gateway and the battlemented tower to the left are meant to be in the background. The artist has no idea, of course, of vanishing points or any such subtleties, and he is unnecessarily careless over his details (the dripstone for example over the balcony of this gateway does not follow the salient and re-entrant angles of the bastions, and the two gable arches at the right and left extremities of the main roof are obviously not parallel); nevertheless he understands enough of the rudiments of perspective drawing to portray the essential features of his buildings, and in a relief of this kind that is as much as is needed. Of the science of perspective he and his colleagues knew no more than the sculptors of Imperial Rome. Such limited knowledge as they possessed of the subject was the outcome of experience and tradition, not of scientific observation. That is why it was entirely beyond their powers to give a correct tridimensional effect to a

Portrayal of architecture

Perspective

landscape or a large group of buildings, and that is why, when confronted by a problem of perspective, they found themselves hopelessly at sea. Look, for example, at their attempts to portray the drum and dome of a stūpa. This was an object more or less new to art, and hence there is only their own ingenuity to help them. How do they do it? In a few cases, as in Pls. 46 and 63, their drawings come near to the truth, but one suspects that this is by accident only; for in the majority of cases they are sadly at fault. What evidently they could not grasp, was how to show curved horizontal lines in elevation. It seemed to them that somehow or other a curved line must always be curved, a straight line always straight, and hence, in drawing a stūpa, they show the crowning *harmikā* as straight, but the railings round the drum and the swags round the dome as curved; in other words, they endeavour to combine perspective and elevation in one. An outstanding example of this misunderstanding of the problem is to be seen in Pl. 36 *c*, 1, illustrating the worship of the Buddha's relic-stūpa by the Mallas of Kuśinagara. The sculptor of this panel is evidently an experienced craftsman; for his little figures are full of life and charm, but when he comes to set out the three circular balustrades around the stūpa, his drawing is all at sixes and sevens. He wants to give an idea of the circular form of the balustrades: even to show some of his worshippers in the procession path between them; but the curvilinear perspective quite defeats him, and he can produce nothing better than the oddly erratic drawing that we see. It is just such a novel problem that confronts the author of our Kapilavastu panel, when he comes to put in his buildings. He can depict a traditional gateway with its bastions and vaulted roofs as well as any artist of the day, but his drawing fails him (as in like circumstances it also failed the Roman sculptors of Trajan's column), when he tries to depict the curving wall of the town or the buildings set back at a distance behind the gateway. The latter problem might, perhaps, have been solved with some success, had the space been broader; as it was, the only method known to him was the conventional one of showing the more distant buildings above the nearer ones, but all in one and the same plane. This, then, was the method followed; but it cannot be pretended that it produces illusion of distance, nor is it possible that it should do this without the help of some sort of perspective.

Pl. 36 c, 1: Worship of the Buddha's relic-stūpa at Kuśinagara

The fact is that the resources of art of that age were unequal to the task he had set himself, and the most difficult part of that task still awaited him. With this fictitious scheme of perspective, in which distance was expressed only by height, how was he to show the miracle of the Buddha walking in the air? The Buddha must not, of course, be portrayed in person—that is against the tenets of the Church—but he can be represented well enough by the promenade (*caṅkama*) on which he was accustomed to take his exercise, a symbol understood of all good Buddhists. That, however, is not the difficulty. The problem is, how to make this *caṅkama* appear, as it were, suspended in the air! He does it in two ways: by inserting it among the tree-tops and by making King Śuddhodana and his group of courtiers turn their faces upwards, as they watch the miracle.[1] Truly, it is a brave effort, but one wonders how many of the Buddhists who saw it, had the genius to solve the riddle of its meaning, as M. Foucher has done.[2]

Foreshortening

There remains still the question of foreshortening, and here also the sculptor was much handicapped by the limitations of his art. His picture is so designed that the royal cortege of Śuddhodana has to be shown moving direct towards the spectator; but here comes in another difficulty. He can portray men on foot advancing full-face towards him; the foreshortening in their case is not a serious matter, and he has plenty of precedents to help him. But it is a different matter with the horses and elephants; he can foreshorten their heads and necks, but he cannot manage their bodies as well. That is a thing that none of the sculptors have so far succeeded in doing. To be sure, there are the elephants in that excellent carving on the Southern Gateway, which are coming almost full-face out of the background. But even those are not of any real help, because their sculptor has been clever enough to realize his limitations and to conceal all except their forefronts behind the adjacent riders. And so far as horses are concerned, no one has ever attempted to show more than their heads turned to the front. The only course, then, is to make the best of established precedent, to depict the chariots and elephants winding down obliquely out of the town, and utilize the footmen to fill in awkward spaces. This is what he does, and he does it as successfully as can be hoped. He might perhaps have shown more skill in his handling of the figures outside the city gate by hiding the horses' legs behind the footmen in front of them, and thus giving more coherence to the group, but, apart from this small detail, we must surely admire the way in which he has overcome so many difficulties and, in spite of the peculiarly awkward shape of the panel and the strictly limited resources of his craft, has succeeded not only in unfolding his tale, but in producing a highly decorative piece of work into the bargain.

Continuous narrative

In the telling of this story of Kapilavastu, the sculptor has not, be it observed, followed the practice usual in modern illustrative art of portraying a single episode or scene; he has done what was frequently done by painters and sculptors in the old world, when they wished to unfold a continuous narrative, *viz.*, presented a succession of episodes, not divided off one from another, but all assembled together in the same panel. First, at the top of the relief, he shows the conception of the Bodhisattva. This, however, is not really part of the narrative, for the conception took place forty years before the other events narrated below; it is meant only as a sort of label to let the spectator know that the city depicted is Kapilavastu. For, of course, every Buddhist knew well enough where

[1] Compare with this the figures gazing upwards in the *Mahākapi Jātaka* on the right pillar of the Western Gateway (Pl. 64 *a*, 1).

[2] Dr. Coomaraswamy's view that the meaning of all the reliefs at Bharhut, Bodh-Gayā and Sāñchī must have been self-evident to contemporary Buddhists can hardly be right. Else what was the purpose of the many explanatory labels on the reliefs at Bharhut? *Cf.* Coomaraswamy, *The Origin of the Buddha Image*, p. 8. 'The Art Bulletin,' New York, Vol. IX, No. 4. 1927.

the conception took place. Then comes the royal procession through the town, with King Śuddhodana riding in its midst. Next, the miracle, with the figures of the king and his courtiers repeated. And, lastly, the gift of the banyan grove, symbolised by a single tree. An example of the same continuous narrative occurred, it will be remembered, in the "War of the Relics" on the Southern Gateway, where in one group the same chiefs are shown both advancing to the attack on the city and returning victorious with the captured relics. There are other reliefs, however, in which the successive stages of the story are set out with more method and elaboration than this. A specially instructive one is on the middle architrave in front of the Eastern Gateway (Pl. 40, 2). It illustrates the *Mahābhinishkramaṇa*, that is, Gautama's Departure from his home in Kapilavastu. Gautama, himself, is not of course represented, but we see his horse Kaṇṭhaka, with *devas* supporting his hoofs, attendants at his side, and Chandaka, his groom, holding the royal umbrella above his head to symbolize the Master's presence; and in order to indicate the prince's progress, this group is repeated four times in succession towards the right of the relief; then, at the parting of the ways, we see Chandaka and the horse returning to Kapilavastu, and the further journey of the prince on foot indicated by his sacred footsteps surmounted by an umbrella and fly-whisk. In the middle of the panel is a *jambu* tree (*Eugenia jambu*), which M. Foucher ingeniously suggests was placed there by the sculptor as a reminder of the first meditation of the Bodhisattva, which took place in the shade of a *jambu* tree, and of the path on which it led him to Renunciation and Enlightenment. Such a reminder is quite in keeping with the methods of these early sculptors, who had to resort to every sort of device to make their meaning clear; but again it makes one wonder whether the Buddhists were præternaturally clever at reading these riddles, or whether by this time they were so familiar with the conventions of this religious art, that a mere hint like this was enough to make them grasp the sculptor's idea.[1] Another good illustration of the continuous style is supplied by the Viśvantara Jātaka on the lowest architrave of the Northern Gateway (Pls. 23, 25, 27, 29, 31 and 33), where we see incident after incident in the well-known story recounted in chronological sequence, without any dividing lines between them: first, the gift of the royal elephant and the banishment of the prince; then, the giving away of the horses and chariot, and the life that followed in the seclusion of the jungles; next, the giving away of the prince's children and of his wife Maddī; and, finally, the restoration of both wife and children at the hands of Indra, and the happy reunion of the family in their paternal palace. From start to finish, the whole story is told with an intriguing wealth of detail, and, provided one knows the story beforehand, there is little difficulty about recognising the successive episodes; but, as M. Foucher points out, it is a *sine qua non* that the spectator should be familiar with the Buddhist legend as well as with the conventions of Buddhist art.

Pl. 40, 2: The Mahābhinishkramaṇa

Pls. 23, 25, 27, 29, 31 and 33: The Viśvantara Jātaka

[1] See p. 125, note 2, *supra*. It is tempting to see, in the absence from the Sāñchī gateways of explanatory labels such as they had at Bharhut, an indication that the Buddhists were becoming more familiar with the conventions of iconography, but we must not forget that the balustrade of Stūpa 2 at Sāñchī, which is earlier than Bharhut, is also without labels.

The method of continuous narration in these two reliefs is not, let it be added, identical with that followed in the "War of the Relics" on the Southern Gateway. In that relief, battle and victory are thrown together in the same group, and the two events are so blended as to make of the whole an indivisible artistic unity. In these two reliefs, on the other hand, the several successive episodes are merely co-ordinated side by side in the author's brain as an organic whole; in other words, the connection between them is mechanical, not organic.

Lower standard of workmanship in some reliefs

In our discussion of these sculptures in the foregoing pages we have naturally given precedence to those which are of outstanding merit, since it is by its best work, not by what is mediocre or bad, that the art of any period is to be judged. Although, however, the standard of these reliefs, taken as a whole, is not as high as the examples chosen above might suggest, it is still—considering their diversity and the manifold hands that were engaged upon them—a remarkably high one, and there are singularly few among them of really poor workmanship. Two of these have already been noticed, *viz.*, the *Shaḍdanta Jātaka* on the top architrave at the back of the Northern Gateway (Pl. 29, 1) and the "Relic Scene at Kuśinagara" on the top architrave at the back of the Western Gateway (Pl. 61, 1). Strangely enough, it is in the same position on the Southern Gateway that another strikingly inferior piece of work is found. We say 'strangely,' because this is a position in which the reliefs can be seen particularly well by any one standing on the raised procession path of the stūpa, and we might, therefore, have expected it to be given to the finest rather than to the least attractive of the carvings, though we know, as a fact, that the most important carvings were reserved for the outer, not for the inner, face of the gateway. The relief in question is figured at the top of Pl. 15, where the reader can satisfy himself at a glance how poorly it compares with the two superb panels below. The subject depicted is the worship of the Last Seven Buddhas, including Gautama—three symbolised by their stūpas, and four by the trees under which each respectively attained Enlightenment. Identically the same subject is illustrated on the three other gateways, but in their case on the front instead of the back of the topmost architrave, and it seems virtually certain that the top architrave on the Southern Gateway was turned front to back by mistake, when the gateway was re-erected by Col. Cole.[1] Obviously the subject is not one that lends itself easily to artistic treatment, nor can it surprise us that even the best of these reliefs (which is the one on the Western Gateway) possesses little or no æsthetic value, though neither this nor any of the others display such striking incapacity in the drawing of the figures or such clumsiness in their execution as the one on the Southern Gateway. The same indifferent workmanship extends also to the reverse, *i.e.*, to the present outer side of this architrave, the middle section of which is adorned with an elaborate lotus design, symbolising no doubt the birth of the Blessed One, whose mother,

Pl. 15, 1: Worship of the Last Seven Buddhas

[1] *Cf.* p. 233 *infra*.

Pl. 11, 1: Nativity Scene

Māyā, in the guise of Lakshmī, occupies its centre (Pl. 11, 1). On this side, however, the design, though weak and ill-suited to the position it occupies, is not altogether without merit. What is especially crude and faulty, is the actual chiselling. Once again, we have but to contrast this architrave with the two below it on the same side, to perceive how careless and unrefined the work is, and how entirely devoid of vitality or feeling for plasticity.

CHAPTER XI

GATEWAY SCULPTURES—continued

The human form: its appeal to the sculptors of Sāñchī

IN the above reliefs we have seen that many of the individual figures are characterised by a refinement of detail that it would be difficult to surpass in stone carving. Such miniature figures represent, however, only one aspect of sculpture. They teach us much about the technique, as it was then understood, of modelling on a small scale, about foreshortening, perspective, composition and the handling of light and shade; what we cannot learn from them is the kind of appeal that the human body *per se* made to the sculptors of Sāñchī. Was it to them, as it had been to the sculptors of Greece, a thing of exquisite beauty in itself, worthy to be studied and reproduced in all its subtle refinements of form and feature? Or was man just an item in the landscape—a thing of beauty without doubt, but not more worthy of special and intensive study than the animals or trees or other natural objects? For an answer to this question we must turn to such larger-scale figures as have survived on these gateways, though, unfortunately, these figures are so few that the answer can at best be only an incomplete one. The finest and most instructive of them are the female bracket figures that support the extremities of the lowest architraves. Two of them, with their legs broken, survive in their places on the Northern Gateway (Pls. 25, 27, 31 and 33), and one, quite intact, on the north side of the Eastern Gateway (Pls. 44 and 48); of the others there are two torsos and various other fragments in the museum (Pl. 68),[1] the original location of which it is not possible to determine with certainty. These figures are not merely architectural members, nor are they, as was once thought, representations of dancing girls without any religious significance. They belong to the same class of minor deities as the yakshīs and devatās (Sudarsanā, Culakokā, Sirimā, etc.) sculptured on the balustrades of Bharhut and of the Second Stūpa at Sāñchī. Here, the overhanging branches on to which they are holding, seem to indicate that they are *vṛiksha-devatās*[2] or dryads—descendants of those pre-Āryan tree-goddesses whose effigies are figured on Indus Valley seals of the third and fourth millennia B.C. and whose cult, along with that of the Mother goddesses and Śiva, must be reckoned one of the oldest in India. That this particular form of bracket is appropriate to its position on the gateways, no one with a proper understanding of architectural principles is likely to maintain; for a first essential in such a bracket is that it must be capable of resisting the real or imaginary strain imposed upon it. So far, however, from doing this, the two figures on the Northern Gateway (Pls. 25, 27, 31 and 33) seem rather to be dependent on the architrave for support than themselves to contribute it—an effect for which their own leaning

Female bracket figures

[1] *Cf. Cat. of the Museum of Archaeology at Sāñchī*, Nos. A24-A34, pp. 23-24.

[2] Known more specifically as *Śālabhañjikā*. *Cf.* pp. 37, 232 n. 1.

postures and the outward curve of the trees against which they are resting, are responsible, since, obviously, neither the one nor the other would be effective in withstanding the weight of the ponderous mass above them. The dryad on the Eastern Gateway (Pl. 44) is a much more appropriate support, as there is that in her posture which suggests tension and resistance ; but even in her case the bent mango-tree is little calculated to sustain a heavy weight above its fragile boughs.

Pls. 44 and 48 *b*: The bracket dryad of the Eastern Gateway

Apart, however, from its structural propriety, which is not our immediate concern, there can be no two opinions as to the superb lines of this dryad of the Eastern Gateway, whether viewed from the front or the back (Pls. 44 and 48 *b*). Its keynote is that same naturalness and unaffected simplicity that we noticed in many of the smaller relief figures, only that here, in proportion to the larger size of the sculpture, these qualities stand out more clearly. The difference between this figure and the yakshīs and devatās on the Bharhut balustrade is the difference between art and artifice. In the Bharhut work we are instinctively conscious of the pains the sculptor has taken to master his material and to render, in his own dry and accurate way, every detail that he can of the figure's anatomy. Looking at the Sāñchī dryad, we think of none of these things. We see only the finished form, supple and full, in its entirety : the telling grace of its outlines, the easy repose of its attitude. In this case, it is the sum total of beauty that attracts our gaze, not the minor details, nor yet the means by which the beauty was achieved. Defects there undoubtedly are, that will not escape our closer scrutiny, but for the moment they are obscured by the satisfaction we get from the work as a whole. One such defect is that the neck is too short and thick, and the head set too squat upon the shoulders; another, that the features of the face are all but repellent in their plainness; a third, that the arms are unduly angular; and a fourth, that the modelling of the feet is sketchy and inaccurate. The shortness of the neck can hardly surprise us, seeing that it is a defect common to almost every sculpture of the Early School; nor shall we be over-critical about the angularity of the arms or the sketchiness of the feet; but it might at least have been expected that the faces of this and its fellow dryads on the Northern Gateway would have shown some measure of comeliness. It is not as though the sculptors of this age were insensible to facial beauty. There are hundreds of pretty faces among the smaller relievos, and we have seen how one type of prettiness was evolved by one sculptor, another by another, and how seldom their particular types were varied, even by the most skilful artists. Not all the faces, of course, among these smaller relievos are comely. Many are as ill-favoured as those of the dryads we are now discussing; but there can be no question that prettiness was a thing at which the artists normally aimed, and if they were unsuccessful in depicting it, it was probably because they were lacking in skill. The same remarks apply, also, to the somewhat larger reliefs on the false capitals and dies between them. Take, for example, the six reliefs of Māyā in Pls. 13, 24, 25, 41, 44 and 56, all of which are carved on the dies, and are approximately of the same size. Of these, the one on the Southern

Facial beauty

Figures of Māyā compared

Gateway (Pl. 13) is too damaged for the features of the face to be made out, but, of the remaining five, the one on Pl. 41 has as pretty and charming a face and form as any representation of Māyā or Lakshmī known to us, and the other one on the same gateway (Pl. 44), though not up to the same standard, is nevertheless quite pleasing. On the other hand, the two on the Northern Gateway (Pls. 24 and 25), which are evidently the work of inferior artists, are without beauty of any kind; and the one on the Western Gateway (Pl. 56) is startlingly ugly. Or take, again, the figures of riders on the false capitals. Altogether, there are seventy of them surviving on the four gateways, but only thirty have their faces preserved more or less intact, and of these not more than six—all on the Eastern Gateway[1]—have really pleasant, expressive features, while fifteen have fairly pleasant ones, and nine are strikingly plain, if not definitely ugly. A few of these figures that are riding grotesque and fabulous animals, may have been intentionally provided with faces in keeping with their mounts, but, speaking of these small relievos generally, it is true to say that their standard of good looks depends on the skill of the artists, some of whom were entirely incapable of modelling attractive features. In view of this, it is interesting to observe that, among the larger figures of the Early School, there is not a single one that has any pretensions to possessing a comely face. The reason is not, I think, far to seek. The small relievos in stone were executed, as we have already noticed, by ivory-carvers or others who had behind them generations of experience in the finest kinds of carving, or, if they were not actually executed by these miniature artists in person, they were at any rate indebted to them and to their work for all that was most essential in the matter of style and technique. But when it came to the carving of life-size or bigger statues, the lessons that the new stone sculptors could learn from this old-established miniature art, were of little avail. They were completely at a loss how to reproduce the pleasing expressions of the tiny faces on a larger scale; and, as a fact, it was not until the half-Greek School of Gandhāra had shown them the way, that they learnt how to accomplish this.

Faces of riders on the false capitals

Seeming nudity of dryads and other figures

To return, however, to the dryad of the Eastern Gateway. To all appearances she is represented as nude or virtually nude, but, as a fact, she is supposed to be clad in a thin, transparent garment (*dhotī*) from the waist to below the knees, through which the form is clearly visible. This curiously artificial convention, more suggestive perhaps than complete nudity would have been, is characteristic of many of the sculptures at Sāñchī and Mathurā, but not of those at Bharhut. In this case, the convention is all the more anomalous, because, although the front of the garment is so lightly indicated as to be scarcely perceptible, the back view (Pl. 48 *b*) makes it obvious that the *dhotī* is conceived as passing from front to back through the fork of the legs, and, this being so, the semblance of nudity as viewed from the front becomes an impossibility. In some of the smaller dryad figures (*e.g.*, on Pls. 24, 26, 27 and 30 *a*) the front of this same garment is more evident, notwithstanding that the form is equally conspicuous. In the particular dryad

[1] See Pls. 43, 48 *a*, 2, and 48 *b*.

Treatment of hair

we are discussing the hair is confined in an elaborately folded coif on the top of the head, but allowed to fall loose over the shoulders and back (Pl. 48 *b*); in other examples it is braided with wool after the present-day fashion of Turkomān and Kashmīri women, and festooned in a number of long loops down the back (Pls. 30 *a*, 31 and 33). If the sculptors have been careless or indifferent over the features of the face, they have certainly spared no pains to render with fidelity every detail of the hair and the head-dress, as well as of the armlets, anklets, girdles and other ornaments; and they have shown no scruples about obscuring, where necessary, the shapeliness of arms and legs by covering them with bangles. Doubtless this was an old-established fashion from which it may have been difficult for them to break away,[1] but it is noteworthy how very different is the treatment of these bangles at Sāñchī and Bharhut. In the Bharhut reliefs they are also clearly defined, but with such restraint and refinement that they serve to enhance rather than to detract from the charm of the whole. At Sāñchī, too, the decorative value of jewellery is well understood, but it is not harmonized in the same way with the plastic beauty of the body. The bangles are there as a matter of course, because tradition requires them, but the artist does not attempt to lighten their heaviness for the reason that he is interested less in the finer subtleties of anatomic modelling than in broad decorative effects; and it must be confessed that he succeeds remarkably well in achieving his purpose.

Bangles, girdles, etc.

Limitations of figural art at Sāñchī

Yet, passing over its defects (which might easily have been remedied) and looking only at its undeniably great qualities, one cannot, even so, be wholly satisfied with this figure. Its art is almost too facile; it gives too little promise of the future. In the presence of the larger figures at Bharhut we feel much as we do in the presence of early Attic work. Its power of expression may for the moment be narrowly limited, but it is wholly sincere in its striving after beauty, and we are conscious of the great future that may await it, when the mastery over material and technique shall be gained. For the Sāñchī sculpture there is no such outlook. It marks the end rather than the beginning of a period. Technical difficulties have been overcome; unaffected and dignified realism has been achieved; but that is as far as this art is ever likely to go: it fails in a sense, because it is so clear that it will go no further.

Other figures of dryads

These remarks about the dryad of the Eastern Gateway are generally true of the two corresponding figures on the Northern Gateway (Pls. 25, 27, 31 and 33) and of the broken torsos of two others in the museum (Pl. 68). The latter, indeed, exhibit a flexibility in their modelling and a clearness in their chiselling that would have done credit to a Greek. The former are not so happy. They show the same bigness of conception and the same sense of plastic form, but they lack the decision and stylishness of the others, and from a functional point of view could hardly have been more nerveless.

[1] *Cf.* for this feature, the bronze statuette of a dancing girl from Mohenjo-daro. *Mohenjo-daro and the Indus Civilization*, ed. Marshall, Pl. XCIV, 6-8.

When we turn from these bracket figures to the Guardian Yakshas that stand sentinel inside the gateways (Pls. 36 *a* and *b*, 50 *a*, 52 *b* and 66 *a*), we are struck almost more by the contrast than by the kinship between them. Not that they have not much in common. There is the same short thick neck, the same immobile set of the head, the same plain, emotionless features. These are traits that cannot be mistaken ; but for the moment we forget them in our surprise at the rigidity and awkwardness of these Guardian Yakshas as compared with the easy grace of the Vṛiksha-devatās. Only one among the guardians makes any pretence at being unconstrained in his attitude, *viz.*, the spearman at the Western Gateway (Pl. 66 *a*). In this relief the neck is longer and the poise of the head more natural ; the shoulders are not so square ; the pose easier, with the weight thrown very slightly forward onto the right leg ; and the toes of the right foot are curved over the edge of the plinth on which the figure is standing. In the case of the others, the head, which, be it noted, is disproportionately large for the body, is sunk deep into the shoulders, the shoulders themselves are square, the body and legs stiff and frontal, and the feet turned outwards almost at right angles to the legs. We have said that these figures astonish us by their ungainliness, but it is only for a moment ; for what, after all, should we expect of sentinels in these positions ? Among the smaller reliefs on the gateway jambs, there are a few, as we have seen, that show an unmistakable archaizing tendency, both in the frontality of individual figures and in the schematic grouping of the whole. Here, too, the influence of tradition has no doubt been in some measure responsible for the seemingly archaic appearance of these guardians, but this is not the only reason. If we look at the free-standing figure of the *caurī*-bearer between the *dharmacakra* and the *triratna* on the top of the Northern Gateway (Pls. 22 and 30 *b*), we realize at once why the sculptor has made it so architecturally formal and severe. In such a position it could not be otherwise, if it was to harmonize with the essentially tectonic lines of the other crowning ornaments. The same observation holds good of the guardians of the gateways. The position they occupy in relation to the squared jambs of the structures and their own character as sentinels of the stūpa, demand that they be square of frame, with a firm and erect carriage. This is why they are designed to be as nearly as possible the counterparts in relievo of the free-standing figure on the top of the Northern Gateway ; and, indeed, they are little else than statues in the round cut in half. But there is one marked difference between them and the free-standing figures. As observed above, the sculptors were not yet familiar with the technique of large-scale relief, and when they came to the feet, they did not know how to deal with them, the difficulty being to keep the niches reasonably shallow and at the same time prevent the feet of the guardians projecting in front of the lower edges. The only way they could find out of this difficulty was to turn the feet sideways, as they had been turned in the archaic statues ; and this unnatural turn involved also stiffening the knees and legs and to some extent the trunk as well. Thus, the ultra-rigidity of these figures is traceable, in the main, to the difficulty of disposing of the feet. Were it not for this, they would, from a plastic point of view,

Guardian Yakshas

be closely on a par with the free-standing statue referred to above. In their case, it need hardly be said, much more care and labour have been expended on the modelling of the knees and abdomen and other anatomical details, as well as on the elaboration of clothes[1] and ornaments, but no amount of care on such minor features could redeem these Yakshas from being dull and uninteresting. There is nothing whatever imaginative about them: they miss the refined elegance—the preciousness, if I may use that word—that gives a peculiar charm to the Yakshas and Yakshīs of Bharhut; and, on the other hand, they miss the unconstrained beauty of form that makes the Vṛikshakā bracket on the Eastern Gateway such a joy to behold.

Smaller figures of dryads between architraves

With a single exception, all the smaller figures of Vṛiksha-devatās that stand between the projecting ends of the architraves (four on the Northern and one on the Eastern Gateway) face outwards, and pains have been taken to make them as presentable as possible from the back by carefully finishing off the long loops of their hair and other details. The one exception is the Vrikshakā between the middle and top architraves on the west side of the Northern Gateway (Pls. 21, 26, 28 and 30 *a*), which is so designed as to face both ways without the deception being noticeable. The same Janus-like device is also employed for the other free-standing statues that fill the interspaces between the middle sections of the architraves (Pls. 21, 28, etc.), but there is this difference in the methods adopted that, whereas the dryad consists virtually of two entire figures set back to back, the horses and their riders in the upper row possess but one body with two connected heads, while, in the row below, the elephants are normal and only their riders duplicated.

Animal sculpture

It has sometimes been said that the sculptors of Sāñchī knew more about the carving of animals than of men. The criticism is not merited. Some of the animals on these gateways are undoubtedly very fine—the finest, perhaps, of their kind in India—for the sculptors had a natural gift for understanding the ways of animals and portraying them with faithful and facile touch. It was a gift that they had inherited from their non-Āryan ancestors, and it was doubtless quickened by their own religious outlook, which envisaged all nature as one harmonious scheme, and all living things as equally worthy of attention and love. But it is no disparagement of their animal carvings, if we do not place them on the same level with those of their men and women. To the sculptors of Sāñchī, man was not what he had been to the sculptors of Greece—a thing of consummate physical beauty; nor was he what he was destined to become in the Golden Age of India or in the Renaissance of Italy—an embodiment of ethical or spiritual ideals. On the other hand, he was far more than a mere item in the landscape of the universe. Notwithstanding Buddhism and the philosophic systems which led up to it, man was

[1] Observe that in most of these figures the folds of the *dhotī* are indicated by lines lightly incised on the legs above the knees, but that in the Yaksha of the Western Gateway the drapery is treated much more convincingly. The method of portraying its transparency in the latter relief is similar to that afterwards adopted in the Mathurā School.

already the central figure round which all else revolved. The Sāñchī sculptures have been called "the Jungle-book of India". They are much more than that. They are a compendium of life in all its aspects. If they have graphic pictures to show us of life in the forest, they have equally graphic ones of life in court and city, and we must not be forgetful of the latter in our admiration for the former.[1]

Elephants

What makes many of the animals of Sāñchī so peculiarly attractive, is the same unaffected naturalism that we noticed in the human figures. Most striking among them are the elephants. Some of these we have already discussed: the best on the back of the Southern, the worst on the back of the Northern, Gateway (Pls. 15, 2 and 29, 1). Some fine workmanship, as we have seen, is also put into many of the heads on Pls. 15, 3 and 61, 2 and 3, as well as into the beasts on the lowest architrave in front of the Western Gateway, including the two false capitals. But it should be noted that the beasts in the left half of this architrave show a better understanding of the head and ear structure than those in the right; on the other hand, the pair on the southern false capital are decidedly superior to those on the northern (Pls. 55, 57 and 59). Much less successful are the elephants doing honour to the Rāmagrāma Stūpa on the lowest architrave at the back of the Eastern Gateway (Pl. 46, 3). The five to the left of the stūpa are evidently by a different hand from the rest, and their treatment is more skilful, but the difference is only slight: all are stilted and wooden, especially about the legs, and the modelling lacks both vigour and truth. Moreover, those in the back row, especially on the right side, suffer from an obvious technical defect in the handling of the relief, the fact being that it is impossible to grade such large and ponderous beasts successfully, if all the bodies are to be kept in one plane and the cutting is to be as deep as it is here. That perhaps is why the artist who designed the fine herd on the back of the Southern Gateway (Pl. 15) preferred to keep his relief so shallow.

Deer

Other animals that are portrayed with much fidelity and feeling, are the deer and buffaloes. Of the former, the best examples are to be found in the Deer Park scene on the front of the Western Gateway (Pl. 55, 2); of the latter, in the "Adoration of the Buddha" on the back of the Eastern Gateway (Pl. 46, 2). In each of these reliefs the work was divided between two sculptors, and there is a marked difference between the animals in the right and left halves of the two panels. In Pl. 55, the deer to the right of the sacred wheel are recognisable at a glance as black-buck, with their does behind them; forms and attitudes alike are typical of these animals, and it is clear from the freedom with which they are grouped, as well as from the illusion of depth obtained in the relief, that they are the work of a well-practised hand, though his limitations are disclosed in his

[1] When judging the animals of Sāñchī it is well to remember that the standard for animal sculpture is generally much lower than the standard for human sculpture. That is because man is not accustomed to observe animals as closely as he observes his fellow beings. Every human face that he sees, he discriminates at a glance from its neighbours by the subtle variations of feature that make up its individuality. With animals he does not do this; he notes the characteristics of the species and the traits and habits peculiar to it rather than the features of the individual; and when he depicts them, he inclines to reduce them more to types.

attempt, brave as it is, at foreshortening the crouching buck to the left of the group. What the animals in the left half of the panel are meant to be, it is more difficult to make out. Their horns and heads are seemingly intended for deer, but the bodies and long tails suggest that the sculptor was more familiar with domesticated cattle, and not observant enough to appreciate the points of difference between them. In the panel of the Eastern Gateway (Pl. 46) it is the left half of the relief that is the more successful. The author of the other half has displayed some skill with his two deer at the right-hand bottom corner,

Buffaloes

but the beast to the right of the central tree is recognisable as a buffalo only from the shape of his horns, and even they are wrongly set. The buffaloes on the left side, on the contrary, are first-class bits of sculpture—living images of those uniquely slow and patient-working beasts.

Humped bulls

Another animal that is portrayed with much simplicity and directness, is the humped bull or zebu (*Bos indicus*). A good example is afforded by the pair of seated bulls with riders on the top false capital on the north side in front of the Eastern Gateway (Pl. 43), and other representations may be seen on the corresponding false capital to the left of the same gateway (Pl. 41) and on the lowest false capitals in front of the Northern Gateway (Pls. 25 and 27), but in these latter cases the forms of the beasts are conspicuously fatter and clumsier than in the first-mentioned, and, though perhaps no less true to nature, are far less vital and pleasing to the eye. The bulls and riders on Pl. 43 deserve, indeed, more than a passing glance; for the breadth and directness of their treatment, without any conscious straining after effect, are typical of the traditional spirit of Mālwā art. To appreciate the better what this implies, we have but to place these animals by the side of one of the Brāhmani bulls—the best of the series—engraved on the seals of Mohenjo-daro.[1] In both cases, the artists were keenly alive to the beauties of the animal form, and each in his own way was highly skilled in the portrayal of it, but what a world of difference between them! For the prehistoric engraver, his pre-conceived ideas came first and foremost and effectively dominated the objective beauty of the forms he was delineating, so that the features he selected for emphasis were those, and those only, which lent expression to his own ideals. For his successor of 3000 years later, subjective idealism, except in the decorative field, was subordinated to the beauty of his subject. An artist by instinct, he had a gift for reducing what he saw to broad and simple forms and for giving those forms a natural, unassuming dignity, which contrasts sharply with the more sophisticated style of Mohenjo-daro. That the Sāñchī sculptor was working from direct observation of his subject, there can be no shadow of doubt, but it was not a matter of slavish copying on his part. Compared with the Mohenjo-daro engraving there is little artifice, little of what is commonly called "style", in his bulls and their riders, but he was master enough of his art to understand the full meaning of rhythm and the value of

[1] *Mohenjo-daro and the Indus Civilization*, ed. Marshall, Pl. CXI, No. 337.

eliminating superfluous details, while at the same time bringing out, without undue emphasis, the essential anatomy of his animals; and that is the most that we can look for in the figural art of this school.

Camels Camels (Pls. 47 and 48) were evidently not as familiar to the artists of Sāñchī as some other animals, and, indeed, it is a matter of surprise that they should make their appearance at all on these monuments, considering that they are rarely, if ever, seen in Mālwā. The camel portrayed at Sāñchī, both on Stūpa 2 and Stūpa 1, is the two-humped Bactrian beast (*Camelus bactrianus*), not the single-humped Arabian species (*Camelus dromedarius*). That the sculptors were not at home with these animals, may be judged from a comparison of the two middle false capitals on the back of the Eastern Gateway (Pls. 47 and 48). On the northern one, the relative proportions of the beast are fairly accurately maintained, and the eyes and the ears are reasonably correct, though the drawing of the head is lacking in character; in the other example, the beasts are disproportionate in size to their riders, the ears are out of place, the eyes look more like protuberances on the skull than what they are intended to be, and the two humps are exaggerated. On the other hand, the sculptor has evidently been at pains to show the peculiar bend of the hind legs, when the beast is sitting, and in other respects to bring out its most salient characteristics.

Horses The horse, though no doubt as common as any other animal in this part of India, seems rarely to have appealed to the imagination of the Indian artist, or perhaps it is generally less successful, because more difficult to draw than the more favourite elephant, deer, bull or buffalo. The picture, however, of one horse nuzzling into the neck of another on Pl. 50 *a*, 1 (near top), is a telling piece of work, which has evidently been inserted solely for the sake of its charm, not because the animals were needed at this particular point. But most of the horses in these reliefs are mere stereotyped representations, with little more characterisation than is necessary to distinguish the species and, occasionally, the breed. Figures on such a tiny scale as these (they seldom exceed 5 or 6 in. in height) and carved as they are out of relatively coarse sandstone, cannot obviously be expected to show the same definition of detail or the same degree of realism that reliefs on a large scale might do, but it is evident from the two horses' heads on Pl. 50 alluded to above and from the more successful modelling of other animals on an equally small scale, that the stereotyped appearance of most of the horses is not entirely due to their diminutive proportions. Of the breeds portrayed, two at least are clearly distinguishable, *viz.*, a light riding pony very like the present-day Arab, which is figured at the extreme left end of the bottom architrave at the back of the Northern Gateway (Pl. 29, 3); and a sturdy type of draft horse which is well illustrated on the two middle false capitals in front of the Western Gateway (Pls. 56 and 58). These thick-set, sturdy animals call to mind some modern Flemish breed or the magnificent caparisoned creature with the rider beside him at Konārak.[1] Whether the ordinary chariot horses seen two or four abreast in, for example, Pls. 50 *a* and 23 *a*, are meant to be the same breed as the latter, it would be difficult to affirm. Most of them seem to be of rather lighter build, related perhaps to the present-day Mārwāri pony, but the sculptors of Sāñchī, it must be remembered, were no more concerned with the individual breeds of their horses than with the personalities of their men and women, and it was quite enough for them to model an animal which could be recognised at once as a horse and at the same time satisfy the demands of their art. To attempt, therefore, to identify the stalwart creatures depicted on the false capitals of the Western Gateway (Pls. 56 and 58) with any particular breed, ancient or modern, would probably be waste of labour. Doubtless they resemble generally a type of horse familiar to the sculptor, but we may question whether the latter would have had much hesitation in modifying his models in whatever way he thought best to suit the exigencies of his designs. These pairs of plumed and caparisoned horses, with their picturesque riders, make striking motifs for the square fronts of the false capitals, as do also the pairs or trios of other real and fabulous beasts in corresponding positions on the same or other gateways: winged and horned lions, winged griffins and the like,[2] to say nothing of the humped bulls and camels already discussed. Most of these are evidently stock motifs, which had been used time and again for the enrichment of architectural members, household furniture and the like. We feel instinctively that the sculptors were thoroughly at home with them, and that they knew to a nicety how they could be used to the best advantage; and that is why there is no hesitation, no feeling-of-the-way, about these designs, and why they are so admirably adapted, by their very assured formality, to the positions they occupy.

Pairs and trios of animals on the false capitals

Lion-capitals of Southern Gateway

And this brings us to the animals and other figures on the capitals of the four gateways. The earliest and least successful of these are the Lion Capitals of the Southern Gateway (Pls. 16 *b* and 17 *b*). We are not, however, to suppose that these particular beasts are inferior, because this was the first effort at designing such a capital, and that the sculptors thereafter improved with experience. Long ere this, multitudes of *toraṇas* must have been erected in wood, as well as many other structures for which such capitals would be needed; and in this case they could no doubt have produced capitals as successful as those on the other gateways, where old-established types were adopted, but that, for whatever reason, they felt constrained to copy the Aśoka Capital hard by. That they should do so was natural enough, seeing the sanctity that the Lion Pillar had acquired, but the attempt was doomed to failure, because they were putting aside their own traditional types in favour of something that was novel and strange; and they did not possess the requisite knowledge to make an accurate or even approximately accurate copy of it. The feebleness and insipidity of these lions on the Southern Gateway are only too apparent, when they are compared with the originals on the neighbouring pillar of Aśoka (Pl. 107 *a*).

[1] Illustrated in Pl. XLIII of Havell's *Indian Sculpture and Painting*, 2nd edition.

[2] Compare Pls. 12, 13, 24, 41, 42, 43, 47, 48, 56, 58, 62 and 63.

Mark the clumsy, wooden appearance of the beasts, the shapelessness of their stocky legs, the absence of modelling in their claws (of which there are five fully developed ones instead of four), and the fatuous, unreal expression on their faces. Not only do they travesty the lions on the Aśoka Pillar, but they lack altogether the vigour and stylishness of the traditional winged lions on the Eastern and the Western Gateways (Pls. 41 and 63). Their failure in this respect was due not so much to the fact that the artists were inferior in skill to those who executed the latter, but to the fact that they were trying to copy a strange type of beast instead of making use of one of their own familiar models. Parenthetically, it may be remarked that these Lion Capitals of the Southern Gateway afford one of the strongest proofs that the art of the Early School was anything but mimetic; for if the sculptors of this gateway found so much difficulty in reproducing the four lions of the Aśoka Pillar, which was standing within a few feet of them, how were they likely to make more successful copies of other and less accessible prototypes? On the other hand, they also go far to show that tradition played a more important part than originality in the art of this school; for if the sculptors had been accustomed to rely more on their own initiative and less on recognised prototypes, they could surely have succeeded in producing something more convincing than these lions.

Elephant capitals of Northern Gateway

When the Northern Gateway, which followed the Southern, was built, the sculptors were wise enough to recognise that the lions carved by their predecessors had been a failure, and to return to their own more familiar elephants. These they at first addorsed in the same manner as the lions, that is, with the forefronts of the four beasts facing outwards over the angles of the pillar, and bending forward over the head of each they placed a full-breasted female rider, designed to harmonize with the dryads of the brackets alongside (Pls. 21, 25 and 27). Although, however, a decided improvement on the lions, these addorsed elephants cannot be regarded as really happy. They neither form pleasing groups in themselves, nor are they suited to the position they occupy above the square shafts. Seen from the front, they appear to weaken rather than to strengthen the support of the superimposed architraves, partly owing to the rather cramped position of the elephants forelegs and the deep undercutting of the stone beneath their trunks, partly to the weak lines of the trunks themselves (*cf.* Pl. 25), and partly to the thinning of the square shaft as it emerges above their heads. These defects were not overlooked when the

Elephant capitals of Eastern Gateway

Eastern Gateway (Pls. 42 and 44) came to be erected, and an effort to correct them was made, first, by carrying through the square shafts right to the soffit of the architrave without any hollowing out or undercutting of the surface; secondly, by disposing the four elephants on the faces of each shaft in such a way that they appear to be following one another around it; thirdly, by carrying the trunks of the beasts down to the four corners of the abaci, thus giving a semblance of added strength and squareness to the whole. At the same time, in place of the single female riders of more than human proportions which graced the Northern capitals, they substituted ordinary male riders of normal size: one, who is clearly the master, seated on the neck of the beast he is driving; the other, his attendant, carrying aloft a standard crowned by the Buddhist *nandipada*. The female riders of the Northern Gateway, with their full rounded forms and ample breasts, have no doubt a certain attractiveness of their own, but one cannot blind oneself to their flabbiness and artificiality, or to the immense superiority of the riders on the Eastern Gateway with their flags flying aloft. It was not that the sculptors of the Northern Gateway were lacking in experience or technical skill, but just that they had not the good taste and feeling for rhythm of line, symmetry and proportion which their colleagues who carved the Eastern Gateway, possessed. Turn to Pl. 44 and see how this feeling extends not only to the details of the elephant capital, but to the adjoining features as well: to the dryad, with her graceful lines, to the trio of winged lions on the false capitals, and to the figure of Māyā in the guise of Lakshmī at the top of the plate. Then turn to Pl. 25 and see how the corresponding features of the Northern Gateway miss these qualities of taste and style: how unsatisfying the design of the capital and the bracket figure at its side, how wanting in distinction the reliefs on the false capitals and the figure of Māyā above, to say nothing of the projecting end of the architrave and its volute terminal, which exhibit none of the refined workmanship found on the other.

Dwarf capitals of Western Gateway

On the Western Gateway—the last of the four—the capitals take an entirely different form. Here, the sculptors evidently thought that they could go one better by substituting for the elephants pot-bellied dwarfs (*kumbhāṇḍas*) with arms upraised like true Atlantes, to support the entablature. The conception was no doubt an excellent one. In the capitals of the Eastern Gateway, the only fault, if fault there is, is that there is no apparent resistance on the part of the elephants to the superimposed mass above them. No creature, of course, could be found more appropriate for sustaining weight than the elephant, but in this case the riders with banners floating above the beasts could hardly be more unsubstantial or more calculated to destroy the illusion that they are supporting a ponderous entablature above them. From a structural or organic point of view, therefore, it must be admitted that the dwarf capitals on the Western Gateway are more logical and appropriate than the elephant capitals of the Eastern or Northern Gateways. But if they have this one advantage, they are certainly inferior in all else. Dr. Bachhofer has sought to show that these capitals of the Western Gateway are the most successful of all, and that it was for this very reason that they were subsequently copied on the Gateway of Stūpa 3.[1] We do not think that this view will win acceptance from any one familiar with the originals or, indeed, from any one who takes the trouble to compare together the illustrations on Pls. 39, 44, 54 and 57. The conception underlying these dwarf atlantes is admittedly a sound one, but, as they have been designed, the capitals are altogether too ponderous and cumbersome. Looking at the elephant capitals of the Eastern Gateway

[1] *Op. cit.*, I, p. 40.

from any point of view, we cannot help admiring the delightful way in which they harmonize with the rest of the structure; they are massive enough to take the weight above them, but exhibit just that measure of elegance that is necessary to bring them into accord with the delicate reliefs of the pillars below and the heavier and more bizarre figures of the superstructures. The dwarfs of the Western Gateway, on the other hand, accord with nothing either above or below them. From whatever angle they are viewed they appear excessive in bulk and weight, and out of keeping with the fine relief work adjoining them. The sculptors of the smaller gateway of Stūpa 3, who imitated these capitals, were evidently conscious of this defect, and sought to improve on their models by making their own capitals relatively taller and thinner. But it is a very emasculated type of *kumbhāṇḍa* that they have given us—as far inferior to those on the Western Gateway as the latter are inferior to the older figures from which they in turn had been copied (Pl. 104 *d* and *f*).[1]

Dwarf capitals of gateway of Stūpa 3

Plants and trees

When discussing the original balustrade sculptures of Stūpa 2, we saw that the plants and trees there depicted almost invariably took stylised and conventional forms, and that it was only very rarely, as in the *pīpal* at the top of pillar 5 *b* (Pl. 75), that an effort was made to introduce some measure of realism, and to avoid treating the trees in a merely decorative and formal manner. The same observation holds good of the plants and trees on the Bharhut balustrade, only that, there, they are even more schematic than they were in the older reliefs at Sāñchī. Take, for example, the *pīpal* tree just mentioned and compare it with the one figured on the Prasenajit pillar at Bharhut,[2] which is a fair sample of its kind, and observe how much more rounded is the shape of the latter, how symmetrical its branches, how regular the arrangement of its leaves. When we come, however, to the gateways at Sāñchī, we find a marked change in the handling of tree and plant forms. It is not that the sculptors sense for the decorative has become blunted; on the contrary, it is in many respects more acute and ornamental, and it is certainly far more evolved and elaborate than it was before, but there is now a clearer understanding of when it is proper to treat plants and trees conventionally and when realistically. Thus, in the many scenes of jungle life (*e.g.*, Pl. 29, 3) the artists have rightly understood that naturalism was a thing to strive for, and have done their best to depict their plants and trees as truthfully as their limited powers allow. The results, needless to say, are not always equally successful, but they leave no doubt that the artists were endeavouring to break away from accepted conventions and to give a more faithful picture of what they actually saw. Thus, in the banyan trees (*Ficus indica*) on Pls. 29 (top architrave) and 55 (bottom architrave), it is clear to see with what sincerity the artists have endeavoured to show their characteristic traits—the form of their trunks and branches, their pendent roots, leaves and berries; and in the jungle scenes of the *Viśvantara Jātaka* on Pl. 29, 3 and Pl. 33, 1, it is equally evident that the artists have striven to portray the particular

Naturalism and stylization in the gateway sculptures

[1] *Mss. Cat.*, Nos. 30 and 31.

[2] Cunningham, *The Stūpa of Bharhut*, Pl. XIII, 7.

character of each tree: of the banyan and of the *pīpal*, of the plantain, the tāla-palm, the mango and pāṭali.[1] It is not always, however, that trees are rendered with such truth and freedom as these. Sometimes the sculptor is more concerned about his artistry than the accuracy of his representations. Thus, the banyan in the *Shaḍdanta Jātaka* on the Southern Gateway (Pl. 15, 2), albeit a charming bit of drawing, is by no means so true to nature as the examples of this tree already alluded to, and the tree on the extreme right of the same architrave is difficult of identification, notwithstanding that it is sketched with such a sympathetic touch. Moreover, the tendency to archaize which we noticed in some of the human figures, not infrequently extends to trees also, as in the flood scene of the Nairañjanā river, when the Buddha walked on the waters (Pl. 51 *b*, 1), and in the *Mahākapi Jātaka* of Pl. 64 *a*, 1. In these reliefs, the trees are treated in the strictly conventional manner of two or three generations earlier, and there can be little doubt that the sculptors were influenced in their drawing by older representations which they had seen of these particular stories. But it was when depicting the various Bodhi trees personal to the seven Mānushi Buddhas that the sculptors were specially prone to adhere to the types sanctified by tradition, and it is not surprising, therefore, that we find so much conventionality in the treatment of these trees, and experience more difficulty than usual in identifying some of the species.[2]

Tendency to archaize

Bodhi trees of the Mānushi Buddhas

Decorative designs

While, however, the representations of natural trees and flowers were tending to become more realistic, decorative designs were at the same time becoming more highly stylised. The fresh spontaneous designs, such as the lotus panel on Pillar 23 of Stūpa 2 (Pl. 78 *f*), are now giving place to a richer and more elaborate kind of decoration in which human beings, animals and birds are frequently mingled with the floral and foliate forms, and the whole modelled with a skill and feeling for plastic form which distinguish them at a glance from the ornamental carvings of an earlier age. The finest specimens of this decorative relief work on the gateways (if we may call that decorative which almost invariably conceals an inner religious meaning) are to be found on the outer faces of the gateway pillars (Pls. 19 *a* and *e*; 37 *a* and *b*; 50 *b* and *c*; 66 *b* and *c*) and on the lowest architrave of the Southern Gateway (Pl. 11). The motif underlying all these decorations is the same as we found recurring in varying forms among the reliefs on the balustrade of Stūpa 2, *viz.*, the Tree of Life and Fortune. In its simplest form, this tree is figured on the balustrade of the Second Stūpa as a highly stylised lotus, sometimes with birds resting among its leaves (Pillars 23 *a* and 44 *a*), sometimes without them (Pillar 23 *c*). In another form it appears as the *kalpa-latā* or *kalpa-druma*,[3] *i.e.*, a 'wishing creeper' or a 'wishing tree', and its boughs are hung with garlands and jewels—symbolic of the riches and

The Tree of Life

[1] *Bignonia suaveolens.*

[2] Particularly the udumbara (*Ficus glomerata*) personal to Kanakamuni, and the śāla (*Shorea robusta*) personal to Viśvabhū. The pāṭali (*Bignonia suaveolens*), sirīsa (*Acacia sirisa*), banyan (*Ficus indica*), pīpal (*Ficus religiosa*) and mango (*Mangifera indica*) are not usually so difficult to identify. One of the clearest representations of the Bodhi trees of the Mānushi Buddhas is on the back of the Eastern Gateway (top architrave), where the first of the seven (the pāṭali tree of Vipaśyin) is on the extreme right and the pīpal of Śākyamuni on the extreme left. In some other reliefs (*e.g.*, on Pl. 56, 1) the series starts from the left.

[3] Otherwise *kalpa-taru* or *kalpa-śākhin.*

blessings which it has to confer on mankind (Pillar 5 *b*). In some of the leaves, again, there are animals, usually lions or bulls or deer, emerging from its stem (Pillars 44 *a* and *c*, 49 *a* and *b* and 66 *b*) or ensconced among its foliage like the bull in Pillar 5 *b*; and sometimes in addition to, or in place of, the animals there are male and female figures in the middle or at the top of the tree (Pillars 66 *a* and 71 *a*). Generally, the root or source of the tree does not appear, but in two instances it is shown issuing from the navel of a Yaksha (Pillars 49 *b* and 22 *a*);[1] in another it issues from the mouth of a *makara* (Pillar 71 *b*); and in three others the bottom of the stem is grasped by an elephant, which, in its rôle of Nāga, stands for the water in which all life was believed to have its origin.[2] From the top of the tree emerge, as a rule, one or other of the chief emblems of the Buddhist Faith, *viz.*, the figure of Māyā, symbolising the Birth of the Blessed One (Pillars 49 *a* and 71 *a*);[3] the holy *pīpal* tree symbolising his Enlightenment (Pillar 5 *b*); the *dharmacakra* supported on a pillar, symbolising his First Sermon (Pillars 44 *b* and 66 *b*); and the stūpa symbolising his *Mahāparinirvāṇa* (Pillar 44 *c* and Pl. 93 *i*). Although not specifically Buddhist in origin, these four emblems were recognised as sufficiently representative of the Faith, to give the tree a predominantly Buddhist character. It must not be forgotten that the Tree of Life went back to a time ages before the advent of the Buddha. Among the seals of Mohenjo-daro dating from the third or fourth millennium B.C., is one depicting a stylised *pīpal* tree with two heads of unicorns emerging from its stem,[4] and on others is shown the same tree with a dryad (*vṛiksha-devatā*) standing in its branches. In those remote days we may surmise that the *pīpal* tree, like the sacred cedar of the Chaldeans, was looked upon as the Tree of Knowledge as well as the Tree of Life. In historic times, although commonly regarded as the most holy and protected among the trees, the *pīpal* has functioned in a special sense as the Tree, *par excellence*, of Knowledge rather than as the Tree of Life: the tree beneath whose shadow Gautama himself attained supreme Enlightenment. With the Buddhists, as doubtless with other sects also, the Tree of Life—of birth and immortality—was the lotus, which had scarcely figured at all in the Chalcolithic age,[5] and this plant became symbolic, not only of the birth of the Blessed One but of the religion which he promulgated. What idea originally underlay the animals emerging from the stem of the tree, is uncertain, but it seems likely at least that they were associated with the tree in the same way as animal *vāhanas* were associated with the tree spirits, which they support, for example, on the balustrade of the Bharhut Stūpa. Be this, however, as it may, there can be little doubt that the heraldic-looking lions or bulls or deer, which spring from the side of the lotus stems on the balustrade of Stūpa 2 (Pillars 5*a*, 44 *b* and 66 *b*), are the lineal descendants of the unicorn heads emerging from

Its antiquity and adoption by the Buddhists

Unicorns and other animals associated with the Tree of Life

[1] This is one of the later reliefs on the balustrades, which dated from about the time of Christ, not 100 B.C., as noted by Coomaraswamy, *The Art Bulletin*, Vol. XI, No. 2, Part I, note 1.

[2] On the Bharhut balustrade the Lotus Tree of Life is commonly depicted issuing from the mouth of an elephant. *Cf. The Stūpa of Bharhut*, Pls. XXXIX, 2; XLII, C.E. 6.

[3] In one instance only are the male and female figures previously referred to shown at the top, instead of the centre, of the tree (Pl. 86, Pillar 66 *a*).

[4] *Cf. Mohenjo-daro and the Indus Civilization*, Vol. III, Pl. CXII, No. 387, and Vol. I, p. 64 and note 3, where I have pointed out that, the two ideas of wisdom and life being so closely interwoven in the Mesopotamian myth, there is reason to suspect that in an earlier version of the Eden story there was only one tree functioning for both.

[5] Among all the antiquities of Mohenjo-daro and Harappā there is only one representation of a lotus, and that is not one of a leaf or flower, but of a capsule.

the *pīpal* tree on the Mohenjo-daro seals, and we shall see that the same idea is carried on by the unicorns and other hybrid animals in the reliefs on the gateways. As to the male and female figures appearing among the foliage, the simplest explanation seems to be that they, too, are the lineal descendants of the tree spirits which we first meet with on the prehistoric seals of the Indus, and which two or three thousand years later are still a prominent feature among the sculptures of Bharhut; nor does it require any stretch of imagination to see in the pairs of male and female figures which are so commonly found in association with these trees, an allusion to the fertility and reproductiveness of nature, of which they were the acknowledged guardians. That Yakshas or Yakshīs should sometimes be shown emerging from the foliage of the tree, at others standing beneath its boughs on their animal *vāhanas*, at others as the source from which the tree itself has its being, can hardly occasion surprise; for, as the tree spirits became metamorphosed into human shape, it could hardly have happened but that popular ideas regarding the relation in which they stood to the tree or to their own animal *vāhanas* would take divergent forms, and that seeming anomalies and contradictions would creep into the representations of these figures in plastic and pictorial art.

Tree spirits in human shape

The Tree of Life as variously represented on the four gateways

To revert, however, to the gateways of the Great Stūpa—the decoration on the outer faces of their pillars is in every case some variation of this same lotus Tree of Life, now more than ever elaborated. On the right pillar of the South Gate, which is the oldest of the four, it takes the highly stylised form of a row of full-blown flowers, between borders of sinuous lotus creepers (Pl. 19 *e*); on the left pillar of the same gateway it appears as a creeper with undulating stalk, held at the base by a *kumbhāṇḍa*; and from it hang fruits and flowers, garlands and necklaces, while amidst its foliage are seen pairs of male and female figures, animals, birds, jewelled ornaments and amulets (Pl. 19 *a* and *b*).[1] From an artistic point of view the design could hardly be more inappropriate or feeble. In such a position, a design of this kind with the undulating stem of the lotus standing out so prominently, is entirely out of place. By carrying the spectator's eye from side to side, it has the inevitable effect of weakening, or seeming to weaken, the gateway support, instead of adding to its strength. But this is not its only fault. The figures and objects which fill the embrasures formed by the windings of the stem, are merely a confused medley thrown together by the sculptor, without regard to symmetry or composition, and are strikingly disproportionate to the size of the pillar, so that, even if their composition were more orderly and pleasing, they could not escape appearing insignificant. In the designs of the next (Northern) Gateway, these defects were avoided and another type of decorative Life-Tree resorted to—*viz.*, a series of formalised lotus plants one above the other, with artificial brackets in the borders, from which hang jewelled garlands and necklaces of lucky talismans betokening both worldly and spiritual riches. At the root of the tree are

[1] Note that one of the female Yakshīs is holding a necklace of amulets in her hands, while her companion Yaksha is playing on a musical instrument. In front of their feet are what appear to be two of the magic ring-stones found in such large numbers at Mohenjo-daro and Harappā. Cf. *Mohenjo-daro and the Indus Civilization*, Vol. I, pp. 61-63.

the footprints (*śrīpāda*) of the Buddha ; at its summit, the *triratna* device symbolising the Buddha, the Law and the Church. Just how the whole would have been interpreted by the faithful themselves, we cannot be sure.[1] This much, however, is clear, that the tree is here conceived as having its roots in the Buddha himself—here represented by his footprints at the foot of the tree—just as in some of the other reliefs it has its roots in a Yaksha ; and it is reasonable to suppose, therefore, that the tree itself was taken to represent either the Faith which emanated from the Buddha or the mystic indissoluble Trinity of the Buddha, the Law and the Order, together with all the priceless gifts which they had to offer mankind. On the other hand, we must not forget that this Tree of Life and Fortune went back to an age long anterior to the Buddha and that, like the Yakshas or Yakshīs, Nāgas and a multitude of other elements taken from the popular religion of the people, it was only now in process of being absorbed into Buddhism. It is quite likely, therefore, that at this time the Tree bore virtually the same meaning in the eyes of the Buddhists as it had done for generations past in the eyes of their non-Buddhist ancestors, the only significant difference being that, like the similar trees on the balustrade of Stūpa 2, it was now stamped with the symbolic hall-marks of Buddhism and thereby recognised as belonging to the Faith. The corresponding tree on the right pillar of the Northern Gateway (Pl. 37 *b*), bears no distinctive Buddhist emblems. Its main stem, in the middle band of the panel, issues from a "Jar of Fortune" (*bhadra-ghaṭa*) and among its foliage, and starting out, as it were, from the stem, are pairs of Yakshas and Yakshīs, like those present in the Life Trees on the balustrade of Stūpa 2 (Pillars 23 *c*, 49 *a*, 66 *a* and 71 *a*), but, here, males and females are arranged in alternate pairs,[2] while the two sinuous creepers in the borders spring from the mouths of *makaras*. Both of these panels mark a decided improvement on the serpentine design of the Southern Gateway, not merely because they are free from its inherent weakness, but because of the exquisite refinement of their carving ; for though the details are disproportionately small for the position they occupy, the workmanship is so fine and beautifully finished, that the eye is attracted to notice rather the individual patterns than the effect of the composition as a whole. In the carvings on the Eastern Gateway, the sculptors have reverted to the two types of Life Trees on the Southern Gateway, the one on the north pillar (Pl. 50 *b*) corresponding with the formal, full-blown lotus pattern on the eastern pillar of the older gateway (Pl. 19 *e*), the one on the southern (Pl. 50 *c*) with the serpentine lotus on the opposite side of the same gateway (Pl. 19 *a* and *b*). In executing the second panel, however, the sculptors have evidently been fully aware of the insignificance of their model, and have been at pains to produce a bolder design more in keeping with the proportions of the gateway, and to this end they have had to eliminate the medley of jewelled ornaments, amulets, etc., which

[1] Possibly, as M. Foucher suggests (p. 248), we have here the earliest effort to represent the Buddha himself in symbolic form. Seemingly, it is this "Tree" that is referred to in the contemporary inscription No. 17 *b* (p. 301) which is carved on the balustrade alongside. It is there described as the *Bhagavato pamāṇa-laṭhi*, *i.e.*, as giving the height of the Buddha, not as the Buddha himself.

[2] Most of the Yakshas and Yakshīs bear, in one hand, a sword, in the other what appears to be a fringed tray or basket of lotus buds, like those borne by one of the celestial figures from Haḍḍa in Afghānistān (Musée Guimet, No. 17241). M. Foucher, however, takes these objects to be crested shields (*cf.* his description of Pl. 37 *b* and note *ibidem*). Precisely similar objects are borne by the Yakshas on the back of the middle architrave of Stūpa 3 gateway (Pl. 100, 2).

crowd the earlier composition, and to fill the embrasures between the windings of the lotus stem with leaves and flowers only and a few birds ensconced among them. Although this composition suffers from the same conspicuous shortcomings as the serpentine lotus on the Southern Gateway, seeming by its undulations to diminish the stability of the pillar, nevertheless in point of proportion and symmetry it is far the most satisfactory of the Tree of Life designs that had yet been essayed on the gateways. It was reserved, however, to the designers of the Western Gateway to produce not only the most brilliant of all the decorative designs at Sāñchī, but one of the most notable to be found in the whole field of Indian art (Pl. 66 *c*). In this composition the central stem of the Lotus Tree is straight and thick enough only to link together the component parts, without itself being too obtrusive. Along this stem, flowers and leaves are arranged in five successive groups, and, between them, pairs of heraldic-looking animals and riders. The more to enhance their reality, the lotus blooms are shown as if seen slightly from above, and their leaves are treated in the conventional manner characteristic of the Early School,[1] but with a stylishness and delicacy that has rarely been equalled. The animals comprise unicorns, griffins and lion-like beasts with single or double horns—descendants (who shall doubt ?) of the unicorn heads which are shown starting from the stem of a *pīpal* tree on one of the prehistoric seals from Mohenjo-daro, and of the pairs of animals addorsed against the stem of the Lotus Tree on the balustrade of Stūpa 2. From the latter they differ, in that they are attended by riders, either on their backs or standing at their side, and we thus have here for the first time a logical combination of the Yaksha Tree spirits and their *vāhanas*.[2] What makes this composition so dignified and attractive, is not only the effective modelling of beasts and riders and the admirable taste shown in the stylisation of the lotus flowers and leaves, but the peculiarly happy blending and balancing of plant and animal forms in such a way that neither seems quite to dominate the other. On the corresponding face of the opposite (north) pillar, the design, though slightly different, is evidently a copy of this one, but it falls very far short of it in technical beauty of workmanship (Pl. 66 *b*).

It remains to add that the same Lotus Tree-of-Life is figured on the top and bottom architraves in front of the Southern Gateway (Pl. 11, 1 and 3)—on the former in its simple form, with birds resting among its foliage and Māyā in association with it, as she appears also on Pillars 49 *a* and 71 *a* of Stūpa 2 (Pls. 83 and 87); in the latter, springing from the mouths or navels of Yakshas and laden with a wealth of jewelled ornaments. The former, as we have already pointed out,[3] is a piece of crude, stencil-like carving which has little to commend it. The latter is a composition of a much higher order. Admittedly, the serpentine stalk of the lotus is a defect that detracts from the strength of the composition, and clashes at the same time with the slight curvature of the architrave; but, in spite of this, there is a vigour and freedom about the drawing and a

[1] Particularly characteristic are the sharp angular bends and fine ribbing in many of the leaves.

[2] To the same category of mounted Yakshas and Yakshis may belong many of the riders on fabulous animals figured on the false capitals of the gateways.

[3] See pp. 127-8 above.

vitality about the figures which strike a new note in this class of decoration, and show that the artist who conceived it was a man of no little originality and taste.

Character of the Tree-spirits

That the Yakshas in this and other panels were looked upon as veritable spirits of the magic *kalpa-latās* or rather, perhaps, as the plants themselves transformed into human shape, is clear from the way in which they are depicted, sometimes as the sources from which the plants take their birth, at others as themselves growing like buds from the parent stem and then in turn spouting forth leaves and blossoms from their mouths or holding jewelled treasures in their hands. The idea of a Tree of Life springing from a Yaksha can be traced at least as far back as the Vedic age,[1] but it becomes specially familiar during mediæval times in the representations of the birth of Brahmā, who is shown seated on a lotus flower, the stem of which issues from the navel of Nārāyana.[2] A little later, the same idea finds its way into Christian iconography in the form of the "Tree of Jesse," whose root is sometimes depicted issuing from the recumbent figure of Jesse, while its ultimate flower is the Virgin and infant Jesus,[3] just as in some of our Sāñchī reliefs the ultimate flower is the Nativity of the Buddha.

The carvings of the four gateways compared

From all that has been said above it will be seen that the art of these four gateways is as varied and unequal on the decorative as it is on the figural side, but there are no signs that the art of one gateway, taken as a whole, is either more developed or more retrograde than that of another; nor, indeed, in the relatively short period—probably not more than two or three decades—in which these gateways were erected, is it to be expected that the local school of sculpture could either have advanced or fallen off to any appreciable extent. As a fact, but for the obvious copying that has taken place among these gateway sculptures and the evidence which such copying affords as to their chronological sequence, it would have been difficult, if not impossible, to determine the precise order in which the gateways were erected. The finest carving, both figural and decorative, is found on the first and last of the gateways (Southern and Western), but side by side with it on the same gateways are also found some of the worst. On the other hand, the highest average of workmanship is maintained on the Eastern Gateway. Thus, it is manifest that, whatever inequalities there may be in the style or technique of these carvings, they are to be attributed, not to the rise or decay at this time of local art in Mālwā, but solely to the varying abilities of the sculptors employed. When we come, however, to the fifth of these gateways—the one in front of Stūpa 3—we have to admit

The Gateway of Stūpa 3

[1] Coomaraswamy, "The tree of Jesse and Indian parallels or sources" in the *Art Bulletin*, Vol. XI, No. 2, pp. 2 and 3, where he quotes Ṛigveda, X, 82, 5; Atharva-veda, X, 7, 38; Mahābhārata, III, 272, 44, and XII, 207, 13.

[2] Another closely allied motif, as Dr. Coomaraswamy points out, is that of the tree or creeper (*nārī-latā*), whose fruits are houris. *Op. cit.*, p. 3.

[3] Compare the words of the familiar hymn—

"Fruit of that mystic rose,
"As of that rose the stem,
"The root whence mercy ever flows,
"The Babe of Bethlehem."

Here the infant Jesus is conceived as the root as well as the fruit of the Tree, like the Yakshas discussed above and like the Buddha himself whose footprints are the source of the Tree on the eastern jamb of the Northern Gate, while its fruit is the Trinity.

that the art of the sculptor is beginning to show indubitable signs of decline. The smaller dimensions of this gateway, as compared with its predecessors, and the narrowness of the panels which the sculptors had to decorate, might have tended in any case to cramp the freedom of their designs; but, apart from this, it is only too evident that the sculpture of Sāñchī is becoming more and more mimetic and stereotyped, and that figures and ornament alike have lost a large measure of their vitality. Take, as an example, the top architrave at the back of this gateway, and observe the two long rows of worshippers with nothing but two Bodhi trees to break the monotony. In some of the smaller panels of the older gateways, the figures are disposed, as we have noticed, in strikingly stiff and rigid rows,[1] but there is no other instance of isocephalism being carried as far as it is here, or of its conflicting so obtrusively with the lines of the architecture. Or compare the *kalpa-latā* panel on the bottom architrave of the same face (Pls. 99 and 100) with the panel from which it was copied on the Southern Gateway (Pl. 11, 3). The only substantial alteration in the scheme of the design is that the sculptor of the later relief has introduced an extra curve in the creeper and an extra *kumbhāṇḍa* in the embrasure formed by it; and in this particular he has undoubtedly improved on the original, where the treatment of the creeper at the centre was noticeably weak. But in all other respects what a poor travesty of its prototype is the later copy, what nerveless creatures are the pot-bellied dwarfs, and how ineffective and feeble the lotus flowers and leaves! It is the same also with the dwarf capitals of this gateway (Pls. 101 and 102). No doubt the sculptor recognised, and rightly recognised, the shortcomings of the capitals of the Western Gateway (Pls. 57 and 59) which he proposed to take as his model, and he endeavoured to improve on them by making his own less ponderous and cumbersome; but he succeeded only in producing a colourless imitation devoid of any character—which, at the best, was not much—possessed by the original. It is the same, too, with the Yaksha sentinels on the inner side of the gateway pillars (Pls. 103 *c* and *d*, at foot). Compared with the corresponding Yakshas on the older gateways (Pls. 36 *a* and *b*, 50 *a*, 52 *b* and 66 *a*) they are mere doll-like puppets, lacking all virility. We need not, however, pursue this subject further. The reader has but to turn over the illustrations to see for himself how stereotyped and decadent the sculpture of Mālwā was now becoming. It was not merely that the artists were imitating the designs of their predecessors—this happened even when the School was at its zenith, and indeed in ecclesiastical art like this, with its limited range of standard subjects, such repetition was more or less inevitable—but the fact was that, apart from all question of creative genius, their standards were being debased; they were losing their grip on truth and sincerity, and with it their ability to express themselves convincingly.

Later reliefs on ground balustrade of Stūpa 2

The only other sculptures of this period that remain to be considered are a few reliefs already alluded to,[2] which were carved on Pillars 22 *a* and 27 *a* and *b* of the ground

[1] See pp. 109-10 *supra*.

[2] See p. 101 *supra*.

balustrade of Stūpa 2 (Pls. 78 and 79).[1] Of the sculptures on these pillars, the two half circles at the top and bottom of Pillar 22 *a* and the half circle at the bottom of 27 *a* belong to the original decoration; the remainder were added some generations later, at the time when the *toranas* of Stūpas 1 and 3 were being erected. Dr. Bachhofer has attempted to show that these later reliefs appertain approximately to the same age as the balustrades of Amarāvatī, that is, to the latter part of the second century A.D., but in this he is clearly in error, and no one who has studied these sculptures on the spot is likely to be misled by his criticism or conclusion.[2] The sculptures of Pillar 27 *a* and *b* are identical in style and workmanship with those of the *toraṇas*, and closely resemble them in subject matter also. Thus, the scene of the nobleman's wives bathing from the back of his elephant (Pillar 27 *a*, 3) is paralleled by similar groups on the Northern Gateway (Pl. 34 *b*, bottom), as well as on the Gateway of Stūpa 3 (Pls. 101 and 102—projecting ends of lowest architrave), but in respect of drawing and modelling the carving we are discussing on the balustrade of Stūpa 2 is superior to any of these, and is unquestionably earlier than the carving on the gateway of Stūpa 3. Again, the scene on the middle panel of Pillar 27 *b* is very similar to that on the left pillar of the Southern Gateway (Pl. 18 *b*, 2), where the royal Aśoka (?) is seen supported by two of his queens with other females in attendance. As to the motifs of the other panels on this pillar, they occur so frequently on the gateways that it is superfluous to mention parallels, but it is to be remarked that in point of style and in the freedom and boldness of their treatment they approach nearer to the reliefs on the west pillar of the Southern Gateway (Pl. 18 *a*)[3] than to any of the others, and it is by no means unlikely that they may antedate the earliest of the gateways, though it is more probable that they are comtemporary with it. The reliefs on Pillar 22 *a* (Pl. 78) may be somewhat later than those on Pillar 27, since there is rather more stylisation about the Tree of Life designs, and the female figures have a more formal—quasi-classical—appearance. We must beware, however, of stressing these features overmuch; for if we turn to Pl. 37, we see how stylised the Lotus Tree had become on the North Gateway, and as to the female figures framed in the shrine doorways, they may owe their unusual and somewhat un-Indian appearance to the influence of one or other of the Aphrodite types which were undoubtedly familiar at this time in the Panjāb, rather than to any changes which time was bringing about in the formalisation of local art in Mālwā. But, in any case, there is no reason for assigning this relief to a later date than the *toraṇa* of Stūpa 3.

[1] To which may be added the vertical band between the middle and bottom medallions on Pillar 22 *b* (Pl. 78), and the Yaksha and Yakshī on Pillar 25 *b* (Pl. 79).

[2] *Early Indian Sculpture*, Vol. I, p. 61. Dr. Bachhofer says: "The wildly agitated ornamentation, the slim figures, distinguished from the somewhat plump, stumpy ones of the Great Stūpa, the unconstrained conduct of these men, the successful use made of contrast, a certain breadth in the composition suggesting a beautiful freedom: all this inevitably reminds us of Amarāvatī. One may, therefore, safely assume that the time of origin of the two jambs lies in the first half of the second century." There is certainly nothing more agitated in these reliefs than there is, for example, in the worship of the Bodhi Tree by the Nāgas and Nāgīs on the north pillar of the Western Gateway (Pl. 65 *a*, 2) or in the procession of the devas on the west pillar of the Southern Gateway (Pl. 18 *a*, 3) or in the flight of Māra's army on the back of the Western Gateway (Pl. 61, 3, right); nor are the figures in these reliefs slimmer than those, for example, in the top panel of the left pillar of the Southern Gateway (Pl. 18 *a*, 1) or on the top die (north side) in front of the Eastern Gateway (Pl. 43) or than most of the Yakshas and Yakshīs in the Tree of Life on the west pillar of the Northern Gateway (Pl. 37 *b*) or than many on the small *toraṇa* of Stūpa 3 (*e.g.*, Pl. 103 *c* and *e*, top).

[3] A noteworthy detail in the two top panels of 27 *a* is the unusually free postures of some of the worshippers. The same trait is observable in the attitudes of two of the women worshippers in the adoration of the *dharmacakra* on the South Gateway (Pl. 18 *a*, 1).

CHAPTER XII

SOME FURTHER CHARACTERISTICS OF THE GATEWAY SCULPTURES AND THE PROBLEM OF FOREIGN INFLUENCE

Calm, dignified composure of gateway sculptures

AN outstanding feature of the gateway sculptures, which accords well with their religious purpose, is their pervading spirit of calm and dignified composure. Be the figures at rest, or borne along in surging crowds, or dancing with exuberant joy, the effect they produce is invariably one of quiet, assured orderliness, which adds immeasurably to the impressiveness of the whole. And this effect is all the more remarkable, because, among the whole galaxy of sculptures, there are scarcely two by the same hand, and there is not a question, moreover, but that their execution must have been spread over a number of years. The secret of this ordered dignity and composure is not hard to discover. It lies partly in the methods of technique in vogue at this time, especially in the flatness of the bas-relief and the colouristic effect produced by keeping the figures religiously in one plane and so spacing them that they appear as bodies of light alternating with the dark shadows between them; for this is a treatment of relief which, though sometimes tending towards monotony, is more restful to the eye than the cleverest attempts at spatial illusionism, and in a situation such as this it is bound to be more truly decorative. Partly, too, it lies in the naïveté and unaffected ingenuousness of all these compositions, which have something in them akin to the tranquillity of nature itself, and inevitably bring back that tranquillity to our minds. Partly, however, it may be traced to the essentially tectonic character of the gateway decorations, which, with their massive capitals and solid-looking statues in the round, possess a dignity and strength to which it is not easy to find a parallel in Indian art.

Comparison with the sculptures of Amarāvatī

To appreciate more clearly what this quality of dignified composure means in these gateway sculptures, we have but to compare them with the sculpture of the Amarāvatī Stūpa, executed some two centuries later. Between the two there is much in common: the same radiant fancy, the same poetic instinct for the decorative, the same sensuous love of life. So close, indeed, is the affinity between these two schools, that it is impossible to doubt that the one was a lineal descendant of the other, notwithstanding the extraneous influence exerted on Amarāvatī by Gandhāra and Mathurā. But mark, on the other hand, the signal difference between them—a difference for which neither Gandhāra nor Mathurā is accountable. Sculpture at Amarāvatī no longer has the stately tranquillity that it had at Sāñchī; it is restless and worried; its idea of glorifying humanity is to picture the crowded life of court and city, to pack each scene with countless figures, and often to portray them in attitudes of wild emotion. In some scenes, indeed, the figures might be taken to be mænads rather than devout worshippers of the Buddha, so distraught are their poses, so frenzied their movements. Of the pictorial charm and rhythm of these compositions, there is no question; in these respects Sāñchī has nothing to equal them; but their beauty is of a conscious, sophisticated order; it misses the springtime freshness of the Sāñchī work, and with that freshness it misses also the quality of assured repose and strength that gives the latter its peculiar distinction; incidently, too,—though this is beside the point at issue—it is farther than ever divorced from the cloistral spirit of the Śākya faith, which might have found common ground with art in the exaltation of humanity but not in humanity's surrender to intense physical emotions. It seems, as Dr. Bachhofer has pointed out, almost as if the mundane art of the early school were indulging at Amarāvatī in a final outburst of sensuousness before resigning itself to the spiritual impulses which came over Buddhism in the early Gupta age. As a fact, however, the violent emotionalism that distinguishes the sculpture of Amarāvatī was characteristic rather of Dravidian than of Aryo-Dravidian art, and did not penetrate as far north as Central India; so that it is not surprising to find that the paintings of Ajaṇṭā are in many ways nearer akin to the sculptures of Sāñchī than to those of Amarāvatī. Like the former, these paintings rejoice in voluptuous beauty, but they never allow this beauty to run riot and degenerate into extravagance, as it does so often at Amarāvatī. Where the art of Ajaṇṭā parts company with that of Sāñchī is neither in its love of the human form nor in its tranquillity, but in the concrete representation of the Buddha and the Bodhisattvas, and—more important still—in its effort to incarnate in them something of the soul of Buddhism: of its lofty thought and divine compassion. In the age when these paintings were executed, art was no longer content to portray the outward phenomena of life, to perform only the function of illustrating the sacred legends of the Faith or episodes in the history of the Church. It was striving more earnestly than ever to reconcile the flesh and the spirit. Whereas its first endeavour had been to humanise the pietism of the cloister, it was now seeking to elevate humanity into the sphere of the spiritual. Its efforts were only partially successful, because it could not rise superior to its deep-rooted love of carnal beauty. That beauty still constituted the basic warp of Indian art, into which the weft of spiritualism was beginning to be woven, imparting here and there flashes of a divine serenity which had been wanting in the earlier art of Sāñchī and which now showed all the brighter by contrast with a profane and sensuous background.

and with the paintings of Ajaṇṭā

Mundane and sensuous character of many of the scenes

And this brings us to the most remarkable feature of all in these gateway sculptures, *viz.*, to the secular or sensuous and wholly un-Buddhistic character of many of the scenes; and a question we have to endeavour to answer is how it came about that this professedly sacred art so flagrantly misinterpreted the first principles of that religion. In the two centuries that had elapsed from the time of Aśoka, Buddhism had been undergoing a fundamental change. From being an ethical philosophy with an 'idealised nihilism as its goal---a philosophy which appealed mainly to the educated few---it had developed into a popular, cosmopolitan faith for the masses, in which emotionalism was already to a large extent taking the place of abstract reasoning, and idolatry, mysticism and superstition were probably almost as prominent as in contemporary Hinduism. But while this advanced catholicity of outlook accounts for much in these sculptures that conflicts with the old-time spirit of Buddhism, it does not account for everything. It explains---and quite adequately---the presence among them of manifold minor deities belonging to the Hindu Pantheon: of Yakshas, Yakshīs and Vṛiksha-devatās; of Māyā appearing in the guise of Lakshmī; of Nāgas and Nāgarājas; of sacred trees and amulets; and of a host of real or mythical beasts whose cults had come down as a legacy from pre-Āryan times. On the other hand, it fails to explain the genre and mundane scenes, with their sensuous associations. If we would discover the reason for these, we must seek it, not in the altered outlook of the Church, but in the essentially secular nature of the art which the Church had brought into its service; for let it be emphasized once more that the Church had done little up to the present to institute an ecclesiastic art of its own. During the century or thereabouts that separated these gateways from the balustrade of the Second Stūpa, sculpture at Sāñchī had passed with surprising rapidity from archaism to maturity; but there is no reason to suppose that the striking progress it had made was due to sustained patronage on the part of the Church. On the contrary, it is abundantly evident from the character of the sculpture itself as well as from the dearth during this period of other ecclesiastic monuments, that art must have been patronised and encouraged mainly by the ruling or wealthy classes of Vidiśā, Ujjayinī and other cities of Central India, and that the Church only stepped in on occasions to make use of it. This is why we find the guild of ivory-workers of Vidiśā carving the reliefs on the Southern Gateway; for while ivory carvings no doubt found a ready market among the rich of Vidiśā, stone-carvings would seldom be required, and when they were required ---which was chiefly by the Buddhists---they would as often as not have to be executed by craftsmen accustomed to work in other materials.

Changing spirit of Buddhism

Art not ecclesiastic, but secular

We can readily understand, therefore, that on the rare occasions when this secular art was called in to the service of the Church, the task it had to perform was anything but an easy one. The world which was its domain was a world of pomp and pageantry; of music and dance; of laughter and of dalliance in cool arbours or by running streams; of bright lotus blossoms and gay flowering trees. It was a world of sensuous delight, in which monasticism had no part. The pleasures which art extolled, the Church forbade;-the humanity which it sought to glorify, the Church disdained. The highest virtue of the Buddhist was to observe a rigid chastity and abstain from all gratification of the senses or the mind; he must hold himself severely aloof from song and from dance; must avoid the use of ornaments and perfumes, and take no joy even in the contemplation of the beautiful. How were these two worlds—the world of austerity and pietism and the world

Difficulty of accommodati[ng] this secular art to the needs of the Church

of sensuousness—to be reconciled in art? One thing was certain: art could not hope to expound the vital truths of Buddhism. In the sphere of philosophy, art is, by its very nature, inarticulate. There is no common ground between the two. The one is concerned with the visible and the concrete; the other with the invisible and the abstract. With the limitations under which sculpture was still labouring, the most that it could hope to do was to illustrate scenes chosen from the sacred legends of the Church, even as it had been accustomed to illustrate those of everyday life. The only question was whether, in doing this, it was to endeavour to accommodate itself to the orthodoxy of the Church or to maintain its own integrity. We do not suppose that the problem ever actually presented itself in this form to the sculptors who were called upon to execute the reliefs of Sāñchī; probably it never occurred to them that their art could speak in any other accents than those which they had learnt to make their own. But, however this may be, they certainly attempted no compromise with the Church. Their art was at the service of religion, if religion required it; but if there was to be any surrender of principles, it was for the Church, not for themselves, to make it. Whatever the risk of encouraging sensuality or of imperilling the cherished dogmas of the Church, art must pursue its own unfettered way. Of course they did their best to give a Buddhist complexion to their sculptures by making free use of all the mystic signs and emblems of the Faith—these naturally were indispensable—and they were ready even to make shift with a symbol in place of the Buddha's own person. But the essence of their art—its manner and its style—remained virtually unchanged.

Compromise made by the Church, not by the sculptor

Reasons for compromise on the part of the Church

That the Church should have so relaxed its principles as to identify itself with such flagrantly mundane art appears, at first sight, inexplicable, but we must bear in mind that, at the time the gateways were erected, the idea of an hieratic art—an art that should interpret the spirit of the Church as this popular art interpreted the spirit of the world without—did not present itself either to the Church or to the artists of Mālwā.

The nearest approach to such an art had been in the reliefs of Bharhut, but they belonged to an earlier generation, when sculpture in stone was in its infancy. Since then it had developed almost out of recognition, and, so far as Mālwā was concerned, had taken on a purely secular aspect. It was not a question, therefore, of modifying and adapting this secular art to suit the environment of the saṅghārāma, but either of rejecting it altogether or of using it, virtually as it stood, for the edification of the faithful. And we must not lose sight of the solid advantages that, from the Church's point of view, were to be gained by enlisting the fine arts in her service. For picture some of the problems by which she must have found herself confronted at this time. Buddhism was still in the heyday of its prosperity; the numbers of its adherents were continuously growing, and the more they grew, the more insistent became the need, not only for encouraging their interest and instructing them in the history of the Faith, but for a new catholicity in the

Value of the new art for popularising Buddhism

Church's own outlook. How was this interest to be awakened, this instruction given? In those days few could write or read, and since the brethren had largely given up their old habit of wandering from place to place during the greater part of the year and disseminating knowledge as they went, there was less teaching by word of mouth than there had been. In these circumstances, the part that the figurative arts could play in the religious education of the masses was an all-important one; and the more popular and attractive their mode of expression, the wider was their appeal likely to be. But there was another argument in favour of bringing in art as the handmaid of religion. Ever since the days of Aśoka the cult of the relic-stūpa had been steadily and surely supplanting the older Śākya Faith, and by this time the stūpa itself had come to be worshipped as much for its own sake and the inherent virtue that it was supposed to possess as for its associations with the death of the Great Teacher. If there was little in its simple tumulus-like form to stir the imagination or to inspire the love of the masses, it had the incalculable advantage of being a visible and solid body, to which the worshipper could address his prayers. So popular, indeed, had this cult of the stūpa become and so alien was it from the essential spirit of Buddhism, that there must have been a very real danger of its becoming a rival to the parent faith—a danger that was all the greater, because the cult was already gaining ground among the rival sect of the Jainas. It was imperative, therefore, that something should be done to assert the essential unity between this cult and Buddhism, and no better way could be found than by embellishing the stūpa itself with scenes taken from the sacred legends that had grown up round the name of the Teacher and thus, at one stroke, humanising the cult of the stūpa and stamping it as an integral and inalienable part of Buddhism.

Need of asserting essential unity of stūpa-cult and Buddhism

Whether the attitude of the Saṅgha at Sāñchī towards this question of the graphic arts was the attitude at this time of the Church at large or confined only to a certain section of it, is a moot point. In the first century B.C. the Buddhist Church was not an undivided body, organised under a single head; it had already broken up into many sects —among others, into the Sthaviras or Haimavatas, the Vibhajyavādins, the Sarvāstivādins, the Vatsīputrīyas and the Mahāsāṅghikas; and these sects may have taken very diverse views on such a crucial matter. The particular sect established at Sāñchī appears to have been the old and generally orthodox Theravādin, closely connected, among others, with the Sthaviras or Haimavatas and the Sarvāstivādins, and it is likely enough that rival sects, such as the Mahāsāṅghikas, did not share their progressive ideas in regard to figurative art. A significant fact, of which we must not lose sight, is that there are singularly few stūpas known to us either of this or any other period which are embellished with this kind of figural sculpture; and it is impossible to explain this on the assumption that the sculptures have disappeared in the course of the ages. Time and decay may account for the destruction of multitudes of paintings, such as those on the walls of the halls and chapels of Ajaṇṭā, but stone sculpture cannot so easily be disposed of, and the almost total absence

Attitude of the Church towards figural art

Absence of figural sculptures from majority of Buddhist stūpas of it at this period at the great centres of the Faith which have been extensively excavated during the last thirty years, points clearly to the conclusion that the fashion set by the Theravādins at Sāñchī found little favour with the rest of the Church.[1] Had sculpture preserved the more modest and restrained character that distinguished it on the earlier monuments at Sāñchī and Bharhut, it might perhaps have become more fashionable. As it is, the only surviving monuments in which the example of sensuousness set at Sāñchī has been followed, are a few belonging to the Mathurā and Amarāvatī Schools; while, on the other hand, there are multitudes that are entirely destitute of figural carvings. In this matter the influence exerted by Gandhāra art was as wholesome as it was far-reaching; for if Gandhāra art was academic by comparison with the free and naturalistic art[2] of Mālwā, it had the advantage of being an exclusively ecclesiastical development and innocent of any suspicion of worldliness.

Influence of Gandhāra art

* * * * * * * * *

The problem of foreign influence on the art of the gateways

The problem of foreign influence at Sāñchī has twice already claimed our attention, first in connexion with the pillar of Aśoka and afterwards in connexion with the balustrade of the Second Stūpa. As to the former, there was strong evidence, as we pointed out, to support the view that the finest of Aśoka's monuments—the pillars at Sārnāth and Sāñchī—were the work of Yavana sculptors trained in the traditions of Hellenistic or Perso-Hellenistic art. In the reliefs of the Second Stūpa we found no such evidence of Yavana workmanship. We remarked on the presence of some typical Western Asiatic motifs—centaurs, human-headed lions, griffins and the like—and we noticed also that while most of the carvings were still in the archaic stage, a few among them exhibited a noticeably more mature type of relief-work; and we ventured the suggestion that this more advanced technique may have been imitated from examples of Yavana art which at this period were doubtless familiar in the bazaars of Central India. The same problem now recurs in connexion with the sculptures of the gateways, but not in quite the same form. Here, there is no such disparity in workmanship as we observed among the reliefs of the Second Stūpa. Diversity there is, and great diversity, both in style and technique, but it is no more than can be accounted for by the varying abilities of the sculptors engaged on them or by the force of religious conservatism with its archaizing tendencies. What we are concerned with here, is the remarkable advance which relief-work had made in the three generations since the erection of the Second Stūpa, and the problem is whether this advance was due exclusively to the independent development of indigenous art or was the result, in part, of extraneous teaching. Now, it must be made clear, at the

[1] In regard to alien sects, *cf.* Inscrs. 389, 396, 404 *infra*. From a passage in the *Sarvāstivādin Vinaya* it appears that the Sarvāstivādins themselves respected the prohibition against making a likeness of the Buddha. Mr. Waley suggests that this prohibition may have been peculiar to their sect alone, and that, if sculptures should happen to be discovered belonging to other sects, it would not be surprising to find among them scenes in which the figure of the Buddha is represented without compunction. If Mr. Waley's conjecture is right, it would seem that in this particular the Sarvāstivādins were more orthodox than their rivals; but the omission of the Buddha's figure may, after all, have been in the nature of a concession to the members of the Saṅgha and the public who were still opposed to any kind of figurative art. *Cf.* A. Waley in *J. R. A. S.*, April 1933, p. 441.

[2] I confess that I am unable to follow Dr. Coomaraswamy when he says that the only naturalistic style in ancient India was that of Gandhāra. The art of the Sāñchī gateways seems to me in every sense more naturalistic than the academic art of Gandhāra. *Cf.* Coomaraswamy, *The Origin of the Buddha Image*, p. 8, note 7.

outset, that there is no question here, any more than there was over the reliefs of Stūpa 2, of whether the art of these gateways is Indian or foreign. It is just as truly Indian as the art of the Sārnāth and Sāñchī pillars is truly foreign. Here and there, one can detect motifs and concepts borrowed from other countries, notably from Western Asia ; but these borrowings are of an essentially superficial nature and do not affect the real character and substance of the art. The point at issue, therefore, is not whether the sculpture of Mālwā took its inspiration from foreign art, but only whether it derived from that art any help over technical difficulties. The motifs referred to above as coming from a foreign source are not numerous. In addition to those already alluded to on the balustrade of Stūpa 2 there are "Persepolitan" columns, the Persian origin of which is beyond dispute, and there are winged lions and other fabulous creatures, which it is generally agreed were derived from a Western-Asiatic source, while other reminiscences of Western art are to be found in the Yavana wreath worn by one of Māra's host in the Temptation Scene on the back of the Northern Gateway (Pl. 29 *b*),[1] in the grape-vine incorporated into the Tree of Life design on the south pillar of the Western Gateway (Pl. 66 *c*),[2] and perhaps also in the Aphrodite-like figure in one of the later panels on the balustrade of the Second Stūpa (Pillar 22 *a*). Granted, however, that these few features originated in the West, they are certainly not such as to imply that any Yavana or other foreign artists had found their way to Mālwā in the second or first century before Christ. Some of them, such as the Persepolitan columns and the winged lions, may well have been a legacy from Mauryan times, when Yavana artists were employed by Aśoka ; but even if their advent into India took place at a later age, their presence implies nothing more than that foreign *objets d'art* of one kind or another had strayed into the workshops of Central India and there furnished the local sculptors with a few novel motifs or ideas. That Yavana influence on Central Indian art took at this period a more direct form than this, there are no grounds for supposing. All that we know of the Greek settlers in the Panjāb points to their having been engaged in almost incessant strife either among themselves or with their Indian neighbours, and to their having been famous rather for the arts of war than of peace ; nor does it appear that they occupied themselves with the setting up of sculptured monuments even in their own territories. No remains, at any rate, of any such monuments nor, indeed, of any stone carvings at all have been found in the Greek city at Taxila, the foremost of all the Greek settlements of the Panjāb. And even the pillar set up at Vidiśā by Heliodorus, ambassador from Antialcidas, King of Taxila, betrays no trace of Greek feeling in its design. On the other hand, there is plenty of evidence to show that the minor arts were not neglected by the Greeks. Admirable coins, for example, were struck

Foreign motifs very few

Yavana antiquities in the Panjāb and North-West

[1] It is tempting to see Yavana influence in the un-Indian attire of some of the figures in Pl. 36 *c*, *l*, comprising a tunic (=Gr. *chiton*), short cloak (=Gr. *chlamys*), and fillet for the hair (=Gr. *tænia*) ; and even the pointed, Phrygian-looking caps worn by two of the figures in this relief would be appropriate to Yavanas hailing from the region of Bactria or thereabouts. But sleeved tunics, which these appear to be, leggings (*paṭṭīs*) and pointed caps are still worn in the hills of Western Nepal and Tibet, and it is reasonable to infer that in the first century B.C. they may have constituted the national costume of the Mallas, who came perhaps from the hill country.

[2] The attempt made by Vincent Smith to show that the vine was indigenous in India is not convincing. It was never a characteristic motif of Indian art, as it was of Hellenistic art. In the second-first century B.C. it is found beautifully figured on Hellenistic terra-cotta reliefs at Taxila. *Cf.* Vincent Smith, *A History of Fine Art in India and Ceylon*, pp. 74-5.

by the Greek rulers in the North-West, which had a distribution far beyond the limits of the Greek kingdoms. It is safe, too, to conclude, from specimens found on far-distant sites, that export trade was done by the Greeks in small objects such as terra-cotta figurines, vases, gems and the like.[1] Such objects would, as previously stated,[2] be quite sufficient to disseminate a knowledge of Hellenistic methods of relief, and it seems highly probable that it was, in some measure at least, due to them that the sculpture of Mālwā was able to make such phenomenal headway during the Śuṅga and early Andhra domination in the modelling of the human figure, as well as in the development of technique generally.

Dissemination of examples of Yavana art

An alternative but less likely explanation

There is another possible explanation, however, which cannot be left entirely out of account. At the time when this rapid advance took place in the art of Mālwā, stone had only recently come into fashion for purposes of sculpture. Possibly it was the Yavanas themselves who were responsible for introducing it, but, however this may be, there can be no doubt that Indian sculpture must have had a long anterior history, and that reliefs of great decorative merit had been produced in wood and ivory, terra-cotta and metal. This being so, it is open to us to suppose that, when stone came into vogue, the sculptors found themselves hampered by its refractory nature and unable at first to produce such high-quality work as they had been wont to do in other mediums. Then, as they gained the mastery over the new material, their workmanship would quickly improve and in a very short space of time would be likely to reach a stage of relative perfection which would have been impossible, but for their long experience with other mediums. Thus it is possible that sculpture in stone passed with unexampled rapidity and without any adventitious aid from its crude beginnings to the highly developed state in which we know it at Sāñchī. But a serious objection to this explanation is that it takes no account of the technical affinity which exists between these early Indian and Græco-Roman reliefs, and which makes it difficult to believe that they could have been wholly independent one of the other. If we could point to any other country where relief-work of an analogous kind was evolved independently of Græco-Roman traditions, there would be a much stronger argument for predicating an independent growth for the Mālwā School, but nowhere else in the ancient or mediæval world is such sculpture to be found; and even in India itself it is only at this one particular period that reliefs of this quality were produced—reliefs wholly Indian in inspiration and substance, and yet with a distinct quasi-classical flavour in their mode of treatment. Had we more examples of Hellenistic art in Western Asia during the second and first centuries B.C., they would probably throw interesting light on this problem; failing such light, the question must remain an open one. Let it be added that the emphasis laid above on the limited scope of the influence exerted by Yavana art in Central India and Hindustān

Revival of Hellenistic art

[1] Such trade probably included woven and embroidered textiles, all trace of which has necessarily vanished in the destructive climate of India.

[2] See p. 103 above.

uring the last two centuries before the Christian era, is the more necessary because of he prevailing idea that the Indo-Hellenistic art of Gandhāra is directly traceable to he Greek conquerors of the North-West. Excavations at Taxila have now shown that his view must be modified. The conquerors who were largely responsible for the wave of Hellenism which swept over the North-West in the first century A.D., were unquestionably he Parthians, and it is probably to the same agency that the beginnings of the Gandhāra school must also be ascribed. We must beware, therefore, of assuming, on the strength f this later art, that the influence exerted by the Bactrian Greeks in India was wider than t really was. **in the Panjāb under the Parthians**

CHAPTER XIII

TOOLS AND PROCESSES EMPLOYED BY THE SCULPTORS OF SĀÑCHĪ

OF the tools and processes employed in the cutting and carving of the stūpa balustrades and gateways, little can be affirmed, since no specimens have been preserved either of the sculptor's tools or of unfinished sculptures which, *faute de mieux*, might contribute useful light on the subject. So far as the quarrying of the local sandstone is concerned, it appears that it was done by a process which is still generally practised in this country, *i.e.*, by sinking in the face of the stone and along the line of intended cleavage a series of small cup-like depressions, filling them with water and building a fire over them, the heat of which acting on the water causes the stone to split.[1] Thus quarried, the sandstone seems to have been dressed with a pointed hammer or punch and afterwards with a claw tool, the marks of which are clearly visible on many of the rough-dressed blocks. Flat chisels, such as were generally used for rough dressing by the sculptors of Gandhāra, do not appear to have been in fashion at Sāñchī, but for the finer kind of dressing and carving, there is no doubt that both flat and concave chisels of various sizes and curvature must have been employed, though owing to the use of abrasives for the subsequent smoothing and polishing of the surface, it is seldom that the marks of these tools can be detected. That the saw was also employed for cutting up rectangular blocks is also highly probable, but there is no evidence of its having been used for any such purpose as the cutting of folds in the drapery of figures; nor are there any marks among the carvings of the drill, whether pointed, running or tubular, though the pointed drill appears to have been used in the Andhra period by the engravers of the later class of Brāhmī inscriptions.[2] **Quarrying, dressing, cutting and drilling**

For certain kinds of undercutting and finishing work, the file would be the most convenient tool, while for the final smoothing of the surface the abrasive most ready to hand would be river-sand. **Use of file and abrasives**

For polishing, the traditional materials in India are powdered emery, corundum or other hard stone mixed with lac and used in grades of increasing fineness; and these, it may be conjectured, were the materials also employed by the sculptors at Sāñchī. This conjecture, however, applies only to the sculptured gateways and such of the later carvings as were polished, not to the pillar or other monuments of Aśoka. By what **Polishing of sculptures**

[1] Another method also common in India and which may have been used at Sāñchī, though there is no direct evidence for it, is to cut a line of somewhat deeper cavities, drive in wooden wedges and pour water over the latter, thus causing the wood to swell and split the stone.

[2] That chisels and other sculptors' tools were of tempered steel seems likely in view of the fact that steel is known to have been manufactured at this time in Vidiśā. *Cf.* p. 95 and n. 7 *supra*, and *A. S. R.*, 1913-14, pp. 203-4. Sir Robert Hadfield, F.R.S., who analysed for me the pieces of steel found beneath the Heliodorus pillar (*circa* 100 B.C.) was convinced that the metal could not have been produced by any accidental process, but must have been knowingly manufactured as steel.

process these latter were given their intensely lustrous polish, has not been discovered, though microscopic examination of the stone seems to show that it was achieved with the help of abrasives only. Be this, however, as it may, the secret of this process, which was probably introduced by the foreign sculptors of Aśoka, seems to have been quickly forgotten; at any rate there is no trace of any kind of polish, whether Mauryan or other, on the monuments of the Śuṅga age, either at Sāñchī or Bharhut or elsewhere; nor was it until the *toraṇas* of the Great Stūpa were erected under the Andhras that an effort was made to imitate the Mauryan method of finishing the surface. By that time experience had presumably taught the local sculptors the value of polish as a safeguard against weathering, of which there could hardly have been a better demonstration than that offered by the Aśoka Pillar, but whether for this reason or because they preferred the appearance of polished to unpolished stone, they set about polishing their sculptures in the best way they could, and though they were unable to reproduce the unique glaze of the older monuments, they succeeded in producing as good a one as can be obtained by modern methods on sandstone, and in giving by this means a much more extended life to their handiwork than it would otherwise have enjoyed. Time and the elements have long since effaced most of the polish as well as the colour on these sculptures, but patches of both are visible here and there, especially on the Eastern Gateway, where the figure of the sentinel Yaksha inside the north pillar is remarkably well preserved.

Red staining and colourwashing of surface

When polished, the surface of the stone was reddened with a translucent stain, which had the advantage of not obscuring the texture of the stone or the delicate details of the carvings. At a later date, gateways and railings were covered with a coat of creamy white lime followed by a thin red wash, which hid from view much of the fine finish of the carvings and gave the stone a dull, dead appearance. These later coats are still most clearly visible on the Eastern Gateway[1] and balustrade adjoining it on the south, but may also be detected here and there on other parts of the balustrade and on the other gateways. Red, it will be recalled, was the orthodox colour for the walls of cells, *kaṭhina*-hall and other rooms in the early monasteries, black being reserved for the floors. This red colouring was known as *geruka*[2] and seems to have been made by mixing red ochre with limewash, which was also the composition of the later opaque wash used on the gateways and balustrades at Sāñchī. How the original red stain was prepared has not yet been discovered. The practice of colouring the surface of marble statues and reliefs was of course a familiar one among Greek sculptors and known to them as *ganōsis*, but there is no reason to suppose that Yavana influence was in any way responsible for the colouring of these *toraṇas* and balustrades. The application of red colouring matter—usual red lead or minium—to cult or other sacred objects was as common in ancient as it is in modern India and as it was in ancient Rome, and probably derived from pre-Āryan

[1] *I.e.*, on the front face of the north pillar and at the base of the south pillar on its east and south faces.

[2] *Cullavagga*, V, 11, 6; VI, 3, 1 and VI, 17, 1; VIII, 3, 1, and *Mahāvagga*, I, 25, 15, *S. B. E.*, Vol. XX, p. 218, footnote 5. Red, white and black were the only colours allowed in the monastic quarters.

times. It would be only natural, therefore, for the Buddhists to adopt a practice which had been consecrated by long usage among their own people, and for us to look further afield for its origin is needless.[1] It has also to be borne in mind that the balustrades and *toranas* of stone took the place of earlier ones of wood, on which red paint had probably been used as a preservative, and that the paint was afterwards perpetuated on stone long after the practical need for it had passed.

Use of ... ques

Whether the sculptors of Sāñchī made preliminary sketches of their subjects in clay or wax and used these models to guide them in cutting the stone, is a moot point. Modelling in clay is one of the oldest of Indian crafts, and nothing is more likely than that the sculptors would first rough out their ideas in this material. If they did so, their models would have been merely sun-dried, not kiln-baked, and it is hardly likely, therefore, that any of them would have survived. On the other hand, in a technical matter of this kind it might be misleading to draw inferences from the processes employed by western artists. Indian artists are accustomed to rely far more than their European confrères on their powers of memory and visualisation, and they are much less dependent, therefore, on the assistance that models can give them. Moreover, Indian art has at all times been intensely conservative, and the art of Mālwā was no exception to the rule. Types and motifs were so often repeated, that the sculptor must have known many of them, as it were, by heart, and could have experienced little difficulty in modifying them, without the help of models, to suit the exigencies of his subject or his own artistic predilections; and even when he was producing what may be regarded as an original composition, he drew so freely on familiar stock motifs, that his difficulties were probably far less than one is now apt to suppose. Whatever use, however, he may have made of clay or wax models—and we are far from arguing that he did not use them at all—there is certainly nothing in the shape of *puntelli* or other marks on the sculptures themselves to indicate that they were mechanically copied by means of pointing or any other system from the models. Our own view is that working models made of some perishable material were probably in common use, but rather as rough sketches than as finished and exact studies for the final work.

---

[1] As to the appearance of the Sāñchī stūpas in old days, see p. 36 above.

PART THREE

THE MEANING OF THE SCULPTURES

CHAPTER XIV

INTERPRETATION OF BAS-RELIEFS ON THE OLDER BALUSTRADES

Prefatory remarks: changing phases of Early Indian Art

THE many and varied monuments described in Part I are distributed, as Sir John Marshall has pointed out, over a dozen centuries, from the third B.C. to the tenth A.D. They cover, that is to say, the whole history of Indian Buddhism, and in their carved stones may still be read the changing story of the Buddhist Faith no less than the story of Buddhist art. It is on the latter that the eminent archæologist has particularly dwelt, and has shown how the Sāñchī School of Sculpture gradually freed itself from the universal laws which weigh upon primitive art. In the earliest works of this school that are preserved to us, all the figures are still shown full-face and designed from memory. But soon the workmen begin to improve their craft. On the Gateways of Stūpa 1, they have already grasped the difficult secret of foreshortening, learnt to group their actors and make them move, devised a mode of perspective, and acquired the power of composing striking pictures. In the time of the Guptas their architecture preserves a truly classic elegance and sobriety; and though their sculpture has lost certain of its old-time qualities—notably its naïveté and sense of the picturesque—it has taken on a new refinement in spiritual expression and idealistic beauty. It is not till quite late that these qualities give place to architectural grandiloquence, decorative prolixity and the stereotyped repetition of images. For two very good reasons we shall not refer to these questions again. In the first place, we should be able to add nothing to the convincing and illuminating account of Sir John Marshall, and, in the second, our concern here is with the inner meaning rather than with the outward form of this decoration. The historian of art has consented to give place to the professional iconographer, and our particular task in the chapters that follow will be primarily to interpret symbols and bas-reliefs and to identify statues. But it may be useful to point out at the start that a transformation parallel to that found in the technical evolution of sculpture is revealed likewise in the choice of subjects treated, and that in this respect, too, very plainly-marked periods may be distinguished in the evolution of the local school of Mālwā, as they can be in that of Buddhist art in general. At first, we get the impression of an overwhelming flood of motifs of every kind, borrowed wholesale from the repertoire of pre-Buddhist art. This diversity—bewildering at first sight—reminds us that, like the Christians in the Mediterranean world, the Buddhists were, after all, late-comers in India and that they, too, had to adopt and adapt to their religious needs a number of ornaments and emblems invented neither by them nor for them. On the oldest

Character of art increasingly Buddhist

balustrade at Sāñchī—that of Stūpa 2—the frequent recurrence of the "Four Great Miracles" is the only indication we get of a deliberate effort to produce specifically Buddhist themes. This tendency to portray, or at least to suggest, none but scenes taken from the legendary history of the founder of the sect becomes more and more marked; for donors or pilgrims naturally looked only for themes of edification on their religious buildings. This kind of leading idea shows itself with increasing clearness on the balustrades of intermediate date at Bodh-Gayā and Bharhut, and ends by asserting itself completely on the gateways of Stūpa 1 at Sāñchī. There, whether we have penetrated their inner significance or not, we may be sure of having to do only with subjects of Buddhist meaning or intention, to the virtual exclusion of every other theme.

Introduction of the icon into Buddhist Sculpture

Now, these pictures of the former lives or of the last life of the Master, however fully developed in treatment they may be, are always executed in the manner of the Old Indian School, and continue to present the story of the Buddha without ever portraying the Buddha himself. We have to go to Mathurā, if we want to witness the actual introduction into India proper of the new models which the sculptors of Gandhāra, strangers to the traditions of Central India, had just created in the far North-West. These models are especially distinguished by the presence of the actual image (not merely the symbol) of the Master in the centre of the composition. At Sāñchī itself—doubtless because no gateway or balustrade later than the beginning of our era has been found there—we cannot watch this gradual substitution of the Gandhāra formulas, which little by little supplanted the old indigenous themes, till they reigned undisputed over the Gupta and all later bas-reliefs or paintings. We should observe, however, that the curious stele representing the "Subjugation of the Infuriated Elephant", in which the figure of the Buddha is disproportionately large compared with the other actors in the scene (*cf.* Pl. 126 *b*), betrays the double tendency which makes itself felt immediately afterwards alike in Buddhist art and in the Buddhist Church, *viz.*: the tendency, on the one hand, of the bas-relief to transform itself into an icon; and the tendency, on the other, of these icons to monopolize popular devotion to the detriment of the old narrative bas-relief. At Sāñchī, we possess a certain number of these statues—if one can apply the word to figures which, with few exceptions, are never quite finished in the round, but remain attached at the back to the block of stone out of which they have been carved. Soon, too, beside the images of the Master we find an ever-increasing number of Bodhisattvas, and these two groups together come to form what is commonly termed the Mahāyāna pantheon. Finally, the appearance of some idols of Tantric character proclaims a decadence to which the Musulman invasion was soon to put an end.

Materials available at Sāñchī, and the method

As may be seen from this rapid glance at the standing monuments and sculptures of our Holy Hill, all the most essential stages of Buddhist iconography are represented here by remains that deserve to be taken up and studied with care. Just as there are manifold inscriptions described in the Fourth Part of this work, which illustrate the varieties of alphabets that succeeded one another in Central India, from the *Brāhmī* of Aśoka down to the modern *devanāgarī*, so too there is a multiplicity of sculptures, from the earliest medallions down to the latest statues, that have to be passed in review and deciphered one by one. Most interesting and rarest among these remains, are those naturally which are most ancient, and it is these that are most worthy of complete reproduction and minute examination. These precious bas-reliefs, as we have already noted, fall into two distinct groups, and the actual lapse of time which separates them is stressed by some striking contrasts in both composition and choice of subjects. The first group, which will be the subject of the present chapter, includes all the old decorated balustrades at Sāñchī—both those of Stūpa 2, fortunately preserved almost complete, and the remains of those on the terraces and staircases of Stūpas 1 and 3—the sculptures, that is, ascribed above by Sir John Marshall to the Śuṅga epoch, in the second century B.C. The second group (to which the following chapters will be devoted) consists of the monuments erected and decorated late in the following century under the Andhra dynasty: namely, the four gateways of Stūpa 1 and the small gateway of Stūpa 3. Finally, we shall bring together in a fourth chapter everything relating to the iconography of the Kushāṇa, Gupta and Mediæval periods.

of their examination

Such is the order and such the scheme which we propose to adopt in our study. As for the method to be adopted, it follows clearly from what precedes. Our constant aim must be to discover under the decorative or profane appearance of each piece, what edification it conceals for the tutored eye of a Buddhist devotee; and the further we proceed in our study, the more persistent must this effort be, since the certainty of reward grows correspondingly greater. Only thus is there hope of our making real headway in the task we have undertaken—the compilation of an explanatory commentary on the sculptures. Assuredly no one can be insensible to their plastic beauty and inestimable documentary value. Volumes, we may well believe, will yet be written on all they have to teach us about the folk-lore and manners and customs and art of those days. But we must first take up what calls for immediate attention, and before using them as a mirror of manners and customs, we must begin by understanding what they mean; for there is no mistaking that a message for posterity was entrusted to them, though later generations have lost the key to their silent language.[1] Our most urgent task is to find again the lost meaning of these symbols, legendary scenes or idols. Nor must we forget that the space allotted to us is necessarily limited. Just as Sir John Marshall has had to confine himself to the broad outlines of the æsthetic evolution of the sculpture, so we in our turn will keep to the most general principles of its interpretation and refer the reader, for details, to the descriptive text with which we have thought it expedient to accompany the plates

[1] Far be it from us to impute this as a fault to India! Had not Europe, without the same excuse, forgotten likewise in the course of recent centuries the meaning of reliefs and stained glass in her cathedrals?

The oldest reliefs at Sāñchī

The oldest reliefs at Sāñchī—as their composition, their inscriptions and, as we shall see, their subject-matter suggest—seem to be those which decorate the balustrade of the terrace and steps of the Great Stūpa 1 (*cf*. Pl. 8). Compared with the bas-reliefs on the balustrade which runs round Stūpa 2, they seem even more clumsy and schematic.[1] According to the present state of our knowledge, however, the probable interval of time which separates them appears to be inconsiderable. The same may be said also of the existing fragments of the balustrades which bordered the staircase and terrace of the same Stūpa 2 (Pl. 91) and those of Stūpa 3 (Pl. 93). But there is a special reason for according to the ground balustrade of Stūpa 2 the honours of this chapter; for by a lucky chance it still possesses 85 out of the 88 pillars of which it once consisted (Pls. 74-91). This means that, like the gateways of Stūpa 1, but more than half a century before them, it provides archæologists with an almost entire decorative whole. Nothing, as is well known, is rarer in India and nothing, as may be imagined, could be more useful to guide our researches and give weight to our conclusions. We shall, therefore, make it the centre of our theme and use the medallions on the other old balustrades only for reference and comparison.

Ground Balustrade of Stūpa 2

It is true that our investigation lacks one element of precision which we cannot but regret from the outset: we cannot depend on the present arrangement of the decorations. In the semi-destruction and subsequent restorations which this stūpa underwent in the last century, some of the pillars of the balustrade were thrown down and set up again without sufficient regard for their original order, and sometimes, so far as we can guess,[2] with their outer face turned inwards; but the lack of uniformity in the disposition of the motifs carved on them diminishes the drawbacks due to this possible carelessness. Another and more important reservation concerns the pillars which stand at the four entrances, interrupting the circle of the balustrade at the four points of the compass (*cf*. plan, Pl. 71). If not from the very beginning, at least from a very early date, the old sculptors considered it a duty to ornament these pillars from top to bottom, on one or even three faces, as they also did the newel posts at the foot of the stairways (*cf*. Pl. 8, 24). For example, the ornamentation of Pillar 1 (*cf*. Pl. 74), though designed in this way, nevertheless looks very archaic. Yet some of these angle pillars have evidently been recarved at a relatively late date. It is well to be on one's guard against the tendency, still too frequent, to consider these old balustrades in a body, as if all their component parts were completed on the same day. A moment's reflexion, or better still, a glance at

Reconstruction doubtfully correct

Later carvings on certain pillars

[1] We invite attention particularly to the birds, so awkwardly designed (Pl. 8 *b*, Pillar 2), and the buffalo on Pillar 2, shown (as on Pillar 12 *b* at Bodh-Gayā) with its body in profile and its head seen front-face and from above.

[2] A careful study of the monument and the analogy of the coping-stone at Bharhut (*cf*. Cunningham, Pls. X and XI) have convinced us that the medallions decorated with a plain lotus were meant originally to adorn the outside of the monument. For the ornamentation of the *pradakṣhiṇa-patha* (*i.e.*, the path between the balustrade and the stūpa to allow the worshippers to perform the ancient rite of circumambulation of the building), lively themes were naturally reserved, as being more amusing to the eye and more interesting to the mind. It is this rule which was followed also when Pillars 48 and 50-52, recovered during excavation by Sir John Marshall, were recently put back into place. These four pillars have been left blank on Pl. 71, as well as Pillars 45-47, the only ones still missing.—It may likewise be supposed that the architect had a fancy for having the pillar which marked the middle of the four sections of the enclosure decorated specially on its inner face, by joining the medallion to the two half-medallions with a garland. Such at least is the case of Pillar 13 in the N. E. sector, and of Pillar formerly 79 (now 82) in the N. W. sector; but it must be confessed that there is no trace of such an arrangement in the other two sectors. (The view expressed here regarding the disposition of the plain lotus medallions is personal to M. Foucher. It hardly seems to me to be borne out by photographs taken before the balustrade was restored. See description of Pl. 73*a*.—J. M.)

Pillar 27 (Pl. 79)—to take a typical instance—will suffice to dispose of this error. It is evident that the decoration of the square panels which cover two of the sides of this pillar, is contemporary with the gateway-decoration of Stūpa 1, and not with the balustrade-decoration of Stūpa 2, of which it nevertheless forms a part.[1] In this particular case, the contrast is so striking, indeed, that it compels us to exclude it provisionally from our survey, and to link the study of it to that of the sculptures which are to form the subject of our next chapter.

Scheme of decoration

Apart from these exceptions, all the pillars are uniformly and exclusively decorated in the middle—at the intersection with the central cross-bar—with a complete medallion, and in the upper and lower parts—below and above the point where they are inserted into the ramp or the plinth—with a half-medallion. So there are (we have counted them on the site) 152 medallions and 303 half-medallions: each of them, like the 51 square panels to be found elsewhere on the entrance-pillars, being carved in relief. This makes a total of 506 themes, the classification and interpretation of which devolves upon us. Such a large number cannot fail to throw interesting light upon the beginnings of Buddhist sculpture. Our first care must be to review them rapidly, without mixing any kind of preconceived theory or premature hypothesis with our review; thus we may at once clear the way and elucidate the means for their interpretation.

I. General Survey of Themes

The lotus

At first sight the decoration of the balustrade of Stūpa 2 would seem to be based on the lotus. It is present always and everywhere. It is the first thing which strikes and continues to haunt the visitor's eye. It occurs so often, indeed, that one may ask whether it was not once the only decorative motif of the old wooden fences, long since crumbled away. Later on, one would think, an inevitable and legitimate need for variety must have led to the introduction of other subjects; but while giving way to these new themes, the lotus seems at least to have imposed its circular form on them. This must undoubtedly have been the origin of the endless 'medallions' which occur on the Bodh-Gayā and Bharhut balustrades, as well as on those at Sāñchī, and are later replaced by square panels of the kind just mentioned. Even in the present case, the lotus maintained almost undisputed possession of the whole exterior front of the balustrade of Stūpa 2, and though it has been expelled from several medallions, it has rarely been so thoroughly expelled that no memory of it survives, at least in the shape of a bud or rosette. Of that the reader will be quickly convinced if he glances through Pls. 74 to 91. It must, however, be acknowledged that the themes mingled with it or substituted for

[1] See also p. 148 above. One might compare the similar case of the "Sun Chariot" at Bodh-Gayā; the contrast in the technique and its distance in time from the old balustrade of which it was a part, are hardly less great. Need we point out that on the balustrade of Stūpa 2 at Sāñchī the cross-bars or *sūci* have been left bare—a different treatment from that used a little later at Bodh-Gayā and Bharhut, where the *sūci* are decorated in the same way as the pillars (*stambha*)?

it are already very varied. And though these are more often than not borrowed from the vegetable or animal kingdom, they include also quite a number of human figures and a few symbols.

Symbols

Some of the latter, such as the stūpa, are borrowed direct from architecture, or, like the wheel, are commonly perched on one of those columns which were once the pride and are now the glory of the emperor Aśoka (*cf.* Pls. 74, 82 and 86). The felly of this wheel is trimmed outside, as on the old coins, with an edging of umbrellas, even where it forms the centre of a pseudo-lotus, as on Pillar 13 *b* (Pl. 76). Once it is placed upon the symbol called *nandipada* or taurine, which itself rests on a stone throne supported by genii (Pl. 74, 1 *c*). The *nandipada* itself reappears several times, sometimes set among lotuses (Pillars 12 *b*, 13 *b*, 26 *b*), or lotuses loaded with gems (9 *b* and 25 *b*), sometimes forming a part of this floral pattern (31 *b*, 35 *a*, 56 *b*, 68 *b*, 72 *a*, 82 *b*, 83 *a*, 87 *b*). Another symbol, the shield or *śrīvatsa*, so far enigmatic, is connected with the lotus in various ways (9 *b*, 22 *b*, 40 *a*, 48 *a*, 51 *a*, 53 *b*, 75 *b*, 83 *b*). In a reduced form it combines more readily with variations of the 'palmette or 'honeysuckle' (16 *b*, 17 *b*, 19 *a*, 22 *a*, 32 *b*, 42 *b*, 48 *a*, 60 *a*, 65 *b*, 69 *a*, 72 *a*, 82 *a*, 87 *a*), and once, even, with the latter and lions placed back to back (51 *b*).

Plants

This so-called honeysuckle ornament, the most frequent of the floral patterns after the lotus, is found isolated and in clearly recognizable form on Pillars 13 *b*, 22 *a* and *b*, 27 *a*, 28 *a*, 38 *a*, 44 *c*, 51 *a*, 71 *a*, and the number of these reproductions makes it very probable that the artists invested it with symbolical meaning and sacred character. Of the trees, we shall have more to say anon about the *aśvattha* (pīpal, *ficus religiosa*). The mango is also found several times, either sheltering an elephant (58 *b*), or in the form of isolated branches covered with fruit, which is sometimes being plundered by squirrels (25 *a*) or birds (44 *a*), sometimes placed in the hand of a crouching man (74 *b*) or of a fantastic figure (86 *b*). The middle medallion of Pillar 59 *b* shows what seems to be a palm-tree, together with a tree, strangely cut in the shape of an arbour, just like those which we see on the Western Gateway of the Great Stūpa (Pl. 64 *c*). We shall find, too, in the hands of the Caryatids of the *toraṇa* the same blossoming bignonia as in that of the Yakshī on our pillar 1. As for the bunch of flowers on Pillar 27 *b*, it is too ornate to be true to life.

Real Animals

When we turn to the animals, we have no difficulty in recognizing at once, in the forefront, the lion and the elephant, followed by the horse; the bull, which must be considered as the fourth sacred animal, plays a much less important part.[1] Instead, stags or hinds appear frequently, sometimes isolated and either kneeling down (1 *c*, 14 *b*; *cf.* Pl. 8 *a*, 3) or scratching their muzzles with their hind-feet (Pl. 8 *c*, 4); sometimes face to face (Pl. 8 *a*, 6) or back to back (31 *b*, 40 *b*; *cf.* 5 *a*, 44 *b* and *c*, 49 *a*, 66 *b*); sometimes expiring in the jaws of a lion (8 *a*, 24 *b*, at the top) or pursued by a dog with its tail up (44 *a*). Other mammals appear only sporadically, such as the camel with or without a

[1] We shall have to return to this later, p. 188.

rider (54 *a* and 66 *c*), the buffalo (Pl. 8 *a*, 2 and *b*, 2), the rhinoceros (24 *a*), the boar (86 *a*), the squirrel (25 *a*) and two other rodents not yet identified (24 *b*). The monkey, so frequent later on, is absent, but the bear is seen on Pl. 8 *c*, 2.

Birds

Of the birds, the famous *haṁsa* or Indian goose is most in evidence, generally in pairs (55 *b*, 86 *a*) and often combined with the lotus on the half-medallions (6 *b*), medallions (43 *b*, 52 *a*) or creepers (44 *a*, 49 *b*, 66 *a* and 71 *b*). It might often be confused with the crane (*cf.* 5 *b*), which is also twice represented in pairs (73 *a* and 84 *a*). A peacock, spreading out its tail between its two tiny females, fills a whole medallion on Pillar 10 *b*. The parrot may sometimes be recognized among the creepers (see especially 44 *a*). Of other birds, it would be hard to identify a number, particularly those which, on several half-medallions, are carrying garlands in their beaks or on their necks (*cf.* especially 25 *b*, 73 *b*, 79 *b*, 80 *b*). By analogy with these last, one can guess that the central theme at the top of Pillar 18 *a*, between the two addorsed lions, is again a bird's head thrust through a collar of flowers.

Fish

Even fish may be found on our balustrade, sometimes being trampled underfoot by an elephant (35 *b*), sometimes being swallowed by strange sea-monsters, to which we shall return in a moment (*cf.* 34 *a*, 79 *b*, 86 *b*). We shall also recur (p. 184) to the peculiar part played by the tortoise. As for serpents, we can find only one real cobra, writhing in the beak of an exceedingly conventional vulture (38 *b*). The two other specimens, each with five heads and hoods (32 *a*, 81 *a*), supply the transition to the supernatural beings which remain to be enumerated.

Fantastic Animals

In addition to these polycephalic serpents, we meet with a strange creation of the Indian imagination in the shape of an elephant with stag's antlers or, more accurately, a stag with an elephant's head (84 *b*). As to the stag with the fish-tail in No. 11 *b*, it is the well-known form of a Chaldean god. The sea-monster, whether borrowed from occidental art or not, seems in India to have assumed a crocodile's head (79 *b* and 86 *b*), and owes to the same animal its name of *makara* (now *makar* or *magar*). But the saurian muzzle soon became so inordinately lengthened as to recall quite deliberately the trunk of an elephant (8 *b*), which, to leave no room for doubt, sometimes also displays its tusks (30 *a*). Not only can we thus follow on our balustrade the evolution of this decorative motif which was destined to have such a long and far-reaching success,[1] but we see the *makara* in a new function, vomiting forth scrolls of leaf and blossom, sometimes on medallions (25 *a*, 39 *b*, 64 *b*), sometimes on whole faces of pillars (22 *a*, 71 *b*, 88 *a* and *c*).

The lion, too, served as a theme for numerous fantastic variations (we see it again as a sea-monster in 25 *b*), all of which are obviously suggested by Græco-Persian art. Thus, there are the winged lions, sometimes shown front-face, with such a curiously clumsy

---

[1] *Cf.* the studies by Mr. Henry Cousens in *A. S. R.*, 1903-4, pp. 227-31 and Pl. 65 and by Prof. J. Ph. Vogel in *Revue des arts asiatiques*, t. vi, pp. 133-147 and Pls. 33-39.

attempt at foreshortening (9 *a*, 74 *a*, 75 *a*), sometimes shown in profile and back to back in pairs (62 *a*, 77 *a*, 79 *b*). The borrowing becomes still more obvious in the case of the griffin which, after all, is nothing but a lion with an eagle's (or parrot's) beak, winged or not (7 *a*, 56 *a*, 72 *b* or 14 *a* and 35 *b*). Then, too, we have to acknowledge a distant heritage from Assyria in the lion with the human, long-bearded face in 8 *a*, and another with the curly mane in 9 *a*.

Hybrid Creatures

This combination of human and animal shapes is characteristic also of a whole series of supernatural monsters in which we find the same mixture of classical influence and oriental fantasy. Not without surprise do we meet, on the railing of this old Buddhist monument, with the type of the centaur and even of the she-centaur, so exceedingly rare in Greek art: the first ridden by a woman (7 *b*; *cf.* Pl. 8 *f*, 5), and the second by a man (81 *b*). The adornment of their human busts and the trappings on their horse-bodies are, however, treated in the Indian style. Once let loose, indeed, the imagination of the old designers seems to have tried every possible combination of human and equine elements: thus, we can point out a horse with a man's head (82 *a*) and a woman with a horse's head (86 *b*; *cf.* Pl. 27). The former, evidently suggested by the creations of Assyria, has survived in Persian imagery to serve as a mount for Mohammed ascending to the skies. The latter is no less probably a native of the Near East, and no more represents a truly Indian creation than the precisely analogous model of the Demeter of Phigalia was properly a Greek conception; yet its type became acclimatised to India, whence it even passed to Cambodia, and such figures are still found in Hindu mythology under the name of *kinnara*.

In old Buddhist mythology this very vague term (to be translated by 'human monster') is more especially applied to another class of hybrid beings. As in the case of the true classical siren as portrayed at Pompeii, we are here concerned with the combination of a man's trunk grafted onto a bird's body. It should be noticed, however, that we can discover no allusion to the melodious song of these Indian 'sirens' on our old balustrades, though their musical talents are vaunted in literature and constantly confirmed by the later art of Ajaṇṭā, Borobudur and Central Asia, not to mention Siam and Cambodia. Isolated (84 *a*) or associated with some miracle (5 *b* and 74 *b*; *cf.* 27 *a*), their function in the old school is to carry celestial garlands and not, as later, to play the lute. Their bird-like wings, tail and feet ought to have won for them the name of *suparṇa*; but on our medallions (38 *b*) as on the lintel of the Eastern Gateway (Pl. 46), the vulture Garuḍa, king of "those which have fine plumage", always appears simply in the form of a great bird, more or less conventionalized[1].

With the hereditary enemy of the latter—the *Nāga*—we enter finally on an order of beliefs and images more properly Indian. We have mentioned (p. 173) the animal shape

[1] Compare, by the way, with the *kinnara* and *suparṇa*, a fantastic creature (75 *a*) whose bust and stumps of wings end in scrolls. His loin-cloth of leaves, recalling the stylised pleats of the *dhotī* of some other decorative figures on our balustrade (*cf.* 73 *b* and 88 *a*), is found again in Gandhāra and at Mathurā (*cf.* *Art Gréco-bouddhique du Gandhāra*, I, pp. 212 and 252).

of these serpent-genii; but on occasion they can assume human form. Nevertheless, on Pillar 6 *b*, a reptile's tail continues to fill the whole surface of the medallion with its coils, up to the height of the shoulders, whilst a five-headed hood is curved above the turban, and on Pillar 88 *c* the *Nāgī* is distinguished by her three-headed hood.

Human Beings

From these hybrid creatures we pass to the purely anthropomorphous figures. As a matter of fact, we still come upon a certain number of deformed creatures in which we must recognize various classes of inferior genii. Sometimes, as pot-bellied dwarfs, they act as Atlantes under a stone throne (1 *c* and 5 *b*), and we shall find them filling the same rôle on the capitals of the Western and Small Gateways (*cf.* Pls. 54 and 95). More often than not, they are decoratively combined with lotuses, either in a medallion (6 *a*, 9 *a*, 41 *a*, 73 *b*, 85 *a*) or in rectangular panels (23 *a*, 49 *b*, 88 *a*). Special mention must be made of the curiously pleated jerkin of the one decorating the top of Pillar 23 *b*. But what are we to say of the figure seated on a rattan stool in the central medallion of 14 *a*, whose peculiarly shaped headdress proclaims him a king? What do we know of those numerous riders on horse-back, elephant or camel, not to mention the one on the she-centaur? And what are we to make of the scene in which we see an elephant, ridden by two men, trampling underfoot a third, whose hair is caught up in the elephant's trunk (1 *b*)? And though the lion-hunter in 14 *b* looks like an Indian, the big boots and Scythian cap of the one on 88 *b* surely betray at once his foreign origin.

And if we turn to the women, the same uncertainties crop up. On Pillar 1 *a*, the analogy of some inscribed figures at Bharhut allows us to recognize a Yakshī; on the other hand, at the top of face *b* of the same pillar, we shall have decisive reasons (*cf.* Pl. 32) for recognizing Māyā, the Buddha's mother at the sacred moment of child-birth. But what are we to do, for instance, with the crouching woman seen from the back on face *c*, or with the child standing opposite her? And who precisely are the two couples portrayed on this and the preceding face? Here, again, the analogy of Bharhut gives grounds for concluding them to be pairs of *Yakshas*, and the same impression is given by the two couples on Pillar 88 *b*, also at the Northern Entrance, and the erotic group on 20 *a* (*cf.* Pl. 8 *e*) or the merely decorative one on 66 *a*. But when the two partners stand in pious attitudes at the foot of the Bodhi tree (66 *c*) or of the column surmounted by the wheel of the First Sermon (3 *a* and 66 *b*), how can we decide whether we have still to do with supernatural beings or simply with humans, as the fact that their feet tread the ground would lead one to think?

II. Ornamental motifs

These perplexities would be still worse, if we tried to give names to the human figures,[1] to discover the reason for the fantastic creatures, or to justify the presence of the

[1] We shall return to these iconographical questions in Chapter XVII, p. 243.

ordinary animals. Nevertheless, after a careful survey of this balustrade which we made in January 1919, we came to certain conclusions that may be summarily stated.

Traditional designs

(*a*) The first is that these decorations were not produced merely for the sake of the monument which they adorn. Neither one man nor even one workshop would have had a sufficiently fertile imagination to create such a collection of themes in so short a time. The oldest designers (*rūpa-kāraka*) of Sāñchī had already a long past behind them, and did not fail to draw largely on the common stock of their guild for the needs of their task. With this traditional heritage, a number of foreign themes originating in the Near East had already mingled, and this western influence was particularly marked by the introduction of hybrid and monstrous creatures.

Buddhist subjects

(*b*) Nevertheless, in the midst of this medley, a fairly large number of specifically Buddhist subjects present themselves insistently to our eyes. It would have been surprising if this were not so. *A priori* it is quite natural to admit a certain relation between an edifice and its decoration. The first being, as the excavations have proved, indubitably a Buddhist shrine, the ornamentation of its surroundings must adapt itself as far as possible to the worship of the Buddha. The patent existence and frequent recurrence of the "Four Great Miracles" are alone sufficient to make this probability a certainty; and we need not enlarge here on this point, since we must come back to it in detail in the last part of this chapter.

Individual taste of sculptors

(*c*) Yet another conclusion to which we came seems to us equally important. Unless we are much mistaken, a mere glance through the plates will have produced on the reader the same impression as our own frequent perambulations of the monument left on us: namely, that the variety of its decoration is more apparent than real. Let us put ourselves for a moment in the place of those old sculptors faced with the task of decorating these 88 pillars on two and sometimes three sides, and we shall readily understand that, whenever they take a subject, they turn it round every way, repeat it in all its aspects, and do not relinquish it till they have exploited all its possibilities. Thus a large part of their compositions are merely variations on a relatively small number of themes.

To sum up: in the interpretation of these sculptures we shall have to take into account, on a more or less equal footing, (*a*) the routine of the workshop, (*b*) the demands of the Buddhist donors, and (*c*) the individual fantasy of the sculptors. Mere common sense would have sufficed to tell us so; all the same, it may not be superfluous to demonstrate it by some concrete examples.

The Lotus

The most striking instance of all, because the most frequent, is the lotus, which fills more than a third of the medallions on our balustrade. That it was a legacy from the old Indian decorators, no one would dream of disputing: the most sober models which we have here (*cf.* 29 *a*) already give evidence of a formalization long since accomplished. Nor can one doubt that the theme took on, if we may so express it, a Buddhist guise. This flower, so pure in colour and so sweet-smelling, which, without apparent connection with the muddy bottom of the pond, emerges suddenly on the surface of the waters, had long been an emblem of immaculate and divine birth; and we shall see in a moment how it was early used to symbolise the Buddha's miraculous Nativity. But—and this concerns our third point—one cannot refrain from remarking by the way that no two of these seventy-odd lotuses are exactly alike, and that our artists have obviously been at pains to fashion them in every imaginable way. For the most part they multiply the number of the petals till they exceed a hundred (*cf.* 19 *b*), or else they encircle the flower in concentric wreaths or cables or necklaces (*cf.* 33 *a*, 42 *a*, 51 *b*, 57 *a*, etc.). Sometimes they curl a certain number of petals back on the heart (*cf.* 67 *b*, 68 *a*, 70 *a*), or curve them into volutes (33 *b*, 50 *a*), or replace them by palm or fern leaves (36 *a*, 43 *a*). Often they compose a floral pattern of small-scale lotuses entwined together (13 *a*, 42 *b*, 65 *b*, 87 *a*) or hanging from a sort of peg (2 *b*, 19 *a*, 69 *a*), etc. To enumerate all the variations in detail would be impossible; moreover, what interests us here, is not so much their remarkable diversity as what we have to look for beneath this diversity—nothing else, apparently, but what the old designers put there themselves, namely a purely fanciful refinement of ornamentation. In short, the lotuses on our old balustrade have certainly a Buddhist meaning, and, as we shall shortly see (p. 183), certain of their variants suggest a supplementary symbolical intention; but it would obviously be absurd to seek in the greater number of them for anything but an exhibition of the remarkable decorative sense of the Indians.

The Elephant

We must draw the same conclusion from our examination of the sacred animals. Take the elephant, for instance: the analogy of an inscribed relief at Bharhut will allow us (p. 182) to recognize a representation of the miracle of the "Conception" of the Buddha in the two upper half-medallions on Pillars 6 *a* and 85 *b*, where this animal plays the principal part, not to mention the subsidiary part which he takes in the "Nativity" on five other pillars. But what are we to do, from the Buddhist point of view, with the other twenty-five elephants which our medallions show us, not to speak of those surmounting the capitals of columns (5 *a*, 66 *b*) or serving as starting points for scrolls (3 *b*, 5 *b*, 44 *a*, 66 *a*)? Assuredly we shall still discern a pious intention in those portrayed *passant* and holding lotuses in their trunks (4 *a*, 8 *b*, 18 *a*, 24 *a*, 35 *b*, 50 *b*, 54 *b*, 70 *b*, 77 *b*), even when we are shown only their forequarters (10 *a*, 18 *b*, 26 *a*). And, again, in those standing in the shadow of a tree of the same species as that of the Bodhi (38 *b*, 41 *b*) we may scent afar something like a faint religious perfume. This, it will be acknowledged, manages to evaporate when we see them associated merely with mango-trees (58 *b*) or fantastic trees (59 *b*) or garlands (54 *a*); and then, what feeling of sanctity could be awakened by the elephant spraying himself with his trunk on Pillar 15 *b*, or by the one ejecting the remnant of his meal on Pl. 8 *f*, 6? Now, if ever, our artists are simply amusing themselves.[1] So far as their works allow us to divine their secret thoughts, the elephant was without doubt a sacred animal to them. But he was also one of the most precious resources of their stock, and they did not fail to use and abuse him according to their whim. They did worse: they seem to have had no scruple about portraying two sacred animals devouring one other, so that we see on Pillar 24 *b* a baby elephant being attacked from the rear by a lion.

Other animals

This, moreover, is not the lion's only misdeed. Sometimes he is not ashamed to prey upon those very deer with which we are to find him in company before the symbol of the 'First Sermon' (p. 190). At other times, by a just revenge, he becomes in his turn the victim of a hunter (14 *b* and 88 *b*). Moreover, representations of the lion are used for any kind of decorative purpose, now singly (34 *b*, 61 *b*, 63 *a*, 74 *a*), now face to face (1 *c*) now back to back on capitals (3 *a*, 5 *a*, 44 *b*; *cf.* 13 *a*), or framed in half-medallions (4 *a*, 18 *a*, 51 *b*, 87 *a*; *cf.* 27 *b*), or combined with scrolls (3 *a*, 5 *a*, 49 *a*, 71 *b*, 88 *a*), etc. Though his image is thus almost as frequent and hackneyed as that of the elephant, we should note in passing that it is far less successful. As a matter of fact, the efforts at foreshortening are equally unsuccessful in both cases: whatever the animal which our sculptors undertake to show front-face,. they think themselves obliged to conceal from us as little of it as possible; and that is why they broaden its hind-quarters so inordinately as to let the hind-feet show on each side of the forefeet. In this respect the pachyderm in 72 *b* has no reason to reproach or to envy the carnivore in 75 *a*. But when it is a question of showing them in profile, it is quite another matter. Whilst the elephants are always drawn correctly, sometimes even with remarkable skill, the lions linger on in a much more archaic and primitive style; though showing them from the side, the stone-carver makes a point of letting us know that they have two eyes, and so he adds on the upper outline of the face the eye which would normally remain hidden.

One can easily see why our artists, having much fewer opportunities of seeing a wild beast than a domestic animal, should continue to give a portrait drawn from memory of the former, whilst they were already sketching the other from life. But to return to our main preoccupation of the moment, the animals portrayed by them, domestic or otherwise, are certainly not Buddhist by nature. Who would have the boldness to affirm that they have all become Buddhist by intention? After the elephant and the lion we may admit the horse and the bull, whose sacred character is averred (*cf.* below, pp. 186 and 188): but one can detect no specifically Buddhist reason for beatifying a cow and her calf (11 *b*) or the buffaloes on Pls. 8 *a*, 2 and *b*, 2. We are not forgetting that

[1] We should willingly think that they are letting themselves be led away into the same realistic vein, when they show on Pillar 86 *a* an elephant coming out of his stable, the door of which is pierced very high in the tiled roof, in order to let the person riding him pass through more comfortably. Note, by the way, that, as always in the old school, it is the master who is seated astride on the elephant's neck with the *aṅkuśa* in his hand, in the place of the modern *mahout* (72 *b*, 76 *a*, 80 *b*), and when there are two riders, the servant hangs on, as best as he can, to the ropes which girth the elephant's trappings (1 *b*, 11 *a*, 52 *b*, 75 *b*). As to the lotuses which persist in filling the background of these last medallions, they are in this case, unless we are much mistaken, merely a mechanical memory of our old sculptors' favourite theme.

the texts sometimes compare the monk in love with solitude to the shy rhinoceros, and this might give a suitable pretext for the lower half-medallion on Pillar 74 *a*; but what edifying inspiration is to be drawn from camels, pigs, or squirrels? We might, too, discover pious allusions in peacocks or geese (*cf.* p. 182), but cranes and parrots call up no special associations. Doubtless the fault lies largely in our ignorance of old Indian folklore. But that this is not the only reason, we have proof in the frequent use of those hybrid creatures which we pointed out above; for, one asks, what bond could there be between the doctrines of the sect and these old Assyrian or Græco-Persian monsters? Let us repeat: if the Buddhist intention escapes us so often in the decoration of this old Buddhist edifice, that is mainly due to the fact that the designers had not always any definite purpose in selecting their subjects. There is certainly much that they have carved for no particular reason, simply for pleasure: it always meant so much more surface covered. Entrusted with filling five hundred or more frames in a short time, they only got out of the difficulty by emptying their whole bag of motives in a heap—native or foreign, religious or profane—at the same time racking their brains to invent the greatest possible number of variations.

Sculpture of balustrade not essentially Buddhist

These first conclusions give us two useful hints: one concerns the method to be followed in the interpretation of the sculptures, and the other the conditions in which these were executed. From the fact that the donors of the old Sāñchī monuments were pious Buddhist zealots, one is tempted to conclude as a rule, by a sort of tacit convention, that all their workmen must have been so too. This is going ahead too fast. On this point only one thing is certain—that founders and stone-carvers were at bottom Hindus and shared the same popular beliefs; indeed, in no other way could one explain the presence at Bharhut and Sāñchī of all those genii and demi-gods who appear already on our oldest balustrades. For the rest, it would be rash to assert anything. Certainly we have not the slightest intention of maintaining the paradox that none of the Sāñchī artists were Buddhists; but nothing gives us reason to think that they were all, or even most of them, recruited in a guild wholly converted to the religion of Buddha. Even had they been so recruited, that would not have prevented them from placing their services at the disposal of donors who belonged to other faiths and demanded, if not another choice of images, at least other applications of the same symbols. We know from an inscription that the ivory-workers of the neighbouring town of Vidiśā (now Besnagar) claimed the honour of decorating one of the jambs of the Southern Gateway of the Great Stūpa. Who is going to imagine that they worked for Buddhist customers only? We must add that, later on, the Jinas of Mathurā, for instance, are obviously the work of the same hands as the Buddhas found in the same city, and again that, at Ellorā, the workmanship of the Brahmanic, Buddhist and Jain divinities betrays the fact that they originated from a common workshop. At Sāñchī itself, is it not evident that the unseemly decorators of the mediæval temple 45, might just as w[illegible]—indeed rather more suitably—have been entrusted with the decoration of a Hindu temple? Whether or not the fault is due to the division formerly adopted by Fergusson in his book on Indian Architecture, we are too ready to forget that in ancient India it is more than probable that artistic handicraft never had a strictly sectarian character. It behoves us to remember this here, if we are to realise what a potpourri of ideas our balustrade supplies.

Buddhist themes and decorative motifs

As we thus gain further familiarity with these sculptures, we feel increasingly more capable of distinguishing among them, under all the adventitious variants, two classes of subjects, which, it must be confessed, are clearly defined only at the two ends of the series—on the one hand, the thoroughly Buddhist scenes, and, on the other, the purely decorative motifs. Between these two extremes stretches the indefinite zone where one class melts into the other by hardly perceptible degrees, and where so many riddles remain to be solved—some fanciful variations on Buddhist themes, and some Buddhist allusions underlying profane ornaments. Such is the kind of classification to which this rapid and quite objective survey has led us, and this classification will serve us as a useful guide in our attempt at interpreting the various reliefs; for, in the first place, it dispenses with the necessity of trying to explain each and every detail. Doubtless, as we have said, the progress of our studies will consist in discovering with greater clarity and in an increasing number of cases the religious meaning or intention hidden under motifs that are seemingly ornamental, and will consequently drive steadily back the shifting boundary of the decorative themes to the gain of Buddhist subjects. But, on the other hand, the very conditions in which this decoration had to be executed—beginning with the necessity felt by sculptors belonging to various sects to turn everything to their own purpose—lead one to think that, even after the identifications have been made, there will always remain a decorative residuum indissoluble in any Buddhist reagent. The thought, at any rate, is a comforting one, though we are probably very far from having identified all that is identifiable. That is not all: our classification, indefinite as it is, not only throws light on our task, but helps us also to fulfil it. Thanks to it, the ground can be considered provisionally cleared, both of the mechanical borrowings from the repertory then in fashion and of the fantasies of pure ornamentation. It remains only (and this will be the object of the next section) to pick out everything in our balustrade which proceeds from the direct inspiration of the donors. But here, for a change, we need not fear to push our efforts at comprehension to the furthest limits; for we must not forget that our old sculptors had a great deal more to say than they could express, and we must often try and understand their artistic stammerings from a mere hint.

III. Buddhist Subjects

The art of any religion is, after all, nothing but one of the outward manifestations of worship. In Buddhism, a religion with a founder, this worship is naturally addressed to the Master. The veneration attached to his relics at once explains the important part played in architecture by the stūpa or funerary tumulus; in sculpture, the pious respect paid to his memory justifies likewise the biographical character which the decoration of the railing round the stūpa (even before it spreads to the stūpa itself) early tends to assume. And in this biography the devotion of the faithful, as we know, fastened at once on the four essential episodes: the Nativity, the Enlightenment, the First Sermon and the Last Decease. On this point the evidence of the texts is clearly corroborated by that of the carved monuments, and it is indeed the four Great Miracles which are represented from the outset on our balustrade. As edification already wavers between the Nativity proper and two other miracles which were also staged in the holy town of Kapilavastu,—the "Conception" and the "Great Departure"—we can count in all six legendary scenes. As for the "Descent from the Sky", the "Donation of the Jetavana", "Indra's Visit" and other incidents which soon became popular, we find no trace of them. We may at most infer allusions to another mine of subjects which was also before long to be regularly exploited—that of the Master's "former Births" or Jātakas. There can be no question of order among these various pictures. Set in their own frames, they are dispersed at random among the four sectors of the enclosure. It is only later, in Gandhāra and at Amarāvatī, that the scenes succeed one another chronologically in the order in which they would meet the eyes of pilgrims doing their *pradakshiṇa,* and this is so until we reach at length the long biographical series of Borobudur. Nevertheless, there are obvious advantages in following a chronological order in our exposition, provided it is understood that only the four Great Miracles form as yet a coherent and well-established series, whilst the other Buddhist subjects are only guessed at.

The Jātakas

We must admit at once that we should never have dreamed of looking on our balustrade for representations of the former Lives of the Buddha, were it not for the striking similarity which exists between the central medallion on Pillar 86 *b* and a half-medallion at Bodh-Gayā, where the Jātakas have already ceased to be rare. On both we see a naked woman with a horse's head, here carrying a human being on her hip and there leading him by the hand. The exceptional type and the duplication of the figure at once recall the text of the Pāli Jātaka (No. 432), where there is also mention of a 'horse-headed fairy' (*Yakshiṇī assa-mukhī*) who was an ogress and whose habit it was to devour travellers. One day she seized a good-looking Brāhman, and this is probably the scene represented at Bodh-Gayā. But this time she falls in love with her captive, makes him her husband instead of her prey, and of this mésalliance the Bodhisattva is born. It is doubtless the latter who appears in this relief, carried Indian-wise on his mother's hip. These two identifications are confirmed by an old medallion found at Patna and now in the Calcutta Museum, on which we see the whole family united—the fairy in the middle, her husband standing on her right, and their offspring astride on her left hip.[1] On our balustrade the mother and child are obviously returning from fruit-picking, and the appearance of the panel is so purely decorative, that (we repeat), were it not for its two replicas, we should never have suspected that it implied any reference to a legend. However, having accepted this first suggestion as valid, we can only keep our eyes open for some other scene of the same kind. Thus we should be tempted to find an allusion to the *Mora-jātaka* (No. 159 of the Pāli collection) in the peacock on Pillar 10 *b* or to the *Mahā-haṁsa-jātaka* (No. 502, etc.) in the geese on Pillars 55 *b* and 86 *a*, and so forth. But this time the allusion, if it exists, is so vague, that it is safer to disregard it. At most, it may be that these decorative representations of animals conceal only the germ from which the first Jātaka pictures probably grew. It was inevitable, in fact, that the sight of them should, by a natural association of ideas, awaken in the Indians of that time (even more than in modern archæologists) the memory of tales of which the Bodhisattva was supposed to have been the hero in the shape of such and such a beast; and, on the other hand, nothing more was needed to fire the artist's imagination and incite him to compose the "stories without words" of Bodh-Gayā and Bharhut.

The Conception

Without the analogy of the latter balustrade we should not have dared to recognize a portrayal of the Conception or, as the texts call it, the "Descent" (*avakrānti*) of the Blessed One into the womb of his mother, in the form of an elephant. The existence of this scene on one of the Bharhut medallions[2] is proved unquestionably by the inscription accompanying it. The scene is not yet, as it was to be in Gandhāra, staged in an architectural frame; but at least it shows us Māyā lying on her Indian bed, attended by three squatting female attendants, one of whom is fanning her; a lamp (to show that it is night) and a ewer complete the furniture of the queen's bedroom. Whether this attempt at showing an 'interior' was first made at Bharhut or not, we do not know, but in its artless naïveté it certainly constituted a notable innovation. The balustrade of our Stūpa 2 takes us back to a much more schematic version, which retains only the person essential to the eyes of the devotees—the Bodhisattva's *avatāra*. When the elephant in 85 *b* holds, as is sometimes written, a lotus in his trunk, it is with intention. It is true that the one in 6 *a* is merely curling his trunk carelessly over his left tusk; but he is floating on clouds, which fact clearly emphasizes his descent from the sky. Both, moreover, are shown crouching and in profile, with the head to the left of the spectator (*cf*. Pl. 8 *b*, 4). Only a person unfamiliar with the extraordinary fixity of tradition in Buddhist art would be surprised to find him depicted in exactly the same attitude and in the same direction at Bharhut, the only difference being that there he is wearing a more ornate cap. At the same time, we discover the reason for a fact which up to now we could

[1] For the Bodh-Gayā medallion, see *Mémoires concernant l'Asie orientale*, 1919, III, Pl. I, 9 and p. 11, and for that of Patna, L. A. Waddell, ***Report on the Excavations at Pāṭaliputra (Patna)***, Calcutta, 1903, Pl. I and p. 36. We may add that the same motif appears on the bottom lintel of the Small Gateway, but in a quite subsidiary manner. *Cf*. Pl. 96 and p. 229, and at Ajaṇṭā, Cave XVII.

[2] A. Cunningham, *Stūpa of Bharhut*, Pl. XXVIII, 2.

only state, *viz.*, that the legend was more correctly represented in Gandhāra than in the old Indian school.[1] At Bharhut, as on the Eastern Gateway at Sāñchī (Pl. 50), the sculptors have placed Māyā with her head to the left of the spectator, with the result that, contrary to the texts, she offers her left instead of her right hip to the Bodhisattva; moreover, they give him a much larger stature than that of his mother elect, a proceeding which obviously does not contribute to increase the probability of the miracle. But what they were doing, we now see, was not through inadvertence or lack of skill, but merely as a matter of routine. They were simply reproducing mechanically (though surrounding it with new accessories) the old traditional model of the elephant of the "Conception", just as he was when he had to fill the whole frame by himself and to face left. When the Gandhāra artists turned Māyā and the elephant the other way, greatly reducing the size of one to the advantage of the other, it was because, being strangers to the native tradition of Central India, they were free to think for themselves and compose their picture of the Conception on new lines. That is why theirs is found to be at once more faithful to the letter of the texts and more convincing to the eyes of the worshippers.

The Nativity

We do not feel we are making any departure from the extreme caution which we have observed so far in proposing for the first of the four Great Miracles (the Jāti) a sequence of identifications the determining reasons and justifications for which we have published elsewhere.[2] In any case, in the present work we cannot evade the necessity of enumerating these afresh, however succinctly, for the good reason that we have drawn them especially from the Sāñchī sculptures; and since, to enumerate them, we must first classify them, the reader will readily give us leave to adopt the coherent order into which they seem to fall spontaneously, particularly as he may judge for himself the conclusions to be drawn from this series of documents. Having once entered on the study of an exotic iconography, he must look for further surprises. The elephant in the "Conception" may have disconcerted him. On coming to the Nativity his first care must be to banish all Christian memories of the manger, and learn to spell out new symbols. To begin with, he must make up his mind never to see, at any rate in the old school, even in the most explicit pictures, the child of this child-birth.

(*a*) The starting point is naturally given by the lotus flowers, simple or composite, whose decorative rôle and symbolical meaning we have expounded above (pp. 167 and 172); to these two points we shall not return. What interests us now is to ascertain how—the original meaning of this floral pattern having doubtless ended by becoming dulled through constant use—the old designers endeavoured in some cases to rejuvenate it with the aid of various artifices, and to give it body by the addition of new elements. The succession of these gradual transformations can be reconstructed with the aid of our documents,

[1] *Cf. Art G-b. du Gandhāra*, I, p. 293.

[2] *Memoirs of the Archæological Survey of India*, No. 46.

the leading idea which rules it being to make the application of the lotus to the representation of the Nativity of the Blessed One more and more precise. It is evidently with this intention, and no longer simply for purely ornamental purposes, as we might have thought just now (p. 177), that on the lotus background, which as usual covers the whole surface of the medallion, our sculptors have decided to draw sometimes a human head (11 *b*)—a model which frequently recurs at Bharhut—and sometimes, in such a way as to recall the Conception, the profile of an elephant holding a *padma* flower (16 *b*). At other times, it will be remembered, they combine either the same elephant in profile or the "lion of the Śākyas" (61 *b*) with a pattern of flowers, buds and leaves.

(*b*) Simultaneously, they follow another channel of variants, whose vogue is likewise attested by the oldest Indian coins: namely, in those eight very ornamental lotuses whose heart is formed of a circle and the petals of four *nandipada* or 'taurines' (*cf.* p. 172). If one remembers that the 'taurine symbol of the constellation of the Bull, contained an allusion to the chief dates in the Buddha's life (*cf.* p. 188), one may gain some idea of the success of this emblem at once decorative and expressive. But we are still uncertain of the reason why the shield or *śrīvatsa* (*cf.* 53 *b* and 82 *b*) enters also into the composition of these conventionalised lotuses.

(*c*) The attempts sketched in these two directions do not lead very far, however. It is otherwise with the connection between the lotus spray and another emblem of good omen in the eyes of the Indians—a pitcher which is understood to be full of water.[1] Springing from this *bhadra-ghaṭa*, a bunch of leaves, buds and flowers lend themselves to the most varied and often most happy arrangement. So our sculptors have adorned no less than fifteen medallions and five half-medallions in this way, not without the occasional addition, as was their wont, of shields, sacred geese, winged lions,[2] etc.

(*d*) The regular development of the theme requires that, when the sculptors were so far emboldened as to show at least the mother in this scene of the Nativity, she should take her seat on one of the flowers issuing from this vase. This is, in fact, what Māyā is doing on the Southern Gateway of Stūpa 1, as we shall see (*cf.* Pl. 13). It may be found surprising that we should seek in vain on our old balustrade for this intermediary link in the chain of transmission, while we light upon two others which, logically, ought to be of later date. To this we can only reply that it is not logic which rules artistic production.

[1] We feel inclined to seek the origin of this theme in a practice of the old decorators, who liked to show a palmette rising up out of a full-blown lotus. Now, the conical pistil of the *pad'ma*, broadening at the top, inevitably recalls the neck and mouth of a pitcher, just as the semi-spherical body of the flower suggests its bowl; in fact, nobody can fail to see, particularly on the lower uprights of Pl. 28 (*cf.* Pl. 37, etc.), how closely the two outlines resemble each other.

[2] As for the *makara* on 39 *b* (*cf.* 25 *a*, 64 *b*), it is to be connected with the ones used as starting-points for sinuous creepers. Twice at least (23 *b* and 70 *a*; *cf.* 49 *c*) the vase of flowers is replaced by a tortoise—an aquatic animal, no doubt, but one whose symbolical meaning, if it has any, escapes us. In the case of this strange variant, too, we might point out that our sculptors always took care, when arranging flowers and leaves in bouquets, to hide the lower extremities of the stems either under a bit of foliage (*e.g.*, 78 *b*) or a half-rosette (*e.g.*, 55 *b*) or a half-shield (*e.g.*, 82 *a*) or a full shield (*e.g.*, 40 *a*). 'By analogy' with the latter, as the linguists would say—but do not all morphologies follow the same laws?—they might have passed to the tortoise: and in fact we see how one forms an exact pendant to the other on Pillars 48 *a* and 51 *b*. However, it is more prudent not to insist upon simple hypotheses, plausible though they be, but to keep to the fact that the *bhadra-ghaṭa* met with great success everywhere and is found again both in Gandhāra and at Amarāvatī, whilst the ephemeral fantasy of the tortoise appears no more.

(*e*) The first of these more advanced models[1] shows a woman—*i.e.*, Māyā—standing and holding a lotus stem. A curious variant worth noting (26 *b*) shows her simply with clasped hands in company with her two attendants, the one on her right carrying the umbrella and ewer, and the one on her left the fly-whisk—attributes of her royalty and at the same time signs of the invisible presence of the infant Buddha ; and all three stand out against a background of lotus. In the usual way, the queen's right hand is occupied holding a lotus stem while the other lifts the hem of her garment (12 *b*, 15 *a*, 21 *b*). Yet contrary to expectation she is not treading on a *padma* : it is only the late restoration of 22 *a* which gives her this flower as a pedestal, in conformity with an interesting coin of Azes.[2] Once again (on Pillar 2 *a*) a lotus bending round our heroine's head is the only suggestion that we may recognize her to be Māyā and not an ordinary *Yakshiṇī*. For we must be on our guard against falling into the absurdity of trying to identify all our female figures with the Buddha's mother (*cf.* p. 246). Yet we must confess that, without the timely warning of the Bharhut inscriptions, we should hardly have escaped the temptation of seeing Māyā again in the fairies hanging by one hand to the branch of a tree (*cf.* 1 *a*, 23 *c*, 25 *b*) : for this was the very attitude which, in accordance with the texts, the Gandhāra School and the whole of later Buddhist iconography were soon to give her.

(*f*) In the most fully developed composition which the old Indian school has left us, the figure of Māyā remains, on the contrary, hieratically treated and subject to the old law of 'frontality'. This composition goes back, moreover, further than might have been expected, and it is certainly worthy of remark that, long before the Azilizes coins,[3] the ground and terrace balustrades of Stūpa 2 already testify to its existence. From that time on, Māyā is always standing on a lotus (49 *a*, 71 *a*, 76 *b* ; *cf.* Pl. 91 *i*) or at any rate on a pedestal from which lotus stems issue (1 *b*, 85 *b*) ; and every time, as it is written in the sacred texts, two Nāgas, here shown in the form of elephants holding round pitchers in their trunks, are supposed to give her invisible offspring his first bath. This is all we see, either at Bodh-Gayā or at Bharhut or even on the Gateways at Sāñchi. The appearance of the infant Buddha would alone mark a new advance in the way of representing the miracle. But for this sensational innovation we must wait for the Gandhāra School.

Though the artists of Central India never took this decisive step, it is nevertheless interesting to watch retrospectively their ever bolder and more successful attempts to graft onto the old traditional theme everything which might contribute to make it clearer. For, this time, it is not simply a question of freshening up themes that had grown stale. It is evident that they are labouring to portray more and more explicitly the miracle which hitherto they had merely suggested. Apparently, the lotus of the Nativity was no longer sufficient to content the donors, and it is to satisfy their demands that our old sculptors

[1] This model appears at about the same time on the two well-known coins of Pantaleon and Agathocles reproduced in *Art Gréco-bouddhique du Gandhāra*, Pl. III, 12 and 14.
[2] *Ibid.*, Pl. IV, 4.
[3] *Ibid.*, Pl. IV, 13. See also *Memoirs of the Arch. Surv. Ind.*, No. 46, Pl. IV, 5-8.

have tried to make its meaning more definite, first by associating it with other symbols, then by the portrayal of the mother, and lastly by the introduction of the two Nāgas, intimating the bath of the new-born.

The "Great Departure"

In other legendary scenes, also, we find this tendency at work to give further definition to the artistic formulas commemorating them. Perhaps we may see an indirect consequence of this sort of natural law even in the three-fold aspect of the first Great Miracle, as if the craftsmen had early been feeling their way towards the best means of showing it. However that may be, on our old balustrade we find two other substitutes for the "Nativity", one in the "Conception" and the other in the "Great Departure"— a total of three marvels, and doubtless also of three sacred sites for the one town of Kapilavastu. One can see how, from the very beginning of the pilgrimage, the devotion of the faithful must have wavered between these three. For, according to Indian ideas, the *Avakrānti*, ten months before the lying-in, marked the real point of departure for the Master's last earthly existence, whilst his "exit from the world" on entering the religious life, was as important to the faithful as his first advent.[1] Had the old manufacturers of objects of piety, even at that early date, taken it upon themselves to commemorate on the site the three great episodes by selling the elephant of the Conception in the vicinity of the ancient royal palace, the lotus of the Nativity at the Lumbinī park, and the horse of the Great Departure at the gate of the town? The later history of Buddhist art makes it more than probable. Not only do the sculptors at Sāñchī and Bharhut repeat these three symbolical mementoes side by side; but later, on the stelæ representing the four Great Miracles, those of Amarāvatī use indiscriminately the Nativity or the Great Departure to fill the panel reserved for Kapilavastu, whilst those of Benares group the two scenes in the same frame, sometimes adding the Conception.[2] Certainly the lotus of the *Jāti*, or birth proper, must originally have played the principal part, and that part it has kept (with what exuberance, we have seen) on the railing of the old stūpa; but the two other great incidents which were likewise staged at Kapilavastu were not slow to take their place beside it. In the third, the only one which remains for us to study, it seems indeed that we can also distinguish, as in the other two, several successive stages of the theme.

(*a*) The oldest seems to be provided by the balustrade on the terrace of Stūpa 3 (*cf.* Pl. 8 *b*, 7). Composed simply of a horse without harness outlined against the bare background of the medallion, it fully realises the schematic, abstract character which the earliest productions of Buddhist art certainly assumed. But in the medallion on Pillar *b*, 11 in the same plate, a rosette of lotus already surmounts the horse.

[1] Should one see an indication of this in the fact that, as Hiuen Thsang tells us (transl. S. Beal, II, p. 15, and Th. Watters, II, p. 14), Aśoka set up a horse, the emblem of the Great Departure, on the pillar (now smashed) which he had erected at the traditional place of the Nativity?

[2] *Cf.* J. Fergusson, *Tree and Serpent Worship*, Pls. 93-98 and J. Burgess, *Ancient Monuments of India*, Pls. 67-68.

(*b*) The identification of such a vague picture can, of course, only be guess-work. But with Pillar 74 *b* of the balustrade of Stūpa 2 we reach more solid ground, thanks once more to the analogy of Bharhut (Cunningham, Pl. 20, 1) and of the Southern and Eastern Gateways at Sāñchī (Pls. 16 *a* and 40, 2). In fact, we see in both places the horse Kaṇṭhaka, all saddled and bridled, and before him the groom Chandaka is raising the umbrella which testifies to the invisible presence of the Bodhisattva; only, as he is holding the umbrella in both hands, he has no hand left for the other traditional accessory, the ewer, and that is why this is placed on the ground between the horse's feet. Finally, that there may be no doubt about the miracle, the artist has suspended one of his *kinnaras* bearing garlands, in the sky, while other garlands and two rosettes (suggesting a rain of flowers?) complete the medallion. This time there is no possible mistake. It is a complete picture of the *Mahābhiniskramaṇa*—as complete, at least, as the procedure and means of the Buddhist 'primitives' admit of—and even the sculptor of the Eastern Gateway can find nothing to add but a graphic indication of the town and the retinue of gods.

(*c*) But the certainty which we have just reached on this point raises a problem whose importance greatly exceeds the apparent interest of the three medallions concerned. (40 *b*, 63 *b*, 84 *b*). All three have this in common, that they show a rider on the horse, which is doubtless the most natural thing in the world; but what unexpected consequences it leads us to! For imagine this as a natural development of the "Great Departure" theme, analogous to the one we have just witnessed in the case of the "Nativity"! Just as our designers ended by setting Māyā on the lotus, here they have ended by clapping the Bodhisattva on his steed; and in this they are simply manifesting once again the tendency which directs them to renew and clarify the old themes, if need be, by the introduction of the human figure. Notice, moreover, that at least two of the medallions show the rider in profile against a background of lotus in which (if in the present case a meaning must be sought) we can only suppose a direct allusion to the Bodhisattva; and their similarity would draw one to the same identification for the third . . . No doubt, and for our part we ask nothing better. But what would then become of the rule observed everywhere else, at Bharhut, on the Sāñchī Gateways, and among the earlier reliefs at Amarāvatī, forbidding any representation of the Bodhisattva from the time of his last birth? Must we admit that among the sculptors of our old balustrade an innovator slipped in, capable of conceiving and executing this stroke of audacity, which would have found neither imitators among the artists nor approvers among the worshippers? Or are the designers of these medallions, far from attempting a revolution in this one particular, simply devising decorative variants of the time-honoured theme of the horse, exactly as in 82 *a* they gave the mounted horse a human head? They have carried their secret to the grave (or, more accurately speaking, to the funeral-pyre), and we cannot at present venture to affirm anything either way. But it must be acknowledged that these horsemen provide the specialist with ample food for thought. Let us not forget that neither the Bharhut sculptors nor those of the Sāñchī Gateways are by any means shy of showing the future Buddha in scenes from the *Jātaka*, at the time of his earlier royal births, in just the same way as would befit the young Bodhisattva in his last life. Thus, without hesitation they give Prince Viśvantara, for instance, during the Buddha's last earthly existence but one, the appearance and costume which they would have given Prince Siddhārtha. Nothing was easier or more tempting for them than to show the latter. But, on the other hand, it is no less certain that, when the Bodhisattva finally bestrides his horse in the sculptures of Amarāvatī, he does so only under direct influence from the School of the North-West. On the whole, it is to be feared that we shall never know the exact identity of the three riders on our balustrade—in which they are less favoured than the horse and *syce* on Pillar 74 *b*.

Before leaving the miracles of the Early Life we ought also to discuss, after the symbolism of the horse, that of the bull (38 *a* ; *cf*. Pl. 8 *a*, 4 [with lotus] and *b*, 5). What we know most definitely about him may be summed up in the two following points. In the first place, on the old coins he seems to serve as a counterpart to the lotus. Of the five punch marks ordinarily found together, namely the lotus, the bull (with or without his zodiacal sign, the taurine or *nandipada*), the tree, the wheel and the stūpa,[1] inasmuch as the last three relate specifically to the three last Great Miracles, it results that the two others can only correspond simultaneously to the first. A second fact comes to the support of this conjecture : a very elaborate Gandhāra sculpture in the Lahore Museum (*Anc. Mon. India*, Pl. 127) does in fact set the Bull between the Sun and the Moon to make him preside at the "Great Departure" of the Bodhisattva ; and we know besides that this latter event took place on the anniversary of the Conception—that is, in spring, during the month of Vaiśākha (April-May), which actually falls in the sign of the Bull. But these, to be sure, are but vague and indirect indications—such only as carved monuments can give in default of texts.[2] For the moment we will merely say that, in all probability, the bull, while joining with the elephant, the horse and the lion, to complete a traditional group of four sacred animals, was brought into relation, under his astronomical *avatāra*, with the date of the double birth, corporal and spiritual, of the future Buddha.

The Enlightenment

But when we turn from the Kapilavastu miracles to the last three Great Miracles, there is at once an end of these perplexities and complications. On the other three holy sites everything is simple from the start. Only one object was offered for the devotion of the faithful, only one claimed the services of the image-makers ; and these images, in turn, have been faithfully transmitted. Of course we must still make allowance, on the one hand, for the inevitable search for purely formal variants, and, on the other, for

[1] *Cf*. D. B. Spooner, 'A New Find of Punch-marked Coins, *A. S. I. Ann. Rep.*, 1905-6, p. 150 *et seqq*.

[2] On this point we come up against silence or contradictions in the texts. The *Lalita-Vistara*, for instance (ed. Lefmann, I, pp. 25, 55 and 217), specifies clearly that the Conception and Great Departure took place the same day of the same month of Vaiśākha, but adds each time "in conjunction with Pushya", which would be astronomically impossible. The Old School could well borrow (see above, p. 92) all "four animals", but it was not so easy to inspire them with a Buddhist meaning.

the irrepressible desire to enrich the picture with significant details; but at least there is never any doubt about the fundamental theme. To seek no further for an example, on the restored panel of Pillar 27 *a* one cannot hesitate to recognize the same subject as on the old Pillars 5 *b* and 66 *c*. The two latter *stambhas*, it is worth noticing, provide perhaps the most archaic representations of the Bodhi-tree which we possess in stone: they are hardly more advanced than those on the old punch-marked coins. In both we find only a picture (at once conventionalized and faithful) of the sacred fig-tree and of the square balustrade which served to enclose all holy places or objects in ancient India. This balustrade, viewed corner-wise and with a downward perspective on 66 *c*, is shown merely in profile on 5 *b*, but, to make up for that, an umbrella of state surmounts the sacred tree, to which two *kinnaras* hovering in the sky are offering worship. Notice, again, that on this latter bas-relief we are shown the throne—purposely brought in front of the railing—on which the Blessed One was supposed to sit at the foot of his *Bodhi-druma*. It is interesting to compare this simple flagstone supported by two little caryatids with the seat which still survives under the sacred fig-tree of Bodh-Gayā.[1]

The First Sermon

A striking characteristic of these old images is, in fact, the anxiety which they evince to give a precise picture of what was actually seen on the site of every Great Miracle in turn. In this they seem to us to remain faithful to the spirit, if not always to the letter, of the old tokens of pilgrimage. The tree on Pillars 5 *b* and 66 *c* is evidently not any chance *ficus religiosa* with its railing and its votive garlands: it is clearly meant for the one which sprang up (and whose off-shoot can still be seen) at Bodh-Gayā. Similarly, the wheel of the "Setting in Motion of the Law" on Pillars 3 *a*, 5 *a*, 44 *b* and 66 *b* is not a mere theoretical *dharma-cakra*; it is the one which stood on the top of the column erected by Aśoka on the site of the "First Sermon" and to which the magnificent capital of lions, recovered at Sārnāth by the excavations of the Archæological Survey (see Pl. 107 *c*), served as pedestal. We do not hesitate to maintain that the detail (neglected on 27 *a*) of umbrellas edging the felly was directly copied from the original. Not only do the old coins reproduce it, but we find it all over our balustrade, even on the lotus-wheel of 13 *b* and on the only fanciful representation which it gives of the *dharma-cakra* (1 *c*). Yet is it altogether fanciful? The proved existence of Aśoka's column by no means precludes that of a stone throne supported by Yakshas, of the same kind as at Bodh-Gayā (*cf.* 5 *b*) and which would have been surmounted by a wheel possibly resting on a *nandipada* (*cf.* Pl. 91 *g* and *h*). Naturally, we do not contend that our old sculptors always aimed at photographic exactitude; to do so would show little understanding of their mania for variety. Thus, for instance, after having shown the authentic capital of lions on Pillars 3 *a* and 44 *b*, they amuse themselves by substituting elephants for them (66 *b*) or even by mixing elephants and lions (5 *a*). We must also take into account their intemperate

[1] *Cf.* A. Cunningham, *Mahabodhi*, Pl. XIII. We must return later (p. 197) to the question of the "temple" round the *Bodhi-druma*.

indulgence in ornamentation; nor shall we go so far as to guarantee the reality of the lotuses curved in the form of pegs, on which they hang garlands at the tops of their columns. On the other hand, there is always room to wonder whether there does not lurk a traditional recollection beneath this exuberant decoration. Thus, the animals set back to back among lotuses, which fill the bases of Pillars 5 *a*, 44 *b* and 66 *b*, are still, wholly or in part, the antelopes which dwelt, so we are told, in the park of the "First Sermon". Once, bulls are joined with them (66 *b*), and another time two lions (5 *a*). With the former the connection seems to us of the loosest; but perhaps a more evident relation may be noted between the lion and the "lion's roar" (*siṁha-nāda*), as the texts deliberately nickname the Master's First Sermon. A fact which would tend to give credit to this, is that we again find lions at the foot of the wheel on 3 *a* and 1 *c*—in the latter, face to face above a crouching deer. We must beware, however, of trying to press matters too far; for a pattern of animals back to back—lions or antelopes—is found more or less mechanically used below the Nativity (*e.g.*, 49 *a*) and even below the Last Decease (44 *c*).[1]

The Great Decease

As may be anticipated, we meet with the same mixture of realism and fantasy in the representations of the last of the four Great Miracles, as in those of the two foregoing ones. The object of the Kuśinagara pilgrimage was naturally the stūpa which marked the place of the Master's death; and in the old Indian School, even at Amarāvatī, the stūpa remains to the end the emblem of the *Parinirvāṇa*. The School of Gandhāra alone, having the figure of the Buddha at its disposal, can take the initiative of showing him lying on his funeral couch. Of course we shall not look to the stūpa shown on the balustrades of Stūpa 2 (44 *c*) or 3 (Pl. 93 *i*) for an exact image of the one which was venerated at Kuśinagara: that would be too naïve on our part, particularly as the two buildings are widely dissimilar. But there is an obvious likelihood that both may resemble those which had already been raised on Sāñchī hill, and those interested in architecture will not fail to notice their characteristic features: in one, the more archaic of the two, a single balustrade on the ground, with another at the top and one umbrella; in the other, a double balustrade at the base, and, at the summit, a merlon-capped pinnacle which already tends to transform the upper balustrade into a regular *harmikā* (*cf.* below p. 199).

With the *Parinirvāṇa* our old sculptors' stock of legends comes to an end. And there, too, our study should stop, but that it remains for us to justify the assertion put forward above that the four Great Miracles form a connected whole, and really constitute the Buddhist nucleus of the entire decoration. Particularly significant from this point of view is the way they are distributed over the balustrade. It is in the place of honour, near each of the four entrances, that we regularly find them grouped. At the eastern gate the restoration of Pillars 22 *a* and 27 has done nothing to alter the rule: as at the western and northern gates, we see the Nativity, the Enlightenment and the First

[1] As regards these pairs of animals, however, see pp. 143-4 *supra*.

Sermon brought close together. At the southern gate the Sambodhi does not appear; but in accordance with an old Indian superstition, which regarded the South as the quarter dedicated to the Manes, it is replaced by the Last Decease, which is, indeed, not to be found elsewhere. We thus arrive at the following table :—

	E. Entrance	W. Entrance	N. Entrance	S. Entrance
Jāti	22 *a* & 26 *b*	71 *a*	1 *b*	49 *a*
Sambodhi	27 *a*	66 *c*	5 *b*	49 *a*
Dharmacakrapravartana	27 *a*	66 *b*	1 *c* & 5 *a*	44 *b*
Parinirvāṇa	27 *a*	66 *b*	1 *b* & 5 *a*	44 *c*

It is scarcely necessary to point out what a degree of certainty this regular association[1] lends our identifications. They corroborate one another and end by forming a coherent whole which defies scepticism. Additional certitude will be given by the examination of the four big gateways of Stūpa 1, where we shall again find the same group of subjects, only at a much more advanced stage of plastic development.

[1] To understand the grouping, please refer to the plan on Pl. 71, where the pillars of the balustrade are numbered.

CHAPTER XV

INTERPRETATION OF THE GATEWAY SCULPTURES

THE *toraṇas*—that is, the four triumphal arches erected at the four entrances of Stūpa 1—are covered with a profusion of sculptures which contrast with the bareness of its old ground balustrade. By adding to them the one of smaller dimensions which stands at the south of Stūpa 3, we are again confronted (*cf.* above, p. 170) with an 'ensemble' altogether unique in India, and constituting a solid basis for the continuation of our iconographical study. And let us observe, once for all, that in the numerous reliefs decorating these gates we shall find our artists more than ever at grips with the problem of showing the biography of the Buddha without portraying the Buddha himself. We know that the School of Central India continued to wrestle with this difficulty without ever managing to overcome it entirely. A downright "coup d'état" was needed for that, and the historical facts now known give us reason to think that this was brought about only in North-Western India, apparently under foreign influence. The question is still disputed whether this artistic revolution took place, as we believe, at Pushkalāvatī (Peukelaotis) or, as others are inclined to think, at Mathurā. The one thing certain is that the sculptors of the Sāñchī gateways, like those of the balustrades at Bharhut or Bodh-Gayā, never attempted it. Assuredly they are fully conscious—the insistent demands of their donors would not have allowed them to ignore the fact—that they are expected to decorate the surroundings of a Buddhist monument with scenes taken from the life (or rather the lives) of the Blessed Śākya-muni. Moreover, the considerable development in the size and richness of the religious buildings sets them a task of which their predecessors, who were hardly required to do more than furnish mementoes for pilgrims, had not the slightest idea; and they realised most fully that the old methods which they had inherited from them, hitherto perfectly suited to their purpose, no longer met the requirements of the new generations. Nevertheless the fact remains that long habit, added to their natural servility towards hallowed models, always prevented them from breaking openly with traditional usage and showing the Buddha otherwise than symbolically.

Continued absence of the Buddha figure

From this well-established fact it immediately follows that their works appear as a kind of compromise between two opposed tendencies: on one side, the need to comply with the growing exigencies of popular devotion, and, on the other, a superstitious respect for the artistic methods then prevailing. Zealous men and women continued to clamour

The art of the gateways a compromise between established precedent and

growing demands of the Church

for more and more numerous, more and more explicit, presentments of the miracles of their Master. And doubtless the craftsmen would have asked nothing better, had not the insurmountable barrier of 'precedent' prevented them from giving full satisfaction to this pious desire. In this conflict between two contrary forces, neither of which gained the upper hand, Buddhist art naturally continued to follow the intermediate direction which we seemed to discern already in the preceding chapter. We witness a slow transformation and gradual enrichment of the themes which the balustrade of Stūpa 2 has already disclosed. Just as before, the symbols of the Great Miracles go on growing more and more complicated with new details, increasingly precise and topical; other representations, conceived along the same lines, of events equally miraculous but less important, soon make their appearance; and finally, to succeed in adorning all the panels placed at their disposal, the sculptors search either in the former lives of the Blessed One or in the scenes following his death, or even in current popular beliefs, for subjects in which they feel more at ease, and freer from the restraints of the past. Inversely, all the old decorative materials, both floral and animal, which the sect had not from the outset appropriated to their particular ends, come to hold a less and less important, more and more accessory position. At the conclusion of this development, Buddhist art in Central India has created a repertory at once original and varied, and fairly well fulfilling the requirements of the moment. But of essential innovations we find no trace on the monuments.

Plan to be followed in describing the Gateway Sculptures

The conception which we have just formed of the evolution of the School determines the principal divisions of the present and following chapters. On the one hand, we shall have, as before, to proceed to a general inventory of all the subjects represented (Secs. I—VIII). This enumeration will relate to all five *toraṇas* at once, without distinction. But, as we shall take care to number each item, these numbers will afterwards permit us to find without difficulty the place of each subject in the schematic drawings which we shall give of each of the gateways. On the other hand, as these gateways are not exactly contemporary with one another, and as their relative order has already been determined, it may be of interest to study the decoration of each of them separately (Sec. IX); after which it will only remain to sum up the iconographical or chronological information which this two-fold examination has allowed us to gather. All this can, however, be done fairly briefly: for, apart from the fact that we refer for details to the particular description accompanying most of the plates, the reliefs on the *toraṇas* have already formed the subject of numerous studies, the result of which has been summed up by Sir John Marshall in his *Guide to Sāñchī*.

Our first care must be to introduce some order and clarity into a decorative whole which at first sight, as one glances through the plates, gives an impression as much of confusion as of profusion. As always happens in Buddhist iconography, the multiplicity and variety of themes is more apparent than real, and a careful review will quickly bring the principal categories of these manifold reliefs under five or six heads at most. First of all, our attention will be drawn to the group of the Four Great Miracles—for which the precedent of the balustrade of Stūpa 2 has already prepared us. To this fundamental tetrad will be added—for the first time at Sāñchī—about ten other famous but secondary miracles belonging both to the youth and to the teaching career of the Buddha Śākya-muni. The very elaborate representation of no less than five *jātakas* or 'former births marks a new departure, at least locally. But the most curious and original extension made in this repertoire is the introduction of some scenes posterior to the *Parinirvāṇa* of the Blessed One and, consequently, borrowed not from his own biography but from the history of his Church. Moreover, we shall have to discuss a number of devotional pictures, some showing (still symbolically) the six predecessors and the future successor of Śākya-muni, and others conveying to the eyes of the faithful the popular beliefs concerning the paradises (but, not yet, by the way, those concerning the hells). As for the decorative themes, plants, animals or human figures, of which we drew up a long list in the preceding chapter and which formed the principal stock-in-trade of the carvers of the Stūpa 2 balustrade, we have already said that they play a much diminished part on the *toraṇas*; moreover, we do not feel by any means sure of their strictly ornamental character, except in the case where they are symmetrically repeated. For the time being, therefore, we must postpone a study of them till after the other sculptures—infinitely more important and numerous—which have a definite religious significance, have been exhaustively examined.

I. The Four Great Miracles

In the forefront of these are the representations of the four Great Miracles. By a natural chain of sequence we shall take them up again one by one at the point where we left them at the end of Chapter XIV; but first we must insist on the dominant rôle which they play in the decoration of the five Gateways. The fact had already struck J. Fergusson and he worked out statistics according to which what he called 'the worship of the tree recurred 76 times, that of the wheel 10 times, and that of the stūpa 38 times.[1] His figures still hold good, though in the course of the last half century and more his interpretations have been superseded. Our special point of view, however, requires us to subtract from these totals no less than 37 trees and 19 stūpas, which, like the others, represent *Sambodhis* and *Parinirvāṇas*, but not of Śākya-muni. This will have the effect of rectifying what at first sight appears a surprising disproportion between the figures of the second and fourth Great Miracles in comparison with the third. And this is not all; among the trees which serve to recall our Buddha, it is advisable to eliminate, first, those which are not properly speaking the *aśvattha* or *ficus religiosa* of his Enlightenment; then, among the *aśvatthas* themselves, those which (as on Pls. 18 *b* and 40, 3) do not specify

Dominant role of the four Great Miracles

[1] J. Fergusson, *Tree and Serpent Worship*, 2nd ed. (1873), pp. 105 and 242.

the precise moment of this Enlightenment;[1] and lastly, among the funeral tumuli which are supposed to cover the relics of the last Master of our æon, they happen at least twice (Pls. 11, 2 and 46, 3) to be expressly distinguished from the one at Kuśinagara.[2] After making all these deductions we finally obtain the following table, which we have completed by the addition in the left-hand column of the first Great Miracle :—

	1 Miracle of Kapilavastu : (Lotus of the *Jāti*)	2 Miracle of Uruvilvā : (Tree of the *Sambodhi*)	3 Miracle of Mṛigadāva : (Wheel of the *Dharmacakra-pravartana*)	4 Miracle of Kuśinagara (Tumulus of the *Parinirvāṇa*)
Stūpa 1, Southern Gateway	3	2 (out of 16)	1	1 (out of 5)
„ „ Northern „	5	3 (out of 19)	2	4 (out of 8)
„ „ Eastern „	4	2 (out of 17)	1	3 (out of 9)
„ „ Western „	1	4 (out of 16)*	2	5 (out of 10)
„ 3, Small „	2	2 (out of 8)*	4	2 (out of 5)*
	15	13 (out of 76)	10	15 (out of 37)*

On the whole,[3] the four Great Miracles of Śākya-muni remain by far the most frequent subjects; for the most favoured after them occur only twice at most on the whole group of five Gateways. They are also the only ones which are invariably figured together on every one of the *toraṇas* without exception. These are precise facts, easily verifiable from the plates, and not to be ignored. Moreover, in exhibiting so many of these votive pictures, the monuments simply reflect the social importance, already vouched for by the texts, of the four great pilgrimages. Thus, we catch a simultaneous glimpse of the two aspects of the same religious phenomenon, one artistic and the other social, and their signal agreement successfully proves that we need have no fear of exaggerating the part it plays either in the worship or in the art of primitive Buddhism.

[1] Here, so far as it concerns the meaning of the symbol "tree surmounting an empty throne", is the exact statement of what we see on each of the five Gateways :—

	Aśvattha of 2nd Great Miracle.	*Aśvattha not marking the precise moment of the Sambodhi*	*Other trees suggesting Śākya-muni*	*Bodhi-trees of other Buddhas*	*Total*
S. Gateway	2	7	..	7	16
N. „	3	..	8	8	19
E. „	2	1	5	9	17
W. „	4	1	4	7	16
Small „	2	..	..	6	8
	13	9	17	37	76

[2] The result of the same statement for the stūpa is as follows

	Stūpa of 4th Gt. Miracle	*Other stūpas of Śākya-muni*	*Stūpas of other Buddhas*	*Non-Buddhist stūpa*	*Total*
S. Gateway	1	1	3	..	5
N. „	4	..	4	..	8
E. „	3	1	4	1	9
W. „	3	..	5	..	8
Small „	2	..	3	..	5
	13	2	19	1	35

[3] Those interested in our statistics, will kindly notice: first, that, like J. Fergusson, we have not felt obliged to take into consideration the symbols ("tree" or "wheel") carved on the uprights which decorate the intervals of the lintels, but are only partially preserved, and only on the Northern and Eastern Gateways; secondly, that 2 of the *Parinirvāṇas* on the Western Gateway, being carved on the back of the pillars, do not appear on our plates; thirdly, that nevertheless those of our figures marked with an asterisk do not correspond, within one or two units, with those of Fergusson. For the Western Gateway (16 trees instead of 15) we are hard put to explain this difference; as for the Small Gateway (8 trees instead of 9 and 5 stūpas instead of 6), the probable reason is that this has lost one of its dies in the meantime. This die is in the Leitner Collection in the Ethnographical Museum in Berlin (*cf.* Grünwedel-Waldschmidt, *Buddhistische Kunst in Indien*, p 119).

1. We must likewise note that the portrayal of the *Jāti* (or at least the composition which we have come to identify as such) has taken decided precedence of the other miracles of Kapilavastu (*cf.* p. 202). The scenes of the Conception and Great Departure (Nos. 6 *a* and *d*) are obviously abandoned for the one which—with an essential element added, the showing of the new-born—was finally to supply later schools with the classical and universal model of the first of the four Great Miracles.[1] We have already pointed out (pp. 184-5) that we find among the reliefs on the old balustrade of Stūpa 2 curious anticipations of the development which the picture of the *Jāti* ought to have shown only on the gateways—supposing that the old sculptors had cared to comply with our mania for arranging all manifestations of art, like those of life, in chronological order. But just as a number of trees bear buds and flowers at once, the monuments often present the rudimentary and the developed forms of the same theme side by side. In fact, on the *toraṇas*, though the simple decorative rosace is not absent (*cf.* Pls. 23 *b* and 50 *b*), one may say that the portrayal of the Nativity opens at the third of the six stages which we distinguished above and scarcely gets beyond the sixth of them. The most archaic type of the "bunch of lotuses issuing from a vase" is found on the Southern Gateway (Pl. 16); and it is this, too, which supplies the intermediate link which we have so far lacked, in showing Māyā seated alone, without her usual attendant elephants, on the middle lotus (Pl. 13); but at the same time, it gives us (Pl. 11) a model developed almost as far as the one on the Western Gateway (Pl. 56). Let us repeat : in this last composition the upright posture of Māyā, the two Nāga elephants which seem to be sprinkling her but which are really bathing her invisible offspring, and the umbrella surmounting the whole, are so many precise details in strict conformity with the texts ; but to give the last touch —and, pending any proof of the contrary, this step will remain the original contribution of the School of Gandhāra—we must be shown the divine babe springing from his mother's right hip.

The Nativity

2. The portrayal of the *Sambodhi*[2] likewise presents itself under forms which a long lapse of time should separate It is true that we no longer find the most archaic model of all—that on the stamped coins and the oldest *stambhas* (*cf.* p. 189)—in which the miraculous tree is still surrounded by its balustrade : this has been finally removed in order to let us see the "diamond throne" (*vajra-āsana*). Yet the simple fact of placing a stone bench at the foot of a "religious fig-tree" is always regarded as a sufficiently explicit way of showing the Perfect Enlightenment of Śākya-muni. Thus, at least, it appears to be on the front (or what should be the front, *cf.* p. 233) of each of the gateways. But we must suppose that the tree of the Great Miracle at Uruvilvā (or, if we prefer it, at Bodh-Gayā) early became associated with the memory of the first royal visit which it received—Aśoka's visit (*cf.* No. 11). This would explain how the custom was so soon introduced of surrounding it, rightly or wrongly, with the curious architectural setting

The Enlightenment

[1] See Pls. 11, 13, 16, 24, 25, 30, 32, 41, 44, 47-8, 56, 98, 102.

[2] See especially Pls. 15, 19*d*, 26, 29, 31, 51*a*, 55, 61, 65, 100, 103.

with which the Emperor's devotion, or at any rate that of votaries almost contemporary with the Emperor, had endowed it; for the agreement between the evidence at Bharhut[1] and Sāñchī (*cf.* Pls. 18 *b*, 40, 51 *a*, 61) is too significant to leave us in any doubt as to the erection of this kind of high encircling gallery, later replaced by the railing and temple now in existence. We must add, however, that this mode of representation was abandoned almost as soon as it was introduced, and the remains of the right jamb of the Southern Gateway (Pl. 19 *c*, *d*) bear witness in a whole series of episodes (*cf.* Nos. 8 and 9) to an iconographical development of much more interest for the future. Finally, the composition destined to remain classic makes its appearance on the Western Gateway (Pls. 61 and 65 *b*); for we know that all the later schools agreed to make the Master's Enlightenment coincide with the incident immediately preceding it, namely his victory over the army of Māra the Tempter. Nobody will be much surprised to find that on Pl. 61, 3 the Bodhi tree already, two centuries too early, has the stone-built enclosure—in fact a sort of roofless temple—which we mentioned just now. Our European "primitives" in their religious pictures have sufficiently accustomed us to anachronisms of even more glaring improbability.

The First Sermon

3. Leaving aside provisionally the numerous trees denoting either the "enlightenments" of Buddhas other than Śākya-muni, or other episodes in his life, we will pass on to the third of his Great Miracles, the miracle of setting the "Wheel of the Law" in motion for the first time, in the Mṛigadāva or Deer Park to the north of Benares.[2] As we have already seen (p. 195), the comparatively small number of "wheels" on our monuments is explained by the fact that this emblem serves only to represent the preaching of our own Buddha, and on the *toraṇas* at Sāñchī his "First Sermon" only.[3] Just as on the balustrade of Stūpa 2 (*cf.* p. 189), the *dharma-cakra* surmounts sometimes a simple throne and sometimes a column; the first arrangement naturally fits better with the decoration of the dies (*cf.* Pl. 26, etc.; once it even covers a whole lintel) and the second with that of the pillars (*cf.* Pls. 18 and 103); but in either case the meaning is exactly the same. It is frequently emphasised by the presence of the deer, apparently tame, which haunted the site of the third Great Miracle; but it must be acknowledged that the laymen who are shown in the act of paying the wheel such devout homage, are by no means in keeping with the particulars which we read in the texts. In their place one would expect, as in Gandhāra, the *pañcavargīyas*, the group of the first five monks. But the old school of Bharhut and Sāñchī never, to our knowledge, showed a *bhikshu* any more than they showed the Buddha himself; and the two facts are evidently not without close connection. It may well be that the thrice-repeated symbol on the throne on Pl. 18 *b* is already meant to suggest the "three jewels" of Buddhism: but the portrayal of the *Saṅgha* or Community, like that of the Master and of his Law, always remained purely allegorical.

---

[1] Cunningham, Pls. 13 and 31.

[2] See Pls. 18, 26, 27, 42, 55, 63, 97, 103

[3] At Bharhut it is used again to depict the sermon which accompanied the "Great Prodigy at Śrāvastī" (*cf.* No. 15

The Last Decease

4. The very numerous stūpas[1] which serve to represent both the fourth Great Miracle of Śākya-muni and the *Parinirvāṇa* of his six predecessors show no very marked architectural advance on those on the balustrade of Stūpa 2 (*cf.* p. 190), except that now they all have a well-drawn *harmikā* or pinnacle. The greater number possess only one ground balustrade. Yet on the lintels of the Southern and Eastern Gateways (Pls. 11 and 15; Pl. 46), five of them—like Stūpa 1 itself since its recent restoration (*cf.* Pl. 6)—already have a second balustrade bordering the terrace. The pinnacle is commonly lined with merlons and surmounted by one or more umbrellas. The dome is decorated with wavy garlands hanging on a series of pegs sunk in the stonework. The slightly curved form of these hooks—perhaps originally made of ivory—has caused them to retain in the language the name of *nāga-danta*, "elephant tusk". Finally, the stūpa shown on one of the jambs of the Northern Gateway (Pl. 36 *c*, 1) is the only one which presents quite an original and lively appearance, with its triple balustrade and approach beneath a double-lintelled *toraṇa*; and the crowd of worshippers seething round it are doubtless the Mallas of Kuśinagara in the act of performing the posthumous worship of the Master (*cf.* p. 213). But it is a far cry from this statement to the conclusion that we have here a faithful picture of the mausoleum which the Mallas actually raised close to their town over their share of the Buddha's relics; and it behoves us still less to embark on hypotheses of this kind since the stūpa, like the tree, was used automatically to symbolise other Buddhas as well as Śākya-muni. These last representations are so frequent, indeed, in their uniformity, that we are obliged to give them a place apart, immediately after the four Great Miracles, with which, from an iconographical point of view, they are so closely connected.

The other Buddhas

5. It is known that the lives of past Buddhas as well as those of future ones were conceived by the Buddhists as having developed along exactly the same lines and passed through the same essential incidents. It is therefore the rule that each of them in turn must have a tree ready to shelter him at the moment of his *Sambodhi*, and one or more tumuli raised above his relics on the morrow of his *Parinirvāṇa*. Thus, if the two emblems, the tree and stūpa, have sufficed to suggest the Buddha of our own age, they can without effort fulfil the same duty for his predecessors and successor. As a matter of fact, the tree will perform this office in a much more able manner than the stūpa, for it lends itself to various representations according to the species to which it belongs, whilst the funeral monument will hardly admit of such differentiation. Each, nevertheless, will play its part. All that it is important to bring out is the natural transition which led the old sculptors, in quest of subjects suitable to sculpture, to apply the same processes to the portrayal of the legendary Buddhas as to that of the historical Buddha. At the same time this explains the surprising abundance of the tree and tumulus symbols on our *toraṇas*.

[1] See specially Pls. 12, 32, 33, 36, 43, 47, 48, 62, 63, 101, 103.

Fortunately for iconography, poetic extravagances are by the very conditions of their art forbidden to the sculptors. So our old artists have confined themselves to introducing in this way, besides Śākya-muni himself, his six nearest predecessors, with or without his successor elect. This fixed and limited number of characters is a sure gauge for our identifications. On two occasions, on the Northern and Eastern Gateways (Pls. 21 and 45) we find the seven trees of the seven Buddhas of our æon set side by side on the same lintel ; but more often, for the sake of variety, trees and tumuli occur alternately.[1] On the other hand, when a lintel shows less than seven symbols—as, for instance, in the case of the Small Gateway (Pls. 95 and 99)—we must necessarily complete the prescribed number by pressing into service those which we shall not fail to find in their immediate neighbourhood. Now, to which particular Buddha each of the stūpas refers, can only be surmised from its position in the series. But so far as trees are concerned, we can, with the help of the texts and the inscriptions at Bharhut, arrive at a more precise result. The fact is that every one of the seven past Buddhas and Maitreya himself are supposed to have a *bodhi-druma* of a particular species, strictly determined, of which the following is the list with the corresponding equivalents :

1. Vipaśyin	(*Pāli* Vipassin)	. .	*Pāṭali* (*bignonia suaveolens*).
2. Śikhin	(,, Sikhin)	. .	*Puṇḍarīka*.[2]
3. Viśvabhū	(,, Vessabhū)	. .	*Śāla* (*Shorea robusta*).
4. Krakucchanda	(,, Kakusandha)	. .	*Śirīsa* (*Acacia sirissa*).
5. Kanakamuni	(,, Koṇāgamana)	. .	*Udumbara* (*ficus glomerata*).
6. Kaśyapa	(,, Kassapa)	. .	*Nyagrodha* (*ficus indica*).
7. Gautama	(,, Gotama)	. .	*Aśvattha* (*ficus religiosa*).
8. Maitreya	(,, Metteya)	. .	*Nāgapushpa* (*Michelia champaka*).

Nothing further is required in order to distinguish, without any possibility of confusion, each of the 'human Buddhas (*Mānushi-Buddha*) as the group came to be called. We know that all eight are found side by side also on the friezes of the Gandhāra School ; and there, naturally, they all have human shapes, and the Seven Past Buddhas are all exactly alike. As we have already had occasion to remark elsewhere,[3] it may seem paradoxical, but it is true to say that the sculptors of Bharhut and Sāñchī, with their rudimentary means, have realised a much more explicit series, in the sense that it makes it possible to put a name unhesitatingly to each of the invisible members of this honourable company.

II. The Cycle of Kapilavastu

Many themes new to Sāñchī

But it is time, after this iconographical interlude, to resume the enumeration of scenes from the last life of the Buddha which our sculptors have attempted to show,

[1] See Pls. 15, 21, 39, 54.

[2] The identification of this single *bodhi-druma* remains uncertain ; *cf.* the description of Pls. 16, 22 and 46.

[3] *Art G.-b. du Gandhāra*, II, p. 330.

always in the same half-abstract, half-picturesque way. The greater part of these scenes are new to Sāñchī and their introduction marks a considerable advance on the decorative essays of Stūpa 2; but there is scarcely one of them which had not, in the interval that elapsed between the execution of the balustrade of Stūpa 2 and that of the *toraṇas* of Stūpa 1, already been realised either on the balustrade at Bharhut or on that at Bodh-Gayā or on both. In some cases—a striking example will be found in connection with the Jetavana of Śrāvastī (No. 15 *a*)—our artists confined themselves merely to alluding to incidents too well known to be set forth at length; and in no circumstances do they condescend to inscribe their work with any explanatory title. Their colleagues at Bharhut have thus kept the monopoly of these engraved labels, which, contemporary as they are with the reliefs which they serve to identify and probably inscribed by the same hand, remain the unshakable foundation of all Buddhist iconography. It is difficult, therefore, not to believe that they likewise took the initiative, and not to see in this the proof that they were conscious of being, and were in fact, innovators. Inversely, at the time of our *toraṇas*, the great period of invention and creation of themes seems to have come to a close; it is even probable that, if we had not lost two-thirds of the balustrade at Bharhut, there would be hardly a scene at Sāñchī of which we should not have found there the first sketch. At all events, the reliefs on the gateways give us the impression of being the work of men who are utilizing not only methods but even compositions which have already become public property, sometimes spinning them out and sometimes abridging them, according to the space at their disposal.[1]

but not original

This impression is further confirmed by the way in which the subjects are found grouped on the jambs (*cf.* Sec. IX). To be sure, the bond which links together the various scenes is not yet chronological, and we are far from the biographical sequences which the Gandhāra friezes will exhibit, even before we come to those at Borobudur[2]. On the gateways of Sāñchī it is mainly topographical links which associate a number of incidents traditionally relating to the same locality or country. None the less, the fact remains that the decorators of our *toraṇas* deliberately conceive and compose in "cycles"; and, as a consequence, this is the mode of classification which it is convenient to adopt in our treatment of their work. As though by chance, this method, directly suggested by the monuments, reveals the fact that all the scenes at Sāñchī, with one or two exceptions, are staged in one or other of the four great original places of pilgrimage, which we already know—Kapilavastu, Bodh-Gayā, Benares or Kuśinagara—or in one of the four secondary places which were not slow to make a place for themselves in the devotions of the Buddhist worshipper, *viz.*: Rājagṛiha, Śrāvastī, Vaiśālī and Sāṅkāśya. This result will surprise only those who prefer to ignore the relation between art and life

Arrangement of scenes in cycles

[1] Contrast, for example, the schematic compositions on the dies with the spinning-out of the Nativity (Pl. 11), the *Sambodhi* (Pl. 29) or the First Sermon (Pl. 55), etc., on the lintels.

[2] It is perhaps worth while to note in this connection that the question of the chronological order of the scenes placed on the jambs of the Sāñchī gateways has not seemed capable of any solution as a whole. It appears nevertheless that the incidents tend to read from top to bottom (*cf.* p. 209, n. 3 and Pl. 19).

To begin at the beginning, the cycle of Kapilavastu naturally associates the Nativity with the two other rival subjects of the Conception and the Great Departure. We shall find besides at least one allusion to two other incidents connected with these: the "First Meditation", which tells of the future Śākya-muni's awaking to the religious vocation, and the four famous "Drives" which, through the four ominous meetings with an old man, a sick man, a dead man and a monk, revealed to the Bodhisattva the three great sufferings of humanity and the sole means of escaping them. Finally, this unity of place links these scenes of childhood and youth with those which celebrated the Buddha's first return to his native town, a particularly pathetic subject and one which later schools did not fail to take up again. These two distinct groups of episodes we shall place under Nos. 6 and 7.

The Conception

6*a*. The *Garbha-avakrānti* (Pl. 50 *a*) is shown exactly as at Bharhut, and here also the Bodhisattva is descending from the sky in the shape of an elephant into the womb of his sleeping mother, who wrongly presents her left instead of her right hip to him (*cf*. p. 183). But the theme, summarily treated, occupies only the left-hand top corner of a large panel, and, as we have already said, is of incidental value only. Evidently it was already familiar, and, far from requiring a label as it did at Bharhut, it now serves as a notice to announce that the place of the principal scene is Kapilavastu (*cf*. No. 7 *a*).

The First Meditation

6*b*. The case of the following incident is much the same. The "First Meditation" (Pl. 40, 2) is suggested merely by a tree placed, mainly for decorative reasons, in the very middle of the mid-lintel, the whole of which (but for this addition) is taken up by the "Great Departure" (*cf*. No. 6 *d*). The "ploughing" scene which should, as at Bodh-Gayā and, later, in Gandhāra, have identified the subject for certain, is lacking; nor do we see the five *rishis* who were supposed to have been stopped in their aerial flight by the young prince's radiancy[1]; so that, we must admit, the allusion remains rather slight. Yet the species of tree, which is certainly a rose-apple tree (*Eugenia jambu*),[2] the short distance which separates it from Kapilavastu, the balustrade which stresses its sacred character, the umbrella which surmounts it and as usual indicates the invisible presence of the Bodhisattva, all combine to render the hypothesis exceedingly probable. In a manner as natural as it is ingenious, the artist might, after all, have combined in the same picture the opening (summarily indicated) and the denouement (treated in great detail) of the Master's religious vocation.

The Four Drives

6*c*. Between these two episodes the texts never forget, but the ancient monuments always omit to insert, that of the "Four Drives".[3] A relief on the Northern *toraṇa* (Pl. 35 *a*, 1) gives us reason to think that it was not altogether absent from the minds of

[1] On these points see *Art G.-b. du Gandhāra*, pp. 340 *sqq*. and figs. 175-7.

[2] To convince oneself of this, one has only to compare it with the tree depicted and named by an inscription in one of the reliefs at Bharhut (Cunningham, Pl. XLVIII, 11): the appearance of trunk and foliage are exactly the same in both.

[3] *Cf*. the remarks on this point in *Art G.-b. du Gandhāra*, I, p. 348; but note that we have since verified the existence of these scenes in a frieze on the façade of Cave I at Ajaṇṭā.

our sculptors. Coming out of the gate of a town which the "context" of the jamb identifies as Kapilavastu, we see in fact a chariot in which the owner's seat remains empty; it is occupied only by the servant entrusted with the umbrella which announces the invisible presence of the Bodhisattva. That this chariot is intended to stand for all the Four Drives, we shall immediately find proved by the fact that it is preceded by the riderless horse of the "Great Departure"; for it is impossible not to recognize the latter as the faithful charger Kaṇṭhaka, accompanied as usual by the no less faithful groom Chandaka, bearing the ewer. We should seem, therefore, to have again—as recently in No. 6 *b* and hereafter in 7 *a*—a sort of blending of two subjects, the conjunction of which serves for their mutual elucidation. For at the sight of the *Abhinishkramaṇa* horse, how can one help guessing that the chariot behind it belongs also to Prince Siddhārtha? And on what occasion would the Prince be going out of his native town in a chariot, under the admiring gaze of his father and the women of the court, not to mention the people in the street, if not for the four famous drives which instigated his resolve to undertake the Great Departure? To read this riddle in stone only a little good will is required, since the sole solution possible is immediately prompted both by the common tradition of the Scriptures and the particular conventions of the workshop. And as we are dealing with the surroundings of one and the same building, the existence of this relief on the Northern Gateway brings further support to a hypothesis on which we ventured long ago,[1] at a time when we were as yet reduced to examining the Eastern Gateway by itself; perhaps the fourfold repetition of the *Abhinishkramaṇa* horse and suite on Pl. 40, 2, on which we shall shortly have to comment, is meant as much to remind us of the "Four Drives" as to cover the whole length of the lintel.

The Great Departure from the House

6*d*. Of the Bodhisattva's final retirement from the world—or, if you prefer, of his taking the religious vows—we have in any case at least two certain representations. One is still over-simplified and the other very elaborate; but in both of them the horse is riderless. The first (Pl. 16 *a*, 1), however, in addition to the composition on the railing of Stūpa 2 (*cf*. p. 187), shows the gate of the town and two praying divinities, while the groom Chandaka precedes the horse instead of following it, as he does in Pl. 35 *a*, 1. As he continues to hold the ewer in his hand, the umbrella and fly-whisk (the insignia of the Bodhisattva in his character of Crown-Prince) have no alternative but to float miraculously in the air above his mount.[2] On the Eastern Gateway (Pl. 40, 2), in the midst of the great company of *devas* which is present at the nocturnal escape of Siddhārtha, these two emblems—and the four hoofs of his horse into the bargain—have no difficulty in finding hands to carry them; but, to judge from the preceding analogies, it is still the ewer-bearer whom we must identify with Chandaka. Four separate times we see the Bodhisattva's charger passing to the right. The first time, he is still only half

[1] *Conférences au Musée Guimet*, Vol. 34, 1901, p. 224 (or *Beginnings of Buddhist Art*, etc., p. 107).
[2] For the scene represented on the other end of the same lintel, *cf*. description of Pl. 17.

way through the gate of Kapilavastu, a detailed picture of which (a downward view, taken from outside, behind its walls and moats) occupies the left of the lintel. The last time, he has stopped, and together with the groom is taking leave of his Master, shown by a huge pair of foot-prints shaded by the fly-whisk and umbrella.[1] Below, the two inseparables, man and beast, are gloomily returning to the town. Chandaka is bearing the royal trappings which the young prince has just laid aside for ever, and is apparently followed by the emissaries whom King Śuddhodana had vainly sent in pursuit of his son. The explicit details of this story in stone are here enough to prove the identification. As for the fact that, reading the panel from left to right, the night which had favoured the prince's flight has given place to day, this must disturb us no more than it disturbed the sculptor himself. Finally, as concerns the central tree on the lintel, we have already given our explanation of its symbolical value (*cf.* No. 6 *b*).

The Return to Kapilavastu

7a. We have not yet done with the native town of our Śākya-muni. Though he forsook it as prince and heir, every one knows that he returned some seven years later as the "perfectly accomplished Buddha"; and this is the occasion on which we see it again on the right jamb of the same Eastern Gateway (Pl. 50 *a*, 1). For any and every city our artists always held in readiness a design no less stereotyped than the descriptive cliché of the texts.[2] That this is again Kapilavastu, we have no indication except the *lakshaṇa* inserted in the left-hand top corner of the scene; but we could have no surer guarantee, since no one is ignorant of the name of the town of the Conception (*cf.* No. 6 *a*). That, moreover, it is far from superfluous to be informed of the place where we are, we shall quickly perceive; for all the rest of the identification proceeds from that. Since the town is Kapilavastu, it follows that those citizens leaning their inquisitive heads over the balconies of the loggias are Śākyas; and the king who is coming out in great pomp in his chariot, preceded by his band and followed by a long suite of foot-soldiers, horsemen and mounted elephants, can be none other than Śuddhodana, the Buddha's father. Hence the long narrow flagstone suspended in the air at the height of the trees, which he and his courtiers, hands clasped and heads raised, are contemplating with so much veneration, is the *ratna-caṅkrama* or "path of precious stone" which the Blessed One created for himself by means of his magic power on his first return to his native town. His reasons for this act were not, moreover, what you might think, and it was not simply to establish his new dignity—no man being a prophet in his own country—by striking the imagination of his compatriots by a great marvel. It was, we are assured, a knotty question of etiquette which constrained him to a kind of exhibition which he disliked and which he forbade to his monks: of the father who was still king and the son who had become Buddha, which should salute the other first? A miracle solved the difficulty, and "for the third time" Śuddhodana prostrated himself before his son.

[1] One may compare the sacred feet depicted at the bottom of the eastern pillar, eastern face, of the Northern Gateway (Pl. 37 *a*): they bear the mark of the wheel, and this mark only.

[2] On the other hand, this picturesque design tells us infinitely more of Indian life than the allegorical figure wearing a turreted crown, which the school of Gandhāra substitutes for it.

The Gift of the Nyagrodha-ārāma

7*b*. He did not confine himself to such demonstrations of respect; of that, the *nyagrodha* (*ficus indica* or banyan fig-tree) surrounded by its balustrade, which is discreetly indicated in the left-hand bottom corner of the same picture, gives us an inkling. The fact was, the religious rule forbade the new Buddha to live in one of his former palaces, or even inside the town. So his father took care to offer him as residence one of his pleasure parks, planted with Indian fig-trees, close to the gates of his capital. This gift, only suggested in Pl. 50 *a*, 1, is shown more explicitly on the western pillar of the Northern Gateway (Pl. 36 *c*, 3). There, a relief next to the one we have already examined (No. 6 *c*) and to the one with which we are going to deal (No. 7 *c*), combines both scenes 7 *a* and 7 *b* in an abridged form. We see, in fact, the aerial path and the throne under the banyan fig-tree at one and the same time: the Buddha is supposed to have already descended from the former to sit down on the latter. This time Śuddhodana's retinue, much reduced as it is, includes the women of the court. Indeed, it requires no great stretch of imagination to take the two queens who precede the king for the adopted mother of the Buddha, Mahāprajāpatī, and his wife Yaśodharā; but for the present it will be more prudent to urge nothing without proof.[1]

The Conversion of the Sākyas

7*c*. This is not all; for, as we have said, the themes go in sets. As a matter of fact, it was not within the power of the Sāñchī artists to portray the other celebrated episodes so often since depicted in Gandhāra as well as at Amarāvatī and Ajaṇṭā—the meeting of the Buddha with his former wife, the abduction and sudden ordination of his son Rāhula or of his handsome cousin Nanda, etc... But the *lakshaṇa* of the banyan fig-tree allowed them more or less to depict in their own way the Master preaching his doctrine to his family and fellow-citizens in the *Nyagrodha-ārāma*. A pious assembly seated around an empty throne under a *ficus indica* will be enough to represent this scene; and this is what our sculptors have not failed to show us alike on the Northern (Pl. 35 *a*, 2) and on the Western Gateway (Pl. 65 *b*, 2). We may note here, besides, that the processional pomp of the royal visits and the calm serenity of the preaching scenes remain to the end subjects for which they have a special predilection.

III. The Bodh-Gayā Cycle

A second cycle, no less luxuriant than the foregoing, is wholly enacted in the neighbourhood of the town of Gayā, not far from the present village of Urel (the old Uruvilvā). The principal feature will naturally be the famous Bodhi fig-tree, an off-shoot of which still stands in the same place, and the central miracle remains the Perfect Enlightenment of Śākya-muni, which we have already discussed (*cf.* No. 2). But round this main event, a number of miraculous incidents preceding (No. 8) or following it

[1] The temptation is great—and we at first gave way to it—to take two other scenes, one on the Eastern Gateway (Pl. 49 *c*) immediately above 7 *a*, and the other on the Northern Gateway (Pl. 64 *a*, 2) in the neighbourhood of 7 *c*, for two variants of the "Gift of the *Nyagrodha-ārāma*"; but see below, No. 9 *f*.

(Nos. 9-11) continued to figure in the guide-book of local religious attractions (in Skt. *māhātmya*) and to be exploited by the syndicate for the reception of pilgrims. We have already had occasion to remark (p. 198) how open allusions to these legendary episodes have sometimes slipped into the representations of the *Sambodhi*.

The Six Years' Penance

8*a*. Such is particularly the case with one of the reliefs on the Western Gateway (Pl. 65 *b*, 1), which shows, grouped round an otherwise very simple representation of the tree of the Enlightenment, an unusual variety of persons. Our attention cannot fail to be drawn towards a second throne (evidently distinct from the *vajra-āsana*) which is placed right at the bottom of the panel, not far from the shady banks of the river Nairañjanā and outside the *toraṇa* leading into the sacred precincts of the *Bodhi-maṇḍa*. From left to right, the three *devas* who surround this throne clearly express by their attitudes adoration, commiseration and grief—and these were the very sentiments felt by the gods when they thought that the future Buddha was dying, exhausted by his fasting and emaciation. The perfect propriety of the poses of the onlookers and the localisation of the scene seems to convey a fairly explicit hint of the long and famous episode of the penance which gives its name (*dushkara-caryā*) to the Seventeenth Chapter of the *Lalita-vistara*.

Sujātā's Offering

8*b*. We expect after that to see the commemoration of the famous dish of rice-pudding which was the last food taken by the Blessed One before he attained omniscience. But in fact it is only on the left of the middle lintel of the Northern Gateway that we seem to recognize Sujātā for certain, with a ewer in her lowered right hand and an offertory tray on her raised left hand (Pl. 29, 2); and even then she is arriving rather late by the entrance *toraṇa* of the Bodhi-maṇḍa, when the future Saviour is already supposed to be seated on the throne under the tree of his Enlightenment; but we are not going to pick a quarrel with her for that. Perhaps it is she again who is figured on Pl. 19 *d*, 4, with her ewer in her hand. Is she accompanied by an attendant exactly like her, or is she portrayed twice over, before and after her alms-giving? The latter supposition is made probable by the fact that the symmetrical repetition of the same figure is a current practice of the School, and that a neighbouring panel (Pl. 19 *d*, 3) affords an indisputable example. So we shall not be surprised if we see her twice on the relief in question,[1] side by side with the double portrayal of the "Grass Cutter", whose offering makes a pair with hers and follows it immediately in time. As for the numerous women bearing ewers, who appear on the little pictures of *Sambodhi*, we are inclined to take them for a stereotype inspired by "Sujātā's Offering", but one whose legendary significance has, so to speak, evaporated.

The Grass Cutter's Offering

8*c*. However that may be, the right jamb of the Southern Gateway gives us already a fairly complete cycle of the Bodhi. As a matter of fact, this unfortunate pillar

[1] After having seen all these reduplications in the pictures, it is hardly surprising that in relatively late texts, like the *Aśoka-avadāna*, the young village girl has been split into two sisters (*Divyāvadāna*, p. 392). Symmetry, thy might is great!

suffered greatly at the collapse of the *toraṇa* and its remains could not be put back into place; but they are now kept in the local museum and have been reassembled (Pl. 19). Their perusal, hasty as it must be, will yet teach us some valuable and precise facts. Thus panel *d*, 3 shows us indisputably, and twice over, the grass-cutter (*yāvasika*) who presented the future Buddha with the bunch of grass which he needed to strew on his seat, as all past Buddhas had done; to the right (of the spectator) he is bending down, busy attending to his sickle; to the left, he is holding the bunch of *kuśa*-grass in his arms and offering it to the invisible Bodhisattva---a humble present, no doubt, like Sujātā's, but considered by tradition as indispensable, and peculiarly meritorious in itself; for in India the merit of a gift is measured by the dignity of the recipient.

Temptation and Assault by Māra

8*d*. Thanks to the humble offerings of the peasant man and woman, Śākya-muni's seat is ready, and his strength has returned to him. But before the final victory, he is still destined to withstand the assaults of Māra---now insidious and now violent. In fact, the temptation, as soon as resisted, was so quickly changed into an attack that the two operations are associated indissolubly in the imagination of the devotees, and are blended both in reliefs and texts. On the Northern (Pl. 29, 2) as on the Western Gateway (Pl. 65 *b*, 1) the spirit of edification---that curse of religious art which crept into Buddhist art and spoilt it like the others---has given Māra and his sons and daughters such a deferential attitude, and made them appear to accept their defeat with such devout resignation, that it is not surprising that such 'pictures of piety' have led to a belief in the subsequent 'conversion' of the Buddhist Satan. But at the same time his formidable army of demons persists in showing itself in one corner of the picture, to support with threats their leader's attempts at corruption. Whether we are dealing with elegant figures or deformed monsters, we are clearly informed by the Scriptures that at the moment of the supreme crisis the Buddha was completely abandoned by gods and men; and so, in these two tableaux which take place inside the *Bodhi-maṇḍa*, we know beforehand that the Master can only be grappling with Māra and his followers. Only on Pl. 61, 3, after the diabolical army has already been routed on the right, do we see on the left the gods advancing to the help of the victor.

Buddha's Walk

9*a*. As we have said above (p. 197) when studying the schematic stereotype of the second Great Miracle (which is reproduced again on Pl. 19 *d*, 1 and *d*, 4), we can watch here some attempts at a more lively, more dramatic representation of the *Sambodhi*. But the texts give no less circumstantial information of the incidents which followed than of those which preceded this ineffable moment; and in this way, too, a purely mystic and psychological crisis, already transformed by writers into a mythological conflict, has ended by being susceptible of portrayal in concrete terms by the sculptors. They are all in agreement that the perfectly accomplished Buddha---like a king newly crowned, who does not leave the place of his coronation for seven days---remained five or seven weeks in the immediate neighbourhood of the *Bodhi-maṇḍa* "to savour the bliss of Deliverance". The third week is generally devoted to a walk, which religious fancy was not slow to extend to the very end of our world and even to prolong over myriads of other worlds; but at the same time the pilgrims were shown, a little to the north of the sacred tree, the *caṅkrama* or "walking-path" running from east to west, where, more prosaically, the new Buddha took his constitutional, and of which traces have been brought to light by modern excavations.[1] To any one who knows the technical language of the School, there cannot be the shadow of a doubt that this is indeed the episode depicted just above the head of the Yaksha, now broken, which, as usual, adorned the bottom of the jamb (Pl. 19 *d*, 5). This long narrow flag-stone, above which waves a wreath and before which stands a line of praying men and women, represents the real walk of Bodh-Gayā, shown in the same way as the magic walk of Kapilavastu (No. 7 *a*). The context of the pillar demands this, and its exigencies do not stop there.

The Nāgarāja Mucilinda and the Goatherd's Fig-tree

9*b*. The Scriptures are likewise in agreement on the point that, of the two other weeks (only their order varies) one was passed by the new Buddha in company with Mucilinda, the king of serpents, and the other in the shade of a *ficus indica*, which a goatherd (since become a *deva*) had formerly planted for this very purpose. These two incidents are evidently combined in the top panel on the other face of the pillar (Pl. 19 *c*, 1): the remains of a broken *nyagrodha* shelter the traditional throne, and in front of the throne a Nāgarāja, spreading his five-headed hood like a fan, is seated amidst the women of his court. The presence of a tree other than the Bodhi saves us from confusing this king of the serpent-genii with the Nāgarāja Kālika who praised the Bodhisattva at the moment when the latter was bending his steps towards the *aśvattha* of Enlightenment.[2] If, moreover, we do not here see Mucilinda doing all that is written—that is, surrounding the body of the Blessed One with his coils, to shelter him from a great storm—only the lack of means at the disposal of the Sāñchī workshop is to blame. That strange fancy will not be realised in sculpture till much later. Here, a suggestion of it is enough; and apparently the two episodes associated together explained each other clearly enough to be reproduced in exactly the same way on the Western Gateway (Pl. 65 *a*, 2); and this time, as far as the mutilation of the jamb allows us to judge, without any context.

The Offering of the Two Merchants

9*c*. With the two bottom reliefs of this face (Pl. 19 *c*) we pass to the incidents which marked the following week. The Blessed One had as yet eaten nothing since the *Sambodhi*, and the first food which he took was given him by two traders, Trapussa and Bhallika, who happened to pass close by. It is they who are arriving from the right at the bottom of panel *c*, 3, seated with their driver in a chariot drawn by splendid oxen and

[1] In view of the novelty of the theme in question, we may here quote *Mahāvastu*, III, p. 281; *Lalita-vistara*, I, p. 377; S. Beal, *Buddhist Records*, etc., I, p. lxxiii and II, p. 122; Cunningham, *Mahābodhi*, Pls. II and V and pp. 8-10. In order not to break the study of Pl. 19, we shall confine ourselves to pointing out here that this episode of the Walk after the Bodhi" (No. 9 *a*) is likewise shown at the top of the left jamb of the Eastern Gateway (Pl. 51 *a*), immediately above the miracle of the *Sambodhi* (No. 2): here the sort of stone bar which certainly represents the *caṅkrama* of the Master, divides the praying figures into two rows.

[2] The confusion is so easy, in fact, that the *Mahāvastu* (III, p. 300) duplicates the invitation of Mucilinda by that of Kāla or Kālika.

covered with an awning made of matting, of a pattern still used in Southern India servant marches ahead, as usual holding a ewer; pedestrians and horsemen escort them, a dog follows the chariot. The action as presented is limited to that. Our artist has not even shown the divinity who was supposed to have warned them of the unique opportunity which was offered them to win exceptional merit. It is enough that the two merchants come into the story at this moment: every one knows well enough what they have come for

Gift of the Four Bowls

9*d*. Further, before their meritorious gesture can be performed, a preliminary condition must be fulfilled. An absolute law, we are told, demands that the accomplished Buddhas accept no nourishment but that placed in their begging bowl; for they are *ipso facto* ordained as monks,[2] and consequently must conform to the monastic rule. But the new Buddha has no begging bowl as yet; and accordingly the four gods who reign over the four points of the compass run to bring him one each. Though the right-hand side is damaged, this is certainly the meaning of the relief wedged in between 9 *b* and 9 *c*.[3] We see there three of the Four Kings of the four regions of the sky (and we can guess at the fourth in the broken part) in the act of handing bowls to the invisible Blessed One. It is, of course, understood that, to avoid offending anybody, he accepts all four, and then reduces them miraculously to a single one. Notice that, in accordance with the texts, the tree which shades the Buddha's throne is no longer the Bodhi fig-tree, but the *Rājāyatana* or *Tārāyaṇa*, which here seems to have been confused with the Goatherd's *nyagrodha*.[4]

The Jewel-house

9*e*. Of the eight reliefs covering what remains of the right jamb of the Southern Gateway, we have thus identified seven, and all seven belong to the Bodhi cycle; it is difficult to imagine that the eighth should be different. But how are we to explain the fact that the throne of the Buddha is placed under a building (Pl. 19 *d*, 2) at a period in the Master's life when, with no roof to shelter his head, he was leading a strictly homeless life as a begging monk? The first hypothesis which occurs to the mind is to identify this building with the very similar one which is likewise in the neighbourhood of the place of the second Great Miracle, namely the "fire-temple" of the Kāśyapas, which we shall consider in a moment (10 *b*). But in that case, other figures would be expected, and, besides, there are no distinguishing details here. So we are forced to wonder whether, after all, this is not the "jewel-house" (*ratna-gṛiha*) built miraculously by the gods, in which the Introduction to the Pāli *Jātaka* says that the Buddha spent his fourth week, resting after the walk which he had just taken on the *ratna-caṅkrama* of No. 9 *a*.[5] Unfortunately, there is no mention of this timely bungalow in the ancient texts,

[1] They may be compared to the chariots shown in the sculptures of Mathurā (*Epigr. Indica*, II, Pls. II and III).

[2] *Cf. Mahāvastu*, I, pp. 2-3, for the four kinds of ordination.

[3] One might discuss endlessly whether the order of reliefs *c*2 and *c*3 on Pl. 19 should be reversed or not. It is in fact the merchants' alms-giving which determines the offering of the bowls by the Four Kings: but the possession of a bowl by the Buddha is the indispensable condition for his acceptance of the alms.

[4] Notice, by the way, that the "Presentation of the four bowls" is found again on Pl. 56, 2, but this time the Buddha Vipaśyin is the recipient—in which there is nothing surprising, since all the Buddhas successively pass through the same adventures

[5] On this "jewel-house", situated close to the Bodhi-tree and the Walk, see *Jātaka*, I p. 78; and *cf.* the passages in Fa Hien and Hiuen Thsang (transl. S. Beal, I, p. LXIII and II, p. 123), and Cunningham, *Mahābodhi*, p. 35.

and we cannot but regret the mutilation of this jamb of the Southern Gateway; were it preserved intact, it would doubtless have thrown light on the contemporary traditions concerning the weeks which immediately followed the *Sambodhi*.

The Adhyeshaṇa

9*f*. It is probable that among the scenes which have been lost, was one to which Buddhist believers rightly attached great importance, since it was supposed to have decided the foundation of their Church. We mean the "Request" which the two great gods Indra and Brahmā with one accord addressed to the Blessed One, that he would consent to preach to the world the Truth which he had just discovered. We know that the fervour of their entreaties overcame the Master's hesitation; and it is sincere fervour which is expressed in the gesture of their clasped hands—a gesture naturally repeated by their suite—on Pls. 49 *c* and 64 *a*, 2. The Buddha himself is again seated under a *nyagrodha* tree, as in the Mucilinda episode (No. 9 *b*) and in the *Nyagrodha-ārāma* of Kapilavastu (No. 7 *c*). This fact teaches us (need we point out?) not to assign a single interpretation to the presence of such and such species of tree on such and such panel. Doubtless this *lakshaṇa* limits the number of possible identifications of the scene; but the same kind of tree grows in more than one spot on earth, and we must take into account, at one time, the nature of the attendants, as in the case of the *Nāga-rāja* of Pl. 19 *c*, 1; at another, their attitudes. It was their passive pose as seated auditors which enabled us to recognize the Sermon to the Śākyas in No. 7 *c*; and it is the earnestness of their gait and their beseeching gesture which here seem to denote the traditional "Request" of the gods.

The Conversion of the Jaṭilas

10. On the left jamb of the Eastern Gateway we shall find another series of reliefs whose subjects are separated from the previous ones by an interval of time, but which likewise form part of the Uruvilvā cycle and may be identified with certainty. We know that after his weeks of relaxation by the tree of Omniscience, the Buddha, having once determined to preach his doctrine, decided first of all to convert—failing his former masters, who were already dead—five of his old fellow-disciples who were then dwelling in the Deer Park north of Benares. The Great Miracle of the First Sermon performed (No. 3) as soon as the end of the rainy season again permitted travelling, he went back to Uruvilvā to win over to his law a whole college of Brahman anchorites, whose superiors were the three Kāśyapa brothers. The monk with the shaven head only succeeded in overcoming the pride of these "wearers of twisted hair-tufts" (*jaṭila*) by dint of a number of miracles, and it is the most important of these miracles which we see represented here for the edification of visitors to Sāñchī.

The Divine Visits

10*a*. The top panel of the inner face (Pl. 52 *a*, 1) shows us Uruvilvā, the scene of so many wonders, and gives us a most charming peep of village life in India, as it was two thousand years ago and still is to-day. Amidst the picturesque bustle of people and animals we can at last pick out—outside and to the left of the village gate, which the sculptor has here made worthy of a big town—the Master's throne, sheltered under an umbrella and framed by two praying figures. The number and attitudes of these attendants remind us of the famous "Request" of Brahmā and Indra (No. 9 *f*); but the landscape and the neighbouring reliefs carry us to the second sojourn which the Blessed One passed at Uruvilvā after his First Sermon, and it is the glorious visits with which the gods constantly honoured him that are suggested here. It must not be objected that these visits, to appear all the more luminous, took place at night: that is a detail which our sculptors had good reasons never to trouble about (*cf*. No. 6 *d*).

Victory over the Serpent

10*b*. The following panel (Pl. 52 *a*, 2) shows in the most circumstantial way the victory which the Buddha won over the wicked serpent which dwelt in the fire-temple of the Kāśyapas. The building bears a strong resemblance to the one we have just seen on the Southern Gateway (Pl. 19 *d*, 2), but this time, as might be expected, it is surrounded by typical Brahman anchorites. Besides, the Nāga rears his polycephalic hood behind the Master's throne, and the flames issuing from the dormer windows are supposed to have been emitted by the dragon, making people believe there was a great fire. In short, all the details best calculated for determining the identification are liberally furnished here: we cannot ask more.

The Wonders of the Wood and the Fire

10*c*. The small bottom panel (Pl. 52 *a*, 3), whilst it manages to lay before our eyes the life and setting of the hermitages, groups together two and even three other manifestations of the Buddha's miraculous power. In turn, as he pleases, the pieces of wood allow themselves to be split or not by the stone axes of the anchorites (right-hand scene); their sacred fires to be lit or not under the wind of their fans (middle scene); and their ritual oblations to be detached or not from the sacrificial ladle (left-hand scene). But this unaccountable alternation of good and ill will on the part of inanimate objects is not yet enough to open the eyes of those wilfully blind.

The Wonder of the Flood

10*d*. The decisive miracle whose importance claimed the honours of the facade, was occasioned by a freak of the local river, the Nairañjanā, now called the Lilañj. As often happens in India, and as may be seen at the top of Pl. 51 *b*, a heavy rain fell out of season and suddenly raised a flood. When the Kāśyapas, anxious about the Master's fate come to his help in a canoe, they perceive that he has created for himself a dry path in the bosom of the raging waters; and this time their inveterate sense of personal superiority is finally shaken. This *caṅkrama* is, of course, represented by an oblong stone, exactly as in Nos. 7 *a* and 9 *a*. As to the throne depicted under a *nyagrodha* in the bottom right-hand corner of the panel, we shall not be far wrong, if we take it for an allusion to the sermon which the Master addressed to his thousand new disciples immediately after their conversion *en masse*. We know that he afterwards led them to the old capital of

Magadha, Rājagṛiha, and in all probability that is the town which we see on the panel just below (Pl. 51 *b*, 2). But we shall return to this point (No. 13 *a*); for the moment, it would take us too far from Uruvilvā, where we still have business.

Aśoka's Visit to the Bodhi-tree

11. Towards the middle of the third century B.C. this small village received a most sensational visit: "doing what none of the past kings, neither Bimbisāra nor the others, had done", Aśoka came in great pomp to pay homage to the tree which had sheltered the Buddha's Enlightenment. A legend, meant to embellish the occasion further, and preserved by the *Divyāvadāna*, has it that, thanks to the jealous witchcraft of the favourite queen, the tree had almost perished, and that the broken-hearted emperor came in the nick of time to restore it to its former splendour by having it watered "with pitchers of perfumed water". An indication that our sculptors had these tales in mind when they were depicting the second of the four Great Miracles, is to be found in the way they surround the Bodhi-tree with a building two centuries later than the *Sambodhi* (*cf.* Pl. 61, 3). As a matter of fact, on the Eastern Gateway (Pl. 51 *a*), as at Bharhut,[1] we find, round the sacred tree, only the usual company of divinities, numerous as they are; but it is not so on the Southern Gateway (Pl. 18 *b*, 2). There we see only a royal personage apparently supported by two of his queens, as if he were about to faint. But if the central figure is really a king, as it has every appearance of being, we must recall that according to Buddhist tradition he can only be Aśoka. Hence we cannot fail to be reminded, by his tottering attitude, either of the immense grief which overcame him when he was told that his beloved tree was perishing—he declared that he would not be able to survive it—or, in another simpler version of the pilgrimage[2], of the emotion which seized him at sight of a spot so sacred, and which expressed itself by a magnificent alms-giving. In unexpected confirmation of this, it is Aśoka again whom we see arriving from the left in his chariot on the adjacent relief, placed on exactly the same level on the jamb (Pl. 18 *a*, 2): and even in the athlete armed with a great club,[3] who marches at the head of the escort, we cannot but recognize one of those body-guards, of prodigious strength, who the legend says were in his service. All this gives support to our hypothesis; and the agreement of these two scenes with one of the lintels of the Eastern Gateway has strengthened our conviction. There, on the right (Pl. 40, 3), we see again the same king accompanied by the same suite (the larger dimensions of the panel have simply increased its size). He is wearily getting off his elephant, supported by his first queen; then both go forward in devout posture towards the same Bodhi-tree surrounded by the same stone-enclosure—which from then on ceases to be an anachronism. From the other side, to the sound of music, people are advancing in procession to the tree; and the figures in the foreground are plainly carrying the pitchers for watering it[4]... We cannot see what more could be demanded of the

[1] Cunningham, Pl. XIV, 1; for the inscriptions *vide* Hultzsch, *Ind. Antiq.*, XXI, p. 231.

[2] On all these points and those which follow, see *Divyāvadāna*, pp. 397-8, 393, 372-3 (trans. in J. Przyluski's *La legende de l'empereur Aśoka*, Paris, 1923).

[3] If, that is, this club is not simply an Indian sword (*cf.* description of Pl. 62).

[4] These pitchers indirectly give a more significant value to the one placed on the ground in the relief on the Southern Gateway (Pl. 18 *b*, 2). *Cf.*, too, the two scenes on Pl. 79, Pillar 27 *b*.

artist, failing an explanatory label. When we add, finally, that this is not the only composition at Sāñchī which may serve to illustrate the text of the *Aśoka-avadāna* (*cf.* No. 12 *c*), it will be admitted that we may consider the proposed identification as practically certain. Notice, moreover, that the contrast in which these exceptional 'historical-pieces' seem to stand to the usual legendary scenes really exists only in our own minds; to the sculptors of Sāñchī, the miracles of their Master were facts no less historical than the imperial tours of Aśoka.

IV. The Benares and Kuśinagara Cycles

Dearth of scenes and reason thereof

Why are the Kapilavastu and Uruvilvā cycles so full, while there is but one scene relating to Benares,[1] and only two relating to Kuśinagara? Two explanations, one general and the other more particular, at once occur to the mind. The fact has long since been brought to light that from earliest times the interest of the faithful seems to have been centred on the childhood and youth of the Buddha at the expense of the monotonous manifestations of his teaching career; and the fact is that this first period of his life lent itself to "romance", as we say, much better than his apostleship. In the second place, we must take into account the poor means at the disposal of the Sāñchī sculptors as well as the special character of the last two Great Miracles. The Miracle of the First Sermon consists essentially in the foundation of the Saṅgha or Community, and, as we have already said, the Old School of Central India never depicts monks. Further, it can be symbolised by a wheel only, as that of the Last Decease by a tumulus only; and neither the *cakra* nor the stūpa are motifs which admit of multifarious variations as the tree does. Thus the direct representations of the *Dharmacakra-pravartana* (No. 3) and the *Parinirvāṇa* (No. 4) are practically sufficient to exhaust the possibilities of these two emblems.

Drama of the Great Decease

All the same, round the Master's end there grew up spontaneously a sort of drama in three acts, or rather in three tableaux: his death, his funeral and the division of his relics. It remains for the School of Gandhāra to show him lying on his death-bed; the old school started from the end of the second act, taking the funeral tumulus as symbol of the Decease. But the Sāñchī workshop had still the resource to tackle the third act, the events of which were of prime interest to the people of their generation. And they turned to this all the more readily since, in all scenes taking place after the *Parinirvāṇa*, they were freed from the usual conventions concerning the portrayal of the Buddha. We have already seen (p. 199) how a relief on the Northern Gateway (Pl. 36 *c*, 1) tries to transform the purely allegorical representation of the Last Decease into a scene based partly on the texts and partly on the life; and we Europeans would regard the noisy, gesticulating demonstrations round the Master's tomb as highly incongruous, were it not written that

[1] Still we wonder (p. 223) whether the greater part of the *jātakas* (particularly the one of the elephant Shaddanta, which covers no less than 3 lintels on as many gateways) ought not to be carried over into the Benares cycle.

the Mallas of Kuśinagara celebrated his funeral with "dances, songs, music, garlands and perfumes". In fact they seem much less struck with grief for the loss of their Master than filled with joy at possessing the priceless treasure of his relics. We know that the celebrations were soon disturbed by seven rival kings or clans, who came, sword in hand, to claim their share; that the ashes of the Buddha had to be divided into eight equal portions (according, at least, to the simplest version and consequently the one our sculptors followed); and that each of the sharers carried back in triumph to his own country the lot which fell to him and finally placed it under a funeral tumulus: for the last word always belongs to the tomb.

The War of the Relics

12*a*. Of these three scenes, which are all clearly distinguished at Amarāvatī —preliminaries for war, division of the relics, and peaceful departure of the seven claimants—the Sāñchī workshop has treated only the first and the last, side by side, in a very attractive lintel of the Southern Gateway (Pl. 15, 3). In the centre rises the town of Kuśinagara, protected by its towers and its ramparts lined with defenders. From two sides, hurling themselves against the closed gates, come the troops of the seven claimants, one of them shown in his chariot and the other six on elephants. Besiegers and besieged exchange a few arrows; but we are in no great anxiety, for we know beforehand that the armistice will soon be concluded and the relics shared out off-stage: which is the reason why left and right in the background, two of the seven chiefs are already turning their backs on the town. Each of them carries his portion of ashes in a round casket, of a pattern with which we are familiar from the excavations, and is holding it reverently on the forehead of his elephant. Now, if you glance at the two ends of the same lintel (Pls. 16 and 17), you will be able to count the five other chiefs, two on your left and three on your right, also quite evidently in the act of returning home. For the sake of symmetry two of them now drive in chariots—but then what have they done with their caskets? They are not to be seen in their hands. The scruple which disturbs us has disturbed not only us. Seized with remorse, the sculptor has thought out an expedient: he has decorated the false capitals of the lintel with two elephants back to back, and on the heads of the two outside elephants he has likewise placed a casket of relics. And now count: all is in order. There are seven aggressors coming, seven returning, and seven caskets altogether. The artist responsible for this composition was not only a man of great talent: he had a strict conscience, and deserves our esteem no less than our admiration.

On the Western Gateway we find no less than two lintels devoted, one to "the war" and the other to "the transport" of the relics; but, as Sir John Marshall has already had occasion to point out when comparing the first of them (Pl. 61, 2) with that on the Southern Gateway,[1] the sculptor has confined himself to a conventional

[1] See *A Guide to Sāñchī*, pp. 75-76, and p. 118 above.

treatment of his subject. His lack of sincere faith has the immediate result of depriving him of any persuasive power. The procession, preceded by its band, no longer has anything bellicose about it, and the town, banished to the left-hand corner, gives no sign of being in a state of siege. We should even hesitate over the identification, if the sculptor had not deigned to make an effort to show—one in a chariot, two on horseback and four on elephants—the "seven before Kuśinagara", each under a royal umbrella.[1]

The Transport of the Relics

12*b*. The incident depicted on the top lintel (Pl. 61, 1) is treated with the same carelessness, as though by a person who thinks: "That will be clear enough!" The gesture of the central figure bearing a casket of relics (not on the elephant's head but, to carry respect still further, on his own head) suffices to place the scene after the death of the Buddha: but that does not tell us who this person is the only one, notice, who is bearing this precious burden. Does he represent all the seven claimants just mentioned? And could the town towards which he is going (always relegated to the left of the tableau) stand at will for any one of their seven capitals? Or is the presence of a *śāla* tree close outside the gates meant to indicate the precise geographical position? As everybody knows that they were *śāla* trees which sheltered the dying Master, we should thus be in front of Kuśinagara; and then the great personage who comes in procession bringing the relics of the Blessed One could only be the chief of the local clan of the Mallas. At the same time, this would have to be the *first* transport of the ashes from the funeral pyre to the town, and the episode would have to be placed before and not after the arrival of the seven claimants? You see in what uncertainty the sculptor of the Western Gateway leaves us groping, when everything was so clear and open on the Southern Gateway. Obviously it would be vain to rack our brains further over compositions patched up in such a slovenly manner.

The Stūpa of Rāmagrāma

12*c*. On the other hand, we cannot pay too much attention to those on the Southern Gateway, always so carefully set up. Now, there is yet another scene there which its central motive, consisting of a stūpa, connects, if not with the Kuśinagara cycle proper, at any rate with the *Parinirvāṇa* (Pl. 11, 2): and that is why we put it in here. But this is not all. At first sight this lintel seems to present the same distribution as one on the Eastern Gateway (Pl. 46, 3), but on looking nearer we see that the connection is even closer than we thought, and that in both pictures we are dealing with the stūpa of Rāmagrāma which the Chinese pilgrims visited, five *yojana* or 300 *li* east of Kapilavastu, and about which they have told us a two-fold legend.[2]

The first version is taken from the *Aśoka-avadāna*. We have just seen on this Southern Gateway how each of the initial sharers carried his portion of the relics into his own country to place it underneath one of those solid shrines which are called stūpas.

[1] The king in the chariot, shown on the right projecting end of the same lintel, is evidently a supernumerary. On this gateway the ends of the lintels do not afford any explanatory help to the central themes.

[2] S. Beal, *Buddhist Records*, etc., I, p. L, and II, p. 26. *Cf. Divyāvadāna*, p. 380.

Now, it should be known that these eight original deposits were excavated by Aśoka to be distributed among his 84,000 sanctuaries; or rather, that was the fate of seven of them, for he had to give up trying to take possession of the eighth. When his pious pilgrimage brought him before the stūpa of Rāmagrāma, he found it, as we see here (Pl. 11, 2), being worshipped by a whole tribe of *Nāga*-serpents, who offered a courteous but implacable resistance to the imperial archæologist's enterprise. The legend even says (and this is shown on a wonderful medallion of Amarāvatī[1]) that they carried Aśoka into their subterranean retreat to allow him to witness the honours with which they surrounded the remains of the Buddha; and the emperor is supposed to have agreed that the pomp of this worship defied all human competition. We do not see as much here; but at least our artist has, in the clearest fashion, shown the two rival troops most convincingly distinguished on either side of the stūpa which is obviously their stake.

This first point gained, one can hardly help thinking that the lintel of the Eastern Gateway (Pl. 46, 3) gives the second form of the legend, as narrated immediately after by Fa Hien and Hiuen Thsang. The land being deserted, they tell us, the stūpa was abandoned in the jungle; but some *Nāga*-elephants continued to come to pay it worship. The supposition that the two variant legends arose from a play on the meaning of the word *nāga* (serpent or elephant) has long been entertained by us, and we have expatiated elsewhere on the matter[2]; here it is enough to state that on the Eastern Gateway we clearly see a herd of elephants carrying lotuses in their trunks and coming to the stūpa to make those offerings of flowers which still constitute one of the most usual rites of the Buddhist religion.

V. The Miracles of the four other Holy Towns

All the scenes from the life of the Buddha which we have just reviewed belong more or less directly to the *māhātmya* or "spiritual guide" of the four great holy places of Buddhism. But neither the two small towns of Kapilavastu and Kuśinagara, nor the hamlet of Uruvilvā, nor even the city of Benares, could hope to monopolise, in addition to the souvenirs or holy "vestiges" of the Master, the visits and offerings of the pilgrims. Four other big cities, as we have said (p. 201)—Rājagṛiha, Vaiśālī, Śrāvastī and Sāṅkāśya—soon constituted four secondary centres of pilgrimage. How this honour fell to them, while it was denied to Mathurā and Kauśāmbī, is not a question to investigate here. The point to note is that, with one or two exceptions,[3] all the scenes from the Master's biography which we have still to notice on the *toraṇas* are supposed to have been enacted in one or another of these four holy towns: this surely cannot be pure chance.

[1] *Cf. Revue des Arts Asiatiques*, 5th year, Pl. XI, 2 and *cf.* Pl. VIII, 2 and pp. 17-18.

[2] See *Bibl. de Vulgarisation du Musée Guimet*, Vol. 34 (1910, pp. 181-2 and 228-9; *cf. Memoirs of the Arch. Survey of India*, No. 46, pp. 3-4). It is known that on a relief now in the Museum at Sārnāth elephants and serpents are associated in the worship of this same stūpa (*A. S. I.*, 1904-5, fig. 12, or *Cat. of the Museum of Arch. at Sārnāth*, Pl. 23 *b*).

[3] Strictly speaking, the "Visit of Indra" (No. 13 c) does not take place in the town itself, only in the district of Rājagṛiha. On the other hand, we have no certain identification or localisation for the reverse of the middle lintel of the Eastern Gate (see description of Pl. 46, 2).

The Miracles of Rājagṛiha

13. After the conversion of the Jatilas of Uruvilvā, the Buddha hastened to lead his new disciples about thirty miles north-east, to the old capital of Magadha; for all is not done when you have ordained a thousand begging friars at a blow; you must also enable them to get their living by their daily collections. Hence we are led to suppose that it is this town which we see depicted just below the final prodigy of "the Flood" (No. 10 *d*). The fact that of the seven scenes decorating the left (or south) pillar of the Eastern Gateway, six have already been localised at Magadha, lends further probability to this hypothesis. On the other hand, as the seventh panel simply reproduces the usual stereotype of the "royal visit", it would be impossible for any one to guess the place of the scene except by analogy with the adjacent reliefs. The good faith of the sculptors, who have nothing to gain by leading our conjectures astray, the general tenour of the jamb, and a precise tradition, thus unite in inviting us to identify the city depicted at the bottom of Pl. 51 *b* with Rājagṛiha.

Bimbisāra's Visit

13*a*. If the town is Rājagṛiha, it follows inevitably that the king who is driving out of it in his chariot, in the midst of the usual escort, can be nobody but that Bimbisāra who was to become and remain the Master's faithful friend. Soon, as etiquette demands, he alights and leaves behind him the insignia of his royalty, and all his companions except one; and thus, at the left above, he pays homage on foot to the Blessed One. The latter, in accordance with established rule, has taken his seat outside the ramparts of the town, which reach right up to the top edge of the picture. Some indications of water and rocks are there, doubtless to remind us that he had established his retreat on the rocky hill of Antagiri, close by the hot springs which still gush out near Rājgir. But after these indications—vague enough, after all—the sculptor gives us the slip and leaves us in great perplexity. For what occasion is all this shown? The texts tell of at least two particularly famous meetings between the Buddha and Bimbisāra. Is it the one which took place immediately after the "Great Departure from the house", when the future Śākya-muni was still but a fugitive prince disgusted with the world? Or is it the second, as the context of the pillar requires, and has the "perfectly accomplished" Buddha come, in accordance with his promise, to preach his doctrines to the king of Magadha? If this is so, one would expect the sculptor to show us, as at Amarāvatī,[1] the Jaṭilas transformed into monks who accompanied the Master; but he never shows monks. At least, you may say, he might have indicated the Bamboo Grove (*Veṇuvana*) which the king gave as a present to the Buddha and his community; but to that he could reply that the gift was not made till the day after the visit shown here, after the solemn entrance of the Master into Rājagṛiha and following on his reception at the royal palace. What he would have been likely to reply, I think, is that our demands are perfectly ridiculous: it is as clear as daylight that the relief completes the Uruvilvā series, and thus the question of knowing

[1] For all these points it is sufficient to refer the reader to *Art G.-b. du Gandhāra*, I, p. 372 (with references) and fig. 228 (according to Fergusson, *Tree and Serpent Worship*, Pl. 70).

which moment in the legend it represents never even occurred to the donors of the jamb. Our modern mania is to want to *see* everything: but in such traditional art it is enough to *know* which episode one is dealing with.

Ajātaśatru's Visit

13*b*. The species of tree shown above the Buddha's throne, in conjunction with another exceptional detail, allows us to reach a greater degree of certainty for one or even two reliefs on the right (east) jamb of the Northern Gateway—a jamb whose inner face seems to be devoted entirely to Magadha (Pl. 35 *b*). The two episodes shown together on Pl. 51 *b*, 2,—the exit from the town and homage to the Buddha—are here depicted separately, the first (Pl. 35 *b*, 2) above the second (Pl. 35 *b*, 3). The same downward perspective shows us, as before, the same town and the same king, accompanied by the same retinue, issuing in his chariot out of the same gate. Below, the said king, after alighting, stands with clasped hands near the stone throne of the Blessed One. But here the throne is placed under a mango-tree, and the king is accompanied by his wives only. Comparison with an inscribed pillar at Bharhut[1] allows us to recognize by these two peculiar signs the visit which Ajātaśatru, the parricide son of Bimbisāra, desirous of recovering peace for his soul, paid to the Blessed One in the mango-grove of their common physician Jīvaka... But, you may object, out of the seven trees in this park only three are mangoes, and the one in the middle is not only flanked by an *aśoka* and a *champaka*, but framed by two tufts of those bamboos which we looked for in vain just now. That is true; but the central tree is the one which counts, and its two neighbours are there merely for the sake of variety; moreover, there is nothing to prevent us from seeing in the bamboos a discreet allusion to the other hermitage which was likewise at the disposal of the Buddhist community at Rājagṛiha, and consequently a further indication of topography.[2]

Indra's Visit

13*c*. In any case, we cannot quarrel with our sculptors for introducing into the Magadha cycle the well-known episode of the visit which "Śakra, the Indra of the Gods" paid to the Blessed One in a grotto situated some six miles east of Rājagṛiha. The same face of the east jamb of the Northern Gateway (Pl. 35 *b*, 1) gives a very characteristic representation of it, and one in which all the traditional stage-setting is found—cave, rocks, more or less fantastic animals, and, in the group of visitors, the herald of the king of the gods, Pañcaśikha with his harp. The only figure we miss in this visit (and this happens even in the best examples) is the receiver of it. The right (or south) jamb of the Western Gateway gives us on the contrary, as is usual on this gateway, an isolated version so much weakened that we hesitated a long time over its interpretation (Pl. 64 *a*, 3). You will look in vain among the attendants for the jungle animals or the indispensable harpist; and one does not quite see how the flowering tree which continues mechanically to shelter

[1] Cunningham, *Stūpa of Bharhut*, Pl. 16, 3.

[2] Or else must we admit that the banal stereotype of the "royal visit" lends itself here to a double meaning? See the discussion in the description of Pl. 35 *b*, 2.

the Buddha's throne, has been able to grow inside a rocky cave. All the same, it is not the only one to take root in the rock, and the cave is indisputably delineated. Apparently the indication of the "rocky grotto" (*śaila-gṛiha*), conventional as it was, sufficed henceforward to identify this hackneyed subject.

The Miracle of Vaiśālī

14. Those to whom Buddhist iconography is more or less familiar will not have failed to notice that we do not find on the *toraṇas*, among the episodes of Rājagṛiha, the one which was to become and to remain the characteristic mark of that capital, *i.e.*, the subjugation of the infuriated elephant, which the traitor Devadatta, with the complicity of the not yet converted King Ajātaśatru, one day loosed in the high street against the Blessed One and his monks.[1] This does not mean that our artists were ignorant of this legend, which so felicitously inspired those of Amarāvatī and so poorly those of Gandhāra: it means only that they did not feel equal to tackling it. However, the other miracle which also demonstrated that the Buddha's empire of benevolence extended to the animals, was not beyond their capacity. It is much less lively, relating to the offering which a monkey is supposed to have made to the Master in the neighbourhood of Vaiśālī (now Basārh, N. W. of Patna). This wonderful animal is said to have spontaneously brought him back his begging bowl, after filling it with the sweet syrup which is extracted from palm-trees and which, before it ferments, monks are allowed to drink. The right-hand (west) jamb of the Northern Gateway has one of its panels devoted to this very scene, so Indian in flavour (Pl. 36 *c*, 2). Near the throne of the Buddha, placed on the left under an *aśvattha* tree, are two monkeys—or rather a reduplication of the same monkey. The one nearest to the Master is presenting him with the bowl, evidently full to the brim, which he holds in both hands; the other, with empty hands and his arms raised in homage, is no less obviously rejoicing that his present has been graciously accepted. The story goes further, but this is all we are told here. Zealous laymen, women and children, watch the scene, highly edified. If you are gifted with imagination, there is nothing to prevent you from recognizing among them the chief celebrities of Vaiśālī, namely two of the noble Licchavis and, at their side, the lovely courtezan Āmrapālī[2] in company with one of her attendants.

The Miracles of Śrāvastī

15. The facade of the left (east) jamb of the same Northern Gateway (Pl. 34 *a* and *b*) brings us now to the capital of the great kingdom of Kośala, the famous city of Śrāvastī (now Saheṭh-Maheṭh, near Balrāmpur). The dark high wall of the Himālaya crested with snow makes such a lovely background, that it is no wonder it became the favourite residence of the Blessed One and the scene of his greatest "prodigy". At least four panels, if not five,[3] are given up to it here. Do not be surprised that we begin the study

[1] *Cf.* Pl. 126 *b* and p. 249, below.
[2] One might be tempted to find this comely lady on Pl. 16, 5: but the schematic banality of these religious pictures discourages the hypothesis.
[3] For the fifth, *i.e.*, the bottom panel (Pl. 34 *b*, 2), see below, p. 229.

of it neither at the top nor at the bottom, but in the middle; since the sculptor has followed no strict order, the safest way through this maze is to seize the first guiding thread which offers.

The Gift of the Jetavana

15*a*. If we are really at Śrāvastī, we cannot fail to notice its most celebrated site, Prince Jeta's park, the purchase and bestowal of which by the rich banker Anāthapiṇḍika was such an exciting event for local gossip and the subject of such detailed representations on the medallions of Bharhut and Bodh-Gayā.[1] So it was; but times have changed, and the picturesqueness of the theme has almost completely faded. We hunt in vain now for the ox-carts laden with the old square coins, the coolies unloading them and the clerks spreading them carefully, so as to cover the whole surface of the garden with them; for it was at this price that the owner consented (when taken at his word) to give up his estate. These entertaining details have disappeared, and the only trace of them which is left—luckily for our identification, which would otherwise have been impossible and which at once becomes certain—is the curious chequer-work which you may observe on the ground in the second panel from the top (Pl. 34 *a*, 2). Further, from the Bharhut composition the sculptor has retained only the few onlookers, the precious trees which (the texts stipulate) had been respected, and the *gandha-kuṭi*—the cells transformed into chapels, where the Buddha had formerly dwelt and which were still fragrant with the memory of his presence; but the whole setting is exceedingly commonplace, and, not finding a donation-ewer in anybody's hand, we cannot even recognize the generous merchant, still less the prince.

Prasenajit's Visit

15*b*. All the same, we must not complain too much. The characteristic *lakshaṇa* of the layer of coins, casually as it is used here, by indicating the Jetavana gives the key to the neighbouring scenes and, first of all, to the royal visit, which we see on the second panel from the bottom (Pl. 34 *b*, 1). Since we are at Śrāvastī, it follows that the king who is riding out of the city on horseback in the stereotyped way which we have seen so often, must be Prasenajit. But here a Bharhut relief[2] immediately comes to our assistance with two inscriptions, the first confirming that we are indeed dealing with King Prasenajit of Kośala, and the second informing us of the errand on which he is going: he is going to listen to a sermon by the Master in an imposing hall (*maṇḍapa*), which, so the texts tell us, the king had erected expressly for this occasion, and which is shown at the top of the picture. After that, we can no longer doubt that at Sāñchī the same king is likewise on his way to the *maṇḍapa* depicted immediately above his capital (Pl. 34 *a*, 3). Why above? you may ask. There is a reason: the hall of the "Great Prodigy at Śrāvastī" had been erected half way between the Jetavana and the town,[3] and it is just that intermediate position that the sculptor has allotted to it here.

---

[1] Cunningham, *Stūpa of Bharhut*, Pls. 28 and 57; *Mahābodhi*, Pl. 8, 8.
[2] Cunningham, *Bharhut*, Pl. 13, 3; *cf. Beginnings of Buddhist Art*, etc., Pl. 28, 2.
[3] *Divyāvadāna*, p. 155.

But the analogy with Bharhut goes no further, and, in default of the support of any other sculpture, we must have recourse to the texts. How do they conceive the "Great Prodigy"? From the examination to which we submitted them long ago[1] they seem to hesitate between two versions (which, however, are not mutually exclusive) and credit the Blessed One in turn with two kinds of miracles. First of all, he goes walking in the air in various attitudes, emitting alternately flames and waves out of the upper or lower parts of his body; in the second place, multiplying images of himself right up to the sky and in all directions, he preaches his law.

The Great Prodigy: First Episode

15*c*. If, armed with these particulars we now compare our Pl. 34 *a*, 3 with Cunningham's (Pl. 13, 3), we perceive at once that the Sāñchī artist has chosen the first and the Bharhut artist the second of the two successive moments: the walking in the air and the transfiguration while preaching. The Bharhut sculptor has raised his *maṇḍapa* upwards, so as to lodge the "Wheel of the Law of the Blessed One" (thus duly labelled) comfortably under its roof. The Sāñchī sculptor, on the other hand, has managed to stretch his *maṇḍapa* sideways, so as to shelter the Master's "walking-path"—evidently an aerial one, since it is shown above the heads of the spectators, even above the tree-tops. The first has chosen the preaching version and the other, what is called in technical terms the "twin prodigies" of fire and water. Each, of course, treats his adopted version according to his artistic means; but their methods remain very similar, even to such details as, for instance, the heavy wreaths which load the nave of the wheel at Bharhut and wave or hang above the *caṅkrama* at Sāñchī (*cf*. also Pl. 19 *d*, 5).

The Great Prodigy: Second Episode

15*d*. But the texts reserve yet another detail which is of particular interest here. In the Pāli tradition the established name of the *mahāprātihārya* at Śrāvastī is the "miracle at the foot of the mango-tree". Surely this must be the reason why the relief (No. 15 *b*, 1) shows us a mango-tree above the roofs of the town. This discreet hint is made even more probable by the fact that on the top of the jamb (Pl. 34 *a*, 1) we find again a representation of the "Great Prodigy" conceived in this manner. Above the throne of the Buddha and topped with an umbrella rises the big mango-tree which the Blessed One was supposed to have caused to grow miraculously for the occasion. All round, sitting or standing on the ground, King Prasenajit and his courtiers are crowding; higher up (from an effect of perspective) the cohorts of the gods float in the air. Here we return to the second form of the legend, which attributed the decisive victory of the Blessed One over the six heretic masters less to his magic feats than to the irresistible power of his preaching.

The Miracle of Sāṅkāśya

16. It will doubtless have been noticed that, on this last relief, two of the *devas* are busy beating two huge horizontal drums with big sticks: this is their way of beating the

[1] *Journ. As.*, Jan. 1909, p. 10 (or *Beginnings of Buddhist Art*, etc., p. 152).

tom-tom to tell the world of the importance of what is happening. The man who decorated the Northern Gateway was in the habit of characterising his pictures of "Great Miracles" in this way, for we find these two *dundubhi* again at the top of the facade of the right jamb (Pl. 34 *c*), always supporting themselves in the air without the aid of any genie.[1] As pendant to the "Great Prodigy" of Śrāvastī we have, in fact, the famous "Descent from Heaven" (*Devāvatāra*) of Sāṅkāśya (now Sankissa in the Farrukhabād district, the western-most of the holy places of ancient Buddhism). The sight of the magic ladder which the Buddha used for this "Descent" would make identification obvious, even if we had not here the support of a whole pillar at Bharhut (Cunn., Pl. 17). The three panels there will help us, all the same, to distinguish the three separate moments which the Sāñchī sculptor has grouped in the same frame. Above, the Master's sermon in the heaven of the Thirty-three Gods is, as usual, displayed as a throne surmounted by a tree (for there are trees in the Indian paradises) and surrounded by six divinities. In the middle, to the thunder of the divine drums, he comes down in company with the gods, who are leading him ceremoniously back to earth. The magic ladder ends close to another throne under a tree, framed by two families of human worshippers of much smaller stature, a man, a woman and a child. Are they the donors of this jamb of the northern *toraṇa*? At any rate they are there to suggest the third episode, the resumption of contact between the Blessed One and his Congregation after his month's stay in heaven. Is it worthy of mention? Such is the force of tradition in Buddhist art that the same three-fold scene reappears on the fresco which decorates the left side of the vestibule of the sanctuary of Cave XVII at Ajaṇṭā; and on the opposite wall it is likewise the "Great Prodigy" which forms a pendant to the *Devāvatāra*.

[1] By the way, the fact that one of these drums likewise surmounts the bottom relief of the west jamb (Pl. 35 *a* bottom) makes the loss of this latter all the more regrettable. We find the same drums on the Ajaṇṭā paintings (Cave XVII).

CHAPTER XVI

INTERPRETATION OF THE GATEWAY SCULPTURES—continued

VI. The Former Lives

WE have now come to the end both of the list of the eight traditional places of pilgrimage and of the scenes taken from the last life of Buddha—not to mention four post-cremation ones which, for topographical reasons, have been annexed to the biography itself, namely the War and the Transport of the Relics and the two Visits of Aśoka, one to the Bodhi-tree and the other to the Stūpa of Rāmagrāma. Accordingly, we can hardly now enter upon the question of his "former lives" without enquiring whether some at least among them are not likewise linked with one or another of the holy towns. The Jātakas, fanciful tales of a distant past, lend themselves to shifting localisation, and we know that several of them were transplanted by Buddhist propagandists from Central India as far as Gandhāra. But the large majority are said, doubtless in accordance with the most ancient popular tradition, to belong "to the time when King Brahmadatta reigned in Benares". Still more precisely, of the five which we meet at Sāñchī, only one—the Viśvantara—is an exception to this rule. The heroes of the four others make, it is true, their usual abode on the Himālayas, but they always deal with a king of Benares or his emissaries. We even learn from the Chinese pilgrims that a memorial stūpa of the *Shaḍdanta-jātaka* (by far the most important of the *jātakas* at Sāñchī) was still to be seen in their time not far from that of the "First Sermon"; so that we should not be over-straining facts, if we were to append this beautiful legend to the "Benares Cycle". Such would be the most obvious way of filling this empty frame (*cf*. p. 213), and of setting up round this town a series of legendary tales similar to those which sprang up round the three other great holy places.

The Jātakas portrayed at Sāñchī

It is perhaps worth while to make one other preliminary remark. To the thirty odd scenes shown of the last life of the Buddha, which we have just pointed out on the *toraṇas* at Sāñchī, the "former lives" add but five more.[1] Such a noticeable disproportion has caused us to wonder elsewhere[2] whether the iconographical rôle of the jātaka, which was so great in the decoration of Bharhut, was not already slipping into the background, awaiting later restoration to favour. Great as was the charm of these illustrated fables, they were naturally somewhat puerile, and that might further explain why among the five

Lessening popularity of the Jātakas

[1] Possibly six. But it would be excessive to count apart the quite accessory representation of the Yakshiṇī Aśvamukhī (*cf*. pp. 181 and 229).

[2] 'Les Représentations de Jātakas dans l'Art bouddhique' (*Mémoires concernant l'Asie orientale*, t. III).

jātakas kept at Sāñchī, the Bodhisattva appears only twice reincarnate in animal shape. Even the interest of his human reincarnations paled before stories borrowed from his real biography. Besides, the novelty of these illustrations had already become perceptibly blunted—that, at least, is the impression given by the way our sculptors treat them.

The Shaddanta-jātaka

17*a*. The rebirth in the shape of the "Elephant with six tusks" is, as we have said, the subject which occupies the greatest space at Sāñchī. At least three lintels, indeed, are given up to it on the Southern, Northern and Western Gateways of the big stūpa (Pls. 15, 29, 55). Sir John Marshall has availed himself of the fact to compare these panels from a technical point of view.[1] From the iconographical standpoint, what strikes us particularly is the vaguely decorative way they are treated, or, if you prefer, their want of narrative directness. Evidently they are no longer intended to relate a still unpublished tale as clearly as possible. Now that the public knows the story beforehand, all the artists care about is that the lintel shall be carved all over. So, with more or less artistic sense and manual skill, they simply try to distribute, round the great banyan fig-tree mentioned in the texts and naturally claiming the centre of the tableau, a more or less numerous herd of elephants grazing, bathing or fanning themselves.[2] Alone the honest sculptor of the Southern Gateway (Pl. 15) makes some effort to distinguish the Bodhisattva for us by the three-fold tusks which he gives him and the royal honours which he makes the others pay him; and he is the only one who considers it incumbent on him to give at least a suggestion of the imminent danger which threatens the noble animal, in the form of a hunter bending down, armed with a bow, in the right-hand corner of his composition. If you know who this hunter is and on what errand the queen of Benares has sent him, and how the Bodhisattva finds in their foul dealing a fresh opportunity of attaining "the height of generosity", well and good. If you know nothing about it, however, apply to the texts or enquire at Bharhut and Amarāvatī, but do not expect Sāñchī to inform you.

Mahākapi-jātaka

17*b*. It remains to be seen how far the oblong shape of the lintels is responsible, in this particular case, for the method adopted by the sculptor of the Southern Gateway and afterwards imitated by the others. Even on the Western Gateway, the latest and most slovenly of all, when it is only a question of filling one of the square panels of the pillars, we find again something of the precision, if not the dryness, of the Bharhut compositions. The analogy between the pictures which the two workshops have left of the *Mahākapi-jātaka* (No. 407 of the Pāli collection) is most striking. In both (Pl. 64 *a*, 1 and Cunn., Pl. 33, 4) the devoted king of the monkeys makes a bridge with his body over the Ganges to enable his people to escape from the archers of the king of Benares; in both, two men stretch a blanket beneath him to catch him the moment he drops, worn

[1] *A Guide to Sāñchī*, pp. 74-5, and p. 120 above.

[2] For the ill-timed fit of devotion with which some of them are seized on Pl. 55, 2, *cf.* the description of this plate.

out; in both we find him in conversation with his "cousin", the king of men. Only, at Sāñchī, the jungle landscape is much more minutely carved, and all the foreground is occupied by the usual stereotype of the royal retinue.

Rishyaśriṅga-jātaka

17*c*. With this increased striving after the picturesque are mingled scruples of delicacy unknown to the older artists. To the latter, everything connected with the Blessed One, either closely or remotely, could only be a source of edification; and thus the Bharhut medallion labelled *Isisiṅga-jātaka* boldly shows us the antelope, which was the Bodhisattva's mother in this existence, in the act of conceiving him, and then of bringing him forth (Cunn., Pl. 26, 7). These indelicate details are spared us on the projecting end of the lower lintel of the Northern Gateway (Pl. 27). Here, in a hermitage much more tightly packed with trees and animals, we see the child twice, on the right bathing in a lotus pool after his birth, and on the left presenting himself before the anchorite who was supposed to be the involuntary author of his being[1]; the hinds are, indeed, present, but if we did not know the story, we should suppose that their only purpose was to fill in the landscape. People who are interested in the origin of tales relative to the Unicorn should notice that the forest-child here already has on his brow the long pointed horn which is shortly to change his name from 'Antelope-horn' to 'Unicorn' (*Ekaśriṅga*).

Syāma-jātaka

17*d*. We find the same method of composition (abundance of minor details, crowded scenes and repetition of persons) in the top panel of the right pillar of the Western Gateway (Pl. 65 *a*, 1). This time it serves to depict the touching story of that model of filial piety, the young anchorite Śyāma. Everything is there: the huts, trees and beasts of the hermitage; the fire and ladle of sacrifice; the two old blind parents; the novice coming down to the water with his pitcher, then bathing in the lotus pond, where the king's arrow strikes him; the king who draws, who has drawn, and who repents of having drawn, his bow; and lastly, in the top left-hand corner, the same four persons reunited round the god Indra who (very properly, since the Bodhisattva takes part in the drama) has come down from the sky on purpose to arrange a happy denouement. It is a "story without words" in the full sense of the term, but with all the episodes grouped in a single frame instead of being divided chronologically, as in Gandhāra, into the successive compartments of a frieze.

Viśvantara-jātaka

17*e*. Lastly, the bottom lintel of the Northern Gateway makes a sort of compromise between the two systems represented in Europe by the altar-screens of the Middle Ages on the one hand, and the antique friezes (or the pictures of Epinal) on the other. On both of its faces the long story of Viśvantara, the prince of charity, has in fact its episodes arranged roughly in chronological order, but with no dividing line between

[1] If we are to go by the indication of the lotus and the little boy's pose, the same scene must have been depicted on the damaged fragment of the Southern Gateway represented on Pl. 67 *d*.

them and not without some overlapping. Both on the obverse and on the reverse they read from right to left. The front shows (Pl. 23 *a*, 1) the capital of the Śibis, the gift of the elephant to the foreign Brāhman, the leave-taking at the gates of the town, the departure into exile (in a chariot drawn by four horses) of the prince and princess and their two children, the gift of the chariot in the foreground, and the gift of the horses in the background. On the left-hand projecting end, Viśvantara with their son, and his wife Mādrī with their little girl, pursue their way on foot through the villages (Pl. 25, 1). At the right end of the back face they are at last arriving within the forest (Pl. 33, 1). The middle part shows their settling down and their life in the hermitage, then the gift of the children to a Brāhman, then that of the wife to Indra disguised as a Brāhman, the revelation of the latter in his usual rôle of *deus ex machina*, and, lastly, the general reunion of the family and their return in a body to their native city (Pl. 29, 3). Meantime, the man who begged the children had already made their grandfather buy them back (on the left-hand projection of the lintel : Pl. 31, 1). These incidents sometimes follow one another and sometimes mingle without too much confusion : you only need to look carefully and to know the story beforehand. But failing the texts, we should defy any one to guess that the indiscretion of his charity has caused the prince to be sent into exile, since everywhere, in town and country, he meets with nothing but tokens of a respect amounting to veneration. Once again the story comes down to us already steeped in devotion and loaded with picturesque accessories. Even without other proofs, this excess of decoration and this overdoing of the edifying side would be enough to show the priority of the sculptures at Bharhut over those at Sāñchī.

VII. Heavens and Paradises

Except for the episodes of the Devāvatāra (No. 16), all the scenes enumerated so far take place on earth. But numerous as they had become in comparison with the themes on the balustrade of Stūpa 2, and in spite of the frequent repetitions which the artists allowed themselves, they were not yet sufficient to cover the surfaces of the five gateways from top to bottom. So it became necessary to have recourse to other kinds of subjects, borrowed not directly from the Buddhist legends this time, but from the popular beliefs which the Buddhists shared with all the Hindus on the subject of the other world. As the sculptors' imagination had no leaning to the macabre, they have had the good taste to spare the faithful the frightful spectacle of hell ; but they have not refused them anticipatory visions of the bliss of heaven. Their pretensions did not, of course, go beyond the region called *Kāma-dhātu*, the world of the desires and pleasures of the senses ; ethereal spheres, in which even forms dissolve, are not within the province of the plastic arts. But, though they have confined themselves to showing the six (or perhaps seven) lower storeys of the divine abodes, they give us tableaux which are sometimes sensual and sometimes chaste: and it is this contrast which justifies to some extent the double title of this paragraph.

The Festival of the cūḍā of the Bodhisattva in Indra's Heaven

18*a*. It is not difficult to guess how they were led to tap this new source of inspiration. Not only did they know that for his last rebirth their Master had descended from the heaven of the Tushitas (No. 6 *a*) and that in his lifetime he had ascended to the heaven of the Trayastriṁśat (No. 16), but they were also aware of what is written in the *Lalita-vistara* as an appendix to the Great Departure (No. 6 *d*) concerning his *cūḍā*—that is, as we learn from the carved monuments, his princely headdress, turban and hair included: "And moreover this came into the mind of the Bodhisattva: How could a *cūḍā* agree with the monastic state? And cutting off his *cūḍā* with his sword, he flung it into the air; and the Thity-three gods seized it in order to pay it worship. And still to-day in the home of the Thirty-three gods they celebrate a festival in its honour".[1] It is this very festival which is depicted first on a duly inscribed relief at Bharhut (Cunn., Pl. 16, 1), and then on one of the panels on the left (west) jamb of the Southern Gateway (Pl. 18 *b*, 3). To all appearances, here as well as on the two panels immediately above (*cf*. No. 11), this scene should be connected with the adjacent relief on the other face of the pillar (Pl. 18 *a*, 3). As token that Indra, accompanied by his wife Śacī, is thus arriving from the left on the threshold of his own heaven, we have his gigantic stature and that of his elephant Airāvata, besides the special type of the dumpy, pot-bellied Yakshas who precede him. Perhaps before the right-hand part of the relief was crushed, one could see that on the forehead of his mount he held the precious relic which he is venerating close by, together with his heavenly companions. In any case there can be no two opinions about the meaning of this latter panel: here, as at Bharhut, the *cūḍā* of the future Buddha holds the place of honour, under an umbrella and on the altar of a temple, whilst the famous *apsarases* of Indra's paradise are celebrating his worship, according to the traditional formula, with dances, music and song.

The First Six Devalokas

18*b*. If we can depict the second of the six storeys of the Kāma-dhātu, there is no reason why we should not depict the five others. Placed one above another, they would do, any way, to cover the whole face of a jamb. Such was the argument of the man who decorated the right pillar of the Eastern Gateway (Pl. 49 *a* and *b*): but satisfied, apparently, by this great effort of imagination, he has not overtasked his brain in putting his plan into execution. We find practically the same tableau repeated six times on end, one above the other. A celestial palace, similar to the one we have just seen on Pl. 18 *b*, continues to shelter the same divine tenants, the only difference being that the facade is now divided into three parts by columns set carefully at even distances, which gives an odd effect of perpendicular style. On each landing, we find, with tiresome monotony, the same king of the gods sitting under the middle bay with his thunderbolt and his flask of

[1] *Lalita-vistara*, ed. Lefmann, p. 225.

ambrosia (*amṛita*) in his hands, his viceroy (*uparāja*) on his right, his dancers and musicians on his left. Only on the ground-floor, the necessity of putting in the Four Kings of the four points of the compass all at once, meant throwing the nymphs into the background (Pl. 49 *b*, 2). Such being the case, it is only from their place in this vertical series that we can recognize in turn, from bottom to top, above the heaven of the Four Guardians of the world, the one (which we have already visited twice in Nos. 16 and 18 *a*) belonging to the Thirty-three gods, of whom Indra is head; then, the heaven of Yama, whence the light of day becomes eternal; next, the heaven of the Tushitas, the gods 'satisfied' with their lot; then, the heaven of the Nirmāṇa-rati, where all desire is transformed instantaneously into pleasure; and finally the heaven of the Paranirmita-vaśavarti, who dispose not only of their own creations, like the former, but also of those of others; for, thanks to the ascensional power of the *devas*, every extra storey marks a superiority over the one below. As always happens with serial pictures of the Buddhists, the numerical lists of texts furnish us with definite identifications. Only one point remains: who are the *devas* on the terrace of the top palace, that is, in the seventh and last storey of all? Did the artist mean to show us the last divinities visible to human eyes, those in Brahmā's heaven, where the form remains but whence desire is banished? Such an attempt would have been within possible range; but the presence of the women and the cup in the hand of the principal figure point rather to Māra, the god of Love and Death and the Master's sworn enemy as lord over the entire kingdom of the senses, enthroned with his viceroy on the pinnacle of his empire.[1]

Scenes of Paradise

18*c*. If we now look carefully over each of these celestial abodes, we perceive that in the main they are faithful to the semi-urban, semi-rural conception, a mixture of palace and park, which the Indians had formed for themselves. Undoubtedly the *vimānas* or aerial pavilions occupy here nearly the whole of the tableau; but at the sides of the columns or through their intervals we see, sure enough, the trees of wonderful gardens—paradises in other words—where the gods were supposed to sport and revel during their infinitely long, but by no means eternal, existence. Thus, all we could see just now of the heaven of the Thirty-three in No. 18 *a* was a palace, and in No. 16 a tree; so that *a priori* it seems highly probable that the decorator of the Western Gateway had also undertaken to cover the right pillar (now unfortunately broken) with storeyed representations of the heavens.[2] Only this time, for the sake of variety, he has chosen to depict the jolly, voluptuous side of the celestial life; and instead of representing the *devas* holding, as we should now say, their *darbar* in their Hall of Audience (which is evidently the subject selected on Pl. 49), he prefers to show them dispersed in couples, each god with his goddess, in the shady haunts of their parks (Pl. 64 *c*). For it goes

[1] Since writing these lines we have noticed that in the *Manual of Buddhist Philosophy* (I, p. 66) Mr. McGovern says of the sixth storey of heaven (without quoting his source): "Strangely enough, either in this heaven or immediately above it is the abode of Māra . ." Observe that in Pls. 34 *a*, 1, 51 *a*, 1 and 103 *a-b* we find no longer heavens but gods simply placed one above another.

[2] Here, however, as we shall have to remark (p. 230), there would have been only three storeys instead of six.

without saying that the pleasures of the kings of the heavens can only be conceived in terms of those of the gods of the earth; and what it is the custom in Europe to call "Mahomet's Paradise" dates from long before Mahomet. On terraces edged Italian-fashion with a balustrade, or on the margin of lotus-ponds, the elect wander or sit in amorous embrace; and sometimes the roof of leaves which shelters them belongs to a tree clipped as curiously as those in a French garden. On the other hand, the landscape placed at the bottom of the right pillar of the Northern Gateway,[1] with its rocks and fountains, reminds one rather of an English park (Pl. 34 *b*, 2). There two couples are amusing themselves drinking or making music, and with them may be compared the ones which are seen on the middle lintel of the Southern Gateway (Pl. 13, 2) or on the bottom lintel of the Eastern Gateway (Pl. 44, 1). Below, two other couples (the slave on the right does not count) are riding on elephants over a flowery pond, as others are doing likewise both on the left extremity of the middle lintel of the Southern Gateway (Pl. 12, 2) and on both ends of the bottom lintel of the Small Gateway (Pls. 101, 3 and 102, 3), according to the well-established fashion of those *jala-krīḍā* or "aquatic sports", to which the Indian climate is so conducive.[2] The two last-quoted reliefs seem to give the final proof that these "genre" tableaux aim, indeed, at giving us visions of paradise.

The Paradise of Indra on Mount Meru

18*d*. It is obvious, too, that, though now placed on the reverse of the lintel, they were meant to continue and complete the middle theme of the facade (*cf*. Pls. 95 and 99). This last composition, uniting the two conceptions which we have seen used in turn, combines a view of parks with one of heavenly palaces, in order to convey to the eye all the traditional ideas about the most popular of the paradises—the paradise of Indra or, if you prefer it, of "Śakra, the Indra of the Gods". Everybody knew that his royal palace, Vaijayanta (so inscribed at Bharhut), rose beyond the Himālayas on the top of Mount Meru, the centre of the universe; and it is this divine mansion which occupies the middle of the lintel. Indra, armed with his thunderbolt, is seated as usual amongst his court; we can even identify his wife Śacī on his left. On each side are the slopes of what we may call the Indian Olympus, inhabited by all kinds of genii; and that is why, amid the trees and rocks of the Nandana-vana, haunted by wild beasts, we see Kinnaras and Yakshas and even the horse-headed Yakshiṇī that we have already met on the balustrade of Stūpa 2 (*cf*. above p. 181). Lastly, at the foot of the mountain, spread the waters of wonderful lakes, well known from the legend—unless we should take these waters to be those of the river Mandākinī. Whichever they are, the sculptor has most fitly made them the abode of two Nāga-rājas; and the ingenious idea has occurred to him of twisting the coils of the snaky bodies of the Nāga with those of the *makaras* on the false capitals, till they finally join with the terminal volutes of the lintels. But at the same time he has had to dismiss to the back face the two series of *jala-krīḍā* which would have been the natural frame for

[1] But *cf*. description of Pl. 34 *b*, 2, where another possible explanation is indicated.

[2] Here, likewise, should come the pretty little tableau on Pillar 27 (re-set) of the balustrade of Stūpa 2 (Pl. 79), which is evidently contemporary with the scenes just quoted.

the Meru of the facade; for it is not only the Nāga-rājas who reside on its slopes, but the three other "Great Kings" as well.

As a result of all the comparisons made above, these "genre" pieces seem to throw mutual light on one another and even assume, as they should, a semi-religious tone. Everything considered, it is probable that at the bottom of the left pillar of the Northern Gateway (Pl. 34 *b*, 2), as well as at the bottom of the right pillar of the Eastern Gateway (Pl. 49 *b*, 2), we are dealing simply with two different versions of the Paradise of the "Four Great Kings". As for the right pillar of the Western Gateway (Pl. 64 *c*), if it had come down to us intact, it is more than probable that it would merely have shown us the three lowest *devalokas* in as many tableaux. We have two reasons for thinking so, one material and the other moral: the first is that the facade of the symmetrical pillar allowed of three panels only, *plus* a decorative theme; the second is that the sensual paradises are only the lowest storeys of the Indian heavens; and the sculptor would certainly have taken care not to show in the same free manner the fourth heaven, that of the Tushita gods, where the Master spent his last life but one, and where his heir presumptive, Maitreya, is now awaiting his hour. In any case, on the Sāñchī gates we are still very far from the licentious postures which were finally to be assumed by the "erotic couples" destined to become so numerous in the later iconography of India (*cf.* below, p. 246).

VIII. Symmetrical Themes

We have now enumerated all, or nearly all, the scenes which the Sāñchī workshop employed for the decoration of the jambs, dies and lintels of their *toraṇas*; but they still had to adorn the capitals and false capitals of the vertical uprights, and finally to fill the intervals of the horizontal architraves. For this, as may be seen, they have used scarcely any themes but those whose essentially decorative character is at once made evident by their symmetrical repetition. This does not mean that many of these so-called ornaments cannot have—and have not, in fact, a symbolical or mythological value, even though it often escapes us; and moreover we have just shown how many a religious scene can be transformed into pure decoration. All the same, the distinction is justified in practice and will spare us needless repetitions. It likewise enables us to obtain a truer view of the development of the repertory between the execution of the round medallions on the balustrade of Stūpa 2 and that of the rectangular panels on the Gateways of Stūpa 1. If we were to close our inventory here, we might imagine that the sculptors of the *toraṇas* had invented a totally new assortment of pious tableaux, that the moment they touched subjects already treated they began at the point where their predecessors had stopped, and that they had contemptuously cast aside, as being out of date and obsolete, the ornamental paraphernalia so dear to the latter. We have already put the reader on his guard against this impression: nothing could be further from the truth. The fact is that all those old themes—geometrical, floral, animal, etc.—which we reviewed above (pp. 171 *sqq.*), reappear almost in full on the gateways; only now they play a subordinate part and are there, in an often disconcerting jumble, chiefly to frame the Buddhist scenes. Consequently we shall not feel bound to give a complete and rigorous classification of them again.

Geometrical and Floral Patterns

19*a*. Scattered here and there on all sides are dog-tooth patterns, merlons and balustrades, together with palmettes and lotuses, whose importance in Indian ornament and symbolism has already been emphasised. If you would look at more palmettes, turn for them to Pls. 25 and 33; and for more lotuses, to Pl. 23 *b*. Together or separate, in rows or in garlands, these two themes cover the outer edges of the pillars (Pls. 37, 50, 66) and sometimes even invade the lintels (Pls. 11 and 99). In these garlands the vine-leaf and grape are sometimes mingled (Pl. 66 *c*), not to mention our old friends, the *haṁsa*, tortoise, *makara*, lion, griffin and goblin. As to the volute ornament, not very happy in its effect, which forms (or formed) the terminal on the projecting ends of all the gateway lintels, it seems to have been originally conceived as a tubular lotus stalk curling round itself; only the decorator of the Small Gateway, as we have seen, once attempted to take it as the continuation of his Nāga-rājas' twisty tail (Pl. 95).

Decorative animals

19*b*. The false capitals corresponding to this lintel are decorated with a *makara* struggling with a goblin, and the sea-monster, well known to the old artists (*cf.* p. 173) is again used elsewhere to vomit garlands (Pl. 50 *c*): but, as a rule, the false capitals are treated in the Iranian manner and decorated with two animals back to back, generally couchant, though occasionally standing or walking. Notice the law of symmetrical alternation observed nearly everywhere (a few aberrations have been committed by the carvers of the Northern and Western Gateways), which demands that, from pillar to pillar, corresponding animals must occupy the fore- and the background in turn. These animals more often than not belong to the traditional tetrad, horse, bull, elephant and lion (the last often winged and sometimes horned); but, for the sake of variety, camels or stags, he-goats or she-goats, are sporadically substituted for them. The projecting ends of the lintels, when they are not invaded by the middle scene or commandeered to complete the number of the seven Mānushi-Buddhas or of the Four Great Miracles, show for preference either wild elephants striving to tear up trees (Pls. 41 and 43), or peacocks, single (Pl. 13) or in pairs (Pls. 30 and 32, 42 and 44). It has long been proposed to regard these birds, on account of their Indian name (Skt. *mayūra*, Pāli *mora*), as a sort of canting badge for the dynasty of the Mauryas to which Aśoka belonged; but this is pure guess-work. Another would be to imagine in them (as we thought of doing above, p. 182) a possible allusion to the *Mora-jātaka*. Lastly, the big capitals of the jambs on the Southern Gateway are made of four lions, on the Northern and Eastern Gateways of four elephants, whilst on the Western and Small Gateways the animals have given place to atlantes (see pp. 138-41).

Human figures

19c. The decorative themes described above are often interspersed, as we have said, with human figures, beginning with the *putti* of the garlands and the riders usually perched on the animals shown back to back on the false capitals. Some of these, both men and women, are such unexpected types that one would be inclined to take them for foreigners, till one remembers that India already contained the most extraordinary medley of peoples. The couple of "jungle-dwellers" on Pl. 43 or the riders on Pl. 48 (Eastern Gateway) are good examples of these ethnographical curiosities. But more often than not we seem to be dealing with "spirits" or genii who are shown under two very different aspects. Some, fat dwarfs with short arms and crooked legs, entrusted with holding up the architraves (Pls. 54 and 95) or spouting out garlands (Pls. 11 and 100), probably belong to the deformed, half-devilish race of the Kumbhāndas. The others, who affect the elegant appearance of great noblemen, mount guard at the bottom of the inner face of the jambs, and their similarity to the inscribed images at Bharhut allows us to recognize them as belonging to a higher species of Yakshas. In the next chapter we shall have to come back to the question of their identification, when we are dealing with the statues and stelæ (*cf.* p. 243).

Detached figures

20. Meantime we incline to make a separate category—though we have to deal once more only with symbols, animals and genii—of the figures in the round which surmount the gateways and fill the intervals of the architraves. Naturally these statuettes were separately executed, and then their pedestals (sometimes their tops too) made to fit by tenons into mortices prepared for them on the edges of the lintels. If we are to judge by the Northern Gateway, which is better preserved than the others (Pl. 21), the emblematic Wheel of the Good Law was erected on the middle of the top of this curious stone scaffolding, on a pedestal made of elephants or lions. Right and left it was attended, just as if it were the Buddha himself, by a divine figure bearing a fly-whisk. On both sides the terminal motif of the two vertical pillars consisted of one of those *nandipada* devices which, as numerous examples testify (*cf.* Pls. 42 and 44), likewise surmounted the flagstaffs. Seeing them combined deliberately with the lotus-wheel and the shield, one can hardly help suspecting an allusion, in the union of these three symbols, to the three jewels of the Buddhist Triad (*cf.* the description of Pl. 24, 4). At the extremities of the top architrave—and of the others as well—is either a lion or an elephant, standing or sitting (*cf.* Pl. 39). Other elephants or horses, generally with drivers and riders carved on both faces, are inserted between the vertical uprights, which are themselves covered with allegorical decoration. Lastly, the most original (though borrowed from Bharhut) and the most artistic note is added by those fairies who "with their pliant bodies bent like a bow" served as brackets to support the projections of the lintels above them.[1]

[1] For the origin and designation of these *śālabhañjikās*, we may now refer the reader to the excellent and conclusive discussion of Prof. J. Ph. Vogel (*Acta Orientalia*, Vol. VII, p. 201 *et seqq.*). See, also, pp. 130 *sqq.* above.

IX. Distribution of themes on the toraṇas

This time our inventory is really and truly ended. But after looking at the five *toraṇas* from all sides and noting or identifying as fully and briefly as possible the decorative motifs and the legendary scenes depicted on them, it now remains for us to examine, gate by gate, how each decorator—either on his own initiative or on the instructions of the donors—conceived and established his plan of decoration; for it is quite certain that at least an approximate scheme must have been made beforehand for each one of them. Let us be clear on this point. After the minute inspection which we have made of them as a whole, it is naturally out of the question to waste time making another complete inventory of each gateway separately. We must, and can, leave aside for the present all the ornaments which we have termed "symmetrical", on account of their reappearing regularly in duplicate on both sides of the *toraṇa*; and for the legendary scenes it will henceforth be enough to indicate them under the short title we have already used for their classification. Thus, by keeping only to the essential features, we have some chance of penetrating fairly deeply into the intentions of our sculptors; and their involuntary confidences cannot fail to throw new and interesting light on the development of Buddhist iconography.

Intentions of the decorators

Unfortunately, this hope is imperilled by a preliminary doubt. Are we quite sure that all the architectural features of the Gateways are in their original place? There can hardly be a doubt about the Northern and Eastern Gateways, but we know that the other three were re-erected in the last century. Now, a comparison of their present state with the two gates remaining more or less intact proves at a glance that this restoration has suffered from mistakes, which are all the more regrettable because a little care would have sufficed to avoid them. We can lay down as a rule that the external facade of the *toraṇas* was always honoured with the most important, most carefully elaborated scenes, whilst the back, more carelessly done, had to be content with decoratively-treated or purely decorative subjects. This simple observation of facts, so well in keeping with what we should have expected, leads at once to the conclusion that the top and bottom lintels of the Southern Gateway, the two bottom lintels of the Western Gateway and the top lintel of the Small Gateway, have been re-erected back to front. We must naturally put them back mentally into place before trying to reconstruct the decorative scheme of the whole.

Errors made in reconstruction of Gateways

The same question arises in connection with the "dies", as we have agreed to call the four cubic stones wedged in, along the line of the two main pillars, below and above the middle lintel. But here the Northern and Eastern Gateways will hardly serve as guides, for the reason that, even on them, we cannot discover what rule has guided the decoration of these features. Yet one fact is obvious; these dies always bear on both faces symbolical representations of one or other of the Four Great Miracles and (except for two lintels, one on the Southern and the other on the Western Gateway) they even possess, so to speak, the monopoly of the Nativity and First Sermon scenes.[1] But either these themes are distributed in a most disorderly fashion, or else they are combined, at the mercy of the carver's fancy, with the trees and tumuli of the lintels to complete the usual numerical series of the four Great Miracles or of the seven Mānushi-Buddhas. We must not, however, lose ourselves among these details, which should rather be postponed till we come to the description of the plates, and to the account of the trees and wheels carved on the uprights of the Northern and Eastern Gateways, the only ones which have been preserved. For the present, our observations will have bearing only on the pillars and lintels, which alone afford a solid basis; nor shall we stop to notice in every case whether the projecting ends of the lintels do or do not prolong the subject treated on the middle part: for there is no perceptible rule for this either.

Southern Gateway

When, after thus clearing the approach, we embark on the study of the Southern Gateway, we meet with a further difficulty. Not only have its upper and lower lintels been reversed, but even its jambs have not come down to us complete. Nevertheless, by restoring the former to their original position and reassembling all the remaining pieces of the latter, it is possible to make out the broad lines of the programme which the decorator had mapped out for himself.

At the top of the facade we must, as on the Northern and Eastern Gateways, put back the row of the seven Mānushi-Buddhas. But here the seven symbols occupy only the middle part of the lintel, so that the projecting ends remain free for a Great Departure on the left and a symmetrical scene on the right. The two other lintels exhibit two magnificent and traditionally connected scenes, the War and Division of the Relics below, and Aśoka's visit to the stūpa of Rāmagrāma in the middle. The three back faces show merely, as usual, two decoratively-treated subjects (the Nativity and the Shaddanta-jātaka) and a plain decorative garland.

Passing on to the jambs, we find them devoted to the Bodh-Gayā cycle and its complementary miracle, the First Sermon at Benares. To the First Sermon is given the honour of the facade on the left (west) jamb; on the inner face of the same is the Enlightenment combined with Aśoka's visit to the Bodhi-tree; and the two other panels extant are concerned with the worship of the Bodhisattva's *cūḍā*. Lastly, what remains of the right jamb (Pl. 19) has only room for the incidents which occurred just before or just after the *Sambodhi*.

Let us now sum up. Apart from a single Jātaka, the Southern Gateway as yet treats only the four Great Miracles, or scenes closely connected with them. Though it shows great progress in comparison with the medallions on Stūpa 2, it marks no real

[1] At Sāñchī, 19 out of the 20 dies of the *toraṇas* are extant; on their 38 faces we can pick out 14 *Jāti* (*cf.* top lintel of Southern Gateway, Pl. 11), 6 First Sermons (*cf.* middle lintel of Western Gateway, Pl. 55), 10 Bodhi trees and 8 stūpas of Parinirvāṇa. In working out these statistics we can hardly escape the impression that the dies were prepared beforehand and sometimes put into place haphazard—unless we are also to take into consideration the donors' caprice.

advance on those at Bharhut, except in its new compositions of the War of the Relics and Aśoka's Pilgrimage.

Northern Gateway

The Northern Gateway, which has remained practically the same as when it was erected some two thousand years ago, brings us on to much firmer ground; but the lack of imagination in its decorators is a great blow. Only the two faces of the bottom lintel attest some attempt at innovation, first by depicting the Jātaka of Ṛishya-śṛiṅga, and secondly by unfolding that of Viśvantara. The two others, both obverse and reverse, show merely series of trees and stūpas, and a decorative treatment of the *Sambodhi* and the Shaḍḍanta-jātaka, both subjects already mentioned.

Matters are a little better on the jambs. They display, indeed, as before, only visiting or worshipping scenes, but at least they reveal an interesting effort at varying the spots. It is annoying for our statistics that we have lost the Great Miracle which was once depicted at the foot of the right pillar, the sole vestige of which is a big divine drum; but in spite of its disappearance, not one of the "eight" places of pilgrimage is absent. Besides the miracles of the four great holy towns (supplemented, in the case of Kapilavastu, by the Four Drives, the Great Departure and the Return) we are shown, side by side, the Jetavana and the Great Prodigy at Śrāvastī, the Descent from Heaven at Sāṅkāśya and the Monkey's Offering at Vaiśālī; while Rājagṛiha is suggested, first, by Ajātaśatru's visit and, secondly, by Indra's. But for the fact that the miracle considered as belonging to this last city was afterwards to become the Subjugation of the Mad Elephant, we already find here in full the programme of the future Gupta stelæ representing the "eight miracles".[1] We may note the fact; but we must not forget to add that the Monkey's Offering is the only subject which we might style new, and which we do not find on the railing, incomplete as it is, of Bharhut.

Eastern Gateway

The Eastern *toraṇa*, which has likewise remained in place, does not bring us as many novelties as its better artistic appearance gave us reason to hope. On its two faces, the top lintel has those evidently very venerable, but drearily mechanical, series of trees and stūpas. The facade of the middle lintel repeats *ad nauseam* the tableau of the Great Departure; and it is largely the carver's own fault, if we are left in doubt about the meaning of the "zoological garden" which loads the back face.[2] The bottom lintel is more instructive: on the obverse side it shows Aśoka's visit to the Bodhi-tree in quite a lively manner, whilst on the reverse it gives a new version (but, as usual, treated like a tapestry cartoon) of the legend of Rāmagrāma; even thus it does no more than take up again subjects of which one had already been sketched and the other suggested on the Southern Gateway.

[1] *Cf. J. As.*, 1909, Pl. I, or *Beginnings of Buddhist Art*, etc., Pl. XIX, 1.

[2] See description of Pl. 46, 2.

On the left (southern) jamb, the Uruvilvā cycle has been enlarged by the introduction of the series of episodes telling of the laborious conversion of the Jaṭilas. The Magadha miracles overflow even onto the other pillar, and the "Request of the Gods" is added to the *Sambodhi* and the "Master's Walk". But the effort to be original ends there. The inner face of the right (north) jamb relapses into repetitions of the Return to Kapilavastu, and, as to the storeys of heaven on its facade, we have already commented on the obtrusive monotony of this tableau.[1]

On the whole, our impression remains the same: the repertory is evolving, but exceedingly slowly. It is evident that the younger members of the workshop, separated by scarcely a generation from the sculptors of the Southern Gateway, remain hypnotised by the productions of their predecessors, and advance but timidly along the way opened by them. But still, they do advance. In the two following gateways it seems, on the contrary, as though they are simply marking time, or even retrogressing.

Western Gateway

Our first care must be to follow the peremptory advice which comparison with the Northern and Eastern Gateways gives us, and to reverse mentally the two bottom lintels on the Western Gateway. And what do we see, then, on the facade? At the top, as before, representations of trees and stūpas as commonplace as they are stylised; in the middle, a weakened version of the War of the Relics, and at the bottom a tableau of the *Sambodhi* drawn out length-wise. On the reverse side, in the same order, we find a Transport of the Relics, which is merely a poor duplicate, another dilution of a Great Miracle (the First Sermon) and a third edition of the Shaḍḍanta-jātaka.

The themes on the pillars are likewise borrowed from all sides. As a matter of fact, the Śyāma-jātaka has not been found at Bharhut, but that of Mahākapi figures among the medallions preserved in the museum at Calcutta. The scenes from the Last Life—Enlightenment, Mucilinda's Homage, Request of the Gods, Indra's Visit and the Return to Kapilavastu—are stale subjects, treated in the most slovenly fashion.[2] The three views of Paradise which, when complete, most probably covered the obverse of the left jamb, are simply a re-hash of themes already found on the Southern and Eastern Gateways. And in the iconographer's eyes the artist, clever as he is, deserves a very bad mark for not even being capable of filling four front panels on each facade with his repetitions, but having to resort to an ornamental design for the bottom one.

The Small Gateway

Thus it seems that the inventive and creative period of the workshop was already at an end with the Western Gateway; and a definite deterioration becomes noticeable on the Small Gateway of Stūpa 3. Here, only the upper lintel has to be mentally put back into place. By analogy with the other gateways we then perceive the familiar

[1] *Cf.* above, p. 227 and below, description of Pl. 51 *a*.

[2] For the panel cut at the bottom of the inner face of the left jamb, see the description of Pl. 65 *a*.—Besides, we shall have to point out many other weaknesses of the carver (or carvers) in describing the plates relating to the Western Gateway.

representations of the Bodhi-trees at the top of the facade. But these, mingled with stūpas, are now repeated all over the second lintel; and, as the three obverses are filled with decorative garlands, we can credit the sculptor's initiative only with an attempt at showing the Paradise of Indra. The ornamentation of the jambs is poorer still, being composed merely of symbols of the last three Great Miracles, with rows of worshippers set one above another.[1] In a word, the decorative scheme of this gate, which we have technical reasons for knowing to be later than the four others, is more archaic in inspiration even than that of the Southern Gateway. This proves once more how delicately criteria of chronology in matters of art require to be handled.

Conclusions

It is time to conclude. But before finally taking leave of the sculptors of the *toraṇas*—and with them, of the old school,—we must congratulate ourselves on the excellent relations which it is possible to maintain with them. The detailed examination of their works has inevitably put us on a familiar footing with them and even allowed us to discern certain nice shades among them.[2] It is certain, for instance, that the carver of the Southern Gateway was infinitely more conscientious than the carver of the Western Gateway: whilst the former is scrupulous not to make the least omission, the other takes the facts of the legend very lightly. But one may say as a general rule that there was confidence—and rightly so—between the artists and their customers. The donors could legitimately count (otherwise their generosity would instantly have dried up) on the perfect good faith of the carvers in their efforts to suggest the Master's miracles to the best of their ability; and the carvers in their turn felt equally justified in depending on the good will of their public; for if the indulgent imagination of their customers had not consented beforehand to see a Buddha everywhere, though they were never shown him, the good *rūpa-kāraka* would obviously have been obliged to shut up shop. Each side had, so to speak, to meet the other half-way; and the reader cannot fail to notice that this remark affects the validity of a number of the identifications we have proposed above. When, to interpret this or that panel, we have relied either on the context of the jamb (*cf.* Nos. 9 *a*, 13, 15, etc.), or on the insertion, by way of label, of a certain episode (*cf.* Nos. 6 *a* and 7 *a*), or on any other subsidiary detail, it was not, as will readily be believed, for the vainglory of increasing by some few instances the number of scenes identified by us. We proceeded simply on the lines of the tacit agreement made of old between the artists and their customers, which laid down as a basis of their transactions a sincere reciprocal effort at mutual understanding. The attitude of modern iconographers on this point should be no different from that of the old donors, whose legitimate heirs they set up to be; for they will recover the full knowledge of this artistic inheritance only on condition that, by long, close acquaintance with the sculptures, they put themselves into a position to understand by a bare hint the intentions of the sculptors.

---

[1] A single panel, as we shall shortly see (p. 245 and description of Pl. 103 *a*), is of special iconographical interest.

[2] See above, Ch. X.

In this spirit we believe that we have, with the help of our predecessors, Cunningham, Fergusson, Burgess, Grünwedel, d'Oldenburg, etc., and in the expectation that our successors will accomplish still more, discerned, besides some twenty decorative themes, four scenes of paradise, five jātakas, four scenes posterior to the Nirvāṇa, and some thirty biographical episodes—a total of about sixty different subjects. It is true to say that the elements making up these pictures, both buildings and persons, are repeated with almost mechanical uniformity: when you have seen one town, you have seen them all; when you have seen one king you have seen all the kings, and all the gods into the bargain.[1] Such as it is, this decoration, executed in square or oblong, but always rectangular, frames, testifies to a considerable progress from the circular medallions on the balustrade of Stūpa 2, which formed the subject of our first chapter. We should pay the highest compliments of all to the Sāñchī workshop, had not chance—luckily for us and unluckily for them—preserved likewise part of the sculptures at Bharhut and Bodh-Gayā (*cf.* above, p. 201). The existence of these valuable remains reduces to insignificance the innovations which we can place to the credit of the stone-carvers of Sāñchī. A single Jātaka (that of Śyāma), a few legendary scenes, such as the Return to Kapilavastu and the Monkey's Offering, and finally the pseudo-historical pictures—that is all that appears to represent their original contribution to the repertory. Moreover, it must not be forgotten that we have lost more than a third of the pillars from Bharhut and Bodh-Gayā, so that none can affirm with certainty that any subject at Sāñchī was completely unknown hitherto. And we have shown how the numerous themes, thus recast, are generally treated in a more and more prolix, less and less convincing, manner. In proportion as these replicas grow staler, the advance noticed in the composition and execution of the first Gateways slackens speed: the Western Gateway is covered merely with prosy repetitions, and the Small Gateway marks a positive retrogression. In short, everything points to the fact that the sap of the old school was spontaneously drying up.

Such is the dominant impression which emerges from our careful examination. But when, as we shall see, this slow but steady decadence is brought to a sudden stop, we must attribute the ensuing blank to exterior causes, notably to the invasions of the barbarians (*mlecchas*), who then, as they have done from time to time, spread over India. At all events, the fact as shown by the excavations is unquestionable. The prosperity of Sāñchī which was so brilliantly maintained during the three centuries immediately preceding our era, subsequently underwent almost as long an eclipse. Had there not been some check in the gatherings of the devotees, in the liberality of the patrons and in the activity of the artists during the first and second centuries of our era, we should not fail to find on the top of the sacred hill important monuments to correspond

[1] We shall have occasion to return to this point (p. 242).

with this transition period; and the decoration of these buildings would inevitably have shown us the effect of the new repertory meanwhile created in Gandhāra. Nothing, indeed, would have been more interesting than to study at Sāñchī the reactions of its workshop to the new fashions, and all that mingled give-and-take which we see in operation both at Mathurā and at Amarāvatī. But this curious spectacle is denied to us here. In vain, for example, do we look for those mixed stelæ in which the new versions of the four Great Miracles creep in little by little among the old formulas, without ever quite supplanting them. Neither on the site nor in the local museum have we discovered any relief which might serve to bridge the gap between the end of the old school, characterised by the absence of figures of the Buddha, and the appearance on the scene of those images of the Buddha which are the trade-mark of the new.

CHAPTER XVII

STATUES AND STELÆ

WITH the balustrades and gateways of the stūpa—which, remember, are all that we have touched upon so far in our study—we are far from having made a survey of all the sculptures at Sāñchī. Collected in the little local museum (an excellent catalogue of which has been published)[1] or scattered over the top and at the approaches of the holy hill, about a hundred stelæ and statues still survive in a more or less fragmentary state, not counting the reliefs which decorate the porches and basements of the late temples. The most interesting as well as the best preserved specimens have been reproduced in the plates,[2] and we have reserved this chapter for their examination. But, at the same time, we should cast a backward glance over the numerous figures in relievo, "double-faced" or even in the round, which the *toraṇas* have already presented. This retrospection is especially necessary, since up to now we have had systematically to neglect the identification of persons and attend mainly to the interpretation of scenes. Yet we must beware of tumbling into another pitfall. If we tried to make an inventory of one and all the figures which swarm over the reliefs, we should have to undertake a complete ethnography of ancient India; and even if the time were ripe for such an enterprise, this would be no place to attempt it. So let us keep within definite bounds and in dealing either with images or reliefs go no further than the part allotted to us, which is to give, as far as possible, titles to the scenes and names to the persons. Just as before, in spite of their overlapping, we deliberately neglected the decorative motifs in favour of the pictures, so now, out of the many figures illustrative of different types, we shall concentrate on those only to which Indian tradition has assigned either a particular rôle or a special worship. This is just the point where the difficulties begin.

Classes of figures on the *toraṇas*

Nothing, in fact, would be easier—or rather, nothing till now has been easier for us—than to class in categories the actors in the hundred-act play which is performed on the *toraṇas*. It was enough to make use of the only criterion which has ever allowed the diverse inhabitants of India to know the status they occupy among themselves, namely, the distinction of castes. By its means and without the slightest effort we have been able to collect, apparently at least, a most encouraging number of unquestionable identifications. On the bottom steps of the social ladder we have discovered barbarians,

[1] *Catalogue of the Museum of Archaeology at Sāñchī, Bhopal State*, by Maulvi Muhammad Hamid, Pandit Rām Chandra Kāk and Mr. Ramāprasād Chanda, with a foreword by Sir John Marshall (Archæological Survey of India), Calcutta, 1922.

[2] See particularly Pls. 67-70, 104-108, 113, 115, 118-120, 124-127.

jungle-dwellers, hunters, Svastika the grass-cutter, coachmen, elephant-drivers (placed on the crupper of their beasts), Chandaka the groom, male and female bearers of umbrellas and fly-whisks, standard-bearers, musicians and soldiers. The middle class of Vaiśyas has won our esteem in the persons of Sujātā the village girl, Trapussa and Bhallika the merchants, Anāthapiṇḍika the banker. But it is above all the noble Kshatriyas, on foot, in their carriages, on horseback, or astride on their elephants' necks, who parade complacently over the reliefs; and we have pointed out the sculptors' evident partiality for court scenes and royal processions. So we have seen, sitting or walking past, always accompanied by their retinues, the father of the Blessed One, Śuddhodana; his great friend Bimbisāra, the king of Magadha; the latter's parricide son, Ajātaśatru; the impartial Prasenajit of Kośala; the great Licchavi lords of Vaiśālī, etc. So much for the laymen. Among the religious figures, though we have had to resign ourselves to the absence of Buddhist monks, we have at least met a number of Brahman anchorites, and even recognized among them the three Kāśyapas. And when we turned from humanity to the 'non-human' (*amānushya*), that is, to supernatural beings, we were able to enumerate not only all the varieties of genii, including the Gandharva Pañcaśikha and the Nāga Mucilinda, but the first seven classes of gods, from the four Guardians of the World up to Brahmā, taking Indra on the way. In short, one would think that we moved about at ease in a familiar land, where nothing would be simpler than to put a name to the figures.

Figures identifiable only from the context

We must swiftly dispel this illusion. The fact is, we have not once been able to identify a single figure by his appearance, only from the context of the relief. Without that help, we are absolutely incapable of distinguishing, for instance, one king from another, or a king from a god, or even a king's court from a god's paradise: there is but one model for them all (physical type, dress and ornaments included), which serves to portray a god of the earth or a king of the sky, till it comes to be applied to the portrayal of the Mahāyānic Bodhisattvas. Before a detached image of a great lord we are thus left completely helpless; or, at least, it is as difficult to give him a proper name as it is easy to recognize his caste. To have a name, the image must also bear either a label (as at Bharhut) or some characteristic attribute or *lakshaṇa*, or some other extrinsic circumstance must come to our aid. The proof that these difficulties were not insurmountable, is that they did not prevent the Buddhist pantheon from being built up little by little till it attained all the amplitude to which the lamaic collections bear witness; but the further back one goes, the more hampering they prove to the iconographer. We will therefore follow very cautiously and within the limits of our own documents the progressive enrichment of this pantheon. To the deities whose cults the Buddhists shared with the Hindus, we shall see successively added the specifically Buddhist images of the Master, and then of the Bodhisattvas. As for the so-called Tantric idols, they hardly succeed in making their appearance.

I. Popular Divinities

The Indian sense of the divine hierarchy is concretely displayed in the tiers of paradises on the left pillar of the Eastern Gateway; and a lintel of the Small Gateway shows, on the slopes of Mount Meru, the wonted abode of the genii: for the demi-gods are no less minutely classed and localised by the scriptures than the gods. All the same, on the very threshold of our study, a great disappointment awaits us. At the bottom of each of the four *toraṇas*, standing at the four points of the compass round Stūpa 1, two genii, facing each other, play the part of door-keepers (*dvāra-pālas*). Their duties cannot be questioned: they are entrusted with stopping evil spirits, disbelievers, and in general, all inauspicious influences against which, before the erection of the Gateways, the crooked entrances of the balustrade already set up a screen.[1] We had some right to hope that, if these kindly porters did not portray the four Guardian Kings of the Four Regions of Space, each accompanied by his viceroy, they would at least offer us a faithful image of the four cohorts enrolled under their command. At any rate this is what we were led to expect by the analogy of the inscribed figures which originally decorated the corners of the Bharhut balustrade; and in the present case, failing inscriptions, their respective positions should have sufficed to reveal their names. Unfortunately, not one of them shows us the characteristic features or attributes which the texts give to the Gandharvas of the East, the Kumbhāṇḍas of the South, the Nāgas of the West, or the Yakshas of the North. You would think they had agreed beforehand to be exactly alike and, moreover, similar to the rest of the gods. And so our hope of complete and precise identification falls to the ground, to the great detriment of our iconographical census. **Guardian Door-keepers**

As a matter of fact, we meet here and there with genii belonging to these various categories, but, failing to find them in the expected place, our classification of them will be fatally lacking in precision. What appellation are we to give, for instance, to the bird-like figures with human bust, and the other flying spirits which fill up the skies of the reliefs, and sometimes even burst out from the ends of the architraves (*cf.* Pl. 17, 7)? Nothing would be more tempting than to unite them under the generic term of Gandharva: and this is probably the decision we should have ended by taking, did we not, by good or ill luck, know an undoubted specimen of this kind of genius, namely the harpist Pañcaśikha—and Pañcaśikha, like all the other gods in Indra's retinue (*cf.* No. 13 *c* and Pl. 35 *b*, 1), has no wings.[2] Besides, it is very probable that the name of Kumbhāṇḍa should be applied to the portly dwarfs who spout forth garlands from their mouths or act as atlantes (Pls. 11, 3; 19 *b*, 57, 59, 95, 99; and *cf.* Pls. 104 *f* and 126 *i*). Since they inhabit the region of the South, we might affirm that they play most suitably the part of atlantes on the pillars of the Small Gate erected on the south of Stūpa 3, but for the fact **Difficulties of nomenclature**

[1] On these architectural arrangements, *cf.* Sir John Marshall's note on p. 36 of *Guide to Sāñchī* and p. 33 above. As is well known, the idea of these screens and door-keepers is Chinese no less than Indian.

[2] The *Kinnaras*, on the other hand, who have wings, have no harps at Sāñchī; on these involved questions *cf.* above, p. 174, and *Guide to Sāñchī*. pp. 40 and 43.

that there they are merely imitating those on the Western Gateway of Stūpa 1, where the reason for their presence escapes us. When, moreover, on the Northern and Western Gateways, the same grotesque and demon-like creatures reappear beside the great god Māra to form the army of the 'Temptation' (Pls. 29, 2; 61, 3; 65 *b*, 1), by what name are we to call them, when the texts give them every name? In fine, there are but two cases where by unanimous consent the word correctly corresponds to the thing, *viz.*: those of the Nāgas and Yakshas; and these are also the two sorts of genii of which we possess the greatest number of detached images.

Nāga and Nāgī

It will be remembered that the serpent-genii are capable of taking on very various forms, sometimes animal, sometimes semi-animal and sometimes nearly human[1]; we have only to notice here, as a morphological curiosity, the single-hooded Nāgīs with forked tails which decorate a fragment of a pilaster of very late date (Pl. 127 *f*; No. 45 in the *Catalogue*). Besides this, we must draw attention to no less than five more-than-life-size statues, one of which is unfortunately incomplete. Three of them represent a Nāga standing and haloed with a seven-headed hood. Of these three, two are kept in the museum (No. A. 102 (Pl. 125 *b*) and No. A. 103), whilst the third and oldest (Pl. 125 *c*) is still the object of a popular cult on the hill of Nāgourī, in the immediate neighbourhood of Sāñchī. In date they range from the first or second to the fifth century A.D. The Nāgī which may have formed a pair with the Nāga of Nāgourī, though of much rougher workmanship, is broken in the middle and only the lower part remains (Pl. 124 *a*); but one almost complete, though very much worn, statue of a Nāgī with a fivefold hood, of slightly later date, was found *in situ* in front of Temple 31 (Pl. 115 *a* and *b*). All these images, though executed on the spot in the grey sandstone of the district, are treated in the manner of those which we know to have been in great vogue at Mathurā, and which Professor Vogel has so well studied: the all-human body is simply backed against the twisting coils and polycephalic hood of the reptile. As no inscriptions give us their name, it is impossible to push our study of them further

Yaksha and Yakshī

We are no more fortunate with the Yakshas whose images have been preserved in numbers on the *toraṇas* (*cf.* also Pl. 67). Whether they play the part of attendants or of door-keepers, their superhuman quality is beyond doubt, but their precise identity escapes us; for uniformly under their big tufted turbans and heavy trappings they all affect the rather conceited air of the *nāyaka* or "leading man" of the Indian dramas. Only two of them do anything to remind us by their martial attire that each of the four Guardian Kings of the World had eight *senāpati* or generals under his command. One, half preserved on a fragment of the west pillar of the Southern Gateway (Pl. 67 *e*; *Cat.* No. A. 12), is wearing the broad Indian sword at his side; the other, still in place on the south pillar of

[1] *Cf.* above, pp. 174-5. At present it is sufficient to refer the reader on all these points to the excellent studies of Prof. J. Ph. Vogel, *A. S. R.*, 1908-9, pp. 159 *sqq.*; *Indian Serpent-Lore*, p. 41.

the Western Gateway (Pl. 66 *a*) is holding a spear in his right hand and has hung his sword on a neighbouring mango-tree. For Yakshas or Yakshīs are always shown with the foliage of trees, which may betoken a paradise, but which in any case are the same as grew in those earthly paradises, the well-watered parks of India.

Kuvera, Hāritī and Pañcika

Among the *senāpati* of Kuvera or Vaiśravaṇa, the guardian god of the North, we know that the so-called Pañcika, as dispenser of riches, was the object of a particularly wide-spread cult, and it would have been more than surprising if none of his images had survived at Sāñchī. One would be equally justified in expecting to find his wife Hāritī, the ogress whom the Buddha's mercy had transformed into a giver of children; for we know from I-tsing that their joint image was placed in evidence in all the monasteries of India. And in fact[1] a whole panel on the gateway of Stūpa 3 is devoted to a picture of their happy family life (Pl. 103 *e*, 3); and this picture contains both the essential features which the Gandhāra School was to preserve and the minor details which later iconography was to develop.[2] In the foreground, the genie of riches and the fairy of fecundity are sitting side by side. He is holding a purse in his hand, she is suckling their last-born, and both are leaning tenderly towards a little boy who is learning to walk and seems to be trying to climb onto his father's knee. Behind them their court is represented by a female attendant, four musicians and a female dancer : for what Indian princeling had not his band and his ballet dancers ?

Isolated statues of Pañcika have likewise been found in the excavations, but they belong to a later date. Two of them appear on the left side of the threshold (Pl. 118 *b*) and in one of the platform panels (Pl. 119 *d*) of Temple 45 (*cf.* Pl. 117 *a*). Big and pot-bellied, just as such an opulent personage should be, the squatting genie is holding a purse in his right hand and in his other probably the lemon to which he owes his nickname of Jambhala. The museum contains two other detached statues, much mutilated (*Cat.*, No. 32 and A. 110); in the latter (Pl. 126 *h*) the ichneumon skin of which the purse is made, has again become a living ichneumon with jewels coming out of his mouth, whilst under the throne and right foot of the image lie inverted pots containing the treasure promised to the devotees.

The reader cannot have failed to notice at the other end of the threshold of Temple 45 another portly personage just like Pañcika, and certainly also a Yaksha in the train of the god of riches. This conjunction is no accident. Even to our knowledge, the two cronies already form a pair at the two ends of some lintels at Sārnāth and Ajaṇṭā—and at Ajaṇṭā again on the facades of two hypogea—when they do not go so far as to occupy fraternally the twin thrones of one sanctuary. Under the verandah of Cave XVII

[1] This identification is due to Madame E. Bazin-Foucher and appeared for the first time in the *J. A.*, juin 1933. As the group is placed below a Bodhi-tree, too rapid a glance had made us think of Māra's usual setting. We may add that Madame E. Bazin-Foucher believes she can recognize the same couple of genii on the right part of Pl. 96, 3.

[2] *Cf. Art Gréco-bouddhique du Gandhāra*, fig. 382-386 et 505.

an inscription suggests the name of Manibhadra for the second, and this identification is quite probable; for this chief of the genii is found likewise in the texts, associated either with Kuvera (whose younger brother he is sometimes considered to be) or with Pañcika himself.[1]

It is to be supposed that the isolated representations of Hāritī at Sāñchī have been unlucky, for we do not possess a single one; and though on Pl. 119 *d* the genie of riches is represented again in company with a woman standing on his left, no particular mark distinguishes her. In dealing with the Yakshī whose "horse's head" is, on the contrary, a most characteristic sign, and who, after being found on the railing of Stūpa 2 (Pl. 90, No. 86 *b*), reappears on the Small Gateway of Stūpa 3 (Pl. 96, 3), the stumbling block is different, but the result is the same; this time it is the texts which give her only a purely descriptive name. What now are we to say of the gentle ladies on the *toraṇas* (*cf.* also Pl. 68) who lean against the trunks or hang on to the boughs of trees which curve round like a vault above their heads? That these, too, are fairies, we are assured by the analogy of their labelled sisters at Bharhut; but for lack of inscriptions we know no more about them. It is especially hard to console oneself for this, since this graceful theme always enjoyed especial favour in Indian art. Without going outside Sāñchī, it appears already on the oldest carved balustrades (*cf.* Pl. 74, 1 *a*); and we find it again mechanically treated under trees formalised into scrolls at the right and left of the principal entrance to Temple 45 (Pl. 118 *b*).

Yakshī and Tree motif

Gaṅgā and Yamunā

On the same doorway, these two Yakshīs stand next to two other female divinities who, not content with acting as their doubles in their rôle as guardians of the gate, usurp this function again on each side of the two side-porches (Pls. 118 *a*, 120 *a* and *b*; *cf.* 113 *c*). Though always escorted by their umbrella-bearers, these are deities of much the same class—in fact, as we should say, a kind of naiad-queen; but thanks to the indication of their respective *vāhanas*, we can for once identify Gaṅgā on the *makara* or crocodile to the spectator's left, and to his right her tributary, Yamunā, on the tortoise (*kūrma*). Yet we must beware of exaggerating the iconographical importance of this meagre success: there is hardly a mediæval temple in all Northern India whose door is not framed by these commonplace images.

Erotic couples

Finally, the reader must have noticed incidentally on these plates a theme whose traditional importance is too great not to be mentioned here, though it remains obstinately anonymous to the very end. It concerns the numerous couples joined in more or less close embrace, which we already observed in the decoration of Stūpa 2 (*cf.* above, p. 175) and which we find again on Temples 18 and 45. Such figures may be seen in abundance, both

[1] See *Catalogue of the Museum of Archaeology at Sārnāth*, p. 233 and Pls. 24 and 29; Ajaṇṭā, *A. S. W. I.*, IV, Pl. 13; 23, 2; 30 and 33, 1; and *cf. J. Hyderabād Arch. Soc.*, 1919-20, p. 96. In support of the identification *cf. Lalita-vistara*, p. 390, l. 20; *Kathāsarit-sāgara*, 13, 165 and 131, 3; Wassiliew, *Der Buddhismus*, p. 198 (216 in Germ. ed.), etc.

on the old balustrades at Mathurā and on the door frames or capitals in the hypogea at Ajaṇṭā and Ellorā, not to mention the modern Brāhmanic temples. Here, at Sāñchī, the usual love duet (Pls. 113 *c*, 119 and 120 *a*) is sometimes transformed into a trio by the addition of another woman (Pls. 118 and 120 *b*). Faced with such erotic scenes, a novice in archæology is apt to be both dumbfounded and shocked; for how is he to explain why pictures so free, sometimes even licentious, are to be found round stūpas or on temples which (as the excavations have proved) enshrined holy relics or images of the Buddha? With a little more experience, he will perceive that it is quite useless to worry his head about this. Neither the Master nor his Law nor his Community could be held responsible for this artistic immodesty. These erotic scenes were no more 'Buddhist' then than they are now, and the explanation of their presence where one would least expect them is doubtless the same for antiquity as for the Middle Ages. If the sculptors had no scruple about decorating religious buildings in this way, that is merely because, being artists and not moral preachers, they were accustomed to flatter public taste, even in what was least commendable, and to follow the fashion in vogue in every workshop.

The Four Lokapālas

But let us leave these purlieus of mundane art and superstition, and clamber up the first stage of the celestial pyramid. At the four corners of our horizon the Four Guardian Kings of the World have their seats, whose subjects are the four categories of genii which we have just enumerated. Their names—Dhṛitarāshṭra (in the East), Virūḍhaka (in the South), Virūpāksha (in the West) and Vaiśravaṇa (in the North)—are well known to us from the texts. Moreover, we see (or at least, if the stone were not mutilated, we should see) all four of them twice or thrice over: perhaps at the foot of the Bodhi-tree on the left jamb (Pl. 51 *a*), certainly in the lowest sky of the right jamb of the Eastern Gateway (Pl. 49 *b*), and on the remains of the Southern Gateway (No. 9 *d* and Pl. 19 *c*, 2; *cf*. Pl. 56, 2). Here is a fresh disappointment; for no distinction of a plastic kind is made among them in the Old School any more than in Gandhāra; once more, they are *devas* like the others.

Devas

We have commented already (pp. 227-8) on the strange monotony of the representations of the first six storeys of Heaven. Only from the numbering of their storeys have we been able to guess the generic name of each of the first six categories of devas; and their superiors, the 'Inhabitants of the Pure Abodes', which we have every reason to locate at the top of Pl. 51 *a* (*cf*. Pl. 103), are exactly like the others. Even where Māra, the sovereign of the world of the senses, is shown in the rôle of Tempter, as on the Northern (Pl. 29, 2) and Western Gateways (Pls. 61, 3 and 65 *b*, 1), he neither displays nor makes anybody beside him display any characteristic *lakshaṇa*, not even the *makara*, which was his ensign in his quality of God of Love as well as of Death.[1] The puzzle is no less great, when it comes to distinguishing Brahmā from Indra in the scenes

[1] On this *makara-ketu*, *cf*. *Art G.-b. du Gandhāra*, II, fig. 400-401 and p. 196.

which claim the presence of both, as in the 'Request' or the 'Descent' (Pls. 49 *c*, 64 *a*, 2, 34 *c*), or to differentiating Indra from the gods in his train on the occasion of his famous 'Visit' to the Buddha (Pls. 35 *b*, 1 and 64 *a*, 3). And if we fail to discover any traits of individual physiognomy, we are scarcely any better off in regard to guiding signs in the attire, though on the occasion of the Viśvantara and the Śyāma-jātaka (Pls. 29, 3 and 65 *a*, 1), Indra has allowed himself to be adorned with the tiara which was to remain his special mark in the School of the North-West. We know, moreover, that this School deliberately gave Brahmā, in his character of eponymous god of the Brāhmans, the special head of hair of the Brāhman anchorites. It is interesting to find that this same characterisation has become traditional on the stelæ of the Gupta period: and so, as the two divinities standing at either side of the Buddha on Pl. 70 *c* have had the good luck to keep the tops of their heads, the round tuft of hair on one declares him to be Brahmā, as surely as the cylindrical tiara of the other shows him to be Indra.[1]

II. The Buddhas

From the Devas we pass in hierarchical order to him who is "above the gods", namely the Buddha. But, to begin with, we must sum up all our previously acquired experience and repeat once more what we have said about the absence of his image in the old Indian school. The unanimity of the monuments on this point has forced the agreement of archæologists, but we must beware of playing on the meaning of words. What is meant is, of course, the anthropomorphous image of the Buddha, for on the Sāñchī Gateways, as at Bharhut, his symbolical image is believed to be everywhere, in all the lotuses, beside all the wheels, on all the thrones, under all the trees. A lover of paradoxes might even maintain without too much exaggeration that we already have a full-length representation of the Master on the east jamb of the Northern Gateway; and to verify the assertion one need only refer to Pl. 37 *a* of the present collection. Obviously the sculptor has taken advantage of the four metres of the pillar's height to show in his own way the Blessed One, with almost his traditional stature, which (as everybody knew) was sixteen Indian feet. Below, he has naturally placed the two sacred foot-prints, marked with the wheel, the direction of the toes showing that the sole is supposed to be planted on the ground. Above, over a sort of long stalk made of palmettes issuing out of lotuses, he has placed the emblem which, as we have seen, often stands for the Buddha on the thrones of the reliefs (Pl. 18 *b*, 1; 40, 3; 51 *a*, 2) and which, for want of a more Buddhist name, we have called *nandipada* or taurine.[2] Finally, he has crowned the whole with an umbrella, another emblematic sign of the noble 'presence,' and from top to bottom, on both sides of the central stalk, he has lavishly scattered, in the shape of necklaces and jewellery, all

---

[1] *Cf.* again, on Pl. 70 *b*, the silhouette left by the smashing of Indra's head. One might also wonder whether it is not he on Pl. 126 *b*, taking the place of Vajrapāṇi.

[2] If one insisted on giving a Buddhist designation, we might call it a *dvi-ratna* (Buddha and Dharma) to distinguish it from the *tri-ratnas* (Buddha-Dharma-Saṅgha) which decorate the tops of the gates (*cf.* Pls. 26 and 43) and where the third element, the Community, is represented by the addition of the 'shield'.

that the world recognizes as most precious.[1] We may be certain from the analogy of a pillar at Amarāvatī (Fergusson, *Tree and Serpent Worship*, Pl. 70) that he meant to carry out, and sincerely believed that he had thus carried out, a veritable icon of the Buddha; for there, too, a sort of column-shaft, surmounting the same sacred feet and surmounted by the same three-cusped symbol, serves to represent the Buddha, now walking and now preaching, on the occasion of the miraculous conversion of the Jaṭilas (*cf.* above, p. 210). We are therefore dealing here, indeed, with a conscious effort, aiming at the plastic portrayal of the Master: and the odd result, not to say miscarriage, of this attempt, only confirms our preliminary observations.

It remains true, then, to say, as we have done above (p. 239), that in the sculptures preserved at Sāñchī we pass without transition from the study of the old aniconic reliefs to that of the icons of the Buddha. For the intermediate period of which we find so many traces elsewhere, particularly at Mathurā and Amarāvatī, there is no evidence here, the erection of no new stūpa having coincided with it. Nowhere, either on the buildings or in the museum do we see the figure of the Buddha supplanting his own symbols little by little, first taking his seat on the empty throne of his miracles, then passing erect through all the various ups and downs of his life, and finally lying down to die on the bed of his *Parinirvāṇa*. Nor is it given to us to watch how his image grows in the legendary scenes at the expense of the other actors, then reduces them to the rôle of tiny attendants, until it relegates them to the pedestal and completes the transformation of a bas-relief into an icon. Or, at least, we find only a very late example of the second stage of this development, in a stele of the seventh century (Pl. 126 *b*; *Catalogue* No. 9), which represents the very one of the eight Great Miracles whose absence we regretted above (p. 219), namely the "Subjugation of the Mad Elephant" at Rājagṛiha. Otherwise, all our Sāñchī representations of the Buddha are either isolated statues or with the onlookers already resigned to their purely passive rôle. It should perhaps be remembered that the greater number are only "detached", so far as the technical and ritual habits of India admit of it. Owing to the fact that these idols were designed to be set with their backs to the wall of a stūpa or temple, the artists have generally felt free from the necessity of completing them in the round. Finally, from the chronological point of view, they are distributed over about ten centuries and spontaneously fall into three principal groups, according as they correspond to the period of the Kushāṇas, the Guptas, or of later dynasties.

Buddhas in the Kushāṇa style: second to fourth centuries A.D.

The slowing down to which we have alluded in the activity of the Sāñchī workshop during the first centuries of our era can be only too easily explained by the invasions of the Śaka-Pahlavas and then of the Kushāṇas, who under Kanishka and his successors penetrated to the very heart of India. In the land of Mālwā, more or less independent condottieri, known in history under the Persian title of kshatrapa, *i.e.*, "satrap", established and

[1] For a somewhat different view, see pp. 144 *sq.* and 145, n. 1.

maintained themselves until the end of the fourth century in constant warfare, first with the Andhras and then with the early Guptas, not to mention their intestine quarrels. It is not hard to imagine how such a troublous period should have left us nothing comparable to the legacy of the previous centuries. Yet this was the time when the thriving workshops at Mathurā were exporting all over the empire of the Kushāṇas works which are easily recognizable as theirs, on account both of the style and of the characteristic appearance of the red, yellow-speckled sandstone of which they are made. Just as they are found at Śrāvastī, Benares and even as far as Magadha, so we find at Sāñchī Buddha and Bodhisattva images which have been brought over from Mathurā to be dedicated; and this necessarily onerous transport leads one to infer that the articles in question could not be procured on the spot. One of them, the statue of a standing Buddha, of which unfortunately only the feet and pedestal remain, might have provided an interesting historical document, since an inscription refers it to the second century. Its donors have had themselves represented on the socle, and all of them—men, women and children—are wearing the characteristic dress of those very barbarian invaders who had come down from the North-West (Pl. 105 *c*; *Cat.* No. A. 83); the boots, breeches and belted cassocks of the men and the characteristic jackets of the women leave no room for doubt on this point.

We place in about the fourth century two other statuettes of the Buddha which form the transition between the Gandhāra style and that of Central India in the time of the Guptas. The first (Pl. 105 *b*; *Cat.* No. 19) again came originally from Mathurā (the Mathurā museum preserves almost a twin image, Vogel's *Cat.* No. A. 21 and Pl. XVI); it is evidently doing its utmost to reproduce, though in the stiffest manner possible, the drapery of the Græco-Buddhist statues. With the small panel on Pl. 124 *e* (*Cat.* No. 20) we probably return to local workmanship and local stone; but the folds of the *saṅghāṭī*, though rather more supple, are even more sketchily treated. Here the head itself is lost, not only the nimbus, as was the case in Pl. 105 *b*. No doubt it would have shown us the same round face and thick lineaments and curled hair—features which were henceforward to become the rule for all idols of the Buddha.

Buddhas in the Gupta style: fifth century

After being incorporated with the empire of the Guptas in the last years of the fourth century, the district of Sāñchī enjoyed a new period of peace and prosperity. In this Golden Age of India we must doubtless place, among other new foundations (such as Temple 17, Pillars 26, 35, etc.), the dedication of four great Buddhas,—originally seated under canopies carved out of the same grey stone—which still decorate, mutilated as they are, the four entrances to Stūpa 1 (Pl. 70).[1] We know from an inscription engraved on the balustrade (No. 834 *infra*) that in the year 450 they were already in place; and, moreover, we find in them all the well-known characteristics of the Gupta style. On the soft, even effeminate shape of the trunk and limbs, the draperies are barely indicated or entirely

[1] For these four images, *cf.* pp. 38-9 above.

obliterated. The fact that the body is not naked—if it had been, we should be dealing with a Jaina, not a Buddhist idol—is revealed only by the mark where the edge of the garment cuts the arms and legs above the wrists and ankles and displays its folds on the pedestal. But the intentional simplicity of the statue is deliberately counterbalanced by the extraordinary richness of the nimbus. It is hardly necessary to draw attention to the point that the refined decoration of these nimbuses is after all merely a development of that on the medallions of the old balustrades; the lotus rosette still continues to fill the centre, and it is by no means rare for its petals to edge the periphery, as on Pl. 70 *c* and *d*. As for the head, a single specimen of which is preserved, it shows, under its cap of stylised curls, just the 'moon face' which precedents lead us to expect; unfortunately, it does not assume, though trying to do so, the expression of serene concentration, nor veils under its lowered eyelids an intensity of gaze fit to compare with those on the famous and doubtless contemporary image at Sārnāth. Even in the 'good period' we must evidently take account of the unequal quality of the workshops; and the brevity of the said 'good period' is the sad lesson always taught by the history of any art.

Later Buddhas: sixth to eighth century

At this moment, however, another of those periodical invasions intervenes, as is the rule in the destiny of India, coming down from the North-West and spreading devastation over the interior of the peninsula: about the year 500 the Huns seized Mālwā and the surrounding lands. Doubtless their empire was but ephemeral, and from the beginning of the seventh century Harshavardhana came and restored some unity and tranquillity to the Ganges basin. It is in his reign that we should be most inclined to place the greater number of the statues of the Buddha which remain to be examined and which are grouped under the general heading of 'late Gupta'. It is in fact still the continuation of the Gupta style, but the charm is broken and the idealistic aura which throbs and quivers round works of the fifth century has vanished. In seeking to represent the soul at the expense of the body—an attempt contrary to the genius of sculpture—the sculptors have foundered in lifelessness, both bodily and spiritual. Thus, for instance, the Buddhas standing on Pl. 126 *a* and *c* reproduce all the general features of those at Sārnāth, even to the stylised fall of the folds of the *saṅghāṭī*: only the mechanical heaviness of the execution unmistakably places these sawdust dolls in the seventh century.

The most instructive, however, because the most extensive, is the series of our seated images, which seems to reflect fairly well the later evolution of the Buddha type from the end of the fifth to the end of the eighth century. The transition from the Gupta statues on Pl. 70 is supplied by the one on Pl. 125 *e*; his nimbus is lost, but he has the same meditative attitude, the same kind of hair, the same roundness of face, the same obliteration of draperies save at the edge of the garments and in the fan of fluted pleats, which, as on Pls. 105 *b* and 70 *b*, covers the plain cushion on the seat. Under the crossed legs of the idol, probably a teaching one, in Temple 31 (Pl. 115 *c*), one can notice the original and much more rational, though less graceful, manner in which the artist has arranged the gathered skirts of the monastic gown; but this is only an individual experiment, without a future; what must be particularly noted is that the lotus which was already sketched on Pl. 70 *c* and which is here doubled with a second row of symmetrical petals, is henceforward to become the stereotyped seat of the Master. With Pl. 125 *d* we take one step further; for not only does the *saṅghāṭī* leave the right shoulder uncovered, but to the lotus the pedestal adds two lions with one paw raised, which are also to become the rule, no doubt to mark more clearly the throne (*siṁha-āsana*) of the Śākya-siṁha. Finally, the relatively late date of the idols in Temple 45 (Pl. 120 *c* and *d*) is confirmed by the fact that they add to these signs the gesture of "Calling the Earth to witness", and the ovalisation of the nimbus. Against this conjunction of chronological criteria, the reappearance on the statue in the central sanctuary (Pl. 120 *c*) of the apparently archaic indication of the draperies could not prevail, even if the fall of the cloak on the left shoulder, with its three rows of little folds, did not betray a very late period; and as for the statue in the right vestibule (Pl. 120 *d*), though this fall is wanting, the *makara* head which joins the back-slab to the oval of the nimbus is already a mediæval motif.

We thus come down in stages to the late mediæval period; but there our specimens stop, and consequently our study: the rest of the history of the Buddha type is to be found further East. At Sāñchī, the clay ex-votos (Pl. 113 *a* and *b*) themselves go back—or at any rate their moulds go back—to the sixth-seventh century, to judge by the script of their *credo*. In fact, of the latest Buddhas, we find only a few mediocre icons carved in the niches of some tiny stūpas (Pl. 127 *a*, *c* and *d*). If we keep to the only statues which count, two remarks must be made: first, that none appears to be much later than the eighth century,[1] and second, that all aim only at showing the Blessed Śākya-muni. The six other past Buddhas, for which the *toraṇas* had still so much room to spare, seem to have been put aside in favour of the only one who had left historical souvenirs; and as for their metaphysical counterparts, the five Dhyāni-Buddhas, we must suppose that their iconographical codification was brought about, if not too late, at least too far from Mālwā to have left any trace here. Of this fact we seem to find an immediate and incontestable proof in the absence of variety in the *mudrās* assigned to the statues we have just reviewed. The standing figures, as we have seen, exhibit only that of the "Gift", and the old seated images only that of the "Meditation"; those in Temples 31 and 45 alone show the gesture of "Teaching" or, as in the famous sanctuary at Mahābodhi, that of "Calling the Earth to witness". On the whole, these are all traditional attitudes of the last Buddha of our æon, and nothing authorises us to suspect that the Sāñchī hill has ever mustered, like that at Borobudur, any groups of five Buddhas distinguished by five different *mudrās*.

[1] See, however, p. 73 *supra*, as to the cult statue in Temple 45.

III. The Bodhisattvas

If we turn now to the Bodhisattvas, we shall not be long in perceiving that they are distributed chronologically over the same great periods of the Kushāṇas, the Guptas and the later dynasties. People familiar with the development of the Buddhist pantheon will not be surprised that the first of these has left us—as usual carved out of red Mathurā sandstone—only images of the two Bodhisattvas who alone were recognized by the primitive Church, the one who became the Buddha Sākya-muni and the one who is to become the Buddha Maitreya. It is only in the Gupta period that the so-called Mahāyānic Bodhisattvas, like Avalokiteśvara and Vajrapāṇi, make their appearance. As for the later periods, the rare fragments which remain have too little artistic or documentary interest to be worth reproducing here.

The pious lady-donor who bought at Mathurā the statuette on Pl. 124 *b* (*Cat.* No. A. 82) and had it carried at her own expense to Sāñchī, fortunately took care to have an inscription[1] engraved which dates it at the middle or end of the second century A.D., and identifies it as the image of the Bhagavat at the moment when he sat down under the *jambu* tree. It thus portrays the Blessed One at the time when, being as yet only the young heir-apparent Siddhārtha, he fell into the ecstasy of his "First Meditation" at the foot of the rose-apple tree, whose shadow, in order to continue sheltering him, miraculously ceased to turn with the sun (*cf.* above, p. 202). Thus, whilst wearing the dress and ornaments of a high-caste layman, he assumes the traditional pose and gesture of the Indian monk. It is deeply to be regretted that such a well-authenticated image has come down to us so mutilated, and that the condition of the similar statue preserved in the Mathurā museum (*Math. Cat.* No. A. 45, Pl. X) is not much better. Yet we can complete them both without too much uncertainty by giving them the head, big earrings and rich turban of their double, the personage who sits enthroned in the centre of the pedestal of Pl. 105 *c*; for in all probability it is the image of Prince Siddhārtha which the sculptor, in agreement with his clients, has placed here under that of the Buddha Śākya-muni, just as in a Natural History museum the chrysalis is exhibited underneath the perfect insect. **Siddhārtha**

A still more cruel fate has annihilated the precautions taken in exactly the same manner, for the sake of posterity, by another lady donor. Of a statuette inscribed as Maitreya, also originally coming from Mathurā, only three-fifths of the pedestal and a fragment of the right foot have been left (Pl. 124 *d*; *Cat.* No. A. 86)[2]. As the Bodhisattva was represented standing, this foot is naturally shod with the sandal which princes and noblemen commonly wore. But the image carved on the pedestal, seated in the pose of a *yogī*, is barefoot. Minute and sketchy as it is, it is still possible to recognize Maitreya by the water flask which he is holding in his left hand and which doubtless means here, as in **Maitreya**

---

[1] No. 828; pp. 385-6 *infra*.

[2] *Cf.* pp. 47 and 387.

the Gandhāra School, that he is destined to be reborn for the last time as a Brāhman. For in these sculptures too, as on the *toraṇas*, the symbols continued to speak their mute language and to keep more confidences for the initiated than might be imagined.

Avalokiteśvara

A small head in yellowish sandstone (Pl. 126 *d*; *Cat.* No. B. 30) supplies the transition to the work of the Gupta period. Alike in the thick features of the face and in the rounded tuft of the turban which is held in place by a diadem, it recalls the Kushāṇa type of Mathurā; but it already displays a tiny figure of a Dhyāni-Buddha in the headdress. The dhyāni-mudrā of this latter declares him to be Amitābha and at once identifies the head as having belonged to an image of Avalokiteśvara. We possess two further statues of this Bodhisattva, both larger than life, obviously in Gupta style, and apparently the work of the same hand (Pl. 125 *a* and *c*; *Cat.* Nos. A. 100 and 101). They show him standing, the right arm bent near the shoulder and the left hand resting on the knot of the shawl which he has carelessly thrown round his loins in the form of a very loose girdle. As one of them has the right knee and the other the left knee bent slightly forward, they were probably meant to form companion-pieces. Both are wearing bracelets, necklaces and earrings, but there is no image of Dhyāni-Buddha emerging from their high, richly-decorated tiaras. If, none the less, we succeed in identifying them, it is because both are holding up in the right hand the pink lotus (*padma*) to which Avalokiteśvara owed his surname Padmapāṇi.

Vajrapāṇi

It is, again, thanks to his special *lakshaṇa* that we can identify another statue, very similar both in attitude and in style, only of smaller size and in a worse state of preservation (Pl. 108 *b* and pp. 51 and 391; *Cat.* No. A. 99). Though the right hand has been destroyed, the trident end of a thunderbolt has been left on the hip. Now, on the Gandhāra reliefs this *vajra* had long been borrowed from the god Indra by the protecting genie of the Master, who had thence taken the name of Vajrapāṇi. This was the attribute and name which he still kept, when from a common Yaksha he was promoted by the Community, in reward for his good and loyal services, to the dignity of Bodhisattva. A technical detail, perhaps, deserves to be stressed here. The two Avalokiteśvaras on Pl. 125 already wear, inserted between their tiara and their nimbus, a sort of fluted frill apparently belonging to their headdress. The Vajrapāṇi on Pl. 108 has no halo except this sort of 'Medici collar' (if one may so call an ornament which does not surround the neck, but only the nape); but its frills are pierced with holes into which were once fixed the tenons of a metal halo, probably gilded, whilst these rays were simply delineated with a brush on the plain nimbuses of the two other statues.

Mediæval Images

The contingent of Buddhist deities at Sāñchī is reduced to these few big idols. In spite of what the excavations at Sārnāth might have led us to hope, we find no other Bodhisattva, not even Mañjuśrī, nor any female Bodhisattva, not even Tārā. Not that we do not guess at her image in No. A. 111 in the museum, but this statuette is decapitated; and we do not know with whom to connect the two feminine heads reproduced on Pl. 126 *e* and *f* (*Cat.* B. 42 and 43), both of late date. Among the other fragments dating from the Middle Ages which have also been recovered, several more may be distinguished which must have belonged to Avalokiteśvaras (*cf. Cat.* A. 109 and 124; B. 44 and 47), but the majority of these pieces are useless from an iconographical point of view. One remark emerges, however, which is of importance. In all this collection of mutilated statuettes there is but a single figure with multiple arms, and even this one has only four (Pl. 126 *j*). The jar which it is turning over with its left hand seems to connect it with the Jambhala we have already discussed (p. 245); but the little bull crouching between its legs peremptorily identifies it as Śiva—a particularly acceptable attribution, since Śiva would find himself in the bosom of his family, not far from Durgā his wife (*cf. Cat.* Nos. B. 69-70) and their son Gaṇeśa (*Cat.* No. A. 123). The question in itself is of little importance; the fact on which we must insist is that the latest of the images at the local museum offer us nothing really tāntric.

Perhaps the most interesting result obtained from our general survey of the images at Sāñchī is that the Buddhist pantheon which they reveal is conspicuously incomplete. None of those monstrous idols which throng the lamaic temples to-day; no other images of Mahāyānic Bodhisattvas but those of Avalokiteśvara and Vajrapāṇi; no series of Dhyāni-Buddhas, though Amitābha is found in the headdress of his spiritual son: for each category of divinities our observations are the same—they give us the impression that the development of Buddhist archæology was cut short in Western India. We had already learned from the Mathurā Catalogue of Prof. J. Ph. Vogel that the great productive period of the workshops of this town came to an end in the sixth century A.D., probably with the invasion of the Huns; and it now seems apparent that the artistic activity of Sāñchī, rekindled somewhat by the zeal of Harshavardhana, and under his ægis, scarcely continued beyond the eighth century. The eastern part of the Ganges basin was more fávoured. The Sārnāth Catalogue of Prof. Vogel and Rai Bahadur Daya Ram Sahni occasionally comes as far down as the eleventh century; but it was particularly in Magadha and Bengal that the theory and technique of the purely Buddhist heavens and gods were worked out. Yet their novelty is at bottom less new than might have been supposed. Plastically speaking, the Dhyāni-Buddhas are still plain Buddhas, while as for the Bodhisattvas, they can only be great lords, all of the same type, differing from one another in nothing but their attributes. The supernatural images alone, with their multiple heads, arms and even legs, with their stylised contortions or licentious attitudes, seem to bear witness to a new bent—wildly extravagant, no doubt, but original—of the Indian imagination. And even that is only half true. Indeed, the deforming mania which is set on dehumanising the bodies given to divinities, seems to be a comparatively recent malady in India, at least in its most virulent form,[1] though many people both in Europe and in America continue to consider it as the basic characteristic of Indian art. But we must not forget that what is called 'Tantrism' is tantamount to the enthroning of the old popular deities (till then kept outside the bounds of the official cults) on the altars of the sanctuaries. A number of the monstrous or obscene images apparently created in the east of Gangetic India and so complaisantly adopted by the Tibetans, are nothing at bottom but the revival, exaggerated and aggravated, of the grotesque genii and erotic couples of earlier days.

General Conclusions

The partial conclusions at which our last chapter has arrived accord also with the general conclusions of our study. Upon the whole, what can Sāñchī offer to any one undertaking to study the evolution of Buddhist art in India? The reply is now ready: for the mediæval period, almost nothing; for the Gupta and Kushāṇa periods, very little; for the ancient period, almost everything. We shall not, of course, be suspected of wishing to minimise the priceless utility of the inscribed documents at Bharhut (*cf.* above, p. 201); but at Sāñchī, we repeat, the fates have granted us the exceptional favour of possessing *in situ* and practically intact, an incomparable ensemble of monuments. This is what gives this hill its eminent dignity and prime importance in Indian archæology; this is what justifies the special care which, after so many outrages at the hands of amateurs during the last century, has been lavished upon it by the Archæological Survey under the direction of Sir John Marshall; and this is what renders a complete publication of it so necessary. May we be allowed to add further, this is also what explains our having devoted the major part of our study to what is called the "Old School". From the iconographical point of view, Sāñchī's two substantial contributions are the sculptures which decorate, first, the balustrade of Stūpa 2, and, secondly, the gates of Stūpas 1 and 3. As the interval separating them is fortunately made good by the fragments preserved from Bharhut and Bodh-Gayā, we have an uninterrupted vista of the same artistic development. It will be long before historians have exhausted this precious mine of information.

So far as we have been able to see and without prejudice to what future scholars may look for, this information falls into three principal categories according as it concerns the technique of sculpture, the identification of the subjects represented, or the illustrations of the old Indian civilisation.

It will easily be seen that in dealing with reliefs which pass from a simple decorative pattern, through memory drawing, up to 'genre' and historical pieces,

[1] It should not be forgotten that four-armed images of Śiva appear as early as the first century A.D. on the back of coins of the Kushāṇas.

innumerable questions relating to modelling, foreshortening, and perspective cannot fail to crop up : but we have steered clear of them from the beginning. It is not that we fail to recognize their interest, as well as their extreme difficulty : but these knotty problems have already been treated in the second part of this work by Sir John Marshall.

The task which we have essayed, has consisted in following up the identification of scenes and persons ; for, as it presupposes some knowledge of the texts, this task devolves on a philologist. Far be it from our mind to exaggerate the importance of the results, obtained in this sphere in the course of the last fifty years, which we summed up above (p. 238) ; yet we consider that, to write the history of a School of Art, it is indispensable to possess an intimate knowledge of its repertory and to be able to follow its evolution step by step. Let it suffice here to note that, from our detailed survey of the multifarious themes, a law has more and more clearly emerged, which may be formulated as follows : The dominating tendency which directs the minds and hands of donors and artists at Sāñchī is gradually to substitute for purely decorative motifs borrowed from public stock the specifically Buddhist symbol, scene or person. Obviously that is the least that one could expect of their particular devotion to their Master's memory, but it may be useful to have it directly verified by a study of the documents. What we could not avoid intimating at the beginning of this essay, we are now in a position to affirm with full knowledge of the case: for our eyes have seen. In spite of all the difficulties offered by the inadequacy of technical means in the Old School, we have seen the four Great Miracles assert and enlarge their rôle little by little on the balustrades of the stūpas, and each of them organize round itself a sort of cycle ; and to the kernel thus formed, we have seen annexed in turn the former lives, the four secondary Great Miracles, and, finally, the scenes posterior to the *Parinirvāṇa*. Everything considered, there is not a branch of the legendary tradition which has not been laid under contribution. Evidently the order of the day was that the decoration of every Buddhist building must be, as far as possible, given up to the commemoration of the Buddha alone. Nowhere, we may say, can this law be better verified than at Sāñchī. But, at the same time, it is abundantly clear to what an extent the new Gandhāra school, with all its differences of form, is really only continuing the inner evolution of the old school of Central India. Doubtless the Indo-Greek artists of the North-West had received quite a different artistic training, and had methods at their disposal entirely unheard-of till then inside the peninsula ; but they necessarily placed both their talents and their chisels at the service of donors whose *desiderata* remained invariable. When they are bent on composing for their use an illustrated biography of the Master, they merely go on with the task already undertaken by the Bharhut and Sāñchī sculptors. That they marked a decisive advance in being the first to instal the bodily image of the Master in the centre of their compositions, is a point which, in the light of all the facts now known, it seems impossible to call in question. But, at the same time, we must recognize that, on a number of their panels, the old school had set up and prepared the throne on which it only remained to seat the Buddha's icon. If we may be allowed to use a term which Renaissance Italy did not blush to employ, in the 'bottega' of Buddhist art the staff of the workshop changed, but not the firm's trade. A new gang, indeed, succeeded the old craftsmen and revised their technique, but only the better to respond to the demands of the same customers. The vogue of the new fashions was so prompt, so wide and so lasting, only because their promoters knew how to gratify from the first the wishes of the clientèle by serving them with images and scenes still more expressly Buddhist than those created by their predecessors.

The attentive examination to which we have subjected the Sāñchī sculptures seems, therefore, to throw some light on the general evolution of Indian art and to indicate in what direction the future progress of Buddhist iconography will be made. But, though this task seemed to us the most imperative, it was not without regret that we renounced a further study of these sculptures bearing on the complete and vivid picture which they present of the old Indian civilisation. Such a study would have led us too far afield, and, apart from the fact that the collection of these *realia* ought to be made with the draughtsman's pencil in hand, this is not the place to compile a 'Dictionary of Indian Antiquities': for such is the documentary wealth of these reliefs, that that virtually is what the enterprise would amount to. If you are interested in architecture, here are ramparts and city gates, rich palaces and village huts, temples and stūpas, domed or vaulted roofs, terraces and loggias, square and horse-shoe windows. If you have antiquarian propensities, here is a whole collection of weapons, utensils, musical instruments, standards, chariots, boats, horses' and elephants' harness, etc. If you are drawn towards ethnography, we have already enumerated (p. 242) the whole gamut of types from the king to the slave, adults and children of both sexes, with all the details of their dress and ornaments. Apart from this material but most valuable information, how much we can gather about the life itself in towns and hamlets, in courts and hermitages, by looking at these anchorites busying themselves around the sacrificial pyres, bringing water, cutting wood, fanning fires or pouring out oblations, or meditating as they sit at the threshold of their leaf-roofed huts; at those kings holding *darbar* in their palaces or marching in pomp through the streets under the curious eyes of their subjects; at those peasant men and women attending to their domestic occupations, going to draw water, and wielding the pestle to husk the rice, or the roller to crush spices; at those soldiers approaching a besieged town, whose ramparts are lined with defenders . . .! Finally, we might mention the no less important data which these sculptures furnish on the exterior aspects of religious cults, on the shapes in which popular imagination clothed genii and fairies, on the conception formed of the paradises of the gods. But we should never have done enumerating all the points on which we may gather information; for a glance cast through this window opening onto the past of India teaches the onlooker more than a whole library could do.

Before the iconographer, who has received the reader from the hands of the archæologist, passes him on to the care of the epigraphist in Part IV, he may perhaps be allowed one word more. The inscriptions on the railings and gateways of the Sāñchī stūpa reveal no artist's name. Only the left (west) pillar of the Southern Gateway is written down as being the work, as well as the gift, of the guild of ivory-carvers in the neighbouring city of Vidiśā But these short epigraphs have preserved the names of a number of donors, and we may take it as certain that some of them have been represented on the sculptures. We could not readily explain otherwise how the praying figures, which are grouped around almost every sacred tree, wheel or stūpa, not only belong to both sexes, but are sometimes of uneven number and accompanied by children.[1] Now, a curious thing which we wish to bring to notice—and one which says much for the politeness of Indian manners in the first century B.C.—is that in these scenes of worship the women are generally given precedence over the men; at least, it is only on the Western Gateway that we note some regrettable exceptions to this rule. This simple remark induces us, in its turn, to warn the reader *in fine* against a prejudice which is widespread both in Europe and America. In our minds the idea of civilisation is associated, particularly as concerns men, with a sober but, as we say, 'complete' dress, whilst semi-nudity and wealth of ornament immediately give us an impression of savagery. Now, it cannot be denied that, among the leading classes in India two thousand years ago, a great display of jewellery was combined with sketchy and, especially among the women, most transparent garments. But this by no means prevents their civilisation—if by this term we mean women's social status, art and literature, philosophy and morals, just laws and gentle manners—from being already highly refined and in many respects just as advanced as any that the old world has known.

---

[1] See the descriptions of Pls. 15, 1; 22, 2; 26, 1; 43, 1; 48, 1; 57, 1; etc.

PART FOUR

THE INSCRIPTIONS

CHAPTER XVIII

CLASSIFICATION, AGE, PALÆOGRAPHY AND LANGUAGE

Previous publications and new materials

THE inscriptions of Sāñchī were noticed by James Prinsep[1] as far back as 1837. In 1854 General Cunningham[2] published a large number of these records; and in 1880 he gave an account of a further batch of them in his *Archæological Survey Reports.*[3] A critical edition of the Edict on the Aśoka pillar and of four hundred and fifty-six inscriptions of Stūpas 1 and 2, together with English translations, was published by George Bühler[4] in 1892; and in 1912, translations of all the then known records of Sāñchī written in Brāhmī characters, excepting the Aśoka Edict, were incorporated by Professor Lüders in his *List of Brāhmī Inscriptions.*[5] Sir John Marshall's excavations at Sāñchī, carried out between 1912 and 1919, have added extensively to this collection, the total number of the epigraphs discovered up till now being about nine hundred. In all, 842 inscriptions, including also a few of the mediæval period, are dealt with in this volume. They have been numbered serially and classified under four heads, *viz.*, (1) Inscription on the Aśoka Pillar, (2-14) Inscriptions on tne Relic-Boxes and Caskets, (15-827) Early Votive Inscriptions, and (828-842) Selected Inscriptions of the Kushān, Gupta and later periods.

The present edition of the inscriptions is mainly based on estampages prepared by the Archæological Survey of India under the direction of Sir John Marshall. In cases where the estampages have proved to be inadequate or doubtful, the readings have been verified as far as possible from the originals. The transcripts and translations of Cunningham, Bühler and Lüders have been checked, and improvements suggested wherever necessary. The present writer has also availed himself of the readings and translations of about three hundred inscriptions of Stūpas 1 and 2 contained in a rough manuscript which was handed over to him in 1931 by Rai Bahadur Ramaprasad Chanda, late Superintendent of the Archæological Section, Indian Museum, Calcutta. Of the inscriptions edited by Bühler, twenty-one are wanting in the present collection, as they could not be traced and identified. It has, however, been thought advisable to give the missing texts in appendices for the sake of completeness. Reproductions of only a few inscriptions of Sāñchī have up till now been published. To remove this want, facsimiles of almost all the

---

[1] *J. A. S. B.*, Old Series, Vol. VI, pp. 451-463; also *ibid.*, Vol. VII, pp. 562-565.
[2] *Bhilsa Topes*, pp. 235 ff.
[3] *A. S. R.*, Vol. X, pp. 58-59.
[4] *Ep. Ind.*, Vol. II, pp. 87-116 and 366-408 and two Pls.
[5] *Ibid.*, Vol. X, Appendix, Nos. 162-668.

records have been given in the present work. A table[1] (Pl. 141) is also attached to illustrate the successive phases of the development of the Brāhmī alphabet of Sāñchī in relation to the alphabet of other localities in Northern and Western India, from the third century B.C. to the 1st century A.D. The facsimiles and the table have been prepared from estampages and actual photographs.

Classification in groups

The inscriptions are engraved in Brāhmī and its later derivatives. As might be expected, the records do not appertain to the same age; palæographically, they come under the following six groups, which, though not dateable with absolute precision, are nevertheless clearly defined:—

1. The Edict of Aśoka.
2. Inscriptions on the pavement slabs and balustrades (*i.e.*, railings) of Stūpa 1, including the ground, berm, stairway and *harmikā* balustrades. Inscriptions on the relic-boxes and berm and stairway balustrades of Stūpa 3; inscriptions of Temple 40; and those on the relic-box, relic-caskets and balustrades of Stūpa 2.
3. Inscriptions on the gateways and balustrade extensions of Stūpa 1 and on the ground balustrade of Stūpa 3.
4. Inscriptions of the Kushān period.
5. Inscriptions of the Gupta period.
6. Later inscriptions.

Of the above, Groups 4, 5 and 6 are easily distinguishable from one another, as well as from Groups 1 to 3, and do not come within the scope of the present enquiry. A detailed palæographical study is, on the other hand, necessary to determine the chronological order of the first three groups of records. Previous studies on the subject by Cunningham and Bühler had paved the way for such an enquiry, but our special obligations are due to the contribution of Rai Bahadur Ramaprasad Chanda contained in an article entitled 'Dates of the Votive Inscriptions on the Stūpas at Sāñchī',[2] published in 1919.

[1] The table is divided into twenty-two columns arranged in five groups (1, 2, 2 *a*, 3 and 3 *a*) according to their chronological sequence. Groups 1, 2 and 3 correspond with the respective groups of Sāñchī inscriptions mentioned above. Group 2 *a* has been introduced in the table to demonstrate an intermediate stage in the development of the Brāhmī alphabet between Groups 2 and 3, and the last Group, 3 *a*, has been added with a view to complete the series down to the 1st century A.D. The table does not pretend to show all the letters and their varieties, or to exhaust the entire field of early Brāhmī inscriptions; nor does the scheme adopted in this table attempt any finality in regard to dates; it only explains the relative sequence of the groups. It should be specially noted that, for want of sufficient data, it has not been possible to arrange the individual columns within any particular group in strict order of sequence. The epigraphic materials that form the basis of the respective columns are as follows:—Col. I: Sāñchī Edict of Aśoka; Col. II: Girnar Edicts of Aśoka, Nos. 1-22, and Rummindei inscription of Aśoka, No. 23; Col. III: Piprāhwā Relic Casket inscription; Col. IV: Inscriptions of Sāñchī Stūpa 1, ground balustrade, excluding the later extensions; Col. V: Besnagar Pillar inscription of Heliodorus; Col. VI: Ghosundi inscription; Col. VII: Bhilsa Pillar inscription of the 12th regnal year of Mahārāja Bhāgavata; Col. VIII: Inscriptions of Sāñchī Stūpa 2, ground balustrade, Nos. 1-13; Inscriptions of Sāñchī Stūpa 2, Relic-box and caskets, Nos. 14-27; Col. IX: Bharhut Stūpa railing inscriptions; Col. X: Bharhut Stūpa Gate inscription of Dhanabhūti, Nos. 1-14, and later railing, Nos. 15-23; Col. XI: Nānāghāt Cave inscriptions of Queen Nāyanikā; Col. XII: Bodh-Gayā railing inscriptions; Col. XIII: Parkham Yaksha image inscription, Nos. 1-8, Mora Brick inscription of Brahāsvātimitra, Nos. 9-15; Col. XIV: Inscription of the time of King Vishṇumitra, Nos. 1-11; Inscription of Utaradāsaka, Nos. 12-23; Col. XV: Inscriptions of Sāñchī Stūpa 1, gateways; Col. XVI: Inscriptions of Sāñchī Stūpa 1, extensions of ground balustrade Nos. 1-13, Stūpa 3, ground balustrade, Nos. 14-28; Col. XVII: Hāthigumphā inscription of King Khāravela; Col. XVIII: Pabhosa inscription of the time of King Bahasatimitra and Āshāḍhasena; Col. XIX: Ayodhyā inscription of the Kośala king Dhanadeva; Col. XX: Kosam inscription of Gotīputa (*Ep. Ind.*, Vol. XVIII, p. 159 and Pl.), Nos. 1-13; Bhiṭā inscription of the year 18 (*A. S. R.*, 1911-12, p. 44, No. 3), Nos. 14-25; Col. XXI: Amohinī inscription of the time of the Mahākshatrapa Śoḍāsa; Col. XXII: Nāsik Cave inscriptions of the time of the Mahākshatrapa Nahapāna (*Ep. Ind.*, Vol. VIII, Pl. IV, No. 10 and Pl. V, No. 12).

[2] *Mem. A. S. I.*, No. 1, pp. 1-22 and Pls. I-VI.

Groups 1 and 2

Our study must necessarily begin with an examination of Groups 1 and 2 of the inscriptions. Cunningham assumed that the ground balustrade of Stūpa 1 (including the extensions) belonged approximately to the age of Aśoka, since in his opinion the characters of the inscriptions appearing on it were 'exactly similar' to those of the Pillar Edicts.[1] This view was also endorsed by Bühler.[2] But in face of the new light thrown by Sir John Marshall on the sequence of the monuments at Sāñchī, and in face too of more recent studies in Brāhmī palæography, this view now requires substantial modification. As to the former, we have already seen (p. 27 above) that the existence of several floors, between the level of the Aśoka pillar and the ground balustrade of Stūpa 1, proves that many decades—probably not much less than a century—must have intervened between these two monuments. As to the palæographic evidence, the difference between the Brāhmī script on the Aśoka pillar (Group 1) and that on the balustrades of Stūpa 1 (Group 2) can best be seen from a comparative study of the individual forms of letters given in the table. As shown by Chanda,[3] the most noteworthy of these letters are *a*, *dha*, *bha* and *ha*. In this chapter we shall go over the important points in his demonstration in some detail, adding our own remarks wherever necessary.

Inscriptions of Aśoka and those on the balustrade of Stūpa 1 compared

In the inscriptions of Aśoka,[4] the letter *a* has in most cases its two arms meeting at a point. Another type, which was also used, but rather sparingly, in this period, shows a gap between the arms. On the Aśoka pillar at Sāñchī, the letter *a* occurs but once and it is of the latter type; and on the balustrade of Stūpa 1, this type is used almost universally. As first pointed out by R. D. Banerji,[5] it is characteristic of the post-Aśokan writing. It occurs in the Bharhut gate inscription (Table, Col. X, 1) and in the Besnagar pillar inscription of Heliodorus (Table, Col V, 1), both of which belong to the period subsequent to the fall of the Maurya dynasty. The regular use of this type of *a* on the Sāñchī balustrade, in a large number of inscriptions, is therefore very significant. Although a rarity in the time of Aśoka, it seems to have become, during the period that followed, the standard monumental form of the letter. An important difference arises in the case of the letter *dha*. It is not legible in the passage in which it occurs in the Sāñchī Edict, but in other inscriptions of Aśoka it is almost invariably of the shape of the English letter D.[6] In the Sāñchī balustrade inscriptions, the reversed form of the letter, in which the vertical stroke appears to the right of the loop, is uniformly used. That the reversed form of *dha* is typical of the post-Aśokan period, becomes evident from the fact that it is exclusively used in the Bharhut gate inscription, in the Besnagar inscription of Heliodorus, in the Nānāghāt inscriptions of the queen Nāyanikā, in the Hāthigumphā inscription of

[1] *Bhilsa Topes*, p. 271. This view has been upheld also by a recent writer on the subject. *J. A. S. B.*, N. S., Vol. XVIII, 1922, p. 231.
[2] *Ep. Ind.*, Vol. II, p. 88; and *Ind. Pal.*, Trans., p. 32.
[3] *Mem. A. S. I.*, No. 1, pp. 2-3; and *J. B. O. R. S.*, Vol. XI, 1925, p. 75.
[4] See Pls. in Hultzsch, *Corp. Ins. Ind.*, Vol. I, 1925.
[5] *A. S. R.*, 1913-14, p. 111, note 1.
[6] Bühler recognized it as the original form of the letter.—*Ind. Pal.*, Eng. Trans., p. 36. For corrections of his *Tafel* II, 26, see Char [1]a, *J. B. O. R. S.*, Vol. XI, pp. 75-76.

Khāravela and in all later records. As regards the letter *bha*, there are four clear examples of it on the Aśokan pillar at Sāñchī. Each of them shows a projecting horizontal, to which are attached an upper and a lower vertical meeting at an angle on the right. This form with protruding neck is typical of Aśokan Brāhmī, and occurs also on the Piprāhwā casket. In the Girnar recension it occurs in at least thirty-three out of forty cases, and in the Delhi-Topra, Allāhābād-Kosam, Sārnāth and Bairāt inscriptions of Aśoka, in all the twenty-three, six, four and seventeen cases, respectively. This form of *bha* is, however, but rarely found in the inscriptions of Stūpa 1, the only examples being those in Pl. 130, 163 and 179, and Pl. 132, 261. In the majority of Sāñchī inscriptions, it has an unbroken perpendicular on the right, instead of the detached upper and lower verticals, and the middle bar does not show any projection. No doubt this type of *bha*[1] already appears in some of the Aśokan records, but there it is of extremely rare occurrence; thus, there are only three examples of this *bha* in the Girnar Edicts.[2] The letter *ha*, in the inscriptions of Aśoka, has mostly a stroke attached a little below the right end of the curve. There are also a few examples in which the stroke is attached at the very end of the curve,[3] as on the Sāñchī pillar, and it is this form which in the post-Aśokan period becomes universal.

There are two other points of difference to which Mr. Chanda has not alluded. The angular medial *i* sign of the Aśokan documents takes a more cursive shape in the inscriptions of Stūpa 1 at Sāñchī, being very often treated as a slanting stroke, so that it becomes in many cases difficult to distinguish the sign from the medial *ā* (*e.g.*, Pl. 129, 52). In the Aśokan inscriptions, the medial *o*-mark generally preserves the shape of the initial *o*.[4] But in the inscriptions of Stūpa 1, there are many examples in which it is reduced to a single instead of two strokes, attached to the head of the letter,[5] as for instance in *po*, in Pl. 133, 328.

Forms of *bha* and *ra* in early Brāhmī inscriptions

Thus, even on grounds of palæography, the ground balustrade of Stūpa 1 would have to be placed later than the age of Aśoka, but how much later cannot be determined on grounds of palæography alone. Chanda inclines to the view that the records engraved on this balustrade are later than the Besnagar pillar inscription of Heliodorus. He maintains that *bha* with slanting head, which occurs in that inscription, is earlier than the type showing a single vertical on the right, and that the 'cork-screw' *ra*, as Bühler calls it, occurring in the same record, is earlier than the straight-line *ra*. According to Chanda, the Sāñchī inscriptions, inasmuch as they contain these supposed 'later' forms, should be treated as of a later date than the Heliodorus inscription. Now, in the Girnar Edicts of Aśoka there are four examples of the slanting-head *bha*, and, as already noted, there are three in which it has a single vertical on the right, and as many as twenty-seven in which it has an upper and a lower vertical attached to a projecting bar. The first two forms are thus manifestly

[1] According to Bühler, this is a 'secondary' form of *bha*.—*Ind. Pal.*, p. 36.
[2] Bühler recognized these two types as representing respectively the 'primary' and 'cursive' forms of the letter.—*Ind. Pal.*, p. 36.
[3] *E.g.*, Hultzsch, *op. cit.*, p. 22, R. E. IX, *bhatakamhi*.
[4] *Ind. Pal.*, p. 37.
[5] For the survival in the Sāñchī inscriptions of the Aśokan mode of writing medial *o*, see Pl. 132, 265. See also Table, Col. IV, 9.

rare in the Aśokan period. The slanting-head *bha* is used in the Nāgārjunī cave inscriptions of Daśaratha,[1] grandson of Aśoka, along with the other two forms; and in the Besnagar inscription of Heliodorus it is used in all the three instances in which the letter occurs. There are examples of this form of *bha* also in the Sāñchī inscriptions,[2] both at Stūpas 1 and 2, but their number is extremely limited, the prevailing type being, as already pointed out, the one with a single vertical on the right. The rarity of the slanting-head *bha* in Aśokan, as well as in post-Aśokan records, shows that it cannot be regarded as a regular monumental form. It is easy to recognize how, in *bha*, a single line replaced the two lines meeting at an angle, forming the neck of the letter. This line was placed either vertically, so as to coalesce with the lower right vertical, or in a slanting fashion, as on the Besnagar pillar of Heliodorus. In the latter, we can trace the same tendency as in the substitution of a slanting stroke for the older, angular stroke, of medial *i*. As regards *ra*, the cork-screw type no doubt occurs in the Girnar, Siddapur, Brahmagiri and Sopārā Edicts of Aśoka, as well as in one of the Rāmgaṛh cave inscriptions.[3] But it should be remembered that the straight-line *ra* occurs on the Aśokan pillar at Sāñchī, and that, as *la* is substituted for *ra* in the other recensions, it is difficult to ascertain which of the two forms was more current in the Aśokan period. An inscription recently discovered at Barli[4] in Ajmer, which can be assigned to the period of Aśoka on palæographic grounds (*cf.* for instance the extraordinary length of the verticals of such letters as *ca* and *va*), contains the straight-line *ra*. This type of *ra* is used also in the Bhaṭṭiproḷu inscriptions,[5] which are dated by Bühler at about 200 B.C. Even in the Besnagar inscription of Heliodorus it appears at least once (Table, Col. V, 14). On the other hand, in an inscription from Ghosundi near Chitorgarh, the cork-screw *ra* is definitely used. But this inscription[6] has dagger-shaped *ka* in all the three instances in which the letter occurs, *dha* turned to the right, and *a* with space between the arms. In view of these post-Aśokan features, it cannot be referred to a date earlier than the second century B.C. Moreover, the cork-screw *ra* in its original, or modified form, is used instead of, or along with, the straight-line *ra* in certain records which, from other palæographic tests, can be shown to be later than the inscriptions on the ground balustrade of Stūpa 1. These are, among others, the Bharhut gate inscription of Dhanabhūti, the Bodh-Gayā railing inscriptions and the Hāthigumphā inscription of Khāravela.[7] In the face of this evidence it is not possible, therefore, to rely on the tests of the slanting-head *bha* and the cork-screw *ra*.

Thus the slanting-head *bha* and the cork-screw *ra* of the Besnagar inscription of Heliodorus do not necessarily suggest its priority to the epigraphs on the ground balustrade

[1] *Mem. A. S. I.*, No. 1, p. 2.

[2] See, *e.g.*, Table, Col. IV, 12; also Pl. 129, 71, Pl. 131, 209 and *Mem. A. S. I.*, No. 1, Pl. IV, 10.

[3] *Mem. A. S. I.*, No. 1, p. 3, n. 1. Both the cork-screw *ra* and the *bha* with protruding neck occur in this inscription.

[4] *J. B. O. R. S.*, 1930, p. 67 and Pl.

[5] Bühler's *Tafel* II, Col. XIII, 34.

[6] *Ind. Ant.*, 1932, p. 203 and Pl.

[7] *J. B. O. R. S.*, 1917, Pl. IV. It has examples of both types of *ra*.

of Stūpa 1. On the contrary, this inscription shows certain late features[1] which are not shared by many of the inscriptions on this balustrade. It has examples of an almost triangular *va*, and in four out of five examples its *ka* is of the later dagger-shaped type in which the lower half of the vertical is longer than the upper half (Table, Col. V, 17, 2). A very large number of Stūpa 1 inscriptions, however, regularly have the older forms of the letters, as in Aśokan inscriptions, a circumstance that might suggest a somewhat later date for the Besnagar inscription. Taking, however, the majority of letters into consideration it is safer to refer it to the same group to which the ground balustrade of the stūpa belongs (Group 2). The Besnagar record dates from the time of the Greek king Antialcidas of Taxila, who, as stated in it, sent his ambassador Heliodorus to King Kāśīputra Bhāgabhadra, the ruler of Vidiśā. The date of Antialcidas is not yet definitely settled, but Rapson[2] has shown from an exhaustive review of numismatic data that he was the successor of Heliokles, who probably was the son and successor of Eukratides. As Eukratides came to the throne about the same time as Mithradates I of Parthia (171-138 B.C.), Antialcidas may be placed about 150 B.C.; and to about the same date should be assigned the Besnagar pillar inscription of Heliodorus. We shall not therefore be far wrong if we tentatively place the date of the entire group including the ground balustrade of Stūpa 1 and the adjoining pavement slabs at about 175-125 B.C., that is to say, in the earlier part of the rule of the Śuṅga dynasty.[3] The date may have been actually a little earlier or later, but at present there is no means of ascertaining its limits with greater precision.[4] Thus, in the present chronological scheme, the ground balustrade and the latest pavement of Stūpa 1 are next in order to Aśoka's column, but with a gap of about three-quarters of a century intervening between them.

Besnagar inscription of Heliodorus

Later inscriptions on Ground Balustrade of Stūpa 1

A very small number of the ground balustrade inscriptions present, however, certain definitely late features and offer a strong contrast to the archaic writing appearing in the bulk of the records. These features are dagger-shaped *ka*, rounded *ga* (Pl. 128, 3), 'butterfly' or double-looped *cha* (Pl. 132, 306),[5] *pu* in which the *u*-mark is applied in continuation of the right curve of the letter, *pa* and *sa* with equalized verticals, *la* with the left limb hanging down and triangular *va* (Pl. 131, 180, 183 and 190). The parts of the balustrade where these inscriptions occur must undoubtedly have been later insertions, due to subsequent additions and repairs, and they have no bearing on the date of the balustrade as a whole.

---

[1] *Cf.* R. C. Majumdar, *J. A. S. B.*, 1922, p. 232.

[2] *Cambridge History of India*, Vol. I, p. 700. Rapson identifies Bhāgabhadra with Bhāgavata, the last but one Śuṅga king mentioned in the Purāṇas, whose year of accession may be estimated as *circa* 104 B.C. An inscription of the latter which comes from Bhilsa, is in decidedly later characters than those of the Besnagar inscription of the reign of Bhāgabhadra. The two kings, therefore, should be regarded as different.

[3] The commencement of the Śuṅga rule is usually placed at about 185 B.C., on the authority of the Purāṇas. That the date could not be much later is suggested by the fact that a prince of Kośala named Dhanadeva claims in his Ayodhyā inscription to have been the sixth in descent from Pushyamitra, and that the characters of this record (*J. B. O. R. S.*, Vol. X, p. 202 and Pl.) are almost similar to those of the Amohinī inscription of the time of Śoḍāsa (15 A.D.). See my Table, Col. XIX, and *Ann. Bhand. Inst.*, Vol. VII, p. 160.

[4] See, however, pp. 3 and 29 above. It is highly improbable that the stūpa was rebuilt and the railing constructed during the reign of Pushyamitra (184-149 B.C.?). Antialcidas may well have been a decade or two later than the date suggested by Mr. Majumdar.—J. M.

[5] Bühler recognized (*Ind. Pal.*, Trans. p. 35) that from the *cha* consisting of a circle bisected by a vertical, is derived the form with two loops, which Chanda calls the 'butterfly' type. A form somewhat akin to the latter seems to occur, probably only once, in Edict V at Kalsi (Bühler's *Tafel* II, Col. II, 14). But all other examples of *cha* found throughout the inscriptions of Aśoka conform to the earlier type.

Berm balustrade of Stūpa 1

The inscriptions on the berm balustrade of Stūpa 1 are precisely of the same character as those on its ground balustrade, and it is noteworthy that the donors of one sometimes figure among the donors of another. Thus a nun Achalā, from Nandinagara, has to her credit two inscriptions, one on the ground balustrade (No. 170) and another on the berm balustrade (No. 465) of this stūpa. Similar, also, is the case of a *pāvārika* Idadata (Nos. 131 and 472) and of Isidatā, wife of Sakadina (Nos. 142 and 500).[1]

Relic-boxes and berm and stairway balustrades of Stūpa 3

On grounds of palæography, the inscriptions on the relic-boxes of Stūpa 3, and its berm and stairway balustrades, also come under Group 2. The stairways of Stūpas 1 and 3 are to be regarded as contemporaneous, since we know that a person named Arahaguta from Kurara donated certain parts of both (see Nos. 618, 620 and 722). A few inscriptions, palæographically similar to those on the ground balustrade of Stūpa 1, come from Temple 40, which should therefore be referred also to the same age. This also follows from the fact that a donor, Data-Kalavaḍa, who is known from three inscriptions of Stūpa 1 (Nos. 353-355), has left another record of his on a pillar of this temple (No. 790).

Temple 40

Balustrades of Stūpa 2

In the inscriptions on the balustrades of Stūpa 2, we can clearly recognize certain late tendencies. Chanda[2] has drawn attention to the preponderance of roundish *ga* and the appearance of the 'advanced forms' of *cha* and *bha* in these inscriptions. The *cha* tends towards the later double-looped type, instead of the older 'circle bisected by a vertical', and the *bha* has its lower right vertical elongated. As regards *cha*, it may further be pointed out that on the relic-box of Stūpa 2 (Table, Col. VIII, 17) it takes an elliptical rather than circular shape, and on one of the relic-caskets it approaches definitely towards the double-looped form. In the latter case it differs from the *cha* found in the records of Group 3, in so far as its two loops have not yet assumed a perfectly circular form. There are, again, other important palæographic details pointing to a later date for Stūpa 2. On the ground balustrade, the sign for medial *u*, in some cases at least, is added to the letter *ba* in continuation of its right vertical (*e.g.*, Pl. 136, 6), instead of being suspended from the middle of the base (Table, Col. VIII, 8, 9). The latter mode of writing *bu* is characteristic of the Aśoka inscriptions, the Piprāhwā casket inscription and the inscriptions on the ground balustrade of Stūpa 1. In these records, the medial *u* is similarly suspended from the middle of the curves of *pa* and *sa* as well, to denote *pu* and *su* (Table, Cols. II-IV). But on the relic-box and relic-caskets of Stūpa 2, the *u*-mark in such cases is almost invariably applied in continuation of the right limb of the letters (Table, Col. VIII, 20, 27). That these forms of *pu*, *bu* and *su* are late features, is undeniable, since they regularly occur in the Northern Kshatrapa and Kushān inscriptions. Then, again, in the relic-box and casket inscriptions, the letter *va* is of an angular shape and there is a definite tendency to equalize the verticals at their upper ends in the letters

Relic-box and caskets of Stūpa 2

[1] Some of the berm inscriptions, however, show later forms, *e.g.*, roundish *ga* and *bha* with the lower right vertical extended. These are referable to a somewhat later date (*cf.* Pl. 136, 141).

[2] *Mem. A. S. I.*, No. 1, pp. 3-4.

pa and *sa* (Table, Col. VIII, 20, 25, 26). The difference in script between the inscriptions of Stūpa 1 and those of Stūpa 2 would no doubt justify the assumption of a difference in age between the two monuments. But it could hardly have been much more than a generation. This is evidenced by the fact that the screen of the western entrance of Stūpa 1 bears an inscription of one Arahaguta Sāsādaka (No. 310), while a record of his disciple Balaka (No. 671) appears on the ground balustrade of Stūpa 2. Again, the nun Dharmasenā of Kurara, the donor in No. 562 on the berm balustrade of Stūpa 1, is probably identical with the nun of the same name who appears in No. 664 on the ground balustrade of Stūpa 2.

Decorative carvings of Stūpa 2

In this connexion we have also to consider the data supplied by a study of the decorative art of Stūpa 2 which have been discussed at length by Sir John Marshall (pp. 79-80 and 95 ff.). In Stūpa 1 the scheme of decoration was confined to its berm and stairway pillars, which bear panels and medallions in relief, but in Stūpa 2 we find it extended to the pillars of the ground balustrade. The contrast, indeed, between the ground balustrade of Stūpa 1, which is severely plain in character, and that of Stūpa 2, which is richly decorated with panels and medallions, is such that at least a few decades must be supposed to have elapsed between them.

Later forms of *bha, bu, pu*, and *su*

For a more definite estimate of the date of Stūpa 2 we require to know when the late characteristics, like *bha* with elongated lower vertical and the new forms of *bu*, *pu* and *su*, began to appear in the Brāhmī writing of Eastern Mālwā. Although, in the absence of adequate data, this question cannot be answered fully, some light is thrown on it by a Bhilsa pillar inscription of the twelfth regnal year of Mahārāja Bhāgavata, who has been rightly identified with the last but one Śuṅga king of the same name mentioned in the Purānic lists.[1] On the authority of the Purāṇas the twelfth regnal year of Bhāgavata would fall about 104 B.C. The Bhilsa inscription of this king shows the late type of *pu*, and *bha* with the lower right vertical extended. It also shows a tendency to equalization of verticals in the letter *sa*. These characteristics (Table, Col. VII), while absent in the inscriptions on the ground balustrade of Stūpa 1 and the Besnagar pillar, are shared by those on the relic-caskets of Stūpa 2. Taking all these facts into consideration, the date of Stūpa 2 can be safely relegated to the last quarter of the second century B.C.[2] Judging from palæography, the major portion of the balustrade of the Stūpa of Bharhut (Table, Col. IX) would also appear to belong to this period. It should be noted that on this balustrade, as at Stūpa 2 of Sāñchī, some of the late, or transitional, forms of letters often occur side by side with earlier ones. Specially noteworthy are the examples of *cha*, *bu*, *bha* and *sa* (Table, Col. IX, 7, 16, 18, 27). Some of the *cha*'s are midway between the Aśokan *cha* and the later double-looped type. The letter *bha* retains in some cases the older form in which its two verticals are of equal length, but the predominant type is the one with the lower right vertical elongated. Some examples of *sa* show also the tendency

The Bharhut Balustrade

[1] *Mem. A. S. I.*, No. 5, p. 152 and Pl. XXVI, *a*.

[2] Regarding this date, see also above p. 80.

to equalization of the verticals at their upper ends. The inscriptions of Stūpa 2, together with those on the Bharhut railing and the Bhilsa pillar, represent, therefore, the concluding phase of Group 2 of our Table of Alphabets (*circa* 125-100 B.C.)

Later inscriptions at Bharhut

Between Groups 2 and 3, shown in the table, a further stage in the development of the Brāhmī alphabet is witnessed in a number of inscriptions found outside Sāñchī (Group 2 A), the evidence of which has to be considered before we pass on to describe the palæography of Group 3. The records engraved on a gateway pillar (Table, Col. X, 1-14) of the Bharhut Stūpa and some portions of its railing (*e.g.*, Lüders, *List*, No. 766 of Mahila), which appear to have been later additions, fall under this category (Table, Col. X, 15-23). From the gateway inscription we learn that it was erected by Dhanabhūti during the reign of the Śuṅgas (*Suganaṁ rajė*). But this could not have referred to the earlier members of the dynasty, and it is not possible to agree with Bühler in assigning the inscription to such an early date as the middle of the second century B.C.[1] In these later Bharhut inscriptions, the beginning of the serif can be clearly traced in the broadening of the tops of some of the letters. Other features appearing in them are: *ka* with short upper vertical, rounded *ga*, elliptical *cha*, *pa* with nearly equalized verticals, *bha* with right lower vertical extended, a modified form of the cork-screw *ra*, *ma* and *va* with tendency towards angularization, and *pu* and *su* in which the *u*-mark is applied in continuation of the right curve of the letters. Palæographically, the inscriptions should be classed with certain epigraphs on the Bodh-Gayā railing, *e.g.*, those of the time of Brahmamitra and Indrāgnimitra[2] (Table, Col. XII) and with the Mathurā inscriptions (Table, Col. XIV) of Utaradāsaka[3] and King Vishṇumitra.[4] It is important here to follow the sequence of the Brāhmī inscriptions from Mathurā up to the date of the Northern Kshatrapas and allocate the two Mathurā records to their respective places in the series. One of the earliest inscriptions that come from Mathurā is that on the Parkham image of Yaksha Maṇibhadra[5] (Table, Col. XIII, 1-8). Although the inscription contains certain archaic forms, *e.g.*, *ga*, *ta*, *ma* and *va*, yet the occurrence in it of the late type of *pu*, a *da* with short upper vertical, the thick tops of certain letters and the tendency to equalize verticals in *pa*, all point to the conclusion that it cannot be referred to a date earlier than the closing years of the second century B.C. To about the same period must also be referred the inscriptions of Kings Gomitra and Brahāsvātimitra (Bṛihatsvātimitra), from Ganeshra and Mora near Mathurā,[6] respectively (Table, Col. XIII, 9-15). The next group of inscriptions consists of the epigraphs of Vishṇumitra and Utaradāsaka, which frequently have letters with serif, rounded *ga*, elliptical *cha* (in Utaradāsaka's inscription), *ta* still retaining in many cases

Inscriptions from Mathurā

---

[1] Bühler's *Tafel* II, Col. XVIII.

[2] Cunningham, *Mahābodhi*, Pl. X, figs. 1-10. The Bodh-Gayā inscriptions may be somewhat later than the Bharhut gate inscription in view of the fact that the *cha* occurring on one of the Bodh-Gayā pillars consists of two circular loops.

[3] *Ep. Ind.*, Vol. II, p. 195 and Pl.

[4] *Ind. Hist. Quart.*, Vol. II, 1926, p. 442 and Pl.

[5] See Plate in Chanda's 'Four Ancient Yakṣa Statues' in *Jour. Deptt. Letts.*, Calcutta, Vol. IV, 1921. The reading (*Ma*)*nibhada* was first suggested by me. As there has been a good deal of controversy about the reading of the inscription, only letters of undisputed value have been entered in my table.

[6] *A. S. R.*, 1911-12, Pl. LVIII, figs. 16, 18. This Brahāsvātimitra is different from Bahasatimitra of the Pabhosa inscription (*Ep. Ind.*, Vol. II, p. 242 and Pl.), who must have flourished at least half a century later (*circa* 50-25 B.C.).

its angular form and in others its right limb showing slight curvature, triangular or nearly triangular *ma* and *va*, *bha* with extended lower vertical on the right, a modified form of the cork-screw *ra*, and an equalizing tendency in the verticals of *pa*, *ya* and *sa*. As most of these features are shared by the two Mathurā inscriptions and the Bharhut gate inscription, we are justified in referring these epigraphs to the same period. Still later comes the Amohinī tablet of the reign of the Mahākshatrapa Śoḍāsa, which, according to Lüders,[1] is dated in the year 72 of an unspecified era. It seems that the earliest era to which this year could be referred is the Mālava era of 57 B.C. According to this reckoning the date of the inscription is equivalent to 15 A.D. In the accompanying table, the characters of the record have been shown under Group 3 A, for which the tentative date 1-50 A.D. may be adopted. Another Mathurā inscription which palæographically belongs to this group, is that of Kshaharāta Ghaṭaka.[2] The title 'Kshaharāta' connects him with the clan of the Satrap Nahapāna of Western India. The characters of Nahapāna's inscriptions, in view of their close resemblance to those of the time of Śoḍāsa, are also included in the table for comparison. The records of Group 3 A show a further stage in the development of the Brāhmī alphabet, the most striking features of which are the new forms of *ḍa* and *bha*, the former bent towards and opening on the right, and the latter having a continuous curve in place of the angular left limb. Further, the upper verticals of all the letters except *la* are equalized, *cha* consists of two circular loops as a rule, *ta* becomes rounded, the stem of *ra*, which is no longer wavy, is bent to the left at the lower end, the letters *ma* and *va* are fully triangular, the serif marks are more prominent and occur regularly, and many letters show angular forms, *e.g.*, *gha*, *la*, *pa*, *sha* and *ha*.

The difference in palæography between the inscriptions of Dhanabhūti, Utaradāsaka and Vishṇumitra on the one hand, and that of the Northern Kshatrapa inscriptions from Mathurā on the other, is so marked that an interval of at least a century must be assumed to account for it. It is reasonable, therefore, to conclude that the Mathurā inscriptions of Utaradāsaka and Vishṇumitra, and the Bharhut gate inscription of Dhanabhūti belong to about 100-75 B.C. We have already arrived at the conclusion that the approximate date of Stūpa 2 at Sāñchī is 125-100 B.C. This margin of about a quarter of a century is necessary to account for the difference in script between the Bharhut gate inscription, and the inscriptions of Stūpa 2 at Sāñchī and of the older parts of the Bharhut balustrade.

Group 3. Inscriptions on extensions of ground balustrade of Stūpa 1 and on its four gateways

The records engraved on the extensions to the ground balustrade of Stūpa 1, its four gateways, and the ground balustrade of Stūpa 3 come under Group 3 of Sāñchī inscriptions. They are referable to the period of King Sātakarṇi, one of whose officials, Vāsishṭhīputra Ānanda, erected the South Gate of Stūpa 1. Cunningham first recognized that the balustrade extensions and gateways of Stūpa 1 are later than the rest

[1] *Acta Orientalia*, Vol. X, pp. 118-125. [See, however, Rapson in *C. H. I.*, I, pp. 526, 575, for a different date.—J. M.]

[2] *A. S. R.*, 1911-12, Pl. LVIII, fig. 17.

of the balustrade. This he inferred from 'the more recent character of the inscriptions,'[1] and also from the circumstance that, at the northern entrance of the Stūpa, an inscription on a pillar of the main balustrade was found hidden by a pillar of the later extension.[2] Similar overlapping occurs also elsewhere, for instance, at the East Gate, where its left jamb comes in contact with a pillar of the main balustrade in such a manner as almost to cover a two-line inscription (No. 103) on the latter. The inscriptions on the gates of Stūpa 1 belong to one and the same period. The North, East and West Gates bear imprecatory inscriptions which use almost identical forms of expression, and also agree generally in the style of writing. Then, again, the south pillar of the West Gate and the middle architrave of the South Gate were donated by one and the same person, Balamitra, the disciple of Ayacuḍa; and so, too, the south pillar of the East Gate and the north pillar of the West Gate were both gifts of Nāgapiya, a banker of Achāvaḍa and native of Kurara.[3]

Two contemporary scripts

The imprecatory inscriptions and the records of Balamitra and Nāgapiya reveal different styles of writing. Chanda[4] distinguishes three such styles, according as the inscriptions contain 'archaic', 'regular contemporary monumental' and 'irregular advanced forms. Broadly speaking, however, only two styles of writing can be recognized on the gateways, one representing the ordinary script of the age like that found in the imprecatory inscriptions, and the other, an ornate style aiming at beauty and symmetry of form, as exemplified in the records of Balamitra and Nāgapiya, as well as in the Sātakarṇi inscription. Similarly, on the balustrade extension, an inscription of Arahadina (Pl. 129, 90) belongs to the latter category, while an inscription of Nāgila (Pl. 129, 91) exhibits the ordinary writing of the time, without any attempt at ornamentation. The ornate script found at Sāñchī was by no means a purely local feature, but had a much wider distribution. It appears on the coins of a Siri-Sātakani from Mālwā, and on those of certain kings of Mathurā, Ahicchattra and Kauśāmbī.[5] This script seems to have gradually taken the entire field and ultimately developed into the Northern Kshatrapa alphabet of Mathurā and the alphabet of the inscriptions of Nahapāna's reign from Nāsik and other places of Western India. The tendencies of the Kshatrapa alphabet can be traced already in the inscriptions of Group 3. A record of this group, which is nearer in point of time to the Kshatrapa inscriptions, is the Pabhosa inscription, which shows the same type of angular *la* as in the Amohinī tablet.

Ordinary and ornate scripts compared

The principal points in which the two contemporary styles of writing of Sāñchī differ are as follows. In the ornate style (Table : Col. XVI, 1-13; Col. XV, 2, 4, 6, 8, 11, 13, 15, 17, 20, 22, 24, 25, 27, 28-30), the tops of the letters are broadened to form a knob or serif, which in many cases has the shape of a solid triangle pointing downwards. These

[1] *Bhilsa Topes*, p. 272. [2] *Ibid.*, p. 273. [3] *Mem. A. S. I.*, No. 1, p. 5. [4] *Ibid.*, pp. 5-6.

[5] *E.g.*, Cunningham, *Coins of Ancient India*, Pl. V, 18 (Dhanadeva of Kauśāmbī); V. A. Smith, *Catalogue of Coins in the Indian Museum*, Vol. I, Pl. XXII, 1 (Agnimitra), 6 (Bhūmimitra), 7 (Phalgunimitra).

knob-headed letters, which appear first at Bharhut and Mathurā, are more pronounced and developed in Group 3 of the Sāñchī inscriptions, and ultimately become a prominent feature of the Northern Kshatrapa and Kushān inscriptions of Mathurā and of those of the time of Nahapāna in Western India. In the ornate style of Sāñchī, the upper verticals of such letters as *a*, *ka*, *cha*, *ta*, *da*, *va* and *sa*, are necessarily reduced in height, so as almost to merge in the serif. Another ornamental feature is the appearance of the flourish in the medial *i* sign. In the ordinary style (Table, Col. XV, 1, 3, 5, 7, 9, 10, 12, 14, 16, 18, 19, 23, 26, 21, 31), the characters often show a mixture of archaic and transitional forms, the serif does not appear regularly and the upper verticals of letters are retained, although much shortened as compared with those in the earlier records of Stūpa 1. Further, the sign for medial *i* does not show any flourish. There is, however, no essential difference between the two scripts, the distinction being one of style rather than of alphabetic form.

Common elements of the two scripts

A number of important palæographic features are common to both the styles, *viz.*, rounded *ga* and *ta*, double-looped *cha*, *ḍa* with curved lower part and short upper vertical, *bha* with right lower vertical extended, *la* with left limb hanging down (a feature more pronounced in the ornate style), and angular treatment of certain letters, *e.g.*, *gha* and *ha* (in Pl. 134, 'South Gate 1'). Moreover, the letters at this period show a general tendency to equalization of verticals at the upper ends (*e.g.*, in *sa*), which is naturally more pronounced in the ornate style aiming at symmetry of form. Thus in the inscription of Sātakarṇi on the South Gate (Pl. 134, 'South Gate 1') all the *sa*'s which do not bear any medial vowel sign have their right limb drawn up to the top level of the letter. A new method of indicating the subscript *r* appears in the conjunct *tra* in the gateway inscriptions. The component *r*, which practically merges in the stem of *ta*, is distinguished by a curvature at the extended lower end of the letter (Table: Col. XV, 13; Col. XVI, 18). In the earlier records, *e.g.*, in the Besnagar inscription of Heliodorus, and in the inscriptions on the Bharhut railing, the subscript *r* has the cork-screw shape, which, appended to the original letter, can clearly be recognized as a distinct element (Table: Col. V, 6; Col. IX, 2, 11). A subscript *r* of this type appears once also on the ground balustrade of Stūpa 1 (Pl. 131, 240) in the conjunct *ḍra*. Another point to note in this connexion is the lengthening of the stem of initial *a* or its lower arm, at the base, which is a characteristic feature of the inscriptions of Groups 3 and 4. In the earlier records, the lower arm and the stem of this letter are generally at the same level.

Inscriptions on ground balustrade of Stūpa 3

The inscriptions on the ground balustrade of Stūpa 3 are also written in the same ornate style as that found on the gateways and railing extensions of Stūpa 1, and would come, therefore, under Group 3. They exhibit (Table, Col. XVI, 14-28) knob-headed letters, a distinct tendency to equalization of verticals at the upper ends, the later forms of certain letters, *e.g.*, *ga*, *ta* and *sa*, and the medial *i* with flourish. This is quite a contrast to the archaic writing on the relic-boxes and the berm and stairway balustrades of Stūpa 3, which have been shown, on independent grounds, to be of the same age as the berm and stairway balustrades of Stūpa 1, and the inscriptions on which have been classed under Group 2 of our table. The late script and the ornate style at Stūpa 3 are restricted to its ground balustrade, just as the archaic script is restricted to the relic-boxes and the berm and stairway balustrades. It is, therefore, quite clear that the ground balustrade of this monument is a later addition. Stūpa 3 balustrade has a gateway, which, as Sir John Marshall has shown, is adorned with reliefs cut in a slightly later style than those on the four gateways of Stūpa 1. We can, however, reasonably assume that these five gateways, together with the ground balustrade of Stūpa 3, belong virtually to the same period.

Chronology of Groups 2 and 3

The inscriptions on the gateways and balustrade extensions of Stūpa 1, and the ground balustrade of Stūpa 3, written either in the ordinary or in the ornate style, exhibit so many new features, as compared with the inscriptions on the main ground balustrade of Stūpa 1, as also with those on the relic-boxes, and the berm and stairway balustrades of Stūpa 3, that we shall not be far wrong in assuming an interval of about a century between the two groups of records (*viz.*, Groups 2 and 3), the intermediate stage being represented by the Bharhut inscription of Dhanabhūti (*circa* 100-75 B.C.). Again, the inscriptions of Group 3 at Sāñchī, being in characters which are undoubtedly earlier than those of the Mathurā inscription of Śoḍāsa of the year 72, have to be placed between about 100-75 B.C. on the one hand, and about 15 A.D. on the other. The initial point in the date of Group 3 may, therefore, be tentatively fixed at about 50 B.C., which would also be the approximate date of King Sātakarṇi mentioned in the inscription on the South Gate of Stūpa 1.

Identity of King Sātakarṇi

But scholars are sharply divided in opinion as regards the date and identity of this Sātakarṇi. Cunningham identified him with the third Andhra king of the Purānic list, and, following Wilson, placed him in the first quarter of the first century A.D.[1] Bühler agreed with Cunningham in this identification, but assigned him to a date as early as the middle of the second century B.C.[2] In his opinion the characters of the Sāñchī inscription are 'almost identical with those of the Nānāghāt inscriptions of Sātakarṇi I. Accordingly, he would regard Sātakarṇi of Sāñchī to be a contemporary of King Khāravela of Kaliṅga mentioned in the latter's Hāthigumphā inscription which is referred by Bhagwanlal Indraji to the middle of the second century B.C. The synchronism of a Sātakarṇi with Khāravela, the identification of this Sātakarṇi with the king of that name of the Nānāghāt and Sāñchī inscriptions and the date of Khāravela himself have been the subject of much controversy. Rapson[3] and Jayaswal[4] adhere generally to the view of

[1] This was also the view of R. G. Bhandarkar. See *Ind. Ant.*, 1920, pp. 30-31.

[2] *Ep. Ind.*, Vol. II, p. 88; also *Ind. Pal.*, Trans., p. 39.

[3] *Cambridge History of India*, Vol. I, pp. 533, 535.

[4] *Ep. Ind.*, Vol. XX (1932), p. 74 and earlier publications in *J. B. O. R. S.*, since 1917.

Bhagwanlal regarding the date of Khāravela, and also identify Sātakarṇi of the Hāthigumphā inscription with Sātakarṇi I of Nānāghāt. But Rapson[1] pointed out long ago Bühler's mistake in assigning so early a date to the Sāñchī inscription, and suggested that the Sātakarṇi of this inscription should be identified with one of the Sātakarṇis who appear later in the Purānic lists. On palæographic grounds, Jayaswal considers this Sātakarṇi to be the same as Sātakarni II.[2] Chanda,[3] on the other hand, draws attention to the palæographic difference between the Hāthigumphā and Nānāghāt, as well as between the Nānāghāt and Sāñchī, inscriptions. He is of the opinion that Sātakarṇi of Nānāghāt is no doubt Sātakarṇi I of the Purāṇas, but the Sātakarṇis of Hāthigumphā and Sāñchī, who are according to him identical, are the same as Sātakarṇi II of the Purānic lists. In the Purāṇas, the first Sātakarṇi is said to have reigned for ten years, and between him and the second Sātakarṇi there are placed two more kings with a reign period of eighteen years each. To Sātakarṇi II the Purāṇas attribute a long reign of fifty-six years. According to Chanda, this king's reign may be tentatively dated between B.C. 75 and 20. On the other hand, R. D. Banerji[4] has attempted to show that the differences in the forms of letters used in the Hāthigumphā and Nānāghāt inscriptions are in reality very few, so that they cannot be far removed in date from one another. This is not the place to enter into the intricacies of these problems, but certain facts may be briefly stated, as they have a direct bearing on the date of the Sāñchī inscriptions.

The Nānāghāt and Hāthigumphā records

A reference to the plates published by R. D. Banerji as well as to my own table (Cols. XI and XVII) will no doubt reveal that the two records from Nānāghāt and Hāthigumphā agree in a number of palæographic details, *viz.*, *ka* with short upper vertical, rounded *ga*, rounded or nearly rounded *ta*, triangular *ma* and *va*, *u*-mark as attached to *pa* and *sa* in continuation of their right curve, and equalization or tendency to equalization of the verticals in *pa*, *sa* and *ha*. But in certain important points the inscriptions show a remarkable difference: the letter *cha*, in Nānāghāt, is archaic, having the form of an ellipse bisected by a vertical, while the *cha* of Hāthigumphā consists of two circular loops; the letter *bha* of Nānāghāt does not show any extension of the right lower vertical, while in Hāthigumphā it invariably has this feature; and in a number of instances the *i*-stroke in Hāthigumphā presents an ornamental flourish which is absent in Nānāghāt. Again, the Nānāghāt letters rarely show a thickening of the upper ends of their verticals, but the Hāthigumphā inscription contains quite a number of examples showing a definite formation of the serif.[5] In view of these differences, we should be justified in placing the Nānāghāt inscriptions a few decades earlier than the Hāthigumphā inscription. It becomes therefore, necessary to distinguish the two Sātakarṇis and regard the Sātakarṇi of the Hāthigumphā inscription as Sātakarṇi II.

[1] *British Museum Catalogue of Coins*, 1908, Introduction, p. XXIV.
[2] *J. B. O. R. S.*, 1917, p. 442, n. 25.
[3] *Mem. A. S. I.*, No. 1, pp. 7, 10, and *Ind. Hist. Quart.*, 1929, pp. 600-601.
[4] *Mem. A. S. B.*, Vol. XI, No. 3 and Pls. 17-23.
[5] Chanda lays much stress on this feature in determining the order of sequence of the Nānāghāt and Hāthigumphā inscriptions. *Mem. A. S. I.*, No. 1, pp. 7, 10; and *Ind. Hist. Quart.*, 1929, p. 600.

Their approximate dates

Palæographically, Nānāghāt and Hāthigumphā would respectively come under Groups 2 A and 3 of the table. The date of the former may be tentatively fixed at about 100-75 B.C. and that of the latter at about 50-25 B.C. According to the Purāṇas, Sātakarṇi I was the third from Simuka, the founder of the Andhra dynasty. If, therefore, the date assigned to the Nānāghāt inscriptions be approximately correct, it would follow that Simuka began to rule from about the last quarter of the second century B.C., and not earlier,[1] as is generally supposed.

Internal evidence of Hāthigumphā inscription

In support of the above dating of Khāravela there is also internal evidence furnished by the great Hāthigumphā inscription. King Khāravela, according to this inscription, led several victorious expeditions to the North. He fought a battle at Gorathagiri, *i.e.*, Barābar hills near Gayā, defeated a king of Rājagṛiha, drove another ruler as far as Mathurā, brought terror to the *rājās* of Uttarāpatha, *i.e.*, Northern India, and humbled Bahasatimitra, the king of Magadha. The record mentions a Sātakarṇi, the ruler of the West, without taking heed of whom Khāravela sent out an army in the second year of his reign. But it does not mention the Śuṅgas, or any sovereign ruler of Northern India. This document refers, therefore, to a period when there was no centralized power in Northern India, that is, to the time following the overthrow of the Imperial power of the Śuṅgas, when, as coins testify, the country was split up into a number of principalities. The overthrow of the Imperial Śuṅgas could not have occurred before the closing years of the second century B.C. Khāravela should, therefore, be placed after this date. What brings the date within still narrower limits is the mention in a passage of the inscription that 'three centuries' (*ti-vasa-sata*) before him King Nanda had opened out a canal in Kaliṅga, and in the fifth regnal year of Khāravela its course was diverted towards his capital.[2] Three centuries from King Nanda, *i.e.*, Mahāpadma Nanda (accession, *circa* 370 B.C.), brings us roughly to the middle of the first century B.C.

Date of Sātakarṇi of Sāñchī

The characters of the Hāthigumphā inscription and those of the records on the gateways of Stūpa 1 resemble each other in so many respects, that they cannot but be referred to one and the same period. All evidence, therefore, points to the conclusion that Sātakarṇi of the Sāñchī record was no other than Sātakarṇi (II) of the Hāthigumphā inscription and that he was reigning about the middle of the first century B.C.[3] In the order of sequence this Sāñchī record comes after the Bharhut Gate inscription of the time of the Śuṅgas, and coins of a Sātakarṇi have been found in Mālwā bearing the legend *Raño Siri-Sātasa* in serif-headed letters identical with those of the Sāñchī inscription. It is thus clear that in Central India the rule of the Śuṅgas was superseded by that of the Andhras[4] in the reign of Sātakarṇi II, about the middle of the first century B.C.

[1] It may be noted that the Nāsik Cave inscription of Kṛishṇa (*Ep. Ind.*, Vol. VIII, p. 93 and Pl. VI, No. 22), the successor of Simuka, has examples of almost triangular *ma* and *va*, which can be explained only on the ground of a late date as suggested above.

[2] *Mem. A. S. I.*, No. 1, pp. 10-12. Jayaswal contends, however, that *ti-vasa-sata* means 'one hundred and three years' and that in the passage under reference the year 103 of a Nanda era is given as the date of the excavation of the canal (*Ep. Ind.*, Vol. XX. p. 87 and n. 7). But according to the above interpretation we get three hundred years in round number, which seems to be far more natural.

[3] *Cf.*, however, p 5 *supra*.

[4] This is quite in accord with the Purānic statement that the Andhras will "destroy the remains of the Śuṅgas' power".—Pargiter, *Dynasties of the Kali Age*, p. 71.

Two Kushān Inscriptions from Mathurā

There is hardly any inscription at Sāñchī that belongs to the first century of the Christian era, that is to say, to Group 3 A of our table. Two inscriptions which can be definitely ascribed to the Kushān rule have been found at Sāñchī. They are referable to the second century A.D., if we are right in assuming that Kanishka flourished in the beginning of that century. Of these, inscription No. 828 is a record of the year 28, when Vāsishka was reigning. The other inscription, No. 829, is dated in the year 22 and in the reign of a king bearing the curious name Vaskushāna, whose identity has yet to be established. It may be noted that he has none of the Kushān titles like *Devaputra*, etc., but is simply styled *rājan*; he may, therefore, have been a local prince of Kushān extraction. The characters of the two records are similar in every respect to those of the contemporary Mathurā inscriptions and call for no special remarks. A further link with Mathurā is furnished by the red sandstone of the sculptures—a material peculiar to that region—on which the inscriptions are cut. Doubtless, the sculptures were executed at Mathurā itself, and the inscriptions also engraved there. That being so, it does not follow from the evidence of these inscriptions that Sāñchī, that is to say, Eastern Mālwā, came actually under the sway of the Kushāns. Existing evidence rather points to the conclusion that during this period the province was held by the Western Satraps, *viz.*, the family of Cashṭana.

Gupta and mediæval inscriptions

The Gupta period is represented by the two well-known inscriptions of the years 93 and 131 of the Gupta era (Nos. 833 and 834), of which the earlier one mentions Candragupta II of the Imperial Gupta dynasty. Two other inscriptions which are to be referred to about the same period, are No. 839 from the neighbouring village of Kanakhera and No. 835 engraved on a pillar in the courtyard of Stūpa 1. Next come a number of votive records, all dating from the mediæval period. The most important of these is No. 842, which is in characters of about the ninth century A.D. It mentions a certain Vappakadeva and a *Mahārāja* Śarvva, who are described as rulers of Mahāmālava, that is Mālwā, in which region Sāñchī is situated.

Language of Inscriptions

The language of the inscriptions of the Kushān, Gupta and later periods is either a mixture of Sanskrit and Prākṛit or pure Sanskrit. But the language of the early votive inscriptions and the relic-casket and relic-box inscriptions from Sāñchī, of the second and first centuries B.C., corresponds to what Senart calls 'Monumental Prākṛit'.[1] This form of Prākṛit, which has already been considered by Bühler,[2] has the usual feature, namely a double consonant is represented by a single letter—a feature that constitutes its chief difference from Literary Prākṛit. Besides this, there are also other peculiarities: the sibilants *śa* and *sha* are denoted by *sa* throughout, and the letter *ra* is never changed into *la*, in which respects the Sāñchī inscriptions agree with the Girnar and the three Mysore

[1] *Inscriptions of Piyadasi*, Vol. II, trans. by Grierson, 1892, pp. 169 ff.

[2] *Ep. Ind.*, Vol. II, pp. 89 ff.

inscriptions of Aśoka. As regards vowels, the notable changes are: *u* of *upa* becomes *o* in *Opedadata*; *ṛi* becomes *a*, in *Asabha*, but *i* in all names having *ṛishi* as their component; *i* often becomes *ī* in the word *Sīha* (*Siṁha*), as in Pāli, and *au* becomes *o*, in *sotika* (No. 499). Among simple consonants very few are transformed, *e.g.*, *ka* is rendered by *ca* in *Cirātī*, with which we may compare *Cilāa* of Literary Prākṛit[1] and *Cilāta* occurring in a Nāgārjunikoṇḍa inscription;[2] *ta* becomes *ṭa*, in *patikama* (No. 122) and *paṭipajeya* (No. 389), and is elided in *Patiṭhiya*; *da* becomes *ya* in *rudhirupayaka* (*rudhir-otpādaka*), in No. 396; *bha* is changed into *ha*, in *Gohila* and *Suhadadata*, in which latter (as also in *upāḍeya*, No. 396) we have to further notice the change of a *ṭa* into *ḍa*; and *va* becomes *ya* once, in *Kākaṇāye*. In regard to euphony, it should be observed that the combination of *a* with a following *u* results in the dropping of the *a*. Thus are formed *Ayutara*, *Dhamutara*, *Nadutara*, etc. The expression *sa-atevasikasa* in No. 242 represents hiatus as in some of the Pillar Edicts of Aśoka and in later Prākṛit inscriptions.

As a rule, a group of consonants is assimilated to a single letter, the phonetic changes taking place mostly as in the Bharhut inscriptions. The following changes may be noted:

ava is contracted into *o* in *Odatikā*; *ksh* changes into *kh* in the name-component *-rakhita*, and in *Yakha*; *ksh* into *ch*, but less frequently into *kh*, in *bhikhu* and *bhikhunī*; *ksh* into *c* in *Cuḍa*; *ksh* into *jh* (*cf.* Pischel, *Grammatik*, p. 223), in *sejha* (No. 633); *ksh* into *ha*, only once in *sihanā* (No. 7), as in Ardha-Māgadhī; *gn* into *g* in *Agidata*; *gr* into *g* in *gāma*; *jñ* into *ñ* in *ñati* (No. 102) and *rāño-* (No. 398); *ñc* into *c* in *paca* (No. 404); *ñj* into *j* in *Kujara*; *ṇḍ* into *ḍ* in *Koḍiniputa*; *ṇy* into *ñ* in *Puñavaḍhana*; *tṛ* into *ti* in *sa-mātika* (No. 347); *tr* into *t* in *Ahimita*; *dg* into *g* in *Mogalāna*; *ts* into *ch* in *Vāchi*; *ty* into *c* in *Kācāniputa*; *tsn* into *nh* in *Jonhaka*; *dy* into *j* in *paṭipajeya* (No. 389); *dhy* into *jh* in *Majhima*, *Vijha*; *dr* into *d* in *Idadeva*; *ny* into *ñ* in *Dhañā*; *ny* into *n* in *ānaṁ* (No. 396); *pt* into *t* in *Ajitiguta*; *pr* into *p* in *Pasanaka*; *rv* into *v* in *save* (No. 389); *rdh* into *ḍh* or *ḍ* in *vaḍhaki* and *vaḍaki* (Nos. 454, 589), and *Bhogavaḍhana*; *rm* into *m* or *ṁm* in *Dhama*, *Dhaṁma*, and *kaṁmika* (No. 199); *ry* into *riya* in *ācariya* (No. 3) and *ya* in *Aya*; *rh* into *raha* in *Araha*, and *ra* in *Ara*; *lg* into *g* in *Phaguna*; *mb* into *b* in *Kāboja*; *śy* into *s* in *Kasapa*; *śr* into *s* in *Datamisa*; *śv* often remains *sv* and often becomes *s*, as in *Asvadeva* and *Asadeva* respectively; *st* changes into *th* in *thabho* (Nos. 665, 673); *sn* often becomes *nh* and often *n* in *nhusā* and *nusā* (No. 285), whereas *sunhusā* (No. 687) is an example of anaptyxis; *sm* changes into *mh* in *-girimha* (No. 298) regarding which witness a similar change in locative in the Girnar Edicts and Nāsik cave inscriptions.

Nominative singular of masculine *a*-bases ends in *o* as in *thabho* (Nos. 397, 402 and 403). The pronominal form *yaḥ* becomes *yo* in Nos. 396 and 404. The instrumental occurs in *Vedisakehi daṁtakāreḥi* (No. 400). But there are not many examples of case

[1] Pischel, *Grammatik der Prākrit-Sprachen*, p. 164.

[2] *Ep. Ind.*, Vol. XX, p. 22.

terminations other than those of the ablative and genitive. It is particularly in the genitives of feminine stems ending in *i* and *ā* that Bühler detected a mixture of forms used in Aśoka's eastern and western recensions. These forms end in *ya*, *yā* or *ye*, although in some cases the dropping of the medial *ā*-mark may be treated as entirely an orthographical blunder. The ablative of stems ending in *a* is often denoted by the lengthening of the vowel, *e.g.*, *Vedisā*, *Tubavanā*, *Vāḍivahanā*, and *Kaṁdaḍigāmā*, and often by *āto*, *e.g.*, in *Vāḍivahanāto*, *Kurarāto*, *Arapānāto*, *Bhogavaḍhanāto* and *Pokharāto*. These ablative formations are similar to those formed in Literary Prākṛit[1] with the addition of *ā* and *do*, *e.g.*, *vacchā* and *vacchādo*. As Bühler has noticed, the ablative in *āto* is not traceable in Aśoka's inscriptions, but is found in the Jaina inscriptions from Mathurā, and once in a Bharhut inscription. The ablative ending *ā* is of frequent occurrence at Bharhut as well as at Sāñchī. Both the terminations *ā* and *āto* occur also in the Nāsik cave inscriptions.[2] A rare ablative ending is *tu* in *gāmatu* (No. 526), which should be compared with *du* (*e.g.*, in *vacchādu*) of Literary Prākṛit. Another rare ablative form with the ending *mha* is found in No. 298, in *girimha*, which occurs also in the Bharhut inscriptions. As regards orthographic irregularities mention may be made of the frequent omission of *ā* and the *anusvāra*. But the dropping of the nasal, *e.g.*, in *atevāsinī*, *Ida*, etc., cannot be always regarded as due to carelessness. The long *ī* in the names *Budhapālītā*, *Isipālīta* and *Budhapālīta*, in Nos. 197, 362 and 363, is rather unusual.

Prākṛit of Aśoka's Edict and later inscriptions of Sāñchī

In Bühler's opinion, the language of these Brāhmī inscriptions from Sāñchī 'differs very little from the literary Pāli and still less from the dialects of Aśoka's edicts'. But it should be noted that, although it has certain points of resemblance to the Aśokan Prākṛit, it would hardly be correct to say that they are identical in character. The retention of the letter *r* in groups, as in Girnar and the North-Western recensions of Aśoka's edicts, is extremely rare in the Sāñchī and Bharhut inscriptions. They are not characterized by a learned orthography like the records of Aśoka, in which, although Sanskrit conjunct groups are generally assimilated, there are still many examples of such groups being retained. In the Sāñchī and Bharhut inscriptions, on the other hand, assimilation is almost universally carried out. As regards other points of difference, the absence of the ablative termination *āto* in the Aśokan Prākṛit has already been noticed. The influence of Māgadhī in the period of Aśoka can be detected in the inscriptions of North-Western and Central India. Even in the Sāñchī Edict there is a clear instance of Māgadhism in *cila*, for *cira*, in line 8 of the record,[3] although in *-sūriyike*, in line 4, the letter *la* is not substituted for *ra*. But neither in the votive inscriptions of Sāñchī nor in those of Bharhut is there a single instance of such transformation. The absence of Māgadhī elements in the Prākṛit inscriptions throughout Northern India in the first century B.C. is a feature of great linguistic importance. Even at Bodh-Gayā and at Hāthigumphā, which

[1] Pischel, *Grammatik der Prākṛit-Sprachen*, pp. 249-251.
[2] *Cf.* the forms *vijayakhadhāvārā* and *khetāto*, *Ep. Ind.*, Vol. VIII, pp. 71, 77.
[3] Senart, *Inscriptions of Piyadasi*, Vol. II, p. 149.

can be legitimately regarded as having been once within the domain of Māgadhī, *ra* is never transformed into *la*.

Here and there it is possible to recognize some new elements in the language of the later inscriptions of Sāñchī, for instance, those of the gateways and balustrade extensions of Stūpa 1. These elements seem to arise out of a recurrence of the tendency to follow Sanskritic orthography, and, although they do not occur uniformly, are nevertheless worthy of notice. Thus, instances like *Vāsiṭhiputra* (South Gate, No. 398) and *Balamitra* (South Gate, No. 399), instead of *Vāsiṭhiputa* and *Balamita*, now begin to appear. Examples like *Jeṭhabhadra, ūkraṁti*, etc., occur on the Bharhut rail. Even in the Besnagar Pillar inscription of Heliodorus, *r*, as the second letter of a conjunct group, is retained in all the four instances that are found in that record. In the earlier class of epigraphs at Sāñchī, such forms in which *r* is retained in groups are, however, unknown.[1] Another point to note is the non-shortening of an original medial *ī*, *e.g.*, in *Vīra* (balustrade extension, No. 195). In the earlier Sāñchī inscriptions, it is in almost all cases changed into short *i*. As against this, there is *Gāgī* in the Bharhut Gate inscription. Medial *ū* remains also likewise unchanged, *e.g.*, in *Mūla, Bhūtika* and *sūci* (Stūpa 3, ground balustrade, Nos. 726, 734) and in *Dhanabhūti* in the Bharhut Gate inscription. These peculiarities are by no means confined to the later Prākṛit inscriptions of Mālwā and Central India, but are found also in the contemporary documents of other parts of India.

[1] The only exception seems to be *Asāḍra* in Stūpa 1, ground balustrade, No. 250 and No. 336. But in this case *ḍra* probably stands for *ḍha*.

Chapter XIX

INSCRIPTION ON THE AŚOKA PILLAR

No. 1 Aśoka Edict

Previous publications

THIS inscription of Aśoka, which is engraved on the fragmentary column standing near the South Gate of Stūpa 1, has been known since 1838, when Prinsep made an attempt to decipher it.[1] The record was subsequently studied by Cunningham[2] and Bühler.[3] After the discovery of the Sārnāth Edict of Aśoka in 1904-5, with which it has many points in common, it again engaged the attention of scholars, and Hultzsch[4] published a corrected version of the epigraph in 1911. The text and translation, as further amended by him, were later incorporated in his *Corpus Inscriptionum Indicarum*, Vol. I, New Edition, 1925, pp. 160-161.

Subject matter

The text, which originally consisted of 8 lines, is not very carefully engraved and has suffered much from damage : the opening line is entirely lost and some letters of lines 2, 3 and 6 are missing. The subject matter of the inscription is identical with that of the Kauśāmbī and Sārnāth Edicts, *viz.*, penalty for schism in the Buddhist Church (*Saṁghabheda*). Thus says Aśoka : "Whosoever, be it monk or be it nun, creates a division in the Saṁgha, shall be made to wear white garments and to reside outside the (Saṁgha) *āvāsa* (quarters)". He further directs that this order should be carried out in future by his descendants, as it was his wish that the united Saṁgha might long endure. The texts of the three versions of the Edict are independent of one another, although some of the words and phrases are common. The full text of the order (*śāsana*) is given in the Sārnāth Edict, according to which the Mahāmātras were charged with its circulation. The King wanted the monks, nuns and lay-worshippers, as well as his Mahāmātras, to be thoroughly acquainted with the order, and directed that the Mahāmātras and lay-worshippers should renew their acquaintance with it on every Uposatha day. Uposatha was the day of fast observed by the congregation every fortnight, when it was customary to recite the *Pāṭimokkha*, the Buddhist criminal code dealing with offences and penal measures. It is natural, therefore, that Aśoka should insist that his Edict, which was in the nature of a supplement to the *Pāṭimokkha*, be also read on the Uposatha day. The Sārnāth Edict was probably issued from Pāṭaliputra, while the Kauśāmbī Edict was addressed to the Mahāmātras of Kauśāmbī. On the other hand, as will be seen from the observations made below, the Sāñchī Edict did not probably contain any reference to the Mahāmātras at all.

---

[1] *J. A. S. B.*, Vol. VII (Old Series), p. 565 and Pl. XXIII, 46.

[2] *Bhilsa Topes*, p. 261 and Pl. XIX, 177; and *Corp. Ins. Ind.*, Vol. I, 1877, p. 116.

[3] *Ep. Ind.*, Vol. II, p. 367 and Pl.

[4] *J. R. A. S.*, 1911, pp. 167-69.

Restoration of Text

The restoration of the damaged and missing text of the Sāñchī Edict calls for some remarks. There are 13 letters in each of the lines 3 to 7, and 14 letters in line 8, which is the last. There is probably one letter missing at the beginning of line 2, in which the total number of letters, judging from those that are legible and from the traces that remain of the rest, was either 12 or 13. Line 1, which is completely gone, contained probably not more than 14 letters. It may be argued that the opening sentence of this inscription was similar to that in the Kauśāmbī Edict which reads: *Devānaṁ-piye ānapayati Kosāmbiyaṁ mahāmāta*, with this difference, that *Vedisā* or *Ujenī* may have been substituted in it for *Kosāmbī*. But, in that case, the number of letters in this line would be as many as 18, which appears improbable, considering the space that is available and the number of letters in other lines. It is, therefore, unlikely that the first line had any reference to the Mahāmātras of Vedisā or Ujenī. The missing sentence may be restored simply: *Devānaṁ-piye Piyadasi ānapayati*—which would make the line one of 14 letters only.

Restoration of line 2

Hultzsch is quite right in restoring the concluding portion of line 2 as *saṁghe samage kaṭe*, as in the Kauśāmbī Edict. Before the word *saṁghe* there appear to have been at least three letters in succession, of which the first one is clearly *bhe*. The following two are doubtfully supplied as *tave* by Hultzsch on the analogy of . . . . *ye kenapi saṁghe bhetave* of the Sārnāth Edict. Boyer restores this broken sentence as *na sakiye kenapi saṁghe bhetave* (*cf. sakiye khamitave* of Jaugaḍa Separate Edict). But the letter preceding *bhe* in the present inscription is *yā*, which, like the portion *saṁghe samage kaṭe*, shows that the Sāñchī text is different from the Sārnāth one, in so far as this passage is concerned. In Pāli,[1] *samaggi-karoti* means 'to harmonize', and *samagga* means 'being in unity' or 'harmonious'. The phrase *samagga-saṁgha, i.e.*, 'saṁgha in union' is of common occurrence in Buddhist literature.[2] In the Cullavagga, VII 5, 3, the expression *saṁgha-sāmaggī* is used as an antonym of *saṁghabheda*. The passage *saṁghe samage kaṭe*, meaning 'Saṁgha has been united', is, therefore, clear enough. From this it also follows that during Aśoka's reign there had been some dissension in the Church, and unity was later established. It is possible that in the Sāñchī inscription Aśoka draws pointed attention to this achievement. If so, we have to look for other possible restorations of line 2, and the only restoration that appears to me satisfactory is *bhedite* or *bhetite* instead of *bhetave*. Boyer read the second letter as *da* and Hultzsch took it to be *ta*. It is difficult to say which reading is more likely, judging from the traces of the letter that has practically peeled off. But Bühler's facsimile seems to favour Boyer's reading. Thus the passage, as restored, would read *bhedite saṁghe samage kaṭe, i.e.*, 'the Saṅgha (which was) divided is (now) united'. The restoration of the word that ended in *yā* just before this portion of the text, is uncertain. Mr. Dikshit has suggested to me that it might

[1] *Pāli-English Dictionary* (P. T. S.).

[2] *Corp. Ins. Ind.*, Vol. I, 1925, p. 161, n. 8 and p. 162, n. 8.

be the remnant of *mayā*, 'by me', to be taken with *kaṭe*. This conjectural reading sounds very probable.

Construction of lines 3-4

In lines 3-4, the clause *puta-papotike*, etc., which is used adverbially, as in Delhi-Topra, Edict VII, was at first taken by Hultzsch[1] as qualifying *ye saṅghaṁ bhākhati*, etc. But in *Corpus Ins. Ind.*, Vol. I, p. 161, he has taken it to qualify the previous sentence *saṁghe samage kaṭe*. It may, however, be pointed out that the sentence *saṁghe samage kaṭe*, etc., ends with the particle *ti* (Skt. *iti*), and a new sentence commences with *puta-papotike*, etc. The first interpretation of Hultzsch has, therefore, been adopted in the present translation.

Significance of the Edict

It is somewhat strange that Aśoka should have set about promulgating edicts so intimately connected with Church discipline. There was ample provision in the Code of the Buddhist Saṁgha for dealing with *saṁghabheda*, which in the *Pāṭimokkha* is reckoned as one of the Thirteen Minor Priestly Offences (*saṁghādiśesha* or *saṁghāvaśesha*). A member of the Order found guilty of any of these offences had to undergo *parivāsa*, *i.e.*, living apart, and practise *mānatta*, *i.e.*, penance, for a number of days. This meant either banishment from a particular monastic residence (*āvāsa*) or suspension from the Order. If a *bhikshu*, during the period of his *parivāsa*, followed the right path of conduct and was penitent, he could be reinstated. The practices that would qualify him for such reinstatement, as in the case of suspension, are laid down in the Cullavagga (I 27). Among other things, he was not allowed to eat or live with the Saṁgha, or to stay with a regular monk under the same roof. But some cases of *saṁghabheda* would not come under the category of the Thirteen *saṁghādiśeshas*, and evidently required a more severe punishment. In the Cullavagga (VII 5, 2) a distinction is made between creating mere disaffection in the Church (*saṁgharāji*) and schism in the Church (*saṁghabheda*) which was looked upon as far more dangerous. The latter comprises as many as eighteen points, and the Cullavagga states that one guilty of *saṁghabheda* lives in hell for a *kalpa* or cycle of years. This *saṁghabheda* is certainly of a graver nature than what would come under the category of the Thirteen Minor Offences, and is evidently so understood in Mahāvagga, I 67, where it is enjoined that a *saṁghabhedaka* must not be taken into the Order, or, if he is already in it, must be expelled. Expulsion was the highest penalty that could be imposed by the Church, and the Mahāvagga (I 60) mentions ten heinous offences for which this punishment should be prescribed. As these included speaking against the Saṁgha and holding false doctrines, extreme cases of *saṁghabheda* would naturally come under this class.[2]

Aśoka's Edicts do not seem to have been directed against ordinary delinquents, but against those who were deliberate aggressors of a dangerous nature. A case of minor disorder, such as *saṁgharāji*, would, of course, come under the Thirteen Minor Offences, and

[1] *J. R. A. S.*, 1911, p. 168.

[2] *Saṁghabheda* came to be regarded, by the time the gateways of Stūpa I were erected (1st century B.C.), as one of the Five Great Sins. See below p. 341.

ecclesiastical authorities could deal with it in the prescribed way. But the very fact that in the present instance they had to call in the aid of the king, shows the gravity of the situation. The passage *saṁghe samage kaṭe* in the Sāñchī and Kauśāmbī Edicts presupposes, as already stated, the occurrence of a *saṁghabheda* of a somewhat serious nature, which was overcome through King Aśoka's intervention. The precautionary measure, which was enforced by a royal proclamation, at least at three centres of Buddhism, was in all likelihood intended to stop the further progress of an organised schismatic movement at its initial stage. The punishment which Aśoka wanted to mete out to the offending members of the Saṁgha, consisted of segregation in an *anāvāsa* and wearing of white robes. The two words *āvāsa* and *anāvāsa*[1] frequently occur in the Vinaya in the sense of 'residence and 'what is not a residence', respectively. Thus, the monks dwell in *āvāsa* (*e.g.*, Mahāvagga, IV 5, 1), which would no doubt mean the quarters or monastic abode attached to the Saṁgha of a particular place. To live in *anāvāsa*, therefore, means living in a house outside the *āvāsa* which was the regular residence of the fraternity. According to the ordinary rules of the Vinaya, a suspended monk would be required to undergo this punishment. But he need not put on white robes, as that would reduce him to the position of a layman. The Cullavagga (I 25, 1) in fact forbids him to wear the outward signs of a layman. Aśoka's order that the offending member should also be made to put on white robes is, therefore, a new measure involving greater humiliation for the monks and nuns guilty of *saṁghabheda*, as it almost amounted to expulsion. If promulgated by the Saṁgha, this order might have been easily flouted. It was, therefore, natural that the Saṁgha should approach the highest temporal authority for enforcing it on the fraternity. It seems as if a serious cleavage had already occurred, and the Church had to provide for effective safeguards against its recurrence in future.

Directed against dangerous schism

Date of the Edict

In the three Edicts, Aśoka thus appears as a champion of Buddhism and Head of the Buddhist Church, bent upon preventing schism in the Order. This phase of his character has been rightly referred to the closing years of his life. Earlier in his reign, Aśoka promulgated Edicts in which stress was laid on religious toleration in its widest sense. He did not, till then, seem to have been swayed by sectarian ideas, or to have concerned himself with matters relating primarily to the internal administration of the Buddhist Church. In fact, he discouraged those who indulged in the condemnation of other sects and praise of their own. He honoured all sects and wished that they should uniformly prosper (Rock Edict XII). This liberal spirit is quite in contrast with the rigid sectarian attitude revealed by the Edicts of Sāñchī, Sārnāth and Kauśāmbī. The sequence in which the Kauśāmbī Edict occurs after the Pillar edicts on the Allāhābād Pillar shows that it must belong to a date later than Aśoka's twenty-sixth regnal year.[2] It is not unlikely, as some scholars think, that the issue of the three Edicts was connected

[1] A slightly modified form *ānāvāsa* occurs in the Sārnāth Edict.

[2] For the date of the Pillar and Edict, respectively, *cf.*, also, pp. 28-9 *supra*.

with the traditional Third Council of Pāṭaliputra. The object of this Council was the suppression of schism (*bheda*) which, according to the *Dīpavaṁsa* (VII 44), had arisen in the Theravāda, during the reign of Aśoka. A large number of heretics had entered into the Order, who did not follow the tenets of the Buddha, and the orthodox monks refused to hold the Uposatha festival with these heretics. The Council was held in the presence of the king himself, under the presidency of his *guru* Moggaliputta Tissa, the leader of the Theravādins or Vibhajjavādins. Here, at the instance of King Aśoka, the monks who dissented from the Vibhajja doctrine expounded their own views. Thereafter, he expelled from the Order the whole of the dissentient body of monks, numbering in all sixty thousand. When the Saṅgha was thus 'purified', it held the Uposatha festival in concord.[1] Tissa compiled the *Kathāvatthu*, refuting the doctrines of schools other than the Theravāda (*Mahāvaṁsa*, V 228-281). The *Dīpavaṁsa* (VII 53) further adds that Aśoka also destroyed the emblems (*liṅga-nāsanaṁ*) of the excommunicated monks as a punishment. In the introduction to the *Samantapāsādikā*, Buddhaghosha states that the heretical monks were unfrocked, being compelled to put on white robes.[2] This wearing of white robes, instead of the customary yellow ones, seems to have been alluded to in the passage in the *Dīpavaṁsa*.[3] How far this story of the schism and the Third Council as recorded in the Ceylonese Chronicles can be accepted as authentic, we do not know. Some scholars are inclined even to treat the whole story as a myth, invented by the protagonists of the Theravāda at a later period. It is, of course, possible that the Chroniclers have overdrawn the picture in some respects, and exaggerated the importance of the gathering. But, as the inscriptional evidence shows, the account cannot be wholly without foundation, and it is clear that Aśoka had to deal with a serious split, and that the measures he adopted served, temporarily at any rate, to close the ranks of the Orthodox Church.

Council of Pāṭaliputra

Text (Plate 128)

1 . . . .

2 . [y]ā bhe[da] . . [gh]e . mage kaṭe[4]

3 (bhi)khuna[ṁ] ca bhi[khun]inaṁ c[ā] ti puta-pa

4 -(po)tike caṁ[da]ma-[sū]ri[yi]ke ye saṁghaṁ

5 bhākhati bhikhu vā bhikhu[ni] va odātā-

6 ni dus[ān]i sanaṁ(dhāpa)yitu anā-[vā]-

7 sasi vā[sā]petaviy[e] ichā hi me kiṁ-

8 ti saṁghe samage cila-thitike siyā ti

Translation

. . . . The (split-up) Saṁgha, both of monks and of nuns, has been made one united whole. As long as (my) sons and great-grandsons (shall rule) and the moon and the sun (shall shine), the monk or nun who creates a division in the Saṁgha shall be made to put on white robes and to reside out of the (Saṁgha) residence. For what is my desire ?—That the Saṁgha as a united (body) may long endure.

[1] *Saṁgho samaggo hutvāna tadākāsi uposathaṁ*—*Mahāvaṁsa*, V. 274.

[2] Boyer, *Jour. As.*, ser. X, tome 10, p. 130.

[3] In the reference to the compulsory wearing of white robes by delinquents in the Sāñchī, Sārnāth and Kauśāmbī Edicts of Aśoka, Mr. R. P. Chanda finds a partial corroboration of the Ceylonese accounts of the Third Council.

[4] Probable restoration: *mayā bhedite saṁghe samage kaṭe*. See pp. 284-5 *supra*.

CHAPTER XX

INSCRIPTIONS ON THE RELIC-BOXES AND CASKETS

No. 2 Inscription on Stone box from Stūpa 2

THE inscription on the stone relic-box from Stūpa 2, which has already been described (above p. 81), was first published in 1854, together with an eye-copy, by General Cunningham.[1] A translation of the record was published by Professor Lüders[2] in 1912, and subsequently the inscription was re-edited by Pargiter,[3] who also published for the first time a mechanical copy of the inscription. When discovered, the box contained four small caskets of steatite, in each of which were found portions of burnt human bones. The box and three of the caskets which are also inscribed (see Nos. 3-12 below) are now in the British Museum.

Purpose of the Stone box and inscription

The inscription is very neatly engraved on one side of the stone box, and consists of three lines. Its palæography has been already discussed in connexion with the age of Stūpa 2 (above p. 269). Like the casket inscriptions, it is later than the original ground balustrade of Stūpa 1, but earlier than the Gateways. The circumstances of the discovery point to the conclusion that the inscription on the box is related, in some way or other, to the inscriptions on the four caskets. The latter give the bare names and epithets of certain saints (*satpurusha*), all of which are in the genitive case, without any specification of the related word which this case would demand. Since, however, the substance found in each of the caskets was ashes, there cannot be any doubt that the *śarīra*, *i.e.*, the corporeal relics of these saints, are here to be understood.[4] The relics were deposited in the caskets, and the caskets preserved inside the stone box. The saints mentioned in the casket inscriptions are as follows: Kāsapagota, Majhima, Hāritiputa, Mahavanāya, Āpagira, Koḍiniputa, Kosikiputa, Gotiputa, Mogaliputa and Vāchi-Suvijayita. Of these, only the first and the last appear in the inscription on the stone box, from which Cunningham[5] inferred that Stūpa 2 was originally intended for the relics of these two persons only. But this is not borne out by the reading proposed here, which makes it plain that the object of the inscription must have been to indicate briefly the contents of the box.

Reading and interpretation

A few remarks are necessary touching the reading and interpretation of the inscription. Cunningham read an *anusvāra* at four places; but it is omitted in Pargiter's text without any justification. An examination of the photographs and a paper squeeze of the inscription, kindly supplied by the British Museum, leaves no doubt as to

---

[1] *Bhilsa Topes*, p. 286 and Pl. XX. [2] *List*, No. 654. [3] *Ep. Ind.*, Vol. XII, pp. 302-303 and Pl.

[4] Regarding a similar casket inscription from Andher, Fleet remarks that it contains a string of genitives, " without any word to govern them or the principal one of them ..... From the fact that they are all found on unmistakable relic-boxes, we know exactly what was intended; namely, that we should supply some word or words meaning 'relics' or 'a deposit of relics'."—*J. R. A. S.*, 1906, p. 155.

[5] *Bhilsa Topes*, p. 291.

the correctness of Cunningham's reading. The *anusvāra* is rather boldly incised in all the four instances, and cannot be mistaken for any accidental mark. In line 2, the second word is read as *upādiya*, both by Cunningham and Pargiter. The former took it as an equivalent of Sanskrit *upādhyāya* ('professor'), but this is philologically impossible. Pargiter, on the other hand, assumed that it was the personal name of the individual who is called Kāsapagota in the inscription. But the actual reading is *upādaya*,[1] clearly a gerundial form corresponding to Sanskrit *upādāya* (from the root *dā* with the prefixes *upa* and *ā*), which means 'including'.[2] The phrase *savina vināyakana*, *i.e.*, 'of all the teachers', with which the record begins, is analogous to *sapurisasa* of the caskets, both being in the genitive case with the related word understood. This word, which is wanting, must have denoted the corporeal relics of the *vināyakas*, as in the case of the caskets, the *vināyakas* being no doubt the same as the *sapurisas* or saints of the casket inscriptions. Kāsapagota and Vāchi-Suvijayita have the epithet *sapurisa* in Nos. 3 and 6 below. The inscription on the relic-box records, therefore, the deposit of the corporeal relics of the teachers, *including* Kāsapagota[3] and Vāchi-Suvijayita.

Text (Plate 140, g)	Translation
1 savina[4] vināyakāna araṁ Kāsapa-	(Relics) of all the teachers, including *ara*[5] Kāsapa-
2 gotaṁ upādaya araṁ ca Vāchi-	gota (*Arhat Kāśyapa-gotra*) and *ara* Vāchi (*Arhat*
3 Suvijayitaṁ vināyaka	*Vātsi*)-Suvijayita, the teacher (or teachers)[6].

Nos. 3-12 Inscriptions on Relic-caskets from Stūpa 2

The four steatite caskets (Cunningham's Nos. I-IV) from Stūpa 2, referred to above, bear in all ten inscriptions incised in shallow lines, which were published by Cunningham[7] with eye-copies, and noticed by Lüders under Nos. 655-664 of his *List of Brāhmī Inscriptions*. These record the names of saints (*sapurisa*, *i.e.*, Sans. *sat-purusha*) in the genitive case, the significance of which has already been discussed (p. 289). Casket No. I has three inscriptions, one on the inner side of the lid, another on the outer side, and a third at the bottom of the casket. The saints referred to in the inscriptions are Kāsapagota, Majhima and Hāritiputa. There are two inscriptions on Casket No. II, one in the outer circle on the lid referring to Vāchiya Suvijayita, and another in the inner circle recording the donation (*dāna*). Casket No. III bears two inscriptions, one on the inner side of the lid, mentioning Koḍiniputa, and another on the outer side, giving the names of Mahavanāya and Āpagira. Casket No. IV bears three epigraphs, each containing a name: one on the outer side of the lid records the name of Kosikiputa; another on the inner side, that of Gotiputa; and a third at the bottom of the casket, that of Mogaliputa.

[1] In Cunningham's eye-copy, there appears an *i*-like stroke on the head of *da*. But it is absent in the photographs and the paper squeeze.

[2] Childers, *Pāli-English Dictionary*, s. v. *upādiyati*.

[3] Kassapagotta is the name of a *bhikshu* in the *Vinaya-Piṭaka* (Mahāvagga, IX, 1). Fleet, *J. R. A. S.*, 1905, p. 686.

[4] The form *savinaṁ*, *i.e.*, *sarvveshām*, occurs again in No. 102 below.

[5] Cunningham and subsequent scholars have taken *ara* as an equivalent of Sans. *arhat*. The form which occurs in the Sāñchī votive inscriptions is, however, *araha*.

[6] Lüders translates the inscription as: "(Relics) of all teachers (*vināyakas*) beginning with Ara (? *Arhat*) Kāsapagota (*Kāśyapagotra*) and Ara (? *Arhat*) Vāchi-Suvijayita (*Vātsi-Suvijayat* ?), the teacher (*vināyaka*)." The last word of the inscription, *viz.*, *vināyaka*, as Pargiter has also recognized (*Ep. Ind.*, Vol. XII, p. 303), seems to apply to both Kāsapagota and Vāchi-Suvijayita. But he takes the first two words *savina vināyakāna* along with the last word *vināyaka*, and translates the passage as "the teacher of all teachers." This interpretation, in view of the *dūrānvaya* which it involves, cannot be accepted.

[7] *Bhilsa Topes*, pp. 287-89 and Pl. XX.

Relic-caskets from Sonāri and Andher

Similar inscribed reliquaries were found by Cunningham also at Sonāri and Andher,[1] in the neighbourhood of Sāñchī. In the Piprāhwā vase inscription, a deposit of corporeal relics of this nature has been called *salila-nidhana, i.e.*, Sans. *śarīra-nidhāna*. A number of Kharoshṭhī inscriptions, which are posterior to the Christian era, refer to the enshrinement of such remains of the Buddha, specifically called *śarīra* or *dhātu*. As pointed out already (p. 289 above), no such words appear on the reliquaries from the Sāñchī region; nor are the relics in any of them described as those of the Buddha.

Identity of Saints whose names are inscribed on the relic-caskets

Some of the names occurring on the Sāñchī caskets are found also in the inscriptions from the Stūpas of Sonāri and Andher, which undoubtedly points to an actual identity of the persons. Of the ten saints whose relics were found at Sāñchī, the names of Kāsapagota, Majhima, Kosikiputa and Gotiputa appear on the Sonāri caskets, while those of Gotiputa, Hāritiputa and Mogaliputa occur on three other caskets from Andher. As pointed out by Cunningham,[2] Āpagira is to be identified with Ālābagira, whose name is recorded on a Sonāri casket. Vāchiya Suvijayita, described as the pupil of Gota, seems to be identical with Vāchiputa (*Vātsīputra*), pupil of Gotiputa of an Andher casket, *Gota* probably being a shorter form of *Gotiputa*. According to the testimony of another Andher casket, Mogaliputa was also a pupil of Gotiputa. The latter is called Koḍiñagota (*Kauṇḍinya-gotra*) on a third casket from Andher, while he bears the epithet *Dudubhisara-dāyāda, i.e.*, 'an heir and kinsman of Dudubhisara'[3] in a Sonāri inscription. In two other inscriptions from Sonāri, Kāsapagota and Majhima have the epithets Kotīputa (*Kautsīputra*) and Koḍiniputa, respectively. This Koḍiniputa Majhima seems to be different from the Koḍiniputa of Inscription No. 9 below. It should be noted that most of the saints are called after their *gotra* or by their metronym, while in the case of a few both are specified. The saint Mahavanāya of No. 8 is not known from any other inscription.

Cunningham identified Mogaliputa with Moggaliputta Tissa of the Ceylonese Chronicles.[4] But this seems improbable, as Mogaliputa was the pupil of Gotiputa,

[1] *Bhilsa Topes*, pp. 315 ff. and 345 ff. The texts are given below for reference.

Inscriptions from Sonāri Stūpa 2.

(*i*) Lüders, No. 156, on crystal box: (1) *sapurisasa Goti-* (2) *putasa Hemavata-* (3) *sa Dudubhisa-* (4) *ra-dāyādasa*
(*ii*) Lüders, No. 157, on steatite casket No. 2: *sapurisasa Majhimasa Koḍiniputasa*
(*iii*) Lüders, No. 158, on steatite casket No. 3: *sapurisasa Kotīputasa Kāsapagotasa sava-Hemavat-ācariyasa*
(*iv*) Lüders, No. 159, on steatite casket No. 4: *sapurisasa Kosikiputasa*
(*v*) Lüders, No. 160, on steatite casket No. 5: *sapurisa-Ālābagirasa*

Inscriptions from Andher Stūpa 2.

(*vi*) Lüders, No. 681, on steatite casket: *sapurisasa Gotiputasa Kākanava-pabhāsanasa Koḍiñagotasa*
(*vii*) Lüders, No. 680, on earthen casket: *sapurisasa Vāchiputasa Gotiputa-atevāsino*
(*viii*) Lüders, No. 682, on steatite vase: *sapurisasa Mogaliputasa Gotiputa-atevāsino*

Inscription from Andher Stūpa 3.

(*ix*) Lüders, No. 683, on steatite casket: *sapurisasa Hāritīputasa*

[2] *Bhilsa Topes*, p. 318. Both *āpa* and *ālāba* may have been derived from Sans. *alpa*, the name corresponding to *alpagiraḥ*, which would mean 'a man of few words'.

[3] Fleet takes *Dudubhisara-dāyāda* as a Karmadhāraya compound, meaning 'Dudubhisara, who was an heir' (*J. R. A. S.*, 1905, p. 688). Lüders is also of the same opinion (*List*, No. 156). But this view is hardly tenable, because it is not stated in the inscription whose heir he was. The phrase should, therefore, be taken as a Tatpurusha (Shashṭhī) compound, and interpreted as above.

[4] *Bhilsa Topes*, p. 293. This view is accepted by Geiger. *Mahāvaṁsa Translation*, p. XX.

the heir of Dudubhisara. The latter can be identified with Dundubhissara mentioned in the *Dīpavaṁsa* (VIII 10)[1] as one of the five missionaries sent by Tissa to the Himalayan country after the conclusion of the Third Council in the reign of Aśoka. The four other missionaries were Mūlakadeva, Sahadeva, Kassapagotta and Majjhima. It is very likely, as Cunningham suggests, that Kassapagotta and Majjhima are identical with the homonymous persons of the Sāñchī and Sonāri caskets.[2] The saint Kāsapagota is referred to in these caskets as *sava-Hemavat-ācariya*, and some scholars find in this epithet a confirmation of the Ceylonese account of the despatch of missionaries to the Himalayas.[3] In view of this, the phrase is usually translated as 'the teacher of all the Himavat region (or, of all the people of Himavat)'.[4] But as Hemavata was also the name of a branch of the Theravāda School,[5] the expression can be taken to mean 'the teacher of the whole community of the Haimavatas'. A Sonāri inscription (Lüders, No. 156) supports the latter interpretation. In this record Gotiputa is mentioned as a kinsman of Dudubhisara, as stated above, and also as *Hemavata*. Here, *Hemavata* is obviously to be interpreted as 'a member of the Haimavata Order'. This school was so called, probably because it arose in the Himavat region, under the inspiration of the five teachers, though its further development may have taken place elsewhere. These are, therefore, the earliest known references to the Haimavatas. It seems likely that it was Kāsapagota who was primarily responsible for the foundation of this school, as he and none else among the saints is styled 'the *Ācārya* of all the Haimavatas'. In the opinion of Fleet, "the *Dīpavaṁsa* plainly indicates Kassapagotta as the leader of the mission to the Himalayas".[6] The *Dīpavaṁsa* has thus correctly handed down to us the names of three of these early Buddhist teachers, *viz.*, Kāsapagota, Majhima and Dudubhisara, and there is no doubt whatsoever that the account must have been based, partially at least, on genuine tradition.

Meaning of *Hemavata*

Enshrinement of relics at different dates

Although Kāsapagota and Majhima were contemporaries of Aśoka, the inscriptions on the Sāñchī casket which refer to them, like those on the other three caskets, are on palæographic grounds assignable to a decidedly later period. This can be explained only by assuming that the corporeal relics must have been collected subsequently for enshrinement, from places where originally they had been preserved. The fact that in three instances at Sāñchī, the ashes of as many as three persons were deposited in one and the same casket, definitely points to the same conclusion, and it is further corroborated by the evidence of the Andher Stūpa 2 inscriptions which refer to the relics of Gotiputa and his two disciples Mogaliputa and Vāchiputa. If we may judge from Cunningham's

[1] The five missionaries are referred to also in Buddhaghosha's *Samanta-pāsādikā*.—Oldenberg, *Vinayapiṭaka*, Vol. III, p. 317.

[2] *Bhilsa Topes*, p. 120. [3] Geiger, *Mahāvaṁsa Translation*, p. XIX. [4] Fleet, *J. R. A. S.*, 1905, p. 681.

[5] Kern, *Manual of Indian Buddhism*, p. 111. One of the seals unearthed at Saṅkisa bears in early Kushān Brāhmī the legend: *Ayana Hemavatana*, *i.e.*, 'of the venerable Haimavatas'.—H. Sastri, *Sir Asutosh Memorial Volume*, Patna, Part I, p. 234.

[6] The passage in the *Dīpavaṁsa* runs as follows:—

Kassapagotto ca yo thero Majjhimo Duṁdubhissaro

Sahadevo Mūlakadevo Himavante yakkhagaṇam pasādayuṁ.—Oldenberg, *Dīpavaṁsa*, p. 54, VIII, 10 and n.; and Fleet's emendation in *J. R. A. S.*, 1905, p. 691.

eye-copies, these inscriptions present the archaic forms of *a*, *pu* and *bha*, as found in Aśokan Brāhmī: the two arms of *a* meet at a point, the *u* stroke of *pu* is applied at the bottom of the curve, and *bha* shows an extension of the middle bar. In view of these peculiarities, the epigraphs of the three saints from Andher have to be referred to the end of the third or the beginning of the second century B.C. In the Andher Stūpa (No. 2), the casket of Gotiputa was associated with that of Mogaliputa, and in Stūpa 2 at Sāñchī the relics of both were kept in one and the same casket. Since, on palæographic grounds, the Andher inscriptions have to be placed earlier than the Sāñchī record, we must conclude that the relics of Gotiputa and Mogaliputa were deposited at Sāñchī at a date subsequent to those of the Andher Stūpa.

Grouping of the relics

A point that deserves special attention in this connection is that the relics of the various saints were deposited in *four* distinct groups in the Sāñchī Stūpa. The relics of Kāsapagota, Majhima and Hāritiputa were kept together in one casket, those of Gotiputa, Mogaliputa and Kosikiputa in another, those of Mahavanāya, Āpagira and Koḍiniputa in a third, while the fourth casket contained the remains of Vāchi Suvijayita alone. That some system was followed in grouping together these relics of different individuals is almost certain. The three saints of each of the three groups must have been connected with one another in life, either as teacher and pupil, or as members of the same fraternity. The relics of Kāsapagota and Majhima were placed in one casket, and those of Mogaliputa and Goṭiputa in another, as already stated. We know that the first two were actually colleagues of one another in the mission to the Himalayas, and Mogaliputa, being a pupil of Gotiputa, was naturally associated with him.

Mutual relation of the teachers

Generations of teachers

The saints of the Sāñchī, Sonāri and Andher caskets represent *at least three* generations of teachers. Gotiputa, who was a kinsman and heir of Dudubhisara, must have flourished after him. Kāsapagota, Dudubhisara and Majhima, who formed the first group of teachers, were followed by Gotiputa, and Gotiputa by his disciples, Mogaliputa and Vāchiputa or Vāchiya Suvijayita. As regards the position of Mahavanāya, Āpagira and Koḍiniputa, nothing can be said definitely. But they probably came sometime before Vāchiya, who is to be reckoned as the last of the *vināyakas*. At Sāñchī, his relics were not associated with those of any other saint, and it was on his casket that an inscription recording the gift (*dāna*) was incised.

Significance of Inscription No. 2

In the light of the above, the inscription on the relic-box from Stūpa 2 becomes more intelligible. It says (p. 290) that the relics inside the box are those of 'all the teachers', including Kāsapagota and Vāchi Suvijayita. Kāsapagota, being the earliest and also perhaps the most venerated of all, is naturally mentioned first; and Vāchi Suvijayita, representing the third or perhaps the fourth generation, and necessarily also the latest of the deceased teachers, is mentioned next. These three or four generations of teachers

Age of Stūpa 2

might easily have covered a span of a century or a little more, and calculating from the reign of Aśoka (*circa* 250 B.C.) onwards we can get an approximate idea of the age of Stūpa 2, in which the relics were enshrined. This evidence does not militate against the date (125-100 B.C.)[1] we have adopted for the monument on grounds of palæography.

Identity of the donors

The inscription in the inner circle of Casket No. II throws welcome light on the identity of the donors of the caskets. Cunningham read it as *Kākanava-pābhāsa-sāhana dānaṁ*, which he translated as 'the gift of Kākanava Prabhāsana'. Lüders, on the other hand, renders the passage as 'Gift of the Pabhāsasāhas of Kākanava' (*List*, No. 659). But a casket from Andher bears the inscription: *sapurisasa Gotiputasa Kākanāva-pabhāsanasa Koḍiñagotasa*, *i.e.*, '(Relics) of the saint Gotiputa, the *Kākanāva-pabhāsana*, of the Koḍiña-gota'. Here, the expression *Kākanāva-pabhāsana* is used as an epithet of Gotiputa and means 'the Light of Kākanāva'. The phrase *Kākanava-pabhāsa* of the Sāñchī inscription has no doubt to be understood in a similar sense, and may be taken as standing for Gotiputa himself. Gotiputa appears to have held a highly dignified position in the Buddhist Church of Eastern Mālwā, as suggested by the fact that his relics were enshrined at no less than three places, namely at Sāñchī, Sonāri and Andher. But the phrase *Kākanava-pabhāsa-sāhana* does not yield any intelligible sense, although, as it immediately precedes *dāna*, there cannot be any doubt that it bears a reference to the donor or donors. An examination of the photograph of the casket shows clearly that the correct reading of the three letters before *dāna* is *sihanā*, and not *sāhana* as formerly read by scholars. It has undoubtedly to be taken as the genitive plural of *siha*, which can be equated with Arddha-Māgadhī *seha*,[2] corresponding to Sanskrit *śaiksha*, meaning 'pupil'. It may, therefore, be concluded that the casket on which this inscription occurs was the gift of the disciples of Gotiputa, the *Kākanava-pabhāsa*. It is highly probable that the other three caskets, which do not bear any donative inscription but were deposited along with this one in the stone box, were likewise contributed by the same persons. These teachers and their followers belonged, of course, to the Haimavata school. About the end of the second century B.C. the Haimavatas must have set about collecting from various sources the corporeal relics of their former *Ācāryas*, from Kāsapagota down to Vāchi Suvijayita, and proceeded to enshrine them in a stūpa at Sāñchī. The phrase *savina vināyakāna*, *i.e.*, 'of all teachers', appearing in the epigraph on the stone box is, therefore, full of significance, having been used purposely, so as to include *all* the *Ācāryas* of the school who died before the erection of this stūpa.

[1] See above, p. 271.

[2] Pischel, *Grammatik der Prakrit-Sprachen*, p. 222.

Texts and Translations

3. Steatite Casket No. I :[1] *Outside lid.*

Text

sapurisa-Kāsapagotasa sava-Hemavat-ācariyasa

Translation

(Relics) of the saint Kāsapagota (*Kāśyapagotra*), the Teacher of all the Hemavatas (*Haimavatas*).

Lüders, *List*, No. 655.

4. Steatite Casket No. I : *Inside lid.*

Text

sapurisa-Majhimasa

Translation

(Relics) of the saint Majhima (*Madhyama*).

Lüders, *List*, No. 656.

5. Steatite Casket No. I : *Bottom.*

Text

sapurisasa Hāritiputasa

Translation

(Relics) of the saint Hāritiputa (*Hārītīputra*).

Lüders, *List*, No. 657.

6. Steatite Casket No. II : *Outer Circle.*

Text (Pl. 140, *d*)

sapurisasa Vāchiya-Suvijayatasa Gat-ātevāsino[2]

Translation

(Relics) of the saint Vāchiya-Suvijayata, the pupil of Gota (*Gaupta*).

Lüders, *List*, No. 658.

7. Steatite Casket No. II : *Inner Circle.*

Text (Pl. 140, *d*)

Kākanava-pabhāsa-siha[n]ā dana

Translation

The gift of the pupils of the Light of Kākanāva.

Lüders, *List*, No. 659.

8. Steatite Casket No. III : *Outside lid.*

Text (Pl. 140, *e*)

sapurisasa Mahavanāyasa sapurisa-Āpagirasa

Translation

(Relics) of the saint Mahavanāya (*Mahāvan-ārya ?*).

(Relics) of the saint Āpagira.

Lüders, *List*, No. 660.

9. Steatite Casket No. III : *Inside lid.*

Text (Pl. 140, *f*)

sapurisasa Koḍiniputasa

Translation

(Relics) of the saint Koḍiniputa (*Kauṇḍinīputra*).

Lüders, *List*, No. 661.

10. Steatite Casket No. IV : *Outer lid.*

Text (Pl. 140, *a*)

sapurisasa Kosikiputasa

Translation

(Relics) of the saint Kosikiputa (*Kauśikīputra*).

Lüders, *List*, No. 662.

11. Steatite Casket No. IV : *Inside lid.*

Text (Pl. 140, *c*)

sapurisasa Gotiputasa

Translation

(Relics) of the saint Gotiputa (*Gauptīputra*).

Lüders, *List*, No. 663.

12. Steatite Casket No. IV : *Bottom.*

Text (Pl. 140, *b*)

sapurisasa Mogaliputa[sa][3]

Translation

(Relics) of the saint Mogaliputa (*Maudgalīputra*).

Lüders, *List*, No. 664.

---

[1] This casket is not in the British Museum and seems to have been lost. [2] Read *Got-ātevāsino.* [3] The last two letters are written in the centre for want of space.

Nos. 13-14 Inscriptions on Relic-boxes from Stūpa 3

Cunningham[1] sank a shaft in the centre of Stūpa 3, and came upon a large slab of stone over 5 ft. in length. On raising this slab he found two stone boxes of cubical shape, each having a lid with an inscription. The lids of both the boxes are now deposited in the Sāñchī Museum.[2] The inscription on one of them mentions the name of Mahāmogalāna, and that on the other, the name of Sāriputa. In Sāriputa's box was found a steatite casket containing one small fragment of bone and seven beads. The box of Mahāmogalāna yielded another steatite casket, which contained only two minute fragments of bone. "On the inner surface of the lid of each casket", says Cunningham, "there is a single ink letter, half an inch in height. In Sāriputa's casket the letter is *sā*, and in that of Mahā-Mogalāna's it is *ma*; these being the initial letters of their respective names."[3] Lids of relic-boxes bearing the inscriptions *Sāriputasa* and *Mahāmogalānasa* were discovered by Cunningham also at Satdhārā near Sāñchī.[4] As pointed out by him, Sāriputa and Mahāmogalāna were the two chief disciples of the Buddha, and, according to Fa Hien, there existed stūpas erected in their honour at Mathurā.[5] Both these apostles are said to have predeceased the Buddha. Sāriputa died at Rājagṛiha, and "over the spot (where his body was burned) there was built a tope" which was still in existence in the time of Fa Hien.[6] Cunningham thought it likely that the relics of Sāriputa remained undisturbed at Rājagṛiha until the time of Aśoka, who, "when he distributed the relics of Buddha over India, would most probably have done the same with the relics of Sāriputra and Mahā-Mogalāna".[7] The erection of Stūpa 3 was, therefore, attributed by Cunningham to the age of Aśoka. But it has already been shown (see above pp. 43 and 269) that the stūpa cannot be placed earlier than the middle of the second century B.C., and that the ground balustrade, which Cunningham assigned to the same early age, was more than a century later than the stūpa. The indications afforded by the characters of the inscriptions of Sāriputa and Mahāmogalāna are not enough for us to pronounce a definite opinion about their date. But they cannot be referred to a period later than the second century B.C.

13. Pl. 137, Stūpa 3, 1.

Text

Mahāmogalānasa

Translation

(The relics) of Mahāmogalāna (*Mahāmaudgalyāyana*).

Lüders, *List*, No. 666.

14. Pl. 137, Stūpa 3, 2.

Text

[S]ā[r]i[putasa][8]

Translation

(The relics) of Sāriputa (*Śāriputra*).

Lüders, *List*, No. 665.

[1] *Bhilsa Topes*, pp. 297-299. [2] *Catalogue of the Museum of Archæology at Sāñchī*, p. 28, Nos. A 67 and A 68.
[3] *Bhilsa Topes*, p. 299 and Pl. XXII; and Lüders, Nos. 667, 668.
[4] *Bhilsa Topes*, Pl. XXV, figs. 4, 5; and Lüders, Nos. 152, 153.
[5] Legge, *Travels of Fa-Hien*, pp. 44-45. On the two apostles see also Kern, *Manual of Indian Buddhism*, pp. 25, 89.
[6] Legge, *op. cit.*, p. 81. [7] *Bhilsa Topes*, p. 307. [8] Only the upper portions of the letters remain.

CHAPTER XXI

VOTIVE INSCRIPTIONS OF STŪPAS 1, 2 AND 3, TEMPLE 40 AND OTHER MONUMENTS

THE inscriptions dealt with in this chapter occur on the balustrades, gateways, pillars and other architectural members of the stūpas, monasteries and temples at Sāñchī. They are generally votive records, giving briefly the names and places of origin of individuals who donated the various parts of the buildings. Most of the donors have no epithets added to their names to denote their adherence to the Buddhist Order; these probably were lay-Buddhists. Some donors, however, definitely style themselves as monks (*bhichu* or *bhikhu*) and nuns (*bhichunī* or *bhikhunī*), their number being over two hundred in all. In several instances the donors are referred to as the pupils (*atevāsī*, *atevāsinī* or *sejha*) of particular teachers. Such connection with teachers is also sometimes indicated by expressions like *Aya-Bhaḍukyia* (No. 265), that is 'one belonging to Ārya Bhaṇḍuka', used in apposition to the donor. Cases in which a donor actually has the epithet *upāsaka* or *upāsikā* (lay-worshipper) are comparatively rare, the former being found only in four and the latter in fifteen inscriptions. Some of the members of the Order have distinctive epithets, *e.g.*, *Aya*, *i.e.*, 'the Noble Master', *Thera*, *i.e.*, 'Venerable', *Bhadata*, *i.e.*, 'Most Gentle', *Bhāṇaka*, *i.e.*, 'Reciter of texts', *Dhamakathika*, *i.e.*, 'Preacher of the Law', *Sadhivihārī*, *i.e.*, 'Co-resident monk', *Vināyaka*, *i.e.*, 'Teacher', *Sutātika* and *Sutātikinī*, *i.e.*, 'one who is versed in the *Suttantas*', *Pacanekayika*, *i.e.*, 'one who is versed in the Five Nikāyas', and *Sapurisa*, *i.e.*, 'Saint'.

Nos. 15-827 Votive inscriptions

Donors

Amongst the laity mention may be made of a queen Vākalā, mother of Ahimita,[1] a householder (*gahapati*), bankers (*seṭhi*, mentioned 19 times), merchants (*vanija*, mentioned 5 times), a foreman of artizans (*āvesani*) of King Sātakani, a royal scribe (*rājalipikara*), a surveyor (*rajuka*), a trooper (*asavārika*), a writer (*lekhaka*), masons (*vadhaki*), a cloak-seller (*pāvārika*), a weaver (*sotika*), and artizans (*kamika*). Even a foreigner, a Greek (*Yona*) from Śvetapatha, participated in these donations. This shows that people of all ranks contributed to the embellishment of the sacred edifices. In several instances gifts are made in the name of the family (*kula*) of an individual, or jointly by a particular sect or guild. People of the latter class mostly hail from Vidiśā and Ujjayinī, *e.g.*, the ivory-workers (*daṁtakāras*) of Vidiśā, and the Dhamakas, Magalakaṭiyas, Sāphineyakas, Tāpasiyas and the Vākiliyas of Ujjayinī. These names are not known from any other sources, and it is difficult to say whether they represent particular families or guilds. The

Lay-members

[1] He may have belonged to the ruling family of Vidiśā.

gift of the *Bodha-goṭhī* (*Bauddha-goshṭhī*), *i.e.*, the Buddhist Assembly or Committee, of Dharmavarddhana is mentioned in Nos. 96-98, and No. 178 records the gift of the *goṭhī* of the Barulamisas of Vidiśā. Gifts by villages, *e.g.*, Vejaja, Asavatī, Morajabhikaṭa, Pāḍukulikā and Cuḍamoragiri, are recorded in Nos. 308, 345, 359, 635 and 642 respectively. In a few cases gifts are also made by the nuns of a particular place jointly, *e.g.*, in No. 341. In No. 776, the lay-worshippers of Kaṁṭakañuya record a joint donation. Quite in keeping with this practice of joint donation is the fact that a number of consecutive members of the ground balustrade of Stūpa 1 were often contributed by persons either of the same family or belonging to the same locality.[1] Evidently in many cases collective subscriptions were raised from particular families, associations, etc., or from the inhabitants of particular places. On some members of the balustrade the names of the donors were inscribed, while others were left blank, although there is every reason to believe that the latter also were the gifts of pious individuals.

Imprecatory inscriptions

Besides the foregoing class of inscriptions recording gifts, there are also a few on the gateways of Stūpa 1 (Nos. 389, 396 and 404) which are of an imprecatory character. The longest one of these is No. 396 on the East Gate, which enumerates the Five Great Sins of the Buddhists, *viz.*, *mati-ghāta*, *piti-ghāta*, *arahaṁta-ghāta*, *saṁghabheda* and *rudhirupaya*. The last-mentioned term corresponds to *lohituppādo* of the Pāli texts. The inscription proclaims that he who dismantles or causes to be dismantled either a *toraṇa* (arch) or a *vedikā* (balustrade) from Kākanāva, *i.e.*, Sāñchī, or removes any of these to *āna ācariya-kula*, shall have the fate of the perpetrator of the aforesaid five sins. In the two other epigraphs, Nos. 389 and 404, these sins are collectively referred to as *pacanatariya* or *pañc-ānantaryāṇi*. The phrase *ācariya-kula* is a technical expression which means, as in the *Mahāvaṁsa*,[2] a Buddhist School. In this treatise the expression *aññ-ācariyavāda*,[3] that is 'other schools of doctrine', stands in contrast to *Theravāda*, which is believed to have been the earliest of all the schools. Similarly, the expression *āna ācariya-kula*, *i.e.*, *any-ācārya-kula* should be taken to denote a school other than that of the Theravādins. The injunction is evidently against the removal of any property from Kākanāva to a non-Theravāda community like the Mahāsāṁghikas.[4] Thus the epigraph incidently supplies the information that Sāñchī was in the hands of the Theravādins, and that, by the first century B.C., other rival schools were established in this region. In the third century B.C., Aśoka had perceived signs of schism at Sārnāth, Kauśāmbī and Sāñchī, and issued edicts for its suppression. Two centuries later, these dissensions in the Church probably took a more serious turn, so that the Buddhists of Sāñchī, who were evidently Theravādins, even apprehended dismemberment of their sacred edifices. Later on, as the inscribed Buddha and Bodhisattva images of the Kushān period clearly testify, an alien school had already established itself at Sāñchī.

Meaning of *āna ācariya-kula*

[1] The order in which the first 349 inscriptions of the ground balustrade are arranged in the Text follows more or less the actual disposition of them on the balustrade.
[2] Geiger's *Text*, p. 28, and *Translation*, p. 27. [3] *Mahāvaṁsa Text*, p. 29. [4] *Cf.* Kern, *Manual of Indian Buddhism*, pp. 105-6.

Names of donors

The names of the donors are of some interest. As Bühler has shown, these furnish 'valuable information regarding the existence of the Pauranik worship at the time they were inscribed'.[1] Names like Arahadata, Dhamarakhita, Bodhi and Saṁgharakhita are purely Buddhist; Asāḍa, Mūlā, Rohiṇī, Svatiguta, etc., are derived from the names of *nakshatras*; Agidevā, Visvadeva, etc., are connected with the ancient Vedic worship; Nāgā, Nāgila, Nāgadata, etc., bear witness to the prevalence of the Nāga cult; Vihnukā, Opedadata, etc., prove the existence of Vaishnavism; and Nadiguta, Samikā, Sivanadi, etc., testify to the fact that Śaivism was also in vogue. To these groups of names distinguished by Bühler we may now add another, consisting of such names as Yakhadāsī, Yakhadina, Yakhī and Yakhila, which point to the existence of Yaksha cults. The prevalence of these folk cults in the second century B.C. is proved by the presence of figures of Yakshas and Yakshīs on the balustrade of the Bharhut Stūpa.[2] There are, again, a few personal names which seem to have been derived from names of countries, such as Gandhāra, Kāmboja, Kekaṭeyaka, Cirātī and Patiṭhana. Probably such nomenclature is to be attributed to the fact that these donors or their ancestors originally belonged to Gandhāra, Kamboja, Kīkaṭa, Kirāta or Pratishṭhāna.

Place-names

In the absence of sufficient data, the identification of most of the localities mentioned in the inscriptions must remain uncertain. Among donors who mention their domicile the largest number came from Kurara or Kuraghara (Kuraragṛiha). This place is mentioned in the Jātakas,[3] and is identical with Kuraghara in Avantī or Eastern Mālwā, which, according to the *Vinayapiṭaka*,[4] was for some time the residence of Mahākaccāna. Its actual position is, however, not known. Next in order of frequence comes Ujenī, *i.e.*, Ujjayinī in Mālwā. It appears as the name of a district (*āhāra*) in Nos. 164 and 359, which included Navagāma and Morajābhikaṭa. The former occurs in eight inscriptions, and the latter six times under various spellings. Next come Nadinagara or Nandinagara, which Bühler is inclined to identify with Nandner (near Tonk), and Vidiśā, modern Besnagar, both in the Gwalior State. The frequent occurrence of these place-names in the Sāñchī inscriptions shows that the cost of erecting the adjuncts to the stūpas was defrayed largely by the people of Mālwā, as might naturally be expected. Although most of the place-names remain at present obscure, it is extremely likely that a large number of these places were in Mālwā and its immediate neighbourhood.

The *Suttanipāta*[5] describes the route followed by the pupils of Bāvarin from the banks of the Godāvarī in the Aśmaka country to Vesālī in Magadha, through the

[1] *Ep. Ind.*, Vol. II, p. 95.

[2] Early Vaishnavism and the cults of Nāga and Yaksha have recently attracted much attention. See, *e.g.*, Chanda, *Mem. A. S. I.*, No. 5; Raichaudhuri, *Early History of the Vaishṇava Sect*: Vogel, *Indian Serpent Lore*, 1926; Chanda, 'Four Ancient Yakṣa Statues' in the *Journal of the Department of Letters, Calcutta University*, Vol. IV, 1921; and Coomaraswamy, *Yakṣas.*

[3] Fausboll's *Jātaka Text*, VI, 15.

[4] *Vinayapiṭaka* (Pāli Text Society, 1929), Vol. I, p. 194; *Ep. Ind.*, Vol. II, p. 96; and B. C. Law, *Geography of Early Buddhism*, 1932, pp. 22-23.

[5] *Suttanipāta* (Pāli Text Society), 1913, p. 194.

Vindhyas. The various stages of this journey are mentioned in the following order: Patiṭṭhāna, Māhissatī, Ujjenī, Gonaddha, Vedisā and Vanasahvaya or Tumbavana. It is interesting to note that the names of all these places appear in the Sāñchī inscriptions. Patiṭṭhāna, *i.e.*, Pratishṭhāna, which occurs twice, is no doubt Paithan in the Aurangabad district of the Nizam's Territory, and Māhisatī, *i.e.*, Māhishmatī, which is mentioned in ten inscriptions, has been identified with Māndhātā on the Narmadā.[1] Ujjenī and Vedisā have been noticed already. Gonaddha, which is placed by the *Suttanipāta* between Ujjenī and Vedisā, is identical with Gonada, *i.e.*, Gonarda, twice mentioned in our inscriptions. According to one view, the term 'Gonardīya' of the *Mahābhāshya*, which means 'belonging to Gonarda', refers to its author Patañjali.[2] As shown by Sylvain Levi,[3] Gonarda appears in a string of names, Avantī-Gonarda-Vidiśā, in the Buddhist text *Mahāmāyūrī*, exactly in the same sequence as in the *Suttanipāta*. There is, therefore, no doubt that Gonarda has to be looked for somewhere between Ujjayinī and Vidiśā. Tubavana (or Tumbavaṇa) is placed in the 'southern division' along with Daśapura (Mandasor in Mālwā), etc., in the *Bṛihatsaṁhitā* (XIV, 15), and is now known from an inscription of Ghaṭotkacagupta[4] of the Gupta year 116. The inscription comes from Tumain, a village in the Esagarh district of the Gwalior State, which is no doubt identical with Tumbavana. From internal evidence it appears that at this period Tumbavana was included in the province of Airikiṇa. Airikiṇa appears as Erakina once in a Sāñchī inscription, and is the same as modern Eran in the Saugor district, a place well known from coins and inscriptions.

Aboda of our inscriptions may be identical with Mount Abu (Arbuda) in the Sirohi State of Rajputana, and Pokhara the same as Pushkara near Ajmer. A place Bhogavadhana, *i.e.*, Bhogavardhana, is mentioned several times, and is known also from the Bharhut inscriptions and the Purāṇas.[5] From some of the Purāṇas it seems that this place has to be located somewhere in the direction of Aśmaka and Muḷaka, that is, in the Godāvarī valley. An adjectival form *Dakhinājiya*, evidently derived from a geographical name, is mentioned only once. Its probable connection with Dākshiṇātya was suggested by Bühler. If so, it may have to be equated with Avantī-Dakshiṇāpatha, that is, the southern division of the Avantī country mentioned in the *Vinayapiṭaka*.[6] In the Brāhmī inscriptions of Sāñchī, the Sāñchī hill has the name Kākanāva. But in the inscriptions of the time of Candragupta II it is called Kākanāda-boṭa,[7] and in an epigraph of about the eighth century, which mentions the Mālwā country as Mahāmālava, it is referred to as Boṭa-Śrīparvata. It is probably identical with 'Śrīparvata' referred to in Bhavabhūti's *Mālatīmādhava* (eighth century),[8] the scene of which is laid in Mālwā.

[1] *J. R. A. S.*, 1910, pp. 445-46.

[2] Bhandarkar, *Carmichael Lectures*, 1918, p. 4 and n. 4; *cf.* Kielhorn, *Ind. Ant.*, Vol. XV, pp. 81-84.

[3] *Sir Asutosh Silver Jubilee Volumes*, Orientalia, Part 2, pp. 195-205.

[4] *Ind. Ant.*, 1920, pp. 114-15.

[5] Barua, *Barhut Inscriptions*, pp. 130-31.

[6] Text (New Ed.), Vol. I, p. 197. If, however, it has been derived from a word like *Dakshiṇādri*, it could be identified with Dakshiṇāgiri near Ujjayinī, mentioned in the *Mahāvaṁsa* (Geiger's *Trans.*, p. 88, n. 3).

[7] Jayaswal connects Kākanāda with the Kāka tribe.

[8] *esh=āsmi Saudāminī bhagavataḥ Śrī-parvatād=upetya Padmāvatīm=upasṛitya*, etc.—*Mālatīmādhava*, Act IX. The mention of Śrīparvata along with Padmāvatī (Pawaya in the Gwalior State) is significant. The adjective *bhagavat*, *i.e.*, divine, which qualifies *Śrīparvata*, can apply very well to a sacred place like the Sāñchī hill.

Section 1. Nos. 15-630. Inscriptions of Stūpa 1

(A) GROUND BALUSTRADE, Nos. 15-363.

Screen of the Northern Entrance.

15. Pl. 128, 1. On the rail-pillar to the left of Entrance.

Text

Vedisā Arahatarakhita[sa] dānaṁ

Translation

The gift of Arahatarakhita (*Arhadrakshita*) from Vedisa (Vidiśā).

Lüders, *List*, No. 521.

16. Pl. 128, 2. On a cross-bar (outside).

Text

Tubavanā gahapatino Patiṭhiyasa bhātu j[ā]yāya Dhañaya dānaṁ

Translation

The gift of Dhañā (*Dhanyā*), the wife of the brother of the householder Patiṭhiya (*Pratishṭhita*) from Tubavana (*Tumbavana*).

Lüders, *List*, No. 450.

17. Pl. 128, 3. On a cross-bar (outside).

(*a*) Text

Tubavanā gahapatino Patiṭhiya hnusāya Vesamanadatāy[e] danaṁ

Translation

The gift of Vesamanadatā (*Vaiśravaṇadattā*), daughter-in-law of Patiṭhiya (*Pratishṭhita*), householder from Tubavana (*Tumbavana*).

Lüders, *List*, No. 201.

On the same cross-bar just above No. 17 (*a*).

(*b*) Text

Kākaṇāye Bhagavato pamāṇa-laṭhi

Translation

The '(height)-measuring staff '[1] of the *Bhagavat*, *i.e.*, the Buddha, at Kākaṇāya (*Kākanāva*).[2]

Lüders, *List*, No. 200.

18. Pl. 128, 4. On a cross-bar (outside).

Text[3]

Tubavanā gahapatino Patiṭhiyasa dānaṁ

Translation

The gift of the householder Patiṭhiya (*Pratishṭhita*) from Tubavana (*Tumbavana*).

19. Pl. 128, 5. On a rail-pillar to the east of the North Gate (outside).

Text

Vudināye upasikāye dānaṁ

Translation

The gift of the female lay-worshipper Vudinā.

Lüders, *List*, No. 199.

20. Pl. 128, 6. On a cross-bar (outside, turned upside down).

Text

Tubavanā gahapatino Patiṭhiyasa dānaṁ

Translation

The gift of the householder Patiṭhiya (*Pratishṭhita*) from Tubavana (*Tumbavana*).

---

[1] *Cf. lashṭi* of Andhau inscriptions. *Ep. Ind.*, Vol. XVI, p. 23.

[2] According to Mr. Chanda, the inscription probably refers to the installation of a sandal wood staff which must have stood for the 'measuring-staff' of the Buddha, near the part of the ground balustrade where this cross-bar had been fixed; but see p. 145, n. 1, *supra*, where Sir John Marshall suggests that the 'measuring-staff' was the East pillar of the Northern Gateway, the outer face of which is adorned with a peculiarly Symbolic Tree-of-Life, intended perhaps to represent the Buddha himself (*cf.* pp. 248-9 and Pl. 37*a*). As pointed out by Mr. Chanda, two somewhat different stories are found in the Buddhist literature. One of these is narrated in the *Divyāvadāna* (ed. Cowell and Neil, pp. 74-76), which refers to the installation of a sandal wood staff by Indra, who by measuring it wanted to find out the true height of the Buddha, but never succeeded. Another story is told by Hiuen Thsang, who narrates "how an unbelieving Brāhmin doubting the statement that Śākyamuni Buddha was sixteen feet high had a stick of that length made to take his measure. But as the figure always exceeded the height of the stick, he could never learn the true height of Buddha". (Watters, *On Yuan Chuang*, Vol. II, p. 146.) It is to be noted that the inscription 17*b* seems to have nothing to do with 17*a* appearing on the same cross-bar, and that 17*b* is in a different and later hand (*cf. e.g.*, the rounded *ga*). It is curious that a donor, if he had really set up a 'staff', should keep his name unrecorded.

[3] In all there are three copies of this inscription, *viz.*, Nos. 18, 20, and 21, of which Lüders notices two only in his *List*, Nos. 202 and 449.

21. Pl. 128, 7. On a cross-bar (outside).

Text

Tubavanā gahapatino Patiṭhiyasa dānaṁ

Translation

The gift of the householder Patiṭhiya (*Pratishṭhita*) from Tubavana (*Tumbavana*).

22. Pl. 128, 8. On a coping stone (inside).

Text

[Vā]ḍi[va]hanā bhichuninā dānaṁ

Translation

The gift of the nuns from Vāḍivahana. Lüders, *List*, No. 163.

23. Pl. 128, 9. On a cross-bar (outside).

Text

sakaka[ya] ?[1] Asvade . . . .

Translation

(The gift of) Aśvade(vā) . . . .
Lüders, *List*, No. 550.

24. Pl. 128, 10. On a cross-bar (outside).

Text

Vāḍīvahanāto Oḍakasa dānaṁ

Translation

The gift of Oḍaka from Vāḍīvahana. Lüders, *List*, No. 511.

25. Pl. 128, 11. On a rail-pillar (inside).

Text

1 Vajigutasa
2 dānaṁ

Translation

The gift of Vajiguta (*Vajrigupta*).
Lüders, *List*, No. 164.

26. Pl. 128, 12. On a cross-bar (inside).

Text

Sirikāya dana

Translation

The gift of Sirikā (*Śrīkā*).
Cf. No. 27.

27. Pl. 128, 13. On a cross-bar (inside).

Text

Sirikāya da[na]

Translation

The gift of Sirikā (*Śrīkā*).
Cf. No. 26.

28. Pl. 128, 14. On a cross-bar (inside).

Text

Samikāya bhichuniyā dānaṁ

Translation

The gift of the nun Samikā (*Svāmikā*).
Lüders, *List*, No. 534.

29. Pl. 128, 15. On a coping stone (inside).

Text

Sīharakhitāya dā[naṁ]

Translation

The gift of Sīharakhitā (*Siṁharakshitā*).

North-East Quadrant.

30. Pl. 128, 17. On a cross-bar (inside).

Text

Kekaṭeyakasa jamata-Vijitasa dānaṁ

Translation

The gift of Vijita, son-in-law of Kekaṭeyaka. Lüders, *List*, No. 166.

31. Pl. 128, 18. On a cross-bar (inside).

Text

Dhamagirikasa mātu dānaṁ

Translation

The gift of the mother of Dhamagirika (*Dharmagirika*).
Lüders, *List*, No. 165.

[1] Bühler reads *sakakacha* at the beginning, but his *cha* seems to be a damaged *ya*.

32. Pl. 128, 19. On a coping stone (outside).

Text

Budharakhitasa bhichuno Ujenakasa danaṁ

Translation

The gift of the monk Budharakhita (*Buddharakshita*), the Ujenaka (an inhabitant of *Ujjayinī*).

33. Pl. 128, 20. On a rail-pillar (outside).

Text

1 Nava[gā]maka-Disārakhi-
2 tasa dānaṁ

Translation

The gift of Disārakhita, an inhabitant of Navagāma (*Navagrāma*).

Lüders, *List*, No. 203.

34. Pl. 128, 21. On a cross-bar (inside).

Text

Kādasa bhichuno dānaṁ

Translation

The gift of the monk Kāda.

Lüders, *List*, No. 167.

35. Pl. 128, 22. On a cross-bar (outside).

Text

. . . . . . dā[naṁ]

36. Pl. 128, 23. On a cross-bar (outside).

Text

Nadāvuno ca Nādivirohasa ca dānaṁ

Translation

The gift of Nadāvu and Nādiviroha.

Lüders, *List*, No. 204.

37. Pl. 128, 24. On a cross-bar (outside).

Text

Poṭhadevāya dānaṁ

Translation

The gift of Poṭhadevā (*Proshṭhadevā*).

Lüders, *List*, No. 205.

38. Pl. 128, 25. On a rail-pillar (outside).

Text

Ujeniya upāsikāya Pusaya (dāna)

Translation

The gift of the female lay-worshipper Pusā (*Pushyā*) of Ujenī (*Ujjayinī*).

39. Pl. 128, 26. On a coping stone (outside).

Text

Ejāvatasa bhichuno Dhamayasasa dānaṁ

Translation

The gift of the monk Dhamayasa (*Dharmayaśas*) of Ejāvata.

40. Pl. 128, 27. On a rail-pillar (outside).

Text

Ujeniye Dhamakānaṁ dānaṁ

Translation

The gift of the Dhamakas of Ujenī (*Ujjayinī*).

41. Pl. 128, 28 and 29.[1] On a cross-bar (outside).

Text

1 Kaṁdaḍigāmiyasa seṭhino
2 pajāvatiyā Devabhāgāya dānaṁ

Translation

The gift of Devabhāgā, the wife of the banker of Kaṁdaḍigāma.

Lüders, *List*, No. 423.

42. Pl. 128, 30. On a cross-bar (outside).

Text

1 Kaṁdaḍigāmiyasa seṭhino
2 pajāvatiyā Nāgāya dānaṁ

Translation

The gift of Nāgā, the wife of the banker of Kaṁdaḍigāma.

Lüders, *List*, No. 206.

[1] Pl. 128, Nos. 28 and 29 are reproductions of the same inscription.

43. Pl. 128, 31. On a rail-pillar (outside).

Text[1]

1 Kaṁdaḍigāmā seṭhi-
2 no dānaṁ

Translation

The gift of the banker from Kaṁdaḍigāma.

44. Pl. 140, *h*. On a cross-bar (outside).

Text

1 Kaṁdaḍi-gāmiyasa seṭhino
2 pajāvatiya Pusāya dānaṁ

Translation

The gift of Pusā (*Pushyā*), the wife of the banker of Kaṁdaḍigāma.

Lüders, *List*, No. 207.

45. Pl. 129, 32. On a cross-bar (outside).

Text

Kaṁdaḍigāmā Vaḍhasa dānaṁ

Translation

The gift of Vaḍha (*Vṛiddha*) from Kaṁdaḍigāma.

Lüders, *List*, No. 208.

46-48. Pl. 129, 33-35. Identical inscriptions on three cross-bars (outside).

Text

Mulagirino dānaṁ lekhakasa

Translation

The gift of Mulagiri (*Mūlagiri*), the scribe.
Lüders, *List*, No. 209.

49. Pl. 129, 36. On a rail-pillar (outside).

Text

1 Ujāniyā Balikāya
2 mātu dānaṁ

Translation

The gift of the mother of Balikā, from Ujāni (*Ujjayinī*).

Lüders, *List*, No. 411.

50. Pl. 129, 37. On a coping stone (inside).

Text

Devabhāgāya [Ma]dhuva[ni]kāya bhichuniyā danaṁ

Translation

The gift of the nun Devabhāgā, an inhabitant of Madhuvana.

Lüders, *List*, No. 168.

51. Pl. 129, 38. On a rail-pillar (outside).

Text

. . . . . . siniyā . . . . . dānaṁ

52. Pl. 129, 39. On a cross-bar (outside).

Text

1 Samaṇasa bhichuno Ayutarasa atevasino
2 dānaṁ

Translation

The gift of the monk Samaṇa (*Śramaṇa*), the pupil of Aya (*Ārya*)-Utara (*Uttara*).

Lüders, *List*, No. 530.

53. Pl. 129, 40. On a rail-pillar (outside).

Text

1 Ujeniyā Kalūrapu-
2 tasa Bumūsa dānaṁ

Translation

The gift of Bumū, son of Kalūra from Ujenī (*Ujjayinī*).

Lüders, *List*, No. 408.

54. Pl. 129, 41. On a cross-bar (inside).

Text

Visākharakhitasa bhichuno dānaṁ

Translation

The gift of the monk Visākharakhita (*Viśākharakshita*).

Lüders, *List*, No. 518.

[1] It may be identical with Lüders, *List*, No. 422.

55. Pl. 129, 42. On the outer face of cross-bar No. 54 above.

Text same as No. 54.

56. Pl. 129, 43. On a cross-bar (outside).

Text

Yakhadinasa bhikhuno dānaṁ

Translation

The gift of the monk Yakhadina (*Yakshadatta*).

Lüders, *List*, No. 211.

57. Pl. 129, 44. On a rail-pillar (outside).

Text[1]

1 . . . . Kalūra-[pu]
2 . . . . . [dā]naṁ

Translation

The gift of . . . . . Kalūra . . . . .

58. Pl. 129, 45. On a cross-bar (outside).

Text

Ujeniyā upasikāye Sirikāye dānaṁ

Translation

The gift of the female lay-worshipper Sirikā (*Śrīkā*) from Ujenī (*Ujjayinī*).

Lüders, *List*, No. 406.

59. Pl. 129, 46. On a cross-bar (outside).

Text

Ujeniyā upāsikāya dānaṁ

Translation

The gift of the female lay-worshipper from Ujenī (*Ujjayinī*).

Lüders, *List*, No. 212.

60. Pl. 129, 47. On a cross-bar (outside).

Text

[U]jeniyā Dhamayasāyā matu bhichuniya dānaṁ

Translation

The gift of the mother of the nun Dhamayasā (*Dharmayaśā*) from Ujenī (*Ujjayinī*).

Lüders, *List*, No. 410.

61. Pl. 129, 48. On a rail-pillar (outside).

Text[2]

1 Ujenakasa vānejasa
2 Isidatasa dānaṁ

Translation

The gift of the merchant Isidata (*Ṛishidatta*), an inhabitant of Ujenī (*Ujjayinī*).

62. Pl. 129, 49. On a cross-bar (outside).

Text

[A]rapāniyā Sihaya dānaṁ

Translation

The gift of Sihā (*Siṁhā*) of Arapāna.

Lüders, *List*, No. 398.

63. Pl. 129, 50. On a coping stone (outside).

Text

Ijavatiyā[3] Vāhilasa dānaṁ

Translation

The gift of Vāhila from Ijavatī.

Lüders, *List*, No. 418.

64. Pl. 129, 51. On a rail-pillar (outside).

Text

1 (Cuḍa)girikāya[4] . .
2 datasa dānaṁ

Translation

The gift of . . . . .

---

[1] This may be another copy of No. 53 above.

[2] It seems to be identical with Lüders, *List*, No. 213 (*Bhilsa Topes*, Pl. XVI, No. 52) which is there supposed to be of ' Isadāta (*Ṛishidatta*), the *rakasavānodāsa* (?) '.

[3] Bühler reads *Ejavatiya* (*Ep. Ind.*, Vol. II, p. 381). But the three dots of *i* are clear on the estampage.

[4] The reading of the first two letters is not certain.

65. Pl. 129, 52. On a cross-bar (outside).

Text

Ujeniyā Dhamagirino dānaṁ

Translation

The gift of Dhamagiri (*Dharmagiri*) from Ujenī (*Ujjayinī*).

Lüders, *List*, No. 217.

66. Pl. 129, 53. On a cross-bar (outside).

Text

Ujeniyā Rohaṇiya dānaṁ

Translation

The gift of Rohaṇī (*Rohiṇī*) from Ujenī (*Ujjayinī*).

Lüders, *List*, No. 216.

67. Pl. 129, 55. On a cross-bar (outside).

Text

Ujeniyā Sulāsasa dānaṁ

Translation

The gift of Sulāsa from Ujenī (*Ujjayinī*).

Lüders, *List*, No. 415.

68. Pl. 129, 56. On a cross-bar (outside).

Text

Ujeniya Saṁghadatasa dānaṁ

Translation

The gift of Saṁghadata (*Saṁghadatta*) from Ujenī (*Ujjayinī*).

Lüders, *List*, No. 414.

69. Pl. 129, 57. On a cross-bar (outside).

Text

Ujeniyā Sonasa dānaṁ

Translation

The gift of Sona from Ujenī (*Ujjayinī*).

Lüders, *List*, No. 218.

70. Pl. 129, 58. On a coping stone (outside).

Text

Nāvagamikānā upasikānā dānaṁ

Translation

The gift of the female lay-worshippers of Navagāma (*Navagrāma*).

Lüders, *List*, No. 214.

71. Pl. 129, 59. On a rail-pillar (outside).

Text

1 Ujeniyā Tapasiyā-
2 naṁ . . . . . Dhama-
3 [da]tāya dānaṁ

Translation

The gift of Dhamadatā (*Dharmadattā*) . . . of the Tāpasiyas from Ujenī (*Ujjayinī*).

Lüders, *List*, No. 409.

72. Pl. 129, 60. On a cross-bar (outside, turned upside down).

Text

Uje(ni*)ya Tāpasiyanaṁ Isimitasa dānaṁ

Translation

The gift of Isimitra (*Ṛishimitra*) of the Tāpasiyas from Ujenī (*Ujjayinī*).

Lüders, *List*, No. 220.

73. Pl. 129, 61. On a cross-bar (outside, turned upside down).

Text[1]

Uj[e]niya Opedadatasa pajāvatiya Vayudataya dānaṁ

Translation

The gift of Vayudatā (*Vāyudattā*), the wife of Opedadata (*Upendradatta*) from Ujenī (*Ujjayinī*).

Lüders, *List*, No. 223.

[1] For two other copies of this inscription *cf.* Nos. 75 and 77 below.

74. Pl. 129, 62. On a cross-bar (outside, turned upside down).

Text

Uj[e]niyā Tāpasiyāna husā-Najaya dānaṁ

Translation

The gift of Najā, a daughter-in-law of the Tāpasiyas from Ujenī (*Ujjayinī*).

Lüders, *List*, No. 219.

75. Pl. 129, 63. On a cross-bar (outside).

Text[1]

Ujeniyā Upedadatasa pajavataya Vāyadataya dānaṁ

Translation

The gift of Vāyadatā (*Vāyudattā*), the wife of Upedadata (*Upendradatta*) from Ujenī (*Ujjayinī*).

Probably Lüders, *List*, No. 407.

76. Pl. 129, 64. On a cross-bar (outside).

Text

Ujeniya Muladataye dānaṁ

Translation

The gift of Muladatā (*Mūladattā*) from Ujenī (*Ujjayinī*).

Lüders, *List*, No. 221.

77. Pl. 129, 65. On a cross-bar (outside).

Text[2]

U . . . . . .ya [Va]yudataye dānaṁ

Translation

The gift of Vayudatā (*Vāyudattā*) . . . . from U[jeni] (*Ujjayinī*).

78. Pl. 129, 66. On a cross-bar (outside).

Text

Ujeniyā Upedadatasa bhaginiya Himadataya dānaṁ

Translation

The gift of Himadatā (*Himadattā*), the sister of Upedadata (*Upendradatta*) from Ujenī (*Ujjayinī*).

Lüders, *List*, No. 224.

79. Pl. 129, 67. On a cross-bar (outside).

Text

(Uje)n[i]yā Upedadatasa bhaginiye Budhaye dānaṁ

Translation

The gift of Budhā, the sister of Upedadata (*Upendradatta*) from Ujenī (*Ujjayinī*).

Lüders, *List*, No. 225.

30. Pl. 129, 68. On a cross-bar (outside).

Text

Ujeni(yā Upe)dadatasa (duhitu) Ja. [ya] dānaṁ

Translation

The gift of Ja. . . the daughter of (Upe)dadata (*Upendradatta*) from Ujeni (*Ujjayinī*).

81. Pl. 129, 69. On a cross-bar (outside).

Text

1 . . . hātakaniya
2 . . . . sāye dānaṁ

Translation

The gift of . . . .

82. Pl 129, 70. On a cross-bar (outside).

Text

Ujeniya Devalaya(?)[3] dānaṁ

Translation

The gift of Devalā (?) from Ujenī (*Ujjayinī*).

[1] *Cf.* Nos. 73 and 77.

[2] It seems to be another copy of No. 73 above.

[3] Or *Vasulaya*?

83. Pl. 129, 71. On a cross-bar (outside).

Text[1]

Ujeniyā Kāḍiya bhichuniye dānaṁ

Translation

The gift of the nun Kāḍī (*Kāṇḍī*) from Ujenī (*Ujjayinī*).

Lüders, *List*, No. 226.

84. Pl. 129, 72. On a cross-bar (outside).

Text[2]

Ujeniyā Kāḍiye bhichuniye dānaṁ

Translation

The gift of the nun Kāḍī (*Kāṇḍī*) from Ujenī (*Ujjayinī*).

85. Pl. 129, 73. On a coping stone (outside).

Text

Sagharakhitāya Koramikāya bhichuniyā dānaṁ

Translation

The gift of the nun Sagharakhitā (*Saṁgharakshitā*), a pupil of Koramikā.[3]

Lüders, *List*, No. 526.

86. Pl. 129, 74. On a cross-bar (outside).

Text

Ujeniyā Vipulāyā dānaṁ

Translation

The gift of Vipulā from Ujenī (*Ujjayinī*).

Lüders, *List*, No. 231.

87. Pl. 129, 75. On a cross-bar (outside).

Text

Ujeniyā Tāpasiyanā Sihadataya dānaṁ

Translation

The gift of Sihadatā (*Siṁhadattā*) of the Tāpasiyas from Ujenī (*Ujjayinī*).

Lüders, *List*, No. 228.

88. Pl. 129, 76. On a cross-bar (outside).

Text

Ujeniyā Chetamatu[4] dānaṁ

Translation

The gift of the mother of Cheta (*Kshetra* ?) from Ujenī (*Ujjayinī*).

Lüders, *List*, No. 227.

89. Pl. 129, 77. On a pillar (outside).

Text

1 [Sv]etapathasa (Yona ?)sa[5]
2 dānaṁ

Translation

The gift of (Yona ?) of [Sv]etapatha (*Śvetapatha*).

90. Pl. 129, 78. On a cross-bar (outside).

Text

Kuragharā Naraya dānaṁ

Translation

The gift of Narā from Kuraghara.

Lüders, *List*, No. 232.

91. Pl. 129, 79. On a cross-bar (outside).

Text

Kuraghara Isimitaya dānaṁ

Translation

The gift of Isimitā (*Ṛishimitrā*) from Kuraghara.

Lüders, *List*, No. 230.

92. Pl. 129, 80. On a cross-bar (outside).

Text

Ujeniyā Saphineyakānā Isikasa dānaṁ

Translation

The gift of Isika (*Ṛishika*) of the Saphineyakas from Ujenī (*Ujjayinī*).

Lüders, *List*, No. 229.

---

[1] *Cf.* No. 84.
[2] *Cf.* No. 83.
[3] Lüders: 'inhabitant of *Kurama* (?)'. But *cf.* No. 645 below.
[4] Bühler reads *Chetamātu.*
[5] *Cf.* Stūpa 1, Berm balustrade, No. 475 below.

93. Pl. 129, 81. On a cross-bar (outside).

Text[1]

Kuragharā Nāgamitaya dānaṁ

Translation

The gift of Nāgamitā (*Nāgamitrā*) from Kuraghara.

Lüders, *List*, No. 233.

94. Pl. 129, 82. On a cross-bar (outside).

Text[2]

Kuraghara [Na]gamitaya dānaṁ

Translation

The gift of Nagamitā (*Nāgamitrā*) from Kuraghara.

Lüders, *List*, No. 426.

95. Pl. 129, 83. On a rail-pillar (outside).

Text

. . . . sa dānaṁ

Translation

The gift of . . . .

96. Pl. 129, 84. On a cross-bar (outside, facing East Gateway).

Text

Bodhagoṭh[i]ya Dhamavaḍhananā dānaṁ

Translation

The gift of the Bodha (*Bauddha*) Committee[3] of the inhabitants of Dhamavaḍhana[4] (*Dharmavardhana*).

Lüders, *List*, No. 234 ; *cf*. Nos. 97, 98.

97. Pl 129, 85. On a cross-bar (outside, facing East Gateway).

Text

Bodhagoṭhiyā Dhamavaḍhananā dānaṁ

Translation

The gift of the Bodha (*Bauddha*) Committee of the inhabitants of Dhamavaḍhana (*Dharmavardhana*).

Lüders, *List*, No. 351 ; *cf*. Nos. 96, 98.

98. Pl. 129, 86. On a cross-bar (outside, facing East Gateway).

Text

Bodhagoṭhiyā Dhamavaḍhananā dānaṁ

Translation

The gift of the Bodha (*Bauddha*) Committee of the inhabitants of Dhamavaḍhana (*Dharmavardhana*).

Cf. Nos. 96, 97 above.

99. Pl. 129, 88. On a cross-bar (outside, turned upside down ; facing East Gateway).

Text

. . . yanāye dānaṁ

Translation

The gift of . . . . .

100. Pl. 129, 89. On a coping stone (outside, facing East Gateway).

Text

Nagadinasa bhichuno[5] dānaṁ

Translation

The gift of the monk Nagadina (*Nāgadatta*).

Lüders, *List*, No. 171 or No. 235.

Additional balustrade against the right jamb of the East Gateway.

101. Pl. 129, 90. On a cross-bar (inside).

Text

Arahadinasa bhikhuno Pokhareyakasa dānaṁ

Translation

The gift of the monk Arahadina (*Arhaddatta*), the Pokhareyaka (an inhabitant of *Pushkara*).

Lüders, *List*, No. 337.

---

[1] *Cf.* No. 94. [2] *Cf.* No. 93. [3] The word *goṭhī* is evidently used in this sense in the Bhaṭṭiprolu inscriptions, Lüders, Nos. 1332 and 1335.
[4] See Bühler, *Ep. Ind.*, Vol. II, p. 92. [5] In the original, the letter *bh* is written in a reversed form.

102. Pl. 129, 91. On a rail-pillar (inside).

Text

1 Bhadata-Nāgilasa
2 savinaṁ[1] ñātīnaṁ
3 dānaṁ thaṁbho

Translation

The gift of a pillar by all the relatives of the Venerable Nāgila.

Lüders, *List*, No. 338.

Screen of the Eastern Entrance.

103. Pl. 129, 92. On the pillar to the left of the entrance (outside; inscription hidden by the left jamb of the East Gate).

Text

1 Ujeniyā Kakaḍakasa(?) nagare (?)
2 Magalakaṭiyānaṁ dānaṁ

Translation

The gift of the Magalakaṭiyas from the town of Kakaḍaka in Ujenī (*Ujjayinī*).[2]

104. Pl. 129, 93. On a cross-bar (outside).

Text

(Kuraghara) . Ma . sa dā(naṁ)

Translation

The gift of . . . from Kuraghara.

105. Pl. 129, 94. On a cross-bar (outside).

Text

Sadhanasa bhichuno dānaṁ

Translation

The gift of the monk Sadhana.

Lüders, *List*, No. 240.

106. Pl. 129, 95. On a cross-bar (outside).

Text

Cirātiya bhichuniyā danaṁ

Translation

The gift of the nun Cirātī (*Kirātī*).

Lüders, *List*, No. 239.

107. Pl. 129, 96. On a cross-bar (outside).

Text

Datakalavaḍasa dānaṁ

Translation

The gift of Datakalavaḍa.

Cf. Nos. 110 and 355 below.

108. Pl. 129, 97. On a cross-bar (outside).

Text

Asvadevaye Bahadatamātu dānaṁ

Translation

The gift of Asvadevā (*Aśvadevā*), the mother of Bahadata (*Brahmadatta*).

Lüders, *List*, No. 241.

109. Pl. 129, 98. On a cross-bar (outside).

The inscription of the year 93 of the reign of Candragupta II. See No. 833 below.

110. Pl. 129, 98. On a cross-bar (outside).

Text[3]

Datakalavaḍasa dānaṁ

Translation

The gift of Data Kalavaḍa.

Cf. Nos. 107 and 355.

[1] Bühler reads *savānaṁ*. But the mark of *i* on *va* is clear.

[2] The reading seems to be *Kakaḍakasā nāgāre*, which may have been an attempt to write *Kakuḍakasa nagarā*. It is difficult to take a satisfactory estampage of the inscription which is covered by a part of the gateway. Does *Kakaḍaka* refer to a town in Ujjayinī District? *Kākandī* is the name of a city from which the form *Kākandaka* is derived (M. Williams, *Sanskrit-English Dictionary*). It is mentioned in a Bharhut inscription (Lüders, *List*, No. 817).

[3] Inscribed below No. 109, on the same cross-bar.

111. Pl. 129, 99. On the corner pillar of the screen (outside).

Text

[U]gireyakasa Svatigutasa dānaṁ

Translation

The gift of Svatiguta (*Svātigupta*), the Ugireyaka (an inhabitant of *Ugirā*).

Lüders, *List*, No. 242.

112. Pl. 129, 100. On a cross-bar (outside).

Text

Satigutasa [dā]naṁ

Translation

The gift of Satiguta (*Śaktigupta* or *Svātigupta*).

Lüders, *List*, No. 529.

113. Pl. 129, 101. On a cross-bar (outside)

Text

Tāpasasa Gonaṁdakasa dānaṁ

Translation

The gift of the ascetic Gonaṁdaka.

Lüders, *List*, No. 445.

114. Pl. 130, 102. On a cross-bar (inside).

Text

Ujeniya Saghakasa dānaṁ

Translation

The gift of Saghaka (*Saṁghaka*) from Ujeni (*Ujjayinī*).

115. Pl. 130, 103. On a cross-bar (inside).

Text

Ujeniyā Vakiliyānā dānaṁ

Translation

The gift of the Vakiliyas from Ujenī (*Ujjayinī*).

Lüders, *List*, Nos. 172 and 237.

116. Pl. 130, 104. On a cross-bar (inside).

Text

Ujeniyā Gohilasa Visasa ca dānaṁ

Translation

The gift of Gohila (*Gobhila*) and Visa (*Viśva*) from Ujenī (*Ujjayinī*).

Lüders, *List*, No. 238 and *Bhilsa Topes*, Pl. XVII, No. 77 and p. 246. *Cf.* also *Bhilsa Topes*, Pl. XVI, No. 12 and p. 237.

117. Pl. 130, 105. Inscription of the Gupta year 131 on a cross-bar (outside ; outer face of No. 116 above). See No. 834 below.

South-East Quadrant.

118. Pl. 130, 106. On a cross-bar (outside).

Text

Yasilaya atevasini-Sagharakhitāye dānaṁ

Translation

The gift of Sagharakhitā (*Saṁgharakshitā*), the female pupil of Yasilā (*Yaśilā*).

Lüders, *List*, No. 245.

119. Pl. 130, 107. On a cross-bar (outside).

Text

Asvadevāya Samikasa mātu dānaṁ

Translation

The gift of Asvadevā (*Aśvadevā*), the mother of Samika (*Svāmika*).

Lüders, *List*, No. 244.

120. Pl. 130, 108. On a cross-bar (outside).

Text

Arahagutāya dānaṁ

Translation

The gift of Arahagutā (*Arhadguptā*).

Lüders, *List*, No. 243.

121. Pl. 130, 109. On a rail-pillar (outside).

Text

. . . . . . Kaṁtarasa(?) dānaṁ

Translation

The gift of Kaṁtara(?) . . . .

122. Pl. 130, 110. On a cross-bar (outside).

Text

seṭhino paṭikama-kārakānā dānaṁ

Translation

The gift of 'the executors of repairs'[1] of the banker.

Lüders, *List*, No. 248.

123. Pl. 130, 111. On a cross-bar (outside).

Text

Yasilāye dānaṁ

Translation

The gift of Yasilā (*Yaśilā*).

Lüders, *List*, No. 247.

124. Pl. 130, 112. On a cross-bar (outside).

Text

seṭhino matu Kaniyasi(ye*)[2]

Translation

(The gift) of Kaniyasi, the mother of thc banker.

Lüders, *List*, No. 246.

125. Pl. 130, 113. On a rail-pillar (outside).

Text

seṭhino mātu Ateyiyā dānaṁ

Translation

The gift of Ateyi (*Ātreyī*), the mother of the banker.

126. Pl. 130, 114. On a cross-bar (outside).

Text

Upidadatasa dānaṁ

Translation

The gift of Upidadata (*Upendradatta*).

Lüders, *List*, No. 251.

127. Pl. 130, 115. On a cross-bar (outside, turned upside down).

Text

Asagutasa dānaṁ

Translation

The gift of Asaguta (*Aśvagupta*).

Lüders, *List*, No. 399.

128. Pl. 130, 116. On a cross-bar (outside, turned upside down).

Text

Vasulāye dānaṁ

Translation

The gift of Vasulā.

Lüders, *List*, No. 249. *Cf.* Nos. 130, 134.

129. Pl. 130, 117. On a cross-bar (outside, turned upside down).

Text

Tuḍasa Phujakapadiyasa[3] dānaṁ

Translation

The gift of Tuḍa (*Tuṇḍa*) of Phujakapada.

Lüders, *List*, No. 448.

130. Pl. 130, 118. On a cross-bar (outside).

Text (*cf.* Nos. 128, 134).

Vasulāye dānaṁ

Translation

The gift of Vasulā.

[1] The Pāli word *paṭikamma* means repairs. See Childers, *Pāli-English Dictionary*, *s.v.*

[2] Bühler reads *Kaniya[si]ye* - - . But there is no trace of any letter after *si* (or *sa*) on the stone.

[3] Bühler (*Ep. Ind.*, Vol. II, p. 384, No. 263) reads *Phujākapalliya*. But *di* is clear on the impression.

131. Pl. 130, 119. On a coping stone (outside).

Text[1]

Idadatasa pāvārikasa[2] dānaṁ

Translation

The gift of Idadata (*Indradatta*), a cloak-seller.[3]

Lüders, *List*, No. 250.

132. Pl. 130, 120. On a cross-bar (outside, turned upside down).

Text

(Sa)mikaye sadhitikāye dānaṁ

Translation

The gift of Samikā (*Svāmikā*) with her daughter.

Lüders, *List*, No. 382.

133. Pl. 130, 121. On a cross-bar (inside, turned upside down).

Text

nakasa[4] bhichuno dānaṁ

Translation

The gift of the monk . . . . of (Ujenī ?).

134. Pl. 130, 122. On a cross-bar (outside, turned upside down).

Text

Vasulāya dānaṁ

Translation

The gift of Vasulā.

Cf. Nos. 128, 130. Lüders, *List*, No. 510.

135. Pl. 130, 123. On a rail-pillar (outside).

Text

Kujarasa seṭhi-bhātu dānaṁ

Translation

The gift of Kujara (*Kuñjara*), the brother of the banker.

Lüders, *List*, No. 255.

136. Pl. 130, 124. On a cross-bar (outside).

Text

Kurarāye[5] Tāpasiyā mātu dānaṁ

Translation

The gift of the mother of Tāpasī of Kurara.

Lüders, *List*, No. 256.

137. Pl. 130, 125. On a cross-bar (outside).

Text

Yakhiya bhichuniye Vedisā dānaṁ

Translation

The gift of the nun Yakhī (*Yakshī*) from Vedisa (*Vidiśā*).

Lüders, *List*, No. 254.[6]

138. Pl. 130, 126. On a cross-bar (outside).

Text

Vāghumatā Saghadanāya bhichuniya dānaṁ

Translation

The gift of the nun Saghadanā (*Saṁghadattā*) from Vāghumata.

Lüders, *List*, No. 253.

139. Pl. 130, 127. On a rail-pillar (outside).

Text

Dhaṁmakasa Vejajakasa dana

Translation

The gift of Dhaṁmaka (*Dharmaka*) of Vejaja.

Lüders, *List*, No. 455.

140. Pl. 130, 128. On a cross-bar (outside).

Text

Virasenāye dānaṁ

Translation

The gift of Virasenā (*Vīrasenā*).

Lüders, *List*, No. 519.

---

[1] For another copy of this inscription see Stūpa 1, Berm balustrade, No. 472.

[2] For the meaning of *pāvārika*, see *Pāli-English Dictionary* (P. T. S.), *s.v.* It is used as a personal epithet also in a Buddhist inscription from Mathurā.—*Ep. Ind.*, Vol. XIX, p. 97. There was a *Prāvārika-vihāra*, 'the monastery of cloak-makers' at Mathurā.—*Ep. Ind.*, Vol. XIX, p. 65.

[3] Bühler reads *Pāviḍakasa*.

[4] Probably *Ujenakasa*.

[5] Bühler reads *Kurariye* (*Ep. Ind.*, II, p. 101, No. 39), but *Kurarāye* is clear on the estampage.

[6] The text of Lüders, No. 500, is identical with his No. 254. Are these two different inscriptions ?

141. Pl. 130, 129. On a cross-bar (outside, turned upside down).

Text same as No. 140.

142. Pl. 130, 130. On a rail-pillar (outside).

Text[1]

1 (I)[s]idatāye Sakadina-pajāva-
2 (ti)ya dānaṁ

Translation

The gift of Isidatā (*Ṛishidattā*), wife of Sakadina (*Śakradatta*).

Lüders, *List*, No. 257.

143. Pl. 130, 131. On a cross-bar (outside).

Text

Kāpāsi-gāmā Arahasa dānaṁ

Translation

The gift of Araha (*Arhat*) from Kāpāsigāma (*Kārpāsigrāma*).

Lüders, *List*, No. 260.

144. Pl. 130, 132. On a cross-bar (inside, turned upside down).

Text[2]

Aya-Pasanakasa bhichuno dānaṁ

Translation

The gift of the monk Aya-Pasanaka (*Ārya-Prasannaka*).

Lüders, *List*, No. 174.

145. Pl. 130, 133. On a cross-bar (outside).

Text[3]

Erakinā Sātilasa dānaṁ

Translation

The gift of Sātila from Erakina.

Lüders, *List*, No. 259.

146. Pl. 130, 134. On a cross-bar (outside, turned upside down).

Text same as No. 143.

147. Pl. 130, 135. On a cross-bar (outside, turned upside down).

Text

Badhakasa bhichuno Koḍijilakasa

Translation

(The gift) of the monk Badhaka (*Baddhaka*) of Koḍijila.

Lüders, *List*, No. 484.

148. Pl. 130, 137. On a cross-bar (inside, turned upside down).

Text same as No. 144.

149. Pl. 130, 138. On a cross-bar (inside), above No. 148.

Text same as No. 144.

150. Pl. 130, 139. On a cross-bar (outside).

Text

Kaṭakañuyā Arahasa dānaṁ

Translation

The gift of Araha (*Arhat*) from Kaṭakañuya.

Lüders, *List*, No. 420.

151. Pl. 130, 140. On a cross-bar (outside).

Text

Kaṭakañuyā Bhādakasa dāna

Translation

The gift of Bhādaka (*Bhadraka*) from Kaṭakañuya.

Lüders, *List*, No. 262.

[1] *Cf.* Stūpa 1, Berm balustrade No. 500 below.

[2] There are three copies of this inscription, *viz.*, Nos. 144, 148 and 149. One Aya-Pasanaka is known also from Sonāri Stūpa 1 (Lüders, Nos. 154, 155).

[3] Bühler reads *Dharakinā* (*Ep. Ind.*, Vol. II, p. 375, No. 173), but suggests *Erakinā* (*ibid.*, p. 96) · Lüders reads *Dharakina*.

152. Pl. 130, 141. On a cross-bar (outside).

Text

Kaṭakañuyakasa (I)dadevasa dānaṁ

Translation

The gift of Idadeva (*Indradeva*) from Kaṭakañuya (*Kaṇṭaka-nyubja* ?).

Lüders, *List*, No. 419.

153. Pl. 130, 142. On a cross-bar (outside).

Text

Apatnakasa dānaṁ

Translation

The gift of Apathaka.

Lüders, *List*, No. 263.

154. Pl. 130, 143. On a cross-bar (outside).

Text

Mahāgirino bhichuno dānaṁ

Translation

The gift of the monk Mahāgiri.

Lüders, *List*, No. 290.

155. Pl. 130, 144. On a cross-bar (outside).

Text

Madhuvan[ā] Isidataye bhichuniya dānaṁ

Translation

The gift of the nun Isidatā (*Ṛishidattā*) from Madhuvana.

Lüders, *List*, No. 291.

156. Pl. 130, 145. On a cross-bar (outside)

Text

Bhogavaḍhanakasa Ajitigutasa

Translation

(The gift) of Ajitiguta (*Ajitigupta*), an inhabitant of Bhogavaḍhana (*Bhogavardhana*).

Lüders, *List*, No. 264.

157. Pl. 130, 146. On a cross-bar (outside).

Text

Arahadinasa dānaṁ Morajāhikaḍi

Translation

The gift of Arahadina (*Arhaddatta*) from Morajāhikaḍa.

Lüders, *List*, No. 354.[1] *Cf.* 158 below.

158. Pl. 130, 147. On a cross-bar (outside).

Text

Morajāhikaṭa[2] Arahadinasa dānaṁ

Translation

The gift of Arahadina (*Arhaddatta*) from Morajāhikaṭa.

Lüders, *List*, No. 265. *Cf.* No. 157 above.

159 Pl. 130, 148. On a cross-bar (outside).

Text

Mo(rajāhikaṭā) (Si?)[ha]datasa dānaṁ

Translation

The gift of (Si ?)hadata (*Siṁhadatta* ?) from Mo(rajāhikaṭa).

160 Pl. 130, 149. On a coping stone (outside).

Text

Virahakaṭa ghariṇiye Sijhāye dānaṁ

Translation

The gift of the housewife Sijhā (*Śikshā*) from Virahakaṭa.

Lüders, *List*, No. 516.

161. Pl. 130, 150. On a rail-pillar (outside).

Text

1 Subhagapathā
2 Dhanakasa dā(naṁ)

Translation

The gift of Dhanaka from Subhagapatha.

[1] Bühler reads *Ramorajahikaḍi* (*Ep. Ind.*, Vol. II, p. 107, No. 90).
[2] Bühler reads the name of the place as *Morasihikoṭa* (*Ep. Ind.*, Vol. II, p. 101, No. 44), and Lüders as *Morajāhikaṭa* (*List*, p. 175, No. 265).

162. Pl. 130, 151. On a cross-bar (outside).

Text[1]

Bhogavadhana Dhamarakhitāya Sivanaṁdino mātu

Translation

(The gift) of Dhamarakhitā (*Dharmarakshitā*), mother of Sivanandi (*Śivanandin*) from Bhogavadhana (*Bhogavardhana*).

Lüders, *List*, No. 266.

163. Pl. 130, 152. On a cross-bar (outside).

Text same as No. 162.

164. Pl. 130, 153. On a cross-bar (outside).

Text[2]

Navagamaka-Samikāye Ujenihārā dānaṁ

Translation

The gift of Samikā (*Svāmikā*) of Navagama (*Navagrāma*) from Ujenihāra (*Ujjayinī-āhāra*).

Lüders, *List*, No. 268.

165. Pl. 130, 154. On a cross-bar (outside).

Text same as No. 164.

166. Pl. 130, 155. On a cross-bar (outside).

Text

Saghāya dānaṁ

Translation

The gift of Saghā (*Saṁghā*).

Lüders, *List*, No. 267.

167. Pl. 130, 156. On a coping stone (outside).

Text

Mitasiriya dānaṁ bhichuniyā Korariyā

Translation

The gift of the nun Mitasirī (*Mitraśrī*), an inhabitant of Kurara.

Lüders, *List*, No. 499.

168. Pl. 130, 157. On a rail-pillar (outside).

Text

1 Sirigutasa
2 vānijasa dānaṁ

Translation

The gift of the merchant Siriguta (*Śrigupta*).

Lüders, *List*, No. 269.

169. Pl. 130, 158. On a cross-bar (inside).

Text[3]

Nādinagarā Kābojasa bhikhuno dānaṁ

Translation

The gift of the monk Kāboja (*Kāmboja*) from Nadinagara (*Nandinagara*).

Lüders, *List*, No. 176.

170. Pl. 130, 159. On a cross-bar (inside).

Text[4]

Nadinagarā Acalaya bhikhuniya dānaṁ

Translation

The gift of the nun Acalā from Nadinagara (*Nandinagara*).

Lüders, *List*, No. 175.

171. Pl. 130, 160. On a cross-bar (outside).

Text

S[ubā](hitasa). . . . . dānaṁ[5]

Translation

The gift f . . . . of Subāhita.

172. Pl. 130, 161. On a cross-bar (outside).

Text

Subāhitasa pajavati(yā) (Majhimā)ya dānaṁ[6]

Translation

The gift of (Majhimā), wife of Subāhita.

Lüders, *List*, No. 544.

---

[1] There are two copies of this inscription, *viz.*, Nos. 162 and 163.
[2] There are two copies of this inscription, *viz.*, Nos. 164 and 165.
[3] *Cf.* Stūpa 1, Berm balustrade, No. 601 below.
[4] For another copy of this inscription, see Stūpa 1, Berm balustrade, No. 465 below.
[5] This inscription is on a cross-bar, which is the third from the top one, *i.e.*, No. 172, and second from No. 173. The name may be restored as Subāhita.
[6] Restored after No. 173.

173. Pl. 130, 162. On a cross-bar (outside).

Text[1]

Subāhitasa pajavatiyā Majhimāya dānaṁ

Translation

The gift of Majhimā (*Madhyamā*), wife of Subāhita.

Lüders, *List*, No. 270.

174. Pl. 130, 163. On a coping stone (outside).

Text

[Na]ṁdutarāya[2] dānaṁ V(e*)disikaya bhichuniya

Translation

The gift of the nun Naṁdutarā (*Nandottarā*), an inhabitant of Vedisa (*Vidiśā*).

Lüders, *List*, No. 468.

175. Pl. 130, 164. On a rail-pillar (outside).

Text

1 Subāhitasa Gotiputa-
2 sa rāja-lipikarasa
3 dana

Translation

The gift of the 'royal scribe' Subāhita, son of Goti (*Gaupti*).

Lüders, *List*, No. 271.

176. Pl. 130, 165. On a cross-bar (outside).

Text[3]

Tiriḍapadā Nāgāya upāsikāya dānaṁ

Translation

The gift of the female lay-worshipper Nāgā from Tiriḍapada.

Lüders, *List*, No. 272.

177. Pl. 130, 166. On a cross-bar (outside).

Text same as No. 176.

Lüders, *List*, No. 446.

178. Pl. 130, 167. On a rail-pillar (outside).

Text

Barulamisāna goṭhiyā dāna Vedisāto

Translation

The gift of the committee (*goshṭhī*) of the Barulamisas from Vedisa (*Vidiśā*).

Lüders, *List*, No. 273.

179. Pl. 130, 168. On a rail-pillar (outside).

Text

. . . . . ra kasa dānaṁ.[4]

180. Pl. 130, 169. On a cross-bar (outside).

Text

Dhamarakhitasa Kācupathasa bhichuno dāna

Translation

The gift of the monk Dhamarakhita (*Dharmarakshita*) of Kacupatha.

Lüders, *List*, No. 275. *Cf.* No. 181 below.

181. Pl. 130, 170. On a cross-bar (outside).

Text

1 Dhamarakhitāye bhichuniye Kācupathasa
2 dānaṁ

Translation

The gift of the nun Dhamarakhitā (*Dharmarakshitā*) of Kacupatha.

Lüders, *List*, No. 274. *Cf.* No. 180 above.

182. Pl. 130, 171. On a rail-pillar (outside).

Text

Saṁdhānasa bhichu(no*) dānaṁ

Translation

The gift of the monk Saṁdhāna.

Lüders, *List*, No. 276.

---

[1] There are evidently three copies of this inscription, *viz.*, Nos. 171, 172, 173.
[2] The first letter is imperfectly written, so that it appears like *u*.
[3] No. 177 is another copy of this inscription.
[4] The first three letters may be *Barula* (*cf.* No. 178 above).

183. Pl. 130, 172. On a cross-bar (outside).

Text[1]

Pusagirino Nāvagāmakasa dā[naṁ]

Translation

The gift of Pusagiri (*Pushyagiri*), an inhabitant of Navagāma (*Navagrāma*).

Lüders, *List*, Nos. 277 and 182.

184. Pl. 130, 173. On a cross-bar (outside).

Text same as No. 183.

185. Pl. 130, 174. On a cross-bar (outside).

Text same as No. 183.

186. Pl. 130, 175. On a coping stone (outside).

Text

Bhichukasa Pāḍāniyasa dānaṁ

Translation

The gift of Bhichuka (*Bhikshuka*) of Pāḍāna.

Lüders, *List*, No. 278.

187. Pl. 130, 176. On a cross-bar (outside, facing South Gateway).

Text

Dhamarakhitasa bhichuno dānaṁ

Translation

The gift of the monk Dhamarakhita (*Dharmarakshita*).

Lüders, *List*, No. 180.

188. Pl. 130, 177. On a cross-bar (outside, facing South Gateway).

Text

Dhamadināya dānaṁ

Translation

The gift of Dhamadinā (*Dharmadattā*).

Lüders, *List*, No. 457.

189. Pl. 130, 178. On a cross-bar (outside, facing South Gateway).

Text

Subhagāya sa-bhaginikāya dāna

Translation

The gift of Subhagā with her sister or sisters

Lüders, *List*, No. 179.

190. Pl. 130, 179. On a coping stone (outside, facing South Gateway).

Text

1 Kaṭakañ[u]yakasa Aya-Patuḍasa
2 bhichuno dānaṁ

Translation

The gift of the monk Aya (*Ārya*)-Patuḍa of Kaṭakañuya.

Lüders, *List*, No. 361.

191. Pl. 131, 180. On a rail-pillar (outside, facing South Gateway).

Text[2]

Udubaraghariyasa Dhama[kasa] dāna

Translation

The gift of Dhamaka (*Dharmaka*) of Udubaraghara (*Udumbaragṛiha*).

192. Pl. 131, 181. On a cross-bar (outside, facing South Gateway).

Text

Soṇadevāyā Parijayā Agidevāya ca dāna[ṁ]

Translation

The gift of Soṇadevā (*Svarṇadevā*), Parijā and Agidevā (*Agnidevā*).

Lüders, *List*, No. 178.

---

[1] There are three copies of this inscription, *viz.*, Nos. 183, 184 and 185, of which two are noticed by Lüders.

[2] Is it identical with Lüders No. 360?

193. Pl. 131, 182. On a cross-bar (outside, facing South Gateway).

Text

Siharakhitasa pajavatiya Soṇadevaya dānaṁ

Translation

The gift of Soṇadevā (*Svarṇadevā*), the wife of Siharakhita (*Siṁharakshita*).

Lüders, *List*, No. 177.

194. Pl. 131, 183. On a rail-pillar to the right of the Southern Entrance.

Text[1]

Udubaraghariyasa Siharakhitasa dāna

Translation

The gift of Siharakhita (*Siṁharakshita*) of Udubaraghara (*Udumbaragṛiha*).

Additional balustrade against the right jamb of the South Gateway.

195. Pl. 131, 184 On a rail-pillar (inside).

Text

Vīrasa bhikhuno dānaṁ[2]

Translation

The gift of the monk Vīra.

Lüders, *List*, No. 343.

196. Pl. 131, 185. On a cross-bar (inside).

Text

Poṭhakasa bhikhuno dānaṁ[3]

Translation

The gift of the monk Poṭhaka (*Proshṭhaka*).

Lüders, *List*, No. 342.

197. Pl. 131, 186. On a cross-bar (inside).

Text

Budhapālitāya bhikhuniye dānaṁ[4]

Translation

The gift of the nun Budhapālitā (*Buddhapālitā*).

Lüders, *List*, No. 341.

198. Pl. 131, 187. On a rail-pillar (inside).

Text

1 Yakhiya bhikhuniyā Vāḷiva-
2 hanikāya dānaṁ[5]

Translation

The gift of the nun Yakhī (*Yakshī*) of Vāḷivahana.

Lüders, *List*, No. 344.

Screen of the Southern Entrance.

199. Pl. 131, 188. On a rail-pillar behind the left jamb of the South Gateway.

Text

Aṭhasa kaṁmikasa dānaṁ

Translation

The gift of the artizan Aṭha (*Artha*).

Lüders, *List*, No. 181.

200-202. Pl. 131, 189-191. On three cross-bars (outside).

Text[6]

(202) Samikasa vānikasa
(201) putasa ca'sa[7] Siripālasa
(200) dānaṁ 3

Translation

The gift of three (cross-bars) by Samika (*Svāmika*), the merchant and his son Siripāla (*Śrīpāla*).

Lüders, *List*, No. 280.

---

[1] No. 216 below is another copy of this inscription.
[2] After the writing there is a symbol which probably represents 'tree in railing'.
[3] There is a *swastika* at the beginning of line 2 and a *triratna* at the end. For the reading *la*, *cf.* Lüders, *J. R. A. S.*, 1911, p. 1081.
[4] There are a *swastika* symbol at the beginning and a *triratna* at the end of the writing.
[5] There is a *triratna* symbol at the end.
[6] The text begins on the topmost cross-bar (202), is continued to the middle cross-bar (201), and concluded on the lowermost one (200).
[7] The words *ca'sa* stand for Sanskrit *ca asya*, as on the joint coins of Strato I and Strato II.—Whitehead, *Catalogue of Coins in the Panjab Museum*, Vol. I, p. 81, n. 1.

203. Pl. 131, 192. On a rail-pillar (inside).

Text

1 Pusagirino bhichuno
2 dānaṁ

Translation

The gift of the monk Pusagiri (*Pushyagiri*).

204. Pl. 131, 193. On a cross-bar (outside).

Text

Dhanagirino Caḍipiyasa[1] ca bhichunaṁ dānaṁ

Translation

The gift of the monks Dhanagiri and Caḍipiya (*Caṇḍīpriya*).

Lüders, *List*, No. 454.

205. Pl. 131, 194. On a cross-bar (outside).

Text

Visākhasa bhichuno dānaṁ

Translation

The gift of the monk Visākha (*Viśākha*).

Lüders, *List*, No. 282.

206. Pl. 131, 195. On a cross-bar (outside).

Text

bhādata-Rājukasa dānā[2]

Translation

The gift of the Venerable Rājuka.

Lüders, *List*, No. 281.

207. Pl. 131, 196. On a rail-pillar (outside).

Text

Levasa . . . . . .

Translation

(The gift) of Leva . . . .

Lüders, *List*, No. 551.

208. Pl. 131, 197. On a cross-bar (outside).

Text

Siribhāgasa saṁbu (?)

Translation

. . . . of Siribhāga (*Śrībhāga*).

Lüders, *List*, No. 537.

209. Pl. 131, 198. On a cross-bar (outside).

Text

A[ya]-Badhikasa bhikh[u]no dānaṁ

Translation

The gift of the monk Aya-Badhika (*Ārya-Bandhika*).

210. Pl. 131, 199. On a cross-bar (outside).

Text

. . . . . matu De[va]rakhitāya dānaṁ

Translation

The gift of Devarakhitā (*Devarakshitā*), the mother of . . . . .

211. Pl. 131, 200. On a rail-pillar (inside).

Text

1 Sāmanerasa Ābeya-
2 kasa seṭhino dānaṁ

Translation

The gift of Sāmanera (*Śramaṇera*),[3] the banker of Abā.

Lüders, *List*, No. 283. *Cf.* No. 212 below.

212. Pl. 131, 201. On a rail-pillar (outside; same pillar as No. 211 above).

Text

1 Sāmanerasa
2 Abeyakasa
3 seṭhino dānaṁ

Translation

The gift of the banker Sāmanera (*Śramaṇera*) of Abā.

Lüders, *List*, No. 184. *Cf.* No. 211 above.

---

[1] Bühler reads *Caḍipiyasa*, and notes that it may be read also as *Caḍhipiyasa*. *Ep. Ind.*, Vol. II, p. 385, n. 71.
[2] Read *dānaṁ*. The letter *da* is carelessly written and bears an additional curve on the left.
[3] *Sāmanera* means a 'novice' in the Buddhistic sense.

213. Pl. 131, 202. On a cross-bar (outside).

Text

Pusa[sa] dānaṁ [Māhisatiyasa]

Translation

The gift of Pusa (*Pushya*) of Māhisatī (*Māhishmatī*).

214. Pl. 131, 203. On a cross-bar (inside).

Text

Patiṭhānasa bhichuno Hāṭiyasa[1] atevāsino dānaṁ

Translation

The gift of the monk Patiṭhāna (*Pratishṭhāno*)[1], a pupil of Hāṭiya.

Lüders, *List*, No. 185.

215. Pl. 131, 204. On a coping stone (inside).

Text

Devada[siya] bhichuniya upāsaka-
Dhamacuḍa(sa*) bhichuno
Vajino bhichuno . . . .

Translation

Of the nun Devadasī (*Devadāsī*), of the lay-worshipper Dhamacuḍa (*Dharmacūḍa*), of the monk Vajī (*Vajrin*), (and) of the monk . . . .

South-West Quadrant.

216. Pl. 131, 205. On a rail-pillar to the left of the Entrance.

Text

Udubaraghariyasa Siharakhitasa dānaṁ[2]

Translation

The gift of Siharakhita (*Siṁharakshita*) of Udubaraghara (*Udumbaragṛiha*).

Lüders, *List*, No. 186. *Cf.* No. 194 above.

217. Pl. 131, 207. On a cross-bar (outside).

Text

[Be]dakaḍā Naṁdagiri-māt[u] dānaṁ

Translation

The gift of the mother of Naṁdagiri from Bedakaḍa.

Lüders, *List*, No. 372. *Cf.* No. 218 below.

218. Pl. 131, 208. On a cross-bar (outside).

Text

Bedakaḍā Naṁdagiri-mātu dānaṁ

Translation

The gift of the mother of Naṁdagiri from Bedakaḍa.

Cf. No. 217 above.

219. Pl. 131, 209. On a cross-bar (outside).

Text

Na[ṁ]digutasa dānā[3] bhichuno

Translation

The gift of the monk Naṁdiguta (*Nandigupta*).

Lüders, *List*, No. 284.

220. Pl. 131, 210. On a coping stone (inside).

Text

Odatikāye bhichuni(ye*) Vedisikayā dānaṁ

Translation

The gift of the nun Odatikā (*Avadātikā*) of Vedisa (*Vidiśā*).

Lüders, *List*, No. 187.

221. Pl. 131, 211. On a rail-pillar.

Text

1 [Saṁ]dhānasa bhi-
2 chuno dānaṁ

Translation

The gift of the monk Saṁdhāna (?).[4]

[1] Bühler reads *Prātiṭhānasa* and *Hāṭiyasa* (*Ep. Ind.*, Vol. II, p. 98, No. 12). The latter may be read also as *Pāṭiyasa*.
[2] Above this is an inscription in Nāgarī characters : *Rā° Śrī-Sāvadeva praṇamati* (Pl. 131, No. 206), *i.e.*, 'the *Rā(uta)* Sāvadeva makes obeisance.'
[3] Read *dānaṁ*.
[4] *Cf.* No. 182 above.

222. Pl. 131, 212. On a cross-bar (outside).

Text

(Si)hasa bhikhuno dānaṁ

Translation

The gift of the monk (Si)ha (*Siṁha*).

223. Pl. 131, 213. On a cross-bar (outside).

Text

Taṁbalamaḍa Kujarasa dānaṁ

Translation

The gift of Kujara (*Kuñjara*) from Taṁbalamaḍa.

Lüders, *List*, No. 287.

224. Pl. 131, 214. On a cross-bar (outside).

Text

Arāpānāto Arahadinasa

Translation

(The gift) of Arahadina (*Arhaddatta*) from Arāpāna.

Lüders, *List*, No. 286.

225. Pl. 131, 215. On a rail-pillar (outside).

Text

Naṁdasa Kurarāto

Translation

(The gift) of Naṁda from Kurara.

Lüders, *List*, No. 289.

226. Pl. 131, 216. On a cross-bar (outside, turned upside down).

Text

Budharakhitasa bhichuno dānaṁ Ejāvatasa

Translation

The gift of the monk Budharakhita (*Buddharakshita*) of Ejāvata.

Lüders, *List*, No. 304.

227. Pl. 131, 217. On a coping stone (outside).

Text

Isidatāye bhikh[u]niye Kurariye dānaṁ

Translation

The gift of the nun Isidatā (*Ṛishidattā*) of Kurara.

Lüders, *List*, No. 292.

228. Pl. 131, 218. On a cross-bar (outside, turned upside down).

Text

Madhuvanā Dhamagutasa bhichuno dānaṁ

Translation

The gift of the monk Dhamaguta (*Dharmagupta*) from Madhuvana.

Lüders, *List*, No. 288.

229. Pl. 131, 219. On a cross-bar (outside).

Text

1 Patiṭhānasa bhichuno dā(naṁ)
2 aya-Tisakasa atevāsino

Translation

The gift of the monk Patiṭhāna (*Pratishṭhāna*), the pupil of the Venerable Tisaka (*Ārya-Tishyaka*).

Lüders, *List*, No. 303.

230. Pl. 131, 220. On a cross-bar (outside, turned upside down).

Text

Dhamapālasa Kothukapadiyasa dānaṁ

Translation

The gift of Dhamapāla (*Dharmapāla*) of Kuthukapada.

Lüders, *List*, No. 293.

231. Pl. 131, 221. On a rail-pillar (outside).

Text

Naṁdasa Korarasa dānaṁ

Translation

The gift of Naṁda, the Korara (an inhabitant of *Kurara*).

Lüders, *List*, No. 289. *Cf.* No. 235 below.

232. Pl. 131, 222. On a cross-bar (outside).

Text

Mahānāmasa

Translation

(The gift) of Mahānāma.

Lüders, *List*, No. 496.

233. Pl. 131, 223. On a cross-bar (outside).

Text

Upasijhasa Phagunasa bhatu bhichuno

Translation

(The gift of) the monk Upasijha (*Upasiddhya* or *Upaśiksha*), brother of Phaguna (*Phālguṇa*).

Lüders, *List*, No. 294.

234. Pl. 131, 224. On a cross-bar (outside).

Text

Bhogavaḍhanāto Isirakhitāya

Translation

(The gift) of Isirakhitā (*Ṛishirakshitā*) from Bhogavaḍhana (*Bhogavardhana*).

Lüders, *List*, No. 295.

235. Pl. 131, 225. On a rail-pillar (outside).

Text

1 Naṁdasa Korara[sa]
2 dana

Translation

The gift of Naṁda of Korara.
Cf. No. 231 above.

236. Pl. 131, 226. On a cross-bar (outside).

Text

Bhogavaḍhanā . . . .

Translation

. . . . . . from Bhogavaḍhana (*Bhogavardhana*).

237. Pl. 131, 227. On a cross-bar (outside).

Text

[Bhoga]vaḍhanā Dhañiyā [dā]naṁ[1]

Translation

The gift of Dhañi (*Dhanyā*) from Bhogavaḍhana (*Bhogavardhana*).

Lüders, List, No. 296.

238. Pl. 131, 228. On a cross-bar (outside).

Text

Jetasa dānaṁ

Translation

The gift of Jeta (*Jita*).

239. Pl. 131, 229. On a rail-pillar (outside).

Text

Kurarāya Vimalasa dāna

Translation

The gift of Vimala from Kurara.

Lüders, *List*, No. 297.

240. Pl. 131, 230. On a cross-bar (outside).

Text

Pusakasa bhichuno dānaṁ

Translation

The gift of the monk Pusaka (*Pushyaka*).

Lüders, *List*, No. 300.

241. Pl. 131, 231. On a cross-bar (outside).

Text

Samidatasa bhichuno dānaṁ

Translation

The gift of the monk Samidata (*Svāmidatta*).

Lüders, *List*, No. 298.

[1] Bühler reads [*Bho*]*gavaḍhanā Dhañikāya*-.

242. Pl. 131, 232. On a cross-bar (outside).

Text

1 Devagirino pacanekayikasa
2 bhichuno sa-atevasikasa no (?)[1]

Translation

(The gift) of the monk Devagiri, who is versed in the *Five Nikāyas*,[2] accompanied by his pupil or pupils

Lüders, *List*, No. 299.

243. Pl. 131, 233. On a rail-pillar (outside).

Text

Kurarāya Dhamakasa dānaṁ

Translation

The gift of Dhamaka (*Dharmaka*) from Kurara.

Lüders, *List*, No. 432.

244. Pl. 131, 234. On a cross-bar (outside).

Text

Gaḍayā bhich[u]niyā Vedisikāya dā[na]ṁ

Translation

The gift of the nun Gaḍā of Vedisa (*Vidiśā*).

Lüders, *List*, No. 439.

245. Pl. 131, 235. On a cross-bar (outside).

Text

Ujeniye Agisimaye dānaṁ

Translation

The gift of Agisimā (*Agnisīmā* ?) of Ujenī (*Ujjayinī*).

Lüders, *List*, No. 302.

246. Pl. 131, 236. On a cross-bar (outside).

Text

Cuḍasa ca Dhamarakhitasa ca bhichunaṁ dānaṁ

Translation

The gift of the monks Cuda (*Kshudra*) and Dhamarakhita (*Dharmarakshita*).

Lüders, *List*, No. 301.

247. Pl. 131, 237. On a coping stone (outside).

Text

. . . taya dānaṁ Nadinagarā bhichuniye

Translation

The gift of the nun . . . . . from Nadinagara (*Nandinagara*).

248. Pl. 131, 238. On a cross-bar (inside, turned upside down).

Text

. . . [ya] Ujenikāye bhichuniye dānaṁ

Translation

The gift of the nun . . . . an inhabitant of Ujenī (*Ujjayinī*).

249. Pl. 131, 239. On a cross-bar (outside, turned upside down).

Text

Pemutikāye[3] Supaṭhāmāye bhichuniye dānaṁ[4]

Translation

The gift of the nun Supaṭhāmā of Pemuta.

Lüders, *List*, No. 478.

[1] Bühler reads *sa atevasi- -no* (?) and suggests that the writer meant *sa-atevāsino dānaṁ*. (*Ep. Ind.*, Vol. II, p. 104, and n. 74). The last two signs, therefore, stand for *dānaṁ*.

[2] For the term *pacanekayika*, see Przyluski, *Le Concile de Rājagṛha*, 1926, p. 338; and Barua, *Barhut Inscriptions*, 1926, p. 29.

[3] Bühler reads *-kaya*.

[4] The last letter is clear on the stone but not in the Plate.

250. Pl. 131, 240. On a cross-bar (outside).

Text[1]

Arapana Asāḍrasa dānaṁ Ugā . . sa [ca] bhichuno

Translation

The gift of Asāḍra (*Āshāḍha*) from Arapana and of the monk . . . .

Lüders, *List*, No. 396.

251. Pl. 131, 242. On a cross-bar (outside).

Text

Māhisatiya Ji[lānasa] dānaṁ

Translation

The gift of Jilāna from Māhisatī (*Māhishmatī*).

Lüders, *List*, No. 498.

252. Pl. 131, 243. On a cross-bar (outside).

Text

[M]āhisatiya[2] Nāgilasa dānaṁ

Translation

The gift of Nāgila from Māhisatī (*Māhishmatī*).

Lüders, *List*, No. 553.

253. Pl. 131, 244. On a cross-bar (outside).

Text

[Mā]hisatiya Gāgi(?)ya dānaṁ

Translation

The gift of Gāgī (Gārgī ?) from Māhisatī (*Māhishmatī*).

254. Pl. 131, 245. On a cross-bar (outside).

Text

Māhi[sati]ya V[i]sade[vā]ya dānaṁ

Translation

The gift of Visadevā (*Viśvadevā*) of Māhisatī (*Māhishmatī*).

255. Pl. 131, 246. On a coping stone (outside).

Text

Naṁdināgārikaya Isidināye bhichuniye

Translation

The (gift) of the nun Isidinā (*Ṛishidattā*), an inhabitant of Naṁdinagara.

Lüders, *List*, No. 305.

256. Pl. 131, 248. On a cross-bar (outside).

Text

Māhisatiya Bhaga[va]ya danaṁ

Translation

The gift of Bhagavā (*Bhagavatī*) from Māhisatī (*Māhishmatī*).

257. Pl. 131, 249. On a cross-bar (outside).

Text

Isikasa bhikhuno dānaṁ

Translation

The gift of the monk Isika (*Ṛishika*).

Lüders, *List*, No. 356.

258. Pl. 131, 250. On a cross-bar (outside).

Text

Girigutāya bhichuniyā dānaṁ

Translation

The gift of the nun Girigutā (*Giriguptā*).

Lüders, *List*, No. 364.

259. Pl. 131, 251. On a rail-pillar (inside).

Text

Pokha[3].

260. Pl. 131, 252. On a rail-pillar (outside).

Text

. . . . . . sāṇa dāna

[1] The portion after *dānaṁ* is left out by Bühler (*Ep. Ind.*, Vol. II, p. 379, No. 210).

[2] Not read by Bühler (*Ep. Ind.*, Vol. II, p. 395, No. 370).

[3] On the stone there is no letter after *kha*. Evidently the engraver wanted to write *Pokhara*, *i.e.*, 'an inhabitant of Pushkara'.

261. Pl. 131, 253. On a cross-bar (outside).

Text

Pusadatasa Nāvagamakiyasa[1] dana

Translation

The gift of Pusadata (*Pushyadatta*), of Navagama (*Navagrāma*).

Lüders, *List*, No. 477.

262. Pl. 131, 254. On a cross-bar (outside).

Text

Seyasasa dānaṁ Bhādanakaṭiyasa

Translation

The gift of Seyasa (*Śreyas?*) of Bhadanakaṭa.

Lüders, *List*, No. 384.

263. Pl. 131, 255. On a cross-bar (outside).

Text

Arapāna Devakasa dānaṁ

Translation

The gift of Devaka from Arapāna.

Lüders, *List*, No. 353.

264. Pl. 131, 256. On a coping stone (outside).

Text

Vāghumatā Kācāniputānaṁ dānaṁ . . sa[2]

Translation

The gift of . . . . the Kācāniputas (*Kātyāyanīputras*) from Vāghumata.

Lüders, *List*, No. 279.

265. Pl. 131, 257. On a cross-bar (outside).

Text

Aya-Kānasa[3] bhichuno dānaṁ Aya-Bhaṁḍukiyasa

Translation

The gift of the monk Aya-Kāṇa (*Ārya-Kāṇa*), (disciple) of Aya-Bhaṁḍuka (*Ārya-Bhaṇḍuka*).

Lüders, *List*, No. 393.

266. Pl. 132, 258. On a cross-bar (outside).

Text

. . . Dhanadatasa dānaṁ[4]

Translation

The gift of Dhanadata (*Dhanadatta*)

267. Pl. 132, 259. On a cross-bar (outside).

Text

Dhamadatasa bhichuno dānaṁ A[ya]-Bhaḍukiya[sa]

Translation

The gift of the monk Dhamadata (*Dharmadatta*), (disciple) of Aya-Bhaḍuka (*Ārya-Bhaṇḍuka*).

Lüders, *List*, No. 367.

268. Pl. 132, 260. On a rail-pillar (outside).

Text

Pokharā Saṁghakhisa[5] dānaṁ

Translation

The gift of Saṁghakhi (*Saṁghākshi ?*) from Pokhara (*Pushkara*).

Lüders, *List*, No. 482.

269. Pl. 132, 261. On a cross-bar (outside).

Text

Budharakhitasa [bhikhu]no Aya-Bhaṁḍukiyasa dānaṁ

Translation

The gift of the monk Budharakhita (*Buddharakshita*), (disciple) of Aya-Bhaṁḍuka (*Ārya-Bhaṇḍuka*).

Lüders, *List*, No. 488.

270. Pl. 132, 262. On a cross-bar (outside).

Text

1 Yakhilasa bhichuno Aya-Devagirino ate-
2 vāsino dānaṁ

Translation

The gift of the monk Yakhila (*Yakshila*), the pupil of Aya-Devagiri (*Ārya-Devagiri*).

Lüders, *List*, No. 376.

[1] Bühler reads *Navagamakiyasa* (*Ep. Ind.*, Vol. II, p. 387, No. 292), but the *ā* stroke is clear.
[2] Bühler reads *Vāghumatā Kācā* . . . (*Ep. Ind.*, Vol. II, p. 375, No. 297).
[3] Bühler reads *Ayakana* (*Ep. Ind.*, Vol. II, p. 379, No. 207).
[4] The first word looks like *Kurara*.
[5] Bühler reads *Saṁgha(ra*)khi(ta*)sa-* (*Ep. Ind.*, Vol. II, p. 388, No. 297).

271. Pl. 132, 263. On a cross-bar (outside).

Text

[Ma]sakasa[1] dana

Translation

The gift of Masaka.

Lüders, *List*, No. 476.

272. Pl. 132, 264. On a coping stone (outside).

Text

Korariya Saghā[ya] bhi(chu)ni(ya) dānaṁ[2]

Translation

The gift of the nun Saghā (*Saṁghā*) of Kurara.

Lüders, *List*, No. 437.

273. Pl. 132, 265. On a rail-pillar (inside).

Text

1 Pokharā Hima-
2 girino dānaṁ

Translation

The gift of Himagiri from Pokhara (*Pushkara*).

Lüders, *List*, No. 370.

274. Pl. 132, 266. On a cross-bar (outside).

Text

Mahisitiya [Bhū]tikāye dānaṁ

Translation

The gift of Bhūtikā from Mahisitī (*Māhishmatī*).

275. Pl. 132, 267. On a cross-bar (outside).

Text

Ma[hi]satiya Arihadataye dānaṁ

Translation

The gift of Arihadatā (*Arhaddattā*) from Mahisatī (*Māhishmatī*).

Lüders, *List*, No. 497.

276. Pl. 132, 268. On a cross-bar (outside).

Text

Mahisatiya Devabhagasa dānaṁ

Translation

The gift of Devabhaga from Mahisatī (*Māhishmatī*).

Lüders, *List*, No. 375.

277. Pl. 132, 270. On a cross-bar (outside).

Text

Pusaye bhichuniye Nadinagarikāye dānaṁ

Translation

The gift of the nun Pusā (*Pushyā*), an inhabitant of Nadinagara (*Nandinagara*)

Lüders, *List*, No. 369.

278. Pl. 132, 271. On a cross-bar (outside).

Text

Dhama(da*)tāya dānaṁ Puñavaḍhaniyāye

Translation

The gift of Dhamadatā (*Dharmadattā*) of Puñavaḍhana (*Puṇyavardhana*).

Lüders, *List*, No. 366.

279. Pl. 132, 272. On a coping stone (outside).

Text

A[chava]ṭa Mātharasa[3] Dhamarakhitasa bhichuno dānaṁ

Translation

The gift of the monk Dhamarakhita (*Dharmarakshita*), the Māthara (*i.e.*, *Māṭhara*)[4] from Achavaṭa.

280. Pl. 132, 273. On a coping stone (outside).

Text

Siri[mi]tāyā Nādina[ga]rikāya bhichuniya dānaṁ

Translation

The gift of the nun Sirimitā (*Śrīmitrā*). an inhabitant of Nadinagara (*Nandinagara*).

Lüders, *List*, No. 538.

[1] The first letter is broken ; but in view of the two equalized prongs that are left, it should be read as *ma*. Bühler reads *Pusakasa* (*Ep. Ind.*, Vol. II, p. 387, No. 291).

[2] Bühler has [*Ku*]*rariyasa Saghā* . . . (*Ep. Ind.*, Vol. II, p. 383, No. 251).

[3] Actual reading *Mātharāsa*.

[4] *Māṭhara, i.e.*, 'a descendant of Maṭhara'.

281. Pl. 132, 274. On a cross-bar (outside).

Text

Siridinaya bhichunaya[1] Nādināgarikāya dāna

Translation

The gift of the nun Siridinā (*Śrīdattā*), an inhabitant of Nadinagara (*Nandinagara*).

Lüders, *List*, Nos. 383, 536.

282. Pl. 132, 275. On a cross-bar (outside).

Text[2]

Poḍaviḍakasa Isidinasa dānaṁ

Translation

The gift of Isidina (*Ṛishidatta*) of Poḍaviḍa.

Lüders, *List*, No. 483. *Cf.* No. 283.

283. Pl. 132, 276. On a cross-bar (outside).

Text

Poḍaviḍakasa Isidinasa dānaṁ

Translation

The gift of Isidina (*Ṛishidatta*) of Poḍaviḍa. *Cf.* No. 282.

284. Pl. 132, 277. On a cross-bar (outside).

Text

Peḍitakasa(?) . . . ghisasa dānaṁ[3]

Translation

The gift of . . . . of Peḍita(?).

285. Pl. 132, 278. On a rail-pillar (outside).

Text

1 Ujeniyā Tāpa-
2 siyānaṁ nusā-
3 ya Mitāya[4]
4 dānaṁ

Translation

The gift of Mitā (*Mitrā*) from Ujenī (*Ujjayinī*), a daughter-in-law (*snushā*) of the Tāpasiyas.[5]

Lüders, *List*, No. 307.

286. Pl. 132, 279. On a cross-bar (outside).

Text

Poḍaviḍakasa Dhaṁmasivasa dānaṁ

Translation

The gift of Dhaṁmasiva (*Dharmaśiva*) of Poḍaviḍa.

Lüders, *List*, No. 371.

287. Pl. 132, 280. On a cross-bar (outside, turned upside down).

Text

1 Madhuvanikāye Budharakhitaye bhichuniye
2 dānaṁ

Translation

The gift of the nun Budharakhitā (*Buddharakshitā*), an inhabitant of Madhuvana.

Lüders, *List*, No. 374.

288. Pl. 132, 281. On a cross-bar (outside, turned upside down).

Text

haraḍiyasa sapurisasa Yugapajakasa dānaṁ

Translation

The gift of the saint Bharaḍiya, an inhabitant of Yugapaja.[6]

Lüders, *List*, No. 308.

289. Pl. 132, 282. On a cross-bar (outside, turned upside down).

Text

Isirakhitasa dānaṁ

Translation

The gift of Isirakhita (*Ṛishirakshita*).

Lüders, *List*, No. 358.

---

[1] Read *bhichuṇiya*.

[2] There are two copies of this inscription, *viz.*, 282 and 283. Bühler reads *Poḍavijhakasa* (*Ep. Ind.*, Vol. II, p. 388, No. 298), but the fourth letter in both cases is clearly a *ḍa*.

[3] This reading is tentative. [4] There is a composite *triratna* symbol here. [5] The Tāpasiyas appear to be a family or tribe settled in Ujjain (*Ep. Ind.*, Vol. II, p. 94, and n. 28).

[6] Bühler translates *yugapajakasa* as "the path-(*finder*) of the age". (*Ep. Ind.*, Vol. II, p. 105, No. 74.) For *sapurisa* (*satpurusha*), *cf.* above, p. 290.

290. Pl. 132, 283. On rail-pillar (inside).

Text[1]

1 [Go]tiputasa
2 Bhaṁḍukasa
3 bhichuno dānaṁ

Translation

The gift of the monk Bhaṁḍuka, son of Goti (*Gauptī*).
Lüders, *List*, No. 194.

291. Pl. 132, 284. On a cross-bar (outside).

Text[2]

[Jo]nhakasa bhichuno dānaṁ

Translation

The gift of the monk Jonhaka (*Jyotsnāka*).
Cf. Nos. 292, 293.

292. Pl. 132, 285. On a cross-bar (outside).

Text

Jon[ha]kasa bhichuno dānaṁ

Translation

The gift of the monk Jonhaka (*Jyotsnāka*).
Cf. Nos. 291, 293.

293. Pl. 132, 286. On a cross-bar (outside).

Text

Jonhakasa bhichuno dānaṁ

Translation

The gift of the monk Jonhaka (*Jyotsnāka*).
Cf. Nos. 291, 292.

294. Pl. 132, 287. On a coping stone (outside).

Text

Aya-Dhanakasa bhichuno dānaṁ

Translation

The gift of the monk Aya-Dhanaka (*Ārya-Dhanaka*).
Lüders, *List*, No. 309.

295. Pl. 132, 288. On a cross-bar (outside, facing West Gateway).

Text[3]

Dhamarakh[i]tāye Madhuvan(i)kāye dānaṁ

Translation

The gift of Dhamarakhitā (*Dharmarakshitā*), an inhabitant of Madhuvana.
Lüders, *List*, No. 312.

296. Pl. 132, 289. On a cross-bar (outside, facing West Gateway).

Text

Dhamarakhitāya Madhuvanikāye dānaṁ

Translation

The gift of Dhamarakhitā (*Dharmarakshitā*), an inhabitant of Madhuvana.
Lüders, *List*, No. 191 or 460.

297. Pl. 132, 290. On a cross-bar (outside, facing West Gateway).

Text

Dhanagirino dānaṁ

Translation

The gift of Dhanagiri.
Lüders, *List*, No. 315.

298. Pl. 132, 291. On a rail-pillar (outside).

Text

Mah[ā]m[o]ragim[hā][4] Sihagirino dana

Translation

The gift of Sihagiri (*Siṁhagiri*) from Mahāmoragi[ri] (*Mahāmayūragiri*)
Lüders, *List*, No. 189.

299. Pl. 132, 292. On a cross-bar (outside).

Text[5]

Samirakhitasa [da]naṁ

Translation

The gift of Samirakhita (*Svāmirakshita*).

---

[1] For another copy of this inscription, see No. 307 below.
[2] There are three copies of this inscription of which two are given by Lüders under his Nos. 310 and 311.
[3] According to Bühler there are three copies of this inscription, *viz.*, Lüders, Nos. 191, 312 and 460.
[4] As Bühler suggests, the text intended is *Mahāmoragirimhā*. *Moragiri* (*Mayūragiri*) occurs in Bharhut inscriptions; see Lüders, Nos. 778, 796, 798, 808 and 860. According to Bühler, there is another copy of this inscription, *viz.*, Lüders, No. 313.
[5] The letters are very much worn out.

300. Pl. 132, 293. On a cross-bar (outside).

Text

Yasopālasa dānaṁ Bhadanakaḍisa[1]

Translation

The gift of Yasopāla (*Yaśaḥpāla*) of Bhadanakaḍa.

Lüders, *List*, No. 314.

301. Pl. 132, 294. On a cross-bar (outside).

Text

Girikasa prajavatiyā Sutiyā dāna[2]

Translation

The gift of Sutī, the wife of Girika.

Lüders, *List*, No. 440.

302. Pl. 132, 295. On a coping stone (outside).

Text

Pusasa Cahaṭiyasa bhichuno dānaṁ

Translation

The gift of the monk Pusa (*Pushya*) of Cahaṭa.

Lüders, *List*, No. 190.

Screen of the Western Entrance.

303. Pl. 132, 296. On a coping stone behind the left jamb of West Gateway (outside, turned upside down).

Text

Therasa[3] Aya-Nāgasa bhichuno Ujenakasa dānaṁ

Translation

The gift of the Elder Aya-Nāga (*Ārya-Nāga*), a monk of Ujenī (*Ujjayinī*).

Lüders, *List*, No. 451.

304. Pl. 132, 297. On a cross-bar (outside).

Text[4]

1 Avisināye sutātikini[yā]
2 Maḍalāchikaṭi[k]āya dānaṁ

Translation

The gift of Avisinā, who is versed in the *Suttantas*,[5] an inhabitant of Maḍalāchikaṭa.

Lüders, *List*, No. 352. *Cf.* No. 305.

305. Pl. 132, 298. On a cross-bar (outside).

Text

1 Avisinaye sūtātikiniyā
2 Maḍalachikaṭikāye dānaṁ

Translation

The gift of Avisinā, who is versed in the *Suttantas*, an inhabitant of Maḍalachikaṭa.

Lüders, *List*, No. 319. *Cf.* No. 304.

306. Pl. 132, 299. On a rail-pillar (outside).

Text

1 Saghadevasa Verohakaṭasa
2 vāṇijasa dānaṁ

Translation

The gift of Saghadeva (*Saṁghadeva*), the merchant of Verohakaṭa.

Lüders, *List*, No. 320.

307. Pl. 132, 300. On a coping stone (inside).

Text[6]

Gotiputasa Bhaḍukasa bhichuno dānaṁ

Translation

The gift of the monk Bhaḍuka (*Bhaṇḍuka*), son of Gotī (*Gauptī*).

Lüders, *List*, No. 442.

[1] Bühler reads *Bhada[ta]-kaḍi[yasa]*, 'pupil of the venerable Kaḍa' (*Ep. Ind.*, Vol. II, p. 371, No. 133). But *cf.* Lüders, *List*, No. 384 (No. 262 above).
[2] Bühler has not read the last two words.
[3] This word is hidden by the left jamb of the gateway.
[4] There are two copies of this inscription, *viz.*, Nos. 304 and 305.
[5] On this term, see Barua, *Barhut Inscriptions*, p. 15.
[6] For another copy, see No. 290 above.

308. Pl. 132, 301. On a rail-pillar (inside).

Text[1]

Vejajasa gāmasa dānaṁ

Translation

The gift of the Vejaja village.

309. Pl. 132, 302. On a cross-bar (outside).

Text

Kurārā Sa[ṁ]valitasa dānaṁ

Translation

The gift of Saṁvalita from Kurara.

Lüders, *List*, No. 362.

310. Pl. 132, 303. On a cross-bar (inside).

Text[2]

Arahagutasa Sāsādakasa bhichuno dānaṁ

Translation

The gift of the monk Arahaguta (*Arhadgupta*), an inhabitant of Sasāda.

Lüders, *List*, No. 196.

North-West Quadrant.

311. Pl. 132, 304. On a rail-pillar (inside).

Text

. . . . [Pemuta ?] Vajika[sa] dānaṁ

Translation

The gift of Vajika (*Vajrika*) from Pemuta(?).

312. Pl. 132, 305. On a cross-bar (outside, turned upside down).

Text

1 Dhama[si]riya[3] bhichuniye
Maḍalachikaṭikāye
2 dānaṁ

Translation

The gift of the nun Dhamasirī (*Dharmaśrī*), an inhabitant of Maḍalachikaṭa.

Lüders, *List*, No. 318.

313. Pl. 132, 306. On a cross-bar (outside, turned upside down).

Text

Pāḍaya [Maḍalā]ch[i]kaḍayāya
bhichun[i] . . .

Translation

(The gift) of the nun Pāḍā, an inhabitant of Maḍalāchikaḍa.

314. Pl. 132, 307. On a cross-bar (outside, turned upside down).

Text

laya Nadinagarikāye [bhi]chuniye
dānaṁ

Translation

The gift of the nun . . . . an inhabitant of Nadinagara (*Nandinagara*).

315. Pl. 132, 308. On a cross-bar (outside, turned upside down).

Text

1 Balikāye bhichuniyā Maḍalāchika-
2 ṭikāya dānaṁ

Translation

The gift of the nun Balikā, an inhabitant of Maḍalāchikaṭa.

Lüders, *List*, No. 317.

316. Pl. 132, 309. On a rail-pillar (inside).

Text

Kiṭiya bhikhuniya Koraghariya dānaṁ

Translation

The gift of the nun Kiṭi (*Kīrti*) of Kuraghara.

317. Pl. 132, 310. On a cross-bar (outside, turned upside down).

Text

Revāye Ujenikāye upasikāye dānaṁ

Translation

The gift of the female lay-worshipper Revā of Ujenī (*Ujjayinī*).

Lüders, *List*, No. 385.

[1] This text is identical with Lüders, No. 195, but the inscriptions are evidently different, as No. 195 consists of two lines.

[2] For an inscription of Balaka, a disciple of Arahaguta, see Stūpa 2, No. 671.

[3] The letter *si* was originally miswritten as *thi*; and the letter *ri*, which seems to have been first omitted inadvertently, was later introduced above the line.

318. Pl. 132, 311. On a coping stone (outside).

Text

Vedisā M[o]hikāye bhichuniye dānaṁ

Translation

The gift of the nun Mohikā from Vedisa (*Vidiśā*).

Lüders, *List*, No. 524.

319. Pl. 132, 312. On a rail-pillar (outside).

Text

1 Subhagasa
2 Koragharasa dana

Translation

The gift of Subhaga of Kuraghara.

Lüders, *List*, No. 197.

320. Pl. 132, 313. On a cross-bar (outside).

Text[1]

1 [I]sidasiye Nādināgarikāye bhichuniye
2 dānaṁ

Translation

The gift of the nun Isidasi (*Ṛishidāsī*), an inhabitant of Nadinagara (*Nandinagara*).

Lüders, *List*, No. 402.

321. Pl. 132, 314. On a cross-bar (outside).

Text

1 Vedisikaya Pusarakhitasa asavārikasa[2]
2 pā[ja]vati(ya) Nāgadatāya dānaṁ

Translation

The gift of Nāgadatā (*Nāgadattā*), wife of the *asavārika*[3] (*aśvavārika*), *i.e.*, trooper, Pusarakhita (*Pushyarakshita*) of Vedisa (*Vidiśā*).

Lüders, *List*, No. 381.

322. Pl. 132, 315. On a cross-bar (outside)

Text

Palasa Asāvatiya dānaṁ

Translation

The gift of Pala from Asāvatī (*Aśvavatī*).

323. Pl. 132, 316. On a cross-bar (outside, turned upside down).

Text

Vāsavaye Nadinagarā bhichuniye dānaṁ

Translation

The gift of the nun Vāsavā, from Nadinagara (*Nandinagara*).

Lüders, *List*, No. 512.

324. Pl. 132, 317. On a rail-pillar (outside).

Text

Kura[gharā] Ghosakasa dānaṁ[4]

Translation

The gift of Ghosaka (*Ghoshaka*) from Kuraghara.

Lüders, *List*, No. 425.

325. Pl. 132, 318. On a cross-bar (outside, turned upside down).

Text

Nāgadatāya dānaṁ

Translation

The gift of Nāgadatā (*Nāgadattā*).

326. Pl. 132, 319. On a coping stone (outside).

Text

Yakhadāsiyā dānaṁ bhichuniyā

Translation

The gift of the nun Yakhadāsi (*Yakshadāsī*).

Lüders, *List*, No. 329.

[1] This text is identical with Lüders, No. 327, which, however, is in one line.
[2] *Cf.* a Bharhut inscription, Lüders, *List*, No. 728.
[3] Bühler reads *Asavāraka*. But the *i*-stroke is clear on the stone.
[4] There seem to be traces of some letters above this line.

327. Pl. 132, 320. On a cross-bar (outside, turned upside down).

Text

[J]itamitaye bhichuniye Vaḍivahanikāye dānaṁ

Translation

The gift of the nun Jitamitā (*Jitamitrā*), an inhabitant of Vaḍivahana.

Lüders, *List*, No. 365.

328. Pl. 132, 321. On a rail-pillar (outside).

Text

1 Rohaṇipadiyasi[1]
2 seṭhino Nāgadi-
3 nasa dānaṁ

Translation

The gift of the banker Nāgadina (*Nāgadatta*), of Rohaṇipada (*Rohiṇīpada*).

Lüders, *List*, No. 379.

329. Pl. 133, 322. On a rail-pillar (outside).

Text

1 Rohaṇipadiya-
2 sa Nigaḍisa dā-
3 naṁ

Translation

The gift of Nigaḍi of Rohaṇipada.

Lüders, *List*, No. 377.

330. Pl. 133, 323. On a cross-bar (outside).

Text

Pokharāto Isidatāya Levasa pajāvatiyā dānaṁ

Translation

The gift of Isidatā (*Ṛishidattā*), the wife of Leva, from Pokhara (*Pushkara*).

Lüders, *List*, No. 479

331. Pl. 133, 324. On a rail-pillar (outside).

Text

1 Rohaṇipadiya-
2 sa Bulikasa
3 dānaṁ

Translation

The gift of Bulika of Rohaṇipada.

Lüders, *List*, No. 378.

332. Pl. 133, 325. On a rail-pillar (outside).

Text[2]

1 Isikasa Rohā-
2 ṇipadiyasa dā-
3 naṁ

Translation

The gift of Isika (*Ṛishika*) of Rohāṇipada.

Lüders, *List*, No. 357.

333. Pl. 133, 326. On a cross-bar (outside).

Text

Pokharāto Tuḍāya Tuḍasa ca dānaṁ le . . .

Translation

The gift of Tuḍā (*Tuṇḍā*) and Tuḍa (*Tuṇḍa*) from Pokhara (*Pushkara*) . . .

Lüders, *List*, No. 481.

334. Pl. 133, 327. On a coping stone (outside).

Text

Nadinagarā Dupasah(ā)-bhichuniye dānaṁ

Translation

The gift of the nun Dupasahā from Nadinagara (*Nandinagara*).

Lüders, *List*, No. 328.

---

[1] Read *Rohaṇipadiyasa*; *si* is added above the line.
[2] The text begins at the bottom and runs upwards. The last letter *naṁ* is written just above the previous one *dā*.

335. Pl. 133, 328. On a cross-bar (outside, turned upside down).

Text

Pokharāto Isidatāya dānaṁ

Translation

The gift of Isidatā (*Ṛishidattā*) from Pokhara (*Pushkara*).

Lüders, *List*, No. 480.

336. Pl. 133, 329. On a cross-bar (outside).

Text

. . . nā[1] Asāḍrasa mātu dānaṁ

Translation

The gift of the mother of Asāḍra (*Āshāḍha*) from (Arāpāna*).

337. Pl. 133, 330. On a rail-pillar (outside).

Text

1 Koragharasa seṭhino
2 Sihasa dānaṁ

Translation

The gift of Siha (*Siṁha*), the banker of Koraghara.

Lüders, *List*, No. 363. *Cf.* No. 339.

338. Pl. 133, 331. On a cross-bar (outside, turned upside down).

Text

1 Aya-Phagunasa sādhivihārino[2]
2 Khemākasa[3] bhichuno dānaṁ

Translation

The gift of the monk Khemāka (*Kshemaka*), the companion (or co-resident) of Aya-Phaguna (*Ārya-Phalguna*).

Lüders, *List*, No. 395.

339. Pl. 133, 332. On a rail-pillar (outside).

Text[4]

1 Koragharasa seṭhino
2 dānaṁ Sihasa

Translation

The gift of the banker Siha (*Siṁha*) of Koraghara.

340. Pl. 133, 333. On a rail-pillar (outside).

Text

1 . . . . sika . . .
2 . . [Va]radatasa(?) dana

Translation

The gift of Varadata (*Varadatta*) . .

341. Pl. 133, 334. On a cross-bar (outside).

Text

1 Balikāya dānaṁ
2 Maḍalāchikaḍikāna savekhaṇa (?)[5]
3 bhichuninaṁ

Translation

The gift of Balikā, (and) of all (?) the nuns of Maḍalāchikaḍa.

342. Pl. 133, 335. On a cross-bar (outside).

Text

Dhamasiriyā dānaṁ

Translation

The gift of Dhamasiri (*Dharmaśrī*).

343. Pl. 133, 336. On a rail-pillar (outside).

Text

. . . . kārā . . . .

344. Pl. 133, 337. On a cross-bar (outside).

Text

Vedisikaya Vaj[i]niya bhi[chu]niya dānaṁ

Translation

The gift of the nun Vajinī (*Vajriṇī*) of Vedisa (*Vidiśā*).

---

[1] Restore *Arāpānā*. *Cf.* Bühler, *Ep. Ind.*, Vol. II, p. 105, No. 72.
[2] Or *sādha-*?
[3] Bühler reads *Khemaka*.
[4] But for the position of *Sihasa* after *dānaṁ*, this text is identical with No. 337 above.
[5] The meaning of *savekhaṇa* is not understood. Is it a mistake for *savina*, 'of all'?

345. Pl. 133, 338. On a rail-pillar (outside).

Text

1 Asavatiya gāmasa
2 dānaṁ

Translation

The gift of the village Asavatī (*Aśvavatī*).
Lüders, *List*, No. 401.

346. Pl. 133, 339. On a cross-bar (outside).

Text

Viraye bhichuniyā Tobavanikāya dānaṁ

Translation

The gift of the nun Virā (*Vīrā*) of Tubavana.
Lüders, *List*, No. 520.

347. Pl. 133, 340. On a coping stone (outside).

Text

Sihāya samātikaya Vajānikaya[1] dāna[2]

Translation

The gift of Sihā (*Siṁhā*), (and) Vajānikā (*Vajriṇikā*), with (her or their) mother (or mothers).
Lüders, *List*, No. 543.

348. Pl. 133, 341. On a rail-pillar (outside).

Text

1 Bhaḍikiyasa
2 Saṁghilasa dānaṁ

Translation

The gift of Saṁghila, (a pupil) of Bhaḍika.
Lüders, *List*, No. 321.

349. Pl. 133, 342. On a cross-bar (outside).

Text

Arahatapālitasa Bha[ḍi]kiya[sa][3] dānaṁ

Translation

The gift of Arahatapālita (*Arhatpālita*), (a pupil) of Bhaḍika.
Lüders, *List*, No. 322.

350. Pl. 133, 343. On a rail-pillar (outside).

Text

1 Arahakasa Pari-
2 panakasa dānaṁ

Translation

The gift of Arahaka (*Arhaka*) of Paripana.
Lüders, *List*, No. 323.

351. Pl. 133, 344. On a cross-bar (outside).

Text[4]

Dhamagirika-mātu dānaṁ

Translation

The gift of the mother of Dhamagirika (*Dharmagirika*).
Lüders, *List*, No. 324.

352. Pl. 133, 345. On a coping stone (inside).

Text

Aya-Rahilasa Sāphineyakasa mātu dānaṁ

Translation

The gift of the mother of Aya-Rahila (*Ārya-Rahila*), of the Sāphineya (family).
Lüders, *List*, No. 198.

353. Pl. 133, 346. On a cross-bar (outside, facing North Gateway).

Text

Vedasa[5] Datasa Kalavāḍasa dānaṁ

Translation

The gift of Data (*Datta*) Kalavāḍa[6] from Vedisa (*Vidiśā*).
Lüders, *List*, No. 522. *Cf.* Nos. 354, 355.

354. Pl. 133, 347. On a cross-bar (outside, facing North Gateway).

Text

Vedisa Datasa Kalaviḍasa[7] dānaṁ

Translation

The gift of Data (*Datta*) Kalaviḍa from Vedisa (*Vidiśā*).
Lüders, *List*, No. 523. *Cf.* Nos. 353, 355.

[1] Bühler reads *Vajinikaya*. Bühler and Lüders take *Samātikā* as a personal name.
[2] The last letter is shaped like *ka*.
[3] Bühler reads *bhi* after *pālitasa*, and leaves the rest unread before *dānaṁ*.
[4] The text is identical with Inscription No. 31 above, except for *Dhamagirikasa* which occurs in the latter for *Dhamagirika*.
[5] Read *Vedisa*.
[6] A pillar bearing an inscription of evidently this Data-Kalavaḍa comes from Temple 40 (No. 790 below).
[7] Bühler reads *Kalavaḍasa*.

355. Pl. 133, 348. On a cross-bar (outside, facing North Gateway).

Text

[Ve]dasa[1] Datasa Kalavaḍasa dānaṁ

Translation

The gift of Data (*Datta*) Kalavaḍa from Vedisa (*Vidiśā*).

Lüders, *List*, No. 330(?). *Cf*. Nos. 353, 354.

356. Pl. 133, 349. On a rail-pillar (outside, facing North Gateway).

Text

1 Oḍiya
2 Nadinaga-
3 rikaya dana

Translation

The gift of Oḍī, an inhabitant of Nadinagara (*Nandinagara*).

Lüders, *List*, No. 325.

357. Pl. 133, 350. On a cross-bar (outside, facing North Gateway).

Text

Kususiriya danaṁ Arapa(nā)

Translation

The gift of Kususirī from Arapana.

358. Pl. 133, 351. On a cross-bar (outside, facing North Gateway).

Text

[Va]sudataya bhikhuṇiyā Nādanāgarikāya dānaṁ

Translation

The gift of the nun Vasudatā (*Vasudattā*), an inhabitant of Nadinagara (*Nandinagara*).

359. Pl. 133, 352. On a coping stone (outside, facing North Gateway).

Text

Ujenihāre Morajābhikaṭisa dānaṁ

Translation

The gift of (the village) Morajābhikaṭa in Ujenī district (*Ujjayinī-āhāra*).

360. Pl. 133, 353. On a cross-bar (outside, facing North Gateway).

Text

Dhamayasāye upasikāye dānaṁ

Translation

The gift of the female lay-worshipper Dhamayasā (*Dharmayaśā*).

361. Pl. 133, 354. On a rail-pillar (inside) at the entrance of North Gateway.

Text[2]

Kekaṭeyaka-putasa Dhamasivasa dānaṁ

Translation

The gift of Dhamasiva (*Dharmaśiva*), son of Kekaṭeyaka (*Kaikaṭeyaka*).

Lüders, *List*, No. 162.

Additional balustrade against the right jamb of the North Gateway.

362. Pl. 133, 355. On a rail-pillar (inside).

Text

1 Isipālitasa ca
2 Samaṇasa ca dānaṁ

Translation

The gift of Isipālita (*Ṛishipālita*) and Samana (*Śramaṇa*).

Lüders, *List*, No. 336.

363. Pl. 133, 356. On a rail-pillar (inside).

Text

1 Paṁthakasa bhichuno ubhina bhātiṇa[3]
2 Budhapālitasa bhichuno dānaṁ

Translation

The gift of the two brothers, the monk Paṁthaka (*Pānthaka*) (and) of the monk Budhapālita (*Buddhapālita*).

Lüders, *List*, No. 473.

[1] Read *Vedisa*.

[2] Below it is inscribed in Nāgarī characters: *Rā°śrī-Sāvadeva praṇamati nityaṁ*.—"The *Rā*(*uta*) Sāvadeva always makes obeisance."

[3] The last word of line 1 has not been read by Bühler; also he reads *ubheyakā* for *ubhina*. (*Ep. Ind.*, Vol. II, p. 387, No. 288.)

(B) MISCELLANEOUS GROUND BALUSTRADE FRAGMENTS, Nos. 364-388.[1]

364. Pl. 133, 2. On a rail-pillar.

Text

Vāka[lā]ye deviye Ahimita-ma(tu) .

Translation

(The gift) of the queen Vākalā (*Vāshkalā*), the mother of Ahimita (*Ahimitra*).

Lüders, *List*, No. 169.

365. Pl. 133, 3. On a rail-pillar.

Text

Nāgilasa seṭhino dānaṁ

Translation

The gift of the banker Nāgila.

Lüders, *List*, No. 470.

366. Pl. 133, 4. On a rail-pillar.

Text

1 Kaṭaka[ñuya]kasa
2 Ara[ha]dāsasa dānaṁ

Translation

The gift of Arahadāsa (*Arhaddāsa*) of Kaṭakañuya.

Lüders, *List*, No. 261.

367. Pl. 133, 5. On a rail-pillar.

Text[2]

Bhadagutasa Sānuka-gāmiyasa mātu

Translation

(The gift) of the mother of Bhadaguta (*Bhadragupta*) of Sānukagāma (*Sānukagrāma*).

Lüders, *List*, No. 258.

368. Pl. 133, 6. On a rail-pillar.

Text

1 Ujeniyā Visvade-
2 vasa pajāvatiyā
3 Mulāya dānaṁ

Translation

The gift of Mulā (*Mūlā*), the wife of Visvadeva (*Viśvadeva*) from Ujenī (*Ujjayinī*).

Lüders, *List*, No. 359.

369. Pl. 133, 7. On a rail-pillar.

Text[3]

(ga)[ha]patino Budhilasa dā(naṁ)

Translation

The gift of the householder Budhila (*Buddhila*).

Lüders, *List*, No. 193.

370. Pl. 133, 8. On a rail-pillar.

Text

1 Sihāya Devadatāya
2 ca dānaṁ K[u]ragharā bhichu-
3 nīnaṁ[4]

Translation

The gift of Sihā (*Siṁhā*) and Devadatā (*Devadattā*), the nuns from Kuraghara.

Lüders, *List*, No. 542.

371. Pl. 133, 9. On a rail-pillar.

Text

. . . . (bhi)khuno Koragharasa dānaṁ

Translation

The gift of the monk . . . . of Koraghara.

[1] These are lying loose at Sāñchī.
[2] The facsimile is hopelessly indistinct. Bühler reads *Bhadagutasa Sānukagaminasa dānaṁ* (*Ep. Ind.*, Vol. II, p. 375, No. 172).
[3] Above the inscription is inscribed the following in Nāgarī characters : *Rā° Śrī-Sāvadeva praṇamati nityaṁ, i.e.,* " the *Rā(uta)* Sāvadeva always makes obeisance ".
[4] Bühler reads *ni* instead of *nī*, but the ī-stroke is clear.

372. Pl. 133, 10. On a rail-pillar.

Text

1 Piyadhamāya
2 Bodhiya ca
3 Koragharina
4 bhikhuninaṁ dānaṁ

Translation

The gift of the nuns Piyadhamā (*Priyadharmā*) and Bodhi of Koraghara.

Lüders, *List*, No. 368.

373. Pl. 133, 11. On a rail-pillar.

Text

Bha[ḍi] . . (bhi)kh[u]no Ko . . . . . . [1]

Translation

(The gift) of the monk Bhaḍi(ka) from Ko(raghara).

Lüders, *List*, No. 492. *Cf.* No. 469 below.

374. Pl. 133, 12. On a cross-bar.

Text

[Bho]ga[va]ḍhanakasa Mahi[da] . . .

Translation

(The gift) of Mahida (*Mahīndra*) of Bhogavaḍhana (*Bhogavardhana*).

Lüders, *List*, No. 373.

375. Pl 133, 13. On a cross-bar.

Text

. . [ma] . risa dānaṁ

Translation

The gift of . . . .

376. Pl. 133, 14. On a cross-bar.

Text

Nadagirino Kothukapadiyasa dānaṁ

Translation

The gift of Nadagiri (*Nandagiri*) of Kothukapada.

377. Pl. 133, 15. On a cross-bar.

Text

Aya-Jetasa bhichuno dānaṁ

Translation

The gift of the monk Aya-Jeta (*Ārya-Jita*)

Lüders, *List*, No. 394.

378. Pl. 133, 16. On a cross-bar.

Text

Datāye bhichuniyā Ma[2] . . . .

Translation

The gift of the nun Datā (*Dattā*) of Ma(ḍalāchikaṭa).

Lüders, *List*, No. 452.

379. Pl. 133, 17. On a cross-bar.

Text

Ujeniya . . . . .

Translation

. . . . from Ujenī (*Ujjayinī*).

380. Pl. 133, 18. On a cross-bar.

Text

Ujeniya Balakaya dānaṁ

Translation

The gift of Balakā from Ujenī (*Ujjayinī*).

Lüders, *List*, No. 222.

---

[1] Restore *Bhaḍikasa* and *Koragharasa dana* (Bühler, *Ep. Ind.*, Vol. II, p. 389, No. 307).

[2] Restore *Maḍalāchikaṭikāye*. *Cf.* Bühler, *Ep. Ind.*, Vol. II, p. 385, No. 267.

381. Pl. 133, 19 On a cross-bar.

Text

Sidhathasa vi . . . .

Translation

. . . . of Sidhatha (*Siddhārtha*).

Lüders, *List*, No. 326.

382. Pl. 133, 20. On a cross-bar.

Text

[Na ?]gada[ta]ya dānaṁ

Translation

The gift of Na(?)gadatā (*Nāgadattā*)

383. Pl. 133, 21. On a cross-bar.

Text

Gotamiye Isinika . . .

Translation

. . . . Gotamī (*Gautamī*) . . Isinikā (*Ṛishiṇikā*).

Lüders, *List*, No. 441.

384. Pl. 133, 22. On a cross-bar.

Text

. . tasa ca dānaṁ

Translation

The gift of . . . . and . . . .

385. Pl. 133, 23. On a cross-bar.

Text

Devarakhitasa Morajahakaṭiyasa bhichuno dānaṁ

Translation

The gift of the monk Devarakhita (*Devarakshita*) of Morajahakaṭa.

Lüders, *List*, No. 453.

386. Pl. 133, 24 On a cross-bar.

Text

Asvavatiyā Isigutasa vaṇijasa dānaṁ

Translation

The gift of the merchant Isiguta (*Ṛishigupta*) from Asvavatī (*Aśvavatī*).

Lüders, *List*, No. 355.

387. Pl. 133, 25. On a cross-bar.

Text

. . . kasa[1] Ajitiguta-kulasa (dānaṁ)

Translation

(The gift) of the family of Ajitiguta (*Ajitigupta*).

Lüders, *List*, No. 549.

388. Pl. 133, 26. On a coping stone.

Text

S(i)r(i)y(ā) V(e)d(i)sikāya bhichuniyā dānaṁ

Translation

The gift of the nun Siri (*Śrī*), an inhabitant of Vedisa (*Vidiśā*).

[1] The lower part of a *na* is visible before *ka*. Probably the missing word is *Ujenikasa*.

(C) GATEWAYS, Nos. 389-404.

(i) *North Gateway.*

389. Pl. 133, 'North Gate', 1. On left pillar.

This fragmentary inscription is part of an imprecation like those on the East and West Gateways.

Text[1]

1 . . . ka pāpakārina[2] save mala[ṁ] paṭipa[je]yā . . .

2 (pac-ānata)riya-kārakānāṁ ca gatiṁ gacheya yo ito[3]

Translation

. . . . all those sinners shall live in dirt . . . . and he who from here . . . . shall have the same fate as that of the perpetrators (of Five Sins).

390. Pl. 133, 'North Gate', 2. Below the elephants bearing the wheel, facing south.

Text

Dhamagirino bhikhuno dā[naṁ][4]

Translation

The gift of the monk Dhamagiri (*Dharmagiri*). Lüders, *List*, No. 335.

391. Pl. 133, 'North Gate', 3. On the crowning lion, east end.

Text

Balamitāya dānaṁ

Translation

The gift of Balamitā (*Balamitrā*).

392. Pl. 133, 'North Gate', 4. On left foreleg of an elephant facing east, between lowest and middle architraves.

Text

1 Asamitasa

2 dānaṁ[5]

Translation

The gift of Asamita (*Aśvamitra*).

393. Pl. 133, 'North Gate', 5. On foreleg of an elephant facing west, between lowest and middle architraves.

Text

1 Vedi[siki ?]yanaṁ

2 dānaṁ[6]

Translation

The gift of the Vedisikas (?) (*Vaidiśikas*).

394. Pl. 133, 'North Gate', 6. On right pillar.

Text[7]

. . . . Kākaṇā(va) . .

(ii) *East Gateway.*

395. Pl. 134, 'East Gate', 1. On the crowning *Triratna.*

Text

Jivasa dānaṁ

Translation

The gift of Jiva (*Jīva*).

---

[1] *Cf.* East Gate, No. 396, and West Gate, No. 404. See Chanda, *Mem. A. S. I.*, No. 1, p. 21 and Pl. VI, 3. Chanda reads . . . *kapālakārisa Vemalapaḍi?* . . . .

[2] The letter *na* was omitted at first and added later below *ri*.

[3] The portion after *ito* must be *Kākaṇāvāto*, etc., which is continued on the right pillar of the gateway (see No. 394 below).

[4] There is a *triratna* symbol at the end.

[5] This word is written above *Asamitasa.*

[6] This word is inscribed above line 1. The reading of the first word is doubtful.

[7] This appears to be a continuation of the inscription on the left pillar (No. 389 above).

396. Pl. 134, 'East Gate', 2. On left pillar above the capital.

This inscription occurs just above the elephant-capital, on the stone block which bears the representation of a standard-bearer holding aloft a banner adorned with the *Triratna* symbol in relief. The writing commences at the left side, on the plain surface of the block, and runs across the relief. It is obstructed partly by the raised symbol and partly by the lines of the banner, already executed. The text is engraved in bold letters up to the middle of the third line, the words being arranged in their natural consecutive order. Thereafter, the letters become smaller in size, and the writing is carried over wherever convenient, evidently to avoid the symbol and the lines of the banner. Thus, section 3*b* of the text is inscribed above 3*a*, 5*a* below 4*a*, 4*b* a little above 4*a*, and 5*b* below 4*b*. The inscription, of which the concluding portion cannot be fully made out, is in the form of an imprecation, being one of the earliest of its kind. It enumerates the five sins which in Buddhist texts are called *matughāto*, *pitughāto*, *arahaṁta-ghāto*, *lohituppādo* and *saṁghabhedo*.[1] The inscription enjoins that he who may be directly or indirectly responsible for the dismantling of an arch or a rail from Kākaṇāva, or for its transfer to another (heretic) Church, shall have the same fate as the perpetrator of the 'five sins' (see above, p. 298). It is interesting to note that Saṁghabheda, or schism in the Buddhist Church,[2] had come to be recognized, after Aśoka, as one of the 'five great sins'. Similar imprecatory inscriptions occur also on the North and West Gates of Stūpa 1.

Text[3]

1 [yo] ito Kākaṇā[vā]to toraṇa vedika vā
2 upāḍeyā upāḍā[peyā][4] vā ānaṁ vā ācariya-kulaṁ
3*a* saṁkāmeyā so ma-
3*b* ti-ghātina piti-ghātina
4*a* arahaṁta-ghātina
5*a* rudhir-upāyakāna[5] sa-
4*b* gha-bhe(dina)[6] . . . . . . te du. cita . .
5*b* nasa pāpā . . . . .
6 kārina sav[e] ma. paṭipae.[7]

Translation[8]

He who dismantles,[9] or causes to be dismantled, an arch or a rail of this Kākaṇāva, or causes it to be transferred to another Church (*Ācaryia-kula*),[10] (shall incur the sin) of the murderers of mothers, murderers of fathers, murderers of *Arhats*, of those who create schism in the Community, and of those who cause bloodshed[11] . . . . . all such sinners (shall live in dirt).

397. Pl. 134, 'East Gate', 3. On left pillar above third compartment.

Text[12]

Korarasa Nāgapiyasa Achāvaḍe seṭhisa dānaṁ thabho

Translation

The gift of a pillar by Nāgapiya (*Nāgapriya*) of Kurara, the banker at Achāvaḍa.

Lüders, *List*, No. 339.

[1] Childers, *Pāli Dictionary*, s.v. '*Abhiṭhānaṁ*'. These five sins are mentioned in the *Vinayapiṭaka*, Mahāvagga, I, 64-67.
[2] See *ante* pp. 285-6.
[3] *Cf.* Bühler's text, *Ep. Ind.*, Vol. II, p. 396; *cf.* Inscription No. 404 on West Gate.
[4] Bühler reads *da* for *ḍa*.
[5] Bühler reads [*kama*] *upāyakāna*.
[6] Bühler leaves out this portion in his text.
[7] Bühler reads [*sa pāpā kara*]*na sevu* . . . *Cf.* No. 389 on North Cate and restore *pāpakārina save malaṁ paṭipayā*.
[8] *Cf.* Bühler's translation: "He who takes away or causes to be taken away from this Kākaṇā(va) an ornamental arch or rail, or causes it to be transferred to another temple of the teacher (shall incur the guilt) of murderers of mothers, of murderers of fathers, of murderers of Arhats . . . . ." *Cf.* also Lüders, *List*, No. 340.
[9] The root is clearly *utpāṭ*, and not *utpād* as Bühler takes it to be.
[10] Bühler takes *ācariya-kula* to mean 'temple of the teacher' on the analogy of *devakula*. But see my remarks above, p. 298.
[11] *I.e.*, *rudhir-otpāda*, which is mentioned as one of the Five Offences in the *Mahāvyutpatti* (Bib. Buddh.), p. 37.
[12] *Cf.* Inscription No. 403 on West Gate.

(iii) *South Gateway.*

398. Pl. 134, 'South Gate', 1. On top architrave facing the Stūpa.

Text

1 Rāño Siri-Sātakaṇisa
2 āvesanisa Vāsiṭhiputrasa
3 Ānaṁdasa dānaṁ

Translation

The gift of Ānaṁda, son of Vāsiṭhī (*Vāsishṭhī*), the foreman of the artisans[1] of the *Rājan* Sirī Sātakaṇi (*Śrī-Sātakarṇi*).

Lüders, *List*, No. 346.

399. Pl. 134, 'South Gate', 2. On the middle architrave (outside).

Text[2]

1 Aya-Cuḍasa dhamakathikasa
2 atevāsino Balamitrasa dānaṁ

Translation

The gift of Balamitra, a pupil of the Preacher of the Law Aya-Cuḍa (*Ārya-Cūḍa* or *Ārya Kshudra*).

Lüders, *List*, No. 347.

400. Pl. 134, 'South Gate', 3. On left pillar, facing east, lowest panel.

Text

Vedisakehi daṁtakārehi rupakaṁmaṁ kataṁ

Translation

Carving done by the ivory-workers of Vedisa (*Vidiśā*).

Lüders, *List*, No. 345.

401. Pl. 134, 'South Gate', 4. On the threshold of the Gateway.

There seem to have been at least four lines of which only a few letters remain.

Text

1 . . . . s[i]hakāna
2 . . . . hakasa . . . .
3 . . . . ta dāsa u
4 . . . tari . . . .

Bühler, *Ep. Ind.*, Vol. II, p. 110, No. 123.

(iv) *West Gateway.*

402. Pl. 134, 'West Gate', 1. On right pillar (outside) above the first compartment.

Text[3]

Aya-Cuḍasa atevāsino Balamitrasa dāna thabho

Translation

The gift of a pillar by Balamitra, a pupil of Aya-Cuḍa (*Ārya-Cūḍa*, or *Ārya Kshudra*).

Lüders, *List*, No. 349.

403. Pl. 134, 'West Gate', 2. On left pillar (outside), just below the capital.

Text[4]

Kurar[i]ya-Nāgap[i]yasa Achāvaḍa-seṭhisa putasa ca Saghasa [dānaṁ] thabho[5]

Translation

The gift of a pillar by the Kurariya (native of *Kurara*) Nāgapiya (*Nāgapriya*), the banker of Achāvaḍa and (his) son Sagha (*Saṁgha*).[6]

Lüders, *List*, No. 348.

404. Pl. 134, 'West Gate', 3 *a-b*. On left and right pillars, just below the capital.

Text[7]

3 *a* Pac-ānatariya-kārakāna gat[iṁ] gacheya yo ito Kākaṇāvāto selakame upā[ḍeya] upāḍ[ā]peya vā
3 *b* anaṁ vā ācariya-kulaṁ saṁkāmeyā tase te[8] pātakā bhaveya

Translation

He shall have the fate of the perpetrators of Five Sins (*paṁc-ānaṁtarya*), who dismantles, or causes to be dismantled, the stone-work from this Kākaṇāva, or causes it to be transferred to another church (*Ācariya-kula*); on him shall devolve these well-known (five) sins.[9]

---

[1] According to Hemachandra's *Abhidhānacintāmaṇi*, *āveśana* means *śilpiśālā*, *i.e.*, 'artizan's workshop'.
[2] *Cf.* West Gate, No. 402.
[3] *Cf.* South Gate, No. 399.
[4] *Cf.* East Gate, No. 397.
[5] There is a *swastika* at the end, separating Inscrs. Nos. 403 and 404. The last word is left out by Bühler.
[6] Bühler identifies this Nāgapiya with the Nāgapiya who is also called 'Achāvaḍa seṭhi' in an inscription of Stūpa 2 (No. 660 below). But the latter does not call himself an inhabitant of Kurara like the former, and therefore seems to have been a different individual.—Chanda, *Mem. A. S. I.*, No. 1, p. 7.
[7] *Cf.* Bühler's text (*Ep. Ind.*, Vol. II, p. 396): *thabho Paṁ[cā]nagariyakārakāna [gata] gacheya yo ito Kākaṇāvāto se[la]kame upāde(ya*)* *[upā]dāpeya vā anaṁ vā ācariyakulaṁ saṁkāmeyā tasa te pātakā bhaveyu*, which he translates as :—" A pillar (the gift) of the workmen, inhabitants of Paṁchānagara (?) . . . . . on him, who takes away or causes to be taken away from this Kākaṇāva the stone work or causes it to be transferred to another temple of the teacher, shall fall (*the guilt*) of those mortal sins." The first word *thabho* is the concluding word of Inscription No. 403 above. As will be seen, my transcript and translation differ materially from those of Bühler, who is followed by Lüders (*List*, No. 350) and Chanda (*Mem. A. S. I.*, No. 1, p. 5, n. 1).
[8] Franke suggests that here *te* stands for *ete* (*Z. D. M. G.*, Vol. 50, p. 586).
[9] *Cf.* similar imprecations in East Gateway, No. 396, and North Gateway, No. 389. The 'Five Sins' (*pañc-ānantaryāṇi*) occurs also in the Sāñchī inscription of the Gupta year 93 (No. 833 below). See Fleet, *Corp. Insc. Ind.*, Vol. III, p. 34, n. 3.

(D) PAVEMENT SLABS, Nos. 405-462.

405. Pl. 134, 1.

Text

Sonaturaya dānaṁ

Translation

The gift of Sonaturā (*Svarṇottarā*?).

406. Pl. 134, 2.

Text

. . . . na[sa] [dānaṁ].

407. Pl. 134, 3.

Text

Jitamitaya danaṁ

Translation

The gift of Jitamitā (*Jitamitrā*).
Lüders, *List*, No. 443.

408. Pl. 134, 4.

Text

Utarasa rajukasa dānaṁ

Translation

The gift of the Surveyor Utara (*Uttara*).
Lüders, *List*, No. 416.

409. Pl. 134, 5.

Text

Sihaya[1]

Translation

(The gift) of Sihā (*Siṁhā*).
Lüders, *List*, No. 541.

410. Pl. 134, 6.

Text

Bhaḍuno dana

Translation

The gift of Bhaḍu (*Bhaṇḍu*).

411. Pl. 134, 7.

Text

Bhaḍuno pajāvatiya dānaṁ

Translation

The gift of the wife of Bhaḍu (*Bhaṇḍu*).
Lüders, *List*, No. 493.

412. Pl. 134, 8.

Text

Varuṇasa danaṁ

Translation

The gift of Varuṇa.
Lüders, *List*, No. 508.

413. Pl. 134, 9.

Text

Rat[i]naya Mahisatiya[2] dānaṁ

Translation

The gift of Ratinī from Mahisatī (*Māhishmatī*).
Lüders, *List*, No. 501.

414. Pl. 134, 10.
Defaced. Only . . *ta* . . . *dānaṁ* can be read.

415. Pl. 134, 11.

Text

Uta[rā]ya da(na)

Translation

The gift of Utarā (*Uttarā*).
Lüders, *List*, No. 559.

416. Pl. 134, 12.

Text

Naṁdasa upa[sakasa] [da]na

Translation

The gift of the lay-worshipper Naṁda.

---

[1] There are four groups of symbols around this inscription.

[2] Bühler reads *Māhisatiya*. But the *ā*-stroke does not occur.

417. Pl. 134, 13.

Text

Ka . ni(ya) A(cha)va[ṭa] dānaṁ

Translation

The gift of Ka . . from Achavaṭa.

418. Pl. 134, 14.

Text

sa ka ra . . . sa dana

419. Pl. 134, 15.

Text

Dhanamitāye bhichuniya dāna

Translation

The gift of the nun Dhanamitā (*Dhanamitrā*).

420. Pl. 134, 16.

Text

Bodhiyā dāna

Translation

The gift of Bodhī.

Lüders, *List*, No. 490.

421. Pl. 134, 17.

Text

Dhamapalasa Koragharasa[1] dānaṁ

Translation

The gift of Dhamapala (*Dharmapāla*), of Koraghara.

422. Pl. 134, 18.

Text

Isilāya danaṁ

Translation

The gift of Isilā (*Ṛishilā*).

Cf. No. 423.

423. Pl. 134, 19.

Text

Isilāya [dā]naṁ

Translation

The gift of Isilā (*Ṛishilā*).

Cf. No. 422.

424. Pl. 134, 20.

Only the letter *na*.

425. Pl. 134, 21.

Text

Bha[ti]kasa danaṁ

Translation

The gift of Bhatika (*Bhartṛika*).

426. Pl. 134, 22.

Text[2]

Supatha[ma]ya bhichuniya dāna

Translation

The gift of the nun Supathamā (*Suprathamā?*).

427. Pl. 134, 23.

Two masons' marks.

428. Pl. 134, 24.

Text

Vijugutaya dana

Translation

The gift of Vijugutā (*Vidyudguptā*).

429. Pl. 134, 25.

Text

. . pala[sa] [A]matikasa

Translation

Of . . . . . the Amatika (inhabitant of Amata?).

[1] The text up to the letter *sa* runs from right to left; and the next two letters from left to right. The letter *da* is written upside down.

[2] To the left of the inscription there is a *triratna* symbol.

430. Pl. 134, 26.

Text

Nadutarasa dana

Translation

The gift of Nadutara (*Nandottara*).

431. Pl. 134, 27.

Text

Aya-Magilasa

Translation

(The gift) of Aya-Magila (*Ārya-Magila*).

432. Pl. 134, 28.

Text

Yāsogirino

Translation

(The gift) of Yāsogiri (*Yaśogiri*).

433. Pl. 134, 29.

Text[1]

Cuda-yo[vana]kasa bo[2] silayo

Translation

Two slabs of Cuda (*Kshudra*), the *Yovanaka*, *i.e.*, a Greek(?)[3]

434. Pl. 134, 30.

Text

Tuḍasa savakulasa

Translation

(The gift) of the whole family of Tuḍa (*Tuṇḍa*).

435. Pl. 134, 31.

Text

Cudasa Pulaphasa savakulasa[4]

Translation

(The gift) of the whole family of Cuda (*Kshudra*) of Pulapha.

436. Pl. 134, 32.

Text

Dhamarakhita(sa) [danaṁ]

Translation

The gift of Dhamarakhita (*Dharmarakshita*).

437. Pl. 134, 33.

Text

. . . dana Davaya

Translation

The gift of Davā (*Dravā*) . . .

438. Pl. 134, 34.

Only the letters *rija* are clear.

439. Pl. 134, 35.

Text

Dhamasa dana

Translation

The gift of Dhama (*Dharma*).

440. Pl. 134, 36.

Text

Su . lakasa dana

Translation

The gift of Su laka.

441. Pl. 134, 37.

Text

Pusaya dana

Translation

The gift of Pusā (*Pushyā*).

442. Pl. 134, 38.

Text

Nadisarasa dānaṁ

Translation

The gift of Nadisara (*Nandīśvara*).

443. Pl. 134, 39.

Text

-rikasa danaṁ

444. Pl. 134, 40.

Text

Apa[l]iya[sa] danaṁ

Translation

The gift of Apaliya.

[1] The letters are engraved on two slabs set side by side in the pavement.

[2] *Cf. be* (Sans. *dve*) meaning 'two' in Nāsik Cave inscriptions—*Ep. Ind.*. Vol. VIII, pp. 71, 82.

[3] *Yovanaka* perhaps corresponds to *Yenaka*.

[4] There are a *swastika* and a *triratna* at the end.

445. Pl. 134, 41

Text

Apa[li]yasa dana

Translation

The gift of Apaliya.

446. Pl. 134, 42.

Text

. . puranasa danaṁ.

447. Pl. 134, 43.

Only the letters *dana* can be read.

448. Pl. 134, 44.

Text

Abhayasa kamikasa

Translation

(The gift) of the artizan Abhaya.

449. Pl. 134, 45.

Only the letters *kha* and *da* are legible.

450. Pl. 134, 46.

Text

Bohumula-pitu danaṁ

Translation

The gift of the father of Bohumula (*Bahumūla*).

Lüders, *List*, No. 486.

451. Pl. 134, 47.

Text

Khārukasa danaṁ

Translation

The gift of Khāruka.

452. Pl. 134, 48.

Text

Dhamakasa danaṁ

Translation

The gift of Dhamaka (*Dharmaka*).

453. Pl. 134, 49.

Text

B[u]dhasenikaya dana

Translation

The gift of Budhasenikā (*Buddhasenikā*).

454. Pl. 140, *k*.

Text

Piyapasikasa vaḍhakino dānaṁ

Translation

The gift of the mason Piyapasika (*Priyadarśika*).

455. Pl. 140, *m*.

Text

Dhamayasāsa[1] dana

Translation

The gift of Dhamayasa (*Dharmayaśas*).

456. Pl. 140, *n*.

Text

Anaṭhitasa danaṁ

Translation

The gift of Anaṭhita.

457. Pl. 140, *i*.

Text

Nagaya dana

Translation

The gift of Nagā (*Nāgā*).

458. Pl. 140, *o*.

Text

Yugakasa dana

Translation

The gift of Yugaka (*Yugmaka*).

459. Pl. 140, *l*.

Text

Isidasiya

Translation

(The gift) of Isidasī (*Ṛishidāsī*).

460. Pl. 140, *r*.

Text

Kulalasa dana

Translation

The gift of Kulala (*Kulāla*).

461. Pl. 140, *s*.

Text

Bhadabhutino dana

Translation

The gift of Bhadabhuti (*Bhadrabhūti*).

462. Pl. 140, *p*.

Text

Avāḍhiya Vanija[ya] dana

Translation

The gift of Vanijā of Avāḍhī.

[1] Read -*yasasa*.

(E) BERM BALUSTRADE, Nos. 463-606.

463. Pl. 135, 1.

Text

1 ṭiyā[1] bhikhuni(ya)
2 (dā)naṁ

Translation

The gift of the nun . . . .

464. Pl. 135, 2.

Text

1 Varadatasa dānaṁ
2 bhāgineyanaṁ Datamisāna

Translation

The gift of the Datamisas (*Dattamiśras*), the nephews of Varadata (*Varadatta*).[2]

465. Pl. 135, 3.

Text[3]

1 Nadinagarā Aca[la](ya)
2 bhichuniya dā[naṁ]

Translation

The gift of the nun Acalā from Nadinagara (*Nandinagara*).
Lüders, *List*, No. 462.

466. Pl. 135, 4.

Text

1 Nadinagara Rohaṇide[va]-
2 ya [dā]naṁ

Translation

The gift of Rohaṇidevā (*Rohiṇīdevā*) from Nadinagara (*Nandinagara*).
Lüders, *List*, No. 467.

467. Pl. 135, 5.

Text

1 Hālāya Dakhiṇāji-
2 ya dānaṁ

Translation

The gift of Hālā, the *Dakhiṇāji*.[4]
Lüders, *List*, No. 548.

468. Pl. 135, 6.

Text

1 . . . ke . nito . . . .
2 Nā[ga]siriya dā[naṁ]

Translation

The gift of Nāgasiri (*Nāgaśrī*) . . . .

469. Pl. 135, 7.

Text[5]

1 Bhaḍikasa bhikhuno
2 Kuraghari(ya)-
3 sa danaṁ

Translation

The gift of the monk Bhaḍika of Kuraghara.
Lüders, *List*, No. 491.

470. Pl. 135, 8.

Text

Laghaya(?) . sārapādā dāna

Translation

The gift of Laghā from . sārapāda.

471. Pl. 135, 9.

Text

. . . . ya dānaṁ.

472. Pl. 135, 10.

Text

1 Idadatasa pavarikasa
2 dā[naṁ][6]

Translation

The gift of Idadata (*Indradatta*), a cloak-seller.

473. Pl. 135, 11.

Text

1 . . na . . . .
2 Arahasa dānaṁ

Translation

The gift of Araha (*Arhat*) . . . .

---

[1] The letter before *ṭi* may be *pā* or *sā*.
[2] It probably means that the gift was made by Varadata and his nephews.
[3] For another copy of this inscription, see Stūpa 1, ground balustrade, No. 170.
[4] For *Dakhiṇājiya*, see p. 300 above.
[5] For another inscription of Bhaḍika, see Stūpa 1, ground balustrade, No. 373.
[6] For another copy of this inscription, see Stūpa 1, ground balustrade, No. 131.

474. Pl. 135, 12.

Text

1 Dhaṁmapālasa
2 Ma[hi]pālasa dāna[1]

Translation

The gift of Dhaṁmapāla (*Dharmapāla*) (and) Mahipāla (*Mahīpāla*).

Lüders, *List*, No. 458.

475. Pl. 135, 13.

Text

1 Setapathiyasa
2 Yonasa dānaṁ

Translation

The gift of the Yona (*Yavana*)[2] of Setapatha (*Śvetapotha*).

Lüders, *List*, No. 547.

476. Pl. 135, 14.

Text

1 (Kura)[ghariya] Sevāsiriya
2 dānaṁ

Translation

The gift of Sevāsirī (*Sevāśrī*) of Kuraghara

477. Pl. 135, 15.

Text

. . sa Kuthupadakasa da[na]

Translation

The gift of . . . of Kuthupada.

Lüders, *List*, No. 556.

478. Pl. 135, 16.

Text

1 Baladatāya Cuḍa-[Mo]-[3]
2 ragiriyāya dānaṁ[4]

Translation

The gift of Baladatā (*Baladattā*) of Cuḍamoragiri (*Kshudra-Mayūragiri*).

Lüders, *List*, No. 485.

479. Pl. 135, 17.

Text

1 Samikasa vani[ka]sa
2 putasa ca Si[ha]deva-
3 sa [dā]naṁ

Translation

The gift of the merchant Samika (*Svāmika*) and his son Sihadeva (*Siṁhadeva*).

Lüders, *List*, No. 532.

480. Pl. 135, 18.

Text

1 . . data . . . data .
2 dānaṁ Arahadas[i]ya .
3 . . [Kaṭa]kañuyaka . . . .

Translation

The gift of Arahadasī (*Arhaddāsī*) . . . of Kaṭakañuya. . . .

481. Pl. 135, 19.

Text

. . . ya dānaṁ bhikh[uni]ya dā(naṁ)

Translation

The gift of the nun . . . . gift of . . .

482. Pl. 135, 20.

Text

Vi[jiti]-mātu dānaṁ

Translation

The gift of the mother of Vijiti (*Vijitī*).

483. Pl. 135, 21.

Text

1 Gaḍāya bhichun[i]-
2 ya dānaṁ

Translation

The gift of the nun Gaḍā.

Lüders, *List*, No. 438.

[1] The last two letters are inserted at the right-hand margin between the lines.
[2] *I.e.*, Greek or Persian.
[3] This letter is clear on the stone.
[4] Bühler reads *Cuḍa[pha]lagiriyāya*.

484. Pl. 135, 22.

Text

1 Vajiniya bhikhuniya
2 dānaṁ

Translation

The gift of the nun Vajinī (*Vajriṇī*).
Lüders, *List*, No. 504.

485. Pl. 135, 23.

Text

1 (Na)dinagarato [Ta] . .
2 yā dānaṁ

Translation

The gift of . . from Nadinagara (*Nandinagara*).

486. Pl. 135, 24.

Text

1 [Naṁ]dinagara upāsa-
2 [kasa] Yamaḍasa[1] danaṁ

Translation

The gift of the lay-worshipper Yamaḍa (*Yamala*) from Naṁdinagara.
Lüders, *List*, No. 466.

487. Pl. 135, 25.

Text

1 Vāḍi[vahanā ?] Palāya[2] bhikhu(niya)
2 dānaṁ

Translation

The gift of the nun Palā from Vāḍivahana (?).

488. Pl. 135, 26.

Text

Agidataya . . . .

Translation

(The gift) of Agidatā (*Agnidattā*) . . . .

489. Pl. 135, 27.

Text

1 Budharakhatāya bhikhu(ni)-
2 ya dānaṁ

Translation

The gift of the nun Budharakhatā (*Buddharakshitā*).
Lüders, *List*, No. 489.

490. Pl. 135, 28.

Text

1 . . laya [V]irasa (pajā)-
2 vatiya sapu[t]ā[ya]
3 . . sa . dānaṁ
4 . ka . sakasa

Translation

The gift of . . . the wife of Vira (*Vīra*) together with her son or sons . . . .

491. Pl. 135, 29.

Text

Apakarasa

Translation

(The gift) of Apakara.

492. Pl. 135, 30.

Text

1 Varadatasa pajāvatiya
2 Isalaya dānaṁ

Translation

The gift of Isalā (*Ṛishilā*), the wife of Varadata (*Varadatta*).
Lüders, *List*, No. 506.

493. Pl. 135, 31.

Text

1 . . . raṇakarasa
2 [ja]yāya dānaṁ

Translation

The gift of the wife of . . .

[1] Bühler reads *Yamada(ta)sa*, and is followed by Lüders. *Yamaḍa* for *Yamala* occurs in a Mathurā inscription of Śoḍāsa, *Ep. Ind.*, Vol. IX, p. 247.
[2] May be read also *Hālāya*.

494. Pl. 135, 32.

Only the letters *dānaṁ* are clear.

495. Pl. 135, 33.

Text

1 Vijitasa Kapasika[sa]
2 mātu dānaṁ

Translation

The gift of the mother of Vijita of Kapasi (*Kārpāsī* ?).

496. Pl. 135, 34.

Only the letters . . *chuna* . . are clear.

497. Pl. 135, 35.

Text

1 . . . rad[e]viya R[o]ha[ni]-
2 ya dānaṁ

Translation

The gift of Rohani (*Rohiṇī*) . . . .

498. Pl. 135, 36.

Text

1 Revatimitāya Balaka-
2 sa pājavati[yā dā]naṁ

Translation

The gift of Revatimitā (*Revatīmitrā*), the wife of Balaka.

Lüders, *List*, No. 503.

499. Pl. 135, 37.

Text

1 Damakasa soti-
2 kasa Kusuka-pitu
3 dānaṁ

Translation

The gift of the weaver Damaka, father of Kusuka.

Lüders, *List*, No. 331.

500. Pl. 135, 38.

Text[1]

1 (I)sidatāya Sakadina[sa]
2 pa[jā]vatiye dānaṁ

Translation

The gift of Isidatā (*Ṛishidattā*), wife of Sakadina (*Śakradatta*).

501. Pl. 135, 39.

Text

1 Devadāsiyā [bhi](khu)-
2 niya dānaṁ

Translation

The gift of the nun Devadāsī.

502. Pl. 135, 40.

Text

Nāgada[tā]ya dana[ṁ]

Translation

The gift of Nāgadatā (*Nāgadattā*).

503. Pl. 135, 41.

Text

1 Nad[i]nagarasa Bhutaka-
2 (sa) [d]ānaṁ

Translation

The gift of Bhutaka (*Bhūtaka*) of Nadinagara (*Nandinagara*).

504. Pl. 135, 42.

Text

Tisāsa[2] dānaṁ

Translation

The gift of Tisa (*Tishya*).

Probably Lüders, *List*, No. 447.

505. Pl. 135, 43.

Text

1 . . . taka pa . . . .
2 [dānaṁ] . . . . .

[1] For another copy of this inscription, see Stūpa I, ground balustrade, No. 142.

[2] Read *Tisasa*.

506. Pl. 135, 44.

Text

1 Suriyāya bhikhu-
2 niyā dānaṁ

Translation

The gift of the nun Suriyā (*Sūryā*).
Lüders, *List*, No. 546.

507. Pl. 135, 45.

Text

1 Mahikasa Osena-
2 kasa dānaṁ

Translation

The gift of Mahika (*Mahika*) of Osena.

508. Pl. 135, 46.

Text

1 . . . . . naṁ dānaṁ . . .
2 . . Bali[kasa] dānaṁ

Translation

The gift of . . . . the gift of Balika.

509. Pl. 135, 47.

Text

1 (I)sirakhi[ta]sa . . .
2 . . [dānaṁ]

Translation

The gift of Isirakhita (*Ṛishirakshita*) . . . . .

510. Pl. 135, 48.

Only the last two letters *dānaṁ* can be read.

511. Pl. 135, 49.

Text

1 Naṁd[i]na[garā] Ama[taya][1]
2 dānaṁ

Translation

The gift of Amatā (*Amṛitā*) from Naṁdinagara.
Lüders, *List*, No. 463.

512. Pl. 135, 50.

Text

1 Juṭasa Osena[ka]-
2 sa dānaṁ

Translation

The gift of Juṭa of Osena.

513. Pl. 135, 51.

Text

1 da . gutāya (?) bhikhu .
2 . . . .

Translation

The gift of the nun . . . gutā (*-guptā*).

514. Pl. 135, 52.

Three letters in the middle probably read *-datāya*.

515. Pl. 135, 53.

Text

1 Revatimitāya
2 [dā]naṁ

Translation

The gift of Revatimitā (*Revatīmitrā*).

516. Pl. 135, 54.

Text

1 [I]sirakhi[tā]ya Jitamā-
2 (tu) dānaṁ

Translation

The gift of Isirakhitā (*Ṛishirakshitā*), mother of Jita.

517. Pl. 135, 55.

Text

Korariya [u]pasikaya danaṁ

Translation

The gift of the female lay-worshipper of Korara.

[1] The name seems to be Amatā, and not Amagā as Bühler reads it (*Ep. Ind.*, Vol. II, p. 386, No. 278).

518. Pl. 135, 58.

Text

. . datasa dānaṁ

Translation

The gift of . . data (*-datta*).

519. Pl. 135, 59.

Only the letters *tate* are legible. The last two may be *dānaṁ*.

520. Pl. 135, 60.

Text

1 . . [m]itaya E[jā]vati-
2 (ya dā)na

Translation

The gift of . . mitā (*-mitrā*) of Ejāvati.
Lüders, *List*, No. 554.

521. Pl. 135, 61.

Text

. . . . . [kāya] dānaṁ

522. Pl. 135, 62.

Text

Rohanipadasa [dā](naṁ*)

Translation

The gift of Rohanipada (*Rohiṇīpada*).

523. Pl. 135, 63.

Text

1 Varamitayā [sa]dhiti-
2 kayā[1] [dānaṁ]

Translation

The gift of Varamitā (*Varamitrā*) with her daughter (or daughters).

524. Pl. 135, 64.

Text

Apākānāya dānaṁ

Translation

The gift of Apākānā.
Lüders, *List*, No. 392.

525. Pl. 135, 65.

Text

. . . . tasa bhichuno dā[naṁ]

Translation

The gift of the monk . . . .

526. Pl. 135, 66.

Text

1 Utarāyā Kāpāsigā-
2 matu[2] bhikhuniyā dānaṁ

Translation

The gift of the nun Utarā (*Uttarā*) from Kāpāsī (*Kārpāsī*) village.
Lüders, *List*, No. 515.

527. Pl. 135, 67.

Text

Kaḍa-mātu dānaṁ

Translation

The gift of the mother of Kaḍa.

528. Pl. 135, 68.

Text

1 Kāṇasa bhichuno
2 dānaṁ

Translation

The gift of the monk Kāṇa.
Lüders, *List*, No. 424.

[1] The letter *dhi* is clear on the stone.

[2] Bühler reads *Vipulāya Kāpāsigāmatū* (*Ep. Ind.*, Vol. II, p. 391, No. 332);. But *Utarāya* is clear on the stone; *tū* is evidently a misprint for *tu*.

529. Pl. 135, 69.

Text

1 Selakasa bhāṇa-
2 kasa dānaṁ

Translation

The gift of Selaka, a reciter of text.[1]

530. Pl. 135, 70.

In the estampage only three letters are legible : *Viraya*, 'Of Virā (*Vīrā*)'.

531. Pl. 135, 71.

Text

1 Kurarāya Belaviya bhichuni-
2 ya dānaṁ

Translation

The gift of the nun Belavā of Kurara.

532. Pl. 135, 72.

Text

1 Varadata-dihitu
2 Kānāya dānaṁ

Translation

The gift of Kānā, daughter of Varadata (*Varadatta*).

533. Pl. 135, 73.

Text

1 [Kura]rā[2] Saṁghapāli(tāya)
2 bhikhuniya dā[naṁ]

Translation

The gift of the nun Saṁghapālitā from Kurara. Lüders, *List*, No. 557.

534. Pl. 135, 74.

Text

[Pu]siniya dāna[ṁ]

Translation

The gift of Pusinī (*Pushyiṇī*).

535. Pl. 135, 75.

Text

Kurariya[3] Nāgādināya dānaṁ

Translation

The gift of Nāgādinā (*Nāgadattā*) of Kurara. Lüders, *List*, No. 431.

536. Pl. 135, 76.

Text[4]

1 [Kura]riya Arāhagutā-
2 [ya] dānaṁ

Translation

The gift of Arāhagutā (*Arhadguptā*) of Kurara.

537. Pl. 135, 77.

Text

1 Kurarāya Arahāpāli-
2 taya dānaṁ

Translation

The gift of Arahāpālitā (*Arhatpālitā*) of Kurara.

538. Pl. 135, 78.

Text

. nakā(?)ya Sa . . . dana

539. Pl. 135, 79.

Text

1 [Kā]pāsi-[gā](ma-bhi)
2 (khu)niyā dānaṁ

Translation

The gift of (the nun) of Kāpāsī village.

[1] On the term *bhāṇaka*, see Barua, *Barhut Inscriptions*, p. 9.
[2] Bühler reads only *rā*, but traces of *Kura* seem clear enough.
[3] Bühler reads *Kurarāya*.
[4] Evidently the same as Lüders, No. 435. But Bühler's text is of one line.

540. Pl. 135, 80.

Text[1]

1 [Maḍa]lāchikaṭ[i](kāya)
2 Avisana[ye] [dā]naṁ

Translation

The gift of Avisanā, an inhabitant of Maḍalāchikaṭa.

541. Pl. 135, 81.

Text

1 Sāḍilehi Naḍasakhi[ya][2]
2 upas[i]kaya dānaṁ

Translation

The gift of the female lay-worshipper . . . . .

542. Pl. 135, 82.

Text

Cuḍonā(ga ?) . .

543. Pl. 135, 83.

Text

1 . . [va]hanikāya[3] ya-
2 . . . [ya] bhikhuniya dānaṁ

Translation

The gift of the nun . . . . of [Vāḍi ?]vahana.

544. Pl. 135, 84.

Text

Arahad[ās]i[ya] . . . .[4] [dānaṁ]

Translation

The gift of the . . . . Arahadāsi (*Arhaddāsī*).

545. Pl. 135, 85.

Text

Nāgadatāya dānaṁ

Translation

The gift of Nāgadatā (*Nāgadattā*).

546. Pl. 135, 86.

Text

[ti]ṭhānasa[5] dānaṁ

Translation

The gift of (Pa)tiṭhāna (*Pratishṭhāna*).

547. Pl. 135, 87.

Text

(Sa)mikaya dānaṁ

Translation

The gift of Samikā (*Svāmikā*).

548. Pl. 135, 88.

Text

Sivatiye

Translation

(The gift) of Sivatī.

Lüders, *List*, No. 540.

549. Pl. 135, 89.

Text

1 Varadatasa paj[ā]vatayā
2 Rohāya dānaṁ

Translation

The gift of Rohā, the wife of Varadata (*Varadatta*).

Lüders, *List*, No. 507.

550. Pl. 135, 90.

Text

1 K[u]rar[i]ya Achāvitiya[6]
2 bhikhuniya dānaṁ

Translation

The gift of the nun Achāvitī (*Ṛikshavatī*) of Kurara.

Lüders, *List*, No. 430.

[1] *Cf.* Stūpa 1, ground balustrade, Nos. 304, 305.
[2] The reading of this line is uncertain.
[3] Probably a remnant of *Vāḍivahanikāya*.
[4] Probably *bhichuniya* has to be supplied. *Cf.* Lüders, No. 333.
[5] Restore *Patiṭhānasa*.
[6] The letter *vi* was omitted at first and inserted later. Bühler reads *Achāvatiya* (*Ep. Ind.*, Vol. II, p. 382, No. 244).

551. Pl. 135, 91.

Text

1 Kurar[ā]ya Saghārakhitāyā
2 [bhi]khuniya dānaṁ

Translation

The gift of the nun Saghārakhitā (*Saṁgharakshitā*) of Kurara

Lüders, *List*, No. 434.

552. Pl. 135, 92.

Text

Visākharakhitasa dānaṁ

Translation

The gift of Visākharakhita (*Viśākharakshita*).
Lüders, *List*, No. 517.

553.

Text

. . . jiratā (?) mātu . . . .

554. Pl. 135, 94.

Text

. . ra . dināyā . .[1]

555. Pl. 135, 95.

Text

Budharakhitaya sa . . .

Translation

(The gift) of Budharakhitā (*Buddharakshitā*) . . .

556. Pl. 135, 96.

Text

1 Sa[phi]nayāya . . .
2 Ara[hāya ?] dānaṁ

Translation

The gift of Arahā(?), a Saphinayā . . .

557. Pl. 135, 97.

Text

Balagutasa dānaṁ

Translation

The gift of Balaguta (*Balagupta*).
Lüders, *List*, No. 564.

558. Pl. 135, 98.

Text

. . . . dānaṁ Kora . . . .

Translation

The gift of . . . . from Kora(ra).

559. Pl. 135, 99.

Text

Kurarāya Sātilāyā danaṁ

Translation

The gift of Sātilā of Kurara.

560. Pl. 135, 100.

Text

1 Kurariya Kaṇ[ā]ya bhichuniya
2 dānaṁ

Translation

The gift of the nun Kaṇā of Kurara.
Cf. No. 561

561. Pl. 135, 101.

Text

1 Kurarāye K[ā]ṇāya bhichuni-
2 ya dānaṁ

Translation

The gift of the nun Kāṇā of Kurara.
Cf. No. 560.

562. Pl. 135, 102.

Text

1 Kuraraya Dhamase-
2 [na]ya bhikhuniya
3 dānaṁ

Translation

The gift of the nun Dhamasenā (*Ḋharmasenā*) of Kurara.
Cf. No. 564.[2]

[1] Probably *Arahadināyā*, *i.e.*, 'of Arahadinā (*Arhaddattā*)'.

[2] For another inscription of a Dharmasenā from Kurara, see Stūpa 2, ground balustrade, No. 664.

563. Pl. 135, 103.

Text

[Ku]rarā[ya] Siride[vi]ya dānaṁ

Translation

The gift of Siridevī (*Śrīdevī*) of Kurara.

564. Pl. 135, 104.

Text

1 Kurariya Dhamasenāya bhikhu-
2 niya dānaṁ

Translation

The gift of the nun Dhamasenā (*Dharmasenā*) of Kurara.

Cf. No. 562.

565. Pl. 135, 105.

Text

1 Varadata-bhāgineyi-Dā-
2 belāya danaṁ

Translation

The gift of Dābelā, the niece of Varadata (*Varadatta*).

566. Pl. 135, 106.

Text

Sujātāye

Translation

(The gift) of Sujātā.

567. Pl. 135, 107.

Text

Achāvāṭa Cirāti-matu dānaṁ

Translation

The gift of the mother of Cirātī (*Kirātī*) from Achāvāṭa.

Lüders, *List*, No. 388.

568. Pl. 135, 108.

Text

Ujeniye Asvarakhitāye dānaṁ

Translation

The gift of Asvarakhitā (*Aśvarakshitā*) from Ujenī (*Ujjayinī*).

Lüders, *List*, No. 405.

569. Pl. 135, 109.

Text

1 Suriyaya Budhadevaya Pematika-
2 ya dānaṁ

Translation

The gift of Suriyā (*Sūryā*) (and) Budhadevā (*Buddhadevā*), an inhabitant of Pemata.

Lüders, *List*, No. 545.

570. Pl. 135, 110.

Text

. . Bharaṇāya bha . . .

Translation

. . . . of Bharaṇā . . .

571. Pl. 135, 111.

Text

Ujeniyā Mita-mātu dānaṁ

Translation

The gift of the mother of Mita (*Mitra*) from Ujenī (*Ujjayinī*).

572. Pl. 135, 112.

Text

Samikasa Aya-Nagasa atevasino dānaṁ

Translation

The gift of Samika (*Svāmika*), the pupil of Aya-Nāga (*Ārya-Nāga*).

Lüders, *List*, No. 531.

573. Pl. 135, 113.

Text

Samikasa Cuḍa-Moragi[ri] . . . .

Translation

(The gift) of Samika (*Svāmika*) of Cuḍa-Moragiri (*Kshudra-Mayūragiri*).

574. Pl. 135, 114.

Text

. . . tāya bhichuniye

Translation

(The gift) of the nun . . . .

575. Pl. 135, 115.

Text

Katakañuyā Dha . . . .

Translation

(The gift) of . . . from Kaṭakañuya.
Lüders, *List*, No. 421.

576. Pl. 135, 116.

Text

Dhamagirino ca Dhamasenasa ca dā[naṁ]

Translation

The gift of Dhamagiri (*Dharmagiri*) and Dhamasena (*Dharmasena*).
Lüders, *List*, No. 456.

577. Pl. 135, 117.

Text

. . ra[yā] dānaṁ

578. Pl 135, 118.

Text

Kasapasa bhichuno Vejasa dānaṁ

Translation

The gift of the monk Kasapa (*Kāśyapa*) of Veja.

579. Pl. 135, 119.

Text

Kurarāya Vala . . .

Translation

(The gift) of Vala . . of Kurara.

580. Pl. 135, 120.

Text

[1](Sā)midatasa bhichuno dānaṁ

Translation

The gift of the monk (Sā)midata (*Svāmidatta*).
Lüders, *List*, No. 535.

581. Pl. 135, 121.

Text

. . . [sa] dānaṁ

582. Pl. 135, 122.

Text

Kapāsi . . .

Translation

. . . . (from) Kapāsi.

583. Pl. 135, 123.

Text

. . . ḍasa dānaṁ sa-pajāvatikasa

Translation

The gift of . . . together with his wife.
Lüders, *List*, No. 555.

584. Pl. 135, 124.

Text

. . . [Ka]ṭa[ka]ñ[u]ya[sa] . .

Translation

(The gift) of . . . . of Kaṭakañuya.

585. Pl. 135, 125.

Text

Tākārāpadā Saṁgharakhitasa dānaṁ

Translation

The gift of Saṁgharakhita (*Saṁgharakshita*) from Tākārāpada.
Lüders, *List*, No. 444. *Cf.* No. 606 below.

586. Pl. 135, 126.

Text

Nadina(gara) . . . .

Translation

. . . . . from Nadina(gara), *i.e.*, Nandinagara.

[1] A portion of the stone has broken off from here.

587. Pl. 135, 127.

Text

U[jeni]kaya Balikayā . . .

Translation

(The gift) of Balikā of Ujenī (*Ujjayinī*).

588. Pl. 135, 128.

Text

Valikasa bhichuno dānaṁ

Translation

The gift of the monk Valika.

589. Pl. 135, 129.

Text

Manoramasa vaḍakino O.[1] . . .

Translation

(The gift) of the mason Manorama . . .

Lüders, *List*, No. 495.

590. Pl. 135, 130.

Text

Ujeniya . . .

Translation

. . . . from Ujenī (*Ujjayinī*).

591. Pl. 135, 131.

Text

Ujeniye Mitaye bhichu[ni](ya) . .

Translation

(The gift) of the nun Mitā (*Mitrā*) from Ujenī (*Ujjayinī*).

Lüders, *List*, No. 412.

592. Pl. 135, 132.

Text

Puruviḍā Disāgiriputānaṁ dā(na.

Translation

The gift of the sons of Disāgiri from Puruviḍa.

Lüders, *List*, No. 475.

593. Pl. 135, 133.

Text

Achavaṭā[2] Nadiṇiyā dāna

Translation

The gift of Nadinī (*Naṁdinī*) from Achavaṭa.

Lüders, *List*, No. 494.

594. Pl. 135, 134.

Text

1 Isinadanasa dānaṁ
2 Puñavaḍhaniyasa

Translation

The gift of Isinadana (*Ṛishinandana*) of Puñavaḍhana (*Puṇyavardhana*).

Lüders, *List*, No. 403.

595. Pl. 135, 135.

Text

1 Samikayā bhikhuni-
2 ya dānaṁ

Translation

The gift of the nun Samikā (*Svāmikā*).

Lüders, *List*, No. 533.

596. Pl. 135, 136.

Text

1 Dhamadinasa
2 dānaṁ

Translation

The gift of Dhamadina (*Dharmadatta*).

[1] It may be a part of the word *Osenakasa*, *i.e.*, 'of an inhabitant of Osena.'

[2] Bühler reads *Machavaṭā* (*Ep. Ind.*, Vol. II, p. 389, No. 310).

597. Pl. 135, 137.

Text

1 Varadatasa dānaṁ
2 bhagini[yā] Vara[s]enāya
3 dānaṁ

Translation

The gift of Varadata (*Varadatta*) (and) gift of his sister Varasenā.

Lüders, *List*, No. 505.

598. Pl. 135, 138.

Text

1 Vitirinahiya[1] Mahi-
2 rakhitasa danaṁ

Translation

The gift of Mahirakhita (*Mahīrakshita*) from Viṭirinahā[2].

Lüders, *List*, No. 514.

599. Pl. 136, 139.

Text

1 Rebilasa Nadinagārakasa
2 dānaṁ

Translation

The gift of Rebila, an inhabitant of Nadinagara (*Nandinagara*).

Lüders, *List*, No. 502.

600. Pl. 136, 140.

Text

1 Nadinagar[ā][3] Utaradataya
2 dānaṁ

Translation

The gift of Utaradatā (*Uttaradattā*) from Nadinagara (*Nandinagara*).

Lüders, *List*, No. 464.

601. Pl. 136, 141.

Text[4]

1 Nādinagara Kāboja-
2 sa bhichuno dānaṁ

Translation

The gift of the monk Kāboja (*Kāmboja*) from Nadinagara (*Nandinagara*).

Lüders, *List*, No. 472.

602. Pl. 136, 142.

Text

1 Kurarāya Pusa[da](tāya)
2 dānaṁ

Translation

The gift of Pusadatā (*Pushyadattā*) of Kurara.

603. Pl. 136, 143.

Text[5]

1 Dhamutarasa
2 kulasa danaṁ

Translation

The gift of the family of Dhamutara (*Dharmottara*).

Lüders, *List*, No. 461.

604. Pl. 136, 144.

Text

maka[sa]

605. Pl. 136, 145.

Text

Ujeniye Revāye dānaṁ

Translation

The gift of Revā from Ujeni (*Ujjayinī*).

606. Pl. 136, 146.

Text

T[ā]kāripādā Saṁ[gha] . . . .

Translation

(The gift) of Saṁgha(rakhita) (*Saṁgharakshita*) from Tākāripāda.

---

[1] The first letter looks like *Vi*.
[2] There is a superfluous *na* on the top of the first *na*.
[4] For another copy of this inscription see stairway balustrade, No. 626 below.
[3] For this word *cf*. *Vitiriñahaya* in Lüders, No. 513 (p. 362, xiii, *infra*).
[5] There is another copy of the inscription, Stūpa 1, ground balustrade, No. 169.
[6] *Cf*. No. 585 above, and restore *Saṁgharakhitasa*.

(F) HARMIKĀ BALUSTRADE, Nos. 607-610.

607. Pl. 136, 'Harmikā', 1.

Pā va na sa ti dhi ya . .

608. Pl. 136, 'Harmikā', 2.

Text

Nagadatasa dānaṁ Patiṭhanā

Translation

The gift of Nagadata (*Nāgadatta*) from Patiṭhana (*Pratishṭhāna*).

609. Pl. 136, 'Harmikā', 3

Text

Ujeniye Vasulāye dānaṁ

Translation

The gift of Vasulā from Ujenī (*Ujjayinī*).
Lüders, *List*, No. 413.

610. Pl. 136, 'Harmikā', 4.

Text

ye . saya na nada yā
Ayas[iy]e dānaṁ

Translation

The gift of Ayasi(?) . . . . . .

(G) STAIRWAY BALUSTRADE, Nos. 611-630.

611. Pl. 136, 'Stairway', 1.

Text

1 Kāḍaya[1] Subhagāya Pusāya Nāgadatasa Sagharakhitasa Koragharānaṁ[2]
2 dānaṁ[3]

Translation

The gift of Kāḍā, Subhagā, Pusā (*Pushyā*), Nāgadata (*Nāgadatta*) (and) Sagharakhita (*Saṁgharakshita*), of Kuraghara.[4]
Lüders, *List*, No. 558.

612. Pl. 136, 'Stairway', 2.

Text

Vāḍivahanā Chaḍikasa bhichuno dānaṁ

Translation

The gift of the monk Chaḍika from Vāḍivahana.
Lüders, *List*, No. 380.

613. Pl. 136, 'Stairway', 3.

Text

Tākāripadā Nadag[i]r[i] . . .

Translation

(The gift of) Nadagiri (*Nandagiri*) from Tākāripada.

614. Pl. 136, 'Stairway', 4.

Text

[Si]rigutāya bhich[un]iyā dānaṁ

Translation

The gift of the nun Sirigutā (*Śrīguptā*).

615. Pl. 136, 'Stairway', 5.

Text

Anurādhasa Goṇadā bhich[u]no [dānaṁ]

Translation

The gift of Anurādha, the monk from Goṇada (*Gonarda*).

616. Pl. 136, 'Stairway', 6.

Text

bha . . upā[s]ikaye dānaṁ

Translation

The gift of the female lay-worshipper . . . .

617. Pl. 136, 'Stairway', 7.

Text[5]

. nara . . . ṇadā bhichuno dā[naṁ]

Translation

The gift of the monk (Anurādha) from (Goṇada).

[1] This word is not read by Bühler (*Ep. Ind.*, Vol. II, p. 396, No. 375).
[2] The letter *naṁ* is written above. Probably the engraver made a correction here. Bühler reads *Koragharakānāṁ*.
[3] This word is carried over to the top of line 1.
[4] Nāgadata and Sagharakhita of Kuraghara appear together also in inscription x below (p. 362).
[5] Probably another copy of No. 615 above.

618. Pl. 136, 'Stairway', 8.

Text

1 . . . t[o][1] Arahagutasa
2 (dānaṁ)

Translation

The gift of Arahaguta (*Arhadgupta*) from (Kurara).

619. Pl. 136, 'Stairway', 9.

Text

1 Korarasa Datakasa
2 [bh]ichuno dānaṁ

Translation

The gift of Dataka (*Dattaka*), a monk of Kurara.

620. Pl. 136, 'Stairway', 10.

Text

Kurarā[t]o Arahagutasa dānaṁ

Translation

The gift of Arahaguta (*Arhadgupta*) from Kurara.

Lüders, *List*, No. 428.

621. Pl. 136, 'Stairway', 11.

Text

. . gutāya bhichuniya dānaṁ

Translation

The gift of the nun . . . . -gutā (*-guptā*)

622. Pl. 136, 'Stairway', 12.

Text

1 Nadinagarikaya [Pusa ?]-
2 [2] siriya bhichuni-
3 ya dānaṁ

Translation

The gift of the nun (Pusa ?)sirī (*Pushyaśrī ?*), an inhabitant of Nadinagara (*Nandinagara*).

623. Pl. 136, 'Stairway', 13.

Text

1 [Nadinagarā] Araha[ya]
2 bhich[u]niya dānaṁ

Translation

The gift of the nun Arahā (*Arhā*) from Nadinagara (*Nandinagara*).

624. Pl. 136, 'Stairway', 14.

Text

Devagutāya bhichuniya dāna

Translation

The gift of the nun Devagutā (*Devaguptā*).

625. Pl. 136, 'Stairway', 15.

Text

[Saṁ]gh[āya] Dāsaka-mātu dāna

Translation

The gift of Saṁghā, the mother of Dāsaka (*Darśaka*).

Lüders, *List*, No. 528.

626. Pl. 136, 'Stairway', 16.

Text

1 Dhamu(tarasa)
2 kulasa da[naṁ]

Translation

The gift of the family of Dhamutara (*Dharmottara*).

Cf. No. 603 (berm balustrade) above, which is identical in text.

627. Pl. 136, 'Stairway', 17.

Text

V[i]rāye dānaṁ

Translation

The gift of Virā (*Vīrā*).

628. Pl. 136, 'Stairway', 18.

Text

[Ā]ṭhakanagarasa[3] Gagaṁdatasa[4] bhikhuno dānaṁ

Translation

The gift of the monk Gagaṁdata (*Gaṁgadatta*), an inhabitant of Aṭhakanagara (*Ashṭaka-nagara*).

Lüders, *List*, No. 390.

629. Pl. 136, 'Stairway', 19.

Text

Visākhasa

Translation

(The gift) of Visākha (*Viśākha*).

630. Pl. 136, 'Stairway', 20.

Text

Soṇasiriye

Translation

(The gift) of Soṇasirī (*Svarṇaśrī*).

[1] Supply *Kurarāto*. *Cf.* No. 620 below. Probably identical with Lüders, No. 429.
[2] The *sa* is a subsequent insertion.
[3] There is a *triratna* symbol before *si*.
[4] Correct reading probably *Gaṁgadatasa*.

APPENDIX

Nos. i-xv. Some Inscriptions published by Bühler but not included in the foregoing Section.[1]

i. *Dhamarakhitasa bhichuno dānaṁ*, 'the gift of the monk Dhamarakhita (*Dharmarakshita*).'—Lüders, *List*, No. 180.

ii. . . *sa bhichuno dānaṁ Aya-Bhaṁḍukiyasa*, 'the gift of the monk . . . ., pupil of Aya-Bhaṁḍuka.'—Lüders, *List*, No. 386.

iii. *Aja[rā]niya dānaṁ*, 'the gift of Ajarāni'.—Lüders, *List*, No. 389.

iv. *Asabhaye Ujenikāye bhichuniye dāna*, 'the gift of the nun Asabhā (*Ṛishabhā*), an inhabitant of Ujenī (*Ujjayinī*).'—Lüders, *List*, No. 400.

v. *Ejāvatiya u[pā]sikānā* . . , '(the gift) of the female lay-worshippers from Ejāvatī.'—Lüders, *List*, No. 417.

vi. 1 *[Ku]raghariya S[āti]siriya*

2 *(bhi)khuni(ya dānaṁ)*

'(The gift) of the nun Sātisirī, an inhabitant of Kuraghara (*Kuraragṛiha*).'—Lüders, *List*, No. 427.

vii. *Kura[ri]ya [Ara]hadināya dānaṁ*, 'the gift of Arahadinā (*Arhaddattā*), an inhabitant of Kurara.'—Lüders, *List*, No. 436.

viii. 1 *Dhamarakhitasa*

2 . *rakarakasa dānaṁ*.

'The gift of Dhamarakhita (*Dharmarakshita*) . . . .'—Lüders, *List*, No. 459.

ix. *Naṁdinagara [Utara]mitaya dānaṁ*, 'the gift of Utaramitā (*Uttaramitrā*) from Naṁdinagara.'—Lüders, *List*, No. 465.

x. 1 *Nāgadatasa Sagharakhitasa ca Koragharānaṁ*

2 *dānaṁ*.[2]

'The gift of Nāgadata (*Nāgadatta*) and Sagharakhita (*Saṁgharakshita*), inhabitants of Kuraghara (*Kuraragṛiha*).'—Lüders, *List*, No. 469.

xi. *Budharakhitasa [dānaṁ]*, 'the gift of Budharakhita (*Buddharakshita*).'—Lüders, *List*, No. 487.

xii. 1 *[Va]sumitaya bhi-*

2 *chuniya [dānaṁ]*

3 *Ujenikaya*

'The gift of the nun Vasumitā (*Vasumitrā*), inhabitant of Ujenī (*Ujjayinī*).'—Lüders, *List*, No. 509.

xiii. 1 *[Vi]tiriñahaya Bhuta-*

2 *rakhitasa danam*

'The gift of Bhutarakhita (*Bhūtarakshita*) from Vitiriñahā.'—Lüders, *List*, No. 513.

xiv. *Sakarakhitasa danaṁ*, 'the gift of Sakarakhita (*Śakrarakshita*).'—Lüders, *List*, No. 525.

xv. *Siriyā bhichuniyā dānaṁ*, 'the gift of the nun Sirī (*Śrī*).'—Lüders, *List*, No. 539.

[1] Mere fragments or doubtful pieces have not been taken into account.

[2] "The inscription has to be read from below."—*Ep. Ind.*, Vol. II, p. 386, n. 76.

Section 2. Nos. 631-719. Inscriptions of Stūpa 2.

(A) GROUND BALUSTRADE, Nos. 631-695.

Screen of the Northern Entrance.

631. Pl. 136, 1. On a coping stone (outside).

Text

Budharakhitasa sutātikasa Arapānakasa danaṁ

Translation

The gift of Budharakhita (*Buddharakshita*), who is versed in the *suttantas*, of Arapāna.

Lüders, *List*, No. 635.

632. Pl. 136, 2. On a coping stone (inside).

Text

Nāgilasa dānaṁ Ayasa aṁtevasino

Translation

The gift of Nāgila, the pupil of Aya (*Ārya*).

Lüders, *List*, No. 569.

North-East Quadrant.

633. Pl. 136, 3. On a cross-bar (inside).

Text

1 Dhamarakhitasa sejhasa Ku-
2 ḍasa dānaṁ

Translation

The gift of Kuḍa, the pupil of Dhamarakhita (*Dharmarakshita*).

Lüders, *List*, No. 570.

634. Pl. 136, 4. On a coping stone (inside).

Text

Pusarakhitasa dānaṁ Ayasa atevāsino

Translation

The gift of Pusarakhita (*Pushyarakshita*), the pupil of Aya (*Ārya*).

Lüders, *List*, No. 612.

635. Pl. 136, 5. On a rail-pillar (inside).

Text

Pāḍukulikāya gāmasa dānaṁ

Translation

The gift of the village Pāḍukulikā (*Pāṇḍukulikā*).

Lüders, *List*, No. 571.

636. Pl. 136, 6. On a coping stone (inside).

Text

Budhilasa Bhogavaḍhanakasa dānaṁ

Translation

The gift of Budhila (*Buddhila*) of Bhogavaḍhana (*Bhogavardhana*).

Lüders, *List*, No. 572.

637. Pl. 136, 7. On a rail-pillar (inside).

Text

[Dha]madevaya dānaṁ[1] Mitasiriya atevasiniyā

Translation

The gift of Dhamadevā (*Dharmadevā*), a female pupil of Mitasirī (*Mitraśrī*).

Lüders, *List*, No. 573.

638. Pl. 136, 8. On a rail-pillar (inside).

Text

1 Sumanasa bhikhuno
2 dānaṁ

Translation

The gift of the monk Sumana (*Sumanas*).

Lüders, *List*, No. 614.

639. Pl. 136, 9. On a rail-pillar (outside).

Text

kuḍakasa dānaṁ

[1] Actually *danaṁ* in the original.

640. Pl. 136, 10. On a rail-pillar (outside).

Text

1 Sagharakhitasa bhichuno dānaṁ Korara-
2 sa

Translation

The gift of Sagharakhita (*Saṁgharakshita*), a monk of Kurara.

Lüders, *List*, No. 608.

641 Pl. 136, 11. On a cross-bar (inside).

Text

Bhichunikāya dānaṁ

Translation

The gift of Bhichunikā (*Bhikshuṇikā*).

Lüders, *List*, No. 641.

642. Pl. 136, 12. On a rail-pillar (inside).

Text

Cuḍamoragirino gāmasa dānaṁ

Translation

The gift of the village Cuḍamoragiri (*Kshudra-Mayūragiri*).[1]

Lüders, *List*, No. 625.

643. Pl. 136, 13. On a rail-pillar (inside).

Text

. . . dānaṁ Morayahikaṭiyasa

Translation

The gift of . . . . . an inhabitant of Morayahikaṭa.

Lüders, *List*, No. 626.

644. Pl. 136, 14. On a rail-pillar (outside).

Text

. vi . kalasa bhichuno dānaṁ

Translation

The gift of the monk . . . .

645. Pl. 136, 15. On a rail-pillar (inside).

Text

1 Dhamara[khitā]ya . . . . .
2 dānaṁ Korami[kaya ate]vāsininā

Translation

The gift of Dhamarakhitā (*Dharmarakshitā*) . . . the female pupils of Koramikā.[2]

Lüders, *List*, No. 648.

646. Pl. 136, 16. On a rail-pillar (inside).

Text

Isilasa bhikhuno dānaṁ

Translation

The gift of the monk Isila (*Ṛishila*).

Lüders, *List*, No. 574.

647. Pl. 136, 17. On a rail-pillar (inside).

Text

Sagham[i]tasa bhikhuno dānaṁ

Translation

The gift of the monk Saghamita (*Saṁghamitra*).

Lüders, *List*, No. 575.

648. Pl. 136, 18. On a rail-pillar (inside).

Text

[Āvesi]kiṇasa bhichuno dānaṁ

Translation

The gift of the monk Āvesikiṇa.

Probably Lüders, *List*, No. 649.

649. Pl. 136, 19. On a coping stone (inside).

Text

Budhapālitasa seṭhino Paḍukulikiyasa danaṁ

Translation

The gift of the banker Budhapālita (*Buddhapālita*), an inhabitant of Paḍukulikā (*Pāṇḍukulikā*).

Lüders, *List*, No. 576.

[1] Bühler reads *Cuṁ[va]-* for *Cuḍa-*, but suggests the possibility of the latter, *Ep. Ind.*, Vol. II, p. 399, n. 11. The reading *Cuṁvamoragiri* (?) is given by Lüders.

[2] There seem to have been names of two pupils here; Bühler reads (*Ep. Ind.*, Vol. II, p. 402, No. 73) *atevāsiniyā*. For *Koramikā*, *cf.* Inscription No. 85 above.

650. Pl. 136, 20. On a rail-pillar (outside).

Text

Budhagutasa Udubaraghariyasa [dānaṁ]

Translation

The gift of Budhaguta (*Buddhagupta*) of Udubaraghara (*Udumbaragṛiha*).

Lüders, *List*, No. 634.

651. Pl. 136, 21. On a cross-bar (outside).

Text

Kasapiya danaṁ

Translation

The gift of Kasapī (*Kāśyapī*).

652. Pl. 136, 22. On a rail-pillar (outside).

Text

[Ro]haṇikasa Udubaraghariyasa dānaṁ

Translation

The gift of Rohaṇika of Udubaraghara (*Udumbaragṛiha*).

Lüders, *List*, No. 609.

Screen of the Eastern Entrance.

653. Pl. 136, 24. On a rail-pillar (inside).

Text

1 . . kasa bhikhuno mātu Koḍāya
2 . . [y]ā dānaṁ

Translation

The gift of Koḍā, mother of the monk . . . .

Lüders, *List*, No. 647.

South-East Quadrant.

654. Pl. 136, 25. On a rail-pillar to the left of the Eastern Entrance.

Text

Ayasa Pokhareyakasa dānaṁ

Translation

The gift of Aya (*Ārya*), an inhabitant of Pokhara (*Pushkara*).

Lüders, *List*, No. 617.

655. Pl. 136, 26. On a cross-bar (inside).

Text

1 . . . . bhikhuno
2 Budharakhitasa Anaṁmitakasa dānaṁ

Translation

The gift of the monk Budharakhita (*Buddharakshita*) . . of Anaṁmita.

Lüders, *List*, No 578.

656. Pl. 136, 27. On a rail-pillar (inside).

Text

Vijhasa bhikhuno dānaṁ[1]

Translation

The gift of the monk Vijha (*Vindhya*).

Lüders, *List*, No. 579.

657. Pl. 136, 28. On a rail-pillar (inside).

Text

Yakhilasa bhichuno dānaṁ

Translation

The gift of the monk Yakhila (*Yakshila*).

Lüders, *List*, No. 580.

658. Pl. 136, 30. On a rail-pillar (inside).

Text

Visākhasa Pāḍā[ni]yasa

Translation

(The gift of) Visākha (*Viśākha*) of Pāḍāna.

Lüders, *List*, No. 616.

659. Pl. 136, 31. On a cross-bar (inside).

Text[2]

1 Ājanāvā Āvāsikasa
2 dānaṁ

Translation

The gift of Āvāsika from Ājanāva.

[1] Actually *dānāṁ* in the original.

[2] There is another copy of this inscription, *viz.*, Stūpa 2, berm balustrade, No. 718 below.

660. Pl. 136, 32. On a rail-pillar (inside).

Text

1 Nāgapiyasa Ach[ā]va[ḍa]-
2 sa seṭhisa dānaṁ

Translation

The gift of Nāgapiya (*Nāgapriya*), the banker of Achāvaḍa.

Lüders, *List*, No. 581.

661. Pl. 136, 33. On a cross-bar (inside).

Text

Dhamagutasa Pusiniyā ca dānaṁ

Translation

The gift of Dhamaguta (*Dharmagupta*) and Pusinī (*Pushyiṇī*).

Lüders, *List*, No. 615.

662. Pl. 136, 34. On a rail-pillar (inside).

Text

1 Sapakiya Korariya dānaṁ
2 bhikhuniya

Translation

The gift of the nun Sapakī (*Sarpakī*), a Korarī (an inhabitant of *Kurara*).

Lüders, *List*, No. 582.

663. Pl. 136, 35. On a cross-bar (inside).

Text

1 Valiya Korariye bhikhu-
2 niye dānaṁ

Translation

The gift of the nun Valī, a Korarī (an inhabitant of *Kurara*).

Lüders, *List*, No. 583.

664. Pl. 136, 36. On a rail-pillar (inside).

Text[1]

1 Dhamasenaya Korariya dāna bhikhuni-
2 ya

Translation

The gift of the nun Dhamasenā (*Dharmasenā*), a Korarī (an inhabitant of *Kurara*).

Lüders, *List*, No. 584.

665. Pl. 136, 37. On a rail-pillar (inside).

Text

Nāgapālitaya dānaṁ thabho

Translation

The gift of a pillar by Nāgapālitā.

Lüders, *List*, No. 585.

666. Pl. 136, 38. On a cross-bar (inside).

Text

Sihāya dāna

Translation

The gift of Sihā (*Siṁhā*).

Lüders, *List*, No. 613.

667. Pl. 136, 39. On a cross-bar (inside).

Text

Utaradatā[ya] . ḍiyā dih[i]tu dānaṁ

Translation

The gift of Utaradatā (*Uttaradattā*), daughter of . . .

668. Pl. 136, 40. On a cross-bar (inside).

Text

Phagulāya bhikhuniyā dāna

Translation

The gift of the nun Phagulā (*Phalgulā*).

Lüders, *List*, No. 586.

[1] For another inscription of the nun Dhamasenā from Kurara, see Stūpa 1, No. 562.

Screen of the Southern Entrance.

669. Pl. 137, 66. On a rail-pillar (inside).

Text

. . datasa Anaṁmitakasa dānaṁ bhikhuno

Translation

The gift of the monk . . -data (. . -*datta*), an inhabitant of Anaṁmita.[1]

South-West Quadrant.

670. Pl. 136, 41. On a rail-pillar to the left of the Entrance.

Text

Nādutarāya dānaṁ

Translation

The gift of Nādutarā (*Nandottarā*).

671. Pl. 137, 64. On a rail-pillar (inside).

Text

1 [Ba]lakasa ayasa Arahagutasa Sāsā-
2 dakasa atevasino dānaṁ

Translation

The gift of Balaka, the pupil of the Reverend Arahaguta (*Ārya-Arhadgupta*), an inhabitant of Sasāda.

Lüders, *List*, No. 587. *Cf.* Stūpa 1, 310, which is an inscription of Arahaguta himself.

672. Pl. 137, 65. On a rail-pillar (inside).

Text

(Dha)marakhitāyā bhikhuniyā dana

Translation

The gift of the nun Dhamarakhitā (*Dharmarakshitā*).

673. Pl. 136, 42. On a rail-pillar (inside).

Text

Mulāyā dāna thabho Gaḍāya atevāsiniyā

Translation

The gift of a pillar by Mulā (*Mūlā*), the female pupil of Gaḍā.

Lüders, *List*, No. 589.

674. Pl. 136, 43. On a rail-pillar (inside).

Text

1 Sagharakhitāya mātu . . kaḍikāya
2 Isidāsiyā bhichuniyā dānaṁ

Translation

The gift of the nun Isidāsī (*Ṛishidāsī*) from . . . . . . mother of Sagharakhitā (*Saṁgharakshitā*).

Lüders, *List*, No. 590.

675. Pl. 136, 44. On a coping stone (inside).

Text

Ayasa Budharakhitasa Pokhareyakasa dānaṁ

Translation

The gift of the Reverend Budharakhita (*Ārya-Buddharakshita*), an inhabitant of Pokhara (*Pushkara*).

Lüders, *List*, No. 591.

676. Pl. 136, 45. On a rail-pillar (inside), to the right of the Entrance.

Text

1 Viṇhukāye Vā-
2 ḍivahanikāye[2]
3 dānaṁ

Translation

The gift of Viṇhukā (*Vishṇukā*), an inhabitant of Vāḍivahana.

Lüders, *List*, No. 592.

[1] Another inscription from Stūpa 2 (No. 655 above) mentions *Anaṁmita*.

[2] Bühler reads : *Viṇhikāye Vāḍyavahanikāye.* The letter *ḍi* seems to have been put in after erasing a *ya*.

Screen of the Western Entrance.

677. Pl. 136, 46. On a coping stone (inside).

Text

. . . . [bhikhu]no dānaṁ

Translation

The gift of the monk . . . .

678. Pl. 136, 47. On a rail-pillar (inside).

Text

Seḍiya[1] bhikhuniya thabho dānaṁ

Translation

The gift of a pillar by the nun Seḍī.

Lüders, *List*, No. 611.

679. Pl. 1-6, 48. On a coping stone (inside).

Text

Sidakaḍā Tikisasa dānaṁ

Translation

The gift of Tikisa from Sidakaḍa.

Lüders, *List*, No. 594.

North-West Quadrant.

680. Pl. 136, 49. On a rail-pillar to the left of the Entrance.

Text

Avisenāyā dānaṁ

Translation

The gift of Avisenā.

681. Pl. 136, 50. On a coping stone (inside).

Text

. . ya Sidakaḍiyā dānaṁ

Translation

The gift of . . . ya of Sidakaḍa.

Lüders, *List*, No. 595.

682. Pl. 136, 51. On a coping stone (inside).

Text

S(i*)dakaḍiyāya Golāya dānaṁ

Translation

The gift of Golā of Sidakaḍa.

Lüders, *List*, No. 596.

683. Pl. 136, 52. On a coping stone (inside).

Text

Budhapālitā(ya*) Sidakaḍiyāya dānaṁ

Translation

The gift of Budhapālitā (*Buddhapālitā*) of Sidakaḍa.

Lüders, *List*, No. 597.

684. Pl. 137, 53. On a rail-pillar (inside).

Text

Saghamitasa Sonadakasa dānaṁ

Translation

The gift of Saghamita (*Saṁghamitra*) of Sonada.

Lüders, *List*, No. 598.

685. Pl. 137, 54. On a coping stone (inside).

Text

Budhagutāya Sedakaḍiya danaṁ

Translation

The gift of Budhagutā (*Buddhaguptā*) of Sedakaḍa.

Lüders, *List*, No. 599.

[1] Bühler reads *Oḍiya*.

686. Pl. 137, 55. On a coping stone (inside).

Text

Agilasa dānaṁ Adhaporikasa

Translation

The gift of Agila (*Agnila*), an inhabitant of Adhapura (*Ardhapura*).[1]

Lüders, *List*, No. 600.

687. Pl. 137, 56. On a coping stone (inside).

Text[2]

Bhūta[gu]taya Sagareyikāya Dhamadata-sunhusāya dānaṁ

Translation

The gift of Bhūtagutā (*Bhūtaguptā*), an inhabitant of Sagarī, daughter-in-law of Dhamadata (*Dharmadatta*).

Lüders, *List*, No. 646.

688. Pl. 137, 57. On a rail-pillar (inside).

Text

Yasogirino dānaṁ bhichuno

Translation

The gift of the monk Yasogiri (*Yaśogiri*).

Lüders, *List*, No. 601.

689. Pl. 137, 58. On a rail-pillar (inside).

Text

Bahulasa danaṁ

Translation

The gift of Bahula.

Lüders, *List*, No. 603.

690. Pl. 137, 59. On a cross-bar (inside).

Text

Gaḍāya Nādināgarikāya

Translation

(The gift) of Gaḍā, an inhabitant of Nadinagara (*Nandinagara*).

Lüders, *List*, No. 604.

691. Pl. 137, 60. On a coping stone (inside).

Text

Arahakasa bhichuno bhāṇakasa dānaṁ

Translation

The gift of the monk Arahaka (*Arhatka*), the preacher.

Lüders, *List*, No. 602.

692. Pl. 137, 61. On a rail-pillar (inside).

Text

Idāgi[data]sa dānaṁ

Translation

The gift of Idāgidata (*Indrāgnidatta*).

Lüders, *List*, No. 605.[3]

693. Pl. 137, 62. On a rail-pillar (inside).

Text

Aya-Naṁdukasa bhikhuna dānaṁ

Translation

The gift of the Reverend (*Ārya*) monk Naṁduka.

Lüders, *List*, No. 606.

694. Pl. 137, 63. On a coping stone (inside).

Text

Nāgarakhitasa bhichuno Pokhareyakasa dānaṁ

Translation

The gift of the monk Nāgarakhita (*Nāgarakshita*), an inhabitant of Pokhara (*Pushkara*).

Lüders, *List*, No. 607.

695. Pl. 140 *j*. On a cross-bar (inside).

Text

Aya-Kapilasa dānaṁ

Translation

The gift of Aya-Kapila (*Ārya-Kapila*).

[1] It may also stand for *Adhaḥpura*.

[2] Bühler reads : - - - *taya Sagireyikāya Dhama* - - [*saka*]*saya dānaṁ*.—*Ep. Ind.*, Vol. II, p. 402, No. 71.

[3] Lüders gives only the first three letters of the name.

(B) PAVEMENT SLABS, BERM AND STAIRWAY BALUSTRADES, Nos. 696-719.

696. Pl. 137, 'Pavement Slab', 1.

Text

. . . ye dānaṁ

697. Pl. 137, 'Pavement Slab', 2.

Text

Arahakasa Pāthūpaka[sa ?]sa dānaṁ

Translation

The gift of Arahaka (*Arhatka*) of Pāthūpaka(sa).

698. Pl. 137, 'Pavement Slab', 3.

Text

. . niyā dānaṁ

699. Pl. 137, 'Stairway Step', 1.

Text[1]

. . . . . . [2]Sāphineyikaya . .

Translation

. . . . . . a Sāphineyikā .

700. Pl. 137, 'Stairway Step', 2.

Text

Gotamiyā bhi[chu](niya) . .

Translation

(The gift) of the nun Gotamī (*Gautamī*).
Probably same as Lüders, *List*, No. 623.

701. Pl. 137, 'Stairway Rail', 1.

Text

Muḍaka-matu dānaṁ

Translation

The gift of the mother of Muḍaka (*Muṇḍaka*).

702. Pl. 137, 'Berm Rail', 1.

Text

Gaṁdhārasa bhikhun[o] dānaṁ

Translation

The gift of the monk Gaṁdhāra.
Lüders, *List*, No. 622.

703. Pl. 137, 'Berm Rail', 2.

Text

1 Asad[e]vāya bhikhuniya dānaṁ
2 Nadinagarā

Translation

The gift of the nun Asadevā (*Aśvadevā*) from Nadinagara (*Nandinagara*).
Probably same as Lüders, *List*, No. 618. *Cf*. No. 714 below.

704. Pl. 137, 'Berm Rail', 3.

Text

1 Aya-Paḍaniya Ava[m]u
2 ya dānaṁ

Translation

The gift of Avamu . . , the (female pupil) of Aya-Paḍana.

705. Pl. 137, 'Berm Rail', 4.

Text

Asagutaya Dhavadevaya dana

Translation

The gift of Asagutā (*Aśvaguptā*) (and) Dhavadevā.
Lüders, *List*, No. 653; Chanda, *Sāñchī Catalogue*, p. 12.

[1] Is it identical with Lüders, No. 644?

[2] There seems to be a trace of *tu* before *sā*, in which case the missing word may be *matu*.

706. Pl. 137, 'Berm Rail', 5.

Text

1 Budharakhitaya bhichuni[ya]
2 dana

Translation

The gift of the nun Budharakhitā (*Buddharakshitā*).

Lüders, *List*, No. 637; Chanda, *Sāñchī Catalogue*, p. 12.

707. Pl. 137, 'Berm Rail', 6.

Text

Si[d]akasa upāsakasa dānaṁ

Translation

The gift of the lay-worshipper Sidaka (*Siddhaka*).

708. Pl. 137, 'Berm Rail', 7.

Text

Isidataya bhikhuniya dana

Translation

The gift of the nun Isidatā (*Ṛishidattā*).

Lüders, *List*, No. 620; Chanda, *Sāñchī Catalogue*, p. 12.

709. Pl. 137, 'Berm Rail', 8.

Text

Palasa bhikhuno dana

Translation

The gift of the monk Pala.

Lüders, *List*, No. 632.

710. Pl. 137, 'Berm Rail', 9

Text

1 Para . . . .
2 Nagasenasa seṭhino da[na]

Translation

The gift of the banker Nagasena (*Nāgasena*) from . . . . . .

Chanda, *Sāñchī Catalogue*, p. 27.

711. Pl. 137, 'Berm Rail', 10.

Text

Idadatasa upāsakasa dana

Translation

The gift of the lay-worshipper Idadata (*Indradatta*).

Lüders, *List*, No. 621; Chanda, *Sāñchī Catalogue*, p. 27.

712. Pl. 137, 'Berm Rail', 11.

Text

. . nikaya[1] . . . . .

713. Pl. 137, 'Berm Rail', 12.

Text

Ciratiya bhichuniya dānaṁ

Translation

The gift of the nun Ciratī (*Kirātī*).

Lüders, *List*, No. 624; Chanda, *Sāñchī Catalogue*, p. 11.

714. Pl. 137, 'Berm Rail', 13.

Text

1 Nadinagarā
2 Asadavaya bhikhu(ni*)ya dana

Translation

The gift of the nun Asadevā (*Aśvadevā*) from Nadinagara (*Nandinagara*).

Lüders, *List*, No. 629; Chanda, *Sāñchī Catalogue*, p. 11. *Cf.* No. 703 above.

715. Pl. 137, 'Berm Rail', 14.

Text

1 Visakasa Rohanipadiyasa
2 dana

Translation

The gift of Visaka (*Viśvaka*) of Rohanipada.

Lüders, *List*, No. 643; Chanda, *Sāñchī Catalogue*, p. 27.

[1] Nothing more can be made out from the facsimile.

716. Pl. 137, 'Berm Rail', 15.

Text

1 Badhakasa Kurarasa bhichu-
2 [no] dānaṁ

Translation

The gift of the monk Badhaka (*Buddhaka*) of Kurara.

Lüders, *List*, No. 633.

717. Pl. 137, 'Berm Rail', 16.

Text

Patiṭhanasa

Translation

(The gift of) Patiṭhana (*Pratishṭhāna*).

Lüders, *List*, No. 474 ; Chanda, *Sāñchī Catalogue*, p. 11.

718. Pl. 137, 'Berm Rail', 17.

Text[1]

1 Ājanāvā Āvāsi-
2 kasa dana

Translation

The gift of Āvāsika from Ājanāva.

Lüders, *List*, No. 619 ; Chanda, *Sāñchī Catalogue*, p. 27.

719. On 'Berm Rail'.[2]

Text

(Si)harakhitasa bhichuno dāna

Translation

The gift of the monk (Si)harakhita (*Siṁharakshita*).

[1] There is another copy of this inscription, *viz.*, Stūpa 2, ground balustrade, No. 659 above.

[2] Not reproduced in the Plates.

APPENDIX.

Nos. xvi-xxi. Some Inscriptions published by Bühler but not included in the foregoing Section.[1]

xvi. 1 *Dhamaraṣiriya*[2] *upasika-*

2 *ya dana.*

'The gift of the female lay-worshipper Dhamarasirī (*Dharmaśrī*).'—Lüders, *List.* No. 627.

xvii. [*Dha*]*masenasa bhikhuno dana,*[3] 'the gift of the monk Dhamasena (*Dharmasena*).'—Lüders, *List*, No. 628.

xviii. *Naṁ*[*du*]*kasa bhichuno dana,* 'the gift of the monk Naṁduka.'—Lüders, *List*, No. 631.

xix. *Bha*[*ra*]*ṇabhūtino bhikhuno dānaṁ,* 'the gift of the monk Bharaṇabhūti.'—Lüders, *List*, No. 640.

xx. *Vipulasa bhi*[*khu*]*no* [*dā*]*naṁ,* 'the gift of the monk Vipula.'—Lüders, *List*, No. 642.

xxi. *Soṇasiriya bhikhuniya dānaṁ,* 'the gift of the nun Soṇasirī (*Suvarṇaśrī*).'—Lüders, *List*, No. 645.

[1] Mere fragments or doubtful pieces have not been taken into account.

[2] Probably to be corrected as *Dhamasiriya.*

[3] "All the letters are much blurred, and the first is not certain."—*Ep. Ind.*, Vol. II, p. 400, n. 13.

Section 3. Nos. 720-735. Inscriptions of Stūpa 3.[1]

720. Pl. 137, 3. On a berm balustrade pillar.

Text[2]

1 Nadinagarā
2 [i]mitaya bhikh[u]naya dana

Translation

The gift of the nun . . mitā (. . *mitrā*) from Nadinagara (*Nandinagara*).

721. Pl. 137, 4. On a pillar of the stairway balustrade.

Text

. . . sa mātu dānaṁ

Translation

The gift of the mother of . . .

722. Pl. 137, 5. On a pillar of the stairway balustrade.

Text

1 Kurarāto Arahagutasa
2 dāna

Translation

The gift of Arahaguta (*Arhadgupta*) from Kurara.

723. Pl. 137, 6. On a pillar of the stairway balustrade.

Text

1 [Ku]rarato Ga . . .
2 dānaṁ

Translation

The gift of Ga . . . from Kurara.

724. Pl. 137, 7. On a pillar of the ground balustrade.

Text

Bhikh[u]niyā Valāyā dānaṁ thabho

Translation

The gift of a pillar by the nun Valā.

725. Pl. 137, 8. On a pillar of the ground balustrade.

Text

[ni]to[3] Tāpasiyānaṁ Pusiniyā dānaṁ

Translation

The gift of Pusinī (*Pushyiṇī*) of the Tāpasiyas of (Ujenī).

726. Pl. 137, 9-10. On a cross-bar of the ground balustrade.

Text

1 [A]laṇasa bhikhuno dā[naṁ]
2 Mūlasa bhikhuno dānaṁ

Translation

The gift of the monk Alaṇa. The gift of the monk Mūla.

727. Pl. 137, 11. On a cross-bar of the ground balustrade.

Text

Dhaṁmaṁdāsasa dānaṁ

Translation

The gift of Dhaṁmaṁdāsa (*Dharmadāsa*). *Sāñchī Cat.*, p. 10, No. 71.

728 Pl. 137, 12. On a cross-bar of the ground balustrade.

Text

Seḍāya mātu pava[ji][4] . . . .

Translation

(The gift) of the mother of Seḍā, a nun . . .

729. Pl. 137, 13 On a cross-bar of the ground balustrade.

Text

Paḍikāya dānaṁ

Translation

The gift of Paḍikā.

[1] Inscrs. Nos. 720-733 are illustrated in the lower half of Pl. 137 marked as 'Stūpa III'.
[2] This seems to be identical with Lüders, *List*, No. 630, which is included by Bühler in inscriptions from Stūpa 2.—*Ep. Ind.*, Vol. II, p. 400, No. 54.
[3] Restore *Ujenito*. [4] Restore *pavajitaya*.

730. Pl. 137, 14. On a cross-bar of the ground balustrade.

Text

Isimitasa bhikhuno dānaṁ

Translation

The gift of the monk Isimita (*Rishimitra*).

731. Pl. 137, 15. On a cross-bar of the ground balustrade.

Text

Saṁghāya [bh]ikhuniyā dānaṁ

Translation

The gift of the nun Saṁghā.

732. Pl. 137, 16. On a cross-bar of the ground balustrade.

Text

Dhamagirisa bhikhuno Perikupasa dānaṁ

Translation

The gift of the monk Dhamagiri (*Dharmagiri*) of Perikupa.

Sāñchī Cat., p. 9, No. 70.

733. Pl. 137, 17. On a cross-bar of the ground balustrade.

Text

Dhamadināya bhikhuniyā dānaṁ

Translation

The gift of the nun Dhamadinā (*Dharmadattā*).

734. Pl. 140, 9. On a cross-bar of the ground balustrade.

Text

1 Vepakasa Sidharasa dihitu
2 Bhūtikāya dana[ṁ] sūci

Translation

The gift of a cross-bar by Bhūtikā, daughter of Sidhara (*Śrīdhara*), an inhabitant of Vepa.

735. On a cross-bar of the ground balustrade

Text[1]

S[o]ṇamitraya mātu dānaṁ

Translation

The gift of the mother of Soṇamitrā (*Suvarṇamitrā*).

[1] It is not reproduced in the Plates. The text is given by Chanda in a printed note dated 13th March, 1919, submitted to the Director General of Archæology. A fragment of it containing the letters *Soṇamitraya* was found by me in 1931 in the godowns of the Sāñchī Museum. The characters are similar to those of the other inscriptions occurring on the ground balustrade of Sāñchī.

Section 4. Nos. 736-827. Additional Inscriptions from the Stūpas, Temples and Monasteries[1].

(A) PAVEMENT SLABS, Nos. 736-775.

736. Pl. 134, 1. From Stūpa 1.

Text

Naṁdasa

Translation

(The gift) of Naṁda.

737. Pl. 134, 2. From Stūpa 1.

Text

Koraghariyā upāsikāya silā

Translation

The (pavement) slab of the female lay-worshipper of Kuraghara.

738. Pl. 134, 3. From Stūpa 1.

Text

. . . maya Nādināgarikāya bhichuniya . . . .

Translation

(The gift) of the nun . . . an inhabitant of Nadinagara (*Nandinagara*).

739. Pl. 134, 4. From Stūpa 1.

Text

Vedisikāya[2] bhikhuniya Ga . .

Translation

(The gift) of the nun . . . of Vedisa (*Vidiśā*).

Sāñchī Cat., p. 8, No. 55.

740. Pl. 134, 5. From Temple 40.

Text

Ājimuditāye

Translation

(The gift) of Ājimuditā.

Sāñchī, Cat., p. 8, No. 56.

741. Pl. 134, 6. From Temple 40.

Only two letters [*si*]*lā*, 'the slab'.

742. Pl. 134, 7. From Temple 40.

Text

Kurariya Sirikāya . . .

Translation

(The gift) of Sirikā (*Śrīkā*) of Kurara.

Sāñchī Cat., p. 8, No. 57.

743. Pl. 134, 8. From Temple 40.

Only two letters *vāḍa*.

744. Pl. 134, 9. From Temple 40.

Only three letters *tasa* [*da*].

745. Pl. 134, 11. From Temple 40.

Text

. . . lasa dānaṁ

746. Pl. 134, 12. From Temple 40.

Only the letter *ya*.

747. Pl. 134, 13. From Temple 40.

Only the letter *ya*.

748. Pl. 134, 14. From near Stūpa 5.

Traces of *se* and two other letters.

749. Pl. 134, 15. From near Monastery 36.

Text

Viṇhumitasa [dā](naṁ)

Translation

The gift of Viṇhumita (*Vishṇumitra*).

Sāñchī Cat., p. 7, No. 48.

[1] The majority of these kept in the Sāñchī Museum and its godowns are isolated fragments. The findspots of some of the pieces are not known.

[2] The letters *di*, *si* are clumsily written.

750. Pl. 134, 16. From near Monastery 36.

Only two letters . . *yamā* . . .

751. Pl. 134, 17. From Monastery 38.

Text

. . . . putasa bhichuno [dā](naṁ)

Translation

The gift of the monk . . . . . son of . . . .

Sāñchī Cat., p. 7, No. 50.

752. Pl. 134, 18.

Only . . . [*s*]*ikāya Ka* . . .

753. Pl. 134, 19. From Monastery 43.

Text

. . . sa bh[i]chuno dānaṁ

Translation

The gift of the monk . . . . .

Sāñchī Cat., p. 8, No. 54.

754. Pl. 134, 20.

Only two letters . . . (*bhi*)*chuni* . . .

755. Pl. 134, 21.

Text

. . . . . kaya bhichuniya . . .

Translation

Of the nun . . .

756. Pl. 134, 22. From Temple 40.

Text

. . . . (Nadi)nāgarikā[ya] dānaṁ

Translation

The gift of . . . . an inhabitant of Nadinagara (*Nandinagara*).

Sāñchī Cat., p. 8, No. 60.

757. Pl. 134, 23.

Only two letters . . *daka* . .

758. Pl. 134, 24.

Text

1 . . . . kaya . . . . .
2 . . . [ma]tasa Arahadi(na) . . .

Translation

(The gift) of Arahadi(na) . . .

Sāñchī Cat., p. 8, No. 53.

759. Pl. 134, 25. From a stūpa near Stūpa 2.

Text

. . . . dataya ca bhi[ch]uniya daṇā [1]

Translation

The gift of the nun . . . . and . . .

760. Pl. 134, 26.

Text

. . . . ya u[pāsika] . . . .

Translation

(The gift) of the female lay-worshipper . . . . .

761. Pl. 134, 27.

Only two letters . . . . *isa* [2] . . .

762. Pl. 134, 28.

Text

. . . . [u]pāsakasa sa-pajāvatikasa sa[puta]kasa dā[naṁ]

Translation

The gift of the lay-worshipper . . . . together with his wife and sons (or son).

763. Pl. 134, 29.

Text

. . . dava[ya] dānaṁ

Translation

The gift of . . .

[1] Read *dānaṁ*.

[2] The missing name is probably *Isila*.

764. Pl. 134, 30.

Text

Naṁduta[rasa] Toba(vanikasa)

Translation

The gift of Naṁdutara (*Nandottara*), an inhabitant of Tuba(vana).

765. Pl. 134, 31.

Text

. . . . [sa] dānaṁ

Translation

The gift of . . . .

766. Pl. 134, 32.

Text

Bodhi . . .

767. Pl. 134, 33.

Text

Koraghariyā Rohaniyā bhichuni[ya]

Translation

(The gift) of the nun Rohanī (*Rohiṇī*), of Kuraghara.

768. Pl. 134, 34.

Text

1 [Kora]riyā Mitasiriyā
2 . . . . [dānaṁ]

Translation

The gift of Mitasirī (*Mitraśrī*), of Kurara.

769. Pl. 134, 35.

Text

. . . takasa bhātu . . .

Translation

(The gift of) the brother of . . .
Sāñchī Cat., p. 8, No. 52.

770. Pl. 136, 36.

Text

. . . . matu Bhādāsiriya dānaṁ

Translation

The gift of Bhādāsirī (*Bhadraśrī*), mother of . . . . .
Sāñchī Cat., p. 7, No. 49.

771. Pl. 136, 37.

Text

[Ro ?]hanipada [Va] . . . .[1]

Translation

. . . . from [Ro ?]hanipada.

772. Pl. 136, 38.

Text

1 Kapi[la] . . .
2 Budharakhitasa dā(naṁ)

Translation

The gift of Budharakhita (*Buddharakshita*) . . Kapila.

773. Pl. 136, 39.

Text

Dhamakasa

Translation

(The gift) of Dhamaka (*Dharmaka*).
Sāñchī Cat., p. 8, No. 58.

774. Pl. 136, 40.

Text

Māḍukasa dā[naṁ]

Translation

The gift of Māḍuka (*Māṇḍuka*).

775. Pl. 136, 41. From Temple 31, north-east of the Main Terrace.

Text

Devagiriputana dāna

Translation

The gift of the sons of Devagiri.

[1] Chanda reads: *Nehanipada va* . . . . (*Sāñchī Cat.*, p. 7, No. 51). See the first letter in facsimile. It may be an attempt to write *Rohanipada*.

(B) TEMPLE PILLARS, BALUSTRADE FRAGMENTS AND MISCELLANEOUS, Nos. 776-827.

776. Pl. 138, 1. On a pillar of Temple 40.

Text

1 Kaṁṭakañ[uya]kā[naṁ] [u]pā-
2 sakānaṁ d[ā]naṁ

Translation

The gift of the lay-worshippers of Kaṁṭakañuya.
Sāñchī Cat., p. 9, No. 65.

777. Pl. 138, 2. On a pillar of Temple 40.

Text

1 . . . . yasa
2 . . . . . . sa Araha-
3 . . . (bhikhu)no dānaṁ

Translation

The gift of (the monk) Araha . . . .

778. Pl. 138, 3. On a pillar of Temple 40.

Text

1 Mārasa Vesa-
2 datasa dānaṁ

Translation

The gift of Māra (and ?) Vesadata (*Viśvadatta*).
Sāñchī Cat., p. 9, No. 64.

779. Pl. 138, 4. On a pillar of Temple 40.

Text

1 . . . . . lara
2 . . . . . . sa

780. Pl. 138, 5. On a pillar of Temple 40.

Text

1 Ujeniyā bhi(khu)-
2 nina pasa(da)

Translation

(The building) of the nuns of Ujenī (*Ujjayinī*).

781. Pl. 138, 6. On a pillar of Temple 40.

Text

1 . . . māto
2 . . . rakhitasa

782. Pl. 138, 7. On a pillar of Temple 40.

Text

1 Tāpas[i]ya Uje(niya)
2 bhichuniyā (dānaṁ)

Translation

(The gift) of Tāpasī, the nun of Ujenī (*Ujjayinī*).

783. Pl. 138, 8. On a pillar of Temple 40.

Text

1 piḍha . . .
2 thaṁ[bho]

Translation

The pillar . . . .

784. Pl. 138, 9. On a pillar of Temple 40.

Text

1 (tha)bho dānaṁ
2 . . . khasa

Translation

The gift of a pillar . . .

785. Pl. 138, 10. On a pillar of Temple 40.

Text

. . . dāna [tha]bho

Translation

. . . . the gift of a pillar.
Sāñchī Cat., p. 9, No. 62.

786. Pl. 138, 11. On a pillar of Temple 40.

Text

Idadatāya bhi[chu]niyā dānaṁ

Translation

The gift of the nun Idadatā (*Indradattā*).

787. Pl. 138, 12. On a pillar of Temple 40.

Text

1 U[je]niyā . . . .
2 dāna

Translation

The gift of . . . . of Ujenī (*Ujjayinī*).
Sāñchī Cat., p. 9, No. 67.

788. Pl. 138, 13. On a pillar of Temple 40.

Text

1 Salibhu-putasa Bahu-
2 lasa dānaṁ

Translation

The gift of Bahula, son of Salibhu.

789. Pl. 138, 14. On a pillar of Temple 40.

Text

1 Tākāripad[ā]
2 Samikasa dānaṁ

Translation

The gift of Samika (*Svāmika*) from Tākāripada.
Sāñchī Cat., p. 9, No. 68.

790. Pl. 138, 15. On a pillar of Temple 40.

Text[1]

Data-[Ka]lavāḍasa dānaṁ

Translation

The gift of Data (*Datta*)-Kalavāḍa.
Sāñchī Cat., p. 10, No. 77.

791. Pl. 138, 16. On a rail-pillar. From Stūpa 1.

Text

Upāsikāya Himarakhitāya dānaṁ

Translation

The gift of the female lay-worshipper Himarakhitā (*Himarakshitā*).
Sāñchī Cat., p. 8, No. 61.

792. Pl. 138, 17. On a pillar.

Text

. . . . bhichu . . . .

793. Pl. 138, 18. On a pillar of Temple 40.

Text

1 Aboda Barāyasikha-
2 naṁ[2] dānaṁ goṭiyaṁ du thaṁ-
3 bho

Translation

Two pillars, being the gift of the Committee (*goshṭhī*) of the Barāyasikhas from Aboda (*Arbuda*).
Sāñchī Cat., p. 9, No. 66.

794. Pl. 138, 19. On a pillar of Temple 40.

Text

. . . . ma[ṇa]k[u]ṭi . . .

795. Pl. 138, 20. On a pillar of Temple 40.
Only three letters . . . . *vahekā* . . .

796. Pl. 138, 21. On a pillar.
Only three letters . . . *Sihara* . . .
Sāñchī Cat., p. 9, No. 63.

797. Pl. 138, 22. On a pillar of Temple 40.

Text

1 . . . . dhana[mu]
2 . . [k]ulasa dānaṁ

Translation

The gift of the family of . . . .
Sāñchī Cat., p. 9, No. 69.

798. Pl. 138, 23. On a pillar of Temple 40.

Text

. . . tagutasa dā[naṁ]

Translation

The gift of . . . . .

[1] *Cf.* Nos. 353-355, which are inscriptions of a Data-Kalavāḍa from Vidiśā.

[2] Chanda reads *sa* for *naṁ*.

799. Pl. 138, 24. On a rail-pillar. From Stūpa 1.

Text

Araha[d]ā . . . .

Translation

(The gift of) Arahadā(sa ?).

800. Pl. 138, 25. On a pillar of Temple 40.

Text

[S]ihanadasa dā[naṁ]

Translation

The gift of Sihanada (*Siṁhanāda*).

801. Pl. 138, 26. On a pillar of stairway balustrade.

Text

1 Sonadeviye
2 dā[naṁ]

Translation

The gift of Sonadevī (*Svarṇadevī*).
Sāñchī Cat., p. 29, No. A. 75.

802. Pl. 138, 27. On a pillar.

Text

. . . . vasa Kaṭakañu . . . .

Translation

. . . . . from Kaṭakañuya . .
Sāñchī Cat., p. 28, No. A. 72.

803. Pl. 138, 28. On a rail-pillar from berm of Stūpa 2.

Text

1 [Ka]ṇ[ha]lasa[1] bhichuno dāna[ṁ]
2 [A]yasa Nakhatanāmasa
3 [a]tevāsino

Translation

The gift of the monk Kaṇhala (*Kṛishṇala*), the pupil of the Aya (*Ārya*) named Nakhata (*Nakshatra*).

804. Pls. 104*e* and 138, 29. On a pillar.

Text

1 Vasumitasa bhaya[y]e
2 Poṭhi[niy]ā . . .

Translation

(The gift) of Poṭhinī, wife of Vasumita (*Vasumitra*).
Sāñchī Cat., p. 28, No. A. 71 and Pl. VII.

805. Pl. 138, 30. On a sandstone bowl. From near Stūpa 1.

Text

bha[gā]ya pasādo

Translation

The offering for distribution.[2]
Sāñchī Cat., p. 37, No. B. 1 and Pl. XIV.

806. Pl. 138, 31. On berm balustrade. From Stūpa 1.

Text

1 Jālāya Soṇayā . . . .
2 kāya atevāsiniyā
3 dānaṁ

Translation

The gift of Jālā, the female pupil of Soṇā (*Svarṇā*). . .

807. Pl. 138, 32. On a pillar.

Text

Arahadā[si]yā dāna

Translation

The gift of Arahadāsī (*Arhaddāsī*).
Sāñchī Cat., p. 29, No. A. 74.

808. Pl. 138, 33.

Text

(Ro)[ha]ṇimitāya dānaṁ

Translation

The gift of (Ro)haṇimitā (*Rohiṇīmitrā*).

---

[1] Chanda reads *Nakulasa* (*Sāñchī Cat.*, p. 12, No. 114).
[2] It seems to have reference to the food offered in the bowl. Chanda translates the passage as : "For the distribution of food (offered at the shrine)".

809. Pl. 138, 34.

Text

1 Isikasa bhikhuno Vāchipu-
2 tasa dānaṁ

Translation

The gift of the monk Isika (*Ṛishika*), a Vāchiputa (*Vātsīputra*).

810. Pl. 138, 35. From Temple 40.

Text

1 Kurarāya . . .
2 dānaṁ

Translation

The gift of . . . of Kurara.

811. Pl. 138, 36.

Text

1 . . . tasa dānaṁ
2 . . . . na

812. Pl. 138, 37. On a rail-pillar from berm of Stūpa 2.

Text

1 . . . bhikhuniya
2 . . . Kurarāya

Translation

. . . of the nun . . . of Kurara.
Sāñchī Cat., p. 12, No. 115.

813. Pl. 138, 38.

Text

1 . . . [Ku]ra[gha][1] . . .
2 . . sa ma[t]u dā[na]ṁ

Translation

The gift of the mother of . . . . of Kuraghara.

814. Pl. 138, 39.

Text

1 [Ku]rarāto Ara[ha] . . .
2 dānaṁ

Translation

The gift of Araha . . from Kurara.

815. Pl. 138, 40.

Text

[I]sade[vasa] dānaṁ

Translation

The gift of [I]sadeva (*Īśadeva*).

816. Pl. 138, 42

Text

[2]Asāḍa[sa] . . . .

Translation

(The gift) of Asāḍa (*Āshāḍha*).

817. Pl. 138, 43.

Text

1 Saghadinasa
2 . . nikasa[3] dānaṁ

Translation

The gift of Saghadina (*Saṁghadatta*).

818. Pl. 138, 44.

Text[4]

. . . [bhikhuni]yā dānaṁ

819. Pl. 138, 45. On a rail-pillar from berm of Stūpa 2.

Text

Dhutasa[5]

Translation

(The gift) of Dhuta (*Dhūrta*).

[1] The middle bar of *ka* is traceable on the estampage.
[2] There is a *svastika* at the beginning.
[3] Probably remnant of Ujenikasa.
[4] Tentative reading.
[5] The inscription is between two *triratna* symbols.

820. Pl. 138, 46. From Stūpa 2.

Text

Budharakhitasa bhikhuno dāna[ṁ]

Translation

The gift of the monk Budharakhita (*Buddharakshita*).

Lüders, *List*, No. 638.

821. Pl. 138, 47. On berm balustrade. From Stūpa 2.

Text

jadatasa dānaṁ

Sāñchī Cat., p. 12, No. 113.

822. Pl. 138, 48. From Temple 40.

Text

Kaṇhamitrasa dānaṁ[1]

Translation

The gift of Kaṇhamitra (*Kṛishṇamitra*).

Sāñchī Cat., p. 29, No. A. 78.

823. Pl. 138, 49. From Stūpa 5.

Text

1 Mulāya bhikhuni-
2 yā dānaṁ[2]

Translation

The gift of the nun Mulā (*Mūlā*).

Sāñchī Cat., p. 29, No. A. 77.

824. Pl. 138, 50. On a coping stone. From Kachi-Kanakhera, near Sāñchī.

Text

Vāsiṭhiputasa Kusumakasa dānaṁ

Translation

The gift of Vāsiṭhiputa (*Vāsishṭhīputra*) Kusumaka.

Sāñchī Cat., p. 13, No. 127.

825. Pl. 138, 51. On a coping stone. From Kachi-Kanakhera, near Sāñchī.

Text

Raño Suhaḍadatasa Kosagharikasa . .

Translation

(The gift) of the *rājan* Suhaḍadata (*Subhaṭadatta*), the Kosagharika (an inhabitant of *Kuśagṛiha*).

Sāñchī Cat., p. 13, No. 126.

826. On a pillar of Temple 40.

Text[3]

Vedisā Re . . . . (Na)ṁdutarā[yā]

Translation

(The gift) of Naṁdutarā (*Nandottarā*) . . . . from Vedisa (*Vidiśā*).

827. On a pillar of Temple 40.

Text[3]

Pokharā Isi . . .

Translation

(The gift of) Isi . . (*Ṛishi* . .), from Pokhara (*Pushkara*).

[1] Chanda reads *yo* after *dānaṁ*. There are certain marks below *dānaṁ*, which seem to have been scratched by later hands.
[2] The marks after *dānaṁ* seem to have been inserted by later hands.
[3] Not reproduced in the Plates.

CHAPTER XXII

INSCRIPTIONS OF THE KUSHĀN, GUPTA AND LATER PERIODS

No. 828 Inscription of the Reign of Vāsashka, the year 28

THIS inscription is incised on the pedestal of a Bodhisattva image of buff-coloured sandstone, which is now in the Sāñchī Museum (Pl. 124 *b*). It has been edited already by several scholars,[1] the latest readings being those of Vogel[2] and Chanda.[3]

It is in Brāhmī characters of the Kushān period and refers itself to the reign of the *Rājātirāja, Devaputra, Shāhi*, Vāsashka. Its language is what is usually called 'the mixed dialect'. The object of the inscription is to record the installation of an image of the *Bhagavat* (Śākyamuni) in the Dharmadeva-vihāra by Madhurikā, daughter of Vera. It may be noted that, although the term *Bhagavat* is used in the inscription, the image to which this term is applied is that of the Bodhisattva and not of the Buddha. The regnal year is mentioned in line 1, which has been read differently by different scholars. Bühler[4] took it to be 78, but Fleet[5] and Vogel[2] read it as 28. According to Lüders, however, it may be 68, although he remarks that "the date of the year is quite uncertain".[6] As the sign in question has the same looped appearance as the sign for 20, the reading 28 may be adopted.

In lines 1-2, Bühler reads *Bhagava . . . . sya jambuchāyāśailā gra. sya*, whereas Vogel and Chanda would read *Bhagavasya jambuchāyā-śaila-gṛihasya*. This passage is translated by Chanda as "(an image) of Bhagavat (Bodhisattva) sitting on the hill under the shade of the Jambu (rose-apple) tree in the Dharmadeva-vihāra". It bears an allusion, as he points out, to the miracle performed by the Bodhisattva at the time of the Ploughing Festival, under a Jambu-tree, which is related in the *Nidānakathā* (Rhys Davids, *Buddhist Birth Stories*, p. 74 f.) and the *Lalitavistara*, Chapter XI. It may, however, be observed that the construction of the sentence is rather unusual. We should expect the word *Bhagavasya*, which is in the possessive case, to be followed by some such word as *pratimā*, the latter being the object of *pratishṭhāpitā*.[7] Indeed, a word denoting 'image' has to be supplied according to this interpretation. Again, the compound *jambuchāyā-śailagṛihasya* can only mean 'of one who has a stone-built house under the shade of a Jambu-tree,' or 'of one whose house is on a hill under the shade of a Jambu-tree'. But the Buddhist legends do not contain any allusion to the Bodhisattva having sat in meditation in a house during the Ploughing Festival.[8] Further, the

---

[1] Lüders, *List*, No. 161.
[2] *A. S. R.*, 1910-11, p. 42.
[3] *Sāñchī Museum Catalogue*, p. 30.
[4] *Ep. Ind.*, Vol. II, p. 369.
[5] *J. R. A. S.*, 1903, pp. 326 ff.
[6] *List*, No. 161 and *Ep. Ind.*, Vol. IX, pp. 244, 245.
[7] *Cf.* No. 830 below.
[8] *Cf.* M. Foucher's remarks on p. 253 *supra*.

word read as *śaila* seems to be *śilā*, and the letter read as *sya* by Bühler, Vogel and Chanda is unlike the other examples of *sya* in the inscription. Judging from a photograph (*Sāñchī Mus. Cat.*, Pl. II, A. 82) I would read it as *śca* and divide the passage as *jambuchāyā-śilā gṛihaś=ca* (for *gṛihañ=ca*). *Jambuchāyā-śilā* would mean a stone image representing the *Jambu-chāyā* episode, and *gṛiha*, the shrine in which it was installed.

Text (Pl. 124 *b* and Pl. 138, 52)

1 . . . . sya[1] r[ā]jāt[i]rājasya Devaputrasya Sh[ā]h[i]-Vāsashkasya[2] saṁ [20] 8 he 1 [di 5] [e]tasy[āṁ] [p]u[rv]v[āyāṁ] Bhagava[sya]

2 . . . . sya[3] jambuchāyā-śilā[4] gṛi[ha]ś-ca Dharmadeva-vihāre pratishṭāpitā Verasya[5] dhitaro[6] Madhurikā

3 (ane)na deyadharma-pari(tyāgena) . . . .

Translation

(In the reign) of the (*Mahārāja*) *Rājātirāja*, *Devaputra*, *Shāhi*, Vāsashka, the year 28, the first month of winter, the 5th day. On this day, a stone (image depicting) the 'Jambu-shade' (episode) of the Bhagavat (Śākyamuni) and a shrine were established in the Dharmadeva Monastery. By this gift, Madhurikā, the daughter of Vera . . . .

No. 829 Inscription of the Reign of Vaskushāṇa, the year 22

This inscription occurs on the pedestal of an image of the Buddha which is now in the Sāñchī Museum (Pl. 105 *c*).[7] The characters are Brāhmī of the Kushān period, and the language is a mixed dialect similar to that of the Kushān inscriptions from Mathurā. As regards orthography, attention may be drawn to the forms *Śakkyamuneḥ* and *pratishṭāpitā* in line 1.

The inscription records the installation of an image of Śākyamuni (*i.e.*, Buddha) by Vidyāmatī, in the reign of a king whose name is read as *Vasṇushāṇa* by Chanda. I may, however, observe that the letter joined to the bottom of *sa* is composed of a curve crowning an upright terminating, at the lower end, in a horizontal stroke stretched to the right. This portion of the ligature cannot, I think, stand for *ṇu*, but must be read as *ku*. Thus we arrive at the reading *Vaskushāṇa* which was the name of the king. It sounds no doubt somewhat curious, but in all probability the person was of non-Indian origin. The name itself suggests that he was probably of the Kushān lineage.

Text (Pl. 105 *c* and Pl. 138, 53)

1 Rājño Vaskushāṇasya sa 20 2 va 2 di 10 Bhagavato Śakkyam[un]eḥ pratimā pratishṭāpitā Vidyamatiye pu . . . .

2 . . . . . . mātā-pitṛiṇa sarvva-satvanā ca hiṭa-su[8]

Translation

In the (reign) of King Vaskushāṇa, the year 22, the 2nd month of the rainy season, on the 10th day, (this) image of the Bhagavat Śākyamuni was installed by Vidyāmatī for . . . . and for the welfare and happiness of (her) parents and all creatures.

[1] Bühler restores *Mahārājasya*.
[2] Bühler reads *Vāsushkasya*.
[3] Bühler restores *Śākyamunisya*.
[4] The letter *lā*, as read by Bühler, is certain.
[5] *Kharasya*—Lüders and Bühler; *Virasya*—Vogel.
[6] Bühler reads *dhitare*, but the *o* strokes are clear.
[7] Chanda, *Sāñchī Museum Catalogue*, p. 30, and Pl. XII.
[8] Abbreviation of *hita-sukh-ārthaṁ bhavatu*. In Chanda's transcript *hita* is omitted.

No. 830 Inscription on a Bodhisattva Image

This inscription is on the base of a Bodhisattva image of Mathurā sandstone, which was discovered by Sir John Marshall in Stūpa 12 and is now kept in the Sāñchī Museum (Pl. 124 *d*).[1] It consists of 3 lines, at the beginning of each of which some letters are missing. It is in Brāhmī characters of the Kushān period, the language being what is usually called 'the mixed dialect'. It records the installation of an image of the Bodhisattva Maitreya by a lady who is described as the daughter of one Vishakula.

Text (Pl. 124 *d* and Pl. 138, 54)

1 (Bodhi)satvasya M[ai]treyasya pratimā pratisht̩[ā](pitā)

2 . . . sya kuṭubiniye V[i]shakulasya dhitu Vashi-

3 . . (sa)tāna hi[ta]-sukh-artha[ṁ] bhavatu

Translation

An image of the Bodhisattva Maitreya has been installed by Vashi . . . . the wife of the householder . . . . and daughter of Vishakula. May (it) be for the welfare and happiness of (all) creatures !

No. 831 Inscription on a Votive Tablet.

The stone on which this inscription is engraved represents the Buddha's foot (*pada*)[2]. The characters, which are of about the fourth century A.D., occur on three sides of the *pada*. Owing to the damaged condition of the stone and the careless nature of the writing it is only possible to give a tentative reading of the inscription.

Text (Pl. 124 *f* and Pl. 138, 55)

A 1 J(e*)ṭhag(u)ptasya

2 hetave putrehi Māḷatagupten-edaṁ(?)

3 . . . . [mā]tā-pita[ra]-pūrvva(ṁ*)gama(ṁ*) kṛitvā

4 . . . (ā)tmano ca(?) nevānasa(?) prataya bhavata[3]

5 . . . .

B upāsaka-Pisula-[kṛita] . . . . . . Chājjapādila-pārthiye(?)

Translation

A. For the sake of Jeṭhagupta (*Jyeshṭhagupta*), by (his) sons . . . by Māḷatagupta(?) . . . . who is preceded by his parents . . . . let it be also to the attainment of his own Nirvāṇa . . . .

B. The lay-worshipper Pisula . . . . . Chājjapādila . . . . . .

No. 832 Inscription on the Pedestal of a standing Figure

The image, on the pedestal of which this inscription was incised, is missing, and the pedestal itself is also not intact. The inscription cannot, therefore, be restored in its entirety. A transcript of it has already been published by Chanda.[4] The characters represent the Northern alphabet, of about the fifth century A.D. The language is Sanskrit, and the composition is in verse throughout, judging from the fragmentary text. Only three incomplete lines of the inscription have been recovered, containing the broken *pādas* of two verses in *Indravajrā* metre. It seems to record the installation of an image (of the Buddha) by one belonging to the *Śūra-kula*, *i.e.*, the Śūra family.

Text (Pl. 138, 56)

1 jāl-āṅgulir-dīpta-suvarṇṇa-ga[5] . . . . . . (ca)-

2 ndro mayūkhair-iva gharma-taptān tasya tṛi-lok-ārtha[6] . . .

3 lena śailā hem-ojvalāt[7]-Śūra-kul-ātmajena[8] . . . .

Translation

(This) stone (image), which is as resplendent as gold . . . . (who) has webbed fingers,[9] (who is) as . . . as burning gold . . . . . . who like the moon . . . . the sun-burnt (creatures) with his rays . . . . by a scion of the Śūra family.

[1] See above pp. 47 and 253-4. [2] *Sāñchī Museum Catalogue*, p. 31, No. A. 85. [3] What is meant is probably *nirvāṇasya prāptaye bhavatu*. [4] *Sāñchī Museum Catalogue*, p. 31.
[5] Chanda restores *gauraḥ*. [6] Read *tri-*. The letter *lo* is written below *ka*. [7] Read *-ojjvalā*. [8] Chanda reads *Śmara*.
[9] This is one of the characteristic marks of a *mahāpurusha*, 'a superman'. *Cf. jālāṅguli-hasta-pādaḥ* in *Lalitavistara* (Ed. Lefmann, p. 106). Some scholars (Stutterheim, *Acta Or.*, Vol. VII, pp. 232 ff.) take it as 'fingers and toes having a web between', and others as 'fingers and toes marked with *jālas* or uniform and parallel lines such as are to be found in the meshes of a net or the lattice of a window' (J. N. Banerji, *Indian Hist. Quart.*, Vol. VI, pp. 717 and 724-25). A Central Asian manuscript contains the Śaka translation of *jāla-hasta-padatā*, which is rendered as 'between the digits are nets'. This confirms the interpretation of 'webbed fingers'. (Konow, *Acta Or.*, Vol. X, p. 301). The expression *jāl-āṅguli* is here applied evidently to the Buddha.

No. 833 Inscription of the reign of Candragupta II, the year 93

This inscription has already been critically edited by Fleet[1], whom I have generally followed in the account given below. It covers a space of about 2 ft. 6¼ in. long by 1 ft. 9 in. broad, and occurs above a Brāhmī inscription (No. 110 above) on the outer side of a cross-bar of the ground balustrade on the south side of the East Gateway of Stūpa 1. The size of the letters is about ⅝ in. The characters belong to the 'southern class of alphabets'. The language is Sanskrit, and the text is entirely in prose.

The inscription belongs to the reign of the *Mahārājādhirāja* Candragupta and the year 93, *i.e.*, 412-13 A.D. The king referred to is, therefore, identical with Candragupta II of the Imperial Gupta dynasty, who, according to an inscription in the Udayagiri cave[2] near Sāñchī, came to this part of the country for conquest. It records the grant of a village, or a plot of land, called Īśvaravāsaka and of a sum of twenty-five *dīnāras* or gold coins to the Buddhist Saṁgha at the monastery of Kākanāda-boṭa, *i.e.*, Sāñchī,[3] by Āmrakārddava, son of Undāna, for the purpose of feeding mendicants and burning lamps at the *Ratna-gṛiha*. Āmrakārddava was evidently a subordinate of the king; hence the expressions *anujīvī*, etc., used in line 3 of the inscription. The phrase *aneka-samar-āvapta-vijaya-yaśas-patākaḥ*, *i.e.*, 'who has acquired banners of victory and fame in many battles', further shows that he must have been a military officer. He probably accompanied Candragupta II in his expedition to Mālwā. The grant made is partly on behalf of the king and partly on behalf of Āmrakārddava himself. The person called *Devarāja*, in line 7, is identical with Devagupta of the Vākāṭaka copper-plates, which is another name for Candragupta II, as suggested by D. R. Bhandarkar. In the Poona plates of the Vākāṭaka queen Prabhāvatīguptā[4], she is described as the daughter of Candragupta II, and in other Vākāṭaka plates as the daughter of Devagupta. This enables us, as shown by K. B. Pathak and D. R. Bhandarkar,[5] to identify Candragupta II with Devagupta.

Text (Pl. 129, 98)

1 Siddham[6] (*) Kā[kanā]daboṭa-śrī-mahāvihāre śila-samādhi-prajñā-guṇa-bhāvit-endriyāya parama-puṇya-

2 kṛi . . . . . tāya catur-ddig-abhyāgatāya śramaṇa-puṅgav-āvasathāy-āryya-saṅghāya mahārājādhi-

3 rā[ja-ś]r[ī]-Candragupta-pāda-prasād-āpyāyita-jīvita-sādhanaḥ anujīvi-satpurusha-sadbhāva-

4 vri[ttim?] jagati prakhyāpayan aneka-samar-āvāpta-vijaya-yaśas-patākaḥ Sukuli-deśa-Na-

Translation

(Lines 1-7)—Perfection! To the Order of the faithful in the Great Monastery of Kākanādaboṭa,—in which the organs of sense (*of the members of it*) remain absorbed in the virtues of morality (*śīla*), meditation (*samādhi*) and wisdom (*prajñā*), which . . . . deeds of the very highest religious merit, which has assembled from the four quarters, (*and*) which is the abode of most excellent *Śramaṇas*—having prostrated himself together with the group of Five,[7] Āmrakārddava, the son of Undāna,—whose life has been made comfortable by the favour of the feet of the *Mahārājādhirāja*, the glorious Candragupta (II), (*and*) who proclaims in the world the good

[1] *Corp. Ins. Ind.*, Vol. III, pp. 29-34, and Pl. III B.
[2] *Ibid.*, Vol. III, p. 34.
[3] *Cf.* inscription No. 834 below and remarks on p. 300 above and p. 395 below (for *Boṭa*).
[4] *Ep. Ind.*, Vol. XV, pp. 39 ff.
[5] *Ind. Ant.*, 1912, p. 215, and *ibid.*, 1913, pp. 160-161.
[6] Written above the first two letters of line 1, in the original.
[7] This is of doubtful import.

5 shṭi . . . . vāstavya-Undāna-putr-Āmrakārddavo Maja-Śarabhaṅg-Āmrarāta-rājakula-mūlya-krī-

6 tam(?) . . . . . ya . . . Īśvaravāsakaṁ pañca-maṇḍalyā praṇipatya dadāti pañca-viṁśatiś(ñ)-ca dīnā-

7 rān (*) Ta[d-da]tta- . . . . yad-arddhena mahā-rājādhirāja-śrī-Candra-guptasya Devarāja iti pri-

8 ya-nām . . . . [ra ?]tasya sarvva-guṇa-saṁpattaye yāvac-candr-ādityau tāvat-pañca bhikshavo bhuṁja-

9 tāṁ ratna-gṛihe [ca dī]pako jvalatu (|*) mama c-āparārddhāt-pañc-aiva bhikshavo bhuṁjatāṁ ratna-gṛihe ca

10 dīpaka iti (||*) Tad-etat-pravṛittaṁ ya ucchindyāt-sa go-brahma-hatyayā saṁyukto bhavet-pañcabhis-c-āna-

11 ntaryyair-iti (||*) Saṁ 90 3 Bhādrapada di 4 (||*)

behaviour of the excellent people, namely, the dependents (*of the king*), (*and*) who has acquired banners of victory and fame in many battles, (*and*) who is an inhabitant of (*the town of*) Nashṭi . . . . . . in the Sukuli country—gives away (*the village or land called*) Īśvaravāsaka, ... purchased from Maja, Śarabhaṅga and Āmrarāta, members of the royal household, and (*also*) twenty-five gold coins (*dīnāras*).

(Lines 7-10)—Out of the half of (*the interest of the dīnāras*) given by him, let five monks be fed, and let a lamp burn in the Jewel-house,[1] as long as the moon and the sun (*endure*), for the perfection of all the virtues of . . . . of the *Mahārājādhirāja*, the glorious Candragupta (II) whose favourite name is Devarāja ; and with my other half let the same number of five monks be fed, and (*let*) a lamp (*burn*) in the Jewel-house.

(Lines 10-11)—Whosoever shall transgress this arrangement,—he shall become invested with (*the guilt of*) the slaughter of a cow and of a Brāhman, and with (*the guilt of*) the Five Sins.

(Line 11)—The year 90 (*and*) 3 ; (*the month*) Bhādrapada ; the day 4.

No. 834 Inscription of the Gupta year 131

This inscription is on the outer face of a cross-bar on the south side of the East Gateway. It has already been edited by Fleet,[2] and the following is based principally on his account.

The writing, which covers a space of about 2 ft. 5 in. long by 2 ft. broad, is not so neatly engraved as in the foregoing inscription. But it is in a better state of preservation. The size of the letters is between 1 in. and ½ in. The characters represent the southern class of alphabets. It is interesting to note that, at this period, both the northern and the southern varieties of the Gupta alphabet were being used simultaneously at Sāñchī and Udayagiri. Inscription No. 832 above is in the northern class of alphabets, whereas the characters of Nos. 833 and 834 belong to the southern class. Again, at Udayagiri, the inscription of Vīrasena (Śāba)[3] and the inscription[4] of the year 106 represent the northern class, but the inscription[5] of the year 82 is written in the southern class of alphabets.

[1] The term *ratnagriha* occurs also in a Mathurā inscription, Lüders, *List*, No. 125. In the Sāñchī inscription of the year 131, a gift is stated to have been made at the *Ratna-griha*, and another at the *Catur-Buddh-āsana*, that is, in the *pradakshiṇa-patha* inside the ground balustrade of Stūpa 1, where four Buddha images are seated.

[2] *Corp. Ins. Ind.*, Vol. III, pp. 260-62, and Pl. XXXVIII B. [3] *Ibid.*, p. 34. [4] *Ibid.*, p. 258. [5] *Ibid.*, p. 21. *Cf.* inscription No. 833 above.

The inscription is in Sanskrit, and written in prose throughout. It refers itself to the (Gupta) year 131, *i.e.*, 450-51 A.D., the 5th day of the month of Aśvayuj (September-October), and records an endowment of sixteen gold coins (*dīnāras*) to the Buddhist community residing in the monastery at Kākanāda-boṭa (Sāñchī),[1] namely, twelve coins for feeding a monk day by day, and three coins for the Jewel-house (*Ratna-gṛiha*) and one for the Place of the Four Buddhas (*catur-Buddh-āsana*), in both cases for maintaining lamps. The grant is made by the *upāsikā* Harisvāminī, the wife of the *upāsaka* Sanasiddha. The 'four Buddhas are the four images in the *pradakshiṇa-patha* adjoining the ground balustrade, one opposite each entrance (Pl. 70 and pp. 38, 39, 250 and 251). The use of the singular in *āsane* shows that the whole *pradakshiṇa-patha* or passage of circumambulation is here meant.

Text (Pl. 130, 105)

1 S[iddha]m [||*] Upāsaka-Sanasiddha-bhāryyayā upāsik(ā*)-Harisvāminyā mātā-

2 pitaram[2]-uddiśya Kākanādaboṭa-śri-mahā-vihāre cāturddiśāy-āryya-saṁ-

3 ghāya akshaya-nīvi dattā dīnārā dvādaśa [|*] eshāṁ dināraṇāṁ yā vṛiddhi-

4 r-upajāyate tayā divase-divase saṁgha-madhya-pravishṭaka-bhikshur-ekaḥ bhoja-

5 yitavyaḥ [||*] Ratna-gṛihe-pi dīnāra-trayaṁ dattaṁ [|*] (ta)d-dīnāra-trayasya vṛi(d*)dhyā ratna-gṛihe

6 bhagavato Buddhasya divase-divase dīpa-trayaṁ prajvālayitavyaṁ [||*] Catur-Buddh-āsa-

7 ne-pi dattaḥ dīnāra ekaḥ [|*] tasya vṛiddhyā catur-Buddh-āsane bhagavato Buddhasya

8 divase-divase dīpaḥ prajvālayitavyaḥ [||*] Evam-esh-ākshayanīvī

9 ācandr-ārkka-śilā-lekhyā svāmini-Sanasiddha-bhāryyayā

10 upāsik(ā*)-Harisvāminyā pravarttitā iti [||*]

11 Saṁvvat 100 30 1 Aśvayug-di 5 ||

Translation

(Lines 1-4)—Perfection ! By the lay-worshipper Harisvāminī, the wife of the lay-worshipper Sanasiddha, twelve gold coins (*dīnāras*) are given for the benefit of (*her*) parents, (*as*) a permanent endowment, to the Order of the faithful, (*assembled*) from the four quarters, at the Great Monastery of Kākanāda-boṭa. With the interest that accrues from these gold coins, day by day one monk from among the Order should be fed.

(Lines 5-6)—Also, three gold coins are given at the Jewel-house. With the interest of these three gold coins, day by day three lamps of Lord Buddha should be lit in the Jewel-house.

(Lines 6-8)—Also, one gold coin is given in the place where (*the images of*) the four Buddhas are seated. With the interest of this, day by day a lamp of Lord Buddha should be lit in the place where (*the images of*) the four Buddhas are seated.

(Lines 8-10)—Thus this permanent endowment,—written upon stone (*so as to endure*) for the same time as the moon and the sun,—has been established by the lay-worshipper Harisvāminī, the noble lady, the wife of Sanasiddha.

(Line 11) –The year 100 (*and*) 30 (*and*) 1 ; (*the month*) Aśvayuj ; the day 5.

[1] *Cf.* inscription No. 833 above.

[2] Read *mātāpitarau-*

No. 835 Inscription on Pillar No. 26 in the Courtyard of Stūpa 1

Pillar No. 26 which bears this inscription has been described above (pp. 49-50 and Pl. 106 *d*). The inscription consists of two fragments which have now been joined together. The beginning portion was first noticed by Cunningham[1] and later published by Fleet.[2] The second fragment, containing the concluding portion of the text, was subsequently discovered by Sir John Marshall in the course of his excavations.

The inscription is in the southern class of the Gupta alphabet, and consists of a single line written in Sanskrit prose. The object is to record the gift of a 'Vajrapāṇi-pillar', two pillars of a gateway, a *maṇḍapa* or pavilion of a monastery, and a gateway. The donor is Rudrasiṁha(?), son of gośūra-Siṁhabala.[3] The latter's title *vihāra-svāmī, i.e.*, 'Officer in charge of Monastery', is preceded by a word of three letters executed rather clumsily. Fleet could not decipher this word, but tentatively read it as *A(?)ka* . . An examination of the original as well as the estampages shows that the three letters should probably be read as *Araka*. The word *Araka* is used as a title in the Chinna inscription of Śrī-Yajña Sātakarṇi,[4] and has been taken by Bühler and Lüders as an equivalent of Sanskrit *aryaka, i.e.*, 'lord.'

The expression *Vajrapāṇi-stambha* means a pillar surmounted by a figure of Vajrapāṇi, in the same way as a *Garuḍa-stambha* means a pillar surmounted by a figure of Garuḍa. This pillar of Vajrapāṇi, marked as No. 35 in the Plan, stood in front of the North Gateway of Stūpa 1 (Pl. 106 *c* and pp. 50-52). The image of Vajrapāṇi[5], which crowned its summit, is now in the Sāñchī Museum (Pl. 108 *b* and *d* and p. 254). The inscription is not dated, but on palæographic grounds Fleet has assigned it to the fifth century A.D.

Text (Plate 138, 57)

A[raka?]-vihārasvāmi-gośūra-Siṁhabala-puttra-
Rudra(siṁha)sya Vajrapāṇi-stambhaḥ
toraṇa-stambha-dvayaṁ vihāra-maṇḍapaḥ
pratolī c-eti

Translation

A Vajrapāṇi-pillar, two pillars (supporting) an arch, a pavilion (attached to) a monastery and a gateway[6] (are the gift) of Rudras(iṁha?), the son of the Abbot, the *A(raka)* gośūra-Siṁhabala.

No. 836 Inscription on Pillar No. 25 in the Courtyard of Stūpa 1

According to Sir John Marshall, this pillar (No. 25) belongs to the second century B.C., and the inscription which it bears was incised upon it long after its erection.[7] The inscription is a fragmentary one, and may have been another copy of the one on Pillar No. 26 (see above). The characters belong to the southern class of the Gupta alphabet, and the language is Sanskrit. It may be assigned to about the fifth century A.D. like the previous inscription.

Text (Plate 138, 58)

. . . . [ṇḍa]pa[ḥ] pratolī c-eti

Translation

. . . . a pavilion, and a gateway.

---

[1] *Bhilsa Topes*, p. 199 and Pl. XXI, No. 199.
[2] *Corp. Ins. Ind.*, Vol. III, pp. 279-80 and Pl. XLII A.
[3] The word *gośūra* may be identical with *guśura* occurring as a title in the Central Asian Kharoshṭhī documents, *e.g.*, *guśura viharavala* in Stein's No. 187. On *guśura* see Burrow, *The Language of the Kharoṣṭhī documents from Chinese Turkestan*, 1937, p. 87.
[4] *J. A. S. B.*, 1920, p. 329; *E. I.*, I, p. 96.
[5] *Sāñchī Museum Catalogue*, p. 33, A99.
[6] For the meaning of *pratolī* see Vogel, *J. R. A. S.*, 1906, pp. 539 ff., and P. K. Acharya, *Dictionary of Hindu Architecture*, pp. 366 ff.
[7] See above p. 49 and Pl. 106 *b*.

No. 837 Inscription on the pedestal of an image

This inscription, which consists of one line, is in the northern alphabet of about the sixth century A.D. The language is Sanskrit. It records a gift, namely the image on which it is engraved, the donor being one Rekhagupta.

Text (Plate 138, 59)	Translation
deya-dharmo-yaṁ Bhadanta-[R]ekhaguptasya yad-atra puṇyaṁ tad-bhava(tu)	This is the pious gift of the Reverend Rekhagupta. Whatever be the merit in this, let it accrue to . . . .
	Chanda, *Sāñchī Museum Catalogue*, p. 34, A 106.

No. 838 Inscription on a Loose Stone Slab

This is a fragmentary inscription, being part of the Buddhist formula, in characters of about the sixth century A.D. The writing is very carelessly executed.

Text (Plate 138, 60)

1 . . . . hetu-pra . . . .
2 . . . . dat teshāṁ ca yo . . . . . .

No. 839 Inscription from a well at Kanakhera near Sāñchī

The stone bearing this inscription, now in the museum at Sāñchī, came from Kanakhera, a village near Sāñchī, where it was built into a well.[1] It was first edited by R. D. Banerji,[2] and subsequently re-edited by me.[3] The inscription consists of 6 lines of writing, which covers a space of 2 ft. 2½ in. by 6⅝ in. The size of the letters varies between 1¼ in. and ⅜ in. The inscription is in a very bad state of preservation, and a number of letters have become blurred or have peeled off altogether.

The characters belong to the class of Gupta alphabets current in Mālwā, which Fleet calls the 'southern class of alphabets'. Palæographically, the inscription is akin to the Sāñchī inscription of Candragupta II, of 412 A.D. (No. 833 above). Its language is Sanskrit, and the text is partly in prose and partly in verse, containing a few Prākṛitic forms or solecisms, *e.g.*, *vejayike* and *trayodaśame* (l. 2). It is in the regular *Kāvya* style of composition, as found in other records of the Gupta period.

In many respects my reading of the inscription differs materially from that of R. D. Banerji, the chief difference being that in line 1 he reads the name of Jīvadāman, whom he identifies with Svāmī Jīvadāman, father of Rudrasiṁha II, a Satrap of Western India of the third century A.D., and that at the end of the inscription he recognizes a date symbol for 200, which he refers to the Śaka era and thus arrives at 279 A.D. as the date of the record. These readings are open to objection, as I have shown elsewhere. I have since examined the original stone, and may say definitely that there is no mention of Jīvadāman in the inscription. At the end of it there occurs the letter *sa* followed by three signs, of which the first one looks like 200 and the two following are clearly 40 1. This year 241 is referable to the Śaka era, the date of the record thus corresponding to 319 A.D.

---

[1] *Sāñchī Museum Catalogue*, p. 33, A 98. [2] *Ep. Ind.*, Vol. XVI, pp. 230-33 and Pl. [3] *J. A. S. B.*, Vol. XIX, 1923, pp. 337-344.

The object of the inscription is to record the excavation of a well by the *Mahādaṇḍanāyaka* Śaka Śrīdharavarmman, son of Śaka Nanda. It refers itself to the thirteenth regnal year of Śrīdharavarmman, which shows that although styled as 'the general he was enjoying the powers and privileges of an independent ruler. Evidently he belongs to one of those Śaka families that settled in Western India in the early centuries of the Christian era and embraced the Brahmanical faith. He calls himself a *dharma-vijayī*, *i.e.*, 'the righteous conqueror' in line 2, and in line 3 there is reference to *dharm-āsi*, *i.e.*, 'the sword of righteousness'. In all likelihood Śrīdharavarmman originally served under some royal family, and later, throwing off the yoke, assumed the position of an independent ruler.

Text (Plate 139, 61)

1 Siddham[1] Bhagavatas-tr[i]daśa-gaṇa-senāpater-ajita-senasya svāmi-Mahāsena-mahā[tejaḥ-prasādāt ?] viryy-[ār]jj[i]ta-[vija][2] . . . . .

2 dharmma-vijayinā Śaka-Nanda-putreṇa Mahā-daṇḍa-nāyakena Śakena Śrīdharavarmmaṇā var[shsha]-[saha]srāya[3] sva-rājy-ābhivṛiddhikare vejayike saṁvatsare trayodaśa[me]

3 Śrāvaṇa-bahulasya daśamī-pūrvvakam-etad-divasaṁ kalyāṇ-ābhyudaya-vṛiddhy-artham-akshaya-svargg-āvāpti-hetor-ddharmma-yaśo-rtthaṁ dharmmāsi-saṁbuddhayā śrāddha[4] . . . .

4 śāśvata-candr-āditya-kāliko-yaṁ . . . . . . i . . . . ma pi[5] kāyo — ᴗ ᴗ ḥ prasanna-salilaḥ sarvv-ādhigamyaḥ sadā

5 satvānā[ṁ] priya-darśano jalanidhir-ddharmm-āmalaḥ śāśvataḥ . . . . my . . . . prācya . . . . . .

6 [kū]paḥ Śrīdharavarmmaṇā guṇavatā khānāpito-yaṁ śubhaḥ [6] Sa[ṁ] [200] 40 1

Translation

Ll. 1-3. Success! (Given) by the general, the Śaka Śrīdharavarmman, son of the Śaka Nanda, the righteous conqueror whose victory was won by his prowess . . . . (through the mighty power graciously bestowed on him by ?) the god who is the commander of the heavenly forces and whose army is ever victorious, the lord Mahāsena,[7] in the thirteenth year of victory marked by the prosperity of his kingdom, on the tenth day of the dark half of Śrāvaṇa, (to remain in force) for one thousand years.[8]

Ll. 3-4. On this day, this (well was excavated) to last eternally, as long as the sun and the moon endure, for the increase of welfare and prosperity, and attainment of eternal (residence in) heaven, and for the sake of piety and fame, being actuated by a benevolent desire(?) awakened by the sword of righteousness.

Ll. 4-6. This auspicious well contains clear water and is always accessible to everybody, having an appearance pleasing to living beings. It is a perennial store-house of water, and is as pure as *Dharma*. It has been caused to be excavated by the meritorious Śrīdhara-varmman.[9] The (year) 241.

[1] In the original the word stands in the left margin between lines 3 and 4.
[2] Restore *vijaya*.
[3] See Thomas, *Ep. Ind.*, Vol. XVI, p. 232, n. 2.
[4] Probably to be restored as *śraddhayā*.
[5] Metre: Śārdūlavikrīḍita.
[6] Here is a sign of interpunction, which Banerji takes to be a 200 symbol. The sign for 40 is read by him as *stu*.
[7] *I.e.*, the god Kārttikeya.
[8] Cf. *Rudradāmnā varshasahasrāya go-brah[m]a . . . . r[tha]ṁ dharmma-kīrti-vṛiddhy-arthaṁ ca*, etc.—Junāgaḍh inscription of Rudradāman, *Ep. Ind.*, Vol. VIII, p. 44, l. 15; also *vāsa-sata-sahassāya* of the copper-plate of Śiva-Skanda-Varman, *ibid.*, Vol. I, p. 7; and *varsha-sahassāya* of Bhamodra Mohota plate, A.D. 502, *ibid.*, Vol. XVI, p. 18, l. 3.
[9] This portion, which is in verse, repeats what has been stated already in the foregoing prose portion.

No. 840 Inscription on the base of a Buddha image

This is an inscription of one line, in the northern alphabet of about the sixth century A D. The language is Sanskrit. It records a gift, evidently the image itself, by a person named Kulāditya.

Text (Plate 139, 62)	Translation
deya . . . . . . samakhata (?) . . . . hacchava Śrī-Kulādityasya yad=atra puṇyaṁ tad bhavatu sarvva-satvānāṁ	The gift of . . . . . Śrī-Kulāditya ; whatever merit there is in this (deed), may it belong to all creatures.
	Chanda, *Sāñchī Catalogue*, p. 3, No. 22.

No. 841 Inscription on the back slab of a Buddhist image

This inscription occurs on the back slab of an image, of which only a portion bearing the figure of a Dhyāni-Buddha has been found ; the image itself is missing. The epigraph is in Nāgarī of about the 9th century A.D., and contains the well-known Buddhist formula.

Text (Plate 139, 63)	Translation
Ye dhammā hetu-prabhavā hetuṁ teshāṁ Tathāgato=hy=avadatu[1] teshāṁ ca yo nirodha evaṁvādī mahā-śramaṇaḥ	"Of those things (conditions) which spring from a cause, the cause has been told by Tathāgata; and their suppression likewise the Great Śramana has revealed."[2]
	Chanda, *Sāñchī Catalogue*, p. 16, No. 156.

No. 842 Fragmentary inscription from Monastery 43

This inscription is engraved on a slab of sandstone of which fourteen fragments have been recovered. It came from Monastery 43 and is now in the Sāñchī Museum.[3] As a large portion of the slab is missing, it is not possible to restore the text in its entirety or to give a connected translation of it. Such facts, however, as may be gleaned from a study of the fragments, are noted below.

The characters represent an ornamental type of the northern alphabet similar to those of the Jhalrāpāṭan inscription dated Samvat 746 (689-90 A.D.).[4] Its chief peculiarity is the ornamental way in which very frequently the superscript signs of medial vowels are written above the heads of letters. The language is Sanskrit and seems to be in verse throughout.

The text in fragments *a-c* (lines 1-3) is devoted to the praise of Lokanātha, who is described as having a lotus in his hand and bearing Amitābha (on his head)[5], and also of Vajrapāṇi. In line 4 of these fragments is mentioned the lord of Mahāmālava or Mālwā, and a certain ruler Vappakadeva and his son, *Mahārāja* Śarvva[6], appear in fragment *e*. Fragment *e*, line 8, seems to refer to the son of Śarvva. In fragment *i*, a monastery (*vihāra*) with cells (*layana*) is stated to have been built by somebody. There also occurs in it the name of an officer Rudra who is described as *aśesha-mahā-śabda*, *i.e.*, 'holding endless

[1] Read *avadat=teshām*. [2] Kern, *Manual of Indian Buddhism*, p. 25. [3] *Sāñchī Museum Catalogue*, p. 59, No. C 833. [4] *Ind. Ant.*, Vol. V, p. 180, and Pl. [5] *Cf.* Pl 126 *d* and p. 254, Avalokiteśvara. [6] The reading is not *Śarjja*, as given in *Sāñchī Catalogue*, p. 59. *Cf.* the conjunct *rvva* in frag. *e*, 9.

big titles . There seems to be a further reference to this monastery in fragment *n*, which supplies the information that the monastery belonged to a person named Tuṅga and that the benefaction recorded took place at Boṭa-Srīparvvata. In *Boṭa* we must, of course, recognize the name *Kākanāda-boṭa* by which the Sāñchī hill is called in the inscriptions of the Gupta years 93 and 131.

Text (Plate 139, 64 *a-n*)

(*a, b, c*) 1 . . . . kala . laṁ śāśvataṁ tattvam-
e . . . vyāhāra-cintā-kṛiti-vishayaṁ ne
-[i]raṁ yaḥ kṛip-ākṛishṭa-dṛishṭiḥ
satvārth-aika-kriya

2 . . . . [i]sitamalagha . sya sambhāra-
tulyaṁ pāṇau padmaṁ bhav-
āmbhasya . . . . gataṁ yo-Mitābhañ-
ca dhatte taṁ vande Lokanāthaṁ

(*b, c*) 3 . . . . va śuddhaṁ śaśvad-baddha-
cittaṁ vahati tanubhṛitāṁ tat- . . . .
vande Vajrapāṇiṁ parama-pura-dayā
saṁ-

4 . . . . devaḥ patir-atula-Mahā-
Mālava-kshmāpa-Lakshmyāḥ . . . . .
[va]ṅdhyaṁ tanuta su-mahān-
duḥsaho yat-pu-

5 . . . . durvvāra-sainyam prācy-
audīcya-pratī(cy) . . . . . (bhū)bhuj-
ājau vijigye Yena go-

6 . . . . [pṛi]thu-yaśaḥ ślāghya-sad-
. . . . . prakaṭita-mahimā . . . .

(*d*) 1 risa . yaḥ . . . .

2 m-api mahā . . . .

3 ta . . . .

(*e*) 1 . . . . prahaṭa-vika . . . .

2 . . . . kṛitam Tat-puttro-sau
sujanmā pra . . . . . .

3 . . . . n[i]rīkshyamāna-tuṅgatvaṁ
yasy-eśasya kshamābhṛitām Nya
. . . .

4 . . . . . . no hata-para-lokam-api
dharmma-ratam Sa Śrī-Vappaka-dev-
ākhya . . . .

5 . . . . . . d-vanda-pālaḥ kshiti-patir-
akhila-kshmā-visarpa-pratāpo
vikhyātaḥ śuddha . . . .

6 . . . . mūhā yatra saṁkocam-īyun
tat-sutaḥ Śrī-Mahārāja-Śarvva . . . . .
. . . .

7 . . . . rttā niśamy-ākulāḥ saṁtrāsād-
giri-kandar-odara-ga(guhā ?) . . . .
. . . . .

8 . . . . (ki)rttir-yadīy-āgamat Tasy-
ātmajaḥ [sa]

9 . . . . m-ati-prauḍha-garvvaṁ
. . . . .

(*f*) 1 . . . . janma . . . .

2 . . . . yas-trailokyaṁ spardhay-
[e]va . . . .

3 . . . . sahasi mahān-tejasi yaḥ
khyātimān . . . .

4 . . . . tī vikhyāto-ti-ma(hā) . . . . . .
. . . .

(*g*) 1 . . . . sti . . . .
. . . .

2 . . . . bhājāṁ cakāra . . . .
. . . .

3 . . . . cina padavinyā(?) . . . .
. . . . .

(*h*) 1 . . . . ḥ samānaḥ pārāpā . . . .

2 . . . . ma . . . .

(*i*) 1 . . . . na Jala-nidhi . . . .

2 v[i]hāraḥ sal-layanan-tato-tra kāri . . . .

3 tāva(t)-sthitiḥ ślāghanīyā bhāsvan-nakshatra-ma(ṇḍala) . . . .

4 n-āśesha-mahā-śabda-Śrī-Rudra-nāma-dheyen-āsmi(n) . . . .

(*j*) 1 . . . . y-Āṅgi(rasa) . . . .

2 . . . . lokā lokāntara- . . . .

(*k*) 1 . . . . hā mūrdha e . . . .

2 . . . . sundarīṇāṁ vadanam-atı-vivarṇṇam bhi

3 n Sad-vṛittā sad-varṇṇā s alaṅkārā . . . .

4 . . . . virala-maṁṇḍitaṁ vyo . . . .

5 . . . . kāryata . . . .

(*l*) 1 . . . . tpa . . . .

2 . . . . vikāsaṁ bhāsvati snig(dha) . . . .

3 . . . . na . . . ja-kshiti . itthaṁ . . . .

(*m*) 1 . . . . t-āspadā ca vacasi prītā

2 . . . . st[i] vastu t[r]ijagati . . . .

(*n*) 1 . . . . yāvad-Boṭa-Śrīparvvate-yaṁ.

2 . . . . ñcana-Tuṅgasya satka esha vi(hāraḥ)

I

GENERAL INDEX

II

INDEX OF PERSONAL NAMES OCCURRING IN SĀÑCHĪ INSCRIPTIONS[1]

[1] The numbers in this index are the serial numbers given to the inscriptions on pages 283-396.

III

INDEX OF GEOGRAPHICAL NAMES OCCURRING IN SĀÑCHĪ INSCRIPTIONS[1]

[1] The numbers in this Index are the serial numbers given to the inscriptions on pages 283-396.

THE MONUMENTS OF SĀÑCHĪ

THE MONUMENTS OF SĀÑCHĪ

BY

SIR JOHN MARSHALL, C.I.E., Litt.D., F.S.A.

Fellow of the British Academy ; Correspondant de l'Institut de France ;
Hon. Fellow of King's College, Cambridge ; Sometime Director General
of the Archæological Survey of India

AND

ALFRED FOUCHER

Membre de l'Institut de France ;
Professeur à l'Université de Paris

With the texts of inscriptions edited, translated and annotated

BY

N. G. MAJUMDAR, M.A., F.R.A.S.B.

Superintendent of the Archæological
Survey of India

Volume Two : Plate I—LXX

Swati Publications

DELHI

First Reprinted 1982

Second Reprinted 1983

Published by : SWATI PUBLICATIONS, 34, Central Market,
Ashok Vihar, Phase-I, Delhi-110052

PRINTED BY **Shivalik Offset Press Naraina Industrial Area, New Delhi**

PLATE 1

THE HILL OF SĀÑCHĪ AND ITS ENVIRONS

The aspect of the hill, its geological formation, ancient and modern approach roads, tanks and embankments are described on pp. 11-13. For the principal group of remains on the summit, the reader should refer to the description of Pl. 2; for Stūpa 2 and other remains on the western slope, to pp. 16 and 79-82, and to the description of Pl. 71; and for the small isolated hill of Nāgourī on the south, to p. 13.

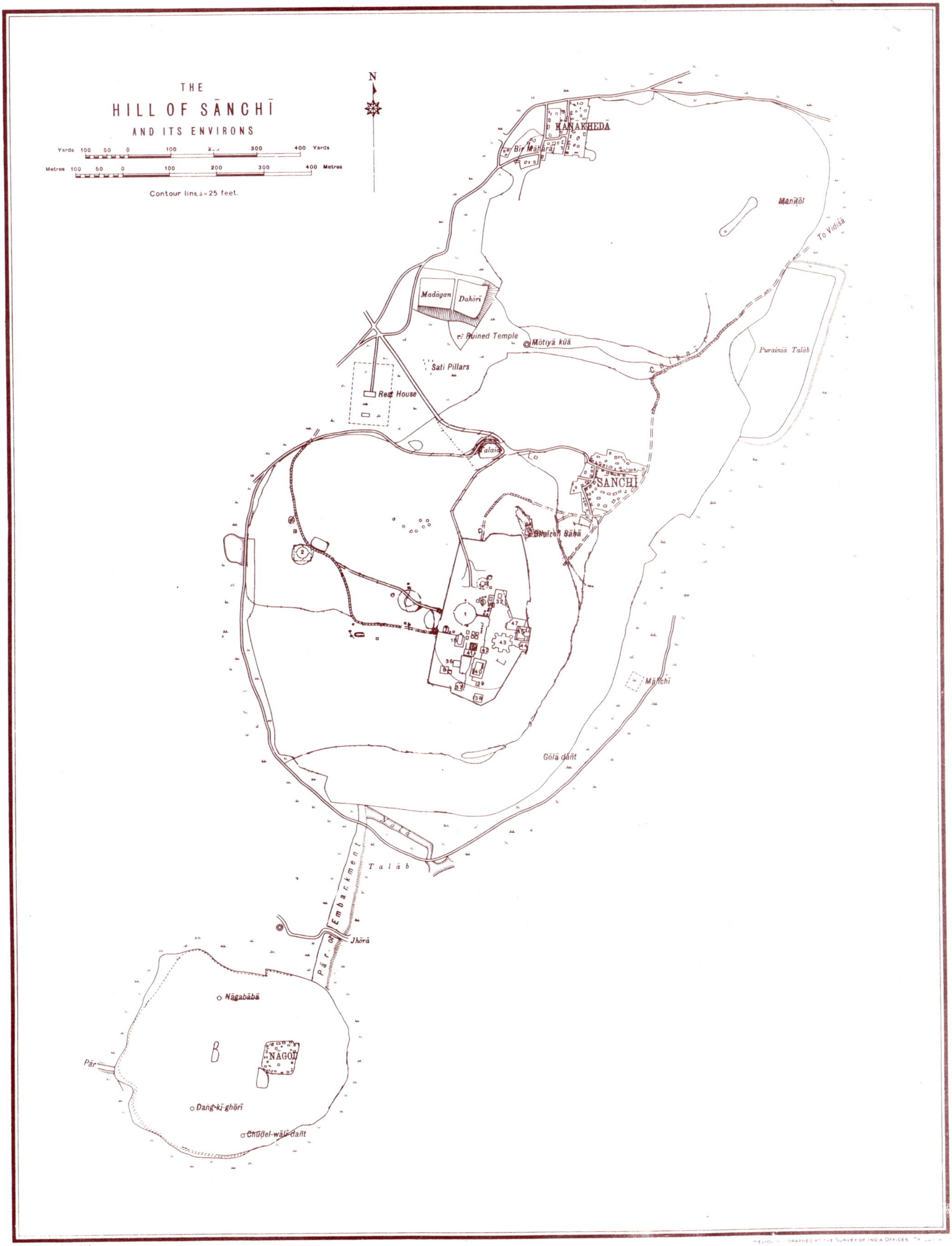

3311 E 33 – 600
SURVEY OF INDIA OFFICES

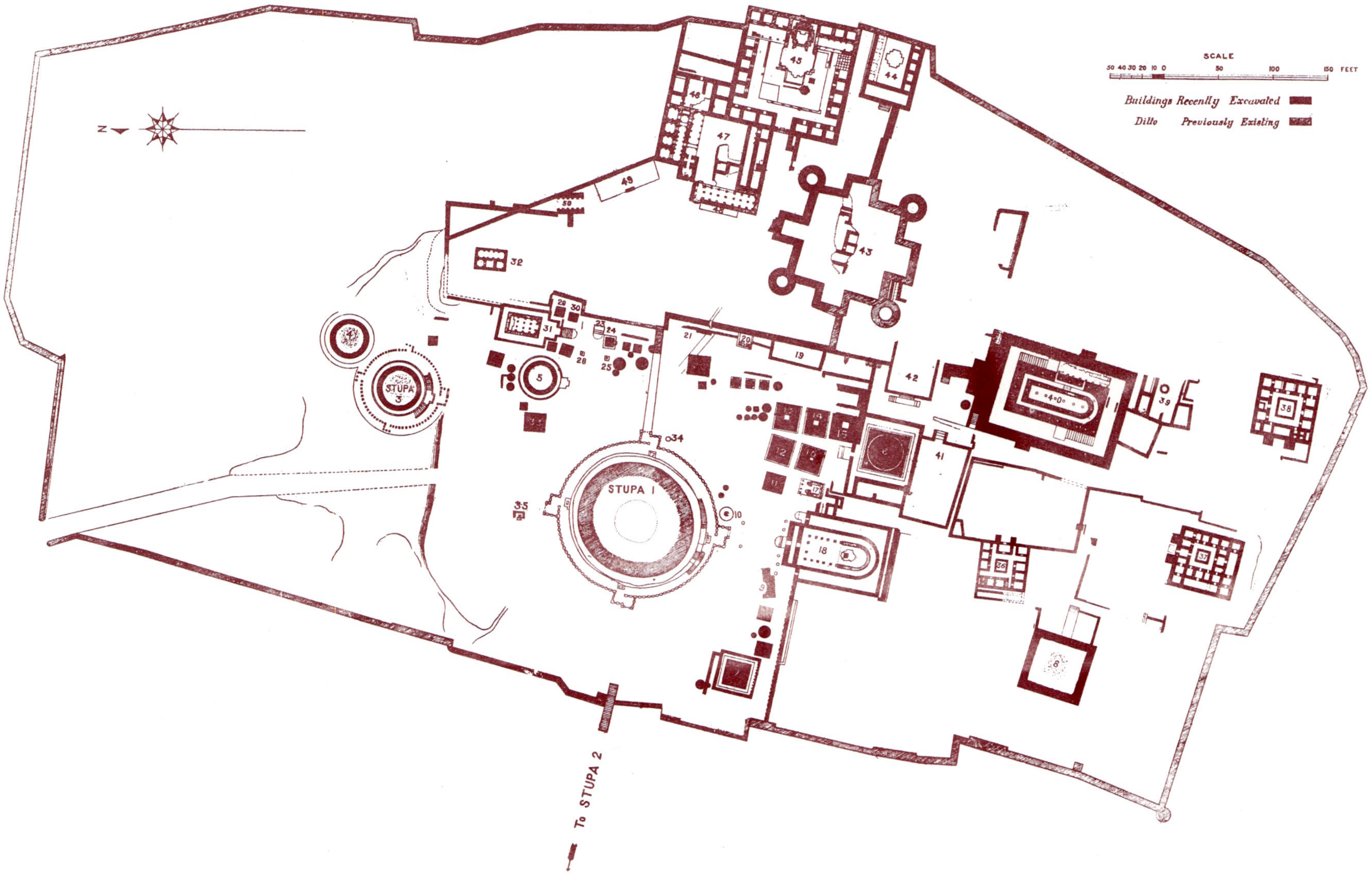

PLAN OF BUILDINGS ON THE HILL-TOP

PLATE 2

PLAN OF BUILDINGS ON THE HILL-TOP

Apart from Stūpa 2, which is situated halfway down the western slope of the hill, all the principal monuments at Sāñchī are comprised in this group on the hill-top, which, along with the encompassing wall, is summarily described on pp. 15 and 16, and in greater detail in Chapters III-IV (pp. 19-60).

Two grades of shading, it is to be observed, are employed in this plan. The darker buildings are those which were unearth Sir John Marshall between the years 1912-20; the lighter or those which had previously been exposed to view.

The dates of the various buildings and of the successive adc or changes made in them are set out in the schedule on p. 18.

PLATE 3

a. VIEW OF HILL FROM THE NORTH-WEST

See the description on p. 11. At the left of the picture, the hill slopes down to the saddle where the modern village of Sāñchī is located. In the middle can be seen, rising above the trees, the dome of the Great Stūpa. To the right, the hill shelves gently away towards Nāgourī.

In the foreground, where the picture shows high standing crops, there used to be a wide expanse of water (p. 13).

b. GENERAL VIEW OF REMAINS FROM SOUTH-EAST

This photograph is taken from the raised plinth of Building 40, the broken pillars of which appear in the foreground (*cf.* Pls. 109 and 110 and pp. 64-68). Beyond them, in the middle of the picture, are the bases of Stūpas 6 and 13-15 (pp. 45-47), and beyond these again, the imposing mass of the Great Stūpa, with three of its gateways visible, the East, South and West (*cf.* Pls. 5 and 6 and pp. 19-40). To the left of the Great Stūpa rise the columns of the Apsidal Temple 18 (pp. 52-56); to the right, the dome of Stūpa 3 (pp. 41-44), with Stūpa 5 in front of it and Temple 31 a little to the right (*cf.* Pl. 115*a* and pp. 45 and 58-59). The wall near the *khirṇi* tree on the right of the picture is the S.-W. corner of Building 43 (p. 78).

a

(a) VIEW OF HILL FROM NORTH-WEST.

b

(b) GENERAL VIEW OF REMAINS FROM SOUTH-EAST

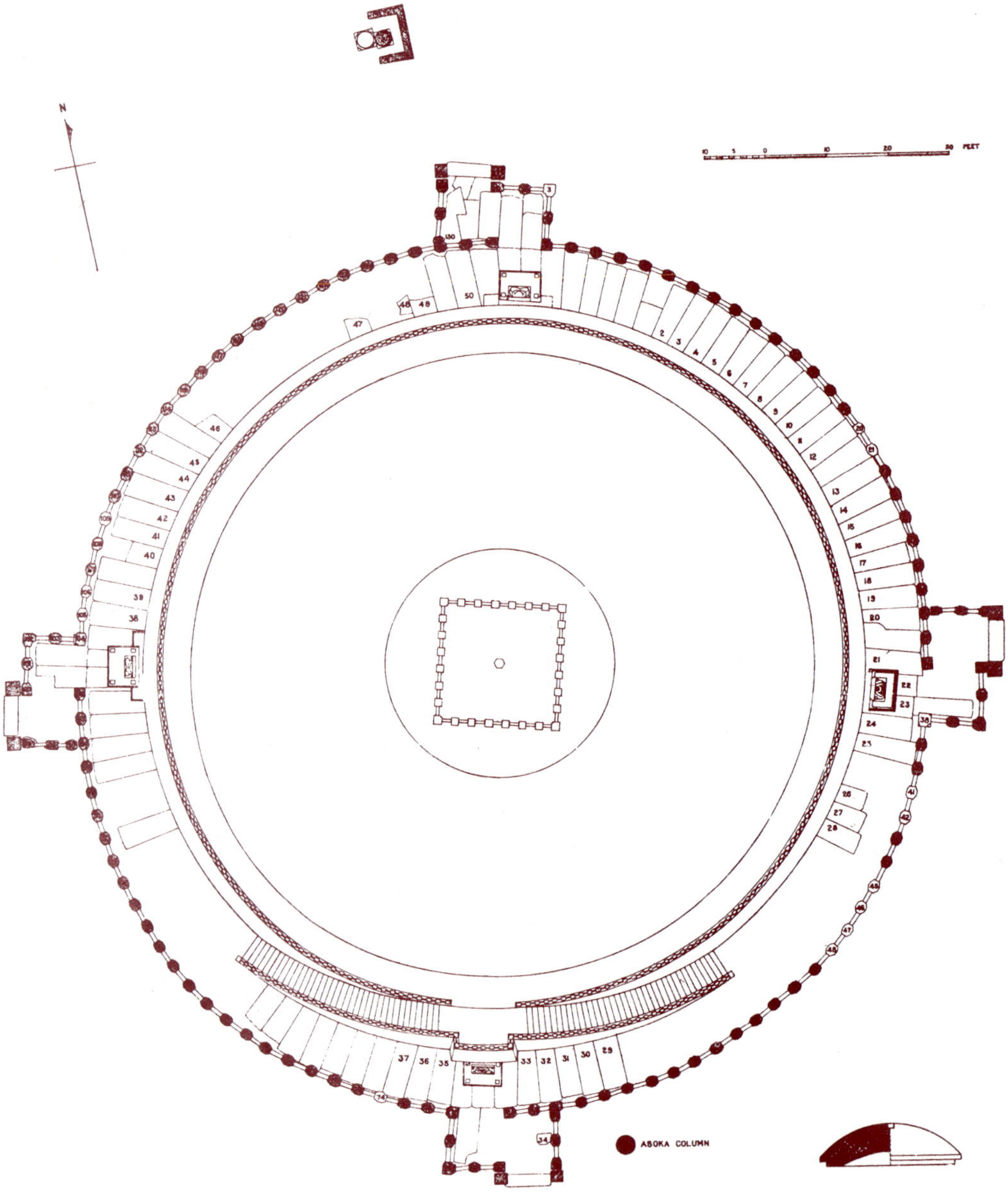

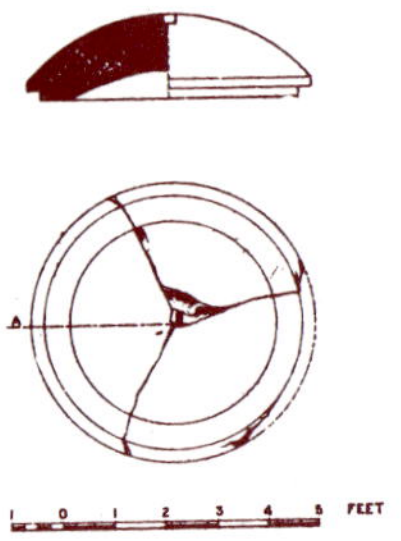

LID OF STONE RELIC BOX.

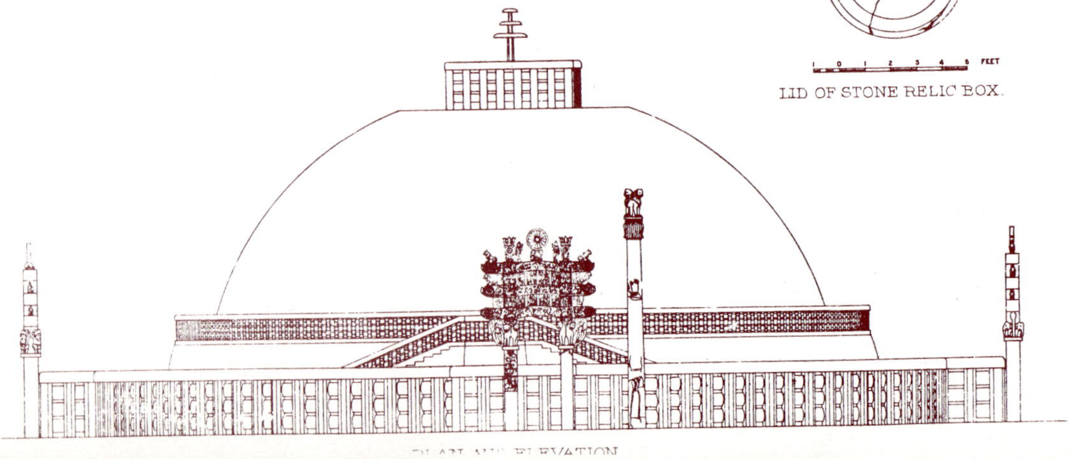

PLAN AND ELEVATION

PLATE 4

PLAN AND ELEVATION OF STŪPA 1

The Stūpa is here shown as enlarged and restored under the Śuṅga régime (pp. 29-36), with the four gateways subsequently added under the Andhras (pp. 36-38). The pillars of the ground balustrade which are shown shaded in the plan, are original pillars still *in situ*; those without shading are modern restorations (*cf.* Pl. 6). Note that the number of steps in each flight of steps should be twenty-five, not as shown in the plan. This error on the part of the draftsman was not discovered until after the Plate had been printed.

The small three-sided plinth a little to the north of the North Gateway belonged to the Gupta Pillar 35 (pp. 50-52). For the ponderous stone lid figured on this Plate, see p. 32.

PLATE 5

VIEW OF STŪPA I, FROM THE NORTH-EAST

This photograph was taken 35 years ago, before the restoration of the berm and crowning balustrades seen in Plate 6. Fortunately, the northern half of the dome was not injured when Capt. Johnson carried out his disastrous excavation of the Stūpa in 1822 (p. 7); it still retains much of its original concrete facing, though no traces are left of any swags or other surface ornaments with which it may once have been embellished (p. 30).

The gateway in the foreground, to the spectator's right, is the Northern—standing as it has stood for two thousand years,—and beyond it, still further to the right, the Western. The low stone foundation on which two Indians are seated, is the plinth of the Gupta Pillar 35 (pp. 50-52). To the left of the picture, the Eastern Gateway is seen in profile only, and a little to the right of it (just visible above the stūpa balustrade) is the roof of the Gupta Temple 17 (pp. 56-58). Beyond is the low jungle in which the ruins of Temple 18 were then enveloped.

VIEW FROM NORTH-EAST

THE MONUMENTS OF SANCHI : STUPA I.

Pl. VI

VIEW FROM SOUTH

PLATE 6

VIEW OF STŪPA 1, FROM THE SOUTH

This picture, taken in 1920, shows the Great Stūpa soon after its southern half had been reconstructed and its balustrades restored (pp. 39-40). The gateway nearest to the spectator is the Southern, which, along with the Western, was re-erected by Major Cole between the years 1881 and 1883 (p. 8). A little to the right of the Southern Gateway appears the stump of the Aśoka pillar set up about 254 B.C.; and lying by its side, the broken sections of its shaft (pp. 25-29). The structure in the foreground to the right is the corner of Temple 18; to the left, the remains of Shrine 9 (pp. 52-56 and 58).

PLATE 7

a. The ground balustrade of Stūpa 1 and the Aśoka column. This sectional drawing shows the foundations of the Aśoka column, the original pavement laid when the column was erected (c. 254 B.C.), and the several pavements which succeeded it, as the ground rose higher and higher, up to the time when the ground balustrade was constructed (c. 145 B.C.). Observe that the Aśoka column rested directly on the bed rock and was maintained in position by a packing of boulders enclosed in retaining walls (pp. 26-27). The words 'red concrete' which appear twice in the drawing are not quite correct. The earliest floor is of broken brick (*bajrī*); the next, immediately above it, of broken brick in clay; the third of pounded brick in lime; the fourth of *bajrī* overlaid with lime plaster; the fifth of stone.

b-e. The remaining figures on this plate show the stairway, berm and harmikā balustrades of Stūpa 1, as well as another section of the ground balustrade, which is of slightly different dimensions from that shown in Fig. *a*. All these balustrades are described on pp. 30-36. Observe that, in each of them, the upright posts (*stambha*) were monoliths. When the ground balustrade was restored, such new posts as were required, were made in two or three pieces, and are therefore readily distinguishable from the original posts (*cf*. Pls. 4 and 6). Observe, also, that the ground and harmikā balustrades of this stūpa are severely plain, whereas the stairway and berm balustrades are adorned with carvings on their outer face.

(a) GROUND BALUSTRADE AND ASOKA COLUMN.

(b) STAIRWAY BALUSTRADE.

(c) BERM BALUSTRADE.

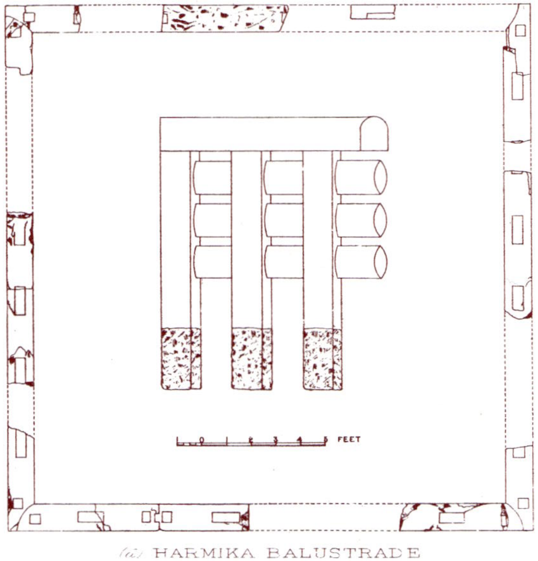

(d) HARMIKA BALUSTRADE

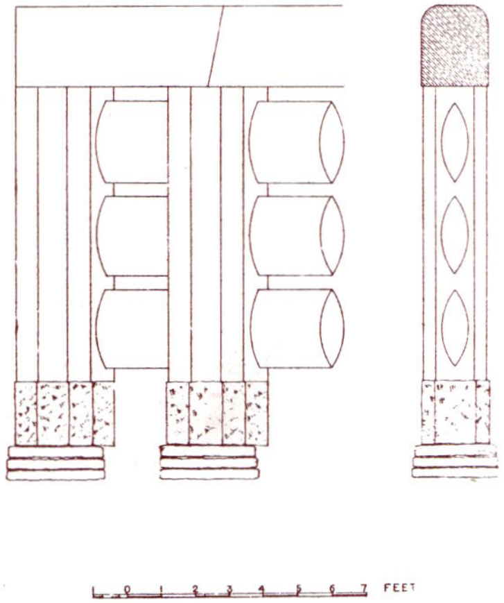

(e) GROUND BALUSTRADE

THE MONUMENTS OF SANCHI: STUPA I.

a

b

c

d

e

f

DETAILS OF BERM AND STAIRWAY BALUSTRADES.

PLATE 8

STŪPA 1.—DETAILS OF BERM AND STAIRWAY BALUSTRADES

The decoration is on the outer face of these balustrades, doubtless in order to brighten up the bareness of the dome. It was not meant for the eyes of the worshippers who made their *pradakshiṇa* on the terrace, but for those who made it on the ground between the big bare balustrade of the stūpa at their left and the decorated balustrade of the terrace at their right (*cf.* Pl. 6). As on the balustrade of Stūpa 2, only the vertical uprights (*stambha*) are decorated, not the horizontal bars (*sūci*), and most of the medallions or half-medallions are patterned with lotuses, variously treated, but most frequently opened rose-fashion. Themes other than the lotus are mainly reserved for the middle row of medallions (but see exceptions under *c* and *f*).

a. Observe the lotus creeper, in a still fairly simple form, up the whole length of the left pillar; then, from left to right on the central medallions, a buffalo whose head is curiously shown from above, an antelope, a bull, a griffin, and two antelopes *affrontés*.

b. In the same order on the middle come an elephant, a buffalo, two more elephants, a bull, a *makara*, a horse, a fourth elephant, a stylised lotus, a fifth elephant and a winged lion: all the 'four animals' are here, but not alone. Above, the second pillar bears two birds *affrontés* holding a garland in their beaks; and the eighth, a vase with lotuses (*cf.* above, p. 184 and note 1).

c. Below will be noticed a single specimen of a bear and a gazelle scratching its muzzle with its hind-foot, both very well sketched; on the middle, an elephant and (at last) two tiny human figures (genie and fairy?).

d and *e*. At the foot of the first pillar of the flight, a male personage standing and holding some flowers looks like a first sketch of the Yakshas of the Gateways (*cf.* Pls. 36, 50, 52, etc.). In *e*, underneath a scroll of lotus creeper, the Yaksha is accompanied by his Yakshī (*cf.* pp. 175 and 244).

f. On the first pillar is a griffin and an elephant; on the fifth, a griffin and a centaur ridden by a woman (*cf.* p. 174); and on the sixth, two elephants.

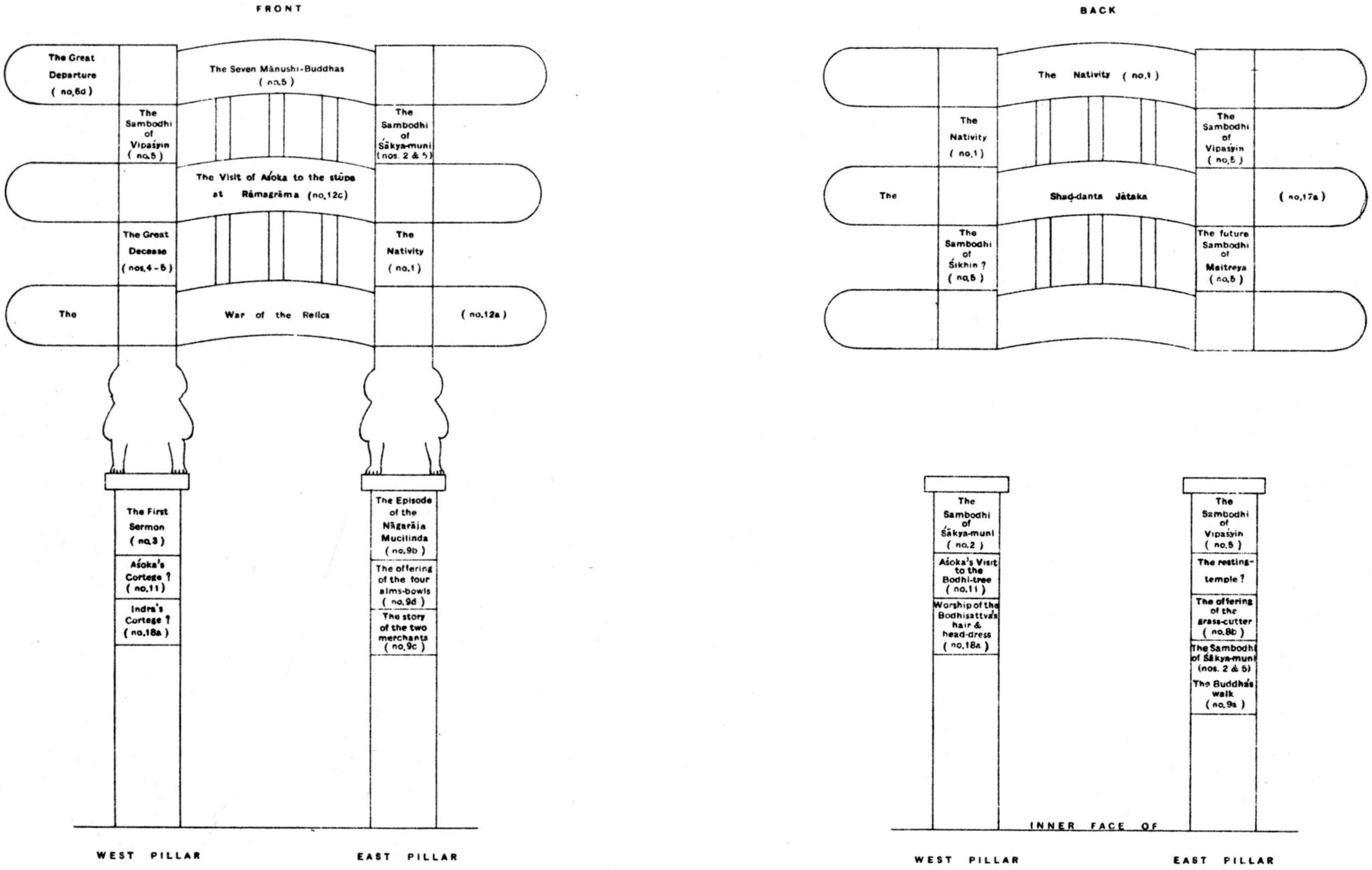

SOUTHERN GATEWAY (Restored) : INDEX-MAP OF THE LEGENDARY SCENES

Reg. No. 3936 E'36-595.

Helio. S. I. O. Calcutta.

FRONT ELEVATION OF SOUTHERN GATEWAY

FRONT FACE OF SOUTHERN GATEWAY

PLATE 10

FRONT OF SOUTHERN GATEWAY

The important thing to notice from the point of view of iconography, besides the serious and much to be regretted gaps in the decoration, is the fact that the top and bottom lintels were reversed when the gateway was set up again in the last century. There can be no doubt that originally the facade presented, minutely executed by a master-hand, three compositions of supreme interest to the eyes of pilgrims, namely :—

(*a*) on the top lintel, the icons of the seven Mānushi-Buddhas;

(*b*) on the middle lintel, Aśoka's Visit to the Rāmagrāma stūpa;

(*c*) on the bottom lintel, the War of the Relics.

The back had merely three decoratively treated themes, namely :—

(*a*) on the top lintel, a Nativity centring a tangle of lotuses[1];

(*b*) on the middle lintel, a spinning out of the Shaḍdanta-Jātaka;

(*c*) on the bottom lintel, pot-bellied dwarfs (*kumbhāṇḍas*) spouting forth the Lotus Tree of Life and Fortune[2].

The modern restoration visible in Pl. 10, upsetting this perfectly well thought out plan, has banished from the front facade the seven Mānushi-Buddhas which the Sāñchī sculptors, as may be seen on the other gateways, had made an absolute rule of portraying on the fronts of all their *toraṇas*, and the magnificent "historical piece" illustrating the siege of Kuśinagara. Only the one bearing the "Visit of Aśoka" has been retained in its original place, and contrasts oddly with the two almost purely ornamental motives between which it is now found inserted. With these reservations, our description will conform to the present arrangement, as shown on the plates.

In addition to one false-capital, two projecting ends of lintels, the uprights and all the separate figures, the restored gateway has lost also half of the west pillar (see Pl. 18) and the whole of the east pillar. The fairly substantial remains of the latter are, however, preserved in the local museum at Sāñchī and are shown on Pl. 19, whilst the two faces of the eastern projecting end of the middle lintel have been put back into place on Pls. 13 and 16.

As regards the capitals, *cf.* Pl. 14.

For the reader's convenience, while looking at Pl. 10, we may again point out :—

(*a*) on the four dies :—a Nativity (Great Miracle no. 1); two Illuminations (G. M. no. 2), one of Vipaśyin and the other of Śākya-muni (that is, of the first and last Buddhas of the series of seven), and lastly a *Parinirvāṇa* (G. M. no. 4)

(*b*) on the western end of the middle lintel, a tableau of paradise, earthly or heavenly (*cf.* pp. 228-229);

(*c*) on the western pillar, a First Sermon (G. M. no. 3) and two 'Visits', one royal and in a chariot, the other divine and on an elephant.

[1] *Cf.* pp. 128 and 146.

[2] *Cf.* p. 146.

PLATE 11

FRONT OF SOUTHERN GATEWAY: MIDDLE SECTION

1. (*Back of*) *Top Lintel.*—As a matter of fact, it is the back and not the front which we see here. In the centre, Māyā, left hand on hip and a lotus in her right hand, standing on a lotus between the two Nāgas, likewise supported by open lotus flowers, gives us an already advanced form of the Nativity (*cf.* p. 197). The whole surface of the lintel is covered from end to end (*cf.* Pls. 12, 1 and 13, 1) with stalks, leaves, buds and flowers of the lotus, among which a couple of Indian geese (*haṁsa*) are set on each side.

2. *Middle Lintel.*—For the general meaning of this scene (which has fortunately been set up again in its original position) see above, p. 215 *sqq.* We must note further here:—(*a*) In the centre, the style of the stūpa obviously analogous to that of Stūpa 1 at Sāñchī (*cf.* Pl. 6). (*b*) On the right, the characteristic details of the royal insignia (turban, ewer, fly-whisk; the umbrella is missing), and the royal chariot and procession. Besides the band, the suite includes all four 'arms', infantry, cavalry, elephants and chariots (*cf.* Pl. 40, 3 and, for the chariot, Pl. 23*a*; but there is here no woman in the retinue). (*c*) On the left, the four Nāgas (*cf.* p. 244) and their families coming to bring the ritual offerings in their hands, in ewers or on plates. The male genii display five-headed hoods, whilst their wives have to be content with a single hood; it is the same with the servant (?) stooping in the foreground at the left of the stūpa; but behind him a young boy—doubtless the heir presumptive of the Nāga-rāja whom he precedes—has already a triple hood. Two of the Nāgas and their Nāgīs are still immersed up to the waist in the lotus-pond which is their home, whilst two others with their female attendants are already seen full-length on the bank. Of the latter, the one nearest the stūpa is the king of the tribe (note his special turban) and the other, standing on a slightly lower level, his viceroy or *upa-rāja* (*cf.* Pl. 49*a*). This may help us indirectly to make out the identity of the great personage who follows Aśoka at the other end of the lintel, and whose stature and elephant, and the two standards which flank him, put him almost on an equal footing with the emperor. This must also be his *upa-rāja* and consequently the second personage in the empire. At the back of the tableau, the row of trees (among which bignonias, mango-trees, champakas and a fan-shaped palm-tree are recognizable) recalls the fact that, according to the legend, the territory of Rāmagrāma had been reclaimed by the forest.

3. (*Back of*) *Bottom Lintel.*—One cannot fail to recall the decoration of the coping stone of the Bharhut Stūpa (*cf.* Cunn., Pl. 39 *sqq.*). At each end of the lintel a pot-bellied dwarf with a big head and short legs, probably a *kumbhāṇḍa* (*cf.* p. 243), is spouting forth a lotus stalk which makes a bending sweep and ends in serpentine coils in the centre. Leaves, buds and flowers of lotus sprout likewise out of the navels of both (*cf.* Pls. 19*b*, 78, nos. 22*a* and 23*a*) and from the mouths of the four other genii, shown from the waist, who are lodged symmetrically in the curves of the stalk. It will be noticed that all six have crinkled hair, with or without a fillet, and carry heavy pearl-necklaces in their hands by way of garlands. At the right, another necklace, made of imbricated scales and presumably of gold or silver, sprouts out of a lotus flower. Observe likewise that one of the genii in the middle (the one on the right) is wearing on his body, instead of the ordinary necklace, two crossed chains connecting six medallions (four of which are visible here); this kind of ornament will be found again elsewhere (*cf.* Pl. 27, 4, etc.)[1].

[1] For further remarks on the significance of this relief, see Part II *supra*, pp. 144-146.

FRONT OF SOUTHERN GATEWAY: MIDDLE SECTION OF ARCHITRAVES

FRONT OF SOUTHERN GATEWAY: WEST END OF UPPER AND MIDDLE ARCHITRAVES

PLATE 12

FRONT OF SOUTHERN GATEWAY: WEST END

1. (*Back of*) *Top Lintel.*—The floral decoration of the middle part reappears, more luxuriant than ever, on the projecting end of the lintel: two *haṁsa* heads are peeping through the lotuses.

2. *Middle Lintel.*—A 'genre' piece without connection with the middle scene. A royal or divine personage, astride on the neck of an elephant, the hook of the aṅkuśa (the handle of which he holds in both hands) resting on the animal's forehead, is riding through a lotus-pond. Behind him his queen brandishes the fly-whisk with her right hand and seems to be holding out her left to another woman to help her to climb up the back of the animal, which is busy tearing up the lotuses with his trunk. In the right-hand corner, a single mango-tree represents all the trees in the 'pleasure park'. In the background, on the terrace-balcony of a palace, two more ladies of the court are watching these 'gambols in the water' (*jala-krīḍā*). We have already hinted (pp. 228-229) at the practical impossibility of guessing whether the scene is conceived as taking place on earth or in heaven.

3. (*Back of*) *Bottom Lintel.*—The decoration is lost. Most likely it represented a peacock (*cf.* Pl. 13). It will be noticed that the ends of the three lintels have protuberances on them; they are the remains of flying figures (*cf.* Pl. 17).

4. *Top Die.*—The usual picture of the second Great Miracle. As proved by a Bharhut inscription and analogy with the back of the Eastern Gateway (Pls. 45 and 47, 1), it represents the *Sambodhi* of Vipaśyin, symbolised by the bignonia.

5. *Bottom Die.*—The stūpa of the *Parinirvāṇa* shown here has the peculiarity that its *harmikā*, adorned as usual with merlons, is surmounted by umbrellas at all four corners, and by a fifth of larger size in the centre.

6. *False-capitals.*—The top and middle false-capitals are decorated with two horses couchant, back to back. Notice in the trappings the richly-plumed headstalls and the girths trimmed with discs. The horse facing left is, in both cases, ridden by a king (note the turban), accompanied on the right-hand horse by his viceroy above, and by his queen below. On the bottom false-capital, the stags substituted for the horses are more simply bridled, but still ridden by the king (in the foreground) and his *upa-rāja*.

PLATE 13

FRONT OF SOUTHERN GATEWAY: EAST END

1. (*Back of*) *Top Lintel.*—As on the west end (Pl. 12), the lotus decoration is continued as far as the volute, and a palmette fills up the space between them.

2. *Middle Lintel.*—The projecting end is one of the detached pieces preserved in the local museum and has been artificially put in place on the plate. As on its companion (*cf.* Pl. 12), there is an elephant grazing in a lotus pond; but the figures here seated on the rocks on the bank are doubtless a couple of genii (*cf.* p. 229). The Yaksha is broken and only his bent left leg is to be seen; the Yakshī has her arms and legs crossed, and between the pair lies their harp. At the left of the fairy, a cylindrical box, resembling a casket of relics (*cf.* Pl. 15, 3), is hung on a peg (*nāga-danta*) and doubtless contains some toilette preparation; below, in a jar, water is cooling.

3. (*Back of*) *Bottom Lintel.*—On a rocky landscape are seen in profile a peacock in the foreground, and in the background a tree apparently burnt by a forest fire and having only the skeleton of its branches left. A water-fall is bursting out of some rocks at the back.

4. *Top Die.*—Stereotype of the *Sambodhi* of the Buddha Sākya-muni, to judge by the tree: for this is the way in which the workshop chose to represent the *aśvattha* or *ficus religiosa*. In the attitude of the two female figures there may be a suggestion of Sujātā's Offering (see p. 206).

5. *Bottom Die.*—Picture, still archaic, of the Nativity (*cf.* pp. 183 and 197): in fact, Māyā is simply seated Indian-fashion on the pericarp of the central lotus and the Nāga-elephants are not yet shown.

6. *False-capitals.*—The middle one is lost. Like the one which surmounts it and the one which forms its companion (*cf.* Pl. 12) it should consist of two horses couchant back to back, ridden by princely personages. The stag in the background on the lower capital has a queen in the saddle. In comparing Pls. 12 and 13 it will be noticed that the orientation of the animals in the fore- and back-ground is symmetrically reversed from jamb to jamb.

As regards the protuberance on the end of the lintels, see Pl. 17.

FRONT OF SOUTHERN GATEWAY: EAST END OF ARCHITRAVES

a FRONT OF SOUTHERN GATEWAY: CAPITAL OF WEST PILLAR

b THE SAME: CAPITAL OF EAST PILLAR

PLATE 14

For the Lion Capitals of the Southern Gateway, see Part II, pp. 138-9.

PLATE 15

BACK OF SOUTHERN GATEWAY: MIDDLE SECTION OF ARCHITRAVES

1. *(Front of) Top Lintel.*—There is no possible doubt that we have to do here with the symbolic representation of the seven Mānushi-Buddhas, or that this representation originally enjoyed the honour of the front view. The only question is how to share out among these Buddhas the four *Sambodhi* trees and the three *Parinirvāṇa* tumuli which symbolize them. A comparison with the Eastern Gateway at Sāñchī and the inscribed reliefs at Bharhut gives us some idea as to the trees: the sculptor has undertaken to show the *bodhi-druma* of the four last Buddhas of the series, namely, from left to right, the *sirīsha* (*acacia sirissa*) of Krakucchanda, the *udumbara* (*ficus glomerata*) of Kanakamuni, the *nyagrodha* (*ficus indica*) of Kāśyapa (it will be noticed that here the pendent roots of the 'banyan fig-tree' are well marked, as also on the middle lintel), and lastly the *ficus religiosa* of Sākya-muni, the leaves of which are very carefully drawn. We are in possession of no facts which would justify any hypothesis as to the distribution of the three *stūpas* among the other three Mānushi-Buddhas.

2. *Middle Lintel.*—On the essentially decorative character of this composition, see Sir John Marshall's remarks above (Part II, p. 120; and *Guide to Sāñchī*, p. 74 *sqq.*), and for the identification of the legend, above p. 224. From the point of view of iconography, the most interesting facts to notice are that the elephant 'Shaḍdanta' is correctly shown with triple tusks and that he recurs no less than four times in the composition. From left to right: (1) he is in his bath, in company with his umbrella- and flywhisk-bearers; (2) he is coming out of his bath and proceeding towards the central *nyagrodha*; (3) he afterwards advances in great pomp, again towards the right, and this time he is preceded by his ewer-bearer; (4) lastly, looking left, but still in profile, he rests aloof in the forest. This is the moment chosen by the hunter, hidden among the rocks, to let fly a deadly arrow from behind: but it is clear that the man is there merely as a reminder, since from that ambush he could never really manage to shoot the elephant (on the Gandhāra frieze, on the contrary, as on the Amarāvatī medallion, the hunter is hiding in a ditch from which he can effectively wound the elephant in the belly). It is likewise surprising that such a careful sculptor should have given his trapper (*vanecara*) the turban of a townsman, though he might claim in his defence that the hunter is a royal emissary and has arrived direct from Benares.

3. *(Front of) Bottom Lintel.*—On the subject of this lintel, see also Sir John Marshall's remarks (Part II, p. 118; and *Guide to Sāñchī*, pp. 75-76) and for identification, above, p. 214. Among the most curious things to be learnt from this picture of a besieged town, we may point out: (1) as regards the town itself, the line of lotuses in the middle of the foreground, marking the ditch in which some of the fighters are standing; the walls made of big bricks or stones, the indication of which is perhaps meant to show by contrast that the two gates and the tower at the left, with their smooth surface, were coated with stucco; the battlements and merlons, the loopholes with or without a dripstone, the loggias with balconies, etc.; (2) as regards the armies, the depiction of the four kinds of troops, on foot, on horseback, on elephants and in chariots; the sort of kamarband (made of a rope wound round the body?) worn by some of the soldiers[1]; the method of defence which consists not only in shooting arrows, but in throwing down stones from the ramparts onto the assailants; the different kinds of weapons: bows, pikes, swords and perhaps clubs (it is difficult to distinguish these two latter from one another on account of the breadth of the swords); the patterns of shields and standards; the trappings on elephants and horses, etc. Finally, we have to point out the shape of the relic-caskets, very like the steatite lathe-turned caskets from the stūpas of Sāñchī itself (see Part I, pp. 44 and 81, *supra*).

[1] This rope-like *kamarband* of the soldiers is still common among Indian chaprasis. In Pl. 64 *a* 1, the soldiers' *kamarband* consists of two broad bands only. *Cf.*, also, Pl. 25, 1.

BACK OF SOUTHERN GATEWAY: MIDDLE SECTION OF ARCHITRAVES

BACK OF SOUTHERN GATEWAY.

PLATE 16

BACK OF SOUTHERN GATEWAY: EAST END

1. *(Front of) Top Lintel*.—The projecting end of the lintel (on what was formerly the front face) is devoted to a distinct subject, the *Mahābhinishkramaṇa* (*cf.* p. 203 *sqq.*). The Kapilavastu gate is here shown as a simple *toraṇa* with two lintels, arched and curled to the form of volutes at both ends. Observe that the two praying figures in the background (probably *devas*) have their hands joined and are *not* carrying the two royal attributes, which float in the air by magic above the horse—both the umbrella (garlanded) and the fly-whisk—whilst the ewer is in the right hand of Chandaka, the groom. The saddle-cloth of Kaṇṭhaka has apparently no girth here.

2. *Middle Lintel*.—Though fractured and mutilated, the decoration has been put back in its place on the photograph. The elephant walking to the right and the baby-elephant following her, evidently represent part of the '84,000' head of cattle over which the Shaḍdanta reigns (*cf.* Pl. 15, 2).

3. *(Front of) Bottom Lintel*.—As above, the middle theme is continued on the projecting end of the lintel, and shows us two of the seven claimants at Kuśinagara (*cf.* p. 214), one riding an elephant and the other in a chariot, with their attendants. It will be noticed that a bearer of bow and arrows (his headdress is most curious: the ends of his turban seemingly surround his face and are drawn like a scarf round his neck) is perched on the elephant between the king and the standard-bearer. Though the umbrella (which here seems to be meant less for the king than for the casket of relics) presumably has a bearer, he is quite invisible. To the right, a plantain is indicated; to the left, down below, a dwarf carrying a pitcher of water in his right hand and with his left leading on the leash a dog with tail erect, marches at the head of the army.

4. *Top Die*.—Archaic representation of the Nativity by the vase of lotuses (*cf.* pp. 183 and 197).

5. *Bottom Die*.—By every analogy we must here have to do with a symbolical representation of one of the seven Mānushi-Buddhas, and the mango-tree could be attributed to Śikhin, if the particular tree dedicated to him (*puṇḍarīka*) has been rightly identified as a kind of mango-tree. We do not, however, know for certain the exact species of this *bodhi-druma* of Śikhin, and the Northern and Eastern Gateways give it rather the appearance of a sort of fig-tree (*cf.* Pls. 22 and 46). This being so, one might be tempted to see on this panel a picture of the gift of the Mango Grove by the courtezan Āmrapālī, and in that case, the two women in the foreground would be the donor herself (with the ewer) and her attendant, whilst the two male figures would stand for two of the Licchavi princes of Vaiśālī: but the identification would, in our opinion, be questionable, since bearers of ewers abound in these little pictures round all the *bodhi-drumas* (*cf.* Pls. 12, 4; 13, 4; 22, 2; 101, 4).—For other mango-trees promoted to the dignity of *bodhi-trees*, see Pls. 96, 2 and 103*d*.

6. *Top false-capital*.—Two Indian bulls couchant, with one knee lifted, recall the bulls set back to back on Persian capitals. Notice their characteristic hump; the head-stall passing through their nostrils, crossing over their muzzles, then folded back round each horn and fixed by a turn or two round the forehead (*cf.* Pls. 41 and 43); the rope round their shoulders, holding the end of the tail forwards, doubtless to prevent it from flicking dust into the faces of the occupants of the chariot (*cf.* Pls. 19*c*; 15, 3; 18*a*; 43, 4, etc., where the same practice is observed with harnessed horses); and lastly the heavy necklaces, still worn by cattle in India. The fastening of these necklaces by means of a big stud passing through a loop, is the same in the case of the men (*cf.* Pl. 36*a-b*), but is better illustrated here. The two riders are evidently great noblemen, if we may judge by their attire; each of them is holding up a tray with a garland, similar to those seen in the hands of the praying figures on the top die of Pl. 17, but here coiled like a snake.

The *middle false-capital*, which should be just like the preceding one (*cf.* Pl. 17), is missing.

7. *Bottom False-Capital*.—The two animals back to back are elephants here, and we have already pointed out (p. 214) the exceptional part which the left-hand one plays in the general subject of the lintel. It will be noticed that the staff of the standard is made of a bundle of sticks bound together at intervals, surmounted by an ensign (*nandipada*), and fitting into a kind of metal butt: the bearer, forced by the weight of these flag-bearing fasces to hold them in both arms, has (to secure his seat) wound round his hips a rope fastened to the elephant's girth. The latter rope holds in place the richly embroidered caparison, decorated with tassels at the corners; a similar cloth, but smaller, forms the saddle; and a third, making a hood over the crown of the beast's head and falling in draped folds on each side of the shoulders above the king's legs, protecting him from contact with the huge flapping ears, is fastened by a rope passing under the neck. What the cord with the bell is hung on to, is not quite clear (*cf.* Pls. 17, 42 and 44).

For the lions of the capitals, *cf.* above, Part II, pp. 138-9.

PLATE 17

BACK OF SOUTHERN GATEWAY: WEST END OF ARCHITRAVES

1. *(Front of) Top Lintel.*—This relief, completely symmetrical with its companion (*cf.* Pl. 16, 1), shows us a royal personage with his groom on his left carrying the umbrella and fly-whisk; in the presence of one of his wives, he is preparing to mount a horse and already holds the reins on its withers with his left hand. In front march a man holding with both hands a staff which rests on his left shoulder, with some indistinct object hanging from it, and a dwarf who has just put down a jar of water (which he was carrying in his hand on the east end of the bottom lintel on Pl. 16). Perhaps he was also holding in leash a dog, which has now disappeared with the fracture of the stone; in that case—the portrayal of the horseman excluding *ipso facto* the *Mahābhinishkramaṇa*—it would be a simple genre piece to be entitled 'Setting out for the Chase'?

2. *Middle Lintel.*—Here, as on the other end of the lintel (*cf.* Pl. 16, 2), the big and little elephant on the march in this landscape of trees and rocks are merely a continuation of the decoration of the middle section (Pl. 15, 2).

3. *(Front of) Bottom Lintel.*—In the same way, the two kings, one in a chariot and the other on an elephant, here forming the companion picture to those marching in the opposite direction on the other projecting end of the lintel (Pl. 16), complete the middle scene (Pl. 15, 3). Here again, the bearer of the bow and quiver is inserted between the king and the standard-bearer on the elephant's back. Behind and half hidden by the streamer floating above the elephant and the umbrella spread over the chariot, one can make out one of the trees cut in the shape of an arbour which we shall have occasion to refer to again (Pl. 64c).

4. *Top Die.*—Miracle of the *Sambodhi* of Vipaśyin symbolised by his *bignonia* above a throne (*cf.* Pl. 12, 4). We have already pointed out, in speaking of the top False-Capital on Pl. 16, the large garlands held by the praying figures. These are made in the Indian manner, by binding together a number of chaplets of flowers strung on threads.

5. *Bottom Die.*—An advance illustration of the *Sambodhi* of the future Buddha Maitreya, shown by his *Nāga-pushpa* or *Michelia champaka*.

6. *False-Capitals.*—The description of those on Pl. 16 may be repeated here almost word for word. But on the upper False-Capital, one of the two riders is holding up a relic-casket and the other (just between the horns of the ox) a blue lotus (*utpala*). On the lower one we should also notice that the hoods of the elephants are adorned with rich pendants; that the standard-bearer has tucked his legs under the caparison and under his left arm is holding the scabbard, covered with criss-cross thongs, of the king's broad-sword; and that the cloth of the standard is divided up by bands into six rectangular compartments, adorned with embroidered emblems in the form of the solar disc and the crescent moon.

7. At the bottom, right hand of this Plate may be seen a specimen of the winged figures, unfortunately damaged, which used to decorate the extremities of the lintels. Represented full-face and foreshortened, the trunk framed between the two wings and the head outlined against the feathers of the tail, they have been conceived exactly on the pattern of those, shown three-quarter face, which fill the upper corners of all the scenes of the Great Miracles.

For the lions of the capital, *cf.* above, Part II, pp. 138-9.

BACK OF SOUTHERN GATEWAY

a. WEST END OF UPPER AND MIDDLE ARCHITRAVES

b. WEST END OF LOWER ARCHITRAVE AND CAPITAL

WEST PILLAR OF SOUTHERN GATEWAY.

UPPER PANELS ON FRONT FACE

UPPER PANELS ON EAST FACE

PLATE 18

WEST PILLAR OF SOUTHERN GATEWAY

*a*1. *Top Panel of Front Face.*—Decorative picture of the third Great Miracle, that of the First Sermon (*cf.* p. 198). The sculptor has forgotten to surmount the Indo-Persian pillar with its usual capital of lions; on the other hand he has given it a pedestal. The Wheel of the Law, topped by a garlanded umbrella, contains 32 spokes, to which the same number of *nandipada* (or should we say *tri-ratna*?) emblems correspond on the outer side of the felly. Below, eight deer make it certain that the place of the scene is the *Mrigadāva*, near Benares. Four kings, each accompanied by his suite and, according to the conventions of the old perspective, supposed to be standing at the four compass points of the monument (*cf.* inscriptions on the Bharhut relief, Cunn., Pl. 14, 1), certainly represent the four *Lokapālas* or Guardians of the World.

*b*1. *Top Panel of East Face.*—Decorative picture of the second Great Miracle—the Enlightenment. The *aśvattha* of the *sambodhi* of Śākyamuni already stands, adorned with streamers and topped with a double garlanded umbrella, in the centre of a temple open to the sky, which the piety of Aśoka is supposed to have erected round it two centuries later. Observe the three dormer-windows and the four pinnacles on the roof, the designs of the columns, and especially the three-fold emblem which the sculptor has likewise anticipated on the Master's *vajra-āsana* (*cf.* p. 197): for in fact there cannot yet be any question of the second and third *ratnas* (jewels), that is, the Buddhist Law and Community (*cf.* Pl. 51*a*).

*a*2. *Middle Panel of Front Face.*—A king in a chariot, accompanied by a suite (reduced in number on account of the smallness of the panel), is going somewhere. It seems natural to suppose that the clue to the riddle is given by the adjacent panel (*b*2), and that we have here King Aśoka going to pay his famous visit to the bodhi-tree. As on Pl. 15, 2, he is accompanied by his viceroy, riding an elephant. For the herald with the club (or sword? *cf.* Pl. 62, 2), see p. 212 and n. 3.

*b*2. *Middle Panel of East Face.*—For the identification which the attitude of the king between his two queens has suggested to us, see above, p. 212. Two more female attendants are holding respectively the umbrella and the pitcher containing the king's drink, with the drinking cup; for the probable purpose of the jar set on the ground, see p. 212, n. 4. In the two women squatting on both sides on *morhas* of rattan, we must doubtless see, as at Amarāvatī, the vendors of offerings and religious articles who are to be found, then as now and in India as everywhere else, round places of pilgrimage; in fact, they are both so unconcerned with the action, that one of them (at the left) has her back turned. In the top right-hand corner, garlands are hung on pegs (*nāga-danta*).

*a*3. *Lower Panel of Front Face.*—There is no inscription here to tell us who is the great lord riding in procession on an elephant with the women of his court; but as the adjacent panel *b*3 seems to show where he is going, we may guess his identity from that; so we have ventured to call him Indra (see above, p. 227). Notice, again, that the woman bearing the umbrella and riding on Airāvata is almost as big as her master; that Queen Śacī is holding a child in front of her on the neck of her elephant; and that the procession is passing under a *toraṇa* with a single lintel, of the type we have already met on Pl. 16, 1.

*b*3. *Bottom Panel of East Face.*—As we have said (p. 227), the analogy of an inscribed relief at Bharhut (Cunn., Pl. 16, 1) banishes any doubt as to the subject and place of the scene. The sculptor has contrived most ingeniously to seat some of the 'Thirty-three' gods on the left, in order to let us see above their heads the orchestra of heavenly nymphs and the contorsions of the lovely dancer with the heavy plaits. It seems to be to the headdress (*cūḍā*) that two of the sky-dwellers are paying the honours of the umbrella and fly-whisk; but we should probably recognize Śakra, the Indra of the gods, in the tall personage standing in the foreground with clasped hands.

On the border of the pillars will be noticed the alternation of Indo-Persian pillars (between *a*2 and *b*2) and floral patterns of stylised lotus (between *a*1 and *b*1), and between *a*3 and *b*3 of a vine with grapes.

PLATE 19

PILLARS OF SOUTHERN GATEWAY

a-b. West Face of West Pillar.—The general conception of the decoration is similar to that of the bottom lintel (Pl. 11, 3); here, too, we see a lotus stalk, issuing probably from the navel (*cf.* Pl. 11, 3 and 78, nos. 22*a* and 23*a*) of the *kumbhāṇḍa* seen in *b*, waving and curling into a volute. The field between the waves is covered with still more varied themes—flowers, fruits, jewels, parrots and other birds, lions and human figures. Compare particularly the couple at the bottom of *a*, sitting in the forest near two lions, with those on Pls. 13, 2 and 44, 1; the genie is playing the harp, whilst the fairy by his side is holding on her knees a heavy necklace of charms, like the one which the Yakshī of the middle wave wears on her breast. For other observations on this panel and for the meaning of the two rings in the lowest register of *a*, see Part II, p. 144 and n. 1.

c. Front of East Pillar.—We know that the pillar is devoted to the Bodh-Gayā cycle (*cf.* p. 205 *sqq.*).

*c*1. The top panel suggests, in the old manner, the repose of the 'completely accomplished Buddha' under the Goatherd's *nyagrodha* and the Mucilinda episode (*cf.* p. 208). It will be noticed that the Nāga-rāja is sitting on his own coils. Around him four of his queens are sitting on *morhas*; at the back, two standing female attendants are waving fly-whisks. Here, again, the Nāgīs have only one hood (*cf.* Pl. 11, 2).

*c*2. The middle panel, though damaged, still reveals three of the four *Lokapālas* or Guardian Kings of the World, standing and each offering a begging-bowl to the invisible seated Buddha. Each of them had his viceroy at his side, and one of the viceroys on the left is playing the harp, exactly as the Gandharva Pañcaśikha does on the occasion of Indra's Visit (*cf.* p. 218 and Pl. 35*b*, 1).

*c*3. The bottom panel shows the merchants Trapusha and Bhallika passing through Uruvilvā. This is an excellent opportunity to study an ox-chariot and its trappings. Observe the way the tails of the oxen are fastened (*cf.* Pl. 16, 1), and for the dog, compare Pl. 16, 3. One might be tempted to see the two merchants once more in the top right-hand corner after dismounting from their vehicle, each with an offering in his right hand; but the resemblance to the figure in the opposite corner and the way servants carry jars of this sort in all the processions (*cf.* Pls. 16, 6; 18*b* 2; etc.) seem to prove that these are subordinate members of the caravan, like the ewer-carrier (below at the left).

d. West Face of East Pillar.—One of the difficulties of interpretation lies in the impossibility of determining with any degree of certainty the chronological order of the subjects on the various panels.

*d*1. The top panel, as a matter of fact, shows in the traditional manner the *sambodhi* of the Buddha Vipaśyin and not of Śākya-muni. The woman that we see piously prostrating herself on each side of the Master's throne may be an allusion to Sujātā's offering. The question crops up again in *d*3 and 4.

*d*2. The identification of this temple has been discussed above (p. 209); there is nothing exceptional about its architecture.

*d*3. Here, thanks to the characteristic appearance of the principal actor, the grass-cutter, the meaning of the scene is clear (*cf.* p. 206). Observe the shape of his sickle. The woman that we see on each side of the throne and who, at the right of the spectator, is raising an offering in her right hand, is perhaps Sujātā.

*d*4. This question should, it seems, be answered affirmatively in the storey below; the ewers held by the two prostrate women are the well-known symbol of donation; moreover, their presence here might, if necessary, be justified by the rule of washing the hands before and after the meal. But, even so, the Sujātā episode ought to precede the episode of the grass-cutter; and the offering of a rice-pudding could not be made in a ewer. It seems much simpler to admit that we have here the ordinary stereotype of the *Sambodhi*, with its usual circle of male and female worshippers, the females with ewers (Pls. 16, 5; 22, 2 [left], etc.).

*d*5. In this case the context of the pillar would, from top to bottom, determine the order of the offering of Svastika (3), the Enlightenment (4) and lastly Buddha's Walk (*cf.* p. 207). It will be noticed that the wreath above the covered walk or *caṅkrama* (*cf.* Pls. 34*a*, 50*a*, 51*a* and *b*) is supposed to be hanging from curved pegs (*nāga-danta*).

e. East Face of East Pillar.—The same design will be found complete on Pl. 50*b*.

a

b

d

e

e. LOOSE FRAGMENT OF EAST FACE.

a. WEST LAR OF SOUTHERN GATEWAY: PA EL ON WEST FACE.

b LOOSE FRAGMENT LOWER PANEL ON WEST FACE.

EAST PILLA RN GATEWAY: LOOSE FRAGME FRONT FACE

WEST FRONT FACE

FRONT ELEVATION OF NORTHERN GATEWAY

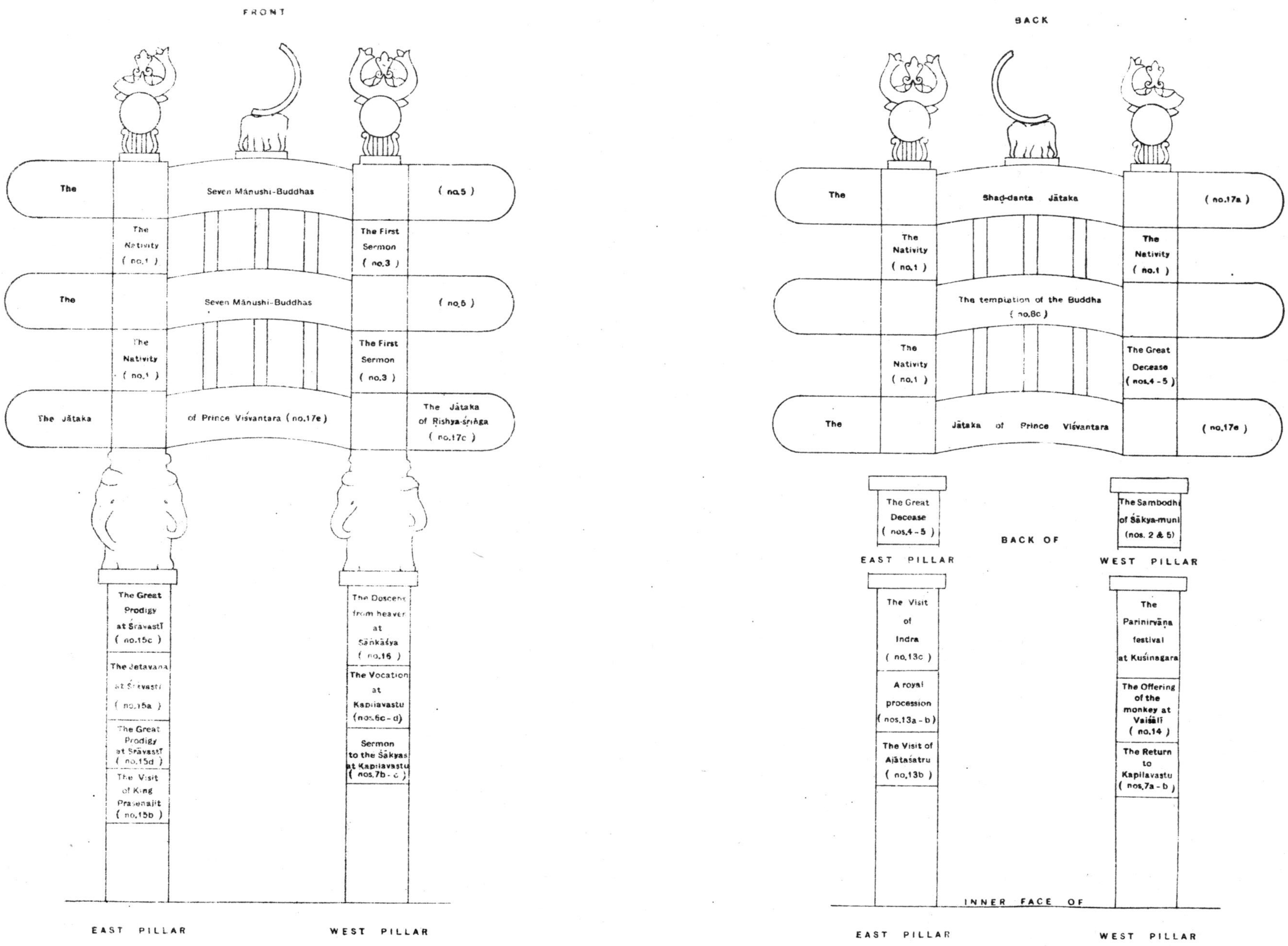

NORTHERN GATEWAY : INDEX-MAP OF THE LEGENDARY SCENES

Reg. No. 3936 E'36 — 595.

Helio. S. I. O. Calcutta.

PLATE 21

FRONT FACE OF NORTHERN GATEWAY

Observe that the Northern Gateway, like the Eastern, and unlike the Southern and Western Gateways, did not have to undergo re-erection in the course of the last century, and that it is the only one that has kept the greater part of its ornamental figures in place.

It is evident that the decoration of the top originally consisted of no less than seven figures: in the centre, a Wheel of the Law and on both sides of it an attendant Yaksha, a *tri-ratna* and a winged lion.

A rapid comparison with Pl. 28 will show that, like the Yakshas on the summit, the lions and (with one exception) the Yakshīs in the spaces between the lintels are carved in the round, whilst the horses and elephants and their riders are carved on both faces in high relief, so that they look in both directions (*cf.* p. 134).

Elephants have taken the place of lions on the capitals here and on the Eastern Gateway; atlantes take their place on the Western Gateway and the Gateway of Stūpa 3.

As on the Southern Gateway, the pillars are edged with small pilasters or with sinuous creepers, including the vine.

The general meaning of the decoration was given on p. 235. We will merely point out for the reader's convenience that this facade shows him:—

(*a*) On the two top lintels the series of the seven Mānushi-Buddhas, whose iconographical importance is thus confirmed; on the bottom lintel the *Ṛishya-śṛiṅga-jātaka* on the right, and in the middle and on the left, the first episodes of the *Viśvantara-jātaka*;

(*b*) On the four dies, the Nativity twice on the left, and the First Sermon twice on the right.

(*c*) On the six uprights between the lintels, a First Sermon above, and a *Sambodhi* below, the Great Miracle being always attended by two genii. It will be noticed that the top right upright has been set back to front: the palmettes belonging to the back have been given the honours of the facade, whilst the genie expected to form a pair with the one on the left is now looking south (*cf.* Pl. 28); but it is to be noted that the mistake was made in ancient, not in modern, times.

(*d*) On the facade of the left (east) jamb, various miracles, the majority of which have the common bond of taking place at Śrāvastī.

(*e*) On the facade of the right (west) jamb, the miracle of the Descent from Heaven at Sāṅkāśya, and two episodes enacted at Kapilavastu. It is hard to determine whether we have lost one or two carved panels by the decay of the stone.

The photograph here reproduced was taken before the restoration of the dome of the stūpa.

FRONT FACE OF NORTHERN GATEWAY.

FRONT OF NORTHERN GATEWAY: MIDDLE SECTION OF UPPER AND MIDDLE ARCHITRAVES.

PLATE 22

FRONT OF NORTHERN GATEWAY

The middle part of the two top lintels can be interpreted iconographically only in conjunction with the two projecting ends.

1. *Top Lintel.*—The front shows, as usual, the seven last Mānushi-Buddhas represented alternately by the trees of their *Sambodhi* and the tumuli of their *Parinirvāṇa*, as on the Southern (Pl. 15, 1), Eastern (Pls. 39 and 45) and Western (Pl. 54; *cf.* Pls. 95 and 99) Gateways. Here we see only five of these symbols, namely two *bodhi-drumas* and three stūpas. Although the facade is blackened and eaten away by the inclemency of the north, we seem to recognize the *aśvattha* or *ficus religiosa* of Śākyamuni at the left, and at the right the *nyagrodha* or *ficus indica* of Kāśyapa—that is, the trees consecrated to the two last Buddhas of the series.

2. *Middle Lintel.*—The designers of the Northern Gateway, apparently sure of public approval, were not ashamed to repeat twice on the facade the same sequence of the seven last Saviours of the world, and for the second time they have symbolised them by their seven trees; on the Eastern Gateway the same repetition is banished to the back (*cf.* Pl. 45), where the series goes in inverse order, from right to left. Here, however, it begins at the left with the *pāṭali* or *bignonia* of Vipaśyin (*cf.* Pl. 24), continuing on the present plate with the fig-tree (unnamed) of Śikhin, the *śāla* or *shorea robusta* of Viśvabhū, the *sirīsha* or *acacia* of Krakucchanda (naturally in the middle in both cases), the *udumbara* or *ficus glomerata* of Kanakamuni, the *nyagrodha* or *ficus indica* of Kāśyapa, and ending on Pl. 26 with the *aśvattha* or *ficus religiosa* of Śākyamuni. The analogy of the inscribed representations at Bharhut (Ćunn., Pls. 29 30), in addition to their place in the series, allows no hesitation in identifying all these trees except that of Śikhin, the only one which has not been found at Bharhut. The evidence of our eyes allows us to assert that here the artist has in mind, not a mango (*cf.* Pl. 16, 5), but a fourth variety of fig-tree (there is no lack of them in India) other than the *religiosa*, *indica* and *glomerata*, and that he meant in fact to suggest the *elastica* or rubber-tree.

3. *Uprights.*—On the centre one, the sculptor has taken advantage of the narrow length of the panel and placed his wheel of the First Sermon at the top of an Indo-Persian column and on a capital made of four lions back to back, like the original set up at Sārnāth by Aśoka on the very site of the third Great Miracle, not to mention its copy, at Sāñchī itself (*cf.* Pl. 107). Notice the garlands and umbrellas and especially the curious shape of the two banners. On the left we have the attendant genie, holding a hem of his *dhotī* in his lowered left hand (*cf.* Pl. 50*a*) and raising (not for his own pleasure, but for a ritual offering?) a long lotus bud in his right, balanced by a hanging garland at the other side of his head. On the right, by mentally turning round the upright, we must replace the Yaksha wrongly figuring on Pl. 29 (*cf.* Pl. 23), and exactly like the former but that his flower is more open.

4. *Detached Figures.*—The crowning piece in the centre was evidently a big *dharma-cakra* or 'Wheel of the Law', the symbol of Buddhist doctrine—probably with 32 spokes like the one on Pl. 18, 1, and supported by a pedestal composed of four elephants arranged as on the capitals of the Eastern Gateway (*cf.* Pl. 42).—The surviving attendant genie is very similar to the *dvārapālas* on the five gates and the Yakshas which we have just seen and shall see again on the uprights. He is holding a fly-whisk in his right hand and in his left what appears to be the end of his *dhotī* folded to the form of an Indian purse (*cf.* Pl. 91*g*). As for the four riders which fill the intervals of the lintels between the three uprights, they are carved on two faces, so as to look towards both the inside and the outside of the monument (*cf.* Pl. 29). One can detect here what is seen more clearly on Pl. 29, the shield-shaped plaque (*Śrīvatsa*)[1] which their steeds wear on the chest.

[1] For this device, see Coomaraswamy, *Notes on Indian Coins and Symbols* (in *Ostasiatische Zeitscrift*, Neue Folge iv, Heft 4), p. 183 *sq*.

PLATE 23

FRONT OF NORTHERN GATEWAY

*a*1. *Bottom Lintel.*—On this lintel, one of Sāñchī's masterpieces, is carved the former rebirth of the Buddha under the name of Viśvantara, the prince of charity (*cf.* p. 225). The story begins at the right in the capital of the Sibis, an excellent excuse for giving us the stereotype of the city (*cf.* Pls. 31, 1; 40, 2; 61, 1 and 2). Behind the battlemented rampart the heir-apparent, riding his elephant, is meeting a foreign Brāhman anchorite in the foreground and receiving his request in the middle-ground; then, in the background, he appears with his family at the balcony and is leaning out, pouring from a ewer onto the hands of this anchorite the water which sanctions the donation of the great Nāga-elephant of the kingdom: so that in all we have three representations, one above another, of the prince and the Brāhman facing each other. Four citizens look passively on at this eminently impolitic action; though it does seem to wrench a gesture of surprise and protestation from the king, who is also observing it from the top of his balcony: and that is the end of the first act.—The section of the lintel between a line passing left of the royal balcony and of the gateway of the town, and another passing in the rear of the chariot, contains the whole of the second scene, namely the farewells of the prince, condemned to exile for squandering the treasures of state. From right to left we see, one behind the other, two female attendants, one carrying a casket and the other a ewer, who, having just come out of the town, link this scene neatly with the foregoing; then the two women bearing the umbrella and (above) the fly-whisk; then the queen-mother, and finally the king, who is raising his right hand in a gesture of grief. Facing this first group stand Viśvantara and his wife Mādrī (P. Maddī), with their two children in front of them; the father and children have hands clasped, as have also the seven citizens who represent the population of the capital. One may notice that the king and his heir have the same peculiar headdress. The left part of the lintel consists of three or, if you like, four episodes concerning the prince's chariot-and-four, and provides an admirable opportunity for studying the body, wheels, shaft and yoke of the quadriga, as well as the harness of the team. (1) First comes the departure of the family: notice that, having no servants, the prince has taken the reins and the stick (it is certainly not a whip and it does not seem to be a goad) in his hands, whilst the princess is herself waving the fly-whisk. As the royal umbrella continues beside the prince's head on the other side, unless it is by a miracle, it must be that the handle is fixed in some socket on the coach. (2) In the left foreground, the prince, according to the required forms, is giving his unyoked chariot to a Brāhman beggar. The two children have remained in the carriage, but Mādrī has alighted and is holding the yoke, while her husband holds the shaft, thus joining him in his act of charity. Notice the indication of the trickle of water coming from the ewer onto the outstretched right hand of the Brāhman, who is holding his ritual jug (*kamaṇḍalu*) in the other. (3) The thread of the story next shifts into the background and is returned towards the right. Left, the same Brāhman is dragging behind him the empty chariot obtained by his shameless begging. (4) Right, another Brāhman, no less impudent, is leading after him the four horses which he has likewise begged, apparently aided in this task by two of his *brahmacārins* or novices, recognizable by their long hair. We will not quarrel with the sculptor for not having repeated for the team of horses the donation scene already shown for the chariot. Indications of trees (bignonia, mango, and banana trees) tell us that we are now in the country. There remains the man seen half-length in the middle of the two groups of four horses? Is he, as we are inclined to believe, their charioteer, or simply a villager acting as a stop-gap? What is certain is that all the other persons are admirably definite. The story continues on Pl. 25, 1.

2. *Uprights.*—The central upright shows the *bodhi-druma* of Sākyamunī forming the companion to his *dharma-cakra* (*cf.* Pl. 22, 3), between the same umbrellas and banners. On each side a Yaksha is paying him homage with a lotus flower. Notice that here the attitudes of the two genii are not identical, but symmetrical, and such that both seem to be turning towards the representation of the second Great Miracle.

3. *Detached Figures.*—The three elephants extant are carved in the round, but the two riders, master and servant, on each of them (*cf.* Pl. 42) are carved in double high relief, so that they face, and are seen equally from, two sides at once (*cf.* Pl. 29).

b. Soffit of Bottom Lintel.—These full-blown pink lotuses (*padma*) framed between blue lotuses (*utpala*) may be compared to those which decorate the outer face of the jambs (Pls. 19*e*, 50*b*, etc.).

(a) FRONT OF NORTHERN GATEWAY: MIDDLE SECTION OF LOWEST ARCHITRAVE

(b) SOFFIT OF THE SAME

FRONT OF NORTHERN GATEWAY : EAST END OF UPPER AND MIDDLE ARCHITRAVES

PLATE 24

FRONT OF NORTHERN GATEWAY: EAST END

1. *Top and Middle Lintels.*—The themes represented are inseparable from those which decorate the rest of these two lintels (*cf.* Pls. 22 and 26). Above, a stūpa stands for the *Parinirvāṇa* of one of the seven Mānushi-Buddhas. Below, a bignonia specifies that we are looking at the *Sambodhi* of the first of the seven, namely Vipaśyin. Notice the inverted goblet on the top of the water-jar standing on the ground at the left.

2. *Die.*—An already very advanced representation of the Nativity (*cf.* pp. 183 and 197): one can discern the umbrella behind the jars held in the two *Nāga*-elephants' trunks.

3. *False-Capitals.*—Iranian in style and formed of two animals couchant back to back: winged stags above and winged lions in the middle. The latter are bridled and mounted by riders who are lashing them with switches; the sleeved tunics and absence of turbans show them to be foreigners.

4. *Detached Figures.*—If the *triratna* on the top of the east pillar is indeed, as it seems to be, the symbol of the three Buddhist Jewels, the full wheel decorated by a lotus must be admitted to stand for the Doctrine or *dharma*; the *taurine* surmounting it, for the Master; and the third element introduced here (absent on Pls. 18*b*, and 51*a* in representations of the *Sambodhi*), the shield (*śrīvatsa*), would then appear to represent the Community (*saṅgha*). The volute horns on both sides of the pedestal are probably intended to consolidate the whole.

The two lions (one winged) and the Yakshī are carved in the round (*cf.* Pl. 32, 5): the latter, much mutilated, is holding by her right hand on to the arched bough of a bignonia; the left hand probably rested on the hip (*cf.* Pl. 25).

PLATE 25

FRONT OF NORTHERN GATEWAY: EAST END

1. *Bottom Lintel.*—Continuation of the *Viśvantara-jātaka* (*cf.* Pl. 23*a* 1): the prince holding their little boy by the hand, and his wife carrying their little girl on her hip, are pursuing the road of exile on foot; with hands clasped the village people are lining their way. Above their heads are scenes of rural life: on the right, two peasant women are sitting with their children in front of their cottages; in the middle, two peasants, shouldering spear or bow, are going hunting; at the left, two others are returning from the forest, and the second is carrying two haunches of antelope balanced on his shoulder at the ends of a stick; notice the shape of the knife stuck in his *kamarband.* A lion finally makes it clear that we are getting deeper and deeper into the jungle. Continuation on the back (Pl. 33, 1).

2. *Die.*—Representation of the Nativity intermediate between those on Pls. 13 and 24 (*cf.* p. 197): Māyā is still seated on the lotus, but the *Nāga*-elephants are already performing their office.

3. *False-Capital.*—Again we find the two zebus (*bos indicus*) ridden by Indian lords, as on Pls. 16, 41, 43, etc.

4. *Capitals.*—The capitals of the jambs, as usual decorated with palmettes, are flanked at the four corners by four elephants, not by lions as on the Southern Gateway; but these elephants, unlike those on the Eastern Gateway, show only their fore-quarters, and consequently do not lend themselves to so complete a description (*cf.* Pl. 42). Yet we already see the hoods with pendants, the double bells and the folds of their saddle-cloths. As for the fact that ladies ride on them, as one is doing here on the left, and sometimes even wield the *aṅkuśa* themselves, we know it is a sport that queens shared with kings (*cf.* Pl. 18*a*). Notice the lithe play of the trunks and the fact that all eight elephants on the two capitals show two empty cavities where the tusks were originally rooted (carried out either in stone or in real ivory?). For further remarks on these elephant-capitals, see Part II, p. 139.

5. *Detached Figures.*—Another general remark which we must make is that the small arched trees under which all the *śālabhañjikā* (*cf.* p. 232 and note) on the Northern Gateway are sheltering, agree in having their trunks on the outer side of the figure (*cf.* Pl. 21). This absolute rule, which the maker of the Eastern Gateway has set aside, here gives the bracket a less decorative appearance than on Pl. 44; but it is more solid and the accident which broke the legs and the right arm did not, as on Pl. 42, carry off the whole figure. Notice the comparative simplicity of the dress and jewels (*cf.* Pl. 33). The tree is a bignonia, whose flowers are, as usual, represented facing front, so that one cannot see the 'trumpet' shape to which they owe their name in Sanskrit and English.

This tree seems to share the fairies' favour with the mango-tree, and it is also a bignonia to which the Yakshī placed between the middle and bottom lintels is clinging, as well as the one above her on Pl. 24; their two opposites, however, have adopted the mango-tree (Pls. 26 and 27). We shall recur (Pl. 27, 3) to their wealth of heavy ornament.

We would point out, once for all, that in the female figures the sex is clearly marked beneath the transparent *dhotī* draped round their lower limbs.

FRONT OF NORTHERN GATEWAY: EAST END OF LOWEST ARCHITRAVE AND CAPITAL

FRONT OF NORTHERN GATEWAY: WEST END OF UPPER AND MIDDLE ARCHITRAVES.

PLATE 26

FRONT OF NORTHERN GATEWAY: WEST END

In obedience to the laws of symmetry in force in the Mālwā School, Pl. 26 forms an almost exact companion to Pl. 24 and requires no individual description, though a few differences of detail may be noted, where these are worthy of remark.

1. *Top and Middle Lintels.*—Of the stūpa above, all that we can say is that it is not that of the last Buddha, Śākya-muni; for he is already represented on the top lintel by his *bodhi-druma* (*cf.* Pl. 22. 1). Contrariwise, the tree on the middle lintel is certainly the end of a series, for it is again the *aśvattha* of Śākya-muni. It will be noticed that from each side worshippers are approaching in families—father, mother and child (donors?). Observe in the right-hand bottom corner a ewer with a spout (*bhṛiṅgāra*) of the pattern already often seen.

2. *Die.*—Corresponding to the first Great Miracle on Pl. 24, we have here the third, namely the First Sermon. The wheel (with 25 spokes) rests directly upon the Master's throne between a king and his viceroy. Must we take this king to be Prasenajit, and see in this little scene a foreshadowing of the way in which this stale cliché passed, as the inscribed relief at Bharhut bears witness (Cunn., Pl. 13, 3), from the representation of the third Great Miracle to that of the Great Prodigy at Srāvastī?

3. *False-Capital.*—Here the riders of the two winged lions, again dressed in close-fitting tunics, are wearing a headdress (topknot with a sort of diadem) resembling that of the jungle-dwellers (*cf.* Pls. 30, 3; 32, 47 and 48).

PLATE 27

FRONT OF NORTHERN GATEWAY: WEST END

1. *Bottom Lintel.*—Representation of the former birth of the Buddha as 'Antelope-horn' (*Ṛishya-śṛiṅga*) or 'Unicorn' (*Eka-śṛiṅga*); for identification, see above, p. 225, and for comparison with the Bharhut and Gandhāra versions, *cf. Mémoires concernant l'Asie orientale*, III, p. 23 and Pl. II, 3 and 4; Pl. IV, 3). The Brāhman anchorite is seated on a stone throne before his hut roofed with leaves (*parṇa-śālā*): notice the cloth band which is tied round his knees and loins for convenience (*cf.* Pl. 52*a*2). The doe, shown with horns, is lying at his feet with raised head: it is the conception. She reappears behind his back, and it is the lying-in, for (already quite big) the new-born is devoutly taking his first bath in a lotus pool. Left of the hut the child appears again, his hands still clasped, and introduces himself to his father, who receives him with some legitimate surprise: for besides the unexpectedness of his birth, he has the oddity of a horn on the brow, inherited from his mother. All the rest, antelopes, lions, elephants, mango-trees, palm-trees, lotuses, etc., and the round temple with dome raised on pillars which shelters the hearth on which the sacred fire in burning (*cf.* Pls. 29 and 52), are inevitable accessories to the scene of the hermitage.

2. *Die.*—This representation of the third Great Miracle is distinguished from that on Pl. 26, 2 by the fact that this time the wheel (with 27 spokes) is placed on the lion-capital of an Indo-Persian column (*cf.* Pls. 22, 3; 40; 74, 3*a*; 103, 2, etc.) between two royal couples, each with a viceroy (?).

3. *Capital and False-Capital.*—For description of the elephants and Indian oxen, the reader is referred to their companions on Pl. 25.

4. *Detached Figures.*—This time, again, the *śālabhañjikā* is partly broken and hanging from an arched bignonia with its trunk on the outer side.

The Yakshī at the top, her head bowed towards the ground as if to greet her visitors, is picking a mango with her right hand and holding the edge of her scarf in her left. Even more clearly than on Pls. 11, 3 and 25, 5 one can see the two chains crossing over the body, joined between the breasts with a medallion, and coupled to four similar medallions placed on shoulders and hips. We know that a sixth medallion corresponding to the one on the chest, was fixed at the crossing of the chains on the back (see Pl. 29, 2).

FRONT OF NORTHERN GATEWAY: WEST END OF LOWEST ARCHITRAVE AND CAPITAL

Pl. XXVIII

PLATE 28

BACK OF NORTHERN GATEWAY

The general remarks concerning Pl. 21 are equally applicable to this. At the left, between the ends of the upper and middle lintels, we notice the only Yakshī that is carved double, so as to face both ways. Remember, also, that the left-hand upright above ought to be turned back to front (Pl. 21 (c)).

The first two lintels are covered with two decorative compositions whose themes are, above, the legend of the six-tusked elephant, and in the middle, the Buddha's Enlightenment. The latter is set between two ornamental motifs in which peacocks appear (*cf.* Pls. 13, 3; 42 and 44, 1). From end to end the bottom lintel continues and concludes the tale of the *Viśvantara-jātaka*.

The dies bear three Nativities, two of them very archaic in style, and a *Parinirvāṇa*.

The uprights were all uniformly ornamented with palmettes issuing from a lotus seen in profile and from above, which resembles, and on the bottom right-hand upright assumes in fact the shape of, a *bhadra-ghaṭa* very similar to those on the two upper dies. Thus we wondered above (p. 184, n. 1) whether the second motif was not after all derived from the first.

Only the false-capitals at the top are like those on the facade the four others bear witness to a praiseworthy effort at variety.

PLATE 29

BACK OF NORTHERN GATEWAY: MIDDLE SECTION

1. *Top Lintel.*—Decorative representation of the legend of the six-tusked elephant (see p. 224 and *cf.* Pls. 15, 2 and 55, 3): it covers the lintel from end to end, but in fact does no more than portray the noble animal twice, grazing with his herd in a lotus pool on each side of the traditional banyan fig-tree (*nyagrodha : ficus indica*). Notice the pendent roots of the fig-tree, among which wander baby elephants. The unusual pose of the elephant in the left-hand top corner, which alone is turning its back to the tree, is perhaps intended to recall the jealous rage of one of the Bodhisattva's two wives. In any case this would be the only allusion to the tragic event which was to interrupt these idyllic gambols, and we get no glimpse of the hunter observed on Pl. 15, 2. (*Cf.* p. 120.)

2. *Middle Lintel.*—The identification of this piece would have been somewhat baffling on account of the extraordinary truculence of the figures in the right-hand half, did not the analogy of the Western Gateway (*cf.* Pls. 61, 3 and 65*b*1) prove incontestably that we are dealing with the demons who formed Māra's army. It follows that the royal personage shown near the middle of the lintel must be Māra himself in his character of god of the sixth heaven (*cf.* Pl. 49*a*). And the presence of the *bodhi-druma* on the left proves that the Buddha is not absent from the scene. Hence we are reminded of the famous incidents of the 'Temptation', which just before the *Sambodhi* brought on a contest between the Sage, abolisher of desire, and the Sovereign Lord of the worlds of Desire; and, indeed, to confirm us in the idea that we are really referred to this episode in the Buddha's career, Sujātā enters at the left with her tray in one hand and a ewer in the other, through the *toraṇa* which acts as porch to the *Bodhi-maṇḍa* (*cf.* Pl. 65*b*1), carrying the famous offering of rice pudding, the last food taken by the Master before his Enlightenment (*cf.* p. 206). Having thus fixed the time and place of the scene, it will be easier to understand the three incidents distinguished by the sculptor: First, he shows us Māra near the centre, seated on his royal throne between female figures bearing the umbrella and fly-whisk, as is the rule for gods as for kings (*cf.* Pl. 49): this is no doubt the moment when fear that the Blessed One may succeed in destroying his empire occurs to his mind; we do not here see him holding a council of war, as some texts relate; but it is curious to notice that near him, with the features of a child (notice the brush-shaped topknot on the head), the sculptor has portrayed one of those *Māra-putras* or 'sons of Māra' known to literary tradition. Next, we see Māra standing in company with this son and doubtless one of his 'daughters' to the immediate right of the tree, proceeding to the Temptation proper, which was only an exchange of more or less uncomplimentary words. Here, it is curious to notice that force of habit has made the sculptor join Māra's hands and treat the group in similar fashion to the praying families in the pictures of the second Great Miracle. The third scene is wedged in between the two former: Māra, his daughter and his son are retiring vanquished and discomfited as their gestures of grief and helplessness show. Meantime his demon court, utterly indifferent to what is happening on the left side of the lintel, continue to drink, sing and dance to music: evidently he has not yet mobilised them as on Pls. 61 and 65 for his 'assault' or 'attack' (*dharshaṇa*). The sculptor has given free rein to his fancy in showing this band of ruffianly genii, enormous, deformed, grimacing; and it is hard to say exactly to what they correspond in the popular mind, and whether they are Asuras caricatured or magnified Rākshasas: all we know is that they still haunt the Indian imagination, now enrolled among the *gaṇas* of Siva. First of all, forming the companion figure to his divine leader, their general (*senā-pati*) is seated Indian-fashion with one of his lieutenants squatting on his right and his 'son' leaning against his left knee: behind him, two horrible demons replace the usual attendants, and the one on his right is handing him a drinking cup. Then, in place of the usual Apsaras or celestial nymphs of the first six *deva-lokas* (*cf.* Pl. 49) a burlesque orchestra (tambourines, harp and sistrum) is accompanying with music and singing the contorsions of a dancer no less grotesque than the musicians. Observe that they are all wearing on their chests the ornament made of medallions and chains which we have already described on Pl. 27, 4. (*Cf.* pp. 116-117.)

3. *Bottom Lintel.*—The middle part takes up the story of the *Viśvantara-jātaka* at the place where it stopped on the east end (Pl. 33, 1) and in four scenes reading from right to left represents:—(*a*) the life in the hermitage; (*b*) the gift of the children; (*c*) the gift of the wife; (*d*) the final reunion. We will consider these scenes in detail; for they are worth the trouble.

(*a*) For the picture of the hermitage, compare Pls. 27 and 52, and observe the hut of leaves; the lotus pool in which an elephant is bathing and two haṁsas are playing, and to which two boars (*cf.* Pl. 90 no. 86*a*) are coming to drink; the groves composed of mango-trees, bignonias, fan-palms and plantains, haunted by buffaloes, antelopes, lions, elephants and monkeys, etc.; the 'bark' dress adopted by the princely pair, as becomes anchorites; the hearth and utensils for sacrifice, etc. The children are playing in the background near the first hut. Notice that Viśvantara (with the supporting thong passing round knees and loins) and Mādrī appear again on the left seated on the threshold of a *parṇa-śālā*. Is this the same hut? More probably it is another; for the hermit's life in the forest required the separation of persons (*cf.* Pl. 65*a*1); at any rate, the presence of the second hut is of no service to the continuation of the story.

(*b*) The second tableau, indeed, begins just to the left of this hut and consists of four scenes only, two in the fore- and two in the background. Chronologically, we should begin at the top left, where the good hunter who watches over the repose of the exiles is trying, with taut bow, to stop the wicked Brāhman beggar; the bottle and the quarter of venison hanging above the hunter's head represent his drink and food and have naturally nothing to do with the usual diet of the prince and princess, who feed on fruits only. Just behind the hunter's back, Mādrī is coming back from her usual fruit-picking, a basket of mangoes on her head. This is the moment chosen by Indra disguised as a lion—here, indeed, as three lions—to block her path. Below, taking advantage of the mother's delay, the wicked Brāhman has the two children irrevocably given to him by the rite of the sprinkling of hands; after which, still in the foreground, he leads them to the left, beating them; we do not know where he is going till we get to Pl. 31, 1.

(*c*) Two scenes, one above the other, suffice now for the supreme sacrifice: in the foreground Viśvantara, as usual dressed as an anchorite, is giving away his wife by the same rite to another Brāhman beggar, whose floating hair distinguishes him from the children's kidnapper. A peacock fills in the space left between the feet of the group. In the background the beggar has changed into Śakra, the Indra of the Gods, recognizable by his thunderbolt, his jar of ambrosia and his tiara, and is presiding at the discreet outpourings of the pair after the cruel trials they have been through.

(*d*) The last tableau on the left of the middle section, with its two processions marching in opposite directions, can only be understood with the aid of Pl. 31, 1, and by remembering that the west end of the lintel shows again, as on Pl. 23, 1, the capital of the Śibis. It is from there that the royal cortege in the foreground is coming. The rider sheltered by a groom under an umbrella, preceded by his bearers of ewer and sandals and his musicians, is none other than the king, Viśvantara's father, who, accompanied by the two little children perched on one elephant, comes to seek the exiles in their retreat. It is also towards their native town that the king in the background, still on horseback, is leading back in triumph the two children, the prince and the princess, who have resumed their secular costume. All's well that ends well. But the happy ending, the rule in Buddhist stories, cannot be considered as quite complete till Pl. 31, 1 is reached.

For the uprights and detached figures, see Pls. 21 and 28.

BACK OF NORTHERN GATEWAY: MIDDLE SECTION OF ARCHITRAVES.

PLATE 30

BACK OF NORTHERN GATEWAY: WEST END

1. *Top Lintel.*—Continuation and end, so far as the western part is concerned, of the elephant herd of the *Shaddanta*, which are also feeding in a lotus pool. Observe that, for the sake of variety and symmetry, they are turned left.

2. *Middle Lintel.*—Fine decorative theme, independent of the middle scene; these peacocks may be compared to the one on the Southern Gateway (Pl. 13) and those on the Eastern Gateway (Pls. 42 and 44). Between them is the outline of a mango-tree above, and below, a tiny plantain; under the beak of each hangs a bunch of grapes between two vine-leaves.

3. *Dies.*—The two dies represent the Nativity: the one above, in archaic fashion, by the lotus bunch issuing from the vase (we have already remarked, Pl. 29, that the back of the neighbouring uprights suggests a plausible origin for this motif); the one below, of a much more elaborate pattern, from which the *bhadra-ghata* has disappeared but which includes the umbrella, though Māyā is still shown seated (*cf.* pp. 183 and 197).

4. *False-Capitals.*—We find at the top the same winged antelopes as on the facade (*cf.* Pls. 24 and 26), here surmounted by a very much stylised bignonia. In the middle, the animals back to back are goats, and their riders with switches in their hands, wear the typical head-dress (topknot rising in a brush on the top of the head and enclosed in a diadem) of jungle-dwellers (*cf.* Pl. 26, 3). The whole motif reappears on the back of the Eastern Gateway (Pls. 47 and 48).

5. *Detached Figures.*—For the *triratna* and the Yaksha at the top, see Pls. 22 and 24. We have already noticed that the Yakshī set in between the two top lintels is the only one carved double (*cf.* Pl. 26). The tree, which was a mango on the facade, has become a bignonia on the back, and the fairy with one leg round the trunk is assuming one of the favourite poses of the Yakshīs at Bharhut (*cf.* Cunn., Pls. 22 and 23), whereas the fairy placed below her is seen from behind. Details of dress will be seen still more clearly on the next Pl. 31, 5.

PLATE 31

BACK OF NORTHERN GATEWAY: WEST END

1. ***Bottom Lintel.***—Here (on the back of Pl. 27) we follow to its denouement the *Viśvantara-jātaka*. Next to the return from exile on Pl. 29, 3, we see, as on Pl. 23, 1, the ramparts, gate and palaces of the capital of the Sibis. If, therefore, one were to set out the two sides of the lintel as on the same frieze, the story of Viśvantara would be framed between two representations of his native town, marking the beginning and end of his adventures. Further, the representations of the two cities are symmetrically reversed: in the present one, it is the royal palace which is on the right, still above the city gate, whilst the palace of the heir apparent has been pushed over to the left; but these buildings evidently correspond from picture to picture, and this fact will help us to identify the details. First scene: the king perceives from his balcony the wicked Brāhman, the children's kidnapper, whose most urgent business seems to be to come and sell them to their grandfather, and who in fact is seen above the merlon-shaped battlements. Second scene: reinstalled in the palace of the heir apparent, the whole exiled family, prince, princess and children, show themselves to the eyes of their loyal subjects. So ends the story. It may be noticed that the city moats are transformed into lotus pools haunted by *haṁsas*, where women come to fill their water jars and their banks into a park of mango-trees and bignonias. Observe the small figure (? watchman) in the corner between the stone gateway and the brick rampart.

2. *False-Capital.*—Here, again, we find the noble riders and richly plumed and harnessed horses of the Southern Gateway (Pls. 12 and 13): notice the shield (*Śrīvatsa*) on the chest and the way the end of the tail is fastened with a band passing under the saddle-cloth.

3. *Capital.*—See Pl. 25. The palmette of lotuses here comes out of a *bhadra-ghaṭa* or auspicious vase.

4. *Panel on back of West Pillar.*—*Sambodhi* of the Buddha Śākya-muni symbolised by his particular tree: one can recognize the tapering point of the leaf of the *ficus religiosa*. What is the nature of the offering being carried on a tray by the two women? Are these to be considered as garlands again, or the three folded pieces of a monastic dress (*tri-civara*)?

5. *Detached Figure.*—The fairy of Pl. 27 is here shown from behind. This allows us to study the details of her hairdressing and costume, as on Pls. 30-33, etc. The tight folds of the *dhoti* are brought up behind between the legs and pass into the girdle. The veil covering the big plaits of hair, with tiers of heavy garlands over it, forms a sort of short cloak over the back.

BACK OF NORTHERN GATEWAY: WEST END OF LOWEST ARCHITRAVE WITH CAPITAL AND PANEL BELOW.

BACK OF NORTHERN GATEWAY: EAST END OF UPPER AND MIDDLE ARCHITRAVES.

PLATE 32

BACK OF NORTHERN GATEWAY : EAST END

1. *Top Lintel.*—For the same reasons as on Pl. 30, the elephants are here passant to the right.

2. *Middle Lintel.*—Same pattern of peacocks, only that single flowers take here the place of the bunches of grapes, whilst a bignonia and another very much stylised tree have replaced the mango-tree.

3. *Dies.*—Above, the same archaic representation of the Nativity as on Pl. 30. Below, the last Great Miracle has taken the place of the first. As an exception, the two praying women, with basket and ewer placed before them, are kneeling in profile, performing the *añjali*, before the terrace of the stūpa, which they partly hide; usually the sculptor is careful that nothing shall stand between the spectator and the elevation of the sacred building.

4. *False-capitals.*—Exact reproduction of their companions on the west side. These decorative pieces give the impression of being the work of the same hand.

5. *Detached Figures.*—For details of the dress and ornaments of fairies seen from the back, *cf.* Pl. 31, 5. In both of them will be noticed the big ankle-ring which, on the one at the bottom supplements those which already cover the leg.

PLATE 33

BACK OF NORTHERN GATEWAY: EAST END

1. *Bottom Lintel.*—The tale of the *Viśvantara-jātaka* is taken up again at the point reached on the front of this same lintel-end (*cf.* Pl. 25, 1). Now we have gone beyond the still inhabited zone between the villages and the jungle. On the right, the prince, princess and children, still on foot, are resolutely entering the lonely forest—deserted except for lions, antelopes and a bird. On the left, they are calling a halt: they have placed their son and daughter at the foot of a mango-tree with some mangoes for food, and themselves are sitting on the rocks, refreshing themselves in the shadow of a neighbouring banyan tree. Below the children flows a small stream with lotuses.

2. *False-capital.*—*Cf.* Pl. 31.

3. *Capital.*—*Cf.* Pl. 25.

4. *Panel on back of East Pillar.*—*Parinirvāṇa-stūpa*, which, as companion (*cf.* Pl. 31, 4) to the *Sambodhi* of the Buddha Śākya-muni, most probably represents his Decease. For what reason has the sculptor, in defiance of all the habits of symmetry observed by this School, planted two praying figures at the left and four at the right, one of whom is a child? We are forced to conclude that in so doing he had to conform to his donors' wishes, and it is but a step further to admit that he has portrayed the donors themselves.

5. *Detached Figures.*—We see here the back of the *śālabhañjikā* of Pl. 25; but the decay of the stone has destroyed the bottom of her locks and garlands (*cf.* Pl. 31, 5).

BACK OF NORTHERN GATEWAY: EAST END OF LOWEST ARCHITRAVE WITH CAPITAL AND PANEL BELOW

b

EAST PILLAR OF NORTHERN GATEWAY *a.* UPPER PANELS ON FRONT FACE; *b.* LOWER PANELS ON FRONT FACE.

PLATE 34

PILLARS OF NORTHERN GATEWAY

a. Front of East Pillar.—As we have said (p. 219) this facade is practically given up to the miraculous scenes which were enacted in the holy town of Śrāvastī. We shall take the reliefs in their order on the jamb, beginning at the top.

a1. Great Prodigy at Śrāvastī: the sermon under the mango-tree.—This is the form that the *mahā-pratihārya* has preserved on modern religious images, particularly in Siam. Here the miraculous mango-tree, weighed down with fruit, already comes to the fore under an umbrella over the throne of the invisible Buddha. In the four persons sitting on cushions in the foreground we must doubtless see King Prasenajit in the right-hand corner (left of the throne), his viceroy in the left-hand corner, and two courtiers in the middle, seen from the back. Do the four personages standing above them, whose feet can touch the ground, belong also to the nobility of the land of Kośala, or are they the four Guardian Kings of the World (*Lokapālas*)? The second hypothesis is the more likely, since above them we surely have to do with gods set in tiers in the heavens. We are at liberty to recognize Indra, with his viceroy on his right, in the first row of six, and above 'the gods of the pure abodes', with Brahmā at their head: but there is no deciding feature to guide us. The most curious detail to point out (which is found again in c1 and Pl. 35*a*3) is the two big drums floating in the air, on which two *devaputras* are beating with heavy clubs held in both hands, to announce the miracle to the whole universe. One need not suppose that the two winged spirits, with which the sculptor felt it indispensable to fill the top of his panel, were entrusted by him with the duty of supporting the two drums in the air: as usual, they are holding a tray of flowers in one hand and in the other a garland which should not be confused (though it may be easily mistaken on the plate) with a sort of hanging strap. Neither must we take the ornament placed on the necks of the two courtiers in the foreground for the knot of a necktie turned back to front; it is the profile of the enormous ear-rings which they wear in common with the other figures (*cf.* Pl. 35*a*2).

a2. Gift of the Jetavana.—It will be remembered that this relief has given us the key to the whole facade of the pillar, thanks to the square coins which are shown edge to edge on the ground and which have remained since Bharhut (Cunn., Pls. 28 and 57) and Bodh-Gayā (Cunn., *Mahābodhi*, Pl. 8, 8) the *lakshaṇa* or special sign of the donation of the Jetavana. The two praying figures who, in defiance of the laws of perspective, appear half-length in the middle of groves of mango-trees, bignonias and champakas, catching the attention by their giant stature, might be taken to be Anāthapiṇḍika the banker, purchaser and donor of the park, on the right, and on the left the former princely owner, Jeta, each with a companion placed below him. But then, what must be done with the two little praying figures in the foreground and the child sitting between them, unless we call them images of donors?[1] Sir John Marshall in his *Guide to Sāñchī* (p. 58) has already identified the three sanctuaries represented with "the three favourite residences of the Buddha, the *Gandhakuṭi*, the *Kosambakuṭi* and the *Karorikuṭi*", of which only the two first are shown and labelled at Bharhut. In front of each the fact that the Master sojourned there is indicated by the presence of his throne.

a3. The Great Prodigy at Śrāvastī: the aerial walk.—On p. 219 will be found the reasons for this identification and the comparison with Pl. 13 of Cunningham's *Stūpa of Bharhut*. For other representations of the *caṅkrama* or Master's 'walk', see above, Pl. 19*d*5, and below, Pls. 36, 50 and 51. Here it is placed under an open hall (*maṇḍapa*) of the same oblong shape, exactly as on Pl. 31, 4, at Bharhut, where the subject is identical. But since, in the foreground of the Bharhut relief, the pillars cut the broad flagstone at regular intervals—a thing our sculptor, sacrificing perspective to clarity in his design, has taken good care not do here—Cunningham took it for a representation, unique of its kind, of the "throne of the four Buddhas". The praying figures standing on the ground among the stylised trees below the aerial *caṅkrama*, if they belong to the legend at all, are again Prasenajit and his court; but what, once more (*cf. a*2), is to be done with the child?

b1. Prasenajit's Visit.—The context of the relief invited us above (p. 219) to recognize, in two tableaux, the king of Kośala, Prasenajit, coming out of Srāvastī, his capital, to betake himself to the site of the Great Prodigy,—a site which stood just half-way between the Jetavana (in *a*2) and the city, above the roofs of which we even seem to see the tip of the mango-tree of the miracle. We must not, however, hide from ourselves the fact that, for lack of a label, we here have no demonstrable proof of this identification. The sculptor has confined himself to reproducing mechanically the double stereotype of the 'city' and the 'royal procession'; the only slightly individual point is that the king and his viceroy are simply on horseback. Indeed, if one were to follow strictly the analogy of the inscribed relief at Bharhut (Cunn., Pl. 13, 3), where King Prasenajit is driving as usual in his chariot, the middle relief on the inside of this pillar (Pl. 35*b*2) would suit the case much better, since its position on the jamb corresponds exactly with that of the Jetavana, and the king would thus enter on a level into the park towards which he is going: nevertheless, after careful consideration, we keep to the reasons which decided us above to study the jamb face by face.

*b*2. But then, as four-fifths of the front of the East pillar in that case relate to Śrāvastī, a logical mind could only see in the bottom panel a worldly aspect of the Jetavana, before its donation to the Buddhist Community, in the days when Prince Jeta and his friends frolicked there with their wives like the thirty "jolly fellows" (*bhadra-vargīya*), of whom a well-known legend of Benares tells us. The hypothesis is tempting and, after all, possible; though the analogies enumerated above (pp. 228-9) all tend to class this panel among the 'pictures of paradise', we have never denied our inability to determine whether several of these paradises are earthly or heavenly. Yet nothing guarantees that this 'genre' scene is anything but a stop-gap here; and, besides, the uneven character of the landscape, with its rocks and little waterfalls, suggests rather the Himālaya, the genii's abode, than the rice flats amid which Śrāvastī stood. Supernatural or otherwise, the person in the top left-hand corner is having a cold drink, for he has a cup in his right hand. To the right, his counterpart is holding a harp in his left hand and apparently teasing his companion with his right, while she is bathing her feet in a rocky basin, where the water from the waterfall is held a moment before dashing into the lotus pool. Again, it is coolness that the elephant-riders and their companions are seeking in this pool, while their elephants are seizing the moment to feed (*cf.* Pls. 12*b*; 79, no. 27*a*; 101 and 102, 3). A peacock and a mango-tree, which has somehow managed to grow in the rock, complete the landscape.

c. Front of West Pillar.—The composition of the plates brings us now to the panels decorating the facade of the opposite (West) jamb. Perhaps the reader would do well to refer at once to the description of the inner facade of the East jamb (Pl. 35*b*) before entering on that of the West jamb.

The upper panel represents the *Deva-avatāra* at Sāṅkāśya; above (p. 221) will be found the details of identification and comparison with the three Bharhut panels (Cunn., Pl. 17). It may be added that the trees shading the thrones are two *ficus*, and that the lower one is set between a champaka (left) and a mango-tree (right); that we have no triple ladder here as at Bharhut, but an attempt at showing in perspective a single staircase edged with two rails, one of which can clearly be seen; that it is impossible to distinguish the one who was the Buddha's mother among the 'Thirty-three' gods to whom he is preaching his doctrine; that we may identify Indra at the left (of the spectator) and Brahmā at the right, once or more represented on each side of the celestial tree, throne and staircase; that the god who is so awkwardly raising his right arm has no other purpose than to let his scarf float in the wind as we wave our handkerchiefs, and that instead of whistling at the same time, as at Bharhut, through the fingers of his left hand, he is holding in them a flower—doubtless of paradise; that, above, two *devas* are beating a drum; and that below on either side of the earthly throne we again find children beside the worshippers (donors?), etc.[2]

The rest of the facade of the West pillar is described opposite Pl. 35*a*.

[1] The disproportionately large size of the figures in the background suggests that, as in Pl. 34c, they may be intended for heavenly beings. See Part II, pp. 109-10.

[2] Observe, here, the distinction in size between the heavenly and earthly figures as in *a*2 above.

PLATE 35

PILLARS OF NORTHERN GATEWAY—continued

a. Front of West Pillar.—For the top panel of the facade of the West jamb, see Pl. 34c.

*a*1. The middle panel reproduces once more the cliché of the city and the royal procession, but this time with the peculiarities which helped us above to divine their double or even triple meaning (p. 203); for it suggests at once no less than three episodes: (1) by the chariot without its principal occupant, the four 'Drives'; (2) by the horse without a rider, the 'Great Departure'; (3) and by the onlookers, all the townswomen whose hearts, as it is written, the charming but invisible Bodhisattva draws after him. One may note that the bearer of the sandals has not been forgotten among the people in the retinue, but that the umbrella-bearer, shown on the chariot, has not been repeated near the horse Kaṇṭhaka; in accordance with the practice of the School, Chandaka is holding the ewer.

*a*2. We shall not be surprised that the next panel brings us back, after a long interval, to Kapilavastu and shows us in its own manner the "perfectly accomplished Buddha" returned to his native town and in the act of preaching his doctrine in the *Nyagrodha-ārāma* (*cf.* p. 205). The central tree alone would not be enough to settle the identification of the scene (*cf.* p. 205, note 1); what finally determines it for us is the aristocratic character and particularly the reverent attitude of the numerous audience. It is clear that all these great personages, sitting Indian-fashion on cushions, are listening most devoutly to a homily. We may add that the upper picture (*a*1) and the side picture (Pl. 36c3) likewise take place at Kapilavastu, and that the latter shows us already, under the same *nyagrodha*, the same throne from the top of which the Blessed One is here supposed to be preaching to the assembly of Śākya nobles, with his father Śuddhodana at their head. But, you may say, which is Śuddhodana? Guess if you can, and choose if you dare, amidst this crowd of stereotyped personages, the one who in the sculptor's mind was the *primus inter pares*.

*a*3. It is probable that the base of the jamb was composed, before its mutilation, of two other scenes: and it is certain that the next one represented again a Great Miracle: for proof we have the big drum (*dundubhi*), which has been preserved at the top together with its drumstick, beside the two winged spirits bearing garlands. We may find consolation in the fact that we shall never know any more about the lost panel by studying the arrangement of the criss-cross thongs which serve to tie the skin on to the case of this 'tom-tom'.

b. Inner face of East Pillar.—We now come back to the inner face of the East jamb, whose facade has been seen and described on Pl. 34*a* and *b*. It consists of three panels only, corresponding in size to the three upper tableaux of Śrāvastī: but it certainly seems as if it is taking us away from the land of Kośala to that of Magadha.

*b*1. *Indra's Visit.*—The fact is, indeed, certain for the top panel (*cf.* p. 218-19 and Cunn., *Stūpa of Bharhut*, Pl. 28, 4, etc.). Here the cave is a semi-artificial hypogeum. Are we to see Indra twice, first in the principal personage (to judge by his size and the shape of his turban) in the foreground, then, in the background, in the 'king' who is looking towards the Buddha and turning his back on the spectator? The Rajputs of India still affect the enormous turbans shown here. The sort of mountain-goats or rams with manes and human faces, which are seen on the right in a cleft in the rocks, are found again, as are the lions on the left, on the Eastern Gateway (Pl. 46, 2).

*b*2. We come again on that hardworked cliché of the city and royal procession; and this time it seems vain to seek information about the town and the king anywhere but in the context of the jamb. But we must choose between two possible ways of reading it. If we read horizontally (as we are expected to do on the Southern Gateway, Pl. 18), the monarch, with music before him, is coming in his chariot right to the Jetavana, and consequently we should have to take him for Prasenajit leaving his goodly town of Śrāvastī. But then we should not know what to do with the royal procession already seen on the facade of the jamb (Pl. 34*b*1), which the other pictures connected with Śrāvastī. We have therefore decided to read vertically; and as the upper tableau on the inner face (*b*1) takes place in Magadha and the lower tableau (*b*3) does the same, we have voted for 'Rājagṛiha' or even for 'Ajātaśatru leaving his capital' (*cf.* p. 218). Yet one would have expected him to be accompanied by the women, who are in fact surrounding him on panel *b*3. On the other hand, it cannot be denied that 'Bimbisāra's Visit' on the Eastern Gateway (*cf.* p. 217 and Pl. 51*b*2), if we leave aside the top left-hand corner, bears a striking resemblance to our Pl. 35*b*2; and as we shall find in *b*3 both the bamboos of the Veṇuvana which Bimbisāra presented to the Master and the mango-trees of the Park of Jīvaka where Ajātaśatru, Bimbisāra's patricide heir, went to seek relief for his remorse, it may be questioned which of the two, father or son, is portrayed on *b*2. Amidst all these perplexities we should not forget to notice a detail not found hitherto, *viz.*, the mirror held in the right hand of the queen, who appears on the balcony on the left between her two attendants (*cf.* Pl. 64c1).

*b*3. For the identification of the scene, *cf.* p. 218. One may state *de visu* that the usual dress of fairies (*cf.* Pl. 31, 5) is exactly the same, back and front, as that of the court ladies. Whatever the implication intended by the presence of bamboos, they are very clear, from the knots on the stalks to the curving plumes of the foliage.

A

WEST PILLAR OF NORTHERN GATEWAY:
LOWER PANELS ON FRONT FACE

B

EAST PILLAR OF NORTHERN GATEWAY:
UPPER PANE[illegible], WEST FACE

EAST PILLAR OF NORTHERN GATEWAY: LOWEST PANEL ON INNER FACE.

b

WEST PILLAR OF NORTHERN GATEWAY
LOWEST PANEL ON INNER FACE.

c

WEST PILLAR OF NORTHERN GATEWAY:
UPPER PANELS ON INNER FACE.

PLATE 36

PILLARS OF NORTHERN GATEWAY—continued

a-b. The composition of the plates has again involved the combination of two jambs; there was moreover an obvious advantage in bringing together the two *dvāra-pāla* genii (*cf.* p. 243) who face each other. Their place on the Northern Gateway permits us to dub them Yakshas with a clear conscience, but no characteristic attribute distinguishes them, any more than the 'Kuvera' at Bharhut (Cunn., Pl. 22, 1). The one on the east pillar has shaken off the 'law of frontality', which still sets the one on the West at 'shoulder arms', so to speak. He has picked a bignonia flower from the tree on his right, whose companion-tree is a mango. The one on the west side having no trees, has had to fill in the space left on both sides of his head by necklaces hanging from *nāga-dantas*; he is holding a bunch of *utpalas* in his right hand. Moreover their clothes, headdress and jewels are, with few variants, the same. The turban, trimmed with a sort of embroidered topknot and held on by fillets, conceals the hair; the *dhotī* drapes the lower limbs, fastened round the waist by a sash whose ends fall in front, whilst the *uttarīya* (shawl or scarf) passes, as here, over the arms or, as elsewhere (Pls. 50 and 52), is carelessly tied round the loins. Notice how the fall of its pleats is stylised. Heavy rings hang from the distended ears, and a broad necklace droops over the chest, fastened on the left shoulder with a big stud passing through a loop; the fore-arms are covered with bracelets, but male persons never wear rings on their legs.

c. These three panels belong to the inner side of the west pillar, whose facade was studied on Pls. 34c and 35*a*.

c1. Just as the representation of the second Great Miracle on Pl. 29, 2, was reinforced by the episodes of Sujātā's offering and Māra's Temptation, so here, that of the fourth Great Miracle is relieved by the picturesque scene of the feast celebrated by the Mallas of Kuśinagara in honour of their share of the Buddha's relics. The stūpa in which they were deposited has no less than two terraces and three railings, the outermost of which is adorned with a *toraṇa* with double lintel. In the air, as many as four *kinnaras* are paying it worship with garlands; as for the human worshippers, they are going round it in procession at a sort of dance step, a few inside but the greater number outside the first balustrade. Some are clasping their hands, one is waving a standard, others are bringing offerings of flowers, while in the foreground thunders an orchestra consisting of a harp, a kettle-drum, two sorts of tambourine (cylindrical and ovoid), a double flute and two curved trumpets, whose mouths are shaped like serpents' heads. Women are severely excluded. Notice the curly hair, tied with a band, and the caps, sometimes round and sometimes pointed; the sleeved tunics bound with a girdle; the little flowing cloaks on the back, knotted under the chin like a chlamys; and finally the sandals and leggings. It is evident that the clan of the Mallas in the eyes of the sculptors of Central India passed for "northerners", otherwise they would not have equipped them thus; perhaps, too, (who knows?) they wanted to flatter the vanity of the pilgrims who were beginning to flock in from the recently converted regions of the North-West by showing them their kinsmen busy celebrating the Master's funeral. *Cf.* also Pt. II, pp. 124 and 157, n. 1, for the drawing of the stūpa and the dress of these figures.

c2. *The Monkey's Offering at Vaiśālī.*—For identification, see p. 219. The tree on the right forming the companion to the Buddha's *aśvattha* is a bignonia: the middle one we have not been able to identify. The monkey is a *langur* (Skt. *go-laṅgula*=ox-tailed). Should the praying figures be connected with the legend or are they the donors? Observe that the follower in the background, whose hair-dressing betrays her subordinate position, is holding garlands on a tray. The representation of the two *upāsikās* and the child kneeling before the throne deserves notice (*cf.* Pl. 32, 3).

c3. *The Return to Kapilavastu.*—The identification seems certain and also the contamination of the two episodes nos. 7*a* and 7*b* (*cf.* p. 204). Behind King Śuddhodana one can see women carrying the umbrella and fly-whisk, a third woman attendant and the heads of two courtiers. Above, one of the three supernatural worshippers, unlike the usual *kinnara*, seems to be a plain *Devaputra* or *Yaksha* in human shape, riding a winged lion: we find this rarer type in Pls. 49c and 64*a*2. For the *caṅkrama*, compare Pls. 19c, 34*a*, 50*a* and 51*a* and *b*.

PLATE 37

PILLARS OF NORTHERN GATEWAY—concluded

This plate unites the reproductions of the two richly decorative designs which cover the outer section of the west and east jambs; the reader should compare them with those on Pls. 19, 50 and 66. In both, the central band is made of palmettes combined with lotuses, and we have already had occasion to see this motif as the origin of the "bouquet issuing from the vase" (*cf.* Pl. 28). A glance at the bottom of *b*, where the lotus is transformed into a *bhadra-ghaṭa*, cannot but help to confirm this impression.

a. We have already (pp. 144-45 and 248-49) discussed the meaning of this curious composition[1]: a detailed description of each motif would take us much too far. Notice only, in the floral pattern, that on the *nandipada* or *taurine* the lotuses give place to the vine; and that among the necklaces of beads and jewellery so variously arranged, which are hung from *nāga-dantas*, two are made of a string of amulets (rosette of lotus, axe-head, elephant-goad, shield, palmette, pair of fish, bunch of grapes (?), barred triangle, etc.), the interpretation of which is still in a large measure obscure.[2] One may compare the sacred feet with those shown on Pl. 40, 2. It is probably to this composition or to the pillar on which it is carved, that Inscr. 17*b* (p. 301) refers as the *Bhagavato pamāṇa-laṭhi*, i.e., 'height-measuring staff' of the Blessed One.

b. The carving on the west jamb does not make the same claim to iconographical importance and seems resigned to its purely decorative role;[1] but it makes up in the details. On the two borders and two intermediate bands are displayed lotus creepers, issuing either from a *bhadra-ghaṭa* or from the mouth of a *makara*-elephant, with or without *haṁsas* on their scrolls. With the *palmettes* on the central band are mingled male or female figures holding a sword in one hand and with the other raising what, by force of habit, one would take for a tray of offerings, but which seems to be a sort of small parade-buckler which was used in the kind of war-dance which Indian fencing still remains. We owe its identification to the fact that on the left, at the bottom, one of the figures has chanced to lower this object, and we see it full-face. We perceive a rectangular tablet edged below with a fringe of tassels (or perhaps bells ?) and surmounted by three crests. Henceforth the optical illusion which made us think that we were looking at the profile of a cylindrical or cubical object behind whose rim the bearer's hand disappeared, is dispelled. This is indeed nothing but a flat oblong *buckler* fitted with an inner handle, which we see on a larger scale on Pls. 100-102. This defensive weapon was normally held in the left hand; but (except in the bottom motif on Pl. 37*b*) the sculptor of the Northern Gateway makes it change hands for the sake of symmetry, thus transforming two of his male and one of his female fencers on the left column into so many left-handers.[3]

[1] For the meaning of these compositions, see also Pt. II, pp. 142-144.

[2] For details of these amulets, *cf.* Maisey, *op. cit.*, Pl. xxxix, figs. 15 and 16.

[3] After repeated examinations of these figures and of those on the gateway of Stūpa 3 (Pls. 100-102) I must confess that I still remain unconvinced that the object held by these Yakshas and Yakshīs of the Lotus Tree is a buckler. It does not seem to be held as a shield should be: nor is it clear why a shield should have a fringe of tassels or bells or three crests in front of it. My personal view, as stated on p. 145 (with footnote 2), is that the objects in question are trays of lotus buds.—J. M.

(a) EAST PILLAR OF NORTHERN GATEWAY : EAST FACE

(b) WEST PILLAR OF NORTHERN GATEWAY : WEST FACE

FRONT ELEVATION OF EASTERN GATEWAY

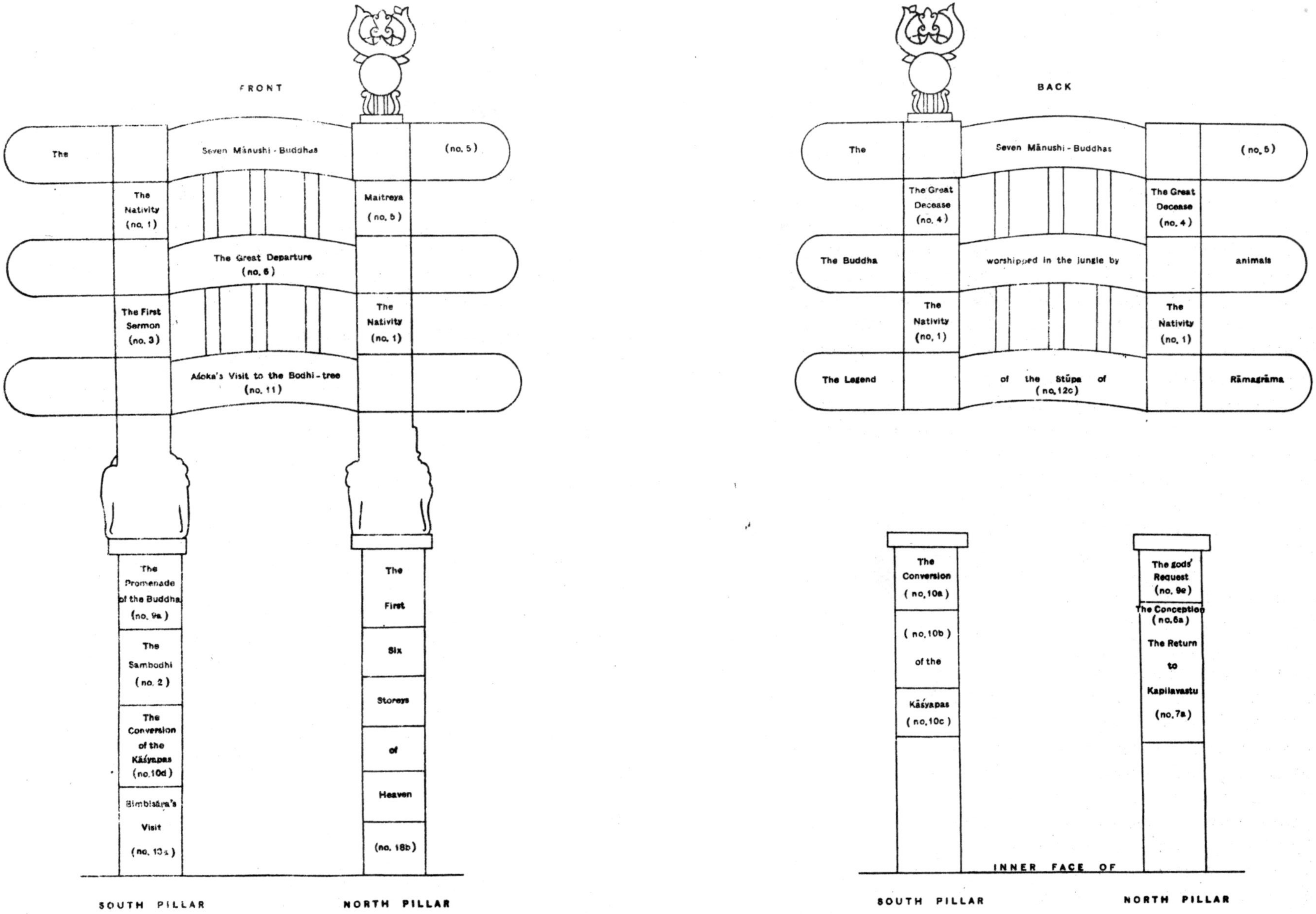

EASTERN GATEWAY : INDEX-MAP OF THE LEGENDARY SCENES

Reg. No. 3936 E'36-595.

Helio. S. I. O. Calcutta.

PLATE 39

FRONT OF EASTERN GATEWAY

Like the Northern Gateway, the Eastern has been preserved in its original position; but, less fortunate than its neighbour and predecessor, it has lost the left-hand *śālabhañjikā* and the majority of the subsidiary figures, the only ones left being one of the two *triratnas* on the top, one *yakshī* and three elephants[1]. The motifs on the capitals and false-capitals are about the same, but are here treated with greater ease and freedom. The lower part of the right-hand jamb has likewise been slightly damaged.

The decoration as a whole has been described on p. 235 (*cf.* the drawing opposite Pl. 38) and the details will be dealt with below. Here, it will be sufficient to indicate briefly for the reader's convenience the meaning of the scenes before him.

On the top lintel are carved the seven last Buddhas of the past; on the middle lintel the "Great Departure" from Kapilavastu; on the bottom lintel, Aśoka's Visit to the Bodhi-tree (*cf.* Pl. 40). The projecting ends of the two latter lintels seem to be given up to purely decorative themes, which have nothing to do with the subjects on the central part.

The four dies represent two Nativities, a First Sermon, and, to complete the series carved on the top lintel, Maitreya the future Buddha (*cf.* Pls. 41-44).

On the six uprights we have, again, three Bodhi-trees and three First Sermons—though on one of the three columns (below, at the left) the wheel which ought to surmount the lion-capital is omitted. Of the three trees, one (above, at the right), belonging to the mango species, should perhaps relate to Sikhin (but *cf.* Pls. 16, 4; 22, 2 and 46, 1); the other two certainly stand for the Enlightenment (above, at the left) of Vipaśyin, and (below, at the right) of Śākya-muni. It may be remarked in passing that the bignonia and the ficus of these last two Buddhas are repetitions of the two trees figured on the top lintel, and consequently do not attempt, as might have been expected, to complete on the facade the list of the seven Bodhi-trees as they are seen lined up on the back of the same top lintel (*cf.* Pl. 45).

The south pillar (left of the spectator; *cf.* Pls. 51-52) is devoted to the Magadha cycle. On the four panels of the front may be seen, from top to bottom, the Buddha's Walk after the *Sambodhi*, the *Sambodhi* itself, the miracle of the flood which unsealed the eyes of the three Kāśyapa brothers, and Bimbisāra's Visit. On the inner face, above the head of a Yaksha door-keeper, are three other panels relating to the arduous conversion of the Kāśyapas.

The north pillar (right of the spectator; *cf.* Pls. 49-50) shows the first six storeys of the world of the gods on its facade, and a lotus decoration on the outer side.

A human figure shows the scale. Through the embrasure of the balustrade one catches a glimpse of half the stele reproduced on Pl. 70*b*. On the left, the ends of the lintels of the Southern Gateway can be seen jutting out.

[1] The diminutive lion on the north end of the lowest architrave does not belong there.

FRONT FACE OF EASTERN GATEWAY

FRONT OF EASTERN GATEWAY : MIDDLE SECTION OF ARCHITRAVES

PLATE 40

FRONT OF EASTERN GATEWAY: MIDDLE SECTION

1. *Top Lintel.*—The series of the seven Mānushi-Buddhas (*cf.* p. 200) is distributed over the whole length of this lintel, represented alternately by their funeral tumulus and the tree of their enlightenment, surrounded as usual (except that none of these is female) by a gathering of praying figures, human or supernatural. The middle part here shown bears only five of these representations, namely three *stūpas* and two *bodhi-drumas*. We can discern no difference between the *stūpas*, but we can immediately recognize the tree of Śākya-muni at the left, and that of Vipaśyin at the right. This proves that the artists' fancy did not always bind himself to follow the traditional order. Having only two trees at his disposal, the sculptor preferred to give the honours of his lintel to those of the first and last Buddhas of the series (*cf.* Pl. 45, and, for the trees decorating the uprights, Pl. 39).

2. *Middle Lintel.*—For the identification of the legend of the *Mahābhinishkramaṇa* or "Great Departure from the House", see p. 203. Note here the curious architecture of Kapilavastu, the loggias of its airy houses, the towers, battlements and gates of its walls. The inhabitants are supposed to be taking the air on their balconies or going about the streets either on foot or on elephants. A postern in the ramparts opens on to the moat, transformed into a lotus pool, where women are coming to draw water. In the retinue which accompanies the Bodhisattva's flight the gods who are not carrying the horse's hoofs are scattering flowers with their right hands, taking them in handfuls from the trays supported by their left, or waving their scarves for joy, or beating celestial drums; but, better bred than those at Bharhut (*cf.* Cunn., Pls. 13, 1, and 17, 3), not one of them is seen with his thumb and forefinger in his mouth, giving vent to a whistle of admiration. The rich and cleverly made trappings of the horse, from the headstall to the crupper, including the embroidered carpet which serves for saddle and is held in place by a girth, are worthy of notice. We may also observe the constancy with which the umbrella and fly-whisk—not to speak of the ewer and sandals—accompany the horse Kaṇṭhaka at each stage, and end by hanging miraculously in the air above the sacred footprints, to signify the invisible presence of the Bodhisattva. The soles of the feet are of course marked with the traditional sign of the wheel. As for the tree, shaded by an umbrella and surrounded by a railing, which stands in the middle of the composition and suggests the "First Meditation", its species is made certain (as we have remarked, p. 202) by comparison with an inscribed bas-relief at Bharhut representing a *jambu*. One appreciates the skill with which the sculptor has managed to distribute at the foot of the tree, so as to frame it in its requisite group of worshippers, three persons who nevertheless continue to join in the principal action, namely: left, the bearer of the sandals; in the background, the ewer-bearer; and on the right, one of the gods throwing flowers. That the four-fold repetition of the horse 'going out' may be meant to remind us of the 'Four Drives', we have already hinted (p. 202) and are inclined to believe it.

3. *Bottom Lintel.*—The facts justifying the identification have been given on p. 212 *seq.* We notice the modesty of Aśoka's headdress, adorned with a simple tuft and much less gorgeous than the usual royal turban. His retinue has its full complement: first Queen Tishyarakshitā, shown twice like the king himself; then the female attendants, two of whom, of course, are carrying the umbrella and fly-whisk; above, a band of flutes, conches and drums; on the right, the guard which would have included the "four corps of troops" if the sculptor had not left out the cavalry; but at any rate he has contrived to show us, besides some infantry armed with swords, spears and bows, a war-chariot and an elephant, both drawn full face and boldly foreshortened. The civilian procession which is arriving from the other side of the Bodhi-tree of Śākya-muni (*cf.* Pl. 51*a*) also includes a band on the left, which in addition to the instruments we have just named includes hand-tabours and a long trumpet. The principals of the procession file past, ceremoniously holding either huge lotus flowers in their hands, or banners whose staves, surmounted by a *triratna* or a wheel, are decorated with heavy garlands (only on the right has the sculptor found room to draw the banner of the standard; *cf.* Pls. 42 and 44). The chief parts are obviously played by the four personages who are advancing in the foreground, carrying in front of their chests pitchers "full of scented water" for watering the sacred tree. Are the person of short stature on whom the king is leaning as he dismounts from his kneeling elephant, and those standing under the galleries of the hypæthral temple, simply court dwarfs, or specimens of those genii (*yakshas*) which the legend ascribes to Aśoka as servants? And ought we to see in the presence of the children, with whom, on the left of the *bodhi-druma*, the sculptor has filled up the gaps in his composition, a proof that the donors of the panels had themselves represented with their families?

For the description of the uprights, see Pl. 39.

PLATE 41

FRONT OF EASTERN GATEWAY: SOUTH END

1. *Top Lintel.*—The stūpa represented belongs to the series of the seven last Buddhas of the past (*cf.* Pl. 40). It is surmounted by no fewer than five umbrellas and two streamers. Three lotuses, seen from the front, indicate a rain of flowers. One of the two female figures holds a tray and the donation-ewer.

2. *Middle Lintel.*—The subject is completely independent of the one shown between the jambs, and in our opinion has no historical or legendary pretensions. Probably it is merely a commonplace of Indian art (*cf.* Pls. 43, 82, 85, 102, etc.) and literature (*cf. Mahāvagga* X, 4, 6-7); some wild elephants are tearing up a mango-tree. Below, left, a conventional indication of rocks.

3. *Die.*—We have here an already advanced form (*cf.* pp. 183 and 197) of the Nativity theme; for Māyā, holding a lotus in her right hand, is seated on a lotus sprouting out of a vase and apparently being given a shower-bath by the two *Nāgas.* In this piece we may relish the happily balanced combination of supple grace and hieratical symmetry (*cf.* Pl. 44 and Part II, pp. 130-1).

4. *Top False-capital.*—Notice the hump, the lyre-shaped horns, the heavy collars and the rope passed through the nostrils of the two Indian oxen, back to back like the bulls on the Persian capitals (*cf.* Pl. 16). The two riders, each holding a lotus, are of the ordinary Indian type.

5. *Middle False-capital.*—Between two winged lions back to back, somewhat Iranian in style, a third lion is thrusting his head and fore-paws. The only tail visible is wound round the hind leg of the lion in foreground.

6. *Detached Figures.*—On the top lintel will be seen a fragment of an elephant's hoofs and above the bottom lintel another elephant with traces of two figures who were riding on it.

FRONT OF EASTERN GATEWAY: SOUTH END OF UPPER AND MIDDLE ARCHITRAVES.

FRONT OF EASTERN GATEWAY. SOUTH END OF LOWEST ARCHITRAVE WITH CAPITAL

PLATE 42

FRONT OF EASTERN GATEWAY: SOUTH END—concluded

1. *Bottom Lintel.*—Against a conventional background of rocks, where two trees are growing (a bignonia and a mango), two peacocks (Pāli: *mora*) are shown in profile. It must be acknowledged that Prof. A. Grünwedel's ingenious hypothesis alluded to above (p. 231), which takes these heraldically treated birds to be the canting arms of the Maurya dynasty, receives some support from the fact that the middle part of this lintel is devoted to an episode from the legend of the Maurya king Aśoka (but *cf.* Pls. 13 and 28).

2. *Die.*—Another wholly schematic representation of the third Great Miracle, the First Sermon (*cf.* p. 198). It is not clear why the sculptor has given the wheel thirty-four spokes. Four men are standing, and in the foreground two women are squatting over the two baskets of offerings which they have brought; all of them worship with clasped hands.

3. *False-capital.*—The same trio of Perso-Assyrian lions as on Pl. 41.

4. *Capital.*—The four elephants, admirably treated, instead of showing only their forequarters as on the Northern Gateway, are shown in profile on four sides in turn, but in so skilful a manner that their heads nevertheless accentuate all four corners of the pillar. We can thus see clearly (*cf.* Pl. 44) every detail of their trappings: caparison girthed with a rope, head-gear with heavy pendants, round bells, etc. Above all we realise perfectly that the elephant's master is sitting in the best place, astride on the neck, with the *aṅkuśa* in his hand; we know that the art of riding an elephant formed part of the education of the sons of good families. Behind him, most insecurely balanced, on the beast's sloping back, the standard-bearer is clinging as best he can. Except for the garlands, the standard is exactly like two of those which we have already seen on the bottom lintel (Pl. 40). For further remarks on this and the corresponding capital at the north end, see Part II, pp. 139-40.

5. *Detached Figures.*—To complete the image of the detached elephant on the projecting end of the lintel, refer to Pl. 41. There is hardly anything left of the fairy on the bracket except fragments of her two feet (*cf.* Pl. 47), two fore-arms covered with bangles and the top of her hair; but for the posture, see Pl. 44.

PLATE 43

FRONT OF EASTERN GATEWAY: NORTH END

1. *Top Lintel.*—The subject is identical with the one which decorates the other end of the lintel (Pl. 41), but the worshipper on the right, and perhaps the one on the left, is followed by a boy (donor and son?). Notice the two offerings' baskets, one inside the other, placed on the ground at the bottom on the right.

2. *Middle Lintel.*—The same remark applies to this panel as to the corresponding one on Pl. 41, 2, and we do not believe that any allusion to the *Shaḍdanta-jātaka* (no. 17*a*) is intended here. Observe, in the background, the pair with curious head-dresses; they are dwellers in the jungle. The woman is holding a bow in her left hand and the man a sheaf of arrows in his right, whilst apparently holding back his wife with his left hand from the dangerous gambols of the two elephants. A bird remains fearlessly perched on the mango-tree, though in the top left-hand corner a monkey is hurrying away. While coming over from one end of the lintel to the other, this 'genre' piece has been enriched with picturesque details (*cf.* Pl. 44, 1).

3. *Die.*—Once again we find, unfortunately damaged, the usual picture of a *Sambodhi* with its ordinary train of worshippers and even, as witnessed by the two ewers in the foreground, donors; but the starry blossoms of the champaka (*nāga-pushpa*) indicate Maitreya. The symbol of the man who is to be the next and eighth Buddha of our æon is evidently intended to complete the series, shown on the top lintel, of the seven who went before him.

4. *False-Capitals.*—The themes on both are the same as their companions on Pl. 41. Only at the top we can see more of the rope which encircled the shoulders and held up the tail of the ox (*cf.* Pl. 16, 6).

5. *Detached Figures.*—The *triratna* standing above the top false-capital, the fairy or Yakshī with the mango-tree and the two mounted elephants (the top one mutilated) are remains of a decorative scheme similar to that on the Northern Gateway, except that the lions have been replaced by elephants. For a description of the latter, the reader is referred to Pls. 42, 4 and 48, 6.

FRONT OF EASTERN GATEWAY: NORTH END OF UPPER AND MIDDLE ARCHITRAVES WITH CROWNING FIGURES

FRONT OF EASTERN GATEWAY: NORTH END OF LOWEST ARCHITRAVE WITH CAPITAL.

PLATE 44

FRONT OF EASTERN GATEWAY: NORTH END—concluded

1. *Bottom Lintel.*—Here again, as on the north end of the middle lintel (*cf.* Pl. 43), we get the impression that the sculptor began his work at the south end and has merely repeated the same theme on the right, embellishing it. Framed between the backward-turned heads of the two peacocks we now observe, in the same rocky landscape as before, a small 'genre' piece (*cf.* pp. 228-9): a genie and his fairy, lovingly embracing, are sitting on the bank of a stream, to which the woman is turning to draw water with a goblet. As supernatural beings, the pair of lovers have nothing to fear from the neighbouring lion or panther, which, moreover, is looking another way (*cf.* Pls. 13, 2, and 19, 1).

2. *Die.*—The Great Miracle of the Nativity is exactly like the one seen on Pl. 41, but much less successful.

3. *The False-Capital* and the *Capital* may be considered as already described on Pl. 42.

4. *Detached Figures.*—In place of the tiny and disproportionate lion on the top of the volute, we must visualize an elephant like those on Pls. 42 and 43. The lion must have been put there at some time after the elephant had fallen. This time the decorative bracket has been preserved complete. Holding with both hands to the arching bough of a mango-tree, the *śālabhañjikā* (*cf.* p. 232) "curves the woodbine of her body" in an attitude which brings out her breasts "like urns of gold". Her locks, spread out over her back (*cf.* Pl. 48), are brought up on the crown of her head into a curious topknot which may be compared to the coiffure of the female servants and jungle-dwellers (*cf.* Pls. 40, 3, and 47, 5). Her transparent *dhotī* is only betrayed by the pleated folds falling at the sides and drawn up at the back between the legs. Her big ear-rings are broken, but the bangles which load her fore-arms almost up to the elbow and her legs almost to the knees, her bead necklace and her girdle of trinkets lend themselves to detailed study. The type presents a pleasing compromise between the court lady and the woman of the woods. (See also pp. 129-30.)

PLATE 45

BACK OF EASTERN GATEWAY

For general description, see pp. 235-6 and *cf.* the drawing opposite Pl. 38.

It will be noticed that the same subject extends over the whole surface in each of the three lintels. Above, each of the seven last Buddhas of the past is represented by the particular tree of his Enlightenment; in the middle, the Buddha Sākya-muni is being worshipped by the jungle animals; below, some elephants are paying homage to a stūpa, which must be that of Rāmagrāma (*cf.* Pl. 46).

The four dies (*cf.* Pls. 47 and 48) are given up to two symbolical representations of the first and last Great Miracles—the last Nativity and the last Decease. One could, if necessary, advance the theory that the two funerary tumuli are meant to be counted with the five shown on the front of the top lintel (*cf.* Pl. 39) to complete the traditional number of seven. The Eastern Gateway would then contain both the seven *Bodhi-drumas* and the seven *Parinirvāṇa-stūpas* of the seven Mānushi-Buddhas.

The backs of the six uprights are uniformly decorated with a combination of palmettes and lotuses, which Sir John Marshall interprets along with those on the outer sides of the Gateway pillars as the Tree of Life and Fortune (*cf.* Part II, pp. 142-4)[1].

This same combination occurs also on the fronts of the capitals (see Pls. 42 and 44), and is found again here on the back of the north capital; on the right, the bare face of the pillar bears nothing but a standard unfurled.

The false-capitals will be described on Pls. 47 and 48.

The background of the photograph shows the site as it was before Sir John Marshall's excavations.

[1] In these and other examples, the palmettes seem to have been regarded as stylised lotus leaves, though they probably had their origin rather in a conventional "Tree of Life" design than in the lotus plant itself.—J. M.

BACK OF EASTERN GATEWAY.

...K OF EASTERN GATEWAY: MIDDLE SECTION OF ARCHITRAVE

PLATE 46

BACK OF EASTERN GATEWAY: MIDDLE SECTION

1. *Top Lintel.*—This time, our sculptors have portrayed the series of the seven Mānushi-Buddhas in chronological order. The south projecting end of the lintel shows the tree of Vipaśyin, the first of them (*cf.* Pl. 47). Reading from right to left (not, as on Pl. 22, 2, from left to right), we therefore see here successively the fig-tree (unspecified) of Sikhin; the *śāla* (*shorea robusta*) of Viśvabhū; the *sirīsha* (*acacia sirissa*) of Krakucchanda; the *udumbara* (*ficus glomerata*) of Kanakamuni, and the *nyagrodha* (*ficus indica*) of Kāśyapa; and lastly, on the north projecting end of the lintel (*cf.* Pl. 48) the *aśvattha* (*ficus religiosa*) of the last Buddha, namely Sākya-muni. In six cases out of seven the identification of the trees presents little difficulty, though the characteristic features of the *udumbara* are hidden under the garlands, and the drawing of the central *sirīsha* is a little surprising at first sight: on the inscribed bas-relief at Bharhut (Cunn., Pl. 29, 3), botanically much more accurate, the branches of the acacia are indeed shown hanging; but *ibid.*, Pl. 14, 3, they are turned up, as here. The Buddha Sikhin is the only one of the series who still suffers from the fact that no inscribed representation of his tree has as yet been found at Bharhut (*cf.* Pls. 16, 5 & 22, 2). As on Pl. 40, 1, all the worshippers are male.

2. *Middle Lintel.*—It seems that for once we must give the credit for this curious tableau to the artist's imagination: at least it illustrates no text known to us. It is, indeed, related that the Buddha, disgusted at the intestine quarrels of his Community, left Kauśāmbī to retire into solitude, and that the beasts waited on him (*cf. Mahāvagga*, X, 4, 6-7); but according to the text the beasts were only wild elephants—and these are just the animals which do not appear on our lintel; so this celebrated episode in the Master's career could at most have supplied the starting point for the composition before us. On the other hand, it is a commonplace of Buddhist legend that the Buddha was able by virtue of his benevolence (Pali, *mettā*) to live without fear in the midst of the wild animals, and perhaps the best commentary on our bas-relief is a passage in the *Cariyā-piṭaka* (ed. R. Morris, *P. T. S.*, Lond. 1882, p. 101), where the Buddha recounts how in a former life, when he was the young anchorite Sāma (Skr. Syāma; cf. *infra*, Pl. 65*a*, 1) he sojourned in the forest in the company of lions, tigers, panthers, bears and the like. Be this as it may, the central *aśvattha* proves that it is the Buddha Sākya-muni, who is receiving homage from this half natural, half supernatural "zoo". The four lions flanking his throne (*siṁha-āsana*), two front-face and two in profile, may be meant to make it clear that we are indeed in the presence of the "Lion of the Sākyas". Buffaloes and antelopes, admirably rendered, represent the real fauna of the jungle. Of the monsters, the two griffins and the two unicorn-lions on the left, and the two bulls with manes, human faces and the horns of a ram (*cf.* Pl. 35 *b*, 1) on the right, come from Assyria *via* Persia; but the many-headed serpent and the bird next to it in the top right-hand corner are autochthonous. The first is a Nāga, a genie-serpent; the second, with its egret, big parrot-beak and ear-rings, must be the hereditary enemy of the first, namely Garuḍa, and both are forgetting their natural enmity in the contemplation of the Blessed One. The bignonia and other trees remind us that the scene takes place in the forest.

3. *Bottom Lintel.*—The identification has been discussed above (p. 215). A herd of ten wild elephants, free of any mark of servitude, with lotus-flowers which they have torn up from the nearest pond and are carrying in their trunks or on their tusks, are performing the ritual worship of the central stūpa. In the right-hand corner at the bottom, a single tree represents the jungle.

For the uprights, see Pl. 45.

PLATE 47

BACK OF EASTERN GATEWAY: SOUTH END

1. *Top Lintel.*—The similarity of an inscribed bas-relief at Bharhut (Cunn., Pl. 29, 1) places it beyond dispute that the *bodhi-druma* represented here between two pairs of human worshippers is that of Vipaśyin. Literary tradition further assures us that this tree is the *pāṭali* (*bignonia suaveolens*) and not, as the highly formalised representation might have suggested, the *aśoka*.

2. *Middle Lintel.*—This scene, comprising buffaloes, antelopes, trees and birds, continues that on the central part: therefore the animals are all facing left. The plantain is here very clearly drawn (bottom, right). It will be noticed that the four birds (parrots?) are shown flying and carrying offerings of fruit (mangoes and grapes) in their beaks.

3. *Bottom Lintel.*—Two elephants and a baby elephant, all turned left, are taking part from afar in the worship of the stūpa, which stands in the centre of the lintel. A bignonia and a mango-tree complete the scenic decoration (*cf.* Pl. 46).

4. *Dies.*—The top die represents, fairly elaborately, a stūpa of the *Parinirvāṇa* (fourth Great Miracle) with the two winged genii who are bringing garlands and the human couple making an offering of lotus; and the bottom die, an archaic form of the first Great Miracle, wherein the Nativity is simply suggested by a bunch of lotuses coming out of a richly decorated *bhadra-ghaṭa*.

5. *False-capitals.*—At the top of the jamb two lions, winged and bridled, their brows adorned with stags' antlers, are walking in opposite directions. The one on the left is ridden by a jungle-dweller with a head-dress like the one on Pl. 43, 2, holding a lotus-bud; the right-hand rider has short curly hair tied with a band, and seems to be emphasizing his foreign origin by carrying a vine-leaf (?) in his hand.

In the middle, two kneeling camels are ridden by a man and a woman: compare the man's heavy necklace with that of the hunter on Pl. 43. The camels are of the Bactrian type, long-haired and with a double hump. The rope is fastened, just as it is nowadays, to a wooden peg fixed in the upper part of the nostrils. Observe the unnaturally protuberant eyes. The two personages seem to be holding, besides the rein, a switch made of twisted stuff. See also Part II, p. 137, and Pl. 48.

Finally, on a level with the bottom lintel, the animals set back to back are plain goats. As the male rider here shown faces right, the sheath of his knife may be seen, thrust into the girdle of his narrow loin-cloth, and his knot of hair shows above the top of his diadem. His female partner wears much the same coiffure, and one may compare the tuft of hair rising like a brush on the top of her head with the topknots of the *śālabhañjikās* (*cf.* Pls. 42 and 44 and also Pl. 48).

For description of the capital, bracket and detached figures, the reader is referred to Pls. 42-44.

BACK OF EASTERN GATEWAY: SOUTH END OF ARCHITRAVES WITH CAPITAL.

BACK OF EASTERN GATEWAY: NORTH END OF ARCHITRAVES WITH CAPITAL

PLATE 48

BACK OF EASTERN GATEWAY: NORTH END

1. *Top Lintel.*—From its place at the end of the series and from the tapering points of its leaves we recognize the *aśvattha* or pipal (*ficus religiosa*) of the historical Buddha Śākya-muni. There are only three human worshippers, two male and one female (donors?).

2. *Middle Lintel.*—Facing in the opposite direction to those which decorate the corresponding end (Pl. 47), all the animals (buffaloes, antelopes with straight or curved horns, and parrots bearing bunches of fruit) are likewise looking at the Buddha in the centre. Note the excellent full-length representation of a date-palm (*phœnix sylvestris*).

3. *Bottom Lintel.*—The remarks that have been made on Pl. 47 apply here to the four elephants of different sizes, all looking right, and to the mango-tree. One must mentally eliminate all the false-capitals which cut up the composition.

4. *Dies.*—Same description as for those on Pl. 47.

5. *False-capitals.*—Here, again, the descriptions of Pl. 47 are applicable, with the exception of a few details. This time the lions at the top are not winged and carry two similar riders of the 'jungle-dweller' type; in the middle the camels are mounted by the ordinary type of riders; and on the goats at the bottom the woman displays a large tuft of hair, whilst the man, whose hair is short, is wearing sandals and leggings. Finally, in the middle false-capital, the rider on the right is clearly brandishing in his right hand a switch made of twisted stuff, which is probably what the right-hand rider on the top false-capital is also doing.

For the *capital*, the reader is referred to Pl. 42.

6. *Detached Figures.*—The *śālabhañjikā* has been described from all sides on Pl. 44; here she is seen from behind, like the Yakshī between the lintels. Notice the difference between her loose hair, and the veil and loops which fall over the back of her elegant counterpart; and observe also that the standard-bearer perched on the back of the detached elephant is a double relief carved in the same attitude on the two sides of a single stone, which fits into a mortice on the top lintel (*cf.* Pl. 43).

PLATE 49

NORTH PILLAR OF EASTERN GATEWAY

a-b. Front of North Jamb.—For the general meaning of the composition see p. 227. From the technical point of view it will be noticed at once that it is divided into seven storeys distributed among four distinct buildings, *viz.*, one storey (which we shall call no. 1) for the bottom palace and two storeys (nos. 2-3, 4-5, 6-7) for the three others. The capitals of the ground-floor columns in each storey are the only ones of Indo-Persian form, surmounted by the usual winged animals back to back (notice by the way that on the fourth storey the animals, from right to left, are lions, horses, elephants and, instead of the expected bulls, goats); the columns supporting the roofs are provided simply with a bracket. The long, keel-shaped roofs are, except on the seventh storey, pierced with dormer-windows of the well-known horse-shoe pattern, sometimes blind (fifth storey) and sometimes partly open and, in this case, closed at the top by a chequered screen (third storey). The whole is crowned by a terrace open to the sky, surrounded on three sides by separate blocks of building. A railing runs along both the ground-floor and the first-floor balcony, above a course decorated with the projecting ends of the joists, which acts alternatively as plinth or as cornice.

1st Storey: The Lokapālas' Heaven.—At the bottom of the hierarchical ladder, where they figure as minor divinities, the "Four Kings who guard the world" occupy a separate building, intermediate between the worlds of men and of gods. Unfortunately, the panel is damaged, but all four of them can still be seen in the foreground in front of a row of female attendants, though one cannot give names to these uniform figures, nor consequently tell which of them is in the seat of honour.

2nd Storey.—The *Trayastriṁśat Heaven*, or the heaven of the "Thirty-Three" is situated on the ground-floor of the next *vimāna* and introduces a series of five court tableaux, all alike; as this is mutilated, we have lost the figure of the president of the group, "Sakra, the Indra of the Gods". We may still note in the top corners the indication of a palm-tree at the left and a mango-tree on the right (*cf.* the plantain on the right of panel no. 1): such indications of trees recur regularly in the background of the two other palaces; for the celestial paradises comprise parks just as they do all the other accessories of royal life.

3rd Storey.—*Yama's Heaven* occupies the first floor of the second palace. We will pass quickly over this panel, on account of its comparatively small dimensions and the mutilations which it has suffered. Besides, the description of the following one applies to this.

4th and 5th Storeys.—The Fourth (*Tushita*) Heaven, where the gods live "in joy", is the one where Śākya-muni, the last Buddha, awaited and where Maitreya, the future Buddha, is awaiting the hour of his last coming upon earth. The fact that the picture contains nothing particularly devotional proves clearly how stereotyped the concept of these paradises was, and already such as we find it today in Ceylon and Indo-China. In accordance with what we have already seen on the 2nd and 3rd storeys and shall see on the 5th (Heaven of the *Nirmāṇa-rati*, that is, of the gods who "rejoice in their own creations"), the "king" of each heaven is seated between the central columns in the pose of the *līlā-āsana*, holding the two divine attributes of the thunderbolt and the flask of ambrosia. Of his heavenly companions, only one is ever seen, apparently the one who performs the functions of his viceroy (*upa-rāja*)—functions well-known from the *Jātaka* texts, and till recently still in existence in some spheres of Indian civilisation such as Nepāl or Cambodia. This viceroy is seated on his right in the same attitude, but with empty hands and on a slightly lower seat, usually a rattan stool (*morha*) covered with a carpet. Behind each of them stand the inevitable women-attendants bearing the royal insignia, the umbrella and fly-whisk. Lastly, the space between the columns on the right is regularly filled with musicians (harp-, flute-, and tambourine-players) and dancers, a ballet being in India an indispensable part of a life of pleasure.

6th and 7th Storeys.—The same description applies to the 6th storey, except that the central figure is not holding the thunderbolt in his right hand. This omission looks to us like a discreet way of letting us know that, though flanked, like his neighbour, with the usual two insignia of royalty, he does not represent the sovereign of the 6th heaven, that of the *Paranirmita-vaśavartin*, and that we must look for Māra, in company with his *alter ego* and their attendants—he with the cup and the other with the flask in his hand—on the balcony of the top gallery (*cf.* above, p. 227).

c. Top Panel of Inner (South) Face of North Jamb.—We were long under the impression that this panel was a sequel to the one which is placed below, and represented in the usual elliptical fashion (Buddha seated on) a throne under a *ficus indica* in the *Nyagrodha-ārāma* which his father Suddhodana had presented to him, receiving the homage of all the aristocracy of the Sākyas, grouped round their suzerain lord. The species of the tree, the odd number of persons, and the striking resemblance which the protagonist bears to King Suddhodana, as he is depicted on the bottom panel (*cf.* Pl. 50), gave strong support to this identification. But the earnest expressions and clasped hands of the personages seem to correspond much better with the famous episode of the *Adhyeshaṇa* (*cf.* p. 210). As a matter of fact, at this time the Buddha Śākya-muni had already left the shelter of his Bodhi-tree (*aśvattha*) for that of a *nyagrodha*, and the royal turban on the central figure would befit Indra, whilst the other principal figure close by would be Brahmā (*cf.* Pl. 64*a*, 2). Each of the two great gods naturally has a retinue of some of his heavenly companions. Notice, in the sky, the two *devaputras* riding on lions, who replace the usual two winged spirits and, like them, fill the accessory role of bearers of offerings.

a.

b

c

NORTH PILLAR OF EASTERN GATEWAY:

a. UPPER PANELS ON FRONT FACE b. LOWER PANELS ON FRONT FACE c. UPPER PANELS ON SOUTH FACE

a.

b

c

(a) NORTH PILLAR OF EASTERN GATEWAY: LOWER PANELS ON SOUTH FACE.

(b) NORTH FACE.

(c) SOUTH PILLAR OF EASTERN GATEWAY: SOUTH FACE.

PLATE 50

PILLARS OF EASTERN GATEWAY—continued

*a*1. *Middle Panel of Inner (South) Face of North Jamb.*—Whatever identification we may adopt for the panel just above, we are here at Kapilavastu. The episode of the Conception (*cf.* pp. 182 and 202) introduced in the top left-hand corner, serves to prove it, and is there for no other purpose: for more than thirty years separate it from the context of the relief, which refers to the return of the 'Perfectly Accomplished Buddha' to his native town (*cf.* p. 204). This is a good opportunity to examine once more (*cf.* Pls. 40, 2 and 51*b*) the architecture of houses and city gates, the make-up of a procession, the appointments of a chariot and the way a royal turban is fixed with a curious spindle-shaped object on the top. And if the identification leaves any reader incredulous, let him compare the long flag-stone of the *caṅkrama* or "walking path" on Pls. 19*d*, 34*a*, 36*c* and 51*a* and *b*. The trees of the park in which the miracle takes place are, above, from left to right, a fan-shaped palm (*tāla*=*borassus flabelliformis*), a bignonia and a mango-tree; and at the bottom on the right, in the same order, a flowering mango-tree (?), a plantain and a bignonia. As for the *ficus indica* in the bottom left-hand corner—whose sacred character, in the absence of the umbrella, is attested by the balustrade round it—it symbolises all by itself a wood of *nyagrodha* (*cf.* p. 204). For the technique and art of this relief, see Part II, pp. 122-123.

a2. *Bottom Panel.*—The guardian genie of the Gate and his counterpart on Pl. 52 ought to represent Dhṛitarāshṭra, King of the Gandharvas, and his viceroy (*cf.* p. 247); but they display no characteristic attribute, not even a harp. We may console ourselves with the thought that, like the Yaksha on Pl. 36, they at least afford us full length illustrations of Indian lords of the first century B.C. (*cf.* Pl. 36). This one is raising in his right hand a many-petalled lotus, whose pericarp is clearly shown, and holding in his lowered left hand the edge of the scarf loosely tied round his waist (*cf.* the Yaksha on Pls. 22, 23 and 29). The trees at the back are a mango at the left and a bignonia at the right. *Cf.* Part II, p. 133.

b. *Outer (North) Face of North Jamb.*—A band of pink lotuses (*padma*=*nelumbium speciosum*), which we have already seen on Pls. 19*e* and 23*b* and shall find again on Pl. 103*f*, is framed between two sinuous creepers of the same flowers, trimmed with buds and leaves. The interval between the rosaques in the middle is filled by leaves or flowers or blue and pink lotuses. *Cf.* Part II, pp. 145-6.

c. *Outer (South) Face of South Jamb.*—It is interesting to compare the corresponding decoration on the outer face of the other jamb. Here, the entire face of the pillar is covered by a sinuous lotus creeper like those which border the opposite one. In this splendid ornamental motif, whose only fault is that it is a little overcrowded, the usual denizens of the lotus pools—geese (*haṁsas*) and, half-way up, a tortoise—are mingled with the flowers, buds and leaves, shown at all stages of development and from every angle. It will be noticed how the stem, which is the tubular stalk, not the rhizome, of a lotus, is coiled round at the top, and at the bottom is issuing from the jaws of a curious *makara* (for which *cf.* Pl. 87, no. 71*b*).

Apropos of this garland, we may notice that it reappears on a reduced scale as a border on all the ornamented sides of the two pillars (except on the facade of the north pillar, where it is replaced by a simple leafy rod), and that in those cases it always comes out of a *bhadra-ghaṭa*. For further observations on these lotus designs, see Part II, pp. 142-6.

PLATE 51

SOUTH PILLAR OF EASTERN GATEWAY

a. Top Panels of Front Face, South Jamb.—It is certainly worthy of note that the two bas-reliefs here shown are found again, one above the other but in inverse order, on the outer face of the so-called Pillar of Prasenajit at Bharhut (Cunn., Pls. 13, 1*a*, and 14, 1). It is evident, even palpable, that these are variants of one and the same theme, so that the Bharhut labels apply also to Sāñchī.

This is what has made it possible to assert definitely (p. 197) that the lower panel (in spite of the anachronism of the hypæthral temple) represents the second Great Miracle in the Master's life—the *Sambodhi*. We notice that here the branches of the sacred fig-tree are coming out through the windows of the encircling gallery. On each side, a mango-tree and a bignonia represent the groves of Uruvilvā. The emblem (here the only one, but twice repeated at Bharhut) surmounting the *vajra-āsana* ought to symbolise the Buddha, or at most the Buddha and his Law (*Dharma*), since the Community (*Saṅgha*) did not come into existence until after the First Sermon; but let it be remembered that the temple itself which is here portrayed, was not built until the time of Aśoka.

It looks as though the four praying figures in the foreground of the lower panel should be identified as the four Lokapālas. In any case the 8 + 10 personages ranged in two lines on the top panel are certainly divinities, and it is even probable, from the analogy of Bharhut, where the inscriptions name them, that they should be divided into two groups (*cf.* Hultzsch, *Indian Antiquary*, XXI, p. 231); the ten, at a rate of two per heaven, represent the *Kāmāvacara* gods, that is, those who still belong to the world of desire and occupy, above the Lokapālas, the five other storeys on the facade of the adjacent pillar (see Pl. 49). The eight at the top we have not yet seen, but in the legend they, too, take an interest in the Master's principal miracles: they are the *Suddhāvāsa-devas* who, beyond the sixth heaven, freed from the tyranny of the senses, dwell in the "Pure Abodes". Here the Sāñchī workmen have contrived to give an occupation to the two rows of supers by making them line up (but without allowing them to turn their backs on the spectator) on each side of the long flag-stone which cuts the picture in two and which can be nothing but the *caṅkrama* or "walking-path" of the Master (*cf.* Pls. 19*d*, 34*a*, 36*c*, 50*a*, 51*b*; and notice that the Eastern Gateway shows this *caṅkrama* always bare and open to the sky, whereas the Southern Gateway has a garland floating over it and the Northern Gateway shelters it under a gallery). Hence the panel assumes a particular meaning: instead of simply showing, as at Bharhut, an assembly of gods hastening hither to pay homage to the newly enlightened Buddha, it portrays in addition the episode of the "Walk" which the Master took soon after the Sambodhi (*cf.* p. 207).

b. Bottom Panels of Front Face, South Pillar.—The other half of the jamb is likewise divided into two panels. The upper one terminates the series of miracles which, not without difficulty, brought about the conversion of the Kāśyapas (*cf.* Pl. 52*a* and p. 210). Here it will be sufficient to notice: the way the flood is represented by wave-like lines; the trees whose trunks are being battered by the water (we can recognize at the left a champaka above and a bignonia below; at the right in the middle, a mango-tree, in which two monkeys are taking refuge; and below, on the bank, a row of plantains); the crocodile, *haṁsas* and cormorants playing among the tuses; the way the planks are jointed and the shape of the paddles of the canoe containing the three anchorites, etc. Are these three extempore navigators the same as the ones we find down below on dry land, with the addition of a young novice (*brahma-cārin*)—namely the "three Kāśyapa brothers"? Some are inclined to think that the personage seen from behind, facing the *caṅkrama* of the Blessed One, is represented prostrate on the ground, and they have given as proof the way the two blossoms beside him are seen from above; but these blossoms, scattered here and there all over the composition, are put there for no other purpose than to indicate, here as elsewhere, the rain of flowers which accompanies the miracle. In any case, this personage can hardly be any other than the eldest of the three brothers, Mahā-Kāśyapa, at last submitting to perform the *añjali* to the invisible Buddha. For the probable meaning of the throne under the fig-tree below at the right, *cf.* p. 211.

For the lower panel, the general context of the pillar, our only guide in the circumstances, has led us to the identification given on p. 217. The bas-relief, reproducing the stereotyped theme of the "Royal Visit", lends itself to the same observations as those on Pls. 18*a*, 34*b*, 35*b*, 50*a*, etc.

It may be remarked that the columns of Indo-Persian style, which sometimes (apparently by a whim of the sculptor's) replace the lotus-creeper on the border, have, in addition to their characteristic capital, a vase-shaped pedestal, which they lack on Pl. 49.

a

b

SOUTH PILLAR OF EASTERN GATEWAY

(*a*) UPPER PANELS ON FRONT FACE

(*b*) LOWER PANELS ON FRONT FACE

a

b

SOUTH PILLAR OF EASTERN GATEWAY.

(*a*) UPPER PANELS ON NORTH FACE. (*b*) LOWEST PANEL ON NORTH FACE.

PLATE 52

SOUTH PILLAR OF EASTERN GATEWAY—concluded

a. Inner (North) Face of South Jamb.—We have already seen that the three upper panels tell the main incidents in the difficult conversion of the Kāśyapas (*cf.* pp. 210-12): it only remains to note here the accessory details, which are abundant.

*a*1. The bas-relief at the top gives us a very lively tableau of the village of Uruvilvā, where herds of cattle, buffaloes and goats are seen among the houses. Above, at the left, on the threshold of their cottages, some women are about their household tasks. Two of them are squatting: one, her attention apparently distracted by the conversation of the man sitting near her, is crushing *cari* powder, and the other is winnowing rice in a *śūrpa*. Two others are standing: one husking rice in a mortar with a big wooden pestle, and the other rolling dough for a cake (*chapatti*). Two others, below at the right, round pitchers on their hips, are going to draw water at what might be taken for a lotus-pool, but which, from the sinuous lines which show the current, seems rather to be the river Nairañjanā, which still waters Urel under the name of Lilañj; and a third is already leaning forward in the act of filling her *ghaṭī*. In front of a building which seems to be the (rather too gorgeous) gate of the village, stands a man, with a bamboo pole on his shoulder and ropes in his hand: right at the top another man shows us how a double burden can be balanced, by hanging a basket or jar by ropes on to the two ends of a bamboo. Such was village life two thousand years ago; such it is today, and there is not one of the utensils represented which is not still in use. The gesture of a villager standing before the gate with hands clasped is the only bond between all these "genre" scenes, so pleasantly treated, and the religious subject, which has undoubtedly been somewhat shelved but which nevertheless represents the third and fourth of the numerous prodigies which led in the end to the conversion of the *Jaṭilas*, in the order given in the *Mahāvagga* (I, 16-18).

*a*2. The sculptor has given more space in the middle panel to the tale of the miraculous victory over the *Nāga*—the first in the *Mahāvagga* version, the last in the *Mahāvastu* version—at the expense of the hermitage picture. However, there is again a rich harvest of picturesque details to be reaped—such as the temple-cupola, raised on pillars; the leafy roof of the round hut (*parṇaśālā*); the dress of bark (beaten into long strands) of the Brāhman anchorites; the rolled mat (*bṛisī*) on which old Kāśyapa is sitting, with a band passing round his knees; the novices coming to draw water, no doubt to put out the fire of the temple, if we are to believe the Gandhāra replicas; the hearths and spoons of Vedic sacrifice; an elephant and two antelopes, one of which is calmly drinking; two buffaloes which, on the contrary, are raising their heads in alarm; three monkeys, frisking or marauding at the left, at the top of a mango-tree and a fan-palm; at the right, a bird resting on a *ficus* near a bignonia; below, some geese playing among the lotuses of the Nairañjanā, whose bank is edged with a row of plantains, etc. It may be wondered, also, whether the sculptor did not, according to his wont, intend to double his subjects. In the middle of the foreground an adult anchorite seems to be taking a chilly plunge in the river, looking out of the corner of his eye at a fire blazing on the bank, near which he has left his pitcher: have we not here an allusion to the miracle of the Buddha creating fires to permit the Brāhmans to warm themselves after bathing (*Mahāvagga*, I, 20, 15)?

*a*3. But it is particularly the bottom panel which, round some new prodigies (*cf.* *Mahāvagga* I, 20, 12-13, and *Mahāvastu*, III, p. 426, ll. 15-18), describes everyday life in the hermitages; the bringing of the offerings and the preparation of fuel for the sacrifice (the anchorites still use primitive axes to split their wood); the curious shape of the hearths and spoons for oblation; the use of fans of matting to coax the fire; and, most interesting detail of all, a stūpa of the most archaic form known—perhaps the mausoleum of a former superior of this Brāhman community. The objects decorating the lower part of the tumulus, seen just above the rectangular balustrade (a double basket(?) between two conches), may be explained—like the oar planted on Elpenor's tomb by the companions of Ulysses—as the instruments which the deceased habitually used in his life-time.[1]

b. Bottom Panel of Inner (North) Face of South Jamb.—Trees and person are just as on Pl. 50. Only the trees have changed sides and the genie, his left hand leaning on his hip, is raising a bignonia flower instead of a lotus in his right hand. *Cf.* pp. 133-4 *supra.*

[1] These objects may, however, be shells, used merely for decorative purposes.—J. M.

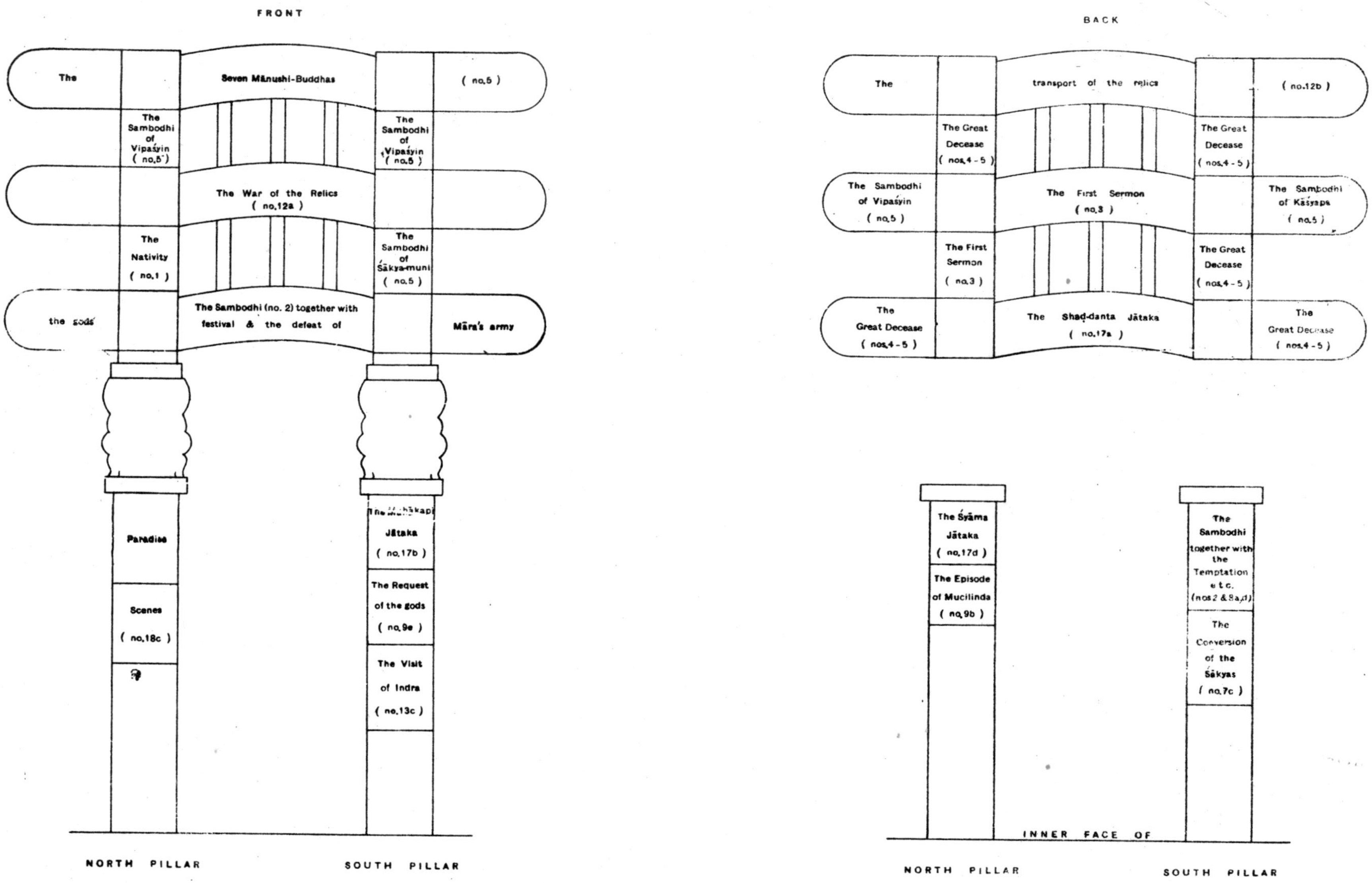

WESTERN GATEWAY (Restored) : INDEX-MAP OF THE LEGENDARY SCENES

Reg. No. 3936 E'36-595.

Helio. S. I. O. Calcutta.

THE MONUMENTS OF SANCHI: STUPA I

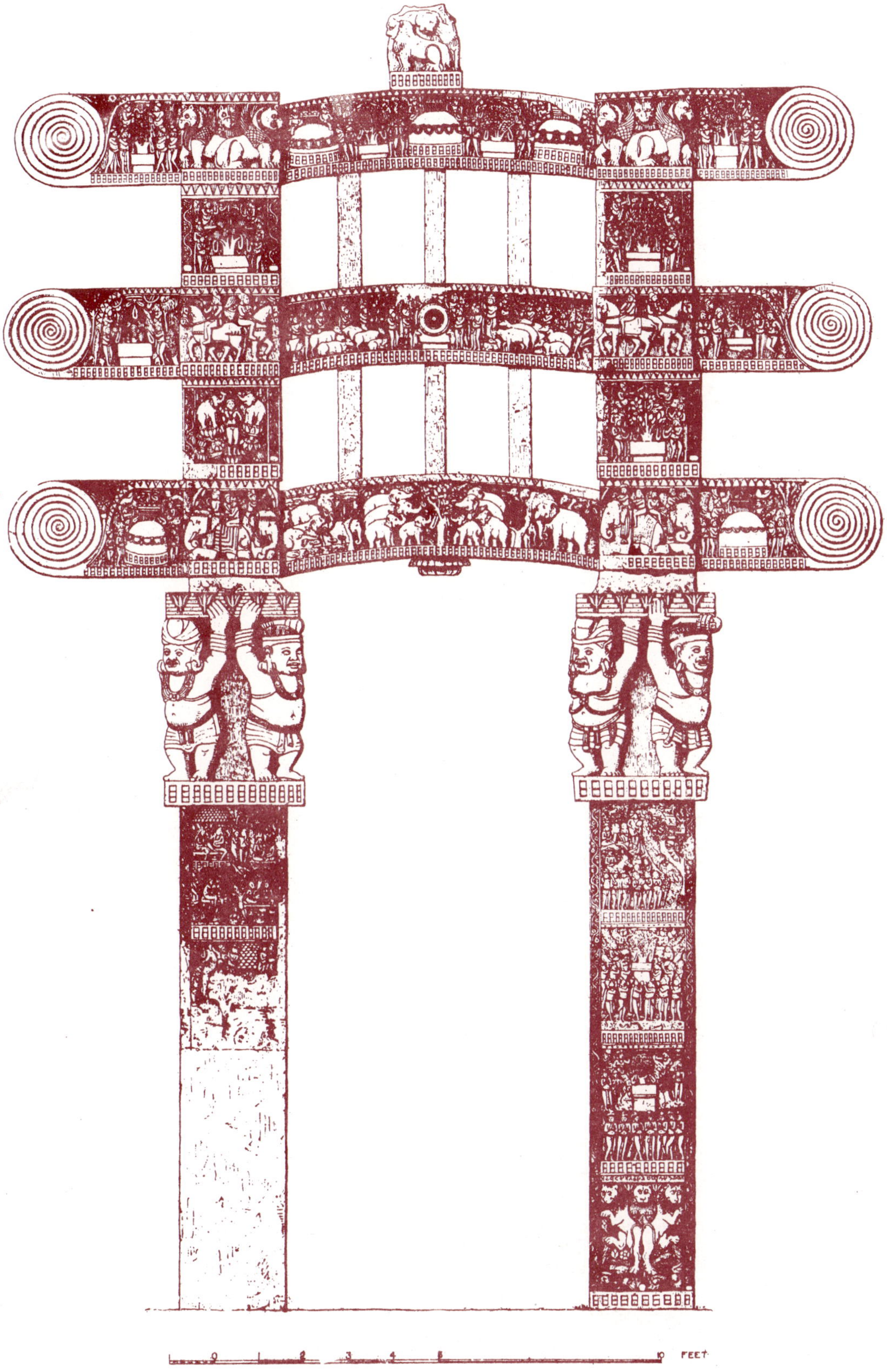

FRONT ELEVATION OF WESTERN GATEWAY

FRONT FACE OF WESTERN GATEWAY

PLATE 54

FRONT FACE OF WESTERN GATEWAY

As we have already said (pp. 233 and 236) and indicated on the drawing facing Pl. 53, the middle and bottom lintels have been put back with the face reversed (*cf.* Pl. 60) during the restoration in the last century. In all probability the original facade was composed as follows:—

a. Top Lintel: Representation of the seven Mānushi-Buddhas;

b. Middle Lintel: War of the Relics;

c. Bottom Lintel: Great Miracle of the Enlightenment;

whilst the back showed in the same order:—

a. a transport of relics which is only an excuse for a procession;

b. a First Sermon stretched out laterally;

c. a decorative (and aberrant) composition of the *Shaḍdanta-jātaka*.

It will be remembered that in our examination, the Western Gateway has always impressed us unfavourably by the slovenliness alike of conception and execution, and the identification of the following scenes is bound to suffer from this indisputable carelessness.

With these reservations we will describe the actual appearance of the Western Gateway as seen on Pl. 53. It will be noticed at once that this Gateway has lost half of its north jamb, its uprights (but see Pl. 57) and all its detached figures except a griffin (Pl. 59) and the pedestal of the central wheel on the top.

This latter was made of four seated lions arranged like the four elephants on its fellow at the Northern Gateway (Pl. 22) and those on the capitals at the Eastern Gateway (Pls. 42 and 44), so that they are seen in profile on each side and their four heads guard the four corners of the pedestal; an additional lion shows his head and paws above their backs as on the false-capitals of the Eastern Gateway (Pls. 41-44) and of this Western Gateway (Pls. 56 and 60).

On the front, as we know, the symbolical representation of the set of the Seven last Buddhas of our æon is the rule for all gateways without exception. Here they are represented by three *stūpas* and four *bodhi-drumas*. Three out of the four dies bear a *bodhi-druma* also on the front face. Had the conscientious carver of the Southern Gateway been at work here, these three trees would no doubt have completed the set of the seven sacred ones; but the artist who designed the Western Gateway had no such scruples: he has merely shown the *bignonia* of Vipaśyin twice over and repeated the *aśvattha* of Sākya-muni. Then—as if there were not enough of these mechanical repetitions—the first tree on the left of the top lintel raises a serious difficulty: it is the *nāga-pushpa* or *michelia champaka* of the future Buddha Maitreya, the last thing one would expect here: for how can the *eighth* Buddha, yet to come, figure in the set of the *seven* last Buddhas of the past? The designer of the Western Gateway is here guilty of a more than ordinary blunder: for we cannot put it down to the last restorers.

There are other marks of carelessness, too: the symbolical pictures of the Enlightenment and Last Decease, which (except for representations of the seven Mānushi-Buddhas) were the monopoly of the dies, have here been pressed into service to fill the ends of the middle and bottom lintels as well; and the entire middle part of the middle lintel has even been given up to the First Sermon, whilst the bottom lintel presents a third and altered edition of the hackneyed legend of the six-tusked elephant.

The four dies show one Nativity to three *Sambodhis*, and, on the back, three *Parinirvāṇas* to a single First Sermon. One may wonder whether this was really the original distribution of motives, or whether two of the dies have not been turned back to front.

On the capitals, atlantes have taken the place of the lions of the Southern Gateway and the elephants of the Northern and Eastern Gateways: they will be found again on the Gateway of Stūpa 3 (Pl. 140).

The mutilated front of the north jamb shows again two common-place pictures of paradise, one of them incomplete. The south jamb has on its inner face an Enlightenment of Sākya-muni and a Conversion of the Sākyas: on its facade, the *Mahākapi-jātaka*, the Gods' Request and Indra's Visit—all but one, motifs already seen above; and as a last confession of impotence, a purely decorative pattern ventures to show itself for the first time on the front of a jamb.

PLATE 55

FRONT OF WESTERN GATEWAY: MIDDLE SECTION

1. *Top Lintel.*—As on the front of the Southern Gateway (Pl. 15), the Seven Mānushi-Buddhas are represented by three stūpas and four *bodhi-drumas*; but here the seven symbols occupy the whole length of the lintel, including the ends, just as on the fronts of the Northern and Eastern Gateways (Pls. 21 and 39), where we have five *stūpas* and only two *bodhi-drumas*. The two trees on the Eastern Gateway are those of the first and last Buddhas of the series; the four trees on the Southern Gateway are those of the last four; the two trees on the Northern Gateway, like the two which here decorate the middle section of the Western Gateway, are those of the last two. At the left of the central stūpa we can clearly recognize the *nyagrodha* of Kāśyapa, and on the right the *aśvattha* of Sākya-muni. The tree at the south end of the lintel seems to be the *udumbara* of Kanaka-muni (*cf.* Pl. 58, 1); on the north end we should have expected the *acacia sirissa* of Krakucchanda as on the Southern Gateway (Pl. 56, 1), instead of the *nāga-pushpa* of Maitreya. As on Pl. 40, 1, we notice the absence of female worshippers.

2. (*Back of*) *Middle Lintel.*—On the middle lintel the sculptor has undertaken without more ado to fill up the long rectangle of the middle section with a motif just big enough to cover a little square panel—namely, the third Great Miracle. As he could change nothing in the principal theme, he has simply planted in the centre the Wheel of the Law (with 32 spokes) on the throne and under the umbrella, but he has made up for this simplicity by repeating the accessories *ad nauseam*. The First Sermon takes place, as we all know, in the Deer Park, in the northern suburb of Benares. As this is a park, he has trimmed all the background of his picture with trees; and as this park contains deer, he shows us, not unskilfully, a whole herd of them (see Part II, pp. 135-6). As for the Master's five first auditors, as his First Sermon turned them into the first five monks, the customs of the School forbade him to show them, for a *bhikshu* must not be depicted any more than a Buddha. Never mind! among the trees and deer he inserts a string of worshippers of the usual aristocratic type, leaving us to guess whether they are gods of the sky, genii of the air, or lords of the earth. That is the whole trick.—Now, Master Donor, pay me for my trouble!

3. (*Back of*) *Bottom Lintel.*—But with these artists of the Western Gateway our surprises are never at an end. On what was and should still be the back of the bottom lintel they have repeated once more the legend of the six-tusked elephant which they could study on the Southern and Northern Gateways (Pls. 15 and 29): without exerting themselves further they show us the noble animal twice—recognizable by his two royal attributes, the umbrella and fly-whisk, as well as by his triple dentition—standing with his people round him on each side of the banyan fig-tree, which, as usual, forms the centre of the picture. It is, indeed, the same composition as on Pl. 29, only more crowded, and we even find again in the top left-hand corner the solitary pachyderm turning her back upon the rest, to remind us of the fatal sulks of the jealous wife. But the odd thing about it is that the elephants and their king no longer know why they are there. On the two other Gateways they are aware that they have only to rest in the shade after their bath, while awaiting the tragic events of which each felt a presentiment and which the sculptor of the Southern Gateway relief even foreshadowed by expressly introducing the hunter. On the Western Gateway they are no longer satisfied with this passive role, and here, with the king at their head, they are all setting about worshipping the banyan tree, offering to it with raised trunks the lotuses which they have plucked from the neighbouring pool (shown, as usual, in the left of the landscape). In the end, the legend transforms itself into a scene of adoration similar to that which is unfolded round a stūpa on the back of the bottom lintel of the Eastern Gateway (Pl. 46, 3), and it looks as if in the sculptor's mind the latter picture had contaminated those on Pls. 15 and 29. Nothing can be clearer than that he is trifling with his subject, or at any rate is only looking upon it as an excuse for decoration. The trees from left to right are an *acacia sirissa*, a jack-tree (*autocarpus integrifolia*), the central *nyagrodha*, a mango-tree, a tree like the one at Bharhut, Cunn., Pl. 45, 10, and a fan-leaf palm. For technical and stylistic details, *cf.* Part II, pp. 120 and 135.

FRONT OF WESTERN GATEWAY: MIDDLE SECTION OF ARCHITRAVES

FRONT OF WESTERN GATEWAY: NORTH END OF UPPER AND MIDDLE ARCHITRAVES

PLATE 56

FRONT OF WESTERN GATEWAY: NORTH END

1. *Top Lintel.*—This stereotyped scene of the *Sambodhi* belongs to the set of seven symbols on the front (*cf.* Pls. 54 and 55); but we may feel some justified astonishment in recognizing its flower as that, not of the *bodhi-druma* of one of the seven last Buddhas of the past, but of the *nāga-pushpa* or *michelia champaka* of Maitreya, the next Buddha to come.

2. (*Back of*) *Middle Lintel.*—Another proof of the decadence of the workshop. Having lost all inventive faculty, they repeat the same clichés mechanically everywhere, and the only attempt at variety is in a contamination of scenes: this is how they try here to relieve the hackneyed representation of the *bodhi-druma* of Vipaśyin by adding a "Presentation of the four alms-bowls" by the Four Guardians of the World—who have performed the same service for all the Buddhas in succession. Finally, the artist borrows two antelopes couchant from scenes of the First Sermon (one on the left behind a plantain, and the other on the right near a mango-tree), animals which have no business here but which serve to fill up space.

3. *Top Die.*—Again the *Sambodhi* of Vipaśyin! One detail, however, deserves to be pointed out; for it gives us very exact information on the nature of the offerings which we have seen so many times borne on trays and merely indicated by a check pattern: they are either flowers or, as here, garlands of flowers, made in the Indian way. Would you like to know the recipe? Detach some flowers from their stem, removing the ends; string the flowers like beads on a thread; join several of these chaplets into a single bundle; arrange the necklaces thus formed round a dish, and carry to th sanctuary, sacred tree or stūpa. Here, the two winged genii ar distinctly seen raising in both hands the rolled-up garlands from th trays held up by the two persons in the middle-ground, whilst th two in the foreground are each holding one. Two other garlands ar seen already hanging from the sacred tree and from the shaft o the crowning umbrella.

4. *Bottom Die.*—Clumsy but advanced representation of the Nativity (*cf.* pp. 183 and 197). The frightful hideousness of Māyā is partly due to a scratch on the stone. (See Part II, pp. 130-31.)

5. *Top False-Capital.*—The two griffins sitting back to back and the third who has his head and forepaws in the embrasure thus formed, recall the arrangement of the winged lions on the Eastern Gateway (Pls. 41-44); notice the curious little curl on the forehead and the serrated juncture of muzzle and beak. The beak is more like that of a parrot than of an eagle.

6. *Middle False-Capital.*—The riders of the two stallions passant (again with riding-whips) are of the aristocratic type. Their shawls or scarves (*uttarīya*) are floating in the wind. We will not revert to the harness of their steeds (whose tails are not fastened). The two ribbons falling upon the saddle-cloth are part of the rider's girdle. We have already seen these horses, lying down, on the false-capitals of the Southern and Northern Gateways (Pls. 10 and 28).

PLATE 57

FRONT OF WESTERN GATEWAY: NORTH END—concluded

1. (*Back of*) *Bottom Lintel.*—On the other Gateways, whenever the scene represented on the middle section of the lintel does not extend to the projecting ends, we have been accustomed to find either some interesting decoration or a genre piece. On the Western Gateway we must learn to content ourselves with an extra religious image: a *Sambodhi* tree as on Pl. 56, 2, or, as here, a *Parinirvāṇa* tumulus (*cf.* Pls. 58 and 59). A curious detail is that the women, who on the other gateways always precede the men, are here placed behind (*cf.* Pl. 58). We knew that the designers of the Western Gateway were not conscientious; now we see that they were not polite either!

2. *Bottom False-Capital.*—These two elephants, lying down in their usual way and back to back, have already appeared on the false-capitals of the Southern Gateway (Pls. 16-17); their splendid harness may also be compared with that of the elephants on Pl. 42. The minute rendering of the pierced and embroidered trappings is especially interesting. The requirements of perspective have placed one of the servants partly above the other: the rope round the loins of the one in the foreground is clearly visible; this allows him, in spite of the realistic slope of the animal's spine, to keep both hands free to hold the handle of the umbrella.

3. *Capitals.*—The four atlas-dwarfs who have here supplanted the lions and elephants, were already familiar to the Bharhut workshop (Cunn., Pl. 15). Their little bandy legs, pot-bellies, huge heads and short arms dispose us to class them among the *kumbhāṇḍas* (*cf.* pp. 232 and 243). In any case there is no connection to be found here between them and the compass point at which their gateway stands: the *kumbhāṇḍas* preside over the South, and we should have expected *Nāgas* at the West. They wear the usual costume and jewels of genii, except that their *dhotīs* are very scanty and that they have no scarves. The ear-rings of the one on the left are curled round in spirals, like ear-rings of this period found at Taxila. For the sake of variety, it seems, the carver has given him a grim look and his neighbour a smile (*cf.* Pl. 59). See Part II, pp. 140 and 141.

b. Upright.—At a glance we see the similarity of the upright, which a lucky chance has preserved and which is here reproduced, to those of the Northern Gateway (Pls. 22, 23 and 29).

FRONT OF WESTERN GATEWAY NORTH END OF LOWEST ARCHITRAVE WITH CAPITAL

FRONT OF WESTERN GATEWAY: SOUTH END OF UPPER AND MIDDLE ARCHITRAVES

PLATE 58

FRONT OF WESTERN GATEWAY: SOUTH END

As this plate is almost the exact fellow of Pl. 56, we need only point out the few divergencies between them.

1. *Top Lintel.*—The *bodhi-druma* (one of the seven symbols of the front) seems to be the *udumbara* or *ficus glomerata* of Kanakamuni, the antepenultimate Buddha of our age. Whenever there are four worshipping noblemen, we are entitled to think of the Four Guardians of the World.

2. (*Back of*) *Middle Lintel.*—The same cliché again. And the tree is again the *nyagrodha* or *ficus indica* of Kāśyapa, the last Buddha but one (*cf.* Pl. 55, 1). Contrary to expectation, the women are placed behind their husbands (*cf.* Pl. 57, 1).—To the front, on the ground, are three trays laden with garlands (*cf.* Pl. 56, 3). At the top are two bignonias; at the bottom, on the right, a plantain.

3. *Top Die.*—The same cliché again and moreover the same *pāṭali* or *bignonia suaveolens* of Vipaśyin, the first of the seven last Buddhas (*cf.* Pl. 56, 2 and 3). The two worshippers must be a king (left of the spectator) and his viceroy.

4. *Bottom Die.*—Same cliché again. Once more we see, with its leaves accurately drawn, the *aśvattha* or *ficus religiosa* of Śākyamuni. The four attendants bearing garlands may again be the four Lokapālas.

5. *False-Capitals.*—We naturally find again at the top the same griffins and, in the middle, the same horses with riders as on Pl. 56. We must not take the thong hanging down the left leg of the rider in the foreground for the strap of a stirrup: it is only the ribbon of his girdle, like that which passed under his leg in Pl. 56, 6. The saddle-cloth conveys a clear impression of being padded.

PLATE 59

FRONT OF WESTERN GATEWAY: SOUTH END—concluded

a. We may refer the reader to the description of Pl. 57; for the differences of detail are insignificant. Even the little plantain decorating the left end of the lintel is repeated (double) on the right end. Only notice, on the torso of the atlas on the left, the same ornament made of little chains crossing breast and back between six medallions, which we pointed out on Pl. 27, 4, and on both of them the tassels at the ends of the girdle. (*Cf.* Part II, pp. 140-41.)

b. This single specimen of a detached figure is an exact reproduction of the griffins which we have already met on the top false-capitals (*cf.* Pls. 56 and 58).

a b

a. FRONT OF WESTERN GATEWAY: SOUTH END OF LOWER ARCHITRAVE WITH CAPITAL.

b. FIGURE FROM SOUTH END OF MIDDLE ARCHITRAVE.

PLATE 60

BACK OF WESTERN GATEWAY (*present state*)

If we replace the procession on the front (which evidently does double duty with that on the middle lintel) by the traditional series of the Seven Mānushi-Buddhas, Pl. 60 will give us the original facade of the Western Gateway.

In its present state, its back exhibits simultaneously:—

Top Lintel: a processional transportation of relics;

Middle Lintel: a would-be "War of the Relics" also treated as a procession.

Bottom Lintel: a *Sambodhi* between two processions of opposite character and going in opposite directions.

This evident abuse of processions has allowed the sculptor to cover his lintels from one end to the other, except perhaps for the left projecting end of the middle one, which, by introducing an extraneous element, only serves to disconcert us.

The dies have replaced the Nativity and the three *Sambodhis* of the other side (Pl. 54) by a First Sermon and three *Parinirvāṇas.* By turning round two of these dies we should certainly obtain greater variety of subjects on both sides.

The false-capitals go back to the winged and sometimes horned lions of the Eastern Gateway (Pls. 41-44 and 47-48).

For the pedestal on the top, *cf.* Pl. 54.

PLATE 61

BACK OF WESTERN GATEWAY: MIDDLE SECTION

1. *Top Lintel.*—We availed ourselves (p. 215) of the data furnished by the *śāla* tree sheltering the Buddha's funeral couch, to recognize Kuśinagara in the "town" cliché at the left. The culminating point in the composition is the relic-casket which the principal personage, mounted on an elephant, is holding on his head with his right hand, while he carries the *aṅkuśa* in his left. His umbrella- and fly-whisk-bearers are both perched on the same beast, and he is followed by a man dressed in the same chlamys as the Mallas on Pl. 36c1. In front, march the band (a tambourine and two kettle-drums in the foreground, two conches and two flutes in the background), a soldier armed with spear and buckler, four standard-bearers, and some riders, three of whom have already got into the town, where we are privileged with a sight of them above the roofs (notice that this sculpture shows the houses filled with onlookers, on both sides of the highroad). Behind the king or chieftain come various great persons mounted on horses or elephants (for the foreshortening of the one on the right, *cf.* Pl. 55, 3, left). The procession continues, as we shall see, on the two projecting ends of the lintels, but there it consists of pedestrians only. (*Cf.* Part II, p. 127.)

2. (*Front of*) *Middle Lintel.*—We refer the reader to pp. 214-215 for identification of this "War of the Relics", which lacks all indication of war or even of relics; for it is not a reliquary but a cup which the man shown half-length on the extreme left is holding. The seven umbrellas of the seven claimants before Kuśinagara are doubtless there to define the place and date of the scene; but there is virtually nothing else, and it is lucky that we have the conscientious composition of the Southern Gateway (Pl. 15, 3) to enable us to identify this imitation. The sculptor of the Western Gateway has reduced the legend to a mere procession preceded by the usual band, but comprising, first, three kings on elephants, then (in the foreground) a king in a chariot, above him two kings on horseback, and a seventh king bringing up the rear on his elephant (an accident has happened to the right-hand bottom corner of the plate and left out another figure on an elephant, but without an umbrella).[1] Of course each sovereign has his own servants bearing umbrella, fly-whisk, ewer or sword. Here and there will be noticed the outline of a shield (on the second soldier in front of the gate), the scabbard of a sword (near the middle), a spear-head (on the right, half way up), etc. All these people, we must confess, are progressing as one man towards the town: for we do not dispute the sculptor's artistic ability. Very effective is the attitude of the servant just in front of the third elephant's forequarters, who is lifting a heavy ewer on to his shoulder. (*Cf.* Part II, pp. 112-14 and 117-18.)

3. (*Front of*) *Bottom Lintel.*—The Great Miracle of the *Sambodhi* spun out into two antithetical processions. In the centre stands the *aśvattha* of Bodh-Gayā, above the *vajra-āsana* and inside its hypæthral temple (*cf.* Pls. 18, 40 and 51). On the right, Māra's vanquished army is fleeing; on the left, the gods (who, as the texts tell us, kept at a respectful distance from the fight) are coming to applaud the Master's victory; and though we must beware of supposing that we are here shown a battle between the forces of good and evil, since the Blessed One triumphed by the strength of his intelligence alone, the dualistic character of the picture is nevertheless striking. As usual, the demoniacal party is much more varied and picturesque than the divine; we can recognise the type of grotesque genii which we have already seen with Māra on the Northern Gateway (Pl. 29, 2) and here, too, on the capitals (Pls. 57 and 59; and *cf.* 65*b*, 1); among this diabolical rout the leaders still retain the appearance befitting *devas* of the sixth heaven (*cf.* Pl. 49*a*). Which of them is Māra? It is hard to guess, but he seems to be the figure armed with a bow, who turns round in his chariot whilst his charioteer is ordered to goad on the team: for Māra is simply another name for Kāma, and in India too the bow is the weapon of Love. The spirit of general panic is undeniably well rendered: among the *senāpati*, some are leaning over the heads of their elephants, others are being thrown by their horses, one of which is stumbling; as for the ordinary demons, letting four of them (two armed with bow and axe) cover their retreat, they are turning their backs and in their hurry to escape fall headlong on the ground. Notice the one in the foreground running his trident into the back of his companion; the flight continues on Pl. 62, 3. In contrast to this stampede, nothing could be more peaceful or solemn than the processional arrival of the gods. In accordance with custom, they are accompanied by a band comprising a kettle-drummer and three tambourine players, also apparently divine; some have simply their hands clasped, others are throwing flowers, bearing garlands, raising standards or waving their scarves—doing, in fact, everything suitable to such an occasion. But the moment we press the identification closer our perplexities begin again. Which is Brahmā?—The first one in the foreground at the head of the Gods of the Pure Abodes?—Which is Indra?—The last one on the left of the foreground (see his royal headdress), with his suite of Thirty-three Gods following him on the south end of the lintel (Pl. 63, 3)?—It would need an acute observer indeed to give a precise answer to these questions, with such elusive sculptors as these. (*Cf.* Part II, pp. 114-15.)

[1] For the missing details, see Pl. 60.

BACK OF WESTERN GATEWAY: MIDDLE SECTION OF ARCHITRAVES

BACK OF WESTERN GATEWAY: NORTH END OF ARCHITRAVE

PLATE 62

BACK OF WESTERN GATEWAY: NORTH END

1. ***Top Lintel.***—End of the procession shown on the middle section. The figures, all on foot in two rows, are proceeding in good order towards the left. As usual on such occasions (see Pl. 61, 3), some are carrying wreathed standards, and others are throwing with their right hands flowers which they are taking out of the tray held in their left. Notice the wheel surmounting the staff of one of the standards.

2. *(Front of) Middle Lintel.*—Once more the end of a procession no less commonplace than the foregoing, though it is far more ably handled. Once again the cliché of the royal procession unfolds: king, royal insignia, chariot, suite—all are there. As it is only a chariot and pair and not a four-in-hand, we get a better view of the collars attaching the necks of the two horses to the yoke of the shaft (*cf.* Pl. 23, 1); notice also that several guards are carrying what look like clubs, but in fact are broad Indian swords, as the crossed thongs on the scabbards show. But who is this king? No one knows. Ought we to connect him with the scene on the middle section (Pl. 61, 2) and class him among the claimants? In that case he would be a surplus figure; for we have already counted seven. Is he, as we are inclined to think, merely a duplicate of the king in the chariot on Pl. 61, 2? Or is this an independent picture relating to another king and another occasion? Once more we must abandon any attempt to fathom the intentions of the sculptors, who seem to have had few beyond covering the spaces they had undertaken to decorate.

3. *(Front of) Bottom Lintel.*—Head of the rout of Māra's army (*cf.* Pl. 61, 3). The picture is conceived in exactly the same fashion as on the middle section. In the background, on account of the great height of their mounts, two fugitives on elephants; in the middle distance, two riders and some horses' heads; in the foreground, the demoniacal foot-soldiers, standing, squatting or fallen, so as to fill up the internal angle of the volute. As usual, none of the figures can be identified, but it is possible to note several interesting details, such as the padding of the saddle-cloths, the breadth of the spear-heads, the gourd from which one demon is refreshing his companion, etc.

3. *Dies.*—The two dies each bear a cliché of the *Parinirvāṇa*, the stūpa of which is being worshipped, on the top die, by four male figures, and on the bottom one by two couples.

4. *False-Capitals.*—Above and below, the triple winged lions and their arrangement are evidently imitated from the Eastern Gateway (Pls. 41-44). In the middle, some variety is introduced by the omission of the third animal and the introduction of two riders; the short hair, tunic and high boots of the one on the left marks him as a barbarian (*mleccha*) and the tuft of hair of the one on the right shows him to be a jungle-dweller (*cf.* Pl. 47, 5).

PLATE 63

BACK OF WESTERN GATEWAY: SOUTH END

1. *Top Lintel.*—Fragment of a procession whose only bond with the principal scene is that it, too, is on its way to Kuśinagara (*cf.* Pl. 61, 1), and whose only excuse for being there is to act as pendant to the one filling the other end of the lintel (*cf.* Pl. 62, 1). At the back, a bignonia and a mango-tree, in the foreground left, a plantain.

2. (*Front of*) *Middle Lintel.*—Here we are faced with the same perplexities as at the opposite end of the lintel (*cf.* Pl. 62, 2). Ought we to link this panel to the middle section? Must we seek another legend, and if so, which one? Or can we take it simply as a genre piece? As we cannot possibly decide, we must confine ourselves to noting down what we see. A king, as the style of his turban proves, is sitting in the park hard by his palace, in a sort of armchair with legs turned on the lathe (already seen at Bharhut: Cunn., Pl. 48, 2) and under it is his ewer; the women bearing the umbrella and fly-whisk are standing at their posts; his queen is seated in front of him on a rattan foot-stool covered with a quilt; with her left hand she is playing with the medallion on her necklace; with her right she is holding out a large cup, or rather standard bowl, into which a third attendant is pouring what appears to be the contents of a little round pot, while the king, leaning with his right arm over the side of the chair, holds a sort of ball in his left hand. Tempting as it is, it would probably be vain to look for an allusion in the urn and ball to the relics over which the seven claimants on the middle section of the lintel are squabbling; on the other hand, it would be no less difficult to admit that this is simply his majesty dining; for the use of the left hand to eat with would seem most surprising to any one familiar with oriental custom. The stereotyped scenery tells us nothing: the palace has of course its verandah and its balconies full of women, and the park has two plantains, a champaka and another tree, which we are unable to identify.

3. (*Front of*) *Bottom Lintel.*—These five persons are evidently the rear of the procession of gods in the middle section, since they are following them and are making the same gestures (*cf.* Pl. 61, 3); but they seem in no great hurry to leave this lovely spot shaded by a mango-tree, a bignonia and a fan-leaf palm, and cooled by a lotus pool in which *haṁsas* are swimming. The second from the right seems even to be loitering to gaze on this spectacle, as though the sculptor could not quite remember why he had put them all there.

4. *Dies.*—At the top, another cliché of the *Parinirvāṇa*, the third on this face of the Gateway (*cf.* Pl. 60).—At the bottom, a cliché of the First Sermon: the *dharmacakra* has no fewer than 38 spokes.

5. *False-Capitals.*—These naturally are the fellows of those on Pl. 62. The middle false-capital adds variety by giving stags' antlers to the lions (*cf.* Pls. 47-48). Here, only the diadems of the two jungle-dwellers are seen, as there was no room left for their topknots; their riding-whips are made of a short piece of rope fastened to a stick.

BACK OF WESTERN GATEWAY: SOUTH END OF ARCHITRAVES.

b

a

c

a. SOUTH PILLAR OF WESTERN GATEWAY: UPPER PANELS ON FRONT FACE.

b. LOWER PANEL ON FRONT FACE.

c. NORTH PILLAR OF WESTERN GATEWAY. UPPER PANELS ON FRONT FACE.

PLATE 64

PILLARS OF WESTERN GATEWAY

a-b. Front Face of South Pillar.—Here the sculptors (or sculptor) have practised great eclecticism and borrowed subjects from all sides, without trying, as on the other three Gateways, to form cycles.

a1. Mahākapi-jātaka.—Jātaka no. 407 of the Pāli collection; not to be confused with no. 516. For identification and brief comparison with the Bharhut medallion (Cunn., Pl. 33, 4), *cf.* above, p. 224; for more detailed comparison, see *Mémoires concernant l'Asie Orientale*, III, Pl. II, 5 and 6. We may note: the strange perspective of the Ganges, flowing right towards us; the manner of indicating the water, and the shape of the fishes; the sword-bearer and bow-bearer in the foreground left; the equipment of musicians and servants, especially of the archer engaged in the quickly ended fight with the monkeys; and, lastly, the fact that, just as at Bharhut, the tree from which the big monkey is hanging by both hands is a *ficus indica* and that there is no mango-tree to be seen. What appears to be a pleated scarf hanging just under the hind-paws of the great ape, is in fact a waterfall dropping into the river from the top of a last spur of the Himālayas.

a2. Adhyeshaṇa.—In support of this identification, see above, p. 210, and note the earnest attitude of the gods—led apparently by Brahmā and Indra. But, as usual on the Western Gateway, the sculptor has been too lazy to characterize his figures. We may again notice the tongues of flame springing out of the rocky ground of the *Bodhimaṇḍa*: this must be understood as an outward manifestation of the *tejas*, not of the gods, but of the Buddha, still burning with the night's struggle which has led to his Enlightenment. A proof that the designer of the present panel was consciously imitating the *Adhyeshaṇa* of the Eastern Gateway (Pl. 49c) is that he has also set the tree between four flying genii, two of whom, astride of lions, are not elsewhere found face to face (only one specimen, isolated, exists on Pl. 36c3, and two female *devatās* on Pl. 65*a*2). He has not, however, made the mistake of showing an odd number of persons.

a3. Indra's Visit.—We have likewise given the reasons (p. 218) which, in spite of the carelessness and omissions of the sculptor, have made us vote in favour of this interpretation. The central tree, set between a bignonia and a mango-tree, is unknown to us; its presence —unexpected, to say the least—can only be explained by the mechanical routine of the sculptor, who could no longer imagine that a throne might be shown without a tree; but the rocky vault of the grotto goes right up to the top of the panel, though it is partly hidden by the crowning umbrella and the arms of the two winged spirits (it will be noticed that the garlands of flowers borne on trays by the latter are not indicated here by the usual check pattern). We shall not be surprised to find, as elsewhere on this Gateway, that the divine spectators are indistinguishable from one another.

b. This decorative motif is evidently closely akin to that on the outer side of the jambs (Pl. 66*b* and *c*), but at the same time influenced by the trios of lions on the false-capitals (Pls. 62-63). We can pick out its origins at Sāñchī itself on the medallions of the balustrade of Stūpa 2, where we find lions face to face (Pl. 74, no. 1c) and lions and other beasts rampant back to back (Pls. 82, no. 44*b*; 83, no. 49*a*; 86, no. 66*b*; 89, nos. 77*a* and 79*b*; *cf.* also Cunn., *Bharhut*, Pl. 37, 3. We need not consider panel 27*b* reproduced on Pl. 79, as it is obviously contemporary with the Western Gateway).

c. Front Face of North Pillar.—The fragments preserved suggest (p. 228) that the sculptor took his inspiration both from the tiers of heavens on the Eastern Gateway (Pl. 49*a* and *b*) and from the erotic representation of a paradise on the Northern Gateway (Pl. 34*b*2). It is clear that the bottom panel was conceived in the same spirit as the one at the top; we see or guess at the same couples, and the same trees, some rounded into arbours and others bearing scarves or jewels hanging from their branches and thus proclaiming their celestial character as "wishing trees".

*c*1. In the top picture we may notice the symmetry of the two arbours, whose leafy roof looks like the rather flattened dome of a *parṇaśālā* (*cf.* Pls. 25, 1; 27, 1; 29, 3; 52*a*2; 65*a*1). Four couples are sitting on low thrones or beds; like good Indians they appreciate their coolness, and when one day these seats grow hot, they will know that they must soon relapse into the vortex of rebirths. At the top left, the lover is helping his mistress with her toilet; she is holding in her left hand a handled mirror (already seen in Pl. 35*b*2); below, he is 'picking' bracelets and necklaces for her from the trees. On the right, the top couple are merely exchanging confidences, and those at the bottom are drinking. The couple standing are coming down the stairway which leads from the garden terrace to the edge of the lotus-pool (unless this is the bank of the river Mandākinī in Indra's heaven, *cf.* Pl. 96, 3) and the woman's gesture, half hiding her face behind her hand, would entitle her in an Italian painting to the nick-name of 'La Vergognosa'.

*c*2. We have not yet come across a harp; but here the male figure in the centre seems to be holding one under his left arm and his partner to be dancing, while the lover to their right is holding his beloved by the chin. Does this mean that we have now left the world of the gods and come down among the genii whose sportiveness is so freely depicted?

PLATE 65

PILLARS OF WESTERN GATEWAY—continued

a. Inner Face of North Pillar.—Only two panels and a half have been preserved; but F. C. Maisey has published a complete drawing of the third. The subjects bear witness to the same eclecticism as on Pl. 64.

*a*1. *The Syāma-jātaḳa* (*cf.* p. 225) brings in an element of novelty. The king on a hunting party has adopted the same equipment as the archer on Pl. 64*a*1; when he reappears for the third and forth times in the middle and at the top of the panel, he has put off his hunter's trappings, the better to show his repentance for his involuntary homicide. But we must not imagine that he is talking to the young ascetic, though they seem to have met face to face: the latter is supposed to have gone down to the pool without seeing him, and the king sees him only after the fatal accident. Sakra, the Indra of the Gods, has his characteristic tiara and bottle of *amṛita*, but has forgotten his thunderbolt. As above (Pl. 29, 3), two *parṇaśālās* are shown side by side, with the father and mother of Syāma seated on the *bṛisī* at the doors of their respective dwellings; for the anchorites' bark garments and the band tied round the knees of the old father, compare Pl. 52*a*2. The trees are a plantain and a bignonia. In the shadow cast by the pillar's capital, on the right, above the space between the two huts (filled by utensils for sacrifice), monkeys are stealing the fruits laid out to dry on a mat.

*a*2. The episode of the Nāga-rāja Mucilinda (*cf.* p. 208) is evidently imitated from the Southern Gateway (Pl. 19*c*1) but treated with greater wealth of personages. The attitude of the Nāga-rāja is the same; his two queens are seated on his right hand and, behind, three attendants are holding a dish, a jar and a fly-whisk, respectively; on his left, his ballet troupe includes a dancing girl and five female musicians (two tambourines, a harp and a flute, the fifth instrument being invisible); as usual, the Nāgīs have only monocephalic hoods. This time, two female divinities are riding in the air on a winged lion and a winged griffin, besides the usual two *ḳinnaras* (*cf.* Pl. 64*a*2).

*a*3. Only the upper part of this panel is now preserved. The lower part was cut away when Col. Cole restored the gateway, but there is a drawing of the whole panel in Maisey's *Sánchi*, Pl. 21, fig. 2, and a description of it on pp. 58 and 59 of the same work. The waters of the river are represented by the usual wavy lines, interspersed with lotus leaves[1] and flowers. Across them, from left to right, passes a barge in the form of a winged griffin bearing on its back a pillared canopy or baldachino, in which is a small basket-like tabernacle covered with a cloth. To right and left of the tabernacle are two attendants, one holding the royal umbrella, the other a fly-whisk (*caurī*). The barge itself is propelled by an oarsman seated in the stern, behind the baldachino; and swimming in the waters alongside are half a dozen other figures, all decked out with jewellery and garlands. Three of them are supported on inflated skins and two on wooden planks, while the sixth with outstretched arms is seemingly trying to get on the barge. Col. Cole took the tabernacle for a throne of the Buddha and interpreted the relief as the miraculous crossing of the Ganges by the Buddha, when he left Rājagṛiha to visit Vaiśālī. A more probable explanation is that it represents the transport across a river of one of the Buddha's body-relics, to which royal honours are naturally being paid, though we might expect the covered tabernacle to be in the form of a stūpa, as it is, for example, in some Gandhāra reliefs (*L'Art Gréco-boudd. du Gandh.*, figs. 289, 290*b* and 291).

b. Inner Face of South Pillar.—The two subjects have been met with already. The first takes us to Uruvilvā (or Bodh-Gayā) and the second to Kapilavastu.

*b*1. The *Sambodhi* or Perfect Enlightenment of the Blessed One shown simply by his *aśvattha* (*ficus religiosa*) above a throne (not surrounded by the roofless temple as on Pls. 18*b*, 51*a* and 61, 3) would hardly be sufficient to fill all the panel, so the sculptor has had recourse to episodes connected with the Bodh-Gayā cycle, and we are left to disentangle the result of this contamination. It looks as if we should begin at the bottom, where we can recognize in the foreground, between three kindly gods, the throne of the 'six years of penance' (*cf.* p. 206) near the edge of the Nairañjanā, shaded by plantains, mango-trees and bignonias, and outside the precincts of the Bodhimaṇḍa. Inside the latter, we know that the persons grappling with the Buddha (in spite of the praying attitude which the sculptor has mechanically given to the principal figure and two of the women) can only be Māra, six of his wives (?), his three "daughters" and two of his "sons"; and finally, on the right, his army, here composed of a horse, a he-goat, a boar, a buffalo, a demon, an elephant and a lion of which only the forequarters and head are seen. In the top left-hand corner is a building, to remind us of the proximity of the village of Uruvilvā.

*b*2. This panel is directly imitated from the Northern Gateway (Pl. 35*a*2), and in both cases only one identification is possible—namely the "Conversion of the Sākyas" (*cf.* p. 205). Here, too, all the spectators are supposed to be sitting on the ground on cushions, even those whom the needs of perspective have lifted into the air, for we have only a human congregation, though of the most elegant kind. The tiny berries on the *ficus indica* are, here too, carefully depicted.

[1] What Maisey calls "a large shell" is only a lotus leaf, with its edges curved inwards, as one commonly sees such leaves in nature and as they are often represented in these and other reliefs.

a

NORTH PILLAR OF WESTERN GATEWAY: UPPER PANELS ON SOUTH FACE.

b

SOUTH PILLAR OF WESTERN GATEWAY: UPPER PANELS ON NORTH FACE.

a

b

c

a SOUTH PILLAR OF WESTERN GATEWAY: LOWEST PANELS ON NORTH FACE.

b. NORTH PILLAR OF WESTERN GATEWAY: NORTH FACE.

c SOUTH PILLAR OF WESTERN GATEWAY: SOUTH FACE.

PLATE 66

PILLARS OF WESTERN GATEWAY—concluded

a. Inner Face of South Pillar.—Bottom panel: only the south jamb has been preserved intact; so we possess only one of the two guardians of the Western Gateway. We should have expected a *nāga* at this quarter: but it is only another *Yaksha*, though of a more than ordinarily belligerent appearance. He is holding his spear in his left hand and has hung his sword on a mango-tree behind him. We can study the detail of both weapons, even to the way the knotted thongs crossing over the broad scabbard of the sword are fastened by a pin with a *nandipada* head[1]; and then the head, the strap(?) on the top, and the socket at the bottom of the spear. We may notice also the comparative simplicity of turban, garments and jewels, befitting a warrior, even though he be a general (*senāpati*). The ear-rings which have been lost must have been of moderate size; an alternating pattern of bignonia (?) and blue lotus hangs from the broad necklace on the chest (see Part II, p. 133).

b and *c*. *Outer Faces of North and South Pillars.*—See Part II, p. 146. The basis of the design is the same lotus tree or creeper which is found on the other gateways and which Sir John Marshall interprets as a Tree of Life and Fortune (*Kalpa-druma* or *Kalpa-latā*), but here it is richer and more elaborate, and the human figures now appear as the riders or attendants of the fabulous animals, that stand rampant and back to back against the tree, the whole making a truly "Renaissance" design of great beauty and variety. Most of the lotus leaves are stylised in the manner peculiar to the Early School, but observe that some of them (near the middle of Pl. 66c) are treated naturally like the buds and flowers; and observe, too, that, besides the lotus blooms, this magic tree of fortune bears also vine leaves and bunches of grapes. The animals starting from the flowers and stem of the tree include griffins, unicorns and horned lions of diverse kinds.

[1] For a similar pin of the 1st century A.D. from Taxila, *cf. A. S. R.*, 1926, p. 113, No. 9 and Pl. XXVI, 11.

PLATE 67

MISCELLANEOUS SCULPTURES

The first three pieces on this Plate (*a*, *b* and *c*) come from the western pillar of the South Gateway. The fragment *d* is from the eastern pillar of the same Gateway, and *f* and *g* from the northern pillar of the West Gateway. The particular gateway from which *e* and *h* come, is not known.

a. Fragment (ht. 2′ 3½″) from the west pillar of the South Gateway of Stūpa 1 (Pls. 18 and 19). The carving of the front face has disappeared. On the inner face is the lower part of a guardian Yaksha, standing, armed with a broad Indian sword and wearing a close-fitting tunic and boots; traces of a sleeve of the tunic are visible on the left forearm. Below, remnants of a lion to left, and uncertain object to right. The outer side, not visible in the photo, is decorated with a flowing creeper (*kalpa-latā*), from which hang jewelled necklaces and fruit, while perched among the foliage are birds eating berries (*cf*. pp. 142-147). In the lower left corner, is the bust of a grotesque *kumbhāṇḍa*, grasping the stem of the *kalpa-latā* in his hand. For other guardian Yakshas, *cf*. pp. 133-134. *Mus. Cat.*, A12.

b. Fragment (ht. 1′ 10″) from the same pillar as above. The carvings on the front and inner faces have disappeared. The outer face exhibits part of the same *kalpa-latā* as the preceding, with pendent necklace and the figure of a monkey seated on one of the branches. *Mus. Cat.*, A14.

c. Fragment (ht. 1′ 1½″) from the same pillar as the above. The relief on the front face shows a headless female figure descending from a couch or chair to left, and the mutilated legs and tail of a horse to right. The lady wears a transparent *dhotī* and scarf, the end of which is held in her uplifted right hand. Behind the horse are what appear to be the legs of a standing human figure. Remains of a *kalpa-latā* with pendent necklace are visible on the outer face. *Mus. Cat.*, A13.

d. Fragment (ht. 12¼″) from the eastern pillar of the South Gateway (*cf*. Pl. 19). On the front face is the lower portion of a relief depicting a mutilated throne of the Buddha, and below it a water-pond with lotuses and ducks. On either side of the throne are small attendant figures, one of which is standing in an attitude of prayer. On the outer face are traces of a flowing *kalpa-latā*. *Mus. Cat.*, A17.

e. Head (ht. 10½″) probably belonging to one of the caurī-bearers on the top of the North Gateway, near which it was found. Observe the large ear-pendants and Indian turban, with a high excrescence in front and a smaller one over the skull behind. For these free-standing caurī-bearers, *cf*. p. 37 and Pls. 22 and 30. *Mus. Cat.*, A55.

f. Fragment in two pieces (ht. 2′ 11½″) from the northern pillar of the West Gateway (Pls. 64 and 65). On the inner face is the mutilated figure of a guardian Yaksha wearing the usual dress and ornaments and standing beside a bignonia tree. The carving on the front face has disappeared. *Mus. Cat.*, A20.

g. Fragment (ht. 1′ 7″) from the same pillar as the preceding one. On the outer face is the fore-front of a griffin facing left, and, above it, part of the same Tree of Life and Fortune that is seen in Pl. 66*b* (*cf*. pp. 142-147). *Mus. Cat.*, A19.

h. Torso (1′ 8¼″) of a caurī-bearer from one of the gateways of Stūpa 1. He wears an elaborate beaded necklace, armlet and *dhotī* fastened by a plain girdle tied in front. At the back are traces of a scarf. *Cf*. p. 37 and Pls. 22 and 30. *Mus. Cat.*, A53.

a

b

c

d

e.

g

h

MISCELLANEOUS SCULPTURES.

a

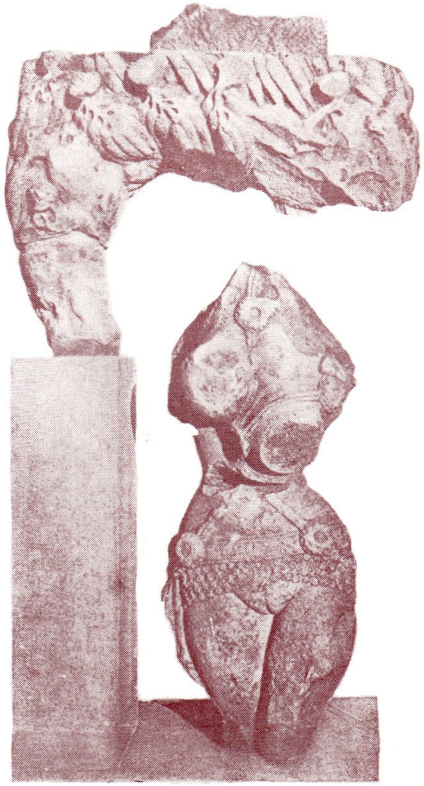

b

c

d

e

f

g

MISCELLANEOUS SCULPTURES.

PLATE 68

MISCELLANEOUS SCULPTURES

With the exception of the small bust *c2*, all the fragments in this Plate belong to the gateway brackets, like those described on pp. 129-132 and illustrated on Pls. 25, 27, 31, 33, 42, 44, 47 and 48.

a. Part of a bracket-arch in the form of a mango branch, similar the one illustrated on Pl. 44. Height, including tenon, 2′ 1″. Below the arch is the torso of a *śālabhañjikā* (ht. 2′ 9¼″), but it does not belong to the bracket above. The mango arch comes probably from the South Gateway and the torso from the south side of the East Gateway. The *śālabhañjikā* wears a transparent *dhotī*, plain hipband, beaded girdle and long necklace falling between the breasts. Hanging down her back are thick loops of hair and garlands resembling those on the bracket figure at the west end of the North Gateway (Pl. 31). For the modelling of this and the following figure, *cf*. remarks on pp. 129-30. *Mus. Cat.*, A25 and 26.

b. The arched bracket above, which represents a bignonia tree, comes probably from the South, the figure below it (ht. 3′ 3½″) from the West Gateway. Observe that the latter is wearing two long chains with medallions hanging from the shoulders and crossing each other below the breasts, as well as at the back. The *dhotī*, hipband, girdle, hair and garlands are treated in the same way as on the previous figure. *Mus. Cat.*, A28.

c. Another bracket arched in the form of a mango branch ht. 3′ 0½″), probably from the West Gateway of Stūpa I. In front of the foliage is the left forearm of a *śālabhañjikā*, wearing bangles and beaded wristlets.

The small bust below (ht. 7″) belongs to a double-faced figure of a *śālabhañjikā*, like that on the middle architrave of the North Gateway (*cf*. Pl. 26). She wears necklaces, heavy ear-pendants, and garlands over her head. *Mus. Cat.*, A27 and B2.

d. Mango-tree bracket (ht. 1′ 0¾″) from between the architraves of one of the gateways. *Cf*. the small mango brackets in Pls. 26 and 27, and the bignonia brackets in Pls. 24 and 25. *Mus. Cat.*, A42.

e. This is the back view of the bignonia bracket in Fig. *b*, but without the smaller broken piece at the bottom.

f. Fragment (ht. 7¾″) of a bignonia-tree bracket similar to that shown in Fig. *b*. *Mus. Cat.*, A34.

g. Fragment (ht. 9¾″) from one of the smaller brackets between the projecting ends of the gateway architraves. The tree is the same as that depicted on Pl. 11, 2 (third from left end and second from right end) and Pl. 50*a*1 (third from right at bottom). Its species has not been identified. *Mus. Cat.*, A45.

PLATE 69

MISCELLANEOUS SCULPTURES

a. Fragment from a shield (*śrīvatsa*) belonging to a *triratna* device, like that surmounting the North Gateway (Pl. 24).

b. Fragment (ht. 9½") of a bull's head, from one of the false-capitals of a gateway.

c. Fragment (ht. 1' 1½") from one of the small balusters between the gateway architraves, *e.g.*, those on Pl. 22. On the front face is the capital of a pillar surmounted by four lions set back to back, supporting a wheel (*dharmacakra*). *Mus. Cat.*, A47.

d. Part of a mango tree (ht. 2' 6") from one of the larger brackets supporting the lowest architrave of the South Gateway. Perched among the foliage at the top is a parrot. *Mus. Cat.*, A24.

e. Elephant (ht. 1' 6¾") with rider and attendant, from between the architraves of one of the gateways, like the elephants illustrated on Pl. 23*a* On the back of the elephant is a plain *uttara-chada*. The master is sitting astride on the neck of the elephant, holding a goad (*aṅkuśa*). The servant crouching at the back holds in his hand the fasces-like staff of a flag ending in a *nandipada* device at the top. The elephant is carved in the round, but the riders have double bodies from the lions upwards, and are facing in both directions. Observe the unusual prominence of the elephant's skull. *Mus. Cat.* A48.

f. Figure in two pieces (ht. 1' 11") of a griffin from the projecting end of an architrave; most probably from the South Gateway. Observe the parrot-like beak, the curious scaly mane and the band of indented moulding round the mouth and base of the beak.

g, *h* and *i*. Statues of winged lions resembling those on the top architrave of the North Gateway (*cf*. Pls. 21, 24 and 26). Heights 2' 1¾", 1' 11½", and 2' 2½", respectively. *Mus. Cat.*, A37 and 38-41.

a

b

c

d

e

f

g

h

i

MISCELLANEOUS SCULPTURES

a. NORTHERN

b. EASTERN

c. SOUTHERN

d. WESTERN

PLATE 70

FOUR STATUES IN THE PRADAKSHIṆA-PATHA OF STŪPA 1

The four images pictured in this Plate are discussed on pp. 38-39 and 250-251. As there stated, they are referred to in an inscription of the year 450-51 A.D. (No. 834); and appear from their style to have been executed in the early years of that century (p. 39, n. 1). Possibly they were intended to represent the four Dhyāni Buddhas, which in mediæval times were commonly set up at the base of stūpas, facing the four cardinal points, *viz.*, Amoghasiddha at the north, Akshobhya at the east, Ratnasambhava at the south, and Amitābha at the west; but *cf.* p. 252. There is nothing in their individual attitudes or in their attributes to help us in determining their identity. The disparity in style and workmanship observable in these images is due, not to any difference in their respective ages, but to the varying ability of the sculptors.

The heights of the four slabs are: *a*, 6′ 2″; *b*, 5′ 4″; c, 3′ 10″; *d*, 5′ 7″.

THE MONUMENTS OF SĀÑCHĪ

THE MONUMENTS OF SĀÑCHĪ

BY

SIR JOHN MARSHALL, C.I.E., Litt.D., F.S.A.

*Fellow of the British Academy ; Correspondant de l'Institut de France ;
Hon. Fellow of King's College, Cambridge ; Sometime Director General
of the Archæological Survey of India*

AND

ALFRED FOUCHER

*Membre de l'Institut de France ;
Professeur à l'Université de Paris*

With the texts of inscriptions edited, translated and annotated

BY

N. G. MAJUMDAR, M.A., F.R.A.S.B.

*Superintendent of the Archæological
Survey of India*

Volume Three : Plate LXXI—CXLI

Swati Publications
DELHI

First Reprinted 1982

Second Reprinted 1983

Published by : SWATI PUBLICATIONS, 34, Central Market,
Ashok Vihar, Phase-I, Delhi-110052

PRINTED BY Shivalik Offset Press Naraina Industrial Area, New Delhi

PLATE 71

ELEVATION AND PLAN OF STŪPA

The design, construction and age of this stūpa are discussed on pp. 79-82 and 270. Though the stūpa is only two or three decades later than Stūpa 1 (as reconstructed under the Śuṅgas), there seems to have been a marked difference in the contours of their domes, the explanation being that the reconstructed dome of Stūpa 1 had to conform to the contour of the original brick dome built by Aśoka a hundred years earlier, whereas the dome of Stūpa 2 followed the more elevated and spherical form in vogue in the 2nd century B.C.

The contour of the dome shown in this Plate is based on the drawings made by Cunningham and Maisey, when the original fabric was still standing to more than half its height. *Cf.* Cunningham, *The Bhilsa Topes*, Pl. XX, and Maisey, *Sánchi and its Remains*, Pl. XXIX, 2.

It should be observed that the stairways of Stūpa 2 are on the east instead of the more usual south side of the monument. This no doubt was merely a matter of convenience, as the old approach road on this side of the hill passed by the eastern entrance of the Stūpa, but it seems to show that in the latter part of the 2nd century B.C., special importance was not attached to the principal entrance being located on the south.

As in the plans of Stūpas 1 and 3 (Pls. 4 and 92), the original pillars of the ground balustrade are indicated by means of shading; the restored ones are without shading.

The pillar-capital shown in Fig. *c* was found a little to the north-west of Stūpa 2, along with some fragments of the shaft (p. 82) and the crowning lion figured in Pl. 104*g*. There is a photo of this capital in Pl. 104*h*. All the pieces appear to be referable to the Śuṅga period. For the design of the capital, *cf.* Pillar 25 (Pl. 106*b* and p. 49), but the contour of this capital is more shapely.

For the stone relic-box (Fig. *d*) and the steatite casket (Fig. *e*), see p. 81; but note that the scale beneath the former is misleading. It should measure 12 instead of 4 inches (*cf.* Cunningham, *The Bhilsa Topes*, Pl. XX). For the inscriptions on the box and casket, as well as on the three other caskets (not figured) which were found inside the latter, see Nos. 2-12 *infra* (pp. 289-95). The box and three of the four caskets are in the British Museum.

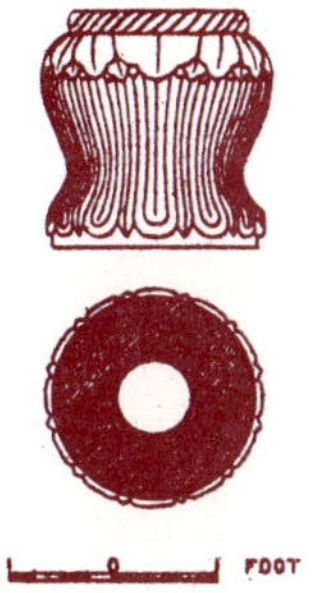

(c) CAPITAL OF COLUMN

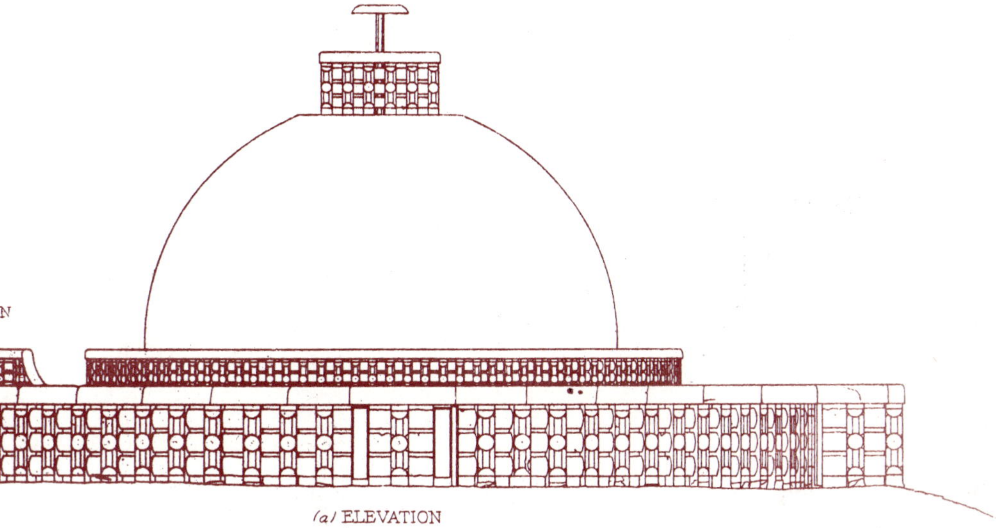

(a) ELEVATION

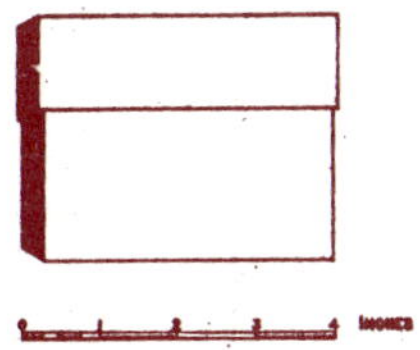

(d) STONE RELIC BOX

(e) STEATITE RELIC CASKET

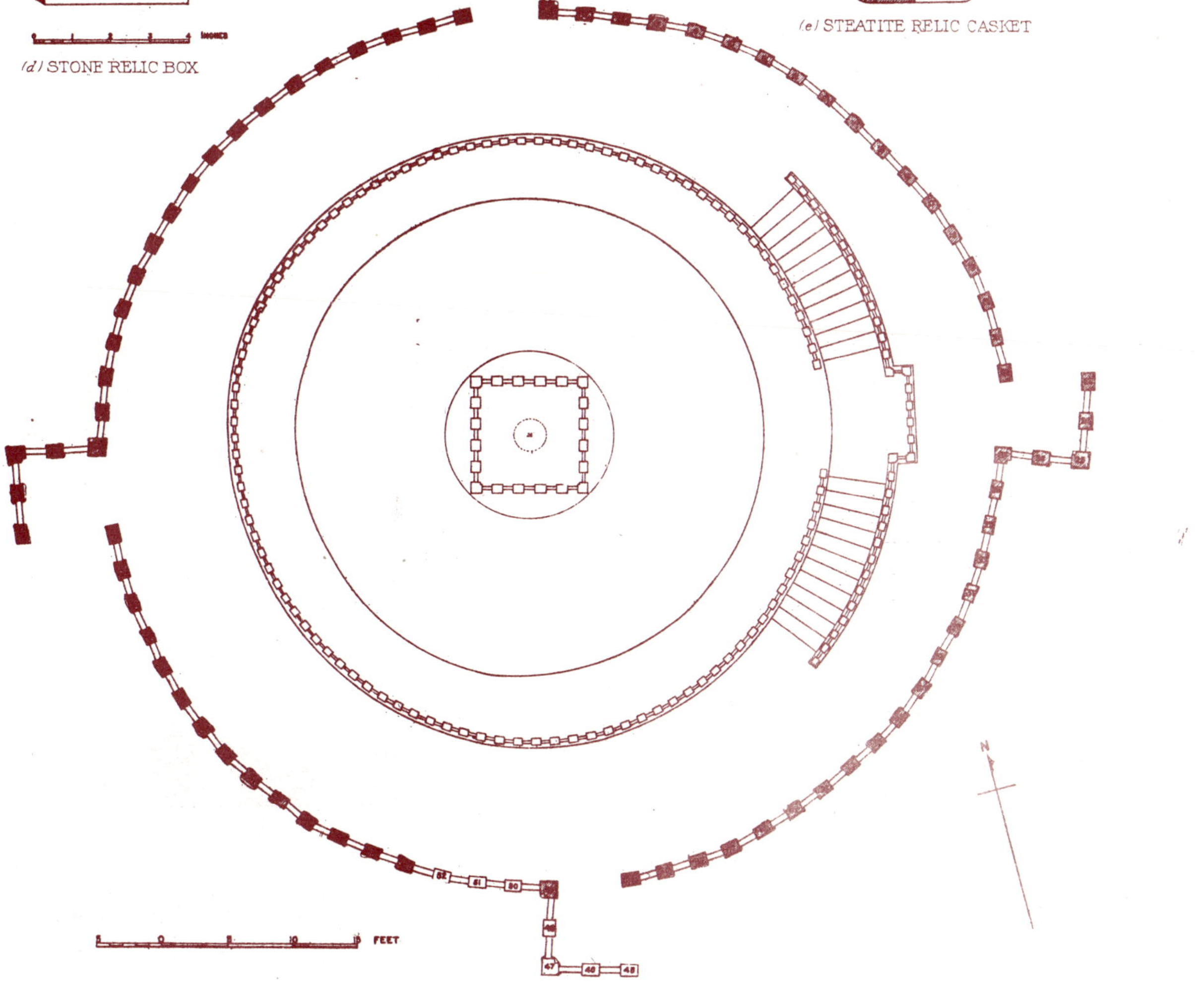

(b) PLAN.

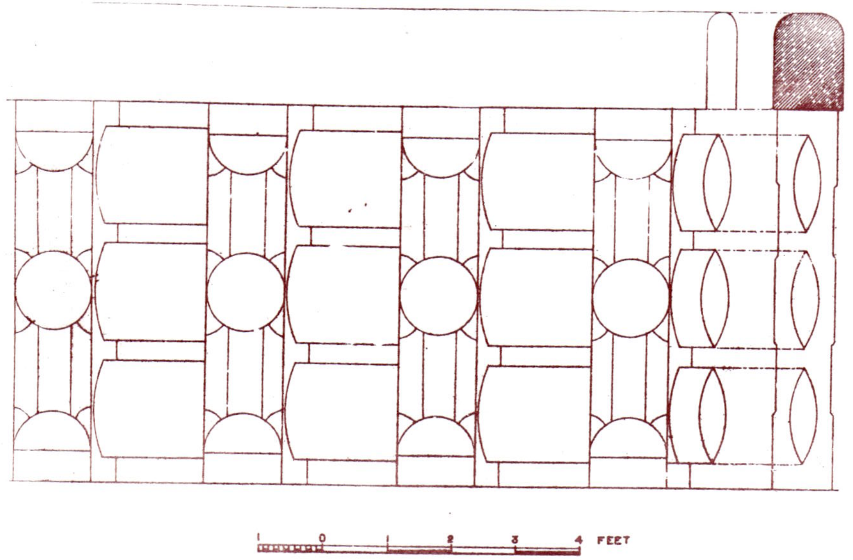

(a) GROUND BALUSTRADE

(c) BERM BALUSTRADE

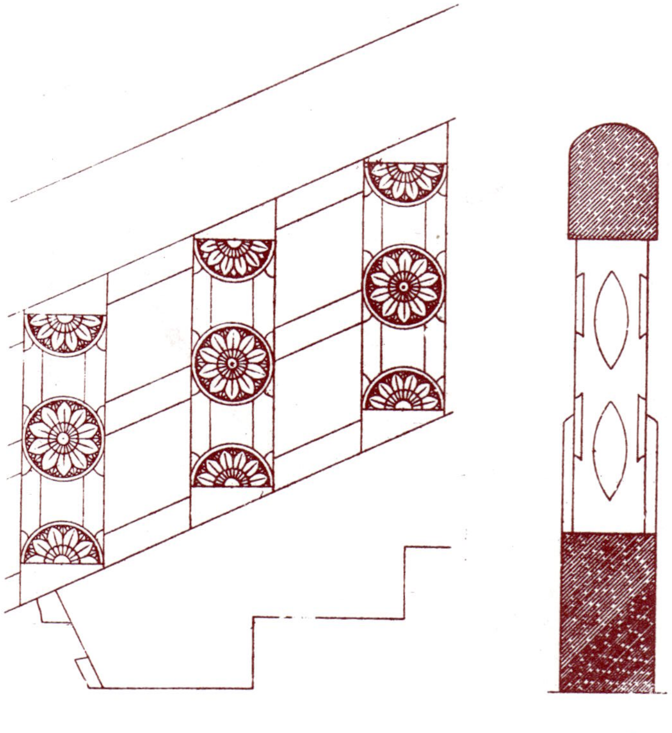

(b) STAIRWAY BALUSTRADE

(d) HARMIKA BALUSTRADE

PLATE 72

THE GROUND, STAIRWAY, BERM AND HARMIKĀ BALUSTRADES OF STŪPA 2, IN ELEVATION AND SECTION

a. Note that in this drawing the ground balustrade (pp. 79-80) is shown without any of the carvings which embellished the discs and half discs on its inner and outer faces. These carvings are reproduced in detail on Pls. 74-91.

The bases of the pillars (not shown in the drawing) were sunk in the ground in the same way as the pillars of the ground balustrade of Stūpa 1 (Pl. 7*a* and *e*), and, like them, supported on stone foundations.

b, c and *d.* The stairway and berm balustrades (pp. 80-81) closely resemble the corresponding features of Stūpas 1 and 3, and, like them, have carvings on the outer face only (*cf.* Pls. 7*b* and *c* and 104*b* and *c*). In the harmikā balustrade, the pillars are quadrangular and plain, as they are in Stūpa 1, not ornamented as in Stūpa 3. On the other hand, the coping (*ushṇīsha*) of this balustrade is enriched by a band of rosettes, as it is in Stūpa 3 (*cf.* Pl. 94*a*).

a. General view of Stūpa 2 before repair.—This picture, taken from the same point of view as the one below, *i.e.*, from a little north of the eastern entrance, is particularly interesting as showing the condition of the ground balustrade before it was repaired. The reader will see that in these two quadrants, the pillars, cross-bars and coping stones, though much displaced, were still intact, and that all that had to be done was to jack up the pillars again and reset them in the vertical, underpinning the foundations, wherever necessary. This, so far as is known, is what was actually done. Indeed, as regards this part of the balustrade, it is hardly possible that any of the pillars could have been turned round, particularly as the construction of the balustrade would have necessitated the cross-bars (*sūci*) being threaded laterally into the uprights—an operation that would have been impracticable without removing and resetting the rest of the pillars (to right or left, as the case might be) in the quadrant.

In the other quadrants, where parts of the balustrade had completely collapsed, the mistake of reversing some of the pillars may easily have been made (*cf.* p. 170, n. 2).

b. General view of Stūpa 2 after repair.—Originally, the dome of Stūpa 2 had the contour shown in Pl. 71*a*, but when rebuilt by a former Political Agent in Bhopal (*cf.* p. 79, n. 2), it was given the characteristic shape of a Muhammadan dome. This faulty restoration has since been corrected, to such extent as was possible without reconstructing the whole fabric: but it should be noted that the shape is still somewhat misleading.

Iconography: The pillars (*stambha*) of the large outer balustrade (Ground balustrade) alone are ornamented; the cross-bars (*sūci*) which are decorated at Bharhut, are here bare.

As many as 85 out of the original 88 pillars have been preserved and are reproduced on Pls. 74-91. Pillars 48, 50, 51, 52, left blank on the plan on Pl. 71, have since been found by Sir John Marshall in the course of excavation. There are thus only three pillars—45, 46 and 47—missing.

It may perhaps be argued that the pillars ought to have been numbered from the east entrance; but as the stūpa was approached by pilgrims of old as well as by modern tourists, from the north, the numbers begin from that entrance. They are in the order in which the pillars are encountered by those making the ritual circumambulation of the monument, in clockwise direction (*pradakshiṇa*). The pillars thus fall into four distinct sectors (*cf.* plan on Pl. 71): North-East (nos. 1-22); East-South (nos. 23-44); South-West (nos. 48-66) and West-North (nos. 67-88).

Several of the pillars flanking the four crooked entrances, whether because they were more exposed to wear than the rest or for other reasons, were recarved at a later date and consequently present notable differences in style (Pillars 22*a* and *b*, 27*a* and *b* and pp. 148-9).

The majority of the pillars (seven-eighths of them, in fact) are ornamented on both sides, with a medallion in the middle and a half-medallion above and below (*cf.* Pl. 72*a*). Only about ten of them display rectangular panels on one or more sides. In eight cases, additional decoration has been inserted between the medallions and the half-medallions. Five pillars are ornamented on three faces.

The reliefs are distributed as follows:—

Sectors.	No. of Pillars.	Medallions.	Half-Medallions.	Panels.	Total.
I	22	38	75	18	131
II	22	40	82	17	139
III	19	34	66	4	104
IV	22	40	80	12	132
Totals	85	152	303	51	506

Before embarking on an examination of the decoration of th i balustrade, it may be interesting, as we have already indicated (pp. 170 *sqq.*), to estimate the exact extent of the task which its contractors had to achieve. If we remember that they were faced with more than 500 frames to fill, we shall not be surprised to find that they resorted to repetitions and variations, or that they used the lotus designs so profusely. Leaving aside for the moment the angle pillars of the entrances, we have come to the conclusion that, as far as medallions are concerned, the lotus was probably their only ornament on the earliest balustrades; and that during a second period it remained the uniform ornament on the outer faces of the pillars (*cf.* p. 170, note 2, and Pls. 72, 93-94). The balustrade of Stūpa 2 appears to be initiating a third period; for the lotus still reigns almost undisputed over the outer face of the pillars, and even on the inner face it has only partially allowed other motifs to fill the circles or half circles into which its shape fitted so naturally, and for which the new intruders were much less well adapted. That this is not a purely subjective impression is proved by the following table, compiled on the spot:—

	Sect. I.		Sect. II.		Sect. III.		Sect. IV.		Total.
	Med.	½-Med.	Med.	½-Med.	Med.	½-Med.	Med.	½-Med.	
Lotus-rosaces	7	38	12	41	13	39	8	35	193
Lotus variants	9	16	13	12	7	11	13	19	100
Lotus with other motifs	17	14	10	18	14	12	18	23	126
Motifs without lotus	5	7	5	11	0	4	1	3	36
Total	38	75	40	82	34	66	40	80	455

Looking through plates 74 to 91 we observe that out of 455 medallions or half-medallions nearly 300 are monopolised by the lotus or its variants. On 126 others it has intruded its presence on one pretext or another, or without any pretext at all. On 36 only has it been completely dislodged by a new motif. Such pertinacity seems to show good proof of an old-established right.

Passing now to the pillars with rectangular (no longer circular) decoration, their case would seem to need a separate and careful examination (*cf.* pp. 170-171). For one thing, a special system of decoration seems to have prevailed on the angle pillars at an early date; and for another, it is certain that at Sāñchī (*cf.* Pls. 8-66 and 93-103), as at Bharhut (Cunn., Pls. 13-20), rectangular frames are found only at the entrances and on the gates of balustrades. Round Stūpa 2 we find them only at the North (nos. 88, 1, 3, 5), East (nos. 23, 27), South (nos. 44, 49) and West (nos. 66, 71) entrances—that is, on ten pillars in all.

A census of the 175 faces of the 85 extant pillars reveals the presence of some 112 human figures and 243 animals, real or mythical. The majority of the latter are lions (57), *haṁsas* (52) and elephants (50). See above, pp. 172-175.

a. GENERAL VIEW BEFORE REPAIR

b. GENERAL VIEW AFTER REPAIR

1 *a*. WEST FACE

1 *b*. OUTER FACE

1 *c*. INNER FACE

2 *a*. OUTER FACE

2 *b*. INNER FACE

3 *a*. NORTH FACE

3 *b*. EAST FACE

4 *a*. OUTER FACE

4 *b*. INNER FACE

5 *a*. WEST FACE

RELIEFS ON GROUND BALUSTRADE

STŪPA 2: RELIEFS ON GROUND BALUSTRADE

North-East Sector

Pillars 1 to 22 belong to the North-East sector of the balustrade. Numbers 1, 3 and 5 (together with 88) mark the four corners of the North entry (*cf.* plan on Pl. 71). These three pillars have thus received special decoration, in which no fewer than three Great Miracles figure (*cf.* p. 186). Of numbers 6 to 22, which run round almost a quarter of the enclosure from north to east, all but the last and 13*b* observe the usual norm.

1. The style of this corner pillar is very archaic and its indecisive characterisation takes us back to a time when the repertoire was not yet stereotyped (*cf.* Pl. 87).

1*a*. On the outer face a Yakshī, already adapting herself, though rather awkwardly, to the plastic poses of Bharhut (*cf.* Cunn., Pls. 22, 3 and 23, 3), encircles the trunk of the bignonia with her arm, but not, let it be noticed, with her leg. Observe the details of her costume and jewels, including the heavy ankle rings, and also the formalised lotus on which the Yakshī stands, which, like that on pillars 3*a* and 5*a*, evidently has the same significance as the more elaborate lotus trees found on other pillars. See Part II, pp. 99-100.

1*b*. Some confusion seems to have been set up at a later date in both literary and artistic tradition between female figures hanging like the Yakshī of 1*a* on to a tree-branch and those which, as here on the outer (north) face of pillar 1, are simply standing between lotus stems (sometimes supporting two Nāga-elephants) and which we have learned to identify as the Māyā of the Nativity (*cf.* pp. 183-6) but at the time when these pillars were carved the two types were quite distinct.—Now, what are we to make of the royal couple standing below Māyā, the queen holding in her left hand the king's right wrist? In our opinion, they are probably a couple of *dvārapāla* genii, such as are found at each of the gateways (*cf.* nos. 23*c*, 49*a*, 66*c*, 71*a*, 88*b*). On the other hand, it would be easy to see in them King Suddhodana and Queen Mahāprajāpatī, that is, Māyā's husband and sister, or, in other words, the Buddha's father and adoptive mother. But, in that case, how are we to understand the picture below? For there is no doubt that this is a scene of capital punishment: the elephant has seized the victim's long hair in its trunk and is trampling him under its feet; and the elephant-driver, clearly a man of low caste, can be none other than the executioner—which explains why his attendant is only hanging on to the elephant's girth instead of displaying the usual insignia of honour, the umbrella, fly-whisk or standard. Since, then, there is no imaginable connection between this group and the two above, there can clearly be no reason for attempting to establish one between the other two. See Part II, pp. 101-2.

1*c*. The inner (south) face presents also a Great Miracle at the top—the First Sermon (*cf.* p. 189); the wheel with 16 spokes, surrounded with umbrellas and perched on a triratna (*cf.* Pls. 97, 4, and 101, 4), surmounts a throne supported, like the *vajra-āsana* of Bodh-Gayā, by two atlas-dwarfs (notice the flowers which decorate the edge of the flag-stone). We might suppose that the two lotuses flanking the *ratna* symbol contain an allusion to the Great Miracle at Śrāvastī, represented at Bharhut also by the wheel (Cunn., Pl. 13, 3), but it seems more natural to interpret them as standing for the Lotus Tree of Life and Fortune, which is found in so many of these reliefs (see Part II, pp. 142 *sqq.*) and to take the two lions rampant and the deer crouching at the bottom, as belonging to the same concept (*cf.* pillars 5*a*, 5*b*, 44*b*, etc.). But what, then, of the four persons intercalated between the atlantes and lions, round a basket seen from above and filled with carefully rolled garlands of the same type as those hanging on the wheel and in the worshippers' hands? Is the seated woman with her back turned, simply the flower-seller (*cf.* Pl. 18*b*2)? And do the man, woman and child represent a family of donors? Or are the man and woman the familiar Yaksha and Yakshī so habitually associated with the Lotus Tree? One point we may notice, is that there is a convention in these older reliefs by which every figure is shown resting on a sort of ledge contrived in the stone, so that the Māyā on no. 1*b* is found without her usual pedestal of lotus.—For the garland-basket, *cf.* Pls. 56, 3; 58, 2; etc.

2*a*. We are inclined to think that face *a* of pillar 2 was once the inner (south) face, since it is the more richly ornamented. At the top, a rosace set between two *utpalas* and two garlands.—In the middle, a composite lotus.—Below, a half-rosace. The three strips combine a number of themes which reappear later on the *toraṇas*: at the top on the edges, and below in the middle, *padmas* set between *utpalas*; and at the bottom on the edges, lotus creepers with undulating stems (*cf.* Pls. 19*e*, 23*b*, 50*b* and c, and 103*f*). These no doubt are the conventionalised Lotus Trees described in Part II, pp. 142 *sqq.* But what of the standing woman? Is she Māyā or a Yakshī of the Lotus Tree? We shall have plenty of opportunities of seeing her again on pillars 12*b*, 15*c*, 21*b*, 22*a*, etc.

2*b*. At top, rosace between *padmas*.—In the middle, a medallion with a central lotus, quartered with four hooks (*nāga-danta*) from each of which hang a flower and leaf of *padma* (*cf.* nos. 19*a* and 69*a*).—At bottom, a half-rosace.

3. Corner Pillar. The two decorated faces are set at right-angles and turned towards the outside (North and East).

3*a*. The north face presents, as companion piece to the Great Miracle of the Nativity on no. 1*b*, that of the First Sermon: the wheel (with 16 spokes) is already (*cf.* Pls. 22, 27, 40, and 103*b*) placed at the top of an Indo-Persian column whose capital of four lions, evidently reminiscent of the Aśoka pillars at Sārnāth and Sāñchī (Pl. 107), ushers in those of the Southern Gateway (Pl. 14). Notice how the shaft of the column is divided into three by two flutes, which may be only a clumsy way of showing an octagonal shaft (*cf.* no. 5*a*). Notice, too, the two lotus branches, with garlands hanging from them, which curl up on either side of the abacus. The identity of the male and female worshipper shown standing on the balustrade which runs round the column (*cf.* Pl. 103*a*) is again known only to the sculptor. For the Lotus Tree at the base, compare Part II, pp. 142 *sqq.*, and for the two lions rampant issuing from the stem, *cf.* Pls. 74, 5*a*, and 66*b* and *c*. Here, the tree is composed of two palmettes only, the lower one of which springs from a sort of half *Srīvatsa* device.

3*b*. The East face is completely covered with a richly decorative Lotus Tree with winding double stem (see Part II, pp. 98-99, and *cf.* nos. 49*b*, 66*a*, 71*b*, 88*a*). At the base, the root of the tree springs from the mouth or trunk of a Nāga Elephant; at the top, the outline of a woman's figure raises the same question as the woman in no. 2*a*.

4*a*. At the top are two lions in profile, couchant back to back under a half-rosace. Notice the effort which has been made to let us see both their ears, and even both their eyes.—In the central medallion, flowers, buds and leaves of a *padma* are issuing from an elephant's mouth, and are brandished in his upraised trunk (*cf.* nos. 8*b*, 18*a*, 24*a*, etc.).—At the bottom, a half-rosace of lotus.

4*b*. A rosace between *padmas*.—A rosace encircled by a garland (*cf.* nos. 21*a*, 36*b*, 51*b*, 56*a*); and here let us notice once for all the peculiar appearance of these garlands (*cf.* no. 3*a*, and *Bharhut*, Cunn., Pl. 36, 7).—A half-rosace of lotus.

5*a*. Pillar 5, as we have said, formed (opposite no. 88) the third corner of the North entrance. As on no. 3, its two ornamented sides are placed at a right angle, but face West and South. Its west face repeats the Great Miracle of the First Sermon in much the same terms and in just the same style as on no. 3*a*. The *dharma-cakra* still has 16 spokes, but an elephant has been introduced among the lions (*cf.* Pl. 93*g*) and somewhat upsets their balance. The worshippers are replaced by two rows of lotus blooms. As for the Lotus Tree at the base, with its rampant animals back to back, see Part II, pp. 143-144 and 146, and compare Pls. 64*b*, 66*b* and *c*.

STŪPA 2: RELIEFS ON GROUND BALUSTRADE—continued

5*b*. Inner (south) face of corner pillar of north entrance. This also bore a representation of a Great Miracle (*cf*. p. 186); this time the third, the Enlightenment. The leaf of the *aśvattha* or *ficus religiosa* of Śākya-muni is clearly drawn. The tree, surmounted by an umbrella between two winged genii, has nothing round it but a railing. Notice that the coping and plinth of the latter are decorated with *padmas*, that its corner pillars lengthen into columns whose tops are lost among the foliage, and that it is flanked with umbrellas and poles loaded with garlands. Below the railing, clumsily shown in plan as it were, is the flagstone of the Diamond Throne (*vajra-āsana*) with two atlas-dwarfs supporting it (*cf*. no. 1c and Cunn., *Mahābodhi*, Pl. 13). The magic Lotus Tree at the bottom of the panel is laden with necklaces and jewellery, like the trees on Pls. 11, 3; 19*a*; 100, 3. It is coming out of the jaws of a scaly, footless *makara*, flattened beneath the feet of a crane or goose and an elephant, the latter of which holds the lotus stalk with his trunk. For the rampant antelope in the bend of the lotus above the elephant, see Part II, pp. 143, 144 & 146, and compare the antelopes on Pillars 5*a* (Pl. 74), 44*a* (Pl. 82), 44*c* and 49*a* (Pl. 83), 66*b* (Pl. 86) as well as on Pl. 66*b*.

6*a*. The upper half-medallion shows us the elephant of the Conception (*cf*. p. 182) moving left on clouds, between two rosettes, representing a rain of flowers. The trunk is resting on the left tusk.—The central medallion, which may be compared to no. 23*b*, shows, set between lotuses, a yaksha of a type intermediate between the *deva* and the *kumbhāṇḍa*; his right hand is raised in the gesture "which removes fear".—At the bottom, a half-rosace.

6*b*. At the top, a bunch of lotus with two *haṁsas*, wings and bills open (*cf*. no. 55*b* and p. 173).—In the middle, a curious type of Nāga-rāja; his five cobra-heads, closely grouped above his turban, make his head-dress inordinately high, and the coils of his serpent-body (ending behind his left foot, just under the hem of his scarf) cover the whole field of the medallion not occupied by two *padmas* and two *utpalas*. Notice how the *padma* stalk held in his right hand passes through the coils.—At the bottom, a half-rosace.

7*a*. Wingless griffin holding a bunch of mangoes in his beak: formalised *padma* buds follow the trend of his tail, and he has the same little curl on his forehead as the griffins on the Western Gateway (Pls. 56 and 58, 5).—Bunch of *padmas* coming out of a vase (*cf*. p. 184).—Half-rosace.

7*b*. Bunch of *padmas*.—Centaur ridden by a woman (*cf*. no. 81*b*). The centaur is holding a garland in his right hand and raises his left on a level with the woman's head-dress. She is seated on a saddle-cloth held in place by a crupper.—Half-rosace.

8*a*. Among lotuses, a man-faced lion with a long beard and twisted, tapering hair.—Among lotuses, a crouching lion in profile, its head facing front, holding an antelope in its jaws.—Palmette.

8*b*. *Makara* with the forequarters of an elephant, a lotus stalk coming out of its mouth (*cf*. nos. 25*a* and 30*a*).—Elephant similar to no. 4*a*.—Half-rosace.

9*a*. In a bunch of lotuses, a lion with curly mane, curiously drawn front-face with the hind quarters spread out on each side of the forequarters (*cf*. nos. 63*a*, 74*a*, 75*a*).—A yaksha with a strange head-dress, framed in a bunch of lotuses on which sit two *haṁsas* (*cf*. no. 73*b* and Part II, p. 144).—Half-rosace.

9*b*. *Śrīvatsa* framed with lotuses.—In a bunch of lotuses trimmed with garlands and necklaces stands a *nandipada* capped with a half-shield.—Half-rosace.

10*a*. Bunch of lotuses coming out of a calyx.—Forequarters of an elephant enveloped in lotuses (*cf*. nos. 18*b*, 26*b*).—Half-rosace.

5 b

6 a

6 b

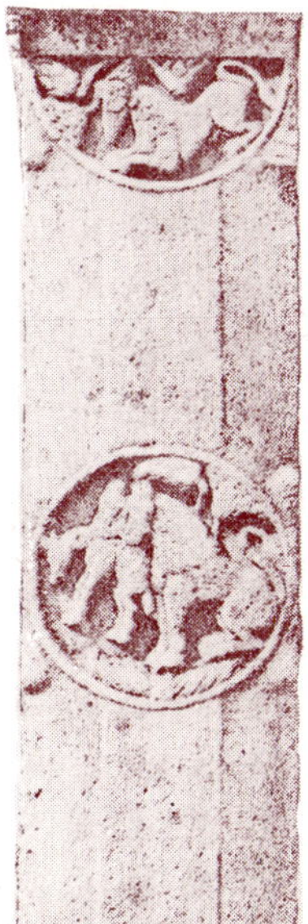

8 a

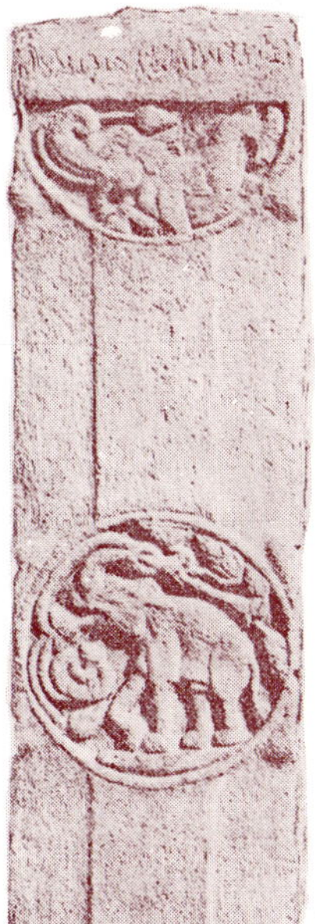

8 b

9 a

9 b

10 a

RELIEFS ON GROUND BALUSTRADE

10 b.

11 a.

11 b.

12 a.

12 b.

13 a.

13 b.

14 a.

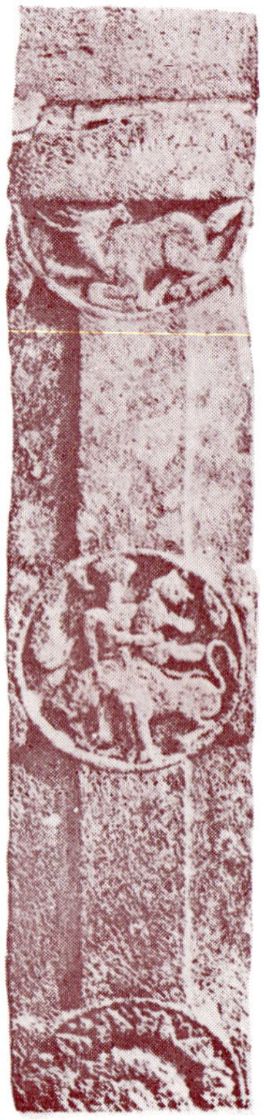
14 b.

15 a.

RELIEFS ON GROUND BALUSTRADE

PLATE 76

STŪPA 2: RELIEFS ON GROUND BALUSTRADE—continued

10*b*. At the top, a lotus rosace between two *utpalas* and two *padma* buds (we may remark at once that this motif will recur on some 30 other top half-medallions).—In the middle, a peacock with tail displayed, between two pea-hens (?) and two formalised *padma* buds; between them, flowerets.—At the bottom, a half-rosace.

11*a*. Half rosace encircled by a garland.—On a rosace, an elephant passant to the right, ridden by a master and servant.—Half-rosace with curving petals.

11*b*. Cow suckling her calf; floweret.—Rosace encircled by two chaplets and framing a man's bust (*cf.* Cunn., *Bharhut*, Pl. 35, 1).—*Makara* with stag's forequarters, and, behind it, a fish.

12*a*. Half-rosace.—Rosace encircled by a garland.—Half-rosace.

12*b*. *Triratna* symbol among lotuses (*cf.* nos. 13*b*, 26*b*).—Woman standing, framed in lotuses (*cf.* p. 183 *sq.* and nos. 15*a* and 21*b*).—Half-rosace.

13*a*. Three lions arranged as on the capital of a column, the fourth remaining invisible (*cf.* no. 3*a*, etc.), and garlands.—Composite lotus.—Half-rosace.

13*b*. Same description as for no. 12*b*.—*Dharmacakra* with 8 spokes surrounded by a border of umbrellas, a cable-moulding and a necklace.—Half-rosace. The middle face of the pillar is adorned with a row of lotus flowers above and a row of palmettes below; *cf.* nos. 2*a* and 22*b* and p. 170, note 2.

14*a*. Winged griffin, crested as usual (*cf.* no. 7*a*).—Figure in royal turban sitting on a rattan-seat, holding a drinking cup in his eft hand and some lotus stalks in his right.—Half-rosace.

14*b*. Antelope couchant.—Man slaying a lioness with his right hand and carrying off a cub in his left arm; in field, lotus buds.—Half-rosace.

15*a*. Bunch of lotuses coming out of a vase.—Woman standing (*cf.* no. 12*b*: the only difference is that here her right arm is raised).—Half-rosace.

PLATE 77

STŪPA 2: RELIEFS ON GROUND BALUSTRADE—continued

15*b*. At the top, a half-rosace surrounded by a garland.—In the middle, an elephant giving himself a shower-bath with his trunk: the jets of the water end in tiny drops; in field, lotus.—At the bottom, a half-rosace.

16*a*. Framed rosace (*cf.* no. 10*b*, etc.).—Rosace encircled by garlands.—Half-rosace.

16*b*. Palmette and lotus coming out of a half-shield (*śrīvatsa*; *cf.* no. 17*b*).—On a rosace encircled by a laurel wreath, an elephant passant to the right and holding a lotus in his trunk (*cf.* p. 177).—Half-rosace.

17*a*. Palmette with *utpalas* coming out of a half-rosace.—Bunc of lotuses coming out of a vase.—Half-rosace (obliterated).

17*b*. Palmette with *padmas* and *utpalas* coming out of a half-shield (*cf.* no. 16*b*).—Rosace.—Half-rosace.

18*a*. Two lions couchant back to back; in the embrasure, a bird's head (?) passing through a garland (*cf.* no. 80*b*).—Elephant and lotuses (*cf.* nos. 4*a* and 8*b*).—Half-rosace.

18*b*. Framed rosace (*cf.* no. 10*b*, etc.).—Forequarters of an elephant brandishing lotuses (*cf.* no. 10*a*).—Half-rosace.

19*a*. *Padma* and *utpala* flowers coming out of a half-shield.—Rosace quartered with four brackets bearing *padmas* hanging from them (*cf.* no. 2*b*).—Half-rosace.

19*b*. Framed rosace (*cf.* no. 10*b*, etc.).—Rosace.—Half-rosace.

20*a*. Framed rosace (*cf.* no. 10*b*, etc.).—Erotic couple (*cf.* pp. 246 and 247) between lotuses; for the attitude of the man holding the woman's chin, *cf.* Pl. 64*c*, 2.—Half-rosace.

15 b.

16 a

16 b

17 a.

17 b.

18 a.

18 b.

19 a.

19 b.

20 a.

RELIEFS ON GROUND BALUSTRADE

20 *b*

21 *a*

21 *b*

22 *a*

22 *b*

23 *a* NORTH FACE

23 *b* OUTER FACE

23 *c* INNER FACE

24 *a* OUTER FACE

24 *b* INNER FACE

RELIEFS ON GROUND BALUSTRADE

STŪPA 2: RELIEFS ON GROUND BALUSTRADE—continued

20*b*. At the top, framed rosace (*cf.* no. 10*b*, etc.).—In the middle, a rosace encircled by a necklace.—Below, a half-rosace. (This was originally the outer face?)

21*a*. Framed rosace (*cf.* no. 10*b*, etc.)—Rosace encircled by a garland.—Half-rosace.

21*b*. Framed rosace (*cf.* no. 10*b*, etc.)—Woman standing (? Māyā) framed in lotus (*cf.* nos. 12*b*, 15*a*, etc.).—Half-rosace.

22*a*. Pillar 22 ends the north-east sector. With the exception of the half medallions at the top and bottom, this face of the pillar was entirely recarved. A lucky chance which has brought nos. 21*b* and 22*a* side by side on the same plate makes this visible at a glance. It is enough to compare the treatment of the standing women in their respective medallions to estimate the transformation in technique which intervened between the two. The flat frontal drawing of no. 21*b* is as archaic as any at Bharhut. whilst the skilled modelling of the middle figure on 22*a* makes it contemporarv with the best period of the Gateways.

At the top, a palmette with *padmas* coming out of a half-shield (*śrīvatsa*). This and the half rosace at the base belong to the original carvings.—In the middle, the image of Māyā (*cf.* pp. 183 *sqq.*), standing on a lotus and framed in lotuses. The ease of the posture, the elegance of the forms and the fluid lines of the scanty draperies combine to make it a little masterpiece. On her right, a female dwarf is holding a ewer, and on her left, another attendant (only half the size of the principal figure) is raising a tray. Observe, too, the flexibility of the stems and the delicacy of the leaves and flowers of the *padma*.—Below, a half-rosace.—Between the top and centre medallions, in middle, a second woman standing framed in vaulted doorway, with balustrade in front; in her left hand she is holding the hem of her scarf, the other end of which falls gracefully over her right arm. One might wonder whether she is not, like some sportive beauties of Mathurā (*cf.* J. Ph. Vogel, *La Sculpture de Mathurā* (Ars Asiatica, XV), Pl. 19*a* and *c*), playing with a pet bird, but what she carries in her right hand, on a level with her head, seems to be only another lotus. Above, on the roof, are two birds.—Between centre and bottom medallions, conventionalised Lotus Tree, formed of repeated palmettes (*cf.* no. 13*b* and Pl. 37). In borders, sinuous lotus creepers. Those above issue from the navels of two squatting *kumbhāṇḍas* (*cf.* nos. 23*a*, 49*b* and Pls. 11, 3, and 19*b*); those below, from the jaws of two *makaras* (*cf.* Pl. 37*b*).

22*b*. Rosace framed in formalised buds (*cf.* no. 10*b*, etc.).—Bunch of *padmas* coming out of a vase: the central *padma*, opening into a rosace, is surmounted by a *śrīvatsa* device.—Half-rosace.—Below, on the middle band, Lotus Tree conventionalised. This band is later work.

East-South Sector.

We now come to a new sector of the balustrade. The four corners of the east entrance are marked by pillars 22 (which we have just described), 23, 25 and 27. Only the last has had to be remade, like 22, its opposite. Nos. 28 to 44 line another quarter of the circular path (*cf.* Pl. 71).

23. Corner pillar, three sides of which are entirely ornamented in the archaic style.

23*a*. A sinuous Lotus Tree with *haṁsas* lodging in it, is held in both hands by a Yaksha facing front and squatting on a tortoise. The main stem, held in his right hand, is probably growing out of his navel (*cf.* 22*a* and see p. 98, Pt. II).

23*b*. At the top, a rosace framed in *padmas* (*cf.* no. 10*b*, etc.).—In the middle a bunch of *padmas* and *utpalas* coming out of the mouth of a tortoise.—At the bottom, a formalised half-rosace.—On the three strips, rows of *padmas* alternating with *utpalas* or sinuous *padma* creepers (*cf.* no. 2*a*); at the top of the middle strip, the same male figure as on no. 6*a*, but his torso and arms are here covered with a tunic gathered into narrow pleats (*cf.* Pt. II, p. 98).

23*c*. Bunch of *padmas* and *utpalas*.—Composite *padma*.—Formalised half-rosace.—The middle strip bears a Yaksha above and a Yakshī (holding the branch and embracing the trunk of a bignonia as in no. 1*a*) below, possibly in their function of guardians of the gates. The two side strips are again decorated with sinuous lotus creepers.

24*a*. Half-rosace.—Elephant and lotuses (*cf.* nos. 4*a*, 8*b*, 18*a*).—Rhinoceros tête-à-tête with a *padma* bud.

24*b*. Lion killing an antelope, which he holds upside down between his forepaws.—Lion attacking an elephant, hardly as large as himself, from the rear.—Two rodents (?) eating a fruit (?) which they are holding in their forepaws.

STŪPA 2: RELIEFS ON GROUND BALUSTRADE—continued

25. This corner pillar is decorated on both outside faces, east and south.

25a. Above, two squirrels rifling mangoes.—In the middle, a bunch of lotuses coming out of the jaws of a *makara* with elephant's forequarters (*cf.* nos. *8b* and *30a*).—Half-rosace encircled by a garland.

25b. Rosace framed between two garlands: the upper garland passes over the necks of three birds, two of which are holding *padma* buds in their beaks.—Bunch of lotuses coming out of a half-rosace and bedecked with four garlands, two streamers and two *haṁsas*, with a *triratna* symbol at top (*cf.* no. *12b*, etc.).—*Makara* with lion's forequarters under a *padma* bud.—The middle band is adorned above with a Yaksha under an umbrella, and below with a Yakshī under the suggestion of a tree (*cf.* no. *23c*). Both Yaksha and Yakshī may be later additions but not so late as the additions on *22a*, *27a* and *27b*, etc.

26a. Framed rosace (*cf.* no. *10b*, etc.).—Forequarters of an elephant among lotuses (*cf.* no. *10a*).—Half-rosace.

26b. *Triratna* symbol and lotus (*cf.* no. *12b*, etc.).—On a rosace background a queen standing praying between two attendants, one holding her umbrella and ewer, the other her fly-whisk (*cf.* pp. 183 *sqq.*).—Half-rosace.

27. This corner pillar, decorated on its north and west sides, was recarved at the time when the *toraṇas* of Stūpa 1 were executed, and this is why it is divided like the jambs of those gateways, into quadrilateral panels separated by railings, and sometimes set between Indo-Persian columns. The technique shows a great advance over the rest of the balustrade, and these reliefs rank among the best at Sāñchī.

27a. In the top panel, the wheel (with 20 spokes) of the third Great Miracle (*cf.* p. 189) perched on a pedestal has its hub bedecked with a garland, as in the representation of the "Great Prodigy at Srāvastī" at Bharhut (*cf.* Cunn., Pl. 13, 3), and is being adored by two couples, the men standing, the women kneeling.—Underneath is the stock illustration of the second Great Miracle, showing (with nothing special to distinguish them) two pairs of worshippers at the Bodhi tree of Śākya-muni and two celestial beings above, with garlands in their hands.—Picture of 'water sports', to be compared to those on the Gateways (*cf.* Pls. 12, 2; *34b*; 101 and 102, 3).—Lotus Tree of Life (*cf.* pillars *1a*, *3a*, *5a*, *5b*, *23a*, etc., and Pls. *66b* and *c*). The half medallion at the base belongs to the original decoration.

27b. The west side has only three rectangular panels. At the top, two lions back to back and half-rampant on two lotus leaves, with a formalised tree between them, remind one of a similar motif on the Western Gateway (Pl. *64b*). In both cases they represent the Lotus Tree of Life.—Underneath, a rājā, leaning on his two queens and surrounded by three attendants, one of whom carries the umbrella, a second the fly-whisk, and the third something no longer distinguishable. They recall the 'Aśoka at Bodh-Gayā' on Pl. 18, 2; the ewer and the jar capped with an inverted goblet are placed on the ground.—No less curious is the general resemblance between the bottom panel and Pl. *18a2*. Here, too, the king, in his chariot, is driving towards the right, accompanied by his viceroy on an elephant; but this time he has only one person with him, and that a woman; he is holding the reins against his left shoulder and has his right arm round the shoulders of his queen, to whom he has entrusted the driving whip or stick. The curved fore-part of the chariot tapers off into a sort of beak which arches over to meet the shaft; a dog with upraised tail (*cf.* no. *44a*, and Pls. 16, 3 and *19c3*) is trotting behind the wheels.

28a. Palmette springing from a leaf.—Rosace encircled by a band of flowerets.—Bunch of *padmas* issuing from a leaf.

28b. Half-rosace.—Rosace.—Half-rosace.

29a. Half-rosace.—Rosace.—Half-rosace.

29b. Half-rosace.—Bunch of *padmas* coming out of a vase.—Half-rosace.

25 a. EAST FACE

25 b. SOUTH FACE

26 a. OUTER FACE

26 b. INNER FACE

27 a. NORTH FACE

27 b. WEST FACE

28 a. OUTER FACE

28 b. INNER FACE

29 a. OUTER FACE

29 b. INNER FACE

RELIEFS ON GROUND BALUSTRADE

30 a

30 b

31 a

31 b

32 a

PLATE 80

STŪPA 2: RELIEFS ON GROUND BALUSTRADE—continued

30*a*. Half-rosace.—*Makara* with elephant's forequarters, out of whose mouth comes a *padma*-stalk (*cf.* no. 25*a*).—Half-rosace.

30*b*. Half-rosace.—Rosace.—Half-rosace. (Originally the outward face?)

31*a*. Half-rosace.—Palmette with *padmas*.—Half-rosace.

31*b*. Two antelopes rampant and back to back under a fig tree (*cf.* nos. 5*a* and 40*b*).—Lotus rosace with four *triratnas*. (*Cf.* nos. 35*a*, 56*b*, 68*b*, 72*a*, 82*b*, 83*a*, 87*b* and Cunn., *Bharhut*, Pl. 38, 2.)—Half-rosace.

32*a*. Half-rosace encircled by a double dog-toothed border.—Nāga serpent with five cobra-hoods (*cf.* no. 81*a*).—Lotus palmette coming out of a half-rosace.

32*b*. Four half-rosaces.—Bunch of *padmas* coming out of a vase.—Palmette with *utpalas* issuing out of a half-shield (*śrīvatsa*).

33*a*. Half-rosace.—Rosace encircled by a laurel wreath and a garland.—Half-rosace surrounded by overlapping half *padmas* (*cf.* no. 87*a*).

33*b*. Half-rosace encircled by a jewelled border.—Rosace with its outer ring of petals curled in the shape of commas.—Half-rosace.

34*a*. Half-rosace.—Starred rosace, encircled by half-rosaces.—*Makara* swallowing a fish; above, another fish (*cf.* no. 86*b*).

34*b*. Lion with open jaws and tongue hanging out, running to the left, surmounted by an *utpala*.—Bunch of *padmas* coming out of a vase.—Half-rosace.

PLATE 81

STŪPA 2: RELIEFS ON GROUND BALUSTRADE—continued

35*a*. Palmette with *padma* buds.—Quadruple *nandipada* (*cf.* no. 31*b*) decked with twelve flowerets.—Half-rosace with curved petals.

35*b*. Winged griffin with big parrot-beak, passant to the left.—Elephant trampling on a fish, from whose mouth comes a lotus garland.—Half-rosace with curved petals.

36*a*. *Padma* rosace framed in leaves and buds (*cf.* no. 10*b*, etc.).—Medallion quartered with petals and *utpala* buds surrounding a small central rosace.—Half-rosace.

36*b*. Lotus palmette coming out of a half-rosace.—Rosace encircled by a garland.—Lotus palmette coming out of a half-rosace.

37*a*. Lotus rosace framed in leaves and buds (*cf.* no. 10*b*, etc.).—Rosace surrounded by a laurel wreath.—Half-rosace.

37*b*. Rosace framed in leaves and buds (*cf.* no. 10*b*, etc.).—Bunch of *padmas* coming out of a vase, with two little *haṁsas* set back to back on leaves (*cf.* no. 43*b* and Cunn., *Bharhut*, Pl. 38, 1). Half-rosace.

38*a*. Indian humped bull kneeling to left, head facing front (*cf.* no. 58*a*) with two flowerets in field.—Rosace.—Palmette.

38*b*. Fantastic bird (Garuḍa?), holding in his beak and under his talons the neck and body of a serpent which is coiling round him.—Elephant facing left, feeding under a fig-tree, from which a garland is hanging on the right (*cf.* no. 41*b*).—Half-rosace surrounded by a garland.

39*a*. Framed rosace (*cf.* no. 10*b*, etc.).—Rosace surrounded by double garland.—Palmette with *utpala* flowers.

39*b*. Half-rosace encircled by double garland.—Small rosace surrounded by a garland of *padmas* issuing from the jaws of a little *makara*.—Half-rosace encircled by a wreath.

35 *a*

35 *b*

36 *a*

36 *b*

37 *a*

37 *b*

38 *a*

38 *b*

39 *a*

39 *b*

RELIEFS ON GROUND BALUSTRADE

40 *a*

40 *b*

41 *a*

41 *b*

42 *a*

42 *b*

43 *a*

43 *b*

44 *a*

44 *b*

RELIEFS ON GROUND BALUSTRADE

PLATE 82

STUPA 2: RELIEFS ON GROUND BALUSTRADE—continued

40*a*. *Srīvatsa* between two *padmas* and two *utpalas*.—Rosace surrounded by a dog-tooth border.—Half-rosace with curled petals.

40*b*. Two antelopes couchant back to back under a fig-tree (*cf.* no. 31*b*).—Rider on richly harnessed horse going left: the rope passing over the rider's knee appears to have served for a stirrup. *Cf.* Nos. 81*b*, 82*a*, 84*b* and for the theme itself, *cf.* pp. 187-188. —Half-rosace.

41*a*. Half-rosace with curled petals.—Yaksha squatting to the front and holding two lotus bunches in his two hands.—Half- sace.

41*b*. Lion going left, head facing front and tongue hanging out, with two *padma* buds in field.—Elephant facing left, feeding under two fig-trees (*cf.* no. 38*b*): notice the roots of the trees.—Half-rosace encircled by double garland.

42*a*. Framed rosace (*cf.* no. 10*b*, etc.).—Rosace surrounded by concentric circles of garland, bead-and-reel border and wreath.—Half-rosace encircled by double garland.

42*b*. Palmette with two *utpalas* and two formalised *padma* buds coming out of a half-*śrīvatsa*.—Rosace surrounded by eight small rosaces and sixteen flowerets.—Palmette with four *utpalas* coming out of a half-*śrīvatsa*.

43*a*. Palmette with two *padma* buds, coming out of a fan-shaped leaf.—Medallion quartered with brackets and fronds around central rosace.—Palmette with two *utpalas* coming out of a half-rosace.

43*b*. Framed rosace (*cf.* no. 10*b*, etc.).—Bunch of *padmas* coming out of a vase with two small *haṁsas* back to back (*cf.* no. 37*b*).—Half-rosace.

44. Pillar 44 marks the end of the east-south sector, at the corner of the south entrance. It is decorated on three sides, and to all appearances it is due to its position (the South being the quarter of the *Manes*) that it bears on side c (Pl. 83) the only representation of the *Parinirvāṇa* which figures on the balustrade of Stūpa 2 (*cf.* p. 190).

44*a*. Outer (south) face: Sinuous Lotus Tree, the base of which is held in the trunk of an elephant passant to left. In addition to the usual leaves, flowers and buds of the *padma*, it includes: in the first bend, bunches of grapes and vine leaves(?), a *haṁsa* and a parrot rifling mangoes; in the second, two birds less clearly characterised (crows?); in the third, two *haṁsas*; in the fourth, three cranes (?) and a parrot; and finally, at the top, an antelope pursued by a dog of the usual type (*cf.* no. 27*b*). On the edges are: left, a reel-and-bead border, and right, a dog-tooth border. For the Lotus Tree design, *cf.* pp. 98 and 99.

44*b*. Inner (north) face: stock illustration of the third Great Miracle, the First Sermon, treated as on nos. 3*a* and 5*a*. Here, the shaft of the column looks cylindrical and its balustrade is shown with a downward perspective. We do not believe that here, any more than on 3*a*, the garlands are conceived as hanging from the jaws of the lions. The lotus flowers and leaves on either side of the column are probably to be regarded as a continuation of the Lotus Tree of Life, flanked by two pairs of rampant antelopes, at the base (*cf.* pp. 99 and 100). The borders resemble those on the south face.

PLATE 83

STŪPA 2: RELIEFS ON GROUND BALUSTRADE—continued

44c. West face: stock illustration of the fourth Great Miracle—the *Parinirvāṇa*. But the stūpa with two balustrades (the second on the terrace, as in the case of the three great stūpas at Sāñchī) leaves no room at its sides for the usual worshippers.—Below the stūpa are four *śrīvatsa* symbols set vertically one above the other, and to either side of them a bead-and-reel border flanked by four *padma* rosettes (*cf.* no. 5*a*). At the base, a Lotus Tree of Life with a pair of lions and a pair of deer rampant. (*Cf.* nos. 5*a*, 44*b*, etc.)

South-West Sector.

It should be remembered that pillars 45-47, which screened the south entrance, are missing: the only remaining pillar at this entrance which admits of particular decoration is no. 49, the fellow of 44 examined above. Nos. 48 and 50 to 52, however, which are shown as missing in the plan on Pl. 71, have now been recovered and replaced. This section of the balustrade is continued, without further interruption, as far as no. 66 inclusive.

48*a*. Palmette with two *utpalas* and two *padmas* coming out of a half-*śrīvatsa*.—Rosace framed by a double garland issuing at the bottom out of the mouth of a tortoise and meeting at the top on each side of a *śrīvatsa* device (*cf.* no. 51*a*).—Missing.

48*b*. Framed rosace (*cf.* no. 10*b*, etc.).—Rosace encircled by a necklace of flowerets.—Missing.

49. Corner pillar with the special kind of ornamentation which is found in this position at the other entrances, composed usually of Great Miracles and the Lotus Tree of Life (*cf.* Part II, pp. 98-99). The two ornamented faces are of course placed at right-angles.

49*a*. East face (opposite no. 44c): Great Miracle of the Nativity as on 1*b*; but here, Māyā's hands are clasped and she is standing on a lotus. Below her, standing between two jars, is the usual couple of Yakshas (*cf.* no. 1*b*), the man here holding a *padma* bud in his right hand.—At base, Lotus Tree of Life with two lions and two deer rampant (*cf.* 5*a*, 44*b* and *c*). Observe the tortoise at the bottom—emblem of water, from which the Lotus Tree issues.

49*b*. North face (looking towards the stūpa). Another form of the Lotus Tree as on 3*b*; at the bottom, instead of an elephant, we have a Yaksha squatting Indian fashion between two cranes, and it is from his navel that the double creeper held in his hands (*cf.* no. 22*a*) is growing; on a level with the three uppermost of the periodic knots in this creeper may be noticed two pairs of cranes (?) face to face, with two lions, back to back, between them.

50*a*. Half-rosace encircled by a border of quatrefoil flowerets.—Rosace with curved petals, surrounded by wreath.—Missing.

50*b*. Rosace framed by two *utpalas* and two *padma* buds (*cf.* no. 10*b*, etc.).—Elephant passant to the right, his head turned back, enveloped in a lotus tree (variant of 8*b*, 18*a*, 24*a*, 35*a*, etc.).—Half-rosace.

51*a*. Palmette coming out of a half-rosace.—Slightly clearer reproduction of the motif on 48*a*.—Palmette with four *utpalas* coming out of a half-*śrīvatsa*.

51*b*. Palmette with two lions rampant back to back, coming out of a half-*śrīvatsa*.—Rosace encircled by a bead-and-reel chaplet and a garland.—Half-rosace.

52*a*. Half-rosace encircled by a wreath and toothed border.—Bunch of *padmas* coming out of a vase between two *haṁsas*.—Half-rosace.

44 c. WEST FACE

48 a. OUTER FACE

48 b. INNER FACE

49 a. EAST FACE

49 b. NORTH FACE

50 a. OUTER FACE

50 b. INNER FACE

5 . OUTER FACE

51 b. INNER FACE

52 a. OU

RELIEFS ON GROUND BALUSTRADE

52b

53a

53b

54a

54b

55a

55b

56a

56b

57a

RELIEFS ON GROUND BALUSTRADE

PLATE 84

STŪPA 2: RELIEFS ON GROUND BALUSTRADE—continued

52*b*. Palmette with buds and leaves of *padma*, springing from a fan-shaped leaf.—Elephant passant to the right, ridden by a turbaned figure holding the *aṅkuśa* and accompanied by his standard-bearer; in field, stalk and buds of lotus.—Missing.

53*a*. Half-rosace.—Rosace with *utpala* intercalated between the petals (*cf.* no. 68*a*).—Half-rosace.

53*b*. Framed rosace (*cf.* no. 10*b*, etc.).—Rosace cantoned with four rosaces and four *śrīvatsas*.—Half-rosace.

54*a*. Camel with two humps kneeling down, head turned left.—Elephant passant to the left under hanging garlands.—Half-rosace.

54*b*. Half-rosace.—Elephant passant to the left under two flowers and bud of *utpala*.—Half-rosace with curved petals.

55*a*. Half-rosace.—Rosace encircled by a chaplet.—Half-rosace.

55*b*. Two *haṁsas* with wings and beaks open (*cf.* 6*b*).—Palmette with an *utpala* flower and two *padma* buds springing from a half-rosace. (*Cf.* Cunn., *Bharhut*, Pl. 37, 1.)—Half-rosace.

56*a*. Griffin lying down, to left; in field, flowerets.—Rosace encircled with a double toothed border and a garland.—Half-rosace with double toothed border.

56*b*. Framed rosace (*cf.* no. 10*b*, etc.).—Lotus rosace with four *triratnas* around and flowerets in field, the whole encircled by double toothed border (*cf.* no. 31*b*, etc.).—Half-rosace.

57*a*. Palmette with two *padma* buds springing from fan-shaped leaf.—Rosace surrounded by two intertwined garlands, within cable-moulding.—Half-rosace.

PLATE 85

STŪPA 2: RELIEFS ON GROUND BALUSTRADE—continued

57*b*. Half lotus rosace; in centre, encirled by a garland, the bust of a turbaned Indian outlined against the back of a throne; in field, flowerets.—Bunch of *padmas* coming out of a vase.—Half-rosace.

58*a*. Indian bullock kneeling down (*cf.* no. 38*a*); behind, stalk and bud of *padma*; in front, flowerets.—Rosace encircled by a wreath.—Half-rosace.

58*b*. Lotus palmette coming out of a fan-shaped leaf.—Elephant passant to the right under the boughs of a mango-tree; floweret in field.—Half-rosace encircled by a chaplet.

59*a*. Half-rosace encircled by dog-tooth border.—Rosace.—Half-rosace.

59*b*. Framed rosace (*cf.* 10*b*, etc.).—Elephant passant to the right under a palm tree; in front of him, a *padma* bud; behind him, tree clipped to form an arbour, like several on the Western Gateway (Pl. 64*c*).—Half-rosace.

60*a*. Lotus bunch coming out of a half-*śrīvatsa* framed in decorative scrolls.—Rosace encircled by toothed border.—Half-rosace.

60*b*. Bunch of *padmas* and *utpalas*, coming out of a half-rosace.—Medallion composed of a central rosace with 8 petals, encircled by 8 palmettes and 8 *utpalas* alternating. Around it, *padma* and garland device surrounded by necklace border.—Bunch of *padmas* coming out of a vase.

61*a*. Half-rosace.—Rosace.—Half-rosace.

61*b*. Half-rosace.—Lion sitting to right, framed between *utpalas* and *padmas*.—Half-rosace.

62*a*. Two winged lions back to back.—Bunch of *padmas* and *utpalas* coming out of a vase.—Half-rosace.

57 *b*

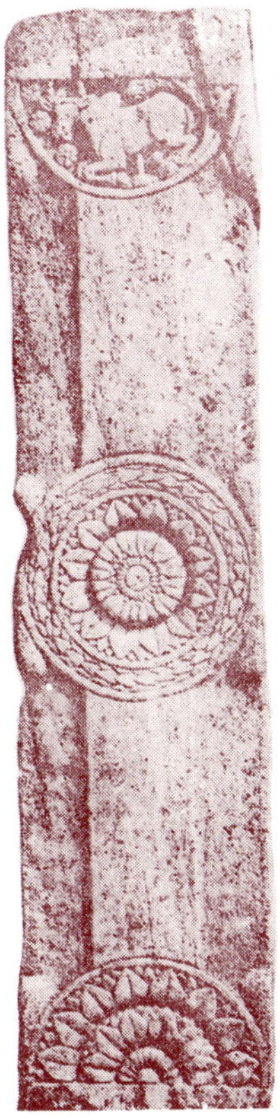
58 *a*

58 *b*

59 *a*

59 *b*

60 *a*

60 *b*

61 *a*

61 *b*

62 *a*

RELIEFS ON GROUND BALUSTRADE

62 *b*

63 *a*

63 *b*

64 *a*

64 *b*

65 *a* OUTER FACE

65 *b* INNER FACE

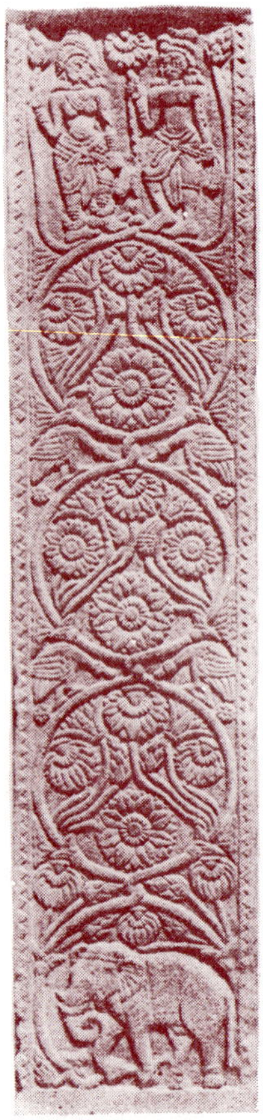
66 *a* OUTER FACE

66 *b* INNER FACE

66 *c* NORTH FACE

RELIEFS ON GROUND BALUSTRADE

PLATE 86

STŪPA 2: RELIEFS ON GROUND BALUSTRADE—continued

62*b*. Framed rosace (*cf.* 10*b*, etc.).—Rosace encircled by a garland.—Half-rosace encircled by toothed border.

63*a*. Lion seated front-face (*cf.* nos. 9*a*, 74*a*, 75*a*) between buds and leaves of *padma*.—Bunch of *padmas* coming out of a vase.—Rosace set between *padma* buds and *utpalas* (*cf.* no. 10*b*, etc.).

63*b*. Half-rosace.—On a rosace background, a horse with rider, carrying a switch in his left hand and going to right (*cf.* nos. 40*b* and 84*b*; and see pp. 187-188).—Half-rosace.

64*a*. Framed rosace (*cf.* no. 10*b*, etc.).—Rosace encircled by a necklace border.—Half-rosace.

64*b*. Half-rosace encircled by a garland and wreath.—*Padma* creeper coming out of the mouth of a *makara* (*cf.* nos. 22*a*, 25*a* and particularly 39*b*).—Half-rosace, encircled by a wreath.

65*a*. Half-rosace.—Rosace.—Half-rosace.

65*b*. Bunch of *padmas* with two *utpalas* coming out of a half *śrīvatsa*.—Formalised lotus made of a rosace surrounded by six other rosaces alternating with the same number of *utpalas*.—Half-rosace surrounded by a double toothed border.

66. This pillar is placed at the corner of the west entrance and elaborately decorated on three sides.

66*a*. The outer (west) face repeats once again the popular motif of the twin Lotus Tree (*cf.* nos. 3*b*, 49*b*, 71*b* and 88*a*). Here, as on no. 3*b*, it takes its root from an elephant (going left); in the interspaces between three of the circles are two pairs of *haṁsas* face to face (*cf.* 49*b*); at the top, the two stalks end in *padma* buds, and frame the couple of yakshas already met with on nos. 1*b* and 49*a* (*cf.* also nos. 66*c*, 71*a*, etc.), and grown hackneyed by so many repetitions.

66*b*. The inner (east) face repeats again, in the same setting, the third Great Miracle, the First Sermon (*cf.* nos. 3*a*, 5*a*, 44*b*), with variations too slight to be worth noticing. We need only observe that here the capital is composed entirely of elephants and that in the Lotus Tree at the base humped bulls have taken the place of the lions back to back.

66*c*. On the north face (the one facing no. 71*a*) is another Great Miracle—the Enlightenment—but treated in a manner even more archaic than on no. 5*b*. The stereotyped couple under the *aśvattha* of Śākya-muni encircled by its railing, has replaced the much more interesting and topical representation of the *vajra-āsana* or diamond throne.—The lower panel shows three pairs of *haṁsas* placed one above another, and below, without any apparent connection, an Indian, turbaned and switch in hand, riding a two-humped camel and going left. For the camel's bridle, *cf.* Pl. 47, 5.

West-North Sector

Pillars 67 to 88 form the fourth and last sector of the balustrade. In addition to no. 66, which we have just seen, the West entrance is flanked at the three other corners by nos. 67, 69 and 71; it is surprising to find that, of these three, only no. 71 has received special decoration. This suggests the query, whether all the pillars of the balustrade were originally made to the same pattern? And if so, whether pillars nos. 1, 3, 5 of the North entrance, 23 of the East entrance, 44 and 49 of the South entrance, and 66 and 71 of the West entrance were subsequent refacimentos, as pillars no. 22 and 27 undoubtedly were, only of earlier date than in the two latter cases?

67. Not only is this corner pillar of the ordinary, normal type, but it shows great decorative simplicity. It may be noted at once that the petals turned in on the hearts of the lotuses in 67*b*, 68*a* and 70*a* are found also at Bharhut (Cunn., Pl. 35, 7).

67*a*. Half-rosace.—Rosace.—Half-rosace.

67*b*. Bunch of *padmas* with two *utpalas* issuing from a fan-shaped leaf.—Rosace with in-turned petals.—Half-rosace.

68*a*. Half-rosace.—Rosace with in-turned petals, and with *utpalas* intercalated between the outer row of petals (*cf.* no. 53*a*).—Half-rosace.

68*b*. Bunch of *padmas* issuing from a vase.—Lotus rosace with four *triratnas*, lotus buds and flowerets around (*cf.* no. 31*b*).—Half-rosace.

69. Corner pillar, but its two exterior faces present only the usual decorative formula—a medallion between two half-medallions, all filled with familiar ornamental motifs.

69*a*. West face: palmette with two *padmas* and two *utpalas* coming out of a half-*śrīvatsa*.—Central rosace quartered with four brackets each supporting a flower and leaf of *padma* (*cf.* nos. 2*b* and 19*a*).—Half-rosace.

69*b*. North face: framed rosace (*cf.* no. 10*b*, etc.).—Rosace surrounded by four smaller rosaces and four *padma* leaves (*cf.* nos. 23*c*, 39*b*, 64*b*, etc.).—Half-rosace.

70*a*. Bunch of *padmas* springing from the mouth of a tortoise.—Rosace with in-turned petals (*cf.* no. 67*b*).—Half-rosace.

70*b*. Framed rosace (*cf.* no. 10*b*, etc.).—Small elephant passant to the left among radiating *padmas* and *utpalas* and holding a big *padma* stalk in his trunk.—Half-rosace.

71. The special decoration on the two faces of this corner pillar is very similar to that on nos. 1, 3 and 49.

71*a*. To match the Great Miracle of the Enlightenment on no. 66*c*, the south face has the Nativity treated as on nos. 1*b* and 49*a*. This time, not only Māyā (*cf.* no. 49*a*) but the two genii also (the woman has gone over to the right) are standing on lotus pedestals. We may notice that one of the two *padmas* which were set above the two elephants on no. 49*a*, has here been replaced by an umbrella, still more explicit sign of the invisible presence of the Bodhisattva.—The base of the panel, as on no. 3*a*, is occupied by two palmettes set one above the other.

71*b*. The east face, fronting on to the circular path, takes up again the Lotus Tree motif, as it is found on nos. 66*a*, 49*b* and 3*a*, but this time the double twining creeper is coming out of the jaws of a *makara* (*cf.* no. 88*a* and Pl. 50c); the angles are filled alternately with lions back to back and *haṁsas* face to face.

67 a OUTER FACE

67 b INNER FACE

68 a OUTER FACE

68 b INNER FACE

69 a WEST FACE

69 b NORTH FACE

70 a OUTER FACE

70 b INNER FACE

71 a SOUTH FACE

71 b EAST FACE

RELIEFS ON GROUND BALUSTRADE

72 a

72 b

73 a

73 b

74 a

74 b

75 a

75 b

76 b

RELIEFS ON GROUND BALUSTRADE

PLATE 88

STŪPA 2: RELIEFS ON GROUND BALUSTRADE—continued

72*a*. Bunch of *padmas* with central *utpala* coming out of a half-*śrīvatsa*.—Lotus rosace with four *triratnas* (*cf.* no. 31*b*), encircled by chaplet border; the two double volutes at the central point of each tricuspid probably represent a *śrīvatsa* simplified to the utmost on account of the want of room, and seem to show some effort to add the third *ratna* to the other two.—Half-rosace.

72*b*. Wingless griffin couchant, to right, between *padma* buds.—On a rosace background, an elephant seen from the front, his hindquarters bulging beyond the forequarters, and showing us at one time both eyes, both ears, both tusks, all four feet, the trunk and the tail: the effect is even more comical than in the lion of no. 74*a*, etc. The turbaned figure seated on the elephant's neck, with *aṅkuśa* in front of his right shoulder, is framed between two rosaces.—Half-rosace.

73*a*. Framed rosace (*cf.* no. 10*b*, etc.).—Double rosace divided by beaded circle.—Two cranes face to face and beaks to the ground.

73*b*. Two birds face to face are holding in their beaks a garland framing a *padma* with two *utpalas* hanging from it; a third bird's head, facing front, is holding two *padma* buds.—A Yaksha of thickset type running to the right and holding in each hand a stem blossoming into a bunch of *padmas*.—Half-rosace.

74*a*. Seated lion facing front between lotuses, his hindquarters showing beyond the forequarters (*cf.* nos. 9*a*, 63*a* and 75*a*).—Bunch of *padmas* coming out of a vase.—Half-rosace.

74*b*. Squatting Yaksha front-face, legs bent in the Indian fashion and heels together; in each hand he holds a mango-bough laden with fruit.—Harnessed horse without rider moving to right; in front of him a groom, bearing a garlanded umbrella and *caurī*; above, a winged genie holding a garland; below, a ewer; rain of flowers and garlands; the purpose of all these accumulated emblems is to depict the "Great Departure from the House" (*cf.* p. 186).—Half-rosace.

75*a*. Female figure with arms and legs in the form of leaves, from which issue the intertwined stems of *utpala* and *padma*; this odd little quasi-Hellenistic figure would be worthy of separate study.—Winged lion seen front-face as on nos. 9*a*, 63*a* and 74*a* (here the sculptor has not even omitted the tail!), between *padma* buds and *utpalas*.—Half-rosace.

75*b*. *Śrīvatsa* between *padmas* and *utpalas*.—On a rosace background, elephant going left, ridden by the usual master and servant. The sculptor has taken care to show both the bells hanging from the elephant's neck (*cf.* Pls. 42 and 44).—Half-rosace.

76*a*. Bunch of *padmas* and *utpalas* coming out of a fan-shaped leaf.—On a rosace background, an elephant moving right, but this time with only one rider (*cf.* no. 80*b*).—Half-rosace.

76*b*. Half-rosace.—Representation (*cf.* no. 85*a*) of the Great Miracle of the Nativity treated (allowing for the difference in the frame) as in nos. 49*a* and 71*a* (*cf.* p. 183).—Half-rosace.

PLATE 89

STŪPA 2: RELIEFS ON GROUND BALUSTRADE—continued

77a. Bunch of *padmas* and *utpalas* coming out of a floweret.—The Lotus Tree of Life abbreviated into a circular medallion with two winged lions back to back (*cf.* no. *79b* and Cunn., *Bharhut*, Pl. 37, 3; and see pp. 142 *sqq*.).—Half-rosace.

77b. The Lotus Tree of Life abbreviated into half circle with two *haṁsas* face to face (*cf.* no. *73b*).—Elephant going left and trampling on two fishes, the first and larger of which has a *padma* garland coming out of its mouth.—Half-rosace.

78a. Framed rosace (*cf.* no. 10*b*, etc.).—Rosace.—Half-rosace.

78b. Same motif as on no. *78a*.—Bunch of *padmas* issuing from fan-shaped leaf.—Half-rosace.

79a. Bunch of *padmas* issuing from fan-shaped leaf.—Rosac encircled by a necklace border.—Palmette of *padmas*.

79b. Swags and garlands, with pendent lotus buds and flowers, suspended over the necks of three birds, one seen front-face (*cf.* nos. *73b*, *77b*, *80b*); each of the two lateral birds holds a *padma* blossom in its beak.—Lotus Tree of Life with winged lions rampant back to back issuing from a fan-shaped leaf (*cf.* no. *77a*).—*Makara* and *padma*.

80a. Framed rosace (*cf.* no. 10*b*, etc.).—Rosace encircled by garland (*cf.* no. 4*b*, etc.).—Half-rosace.

80b. Same motif as on no. *79b*: but (as in no. *73b*) a plain garland replaces the swag and there is a *padma* instead of the central *utpala*.—Elephant going right with a single rider (*cf.* no. *76a*) and holding in his trunk a lotus stalk which issues from the mouth of a small fish under the animal's right forefoot; behind him, a formalised tree covered with flowers; in field, two flowerets.—Half-rosace.

81a. Bunch of *padmas* and *utpalas* issuing from half-rosace.—Bunch of *padmas* issuing from fan-shaped leaf; above, coiled serpent with five heads (*cf.* no. *32a*), darting out five forked tongues. On each side a small genie, holding a garland in both hands.—Half-rosace.

81b. Bunch of *padmas* and *utpalas*.—She-centaur ridden by a man (*cf.* no. *7b*); For the stirrup-rope (?) over the man's knee, *cf.* no. *40b*. The she-centaur holds a garland in her right hand and the handle of a round mirror in her left; in field, flowerets.—Half-rosace.

77 a

77 b

78 a

78 b

79 a

79 b

80 a

80 b

81 a

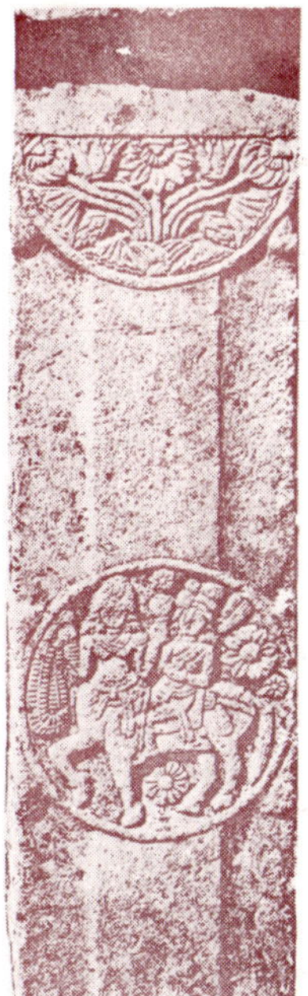
81 b

RELIEFS ON GROUND BALUSTRADE

82 a

82 b

83 a

83 b

84 a

84 b

85 a

85 b

86 a

86 b

RELIEFS ON GROUND BALUSTRADE

PLATE 90

STŪPA 2: RELIEFS ON GROUND BALUSTRADE—continued

82*a*. Bunch of *padmas* issuing from a half-*śrīvatsa*, with central *utpala*.—Framed in *padmas*, a man-faced horse (?) is carrying on his back a rider with a broad Indian sword raised in his right hand. For the stirrup-rope (?), *cf.* nos. 40*b*, 81*b*, 84*b*.

82*b*. Here, as in nos. 13*b* and 25*b*, the middle band is ornamented, in this case with the familiar Yaksha and Yakshī, as in no. 25*b*. The fact that they have *padmas* as pedestals throws no further light on their identity.—At top, bunch of *padmas* and *utpalas* coming out of a fan-shaped leaf.—Lotus rosace (*cf.* no. 31*b*) encircled by four *triratnas*; flowerets and bead-and-reel border. On each of the central points of the *triratnas* is a small *śrīvatsa* symbol. (*Cf.* no. 72*a*.)—Half-rosace.

83*a*. Bunch of *padmas* and *utpalas* springing from a vase.—Same as on no. 82*b*; but here, as in no. 72*a*, the *śrīvatsa* is simply indicated by two double volutes.—Bunch of *padmas* and *utpalas* coming out of a vase.

83*b*. Half-rosace encircled by a lotus creeper enriched with two *śrīvatsas* and two *haṁsas*.—Bunch of *padmas* springing from a vase, with a *haṁsa* on the left and a cock (?) on the right.—Half-rosace framed, as above, with two *śrīvatsas* and two indeterminate birds on a lotus background.

84*a*. Flying to left and carrying a garland in both hands, a winged being with human torso and bird's wings, feet and tail, such as recur so often at the tops of religious pictures, on either side of stūpas or sacred trees; in field, floweret.—Pair of cranes with *utpala* and *padma* bud.—Half-rosace.

84*b*. Fantastic animal (stag with elephant's head); in field, flowerets.—On a rosace background, a horse passant to the left with rider holding the reins in his left hand and raising a switch in his right. For stirrup-rope (?), *cf.* nos. 40*b*, 81*b*, 82*a*.—Palmette of *padmas* and *utpalas*.

85*a*. Bunch of *padmas* issuing from leaf.—Man or genie turbaned, raising his right arm and looking upwards. In field, *padmas* and *utpalas*. (*Cf.* no. 14*a*?.)—Half-rosace.

85*b*. Flying elephant, to left, holding *padma* stalks in his trunk and representing the Miracle of the Conception (*cf.* no. 6*a* and p. 182).—Great Miracle of the Nativity (*cf.* no. 76*b*); here, as in no. 1*b*, the lotus under Māyā's feet has been left out.—Half-rosace.

86*a*. Two boars (?) sniffing each other (*cf.* Pl. 29, 3*a*); in field, floweret.—Elephant with rider coming out of tiled building. Notice the triangular opening in roof to increase the height and allow the rider to pass through.—Two *haṁsas* face to face, remarkably well-drawn.

86*b*. Half-rosace.—The horse-headed fairy (*cf.* p. 181) is coming back from picking mangoes with the Bodhisattva, her son, whom she carries Indian-fashion on her hip; in field, *padma* buds.—*Makara* swallowing a fish; above in field, another fish (*cf.* no. 34*a*).

STŪPA 2: RELIEFS ON GROUND BALUSTRADE—concluded

87*a*. Abbreviated Lotus Tree of Life, with lions back to back, springing from half-*śrīvatsa*.—Rosace encircled by a garland and a ring of half overlapping rosaces (*cf.* no. 33*a*).—Palmette with ***utpalas*** coming out of a half-rosace.

87*b*. Framed rosace (*cf.* no. 10*b*, etc.).—Rosace and four *triratnas* of the same pattern as on no. 35*a* (*cf.* no. 31*b*, etc.).—Half-rosace.

88. This pillar, like nos. 1, 3 and 5, forms a corner of the North entrance. Its three sides (edged with dog-tooth border) are decorated in similar fashion, though without any Great Miracle.

88*a*. The outer (north) face repeats in more sophisticated style the theme of the double Lotus Tree already found at the south and west entrances (*cf.* nos. 3*b*, 49*b*, 66*a*, 71*b*). Here, the stem is issuing from the jaws of a *makara* with elephant's head (*cf.* no. 25*a*). Observe that the circle in the middle encloses a Yaksha similar to the one on no. 9*a*, but squatting on his elephant-feet (*sic*); the whole is surmounted by a *śrīvatsa*. The angles contain in turn a bird (cock?), two lions, two necklaces, two more lions, two *utpalas* and two *padma* buds. For the design, *cf.* pp. 98-99.

88*b*. The inner (south) face—a sign of a new era—is divided into four rectangular panels by strips relieved with necklace patterns. At the top, under hanging garlands, we again find the two genii of no. 1*b*, the woman holding the man's right wrist in her left hand.—Underneath, the same couple appears again. The woman is holding in her right hand a scaly fruit sheathed with leaves, which may be a custard-apple (*annona squamosa*; *cf.* Cunn., *Bharhut*, Pl. 47, 2), and with her left is raising a drinking cup which she has probably filled from the jar at their feet. The man with his left hand is holding the handle of his sword (hanging on a strap going over his right shoulder), while his other is lowered above the jar, as if he were waiting for an opportunity to take a drink. As on no. 1*c*, the figures have under their feet a sort of cushion carved out of the stone. At top, in field, two flowerets, and between the heads of the couple what appears to be a tambourine suspended from a bracket. In the third compartment, a curly-headed man, wearing a Phrygian cap and an embroidered sleeveless tunic, a kind of kilt, and big boots, is defending himself with an ornamented shield and striking at a rearing lion with a short triangular dagger—a clumsy but manifest copy of one of the favourite themes of Persepolis. Three garlands hanging from hooks, three flowerets and a *padma* bud fill up the field.—In bottom compartment, abbreviated Lotus Tree of Life.

88*c*. The east face (opposite no. 5*a*) is divided into three panels only. The top one is partly obliterated. Perhaps the ***makara*** with the elephant's head carried a Yakshī like the one at Bharhut (*cf.* Cunn., Pl. 23, 2).—Below, Lotus Tree issuing from leaf.—In bottom panel, Lotus Tree, with birds bearing garlands at top (*cf.* nos. 73*b*, 79*b*, 80*b*), a Nāgī with three hoods in middle, and two Indian bullocks (*cf.* no. 66*b*) rampant and back to back at bottom.

With pillar 88 we come to the end of our examination of the Ground Balustrade of Stūpa 2 (*cf.* Pl. 72*a*). Sir John Marshall's excavations have recovered fragments of the terrace and pinnacle balustrades.

a-*b*. Fragments *a* and *b* belong to the coping of the ***harmikā***-balustrade (*cf.* Pl. 72*d*): the rosace pattern is framed, in the one, by a twining stem, and in the other by ***utpalas*** (*cf.* no. 2*a*).

Fragments *c* to *i* are remains of the berm balustrade (*cf.* Pl. 72*c*):

c. Lotus Tree with twining stem (*cf.* nos. 23*a* and 44*a*):

d. Lotus Tree (?) of indistinct design (*cf.* nos. 32*b*, 42*b*, etc.);

e. Creeper of vine leaves and grapes (*cf.* no. 44*a*), which a parrot at the top is rifling;

f. Lotus Tree with winding stem; above, a sea-bull ridden by a small Cupid-like genie beneath a row of bells.

g. Great Miracle of the First Sermon. The wheel, with 16 spokes, is set between two garlands hanging from brackets; below it, the seat of a throne, supported on the raised right hands of three little atlantes (*cf.* nos. 1*c* and 5*b*), who carry bags in their other hands (*cf.* Pl. 22, 4); at bottom, a fig-tree.

h. Again the third Great Miracle: the wheel, with 12 spokes crowns the top of an Indo-Persian column (*cf.* nos. 3*a*, 5*a* and 66*b*) at the top, a row of bells. Observe the tendrils of the Lotus Tree on either side, and the abacus in the form of a railing.

i. At top, the Great Miracle of the Nativity (*cf.* p. 183): notic the stiff posture of Māyā and the clumsy arrangement of he feet. Below, Lotus Tree with *haṁsas*.

Fragment *j* is a specimen of the pillars from the Stairwa balustrade (*cf.* Pl. 72*b*): it illustrates what we must come to conside as the normal ancient decoration (*cf.* pp. 171-2), namely a medallio between two half-medallions containing respectively a rosace and tw half-rosaces of the *padma*.

87 a

87 b

88 a

88 b

88 c

RELIEFS ON GROUND BALUSTRADE

a

b

a. b. COPING OF HARMIKA BALUSTRADE

c

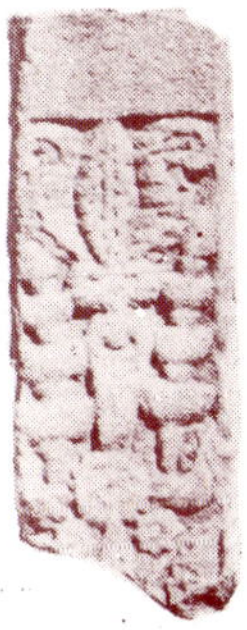
d

e

f

g

h

i

j

c.-i. RELIEFS ON BERM BALUSTRADE. — j SPECIMEN OF STAIRWAY BALUSTRADE

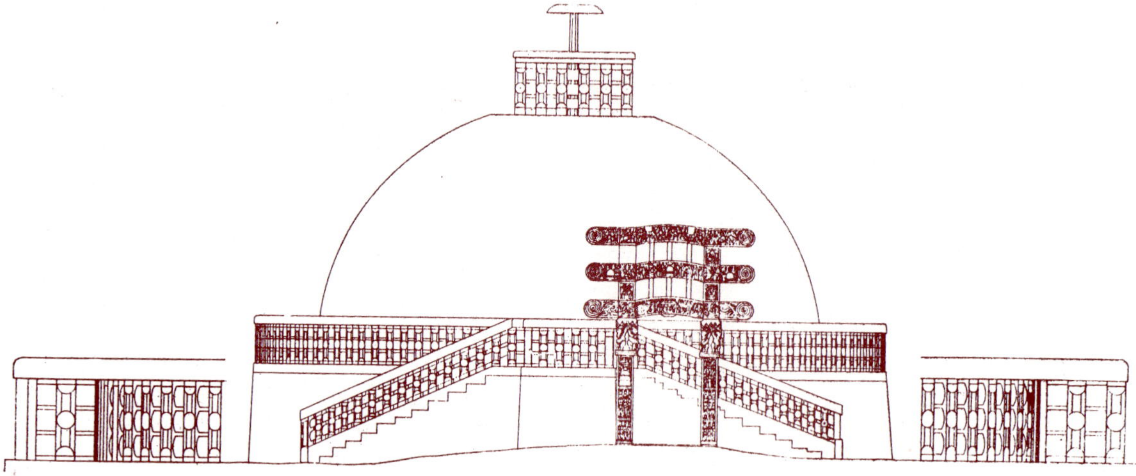

(a) ÉLÉVATION.

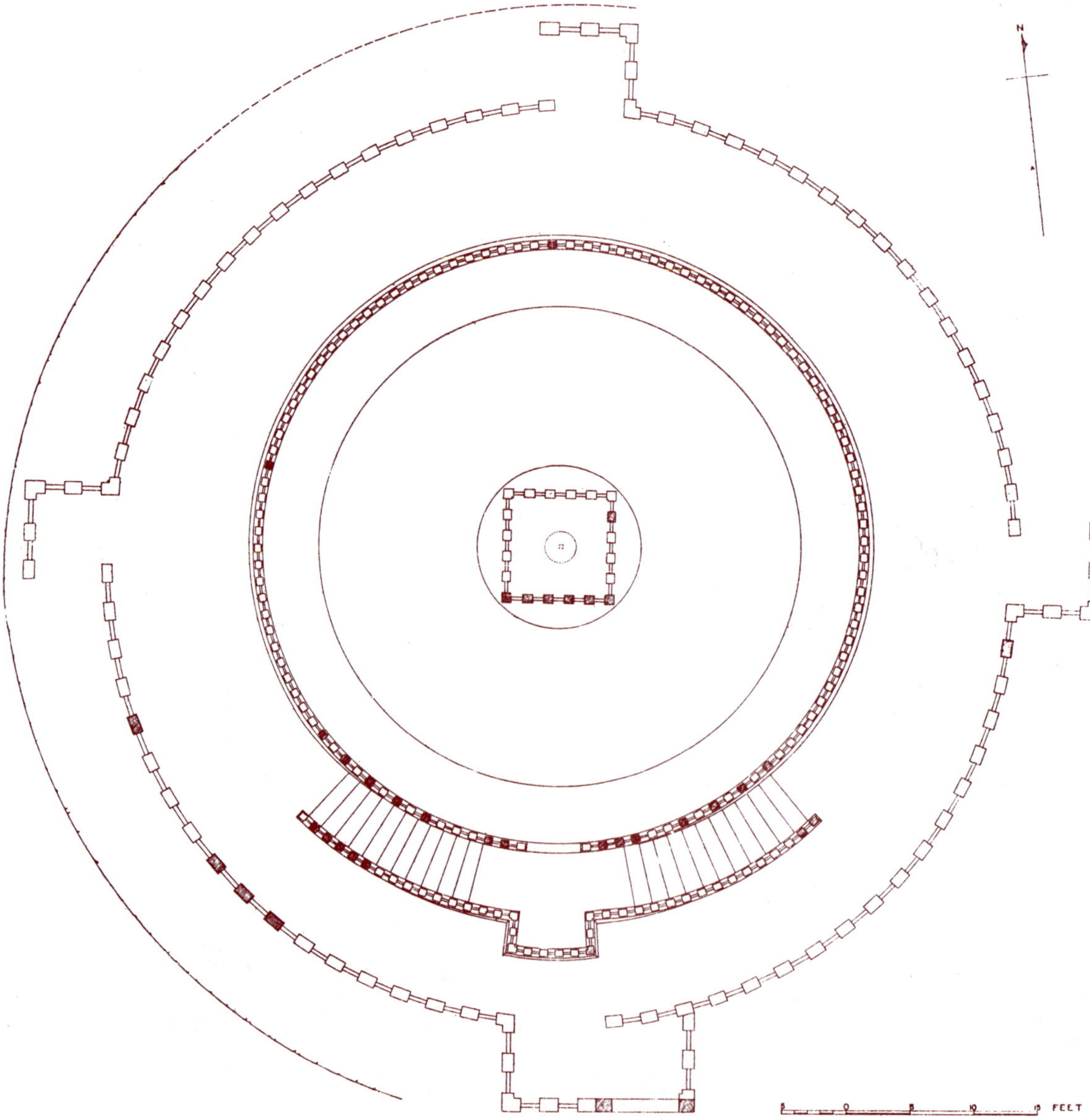

(b) PLAN.

PLATE 92

a-b. ELEVATION AND PLAN OF STŪPA 3

The form, construction and history of this monument are discussed on pp. 41 and 42. As regards the shape of the dome, see the remarks made on Stūpa 2 (Pl. 71). The few balustrade pillars that have survived are distinguished, as usual, by darker shading. Altogether they number no more than 35, *viz.*, 5 of the ground balustrade, 7 on the stairway, 16 on the berm, and 7 on the summit.

At this Stūpa there was only one carved toraṇa, which stood in front of the south entrance. From the style of its carvings it appears to have been erected somewhat later than the toraṇas of Stūpa 2, *i.e.*, in the closing years of the last century B.C. To about the same period also belongs the ground balustrade of this Stūpa. The body of the building, on the other hand, and the smaller balustrades are referable to about the middle of the 2nd century B.C. (p. 43).

PLATE 93

STŪPA 3

a. View of Stūpa 3 from South.—In this illustration, Stūpa 3 is shown as restored by Sir John Marshall out of the heap of ruins seen in the background of Pl. 95. For the state of the monument in 1851, when it was opened by Cunningham and Maisey, *cf.* Cunningham, *The Bhilsa Topes*, Pl. XXII.

To the right of the picture, in the distance, may be seen the remains of Stūpa 4, which was past rebuilding; to the left, the only surviving fragment of the ground balustrade which was still *in situ*. The body of the stūpa is composed of heavy unwrought blocks of stone mixed with broken spalls and faced with ashlar; between it and the masonry of the raised terrace round the base there was no bond, the latter having been added, as the terraces of Stūpas 1 and 2 were also added, after the body of the structure was complete (p. 41 and n. 1). The relic-chamber, which was found intact by Cunningham, was on a level with the terrace berm (p. 44).

For the age of the stūpa, its balustrades and *toraṇa*, see Pl. 92.

b. The threshold of the *toraṇa* has been treated as a pillar of the ground balustrade, unless we prefer to say that one of these *stambhas* has been used for the threshold. The central medallion consisted of four *nandipadas* or taurines mounted on the same *cakra*, with lotuses around; each of the tricuspid ornaments held, it would seem, two *haṁsas*, one on each side of the central point.

c, d, e, f.—Pillars or fragments of pillars from the ground balustrade. Notice how the rosettes and half-rosettes of *padmas* have their pericarps encircled by an aureole of stamens and are framed in blue lotuses (*utpala*).

g and *i.* Corner pillars on the landing of the berm; hence the rectangular form of their panels. The decoration of *g* is divided into two parts. Below, a row of lotuses framed between two rows of rosettes (*cf.* Pls. 50*b* and 83, no. 44*c*) alternating with *utpalas*; above, an attempt at representing the third Great Miracle, for which it lacks only the essential—namely, the Wheel of the First Sermon. Above the rounded roof of an apsidal temple, between two high umbrellas and two garlands, rises the Indo-Persian column on which the *dharma-cakra* ought to have been shown; by a whim of the sculptor's, the capital is composed of two elephants and two lions (*cf.* Pl. 74, no. 5*a*). The temple appears to be of the same form as Temple 18 (pp. 52-55).—The decoration of *i* comprises: at the bottom, a Lotus Tree; in the middle, a *makara*-elephant spouting forth a lotus plant on which are two *haṁsas* face to face (*cf.* Pls. 37*b* and 50*c*); and, at the top, the fourth Great Miracle represented by a very archaic-looking stūpa, the top of which served as a model for the restoration of the monument which it decorated.

h. Specimen of the berm balustrade. With its *stambhas* uniformly decorated with the lotus, and its *sūci* bare, this balustrade goes back to the archaic pattern which we have presupposed (p. 171 and *cf.* Pl. 73).

a. VIEW FROM SOUTH

c

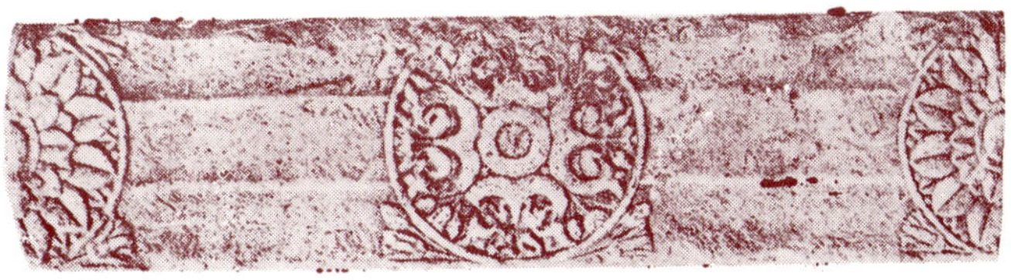

b. THRESHOLD OF GATEWAY

d

e

f

g

h

i

e-i DETAILS OF BALUSTRADES

(a) HARMIKA BALUSTRADE.

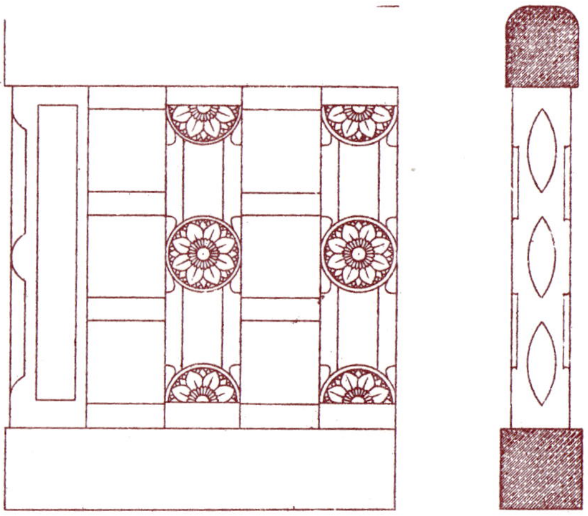

(b) BERM BALUSTRADE.

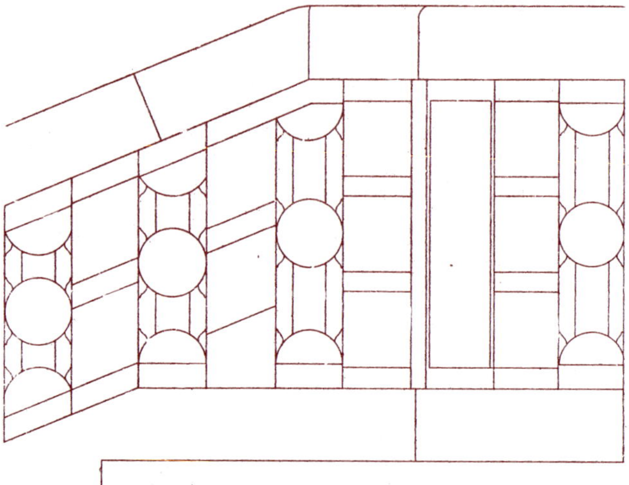

(c) STAIRWAY BALUSTRADE

(d) GROUND BALUSTRADE

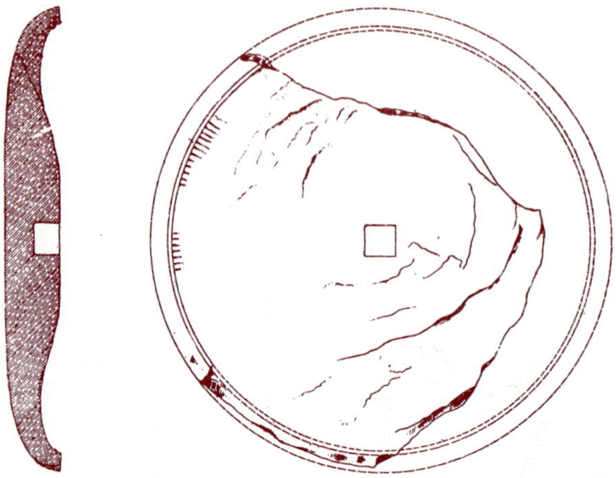

(e) UMBRELLA

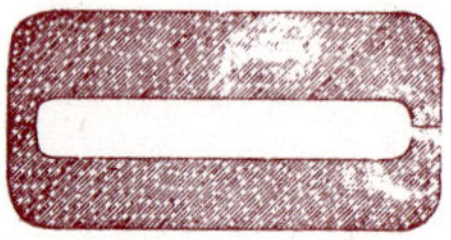

(f) RELIC BOX.

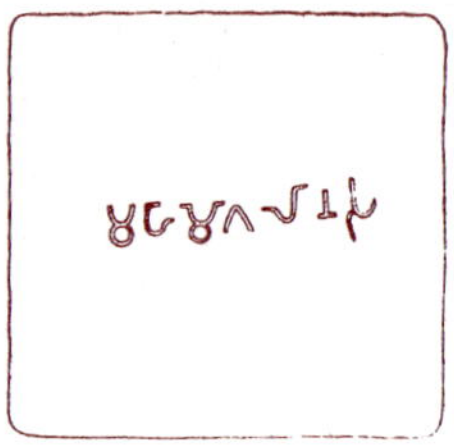

PLATE 94

a-e. The balustrades and umbrella of Stūpa 3 are discussed on pp. 41-43. Here, we need only remark that the decoration of the pillars of the harmikā balustrade is unusual. In the case of Stūpas 1 and 2 (Pls. 7*d* and 72*d*), they are severely plain, only the coping in the latter one being enriched, as here, with a band of lotus rosettes.

The stairway and berm balustrades closely resemble those of Stūpas 1 and 2, but apart from the pillar illustrated in Pl. 93*g* and *i* which was a subsequent addition, their carvings appear to have consisted of lotus medallions only.

As regards the relic-box shown in Fig. *f*, see p. 44 and n. 1. The two caskets found in this stūpa (p. 44) are illustrated in Cunningham, *The Bhilsa Topes*, Pl. XXII.

PLATE 95

STŪPA 3: FRONT FACE OF GATEWAY

The principal point, which comparison with the four *toraṇas* of Stūpa 1 places beyond a doubt, is that, in the course of restoration in the last century, the upper lintel was set up back to front. Originally the facade, according to the invariable rule, presented the symbols of the seven Mānushi-Buddhas, here distributed over two lintels, *viz.*, two *bodhi-drumas* on the top lintel (*cf.* Pls. 99 and 101, 1) and two *bodhi-drumas plus* three *Parinirvāṇa* stūpas on the middle lintel. The bottom lintel showed Indra's paradise. Notice how the serpentine coils of the two *Nāga-rājas* sitting on the extremities of the middle section are supposed to continue through to the end-volutes, which, for once, are joined to the rest of the decoration.

In the same connection we may notice that the design of the bottom false-capitals is the only one of its kind. Instead of two animals back to back, with or without riders, it presents a single personage grappling with a *makara*, whose coils are intertwined with those of the Nāga-serpents.

The dies are as usual devoted to the Great Miracles, and we see the first three here. One die, however, is missing; one of its two carved faces seems to have gone to the Berlin Museum für Völkerkunde with the Leitner Collection (No. I. C. 34. 681; *cf.* E. Waldschmidt, *Grunwedels Buddhistische Kunst in Indien*, Part I, 1932, p. 119 and fig. 61); it represents the last Great Miracle.

On the capitals the same dwarf-atlantes reappear as on the Western Gateway of Stūpa 1.

The poor ornamentation of the jambs (*cf.* pp. 147-8 and 237) contains only gods in tiers below symbolical representations of the third and fourth Great Miracles.

For the decoration of the threshold, see Pl. 93*b*.

On the left of the Gateway are seen fragments belonging to the stairway and terrace balustrades of Stūpa 3. Before its restoration (*cf.* Pl. 93*a*) this stūpa was nothing but the heap of loose stones which fills the back of this picture (pp. 41-43).

FRONT OF GATEWAY: MIDDLE SECTION OF ARCHITRAVES

PLATE 96

STŪPA 3: FRONT OF GATEWAY, MIDDLE SECTION

1. (*Back of*,) *Top Lintel*.—The resemblance between this lotus creeper with its sprites and that on the bottom lintel of the Southern Gateway is most striking: but here there are no jewels, and the *kumbhāṇḍas* (as we have decided to call these grotesque *putti*) have no flowers coming out of their mouths as on Pls. 11, 3 and 100, 3; they are merely waving bunches of lotuses in each hand. The one on the left, less deformed than the others, is the familiar type of 'jungle-dweller' with a brush-shaped topknot; the other three heads extant even go one better for ugliness than the atlantes on the capitals, and try to look like the demons in Māra's army (*cf.* Pls. 29, 2 and 61, 3). For the Lotus Tree motif, *cf.* pp. 144-146.

2. *Middle Lintel*.—The *Parinirvāṇa* stūpa and the two *Sambodhi* trees which flank it, are part of a series of seven Mānushi-Buddhas, to be completed by the two trees on Pl. 100, 1, and the two tumuli on Pls. 97, 2 and 98, 2; altogether, this gives us once more 4 trees + 3 stūpas = 7 symbols of Buddhas. But here the difficulties begin. The old-fashioned artist of the top lintel (Pl. 100, 1), like the one who made the Eastern Gateway (Pl. 40, 1), has rightly given the place of honour to the bignonia of Vipaśyin and the *ficus religiosa* of Sākya-muni, that is, to the first and last Buddhas of the series; but he seems not to have consulted with his fellow-sculptor, the more up-to-date author of the middle lintel, since the latter has again brought out the bignonia of Vipaśyin on the right! Worse still: either the tradition was changing, or else the sculptor scorns it; for the second tree, on the left, is like none of those which, either at Bharhut or on the gateways of Stūpa 1, are devoted to the seven Mānushi-Buddhas; it is depicted as a mango-tree, and this unexpected treatment is deliberate, since it is repeated on Pl. 103*d* (*cf.* Pl. 16, 5). Moreover, the wider spacing of the seven symbols, thus distributed over two lintels, has automatically increased the number of their worshippers. We would draw special attention (*a*) to the palm-leaf fan brandished in the top left-hand corner by one of the female attendants, (*b*) to the two figures, one on either side of the central stūpa, holding in their hands a sort of cornucopia, with flowers coming out of the top—the first examples of their kind that have appeared among these reliefs; (*c*) to the worshipper on the left of the right-hand tree, who is bending down to take some garlands out of a basket.

3. *Bottom Lintel*.—For the general description, see pp. 229-30. Indra has his thunderbolt in his right hand (*cf.* Pl. 49) and the male figure on the right (in spite of the feminine breasts which an accidental light seems to give him) is his harpist, Pañcaśikha (*cf.* Pl. 35*b*1). On either side of the Vaijayanta palace are rocks studded with trees, hollowed with caves and haunted by lions, peacocks and genii; this landscape represents the Nandana-vana on the slopes of Mount Meru. For the horse-headed fairy on the left, who seems to be detaining a man by force, see Pl. 90, no. 86*b* and pp. 174, 181, 223, n. 1, 229; above this group is a 'jungle-dweller' armed with bow and quiver. On the right of the lintel we are left to guess at the presence of Hāritī and Pāñcika, seated not far from one another (*cf.* p. 245 and Pl. 103*e*). Notice the careful symmetry with which the attitudes of the two Nāga-rājas (left or right leg bent) and the arrangement of their two attendants (queen sitting and female servant standing) are reversed. In the waving waters of the river Mandākinī (or the lake Anavatapta?) are fishes, conches, a tortoise and a *makara*.

PLATE 97

STŪPA 3: FRONT OF GATEWAY, WEST END

1. *(Back of) Top Lintel.*—Though the decoration of the middle part of the lintel does not, properly speaking, continue on the projecting end, we have again a grotesque sprite (*kumbhāṇḍa*) running from left to right and waving in each hand a bundle of lotus creepers bearing leaves, flowers and buds (*cf.* Pl. 88, no. 73*b*).

2. *Middle Lintel.*—*Parinirvāṇa*-stūpa of the usual pattern and belonging to the series of the Seven Mānushi-Buddhas (*cf.* Pl. 96, 2).

3. *Bottom Lintel.*—The serpentine coils of the Nāga-rāja, extending beyond the false-capital, are partly submerged in the waters of the river Mandākinī before they end up in the volute which terminates the lintel. In the waters are swimming two otters (?), a tortoise, *makara* and fish (middle), two *haṁsas* and a water-sprite (top).

4. *Bottom Die.*—Only one die remains; it represents the miracle of the First Sermon between two couples of worshippers (*cf.* Pl. 103*b*). The Wheel of the Law (with 24 spokes) is sustained above the throne by the *triratna* device.

5. *Top False-Capital.*—Here we find again the two Indian humped bulls ridden by two Indian noblemen with flowers in their hands—the same that we have already seen on Pls. 16-17, 25, 27 43.

6. *Middle False-Capital.*—We recognize also the two couc horses back to back of Pls. 12-13, 31, 33; but the two riders' heads and tunics make it clear that they are foreigners, and horses, instead of having plain rugs on their backs, are provided proper saddles, held in place front and back by straps, but (?) wit a girth; this is a new feature.

7. *Bottom False-Capital.*—A wrestler clad in a close-fitting t of thick material, with high boots, and wearing round his he fillet with flying ends (*cf.* the Mallas on Pl. 36*b*1) is twisting head of a *makara* and forcibly opening its jaws with both ha while he holds down its body under his right knee. The monst putting out its tongue and its scaly coils are intertwined with smooth serpentine body of the adjacent Nāga-rāja. This mot not found elsewhere at Sāñchī, but we need not seek further Mathurā for parallels (*cf. Art Gréco-bouddhique du Gandhāra*, 94*a* or J. Ph. Vogel, *La Sculpture de Mathurā* (Ars Asiatica, Pl. X*b*).

8. *Capital.*—See Pls. 99; 101, 9; 102, 6.

FRONT OF GATEWAY: WEST END OF AR[illegible] AND CAPITAL

FRONT OF GATEWAY : EAST END OF ARCHITRAVES

PLATE 98

STŪPA 3: FRONT OF GATEWAY, EAST END

1. *(Back of) Top Lintel.*—Same subject as on the west end (Pl. 97, 1); but here, for symmetry, the *kumbhāṇḍa* is going left.

2. *Middle Lintel.*—Stock stūpa (*cf.* Pl. 96, 2), almost exact copy of its fellow on the west side (Pl. 97, 2), but the male and female worshippers have changed places for symmetry.

3. *Bottom Lintel.*—The decorative elements (otters excepted) and their general arrangement are the same as on the other end of the lintel (Pl. 97, 3).

4. *Top Die.*—Intermediate version of the first Great Miracle: the Nativity, with Māyā seated between the two Nāga-elephants (*cf.* pp. 183, 197).

5. *Bottom Die.*—Stock illustration of the second Great Miracle, the *Sambodhi*, utilising once more the *pāṭali* or bignonia of Vipaśyin, a theme much favoured by our sculptors. Notice how carefully the garlands are rolled up on the wicker trays held by the winged genii.

6. *Top False-Capital.*—Same description as for its fellow on the west side (Pl. 97, 5). We may notice once more, since this is the last time we are to see these Indian bulls, the big rosettes under their ears, which served to fasten their collars (*cf.* Pl. 16, 6).

7. *Middle False-Capital.*—We here find again the two couchant horses back to back of Pl. 97, 6; but this time the riders are Indians, and consequently the horses have no saddles.

8. *Bottom False-Capital.*—Same theme as on Pl. 97, 7; but the same care for symmetry, which we have come across several times already, is responsible for reversing the attitudes of the *makara* and the wrestler.

PLATE 99

STŪPA 3: BACK OF GATEWAY

As we have already indicated on Pl. 95, the top lintel was evidently reset back to front; the two *Sambodhi* trees which decorate the middle section (between two decorative motifs imitated from the Eastern Gateway, Pls. 41 and 43, 2) must have figured on the front and been connected with the five symbols on the middle lintel to make up the series of the seven Mānushi-Buddhas. It follows that in the original state of the gateway, the backs of the lintels were adorned only with decorative patterns—all, by the way, copied from the *toraṇas* of Stūpa 1, namely:

Top Lintel: we have already indicated the relation of the lotus creeper with its *kumbhāṇḍas*, at present on the facade (Pls. 95-96), to that on the Southern Gateway (Pl. 11, 3).

Middle Lintel: the lotus palmettes combined with animals and men are a horizontal transcription of the vertical motif on the jambs of the Northern Gateway (Pl. 37), for which see also Pt. II, pp. 142-47.

Bottom Lintel: the middle section is pure plagiarism from the Southern Gateway (Pl. 11, 3); the scenes on the two ends are taken from the Southern (Pl. 12, 2) and the Northern (Pl. 34*b*2) Gateways. We may wonder why the ornamental motif on the middle section does not extend over the whole length of this lintel, as on Pls. 95-98, 1, and what the two 'pictures of paradise' are doing on the projecting ends. Our opinion is that these two last pictures were at first provided to flank Indra's Paradise on the facade (*cf.* Pls. 95-96, 3); when, as an afterthought, the sculptor's fancy suggested linking the serpenting bodies of the Nāgas to the volutes on the ends, he was compelled to banish these paradisal scenes from the facade and to carry them over on to the back, where they are quite unexpected.

The *dies* (we have already remarked that one is gone) are devoted to the three Great Miracles of the Nativity, the First Sermon and Last Decease.

The *false-capitals* repeat in due order the winged lions of the Eastern (Pls. 41-44) and Western (Pls. 62-63) gateways; the elephants of the Southern (Pls. 16-17) and Western (Pls. 57-59) gateways; and the lions with riders of the Northern (Pls. 24, 26) and Eastern Gateways (Pls. 47-48).

Capitals.—The atlas-dwarfs are the exact reproduction of those on the Western Gateway (Pls. 57-59); only their expression is more passive, because the theme has become more stereotyped (*cf.* p. 141). We notice that they, too, are inserted between a balustrade and merlons.

The north face of the *West jamb* shows two Great Miracles, the Enlightenment in the middle, and the First Sermon of Sākya-muni at the top: the bottom panel is of particular iconographical interest (*cf.* Pl. 103*e*).

For the decoration of the threshold, see Pl. 93c.

In the background, we see the balustrade, the Eastern Gateway and part of the dome (before restoration) of Stūpa 1.

BACK OF GATEWAY (LOOKING NORTH)

BACK OF GATEWAY : MIDDLE SECTION OF ARCHITRAVES

PLATE 100

STŪPA 3: BACK OF GATEWAY, MIDDLE SECTION

1. *(Front of) Top Lintel.*—Thanks to the number of attendants lined up (there are no less than 16 of them in the foreground alone, and one notices how they are paraded in the style of Bharhut), two *bodhi-drumas* suffice to fill the whole length of the panel. On the left, we can identify at once the *pāṭali* or bignonia of Vipaśyin, the first of the seven Mānushi-Buddhas; on the right, in spite of its worn surface, we seem to be able to make out the *aśvattha* or *ficus religiosa* of Śākya-muni. We have already seen (Pls. 95-98) how the series of the seven Mānushi-Buddhas is completed on the facade of the middle lintel.

2. *Middle Lintel.*—As already stated (Pl. 99), the motif here is the same as on the jambs of the Northern Gateway (Pl. 37), but here the Lotus Tree is shown undulating across the lintel as on the Southern Gateway (Pls. 11, 3, and 19*a*), while in each of the embrasures formed by its undulations appear, alternately, pairs of Yakshas and lions or griffins rampant, starting up from the lotus flowers. The Yakshas carry drawn swords and trays of lotus buds or bucklers (*cf.* Pl. 37*b* and p. 145, note 2) as on the Northern Gateway. The lions and griffins (*cf.* Pl. 66*c*) are portrayed back to back with heads regardant.

3. *Bottom Lintel.*—Here the artist has cold-bloodedly copied the corresponding panel on the Southern Gateway (Pl. 11, 3) even to the details of the *kumbhāṇḍas*, full or half-length, with stalks of flowers coming out of their mouths and carrying heavy necklaces of pearls or jewels in their hands: only, instead of finishing his two stalks at the top of the lintel, he has stopped their spirals at the bottom, and in the extra embrasure thus left free he has put a seventh figure.

In the face of so much plagiarism we are forced to conclude that originality was now dead or rapidly dying in the workshops of Sāñchī—or rather, of the big neighbouring town of Vidiśā.

PLATE 101

STŪPA 3: BACK OF GATEWAY, EAST END

1. *(Front of) Top Lintel.*—This motif we have already seen on Pls. 41 and 43, 2: wild elephants feeding in the forest and indulging in their favourite game of tearing boughs off the trees. Here the old bull in the foreground is attacking a date-palm, behind which is a plantain.

2. *Middle Lintel.*—Repetition of one of the motifs in the middle section (*cf.* Pl. 100, 2). Nowhere can the objects in the left hands of the Yakshas (*cf.* Pl. 37*b*) be more distinctly seen.

3. *Bottom Lintel.*—Whether the scene takes place in an earthly or a celestial paradise (*cf.* p. 228-229), it represents *jala-krīḍā* or "aquatic sports". The hero of the day (*deva, yaksha* or king, as you please) is riding in the midst of his park (represented chiefly by a bignonia) through a lotus pond, astride the neck of an elephant. Behind him is seated a woman bearing his standard and hanging on by a rope attached to the girth, whilst one of his wives is dangling from the tail and another from the ear of the animal (*cf.* Pls. 12, 2; 34*b*, 2 and 79, no. 27*a*).

4. *Top Die.*—Stock illustration of the third Great Miracle—the First Sermon. This time the Wheel of the Law has only 20 spokes, but rests on the same device as before (Pl. 97, 4). It is set between two couples, both of the women carrying a tray or bouquet (?) and a ewer. Are these to be taken as donors or simply as a mechanical repetition of the usual worshippers and the hackneyed type of Sujātā?

5. *Bottom Die.*—Stock illustration of the fourth Great Miracle, the *Parinirvāṇa*. The same remark as on Pl. 98, 5, holds good for the trays of flowers borne by the winged genii.

6. *Top False-Capital.*—Well-known motif of the three winged lions, one of them with his head and forefeet in the embrasure formed by the backs of the other two (*cf.* Pls. 41-44 and 62-63).

7. *Middle False-Capital.*—Motif of kneeling elephants back to back, already seen on Pls. 16-17, 57 and 59. Here, women are holding the umbrellas for the royal drivers.

8. *Bottom False-Capital.*—Lions seated back to back, similar to those on Pls. 24, 26, 47, 48. Here, the riders are Indian noblemen.

9. *Capital.*—There is nothing specially noteworthy in the stereotyped attitude and costume of the atlas-dwarfs, except perhaps the spiral ear-ring belonging to the one on the right (*cf.* Pls. 57 and 59).

BACK OF GATEWAY: EAST END OF ARCHITRAVES AND CAPITAL

BACK OF GATEWAY WEST END OF ARCHITRAVES AND CAPITAL

PLATE 102

STŪPA 3: BACK OF GATEWAY, WEST END

1. (*Front of*) *Top Lintel.*—Same motif as on the east end (Pl. 101, 1), but the worn state of the stone makes it impossible to determine the species of the tree being maltreated by the elephants.

2. *Middle Lintel.*—Same motif as on the east end (Pl. 101, 2). Here, too, in defiance of symmetry, the sculptor, more faithful to matter-of-fact reality than the author of Pl. 37*b*, has kept the sword in the right hands of his figures.

3. *Bottom Lintel.*—Same motif as on the east end (Pl. 101, 3). Here, however, the elephant is plunged more deeply in the pond. The bearer of the standard (which is decorated with bands in the form of S. Andrew's cross) is holding out her left hand to one of the two queens who is climbing up the animal's hind-quarters, whilst the chief himself is helping the other to scramble up its trunk, by putting his right hand behind the nape of her neck. As usual, the elephant browses placidly on among the lotuses.

4. *Die.*—It has already been seen (Pl. 95) that the top die on this side is missing. The bottom die presents a comparatively ancient, though much formalised, form of the first Great Miracle—the Nativity (*cf.* pp. 183, 197); observe the lotuses which serve as a stool for Māyā's left foot and as pedestals for the two Nāga-elephants.

5. *False-capitals.*—The themes are naturally the same as on the east jamb: at the top, the three winged lions; in the middle, the two elephants (there was no room left to put the umbrella in the attendant's hands); at the bottom, the lions, whose riders, this time, are not noblemen but jungle-dwellers with fillets and brush-shaped topknots. The one on the right is brandishing what ought to be a switch but looks in reality like a lotus flower.

6. *Capital.*—Still the same lifelessness in the atlas-dwarfs. One can detect hardly any point of difference, except in the treatment of the ornaments.

PLATE 103

STŪPA 3: PILLARS OF GATEWAY

As we have already said (pp. 147-148 and 237), the iconographical interest of the scenes on the jambs of the Gateway of Stūpa 3 is of the slightest, with the single exception of the bottom panel on the north side of the west jamb (*e*) first identified by Mme. E. Bazin-Foucher in *J. A.* (8 June, 1933); but we must follow the order of our plate.

Apropos of the first four faces (*a, b, c, d*) one and the same question arises: what identity are we to ascribe to the rows of worshippers lined up, as if on parade, in the representations of the Great Miracles? The fact that in *a* those in the first row at the bottom are pressing hard to show that they are four, indicates, if we are not mistaken, that the sculptor had it in his mind to place again, one above another, the various categories of gods, beginning with the four Lokapālas on the bottom floor (*cf.* Pls. 34*a*, 49, 51*a*). But this excessive zeal apparently serves only to confuse matters: for the hypothesis which the analogy of Bharhut (Cunn., Pl. 13*a*) and our Pl. 51*a* make by far the most probable is this: the balustrade, which in *a* and *b* divides the representatives of the divine hierarchy into two distinct groups, is meant to separate the gods of the lower heavens, still slaves to desire (*Kāma-avacara*) from the gods of the Pure Abodes (*Suddhāvāsa*). In the bottom compartment, all six storeys of the *Kāma-dhātu* (*cf.* Pl. 49*a, b*) would have one representative and one only (except in *a* where, as we have just seen, the sculptor's fancy made them seven); for symmetry in the top compartment the gods of the upper heavens likewise appear six in number, both in *a* and in *b*. Finally in *c* and *d* the sculptor, obliged to reserve the space necessary for the *dvāra-pālas* or guardian genii of the gateway, has been able to put in only two rows of three gods. All these figures are standing in the same attitude and turned out to one type.

The two Yakshas in *c* and *d* reproduce in more constricted form those on the Eastern Gateway (Pls. 50*a* and 52*b*): but the one in *d* is also holding a spray of bignonia flowers on his hip (*cf.* Pl. 36*a*; and see, also, p. 148).

The remaining reliefs will not take long to describe.

a. Stock illustration of the fourth Great Miracle—the *Parinirvāṇa*; the two garland bearers are supposed to be standing on the terrace of the stūpa but appear as if they were walking on a level with the top of the balustrade of this terrace (*cf.* Pl. 74, no. 3*a*).

b. Stock illustration of the third Great Miracle—the First Sermon. The Wheel of the Law (here with 17 spokes) is perched on the lion-capital of an Indo-Persian column, obviously a poor reproduction of those of Aśoka at Sārnāth and at Sāñchī itself (*cf.* Pl. 107). The two worshipping couples (if, as it seems, they are human) are the king and queen on the right, and viceroy and his wife on the left, as on Pl. 97, 4.

c. Stock illustration of the second Great Miracle—the *Sambodhi*. Once more the *bodhi-druma* chosen is the bignonia of Vipaśyin. Notice the elegance of the praying couple.

d. Another stock illustration of the second Great Miracle; but for the second time on this Gateway (Pl. 96, 2) we are surprised to find a mango-tree promoted to the dignity of *bodhi-druma*, shading the throne between the usual worshippers. As on Pls. 16, 5 and 96, 2, the question arises whether this is the tree of the Buddha Sikhin.

e. This side, already seen on Pl. 99, again gives us two clichés of Great Miracles. At the top, the First Sermon (the wheel has 27 spokes; the column has no lion-capital, but garlands are hanging from brackets, as in Pl. 74, nos. 3*a* and 5*a*); the six worshippers (two of whom are women) are, as usual, characterless. Six deer, grouped in threes on each side of a plantain, stress the locale of the Mṛiga-vana. —In the middle, the *Sambodhi* is apparently symbolised by the *ficus religiosa* of Sākya-muni, though one would have expected a more tapering leaf. The six worshippers (a man, a woman, three daughters and a son?) suggest a family of donors.—The bottom panel shows Pāñcika and Hāritī at home (*cf.* p. 245).

f. This garland of pink lotus rosettes framed in blue lotuses seen in profile, is copied directly from those on the Southern, Northern and Eastern Gateways (Pls. 19*e*, 23*b*, 50*b*, respectively).

a. WEST PILLAR
SOUTH FACE

b. EAST PILLAR
SOUTH FACE

c. WEST PILLAR
EAST FACE

d. EAST PILLAR
WEST FACE

e. WEST PILLAR
NORTH FACE

f. EAST PILLAR
EAST FACE

GATEWAY

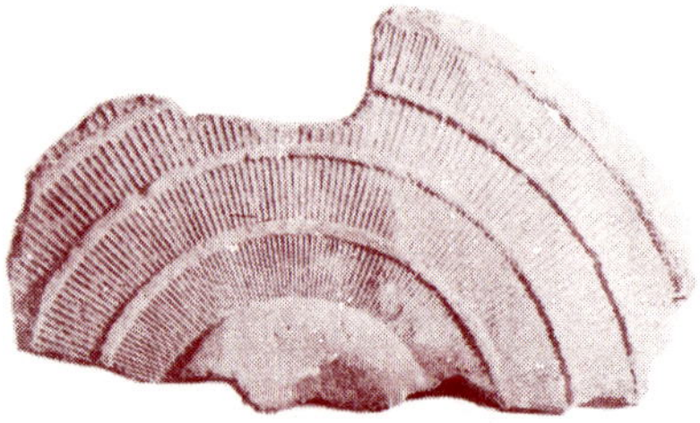

a

b

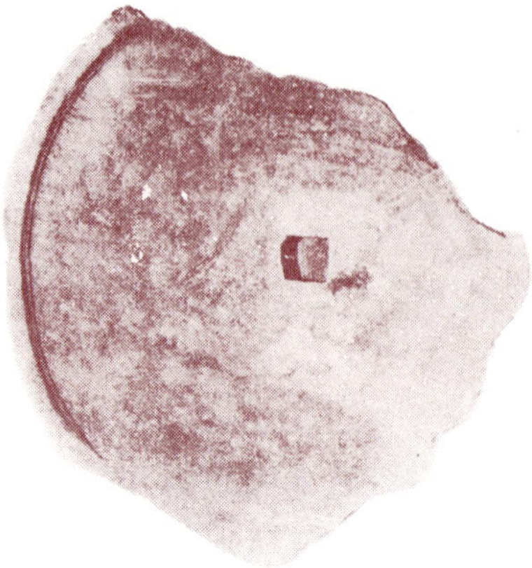

c

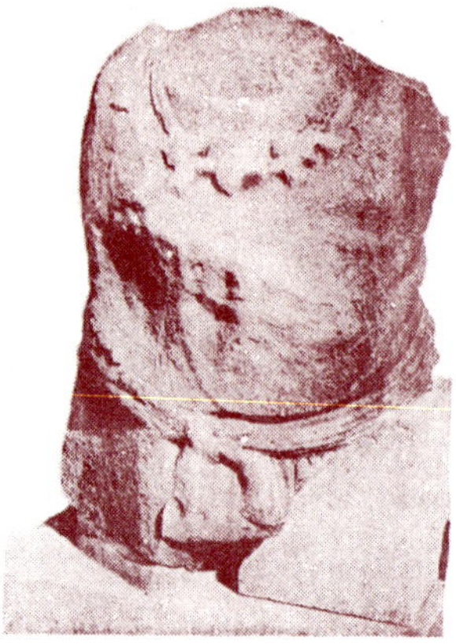

d

e

f

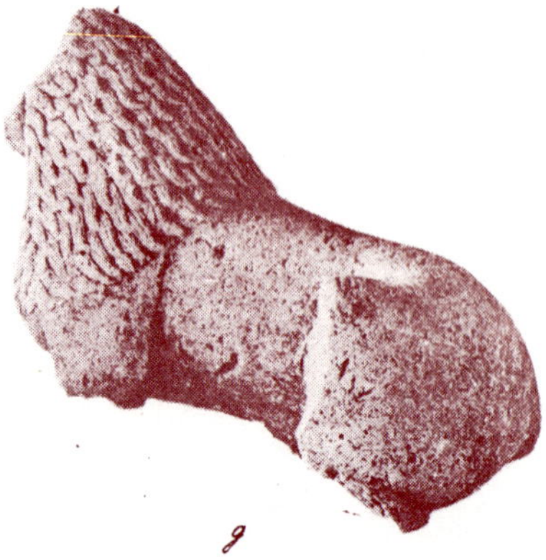

g

h

i

j

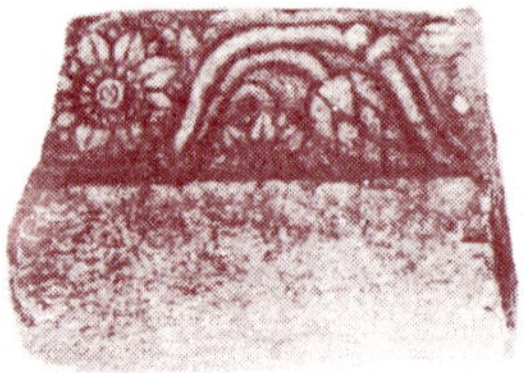

k

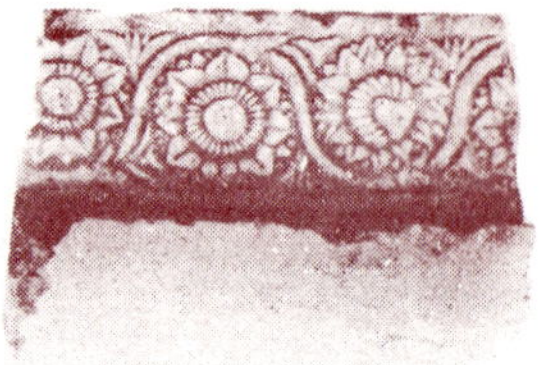

l

MISCELLANEOUS SCULPTURES OF THE EARLY SCHOOL

PLATE 104

MISCELLANEOUS SCULPTURES OF THE EARLY SCHOOL

a. One of several pieces of an umbrella (diam. 1′ 11½″) of highly polished Chunar sandstone. The underside is convex changing to concave near the outer edge; on it are four concentric bands with radiating ribs between; the upper side is plain. The umbrella, which is of typical Mauryan workmanship, was found in the debris on the east side of Stūpa 1, and probably belonged to the original brick stūpa built by Aśoka (p. 24). *Mus. Cat.*, A2.

b. Standard bowl (ht. 2′ 5¼″) of highly polished Chunar sandstone, pieced together from fragments and partly restored. It comprises a square moulded base and octagonal tapering shaft with delicately fluted sides, surmounted by a cup-shaped capital (also eight-sided), on which rested the bowl. The sides of the bowl are missing. This interesting relic dates from the Mauryan period; it was found near Temple 18 (p. 55). *Mus. Cat.*, A10.

c. Broken umbrella of dark purplish sandstone (diam. 3′ 5″), probably from the summit of Stūpa 3. On the underside are traces of radiating ribs.

d and *f*. Two torsos in the round of dwarf atlantes (*kumbhāṇḍa*), with arms upraised as if to support a superstructure. Height 2′ 0″ and 2′ 1″, respectively. They wear *dhotīs* with a loin band tied in front, and necklaces with three pendent charms, two in the form of *nandipadas*. These two figures may well have been the prototypes from which the *kumbhāṇḍas* on the capitals of the Western Gateway were copied (p. 140 and Pls. 57 and 59), but the copies seem very poor and clumsy efforts beside these vigorously modelled figures. They are referable to the Mauryan or Śuṅga period. *Mus. Cat.*, 30 and 31.

e. Fragment of an inscribed balustrade pillar of light grey sandstone (width 8″), with the figure of a he-goat in the centre medallion. Below, is an inscription of two lines in early Brāhmī characters, No. 804 *infra* (p. 381). *Mus. Cat.*, A71.

g and *h*. Figure of a lion of grey sandstone, in the round (length 3′ 6″). It came probably from the top of the column which stood on a platform a little to the N.-N.-W. of Stūpa 2 (p. 82). Śuṅga period. To the same column belongs also the bell-shaped lotus capital *h* (=Pl. 71*c*). For the capital, *cf*. Pl. 106*b*; and for the crowning lion, Pl. 108*c*.

i. This is the forepart of the elephant of grey sandstone (length 2′ 6″) alluded to on p. 68. It was found in Building 40, among the debris packed between the earlier and later structures, and may safely be assigned, therefore, to the Mauryan, or possibly pre-Mauryan period. Though rough and sketchy, the modelling is not without vigour. *Mus. Cat.*, A11.

j. Coping-stone (*ushṇīsha*) of buff-grey sandstone (length 5′ 7″), probably from the harmikā railing of Stūpa 4. On its outer face is an undulating lotus garland with birds here and there among the blooms (p. 45). *Mus. Cat.*, A69.

k and *l*. These are fragments of coping-stones belonging to harmikā balustrades. The latter (length 1′ 2½″) comes from Stūpa 3. From which monument the former comes, is not known; its length is 1′ 4″. Note that both these photos are, by error, shown upside down.

PLATE 105

a. Stūpas 11 to 16 and Temple 17 from the North-West. This picture is taken from the berm of Stūpa 1 and shows the top of its ground balustrade in the foreground. In the distance, to the left of Temple 17, appears the plinth of the pillared Maṇḍapa 40. To the right of Temple 17 is the lion-capital of Aśoka's column, standing on the temporary base provided for it prior to its removal to the museum.

b. Image of Buddha of Mathurā sandstone, seated cross-legged in the *dhyāna-mudrā* (height 2′ 7½″). The head was found broken off and has been refixed. The figure wears a *saṅghāṭī* covering both shoulders; its lower border can be seen on the throne beneath the legs of the Buddha. On the palms is the wheel symbol (*cakra*); on the soles of the feet, the wheel and *triratna*. At the back of the head is a mortice-hole, about 1″ square, for the attachment of a nimbus. The image belongs to the Mathurā School, and is referable to the early Gupta period. It was found in the relic-chamber of Stūpa 14, where it had evidently been enshrined after removal from some older building. *Cf.* p. 47. *Mus. Cat.*, 19.

c. Pedestal of Mathurā sandstone (1′ 4″ wide) surmounted by the feet of a standing Buddha and, to his right, the lower part of an attendant figure. On the front face of the pedestal is a dentil cornice above, and a Persepolitan pilaster to either side; and, framed between them, a group of twelve figures, *viz.*, in the centre, a Bodhisattva seated in the *dhyāna-mudrā*; to the right of him, six male worshippers; to the left, five female. The male figures, both men and boys, wear long tunics of the Kushān pattern held in by a belt at the hips. The women wear *sārīs* and bodices. Some of the worshippers bear lotuses or other offerings; others hold their hands in prayer. On the base of the pedestal is an inscription (No. 829) written in Brāhmī characters of the Kushān period. The ruler Vashkushāṇa, mentioned in it, is not otherwise known, but there is little doubt that he belonged to the Kushān line, and it is evident from the style of the carving that he was not far removed in time from Vāsudeva. *Mus. Cat.*, A83.

d. The reliquary here figured, made of two earthenware cups, one inverted above the other, was found in Stūpa 29. Inside it were a small piece of bone and a broken vase of Maurya or Śuṅga date (*d*, 1), which no doubt had once held some holy relic (p. 48).

a STUPAS 11 TO 16 AND TEMPLE 17 FROM NORTH WEST

b

STATUE OF BUDDHA FROM STUPA 14 ; *c* PEDESTAL OF A STATUE OF BUDDHA

d RELIQUARY FROM STUPA [illegible].

THE MONUMENTS OF SANCHI

MAURYA, SUNGA AND GUPTA COLUMNS

PLATE 106

MAURYA, SUṄGA AND GUPTA COLUMNS

All the four columns figured in this Plate stood on the main terrace, round about Stūpa 1. The first is the Aśoka column near the South Gateway, which is discussed in detail on pp. 25-29 (description and history), 88-89 (art) and 283-7 (edict). The second (*b*) is the Śuṅga Pillar 25, which stood a little to the South of Stūpa 5 (Pl. 2) and is described on p. 49 (*cf.* Maisey, *Sánchi and its Remains*, Pl. 33, 3; and for the short inscription on its shaft, see No. 836, p. 391).

Fig. c is the Gupta Pillar 35 near the North Gateway, which is discussed on pp. 50-51. Its bell-capital and crowning Bodhisattva (Vajrapāṇi) are reproduced on Pl. 108*b* and *d* (*q.v.*).

Fig. *d* is the Gupta Pillar 26 (described on pp. 49-50), which stood near Pillar 25. *Cf.* Maisey, *Sánchi and its Remains*, p. 73. Its capital is figured on Pl. 108*a*; and the inscription on its shaft, which makes mention of the Vajrapāṇi Pillar 35 (Fig. *c*), is discussed on p. 391 (No. 835).

PLATE 107

a–c. CAPITALS OF THE ASOKA PILLAR AT SĀÑCHĪ AND SĀRNĀTH

The two capitals of the Aśoka Pillars at Sāñchī and Sārnāth are shown here side by side, so that the reader may judge for himself of the relative merits of these exceptionally fine pieces of sculpture, which are discussed at length on pp. 88-89 (*cf.* also pp. 25-29). For the Sāñchī capital, *cf. Mus. Cat.*, A1.

b. INSCRIBED STUMP OF ASOKA PILLAR

For the edict engraved on the shaft, see pp. 27-29 and 283-7 (Inscr. 1).

a. CAPITAL OF ASOKA PILLAR

b. INSCRIBED STUMP OF ASOKA PILLAR

c. CAPITAL OF ASOKA PILLAR AT SARNATH

a

b

c

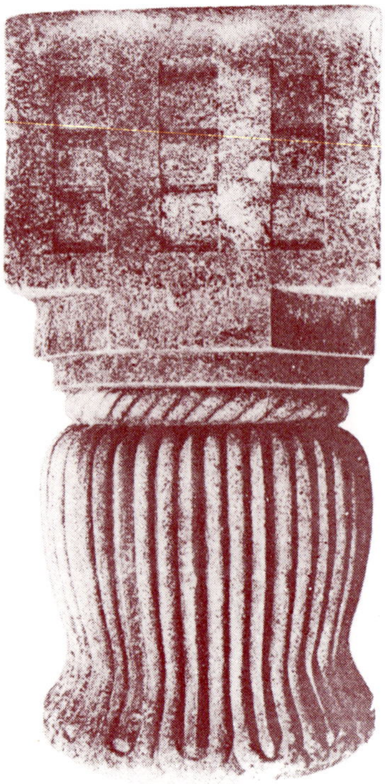

d

CAPITALS AND CROWNING FIGURES OF GUPTA PILLARS

PLATE 108

CAPITALS AND CROWNING FIGURES OF GUPTA PILLARS

Fig. *a* is the lion-capital surmounted by a 'Wheel-of-the-Law from the top of the Gupta Pillar 26 (pp. 49-50 and Pl. 106*d*). The design goes back to the capitals of the Aśoka pillars figured in the preceding plate, but the modelling and workmanship have become crude and clumsy. The *dharmacakra*, which is here the crowning feature, was absent from Aśoka's pillar at Sāñchī itself, but present in the one at Sārnāth (p. 26), and it is frequently seen on the lion-capitals depicted on the balustrades and gateways at Sāñchī (*e.g.*, Pls. 74, 3*a* and 5*a*; 82, 44*b*, etc.).

Figs. *b* and *d*. The latter is the massive bell-capital and abacus which surmounted Pillar 35 near the North Gateway (Pl. 106*c*), and the former is the figure of the Bodhisattva Vajrapāṇi, which stood on its summit (p. 51). Observe that the halo behind the head is incomplete. Its outer rays may be presumed to have been made of metal (probably copper-gilt) and fitted into the twelve small holes pierced round the edge of the stone. *Cf.* p. 254 and *Mus. Cat.*, A100.

Fig. *c* is the winged lion which stood on the top of Pillar 34 near the East Gateway. The pillar, which was set up in the Gupta period, was still standing when Cunningham and Maisey made their drawings in 1851, but all that now remains of it is this crowning ornament. *Cf.* Cunningham, *The Bhilsa Topes*, p. 199 and Pl. 7, and Maisey, *Sánchi and its Remains*, p. 73 (-N) and Pl. 33, 2.

PLATE 109

PLAN AND SECTION OF TEMPLE 40

This very interesting monument is further illustrated on Pl. 110, and discussed at length on pp. 64-68. The remains are of three periods. The original building, erected in the Maurya Age about the same time as the stūpa and pillar of Aśoka, took the form of an apsidal hall or temple raised on a lofty rectangular plinth and provided with a *pradakshiṇa-patha* within and with stepped approaches on its east and west sides. What remains of this early edifice consists only of the plinth (*caya*), with a flight of steps on its western side, and interior foundations. The superstructure, which was of wood, was probably destroyed by Pushyamitra at the same time as the stūpa of Aśoka (p. 25). When rebuilt (about the middle of the 2nd century B.C.), the plinth was much enlarged and the temple was converted into a rectangular maṇḍapa, divided up by rows of pillars and with stepped approaches at its northern end.

The early apsidal temple is readily distinguishable in the plan, but note that the pillars shown over the foundations belong, not to this temple, but to the later and larger maṇḍapa. Note, too: (a) that the rows of these pillars running north and south are not all equidistant from each other; (b) that probably there were other rows of pillars at the sides and ends of the existing group (p. 65).

From the sections it will be seen that the foundations of the pillars descend not more than about 1′ 6″ below the surface, whereas the foundations of the apsidal temple go down 11 feet and more to the bed rock.

The few remains on the east side of the plan, which are differentiated by another kind of shading, belong to a later shrine of the 7th-8th century A.D. (p. 66).

THE MONUMENTS OF SANCHI: TEMPLE 40

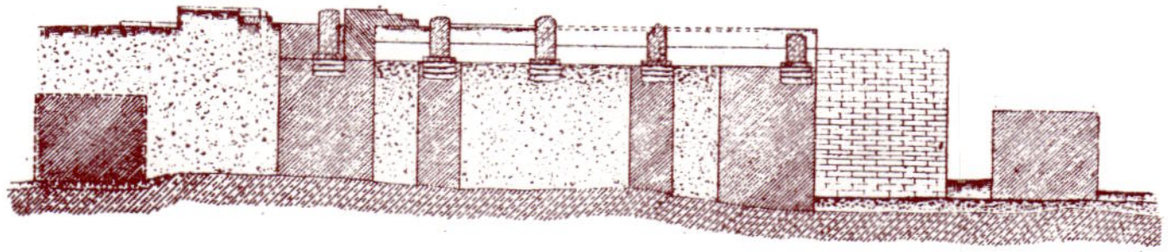

b SECTION ON CD

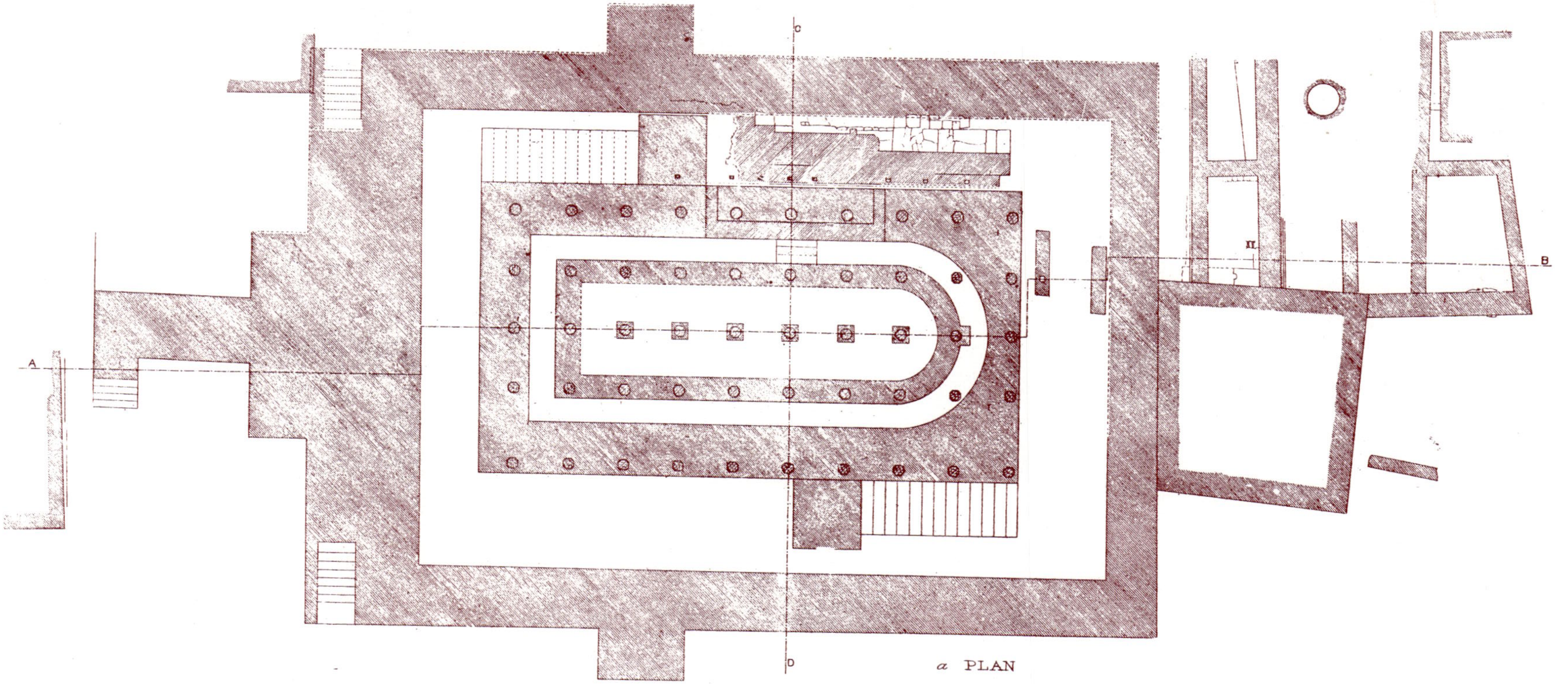

a PLAN

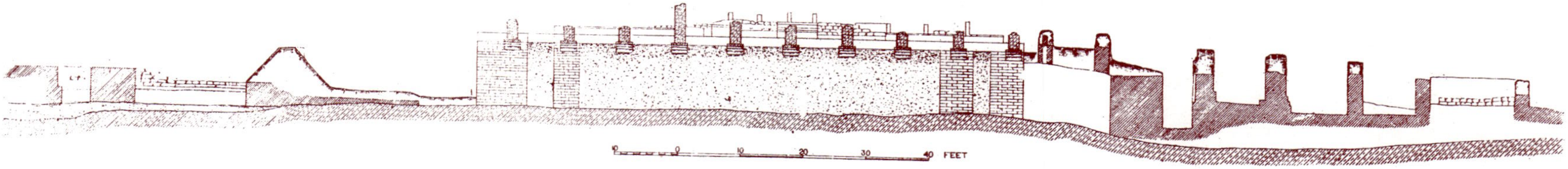

c SECTION ON AB

a. VIEW FROM NORTH-WEST

b. VIEW FROM SOUTH-WEST

PLATE 110

a-b. VIEWS OF TEMPLE 40 FROM THE NORTH-WEST AND SOUTH-WEST

Both pictures clearly show the lofty stone plinth of the early apsidal temple, with the stepped approach projecting from its western side, and the retaining wall of the later maṇḍapa outside it, with a few steps only (seen in the upper picture) let into the thickness of the wall near its north-west corner. Though now much diminished, this retaining wall was once, of course, as high as the original plinth.

As stated in the description of the preceding plate, the stumps of pillars on the top of the inner structure belong, not to it, but to the later maṇḍapa.

It was in the debris packed between the earlier building and the later retaining wall that the broken stone elephant, figured on Pl. 104*i*, was found.

PLATE 111

a-b. SECTION AND PLAN OF TEMPLE 18

This temple is further illustrated on Pls. 112 and 113 and discussed on pp. 52-57. For a drawing of one of the pillars, see also Maisey, *Sánchi and its Remains*, Pl. 33, 5.

Like the Apsidal Temple 40 (Pls. 109 and 110), the original building on this site appears to have been of wood, but to date from Śuṅga rather than Maurya times. Possibly it was intended to take the place of Temple 40 after the latter's destruction in the middle of the 2nd century B.C. The existing structure dates mainly from the 7th century A.D.; it is to this period that the tall square pillars of the nave are referable. The jambs of the inner doorway (Pl. 113*c*) were added in later mediæval times. They are contemporary with the existing Temple 45.

In the apse of this temple there once stood a small stūpa, in the debris of which Maisey, in 1851, found a broken relic-casket of steatite (*Sánchi and its Remains*, p. 74), but all trace of it has since disappeared.

c. This is the hollow block of stone referred to on p. 56, which appears to have been made in mediæval times as a base collar to support one of the pillars of the nave.

d. Specimen of roof tiles found in large numbers at the foot of the temple retaining wall on the west (in the angle seen in Pl. 112*b*). The tiles probably came from the original temple of the 2nd century B.C.

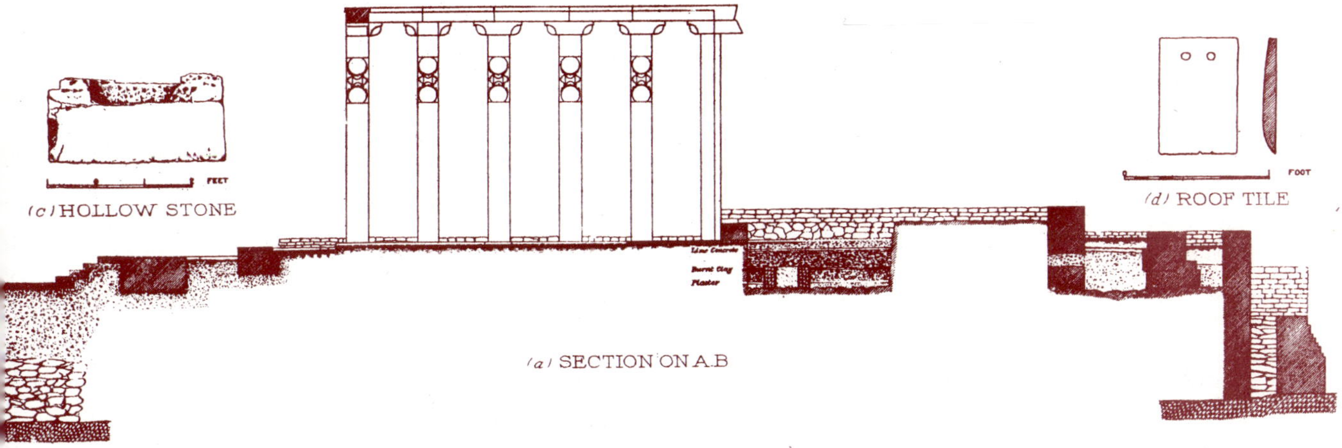

(c) HOLLOW STONE

(d) ROOF TILE

(a) SECTION ON A.B

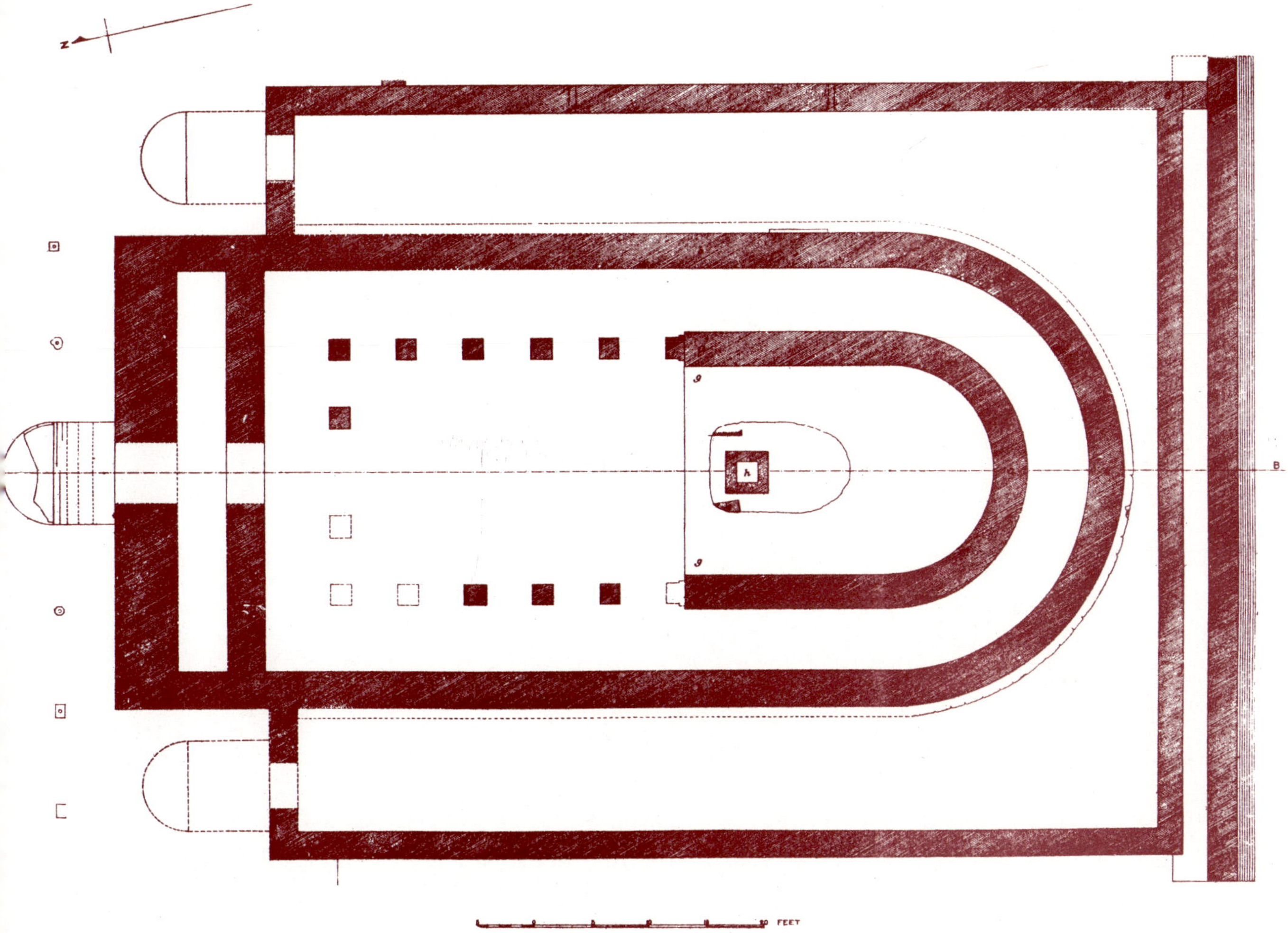

(b) PLAN

VIEW FROM SOUTH-WEST

PLATE 112

a-b. VIEWS OF TEMPLE 18 FROM THE NORTH-EAST AND SOUTH-WEST

Observe, in the upper picture, the curious 7th Century design of the nave pillars. The design is shown more clearly in Pl. 111*a*, and in Maisey, *Sánchi and its Remains*, Pl. 33, 5.

The carved jamb lying on its side at the inner entrance is the same as that figured in Pl. 113*c*. The carvings on it are contemporary with and closely resemble those of Temple 45 (Pl. 118*b*).

In the picture below, taken from the low, rocky ground to the south-west, may be seen the original plinth of the temple (much rebuilt) and the remains of the later retaining wall at its south end, which was added, no doubt, when the plinth showed signs of collapsing.

PLATE 113

a and *b*. These are specimens of 56 terracotta votive tablets of about the 7th century B.C., which were found on the floor of the aisle in Temple 18.

The tablets are leaf-shaped, with a roughly scalloped border and a pointed seal at the top, on which is stamped the familiar creed:—*Ye dharmāḥ hetu-prabhavāḥ*, etc. In the centre, is a figure of the Buddha seated on a lotus throne in the *bhūmisparśa-mudrā*, with an oval halo behind his head and lotus buds to right and left of it. On either side, a little above his shoulders, are two small stūpas surmounted by three umbrellas with flying streamers. Underneath these and filling the vacant space between them and the knees of the Buddha, is a repetition of the sacred creed. Still lower, on a level with the Buddha's knees, are lotus buds springing on long stalks from beneath the throne. A light red slip is still discernible on some of the fragments. *Mus. Cat.*, C752-808.

c. This is the same door-jamb that is seen lying on its side in Pl. 112*a*. The carvings are described on p. 53.

d. In the foreground is the small Temple 17, and behind it, to the right, the columns of Temple 18. The former was erected, probably, in the early part of the 5th century A.D., and is among the most attractive examples of early Gupta architecture. Observe, however, the unduly heavy lion-capitals and how clumsily the junction is effected between the pillared porch and the sanctum behind. The temple is described and its classical affinities discussed on pp. 56-58.

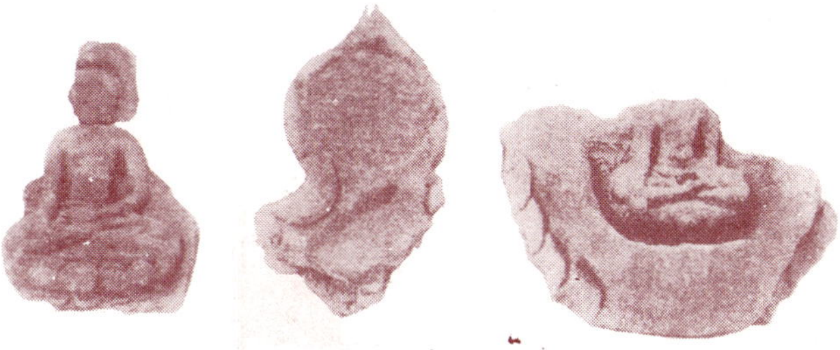

a

b

c

TEMPLE 8 *a, b* TERRACOTTAS *c* JAMB OF DOORWAY

d TEMPLE 17 FROM NORTH EAST

TEMPLE 17

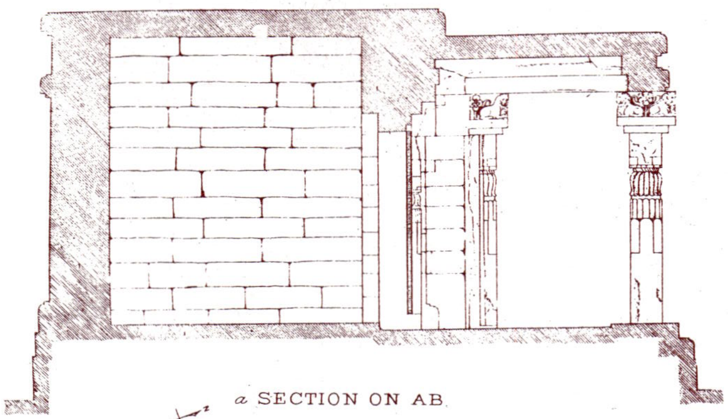

a SECTION ON AB

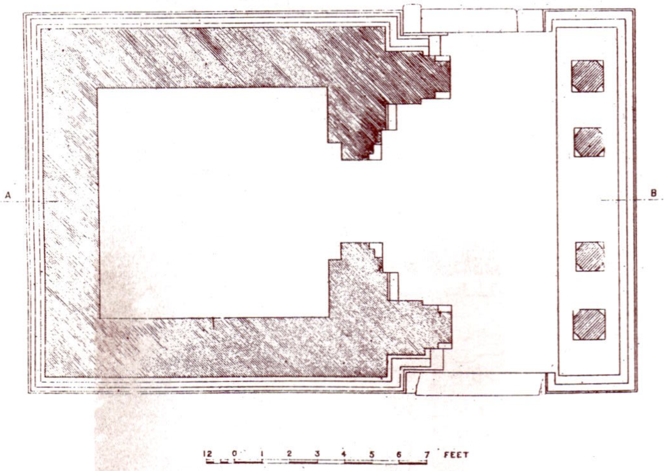

b PLAN

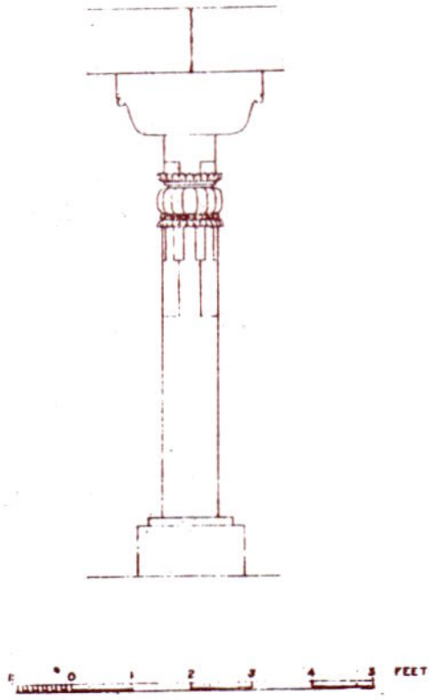

g PILLAR AT F, TEMPLE 31

DETAILS OF ORNAMENT
AT *c* AND *d*, TEMPLE 17

TEMPLE 31

e SECTION ON AB

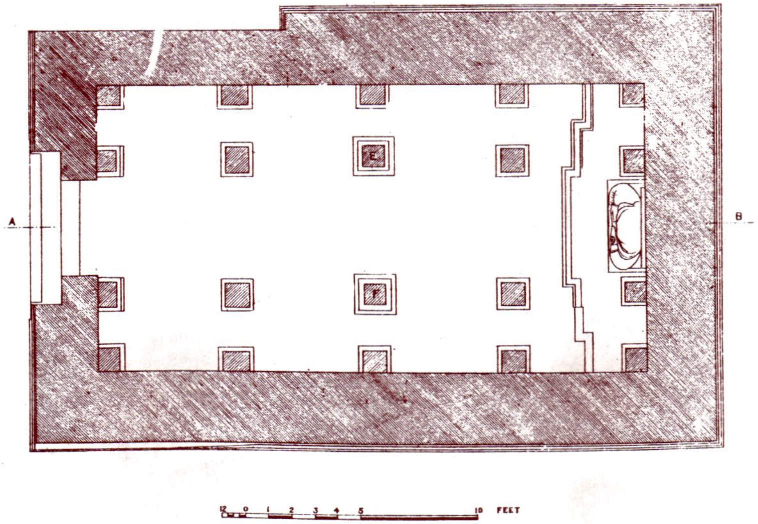

f PLAN

PLATE 114

SECTIONS, PLANS AND DETAILS OF TEMPLES 17 AND 31

a and *b*. Section and plan of the early Gupta Temple 17, illustrated also on Pl. 113*d*, and discussed on pp. 56-58.

c and *d*. These are the vertical bands of carving which decorate the two faces of the innermost angle of the door-jambs on the outside. The design of the former is especially characteristic of the early Gupta period.

e and *f*. Section and plan of Temple 31, described on pp. 58-59 and further illustrated on Pl. 115. The temple was originally built in the 6th-7th century A.D., but reconstructed in the 10th-11th century A.D. To the earlier period belong the broad plinth of the temple (not shown in the plan), the dais or throne, of Nāgourī stone, which extends from side to side of the shrine at its northern end, and probably two pilasters against the east and west walls, which are of the same age and pattern as the pillars of Temple 18 (Pls. 111 and 112). To the later period belongs the rest of the superstructure except the pillars marked E and F on the plan. For the cult statue, see Pl. 115*c*. The two pillars E and F (one of which is illustrated in Fig. *g*) date from the early Gupta period and were presumably taken from some older building.

PLATE 115

a. STŪPA 5, TEMPLES 31 AND 32 AND PILLARS 25 AND 26

Cf. the plan on Pl. 2; and for Stūpa 5 (to the left of the picture), see p. 46. The image which probably occupied the pedestal of Nāgourī stone on the south side of this stūpa is figured in Pl. 125*e* (*q.v.*).

For Temple 31 (to the right of Stūpa 5), see Pl. 114*e* and *f* and pp. 58-59. Temple 32 (on the top of the slope to the right) is discussed on pp. 77-78, and further illustrated on Pl. 116*e*.

To the right and left of the steps in front of Temple 31 can be seen the square plinths of the small Stūpas 28 and 29, which are referred to on pp. 47-48. (*Cf.* also Pl. 105*d*.) Nearer to the foreground are the two pillars Nos. 25 and 26, with their lion-capitals lying beside them. *Cf.* pp. 49-50 and Pls. 106*b* and *d* and 108*a*.

b. This is the same image of a Nāgī that can be seen in the picture above, standing in front of Temple 31. It is of early Gupta date and carved in the round. Probably there was once a corresponding figure on the east side of the steps (p. 59).

c. Image of Buddha in Temple 31. *Cf.* p. 59. This was the cult image of purplish-brown sandstone belonging to the later (10th-11th century) temple, but the image dates from the 7th century A.D., and must evidently have come from some older temple, though probably not from the one on this site. Observe the exceedingly rich carving of the halo, which is in one piece with the rest of the statue. From the marks of breakage on the breast, it appears that the Buddha was in the attitude of teaching (*dharmacakra-mudrā*).

a STUPA 5, TEMPLES 31 AND 32, AND PILLARS 25 AND 26

b NAGI IMAGE IN FRONT OF TEMPLE 31

c BUDDHA IMAGE IN TEMPLE 31

d TEMPLE 45: PILASTER IN SHRINE

c TEMPLE 45: CEILING

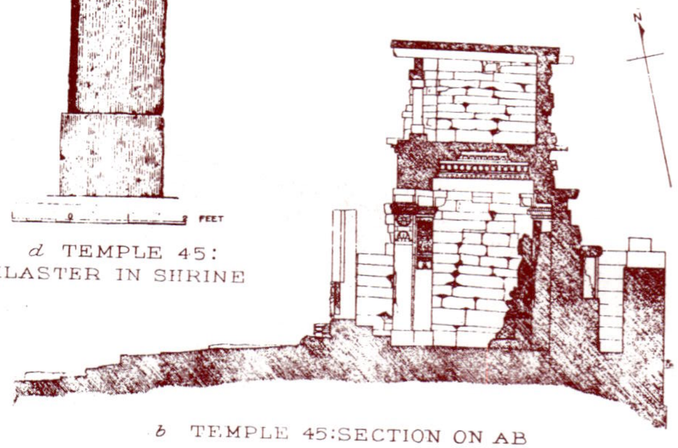

b TEMPLE 45: SECTION ON AB

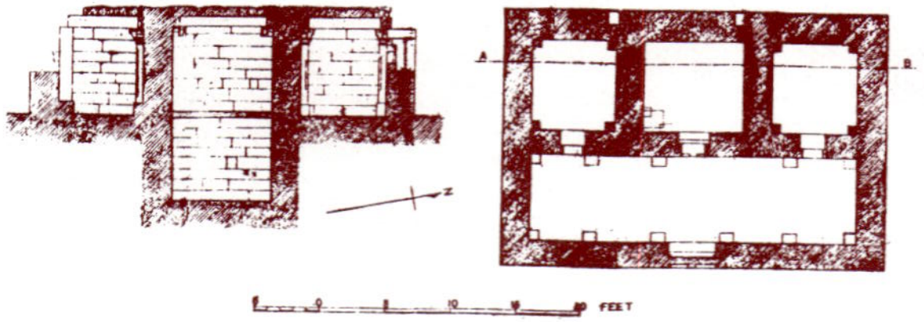

e TEMPLE 32: SECTION AND PLAN

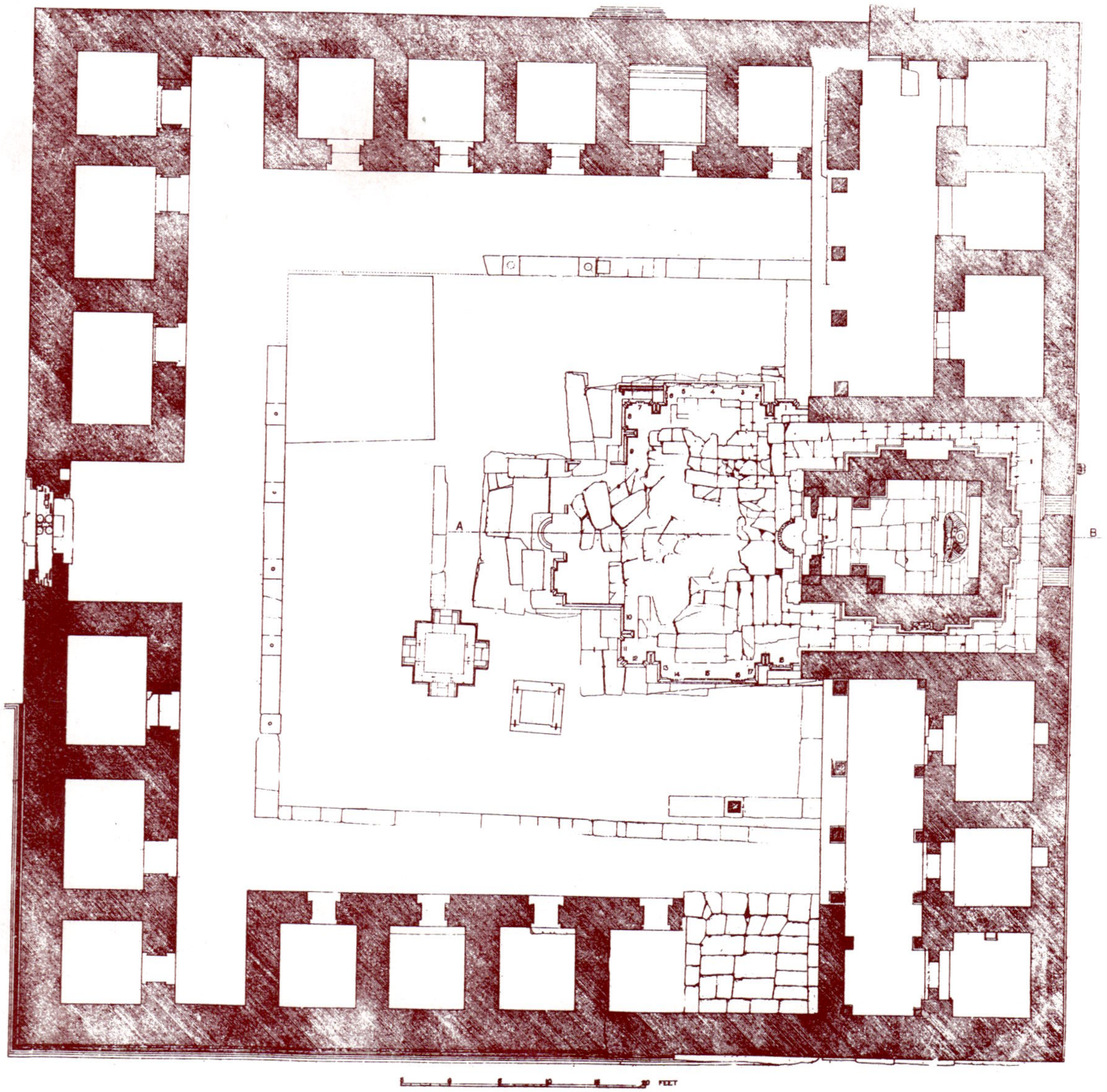

PLATE 116

PLANS, SECTIONS AND DETAILS OF TEMPLES 45 AND 32

a **and** *b*. The remains of Temple 45 belong to two periods: the earlier, so far as can be determined, to the 7th century A.D., or thereabouts; the later to about the 10th century A.D. The earlier comprise the ranges of cells on the north, south and west sides of the quadrangle, the plinths of the three small stūpas in the courtyard, and the low stone kerb at the edge of the verandahs. The later comprise the lofty shrine on the east side of the quadrangle, the raised platform in front of it, and the cells and verandahs flanking it on the north and south. Whatever remains may exist of the original temple, are now hidden beneath the later structures, but small sections of an earlier platform have been exposed to view beneath the foundations of the later one in front of the Temple. For further information about this temple, *cf*. pp. 71-75 and Pls. 117-120.

c. The ceiling of the sanctum (*garbhagṛiha*). It is constructed on the usual principle of diminishing squares, and is a typical example of late mediæval work.

d. This is a specimen of the corner pilasters in the sanctum, which are referable to about the 8th century A.D.; whereas the rest of the structure is more modern by some two centuries. The carvings are described on pp. 72-73.

e. Section and plan of Temple 32. This is the little temple—if temple it was—seen on the rising ground to the right of Pl. 115*a*, and described on pp. 77-78. Observe, in the sectional drawing, the underground cellar beneath the central chamber, and note that the side chambers can be entered only through small windows. No doorways are provided in them.

PLATE 117

a. Temple 45 from west. This view of the temple and its courtyard is taken from outside the entrance on the west (Pl. 116*a*). The remains on the lower level, including the courtyard pavement, the solitary verandah pillar in the S.-E. corner, and the foundations of the cells to the right of it, belong to the earlier period; all the superstructure to the later.

b. In the foreground is the N.-W. corner of the earlier courtyard of Temple 45, with Building 46 adjoining it on the north (right) side, and Building 47 on the west side. Beyond is the dome of Stūpa 3. All the remains in the foreground are of the 7th and 8th century A.D. Observe that the kerb at the edge of the pavement consists of alternate square and oblong blocks of stone. The former, which have mortice-holes at their centres, served as bases for the verandah pillars which encompassed the courtyard. The slightly raised square at the corner of the pavement was the plinth of a small stūpa (Pl. 116*a*).

a TEMPLE 45 FROM WEST

b FORE-COURT OF TEMPLE 45 AND MONASTERY 47

b. ENTRANCE TO CENTRAL SHRINE

PLATE 118

a. SOUTH WING OF TEMPLE 45

The pavement in the foreground belongs to the earlier edifice of the 7th-8th century A.D. The pavement of the later edifice was about 2′ 6″ above it, coinciding with the bottom of the carved plinth on the left of the picture. For the carvings on the latter, see Pl. 119*a* and p. 75; for the doorway in the south wing, with the plain, makeshift lintel, see Pl. 120*b*; and for the seated Buddha image seen in profile at the end of this wing, see Pl. 120*d*. The verandah pillar to the right of the doorway, with the pot-and-foliage base belonged originally to the earlier temple (p. 75).

b. ENTRANCE TO THE CENTRAL SHRINE OF TEMPLE 45

The rich and elaborate carvings which adorn this entrance are discussed on pp. 73-74. Observe how characteristically Hindu all this sculpture is. Just as a thousand years earlier the sculptors of the Early School had adapted the mundane art of the day to the needs of Buddhism, so now they were again adapting the current art of Hinduism; and this art being essentially religious in character, they found it necessary to introduce into it even fewer changes than they had previously done (*cf.* pp. 153-55).

The pilasters with square, fluted capitals of the antechamber came, no doubt, from the same older and unfinished building as the pilasters of the sanctum (Pl. 116*d*).

For the cult image within the sanctum, see Pl. 120c.

PLATE 119

a. Platform in front of Temple 45 from the South-West. This picture clearly shows the respective levels of the courtyard pavements belonging to the earlier and later temples, as well as the filling of heavy stone rubble between them.

b, *c* and *d*. Examples of the figural carvings in the small panels on the vertical faces of the platform (p. 75). Figs. *b* and *c* are the usual amorous couples; Fig. *d*, the pot-bellied Pāñcika or Jambhala (p. 245).

e. Parts of the *kalaśa* and *āmalaka* which crowned the spire (*śikhara*) of this temple.

f. One of the many '*caitya*-and-*āmalaka*' motifs which were used to decorate the faces of the temple spire.

a

b

c

d

e

f

a TERRACE IN FRONT OF SHRINE _ *b c d e f* SCULPTURED DETAILS

a. DOORWAY IN NORTH WING

b. DOORWAY IN SOUTH WING

c. CULT STATUE IN CENTRAL SHRINE

d. STATUE IN SOUTH WING

PLATE 120

a and *b*. Carved doorways in the north and south wings, respectively, of Temple 45. The luxuriant arabesques, highly stylised figures, and erotic scenes closely resemble those on the doorway of the central shrine (Pl. 118*b*), and like them are characteristically Hindu. The doorways were evidently left unfinished, and subsequently covered with lintels taken from some other building.

c. Cult statue of the Buddha in the central shrine of Temple 45. The statue is discussed on p. 73 and illustrated also in Pl. 118*b*. It portrays Buddha in the 'earth-touching' attitude (*bhūmisparśa-mudrā*), seated on a lotus throne, across the lower leaves of which runs the Buddhist creed in letters of about the 10th century A.D. This is the date of the statue also; but the lion-throne underneath belonged to an older statue of the (?) 8th century A.D., and is probably contemporary with the carved pilasters of the sanctum, two of which can be seen in the corners of this picture. As to the small mutilated figures projecting from the centre of the lion-throne, see p. 73.

d. Statue in the south wing of Temple 45. *Cf*. Pl. 118*a*, where the same statue is seen side-face. The statue, which represents Buddha in the *bhūmisparśa-mudrā*, is in a somewhat later style than the preceding one. Where it was originally enshrined, is not known.

PLATE 121

a. PLAN AND SECTION OF MONASTERIES 46 AND 47

The title on the Plate is perhaps misleading, as the two courts belong to one and the same monastery—Court 46 to the east, and Court 47 to the west (*cf.* Pls. 117*b* and 122*a*). The monastery, which is fully described on pp. 76-77, dates from about the 11th century A.D., and is characterised throughout by the plainest kind of masonry. Observe that in the larger Court 47 the remains shown in the open quadrangle appertain to an earlier stratum of buildings (*cf.* section).

b. PLAN AND SECTION OF MONASTERY 38

For the description of this building, see p. 69. Like the neighbouring Monasteries 36 and 37, it dates from about the 7th century A.D.

It was not until the early Gupta Age that this type of self-contained monastery, built around an open quadrangle, was introduced into Hindustān and Central India from the North-West (*cf.* pp. 63-64).

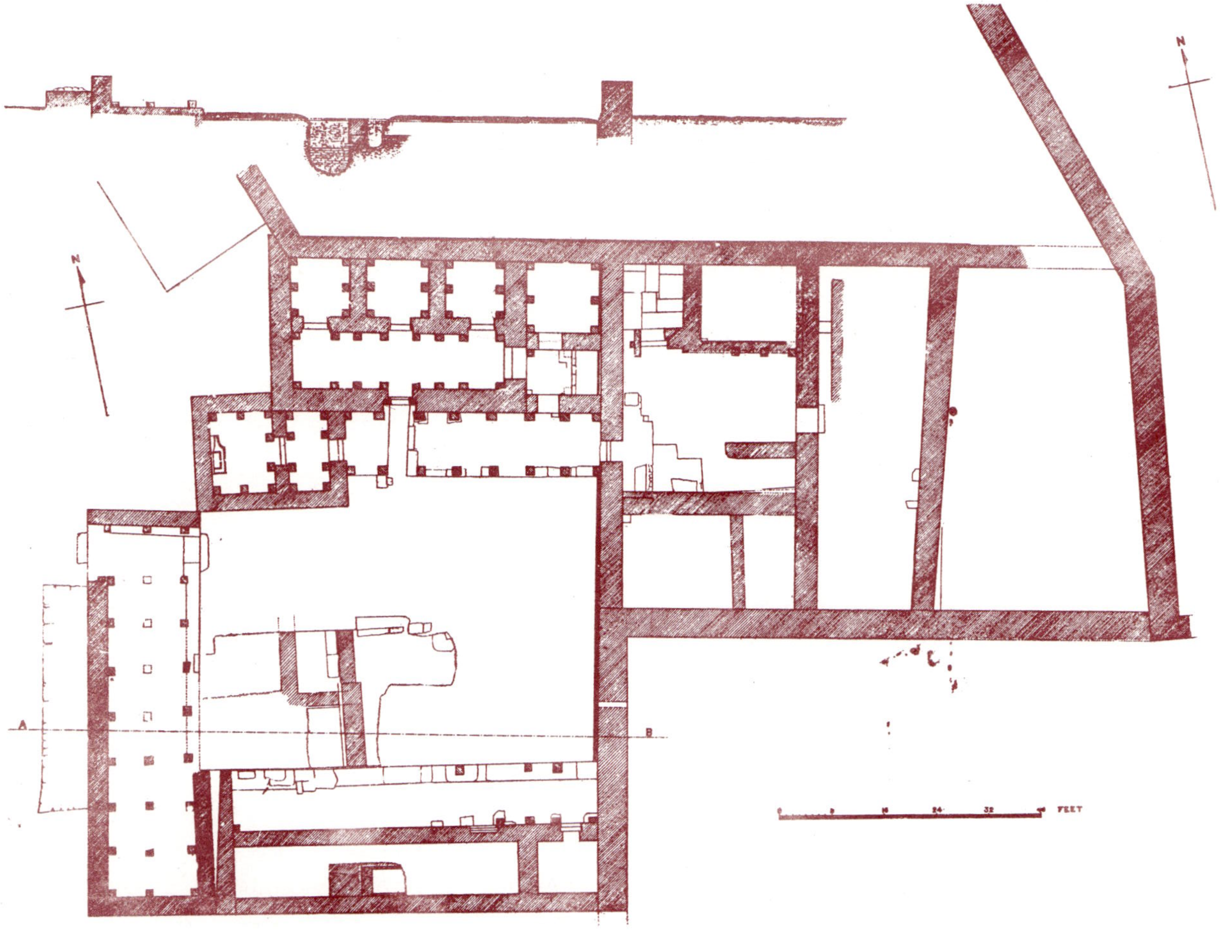

(a) MONASTERIES 46 AND 47 : PLAN AND SECTION.

(b) MONASTERY 38 : PLAN AND SECTION.

a. INTERIOR OF MONASTERY 47

b. MONASTERY 36 FROM SOUTH WEST

PLATE 122

a. INTERIOR OF MONASTERY 47

Cf. Pl. 121*a* and pp. 76-77. The pillared verandah (*ālinda*) seen in the photograph is on the north side of the Court. At its western end is the porch of a small shrine containing an image-pedestal against its back wall. Observe the plainness and rough dressing of the pillars. This is one of the latest structures on the site. At the time it was built (*circa* 11th century A.D.) Buddhism was nearing its final eclipse and no doubt the revenues of the saṅghārāma at Sāñchī had fallen to a low ebb.

b. MONASTERY 36, FROM THE SOUTH-WEST

In the foreground is the small and much ruined Monastery 36, for which, see Pl. 123*a* and p. 69. In the middle distance is Stūpa 6 (pp. 45-46) and beyond it, to the right of the picture, the massive walls of Building 43, with the bastion at its S.-W. corner half shaded by a large khirṇi tree (p. 78).

PLATE 123

a-b. PLANS AND SECTIONS OF MONASTERIES 36 AND 37

Cf. Pl. 122*b* and p. 69. Like the neighbouring Monastery 38, these two buildings are assignable to about the 7th century A.D.

Regarding this early mediæval type of monastery, see description of Pl. 121*b* and pp. 63-64.

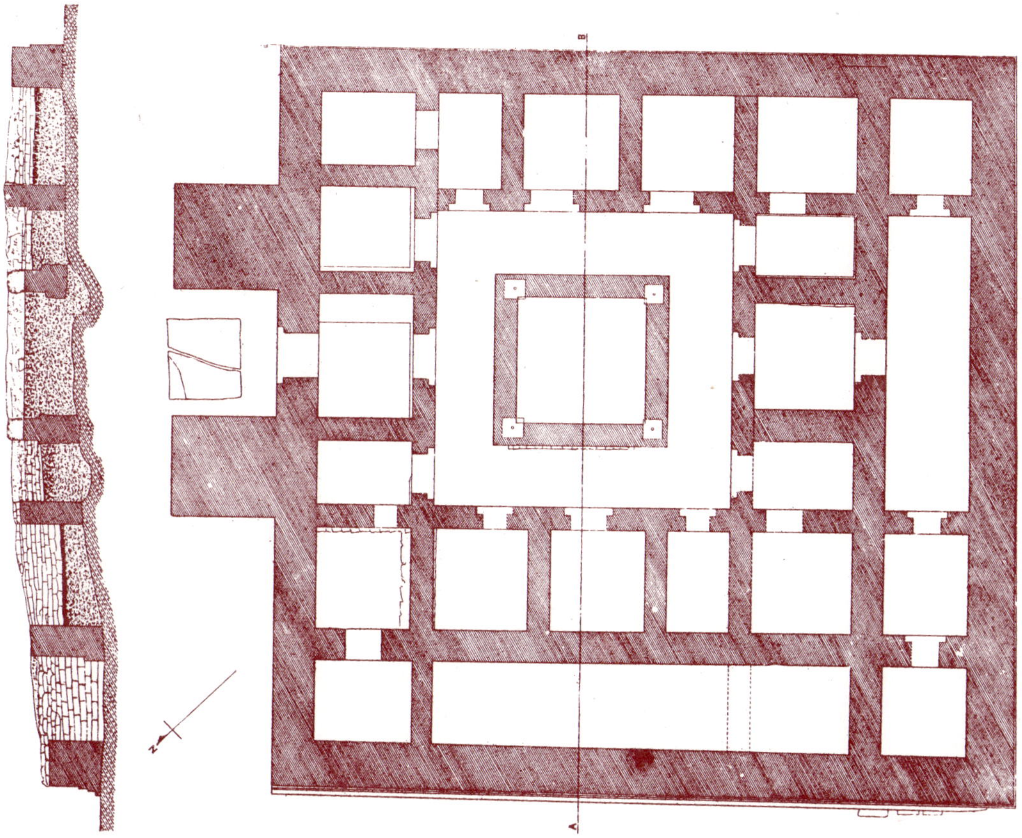

(b) MONASTERY 37: PLAN AND SECTION

(a) MONASTERY 36: PLAN AND SECTION

a

b

c

d

e

MISCELLANEOUS SCULPTURES

PLATE 124

MISCELLANEOUS SCULPTURES

a. Lower part of a Nāgī image in the round, of greyish-white sandstone (ht. 2′ 9″). The Nāgī is standing with left hand on hip, wearing a *dhotī* fastened with a beaded girdle round the hips, scarf, heavy anklets, and a long jewelled cord reaching to the knees. The scarf is bunched at the hips and its ends fall on either side to the ground. Some of the Nāgī's coils are traced on the back. The image, which stands on the hill of Nāgourī (Pl. 1), appears to be a clumsy and expiring effort of the Early School, assignable to the 1st or 2nd century A.D.

b. Image of buff sandstone representing the Bodhisattva seated cross-legged in the *dhyāna-mudrā* (ht. 1′ 6¼″). The figure wears a *saṅghāṭī* over the left shoulder only, a scarf around the loins, jewelled necklaces, pendant and garland. On the front of the pedestal is an inscription in Brāhmī characters of the Kushān period (No. 828 *infra*), from which it appears that the image represents Siddhārtha seated beneath the *jambu* tree on the occasion of his First Meditation (*cf.* pp. 202 and 253). *Mus. Cat.*, A82.

c. Image in the round (ht. 6′ 7″) of a standing Nāga with a seven-headed serpent hood and serpent coils at the back. He wears a *dhotī*, scarf, elaborate head-dress, heavy ear-pendants, bracelets, and a long jewelled cord reaching to the knees. Round his waist twisted snake-like coils take the place of a *kamarband*. The ends of the scarf fall on either side as in Fig. *a*, and the *dhotī* is drawn down into a long point between the feet. In his right uplifted hand was a lotus (*cf.* Pl. 125*b*); in his left, held at the hip, a flask. The image, like Fig. *a*, stood on the Nāgourī hill, and appears to be of about the same age as the latter, though the workmanship is in every way superior.

d. Broken pedestal of Mathurā sandstone (8″×7¾″), with part of the left foot of a standing image, wearing sandals. To the right of the pedestal is a dwarf pilaster with foliate cap. In sunk panel, the partly mutilated figure of the Bodhisattva Maitreya, seated cross-legged and holding a small flask in his left hand. To his left, two female votaries clad in *sārīs*, each holding a lotus stalk in the right hand, and the hem of the *sārī* in the left. On the borders above and below the panel, an inscription in Brāhmī characters of the Kushān period (No. 830 *infra*), from which it may be gleaned that the image was originally dedicated by the daughter of a certain Vishakula. Subsequently it was broken, and this fragment was enshrined in the relic-chamber of Stūpa 12 (p. 47). *Mus. Cat.*, A84.

e. Part of a niche of buff sandstone (ht. 1′ 3″) containing a headless figure of Buddha seated in meditation on a lotus throne, with *saṅghāṭī* covering both shoulders. The sculpture is referable to the 4th-5th century A.D. *Mus. Cat.*, 20.

f. Broken slab of Mathurā sandstone (11¼″×8½″) impressed with foot-print (*pada*), of which the heel only remains. In the heel is a *nandipada* symbol in relief; around it, an inscription in early Gupta lettering (No. 831 *infra*, p. 387); and at the edge, remnants of quatrefoil border. *Mus. Cat.*, A85.

PLATE 125

MISCELLANEOUS SCULPTURES

a. Statue of greyish-white sandstone (ht. 8′) representing the Bodhisattva Padmapāṇi (Avalokiteśvara) standing, with weight on left leg. He wears a short *dhotī* with girdle tied in front, scarf bunched at the left hip, tiara, jewelled necklace, armlets and bracelets. His right hand, raised to the shoulder, holds a lotus; his left rests on the scarf at his hip. In front of the tiara is a *kīrttimukha* mask spouting out garlands. The halo is unusual. Probably the outer rays, which in the case of the figure on Pillar 35 (Pl. 108*b*) were made of metal, were here painted on the plain border of the halo. The statue, which is referable to the 5th century A.D., is markedly inferior to the one on Pillar 35, of which it appears to have been a copy. *Cf.* p. 254 and *Mus. Cat.*, A100.

b. Statue in reddish-grey sandstone (ht. 6′ 10″) of a standing Nāga with a seven-headed serpent hood and schematic coils, worked in the round, behind. The Nāga wears a *dhotī* with girdle tied in front, a scarf passing over the left arm and knees, tiara, jewelled necklace, ear-pendants and bracelets. In front of the tiara is a *kīrttimukha* mask spouting out garlands. The reader should compare this Nāga, which is fifth century work, with the Nāga illustrated on Pl. 124*c* and mark the changed mannerisms and the great differences in style which had crept in during the 3rd and 4th centuries. *Mus. Cat.*, A102.

c. Statue of the Bodhisattva Padmapāṇi (ht. 7′ 6″) similar in all respects to Fig. *a*. *Mus. Cat.*, A101.

d. Image of buff sandstone (ht. 2′ 10″) representing the Buddha seated cross-legged on a lotus throne supported by two lions. The *saṅghāṭī*, which he wears, passes over the left shoulder only, leaving the right shoulder bare. The left hand, which rests, palm upwards, in the lap, holds the end of his girdle. The right hand appears to have been raised in the *abhaya-mudrā*. On the sole of the right foot is a lotus symbol. Between the lions on the pedestal kneel a male and a female devotee, the former with hands raised in prayer, the latter holding a garland. The image is referable to the 5th century; from the waist upwards it is a gracefully-modelled piece of work, but the legs, be it noted, are disproportionately large. *Mus. Cat.*, 23.

e. This is the image which probably occupied the plinth on the south side of Stūpa 5 (*cf.* p. 46). It is of reddish-buff sandstone (ht. 5′ 3″) and represents Buddha seated on a cushioned seat (*cf.* Pl. 70*a-d*) in the *dhyāna-mudrā*. Both shoulders are covered by the *saṅghāṭī*. Behind are the remnants of a halo, and beneath each ear a small mortice-hole, showing where the protracted ear-lobes were at one time repaired. In style, this image is not far removed from the Maṅkuwār image of 448-49 A.D. (*cf.* Coomaraswamy, *History of Indian and Indonesian Art*, Pl. XLIII, 162).

a

b

c

d

e

MISCELLANEOUS SCULPTURES

a

b

c

d

e

h

i

MISCELLANEOUS SCULPTURES

PLATE 126

MISCELLANEOUS SCULPTURES

The first three figures on this Plate are approximately of the same age—6th to 7th century A.D.

a. Image in greyish-white sandstone (ht. 5′ 5″) of the Buddha standing in the 'gift-bestowing' attitude (*varada-mudrā*). The upper garment (*saṅghāṭī*) covering both shoulders and arms is spread out on either side of the figure and held at the shoulder by the left hand; the under garment is visible above the ankles. *Mus. Cat.*, 1.

b. Relief of buff-red sandstone (ht. 5′ 1″) depicting the subjugation of the mad elephant at Rājagṛiha. The right hand of the Buddha rests on the head of the elephant, behind which stands Indra holding a *caurī* in his right hand and *vajra* in his left. The other attendant on the left, where we should expect Brahmā, holds a long staff in his right hand, but in other respects is more like a Buddha figure. Behind the Buddha's head is a disproportionately large halo, with lightly incised ornamentation and garland-bearing Gandharvas on clouds. On the inner circle of the halo is an inscription in one line containing the Buddhist creed. *Mus. Cat.*, 9.

c. Image of Buddha (ht. 4′ 4″) very similar to Fig. *a*, but of dark purplish sandstone. An inscription of one line on the left margin of the slab contains the Buddhist creed. *Mus. Cat.*, 7.

d. Head in buff sandstone of the Bodhisattva Avalokiteśvara (ht. 10″). The hair is disposed in ringlets bound by a fillet with a large rosette in front, on which is a figure of the Dhyāni Buddha, Amitābha. The head is a striking example of Gupta work. *Cf.* p. 254 *supra* and *Mus. Cat.*, B30.

e. Head of dark purplish sandstone with mutilated halo (ht. 10½″). The hair is combed back from the forehead and bound by a wreath with medallion in front. On the forehead is a small *tilaka* mark. The head, which is in the later Gupta style, was found in the debris of Temple 20. *Cf.* p. 255 and *Mus. Cat.*, B42.

f. Head of greyish-white sandstone (ht. 9¾″). The hair is combed back from the forehead and arranged in a high, triple chignon, bound round by a beaded wreath with medallion in front and pendent strings of beads. In the left ear is a large spiral ornament. The head is probably of the later Gupta period, but the date is uncertain. *Cf.* p. 255 and *Mus. Cat.*, B43.

g. Mask of head of dark purplish sandstone (ht. 3¾″). The hair is combed back from the forehead and divided at the centre by a double plait. The head appears to have belonged to an attendant figure, which stood on the left of a group. It is a work of the later Gupta period. *Mus. Cat.*, B32.

h. Headless image in dark purplish sandstone (ht. 1′ 4″) of Pāñcika (Jambhala) seated in an easy posture (*līlāsana-mudrā*) on a seat supported on a row of short balusters. He wears necklaces, armlets, anklets and a long jewelled cord hanging from the shoulders. In his left hand is a purse (made of mongoose skin); under his right foot are two small vases containing treasure for his votaries. *Cf.* p. 245 and Pls. 118*b* and 119*d*. *Circa* 10th century A.D. *Mus. Cat.*, A110.

i. Square capital of a pilaster (ht. 11½″), with bunch of lotuses on three faces and a Yaksha at each of the front corners. Early 5th century. *Cf.* the capitals of Temple 17 (Pl. 113*d*). *Mus. Cat.*, A96.

j. Four-armed image of Śiva (?) seated in the *līlāsana-mudrā* on a double lotus throne supported by a bull. The lower right hand is in the *abhaya-mudrā*; the lower left rests on a vase like those in Fig. *h*. Twined round his right leg and shoulder is a lotus stalk. *Circa* 10th century A.D. *Mus. Cat.*, A112.

PLATE 127

MISCELLANEOUS SCULPTURES

a. Votive stūpa of dark purplish sandstone (ht. 2′ 8¼″) with octagonal base. On each face is an image of the Buddha standing within a pillared shrine, in the *abhaya-* or *varada-mudrā.* In the architectural decoration, observe the *caitya* and *āmalaka* motifs, characteristic of later mediæval work. The crowning umbrella above the harmikā is missing. *Mus. Cat.*, 171.

b. Upper part of a pillar of dark purplish sandstone (ht. 2′ 7¾″) octagonal below and sixteen-sided above, the sides being alternately fluted and flat. The capital is a fluted vase standing on a wreath, with a band of lotus leaves below and another issuing from its mouth. 5th—6th century A.D. *Cf.* the pillar in Temple 31 (Pl. 114*g*). *Mus. Cat.*, 138.

c. Votive stūpa of dark purplish sandstone (ht. 1′ 5½″) without harmikā or umbrella. Spaced at equal intervals round the circular drum are four niches, each containing a figure of the Buddha in the *dhyāna-* or *bhūmisparśa-mudrā.* Between the niches is a rosette-and-lozenge moulding; above, a frieze of swags; and below, a double lotus base.

d. Votive stūpa of dark purplish sandstone (ht. 3′ 4½″) without harmikā or umbrella. Around the drum, divided from one another by pilasters, are four Buddhas seated on conventional rocks, under their Bodhi trees. Two of the Buddhas are in the *bhūmisparśa-mudrā* and a third in the *dhyāna-mudrā.* The fourth is mutilated. Late mediæval period.

e. Door jamb of reddish-brown sandstone (ht. 3′ 1½″) enriched with slender pilaster and two vertical bands with foliate and jewelled designs. The pilaster has a 'pot-and-foliage' base and cap, and between them a band adorned with *kīrttimukha* masks. Early Gupta period.

f. Part of a pilaster of grey sandstone (ht. 4′ 6½″). The carvings are divided horizontally into three registers by a rosette-and-lozenge band above and an *āmalaka* band below. In the lowest register are half and quarter circles with beaded borders and stylised arabesques; in the middle, Buddha, Bodhisattva or other figures in rectangular panels; in the uppermost, *kīrttimukha* masks spouting forth nāgīs with serpent hoods and fish tails and with hands clasped in prayer. *Mus. Cat.*, 45.

a

b

c

d

e

STUPA I: GROUND RAILING.

PLATE 128

INSCRIPTIONS

Aśoka Pillar—

Plate 128 (upper half)	.	Inscription No. 1

Stūpa 1 : Ground Railing—

Plate 128, 1 .	. .	Inscription No. 15
,, 128, 2 .	. .	,, ,, 16
,, 128, 3 .	. .	,, ,, 17
,, 128, 4 .	. .	,, ,, 18
,, 128, 5 .	. .	,, ,, 19
,, 128, 6 .	. .	,, ,, 20
,, 128, 7 .	. .	,, ,, 21
,, 128, 8 .	. .	,, ,, 22
,, 128, 9 .	. .	,, ,, 23
,, 128, 10 .	. .	,, ,, 24
,, 128, 11 .	. .	,, ,, 25
,, 128, 12 .	. .	,, ,, 26
,, 128, 13 .	. .	,, ,, 27
,, 128, 14 .	. .	,, ,, 28

Stūpa 1 : Ground Railing—contd.

Plate 128, 15 .	. .	Inscription No. 29
,, 128, 16 .	. .	Letters too much worn and indistinct ; *va sa da* can be read
,, 128, 17 .	. .	Inscription No. 30
,, 128, 18 .	. .	,, ,, 31
,, 128, 19 .	. .	,, ,, 32
,, 128, 20 .	. .	,, ,, 33
,, 128, 21 .	. .	,, ,, 34
,, 128, 22 .	. .	,, ,, 35
,, 128, 23 .	. .	,, ,, 36
,, 128, 24 .	. .	,, ,, 37
,, 128, 25 .	. .	,, ,, 38
,, 128, 26 .	. .	,, ,, 39
,, 128, 27 .	. .	,, ,, 40
,, 128, 28 } ,, 128, 29 }	. .	,, ,, 41
,, 128, 30 .	. .	,, ,, 42
,, 128, 31 .	. .	,, ,, 43

PLATE 129

INSCRIPTIONS

Stūpa 1: Ground Railing—

Plate	129, 32	Inscription No. 45
,,	129, 33	,, ,, 46
,,	129, 34	,, ,, 47
,,	129, 35	,, ,, 48
,,	129, 36	,, ,, 49
,,	129, 37	,, ,, 50
,,	129, 38	,, ,, 51
,,	129, 39	,, ,, 52
,,	129, 40	,, ,, 53
,,	129, 41	,, ,, 54
,,	129, 42	,, ,, 55
,,	129, 43	,, ,, 56
,,	129, 44	,, ,, 57
,,	129, 45	,, ,, 58
,,	129, 46	,, ,, 59
,,	129, 47	,, ,, 60
,,	129, 48	,, ,, 61
,,	129, 49	,, ,, 62
,,	129, 50	,, ,, 63
,,	129, 51	,, ,, 64
,,	129, 52	,, ,, 65
,,	129, 53	,, ,, 66
,,	129, 54	Only a single letter *ha*
,,	129, 55	Inscription No. 67
,,	129, 56	,, ,, 68
,,	129, 57	,, ,, 69
,,	129, 58	,, ,, 70
,,	129, 59	,, ,, 71
,,	129, 60	,, ,, 72
,,	129, 61	,, ,, 73
,,	129, 62	,, ,, 74
,,	129, 63	,, ,, 75
,,	129, 64	,, ,, 76
,,	129, 65	,, ,, 77
,,	129, 66	,, ,, 78
,,	129, 67	,, ,, 79

Stūpa 1: Ground Railing—contd.

Plate	129, 68	Inscription No. 80
,,	129, 69	,, ,, 81
,,	129, 70	,, ,, 82
,,	129, 71	,, ,, 83
,,	129, 72	,, ,, 84
,,	129, 73	,, ,, 85
,,	129, 74	,, ,, 86
,,	129, 75	,, ,, 87
,,	129, 76	,, ,, 88
,,	129, 77	,, ,, 89
,,	129, 78	,, ,, 90
,,	129, 79	,, ,, 91
,,	129, 80	,, ,, 92
,,	129, 81	,, ,, 93
,,	129, 82	,, ,, 94
,,	129, 83	,, ,, 95
,,	129, 84	,, ,, 96
,,	129, 85	,, ,, 97
,,	129, 86	,, ,, 98
,,	129, 87	Letters too much worn and indistinct
,,	129, 88	Inscription No. 99
,,	129, 89	,, ,, 100
,,	129, 90	,, ,, 101
,,	129, 91	,, ,, 102
,,	129, 92	,, ,, 103
,,	129, 93	,, ,, 104
,,	129, 94	,, ,, 105
,,	129, 95	,, ,, 106
,,	129, 96	,, ,, 107
,,	129, 97	,, ,, 108
,,	129, 98	,, ,, 109 (same as No. 833)
,,	129, 98 (bottom line only)	,, ,, 110
,,	129, 99	,, ,, 111
,,	129, 100	,, ,, 112
,,	129, 101	,, ,, 113

32
33
34
35
36
37
38
39
40
41
42
43
44
45
46
47
48
49
50
51
52
53
54
55
56
57
58
59
60
61
62
63
64
65
66
67
68
69
70
71
72
73
74
75
76
77
78
79
80
81
82
83
84
85
86
87
88
89
90
91
92
93
94
95
96
97
98
99

102
103
104
105
106
107
108
109
110
111
112
113
114
115
116
117
118
119
120
121
122
123
124
125
126
127
128
129
130
131
132
133
134
135
136
137
138
139
140
141
142
143
144
145
146
147
148
149
150
151
152
153
154
155
156
157
158
159
160
161
162
163
164
165
166
167
168
169
170
171
172
173
174
175
176
177
178
179

PLATE 130

INSCRIPTIONS

Stūpa 1: Ground Railing—

Plate 130, 102 . . Inscription No. 114
,, 130, 103 . . ,, ,, 115
,, 130, 104 . . ,, ,, 116
,, 130, 105 . . ,, ,, 117 (same as No. 834)
,, 130, 106 . . ,, ,, 118
,, 130, 107 . . ,, ,, 119
,, 130, 108 . . ,, ,, 120
,, 130, 109 . . ,, ,, 121
,, 130, 110 . . ,, ,, 122
,, 130, 111 . . ,, ,, 123
,, 130, 112 . . ,, ,, 124
,, 130, 113 . . ,, ,, 125
,, 130, 114 . . ,, ,, 126
,, 130, 115 . . ,, ,, 127
,, 130, 116 . . ,, ,, 128
,, 130, 117 . . ,, ,, 129
,, 130, 118 . . ,, ,, 130
,, 130, 119 . . ,, ,, 131
,, 130, 120 . . ,, ,, 132
,, 130, 121 . . ,, ,, 133
,, 130, 122 . . ,, ,, 134
,, 130, 123 . . ,, ,, 135
,, 130, 124 . . ,, ,, 136
,, 130, 125 . . ,, ,, 137
,, 130, 126 . . ,, ,, 138
,, 130, 127 . . ,, ,, 139
,, 130, 128 . . ,, ,, 140
,, 130, 129 . . ,, ,, 141
,, 130, 130 . . ,, ,, 142
,, 130, 131 . . ,, ,, 143
,, 130, 132 . . ,, ,, 144
,, 130, 133 . . ,, ,, 145
,, 130, 134 . . ,, ,, 146
,, 130, 135 . . ,, ,, 147
,, 130, 136 . . Modern writing; not included in Text
,, 130, 137 . . Inscription No. 148
,, 130, 138 . . ,, ,, 149
,, 130, 139 . . ,, ,, 150
,, 130, 140 . . ,, ,, 151

Stūpa 1: Ground Railing—contd.

Plate 130, 141 . . Inscription No. 152
,, 130, 142 . . ,, ,, 153
,, 130, 143 . . ,, ,, 154
,, 130, 144 . . ,, ,, 155
,, 130, 145 . . ,, ,, 156
,, 130, 146 . . ,, ,, 157
,, 130, 147 . . ,, ,, 158
,, 130, 148 . . ,, ,, 159
,, 130, 149 . . ,, ,, 160
,, 130, 150 . . ,, ,, 161
,, 130, 151 . . ,, ,, 162
,, 130, 152 . . ,, ,, 163
,, 130, 153 . . ,, ,, 164
,, 130, 154 . . ,, ,, 165
,, 130, 155 . . ,, ,, 166
,, 130, 156 . . ,, ,, 167
,, 130, 157 . . ,, ,, 168
,, 130, 158 . . ,, ,, 169
,, 130, 159 . . ,, ,, 170
,, 130, 160 . . ,, ,, 171
,, 130, 161 . . ,, ,, 172
,, 130, 162 . . ,, ,, 173
,, 130, 163 . . ,, ,, 174
,, 130, 164 . . ,, ,, 175
,, 130, 165 . . ,, ,, 176
,, 130, 166 . . ,, ,, 177
,, 130, 167 . . ,, ,, 178
,, 130, 168 . . ,, ,, 179
,, 130, 169 . . ,, ,, 180
,, 130, 170 . . ,, ,, 181
,, 130, 171 . . ,, ,, 182
,, 130, 172 . . ,, ,, 183
,, 130, 173 . . ,, ,, 184
,, 130, 174 . . ,, ,, 185
,, 130, 175 . . ,, ,, 186
,, 130, 176 . . ,, ,, 187
,, 130, 177 . . ,, ,, 188
,, 130, 178 . . ,, ,, 189
,, 130, 179 . . ,, ,, 190

PLATE 131

INSCRIPTIONS

Stūpa 1 : Ground Railing—

Plate 131, 180	. . Inscription No. 191
,, 131, 181	. . ,, ,, 192
,, 131, 182	. . ,, ,, 193
,, 131, 183	. . ,, ,, 194
,, 131, 184	. . ,, ,, 195
,, 131, 185	. . ,, ,, 196
,, 131, 186	. . ,, ,, 197
,, 131, 187	. . ,, ,, 198
,, 131, 188	. . ,, ,, 199
,, 131, 189	. . ,, ,, 200
,, 131, 190	. . ,, ,, 201
,, 131, 191	. . ,, ,, 202
,, 131, 192	. . ,, ,, 203
,, 131, 193	. . ,, ,, 204
,, 131, 194	. . ,, ,, 205
,, 131, 195	. . ,, ,, 206
,, 131, 196	. . ,, ,, 207
,, 131, 197	. . ,, ,, 208
,, 131, 198	. . ,, ,, 209
,, 131, 199	. . ,, ,, 210
,, 131, 200	. . ,, ,, 211
,, 131, 201	. . ,, ,, 212
,, 131, 202	. . ,, ,, 213
,, 131, 203	. . ,, ,, 214
,, 131, 204	. . ,, ,, 215
,, 131, 205	. . ,, ,, 216
,, 131, 206	. . See p. 321, n. 2 for reading
,, 131, 207	. . Inscription No. 217
,, 131, 208	. . ,, ,, 218
,, 131, 209	. . ,, ,, 219
,, 131, 210	. . ,, ,, 220
,, 131, 211	. . ,, ,, 221
,, 131, 212	. . ,, ,, 222
,, 131, 213	. . ,, ,, 223
,, 131, 214	. . ,, ,, 224
,, 131, 215	. . ,, ,, 225
,, 131, 216	. . ,, ,, 226
,, 131, 217	. . ,, ,, 227
,, 131, 218	. . ,, ,, 228

Stūpa 1 : Ground Railing—contd.

Plate 131, 219	. . Inscription No. 229
,, 131, 220	. . ,, ,, 230
,, 131, 221	. . ,, ,, 231
,, 131, 222	. . ,, ,, 232
,, 131, 223	. . ,, ,, 233
,, 131, 224	. . ,, ,, 234
,, 131, 225	. . ,, ,, 235
,, 131, 226	. . ,, ,, 236
,, 131, 227	. . ,, ,, 237
,, 131, 228	. . ,, ,, 238
,, 131, 229	. . ,, ,, 239
,, 131, 230	. . ,, ,, 240
,, 131, 231	. . ,, ,, 241
,, 131, 232	. . ,, ,, 242
,, 131, 233	. . ,, ,, 243
,, 131, 234	. . ,, ,, 244
,, 131, 235	. . ,, ,, 245
,, 131, 236	. . ,, ,, 246
,, 131, 237	. . ,, ,, 247
,, 131, 238	. . ,, ,, 248
,, 131, 239	. . ,, ,, 249
,, 131, 240	. . ,, ,, 250
,, 131, 241	. . Wrongly placed upside down in Pl.: letters worn; *seṭhino* ('of the banker') can be read
,, 131, 242	. . Inscription No. 251
,, 131, 243	. . ,, ,, 252
,, 131, 244	. . ,, ,, 253
,, 131, 245	. . ,, ,, 254
,, 131, 246	. . ,, ,, 255
,, 131, 247	. . Illegible
,, 131, 248	. . Inscription No. 256
,, 131, 249	. . ,, ,, 257
,, 131, 250	. . ,, ,, 258
,, 131, 251	. . ,, ,, 259
,, 131, 252	. . ,, ,, 260
,, 131, 253	. . ,, ,, 261
,, 131, 254	. . ,, ,, 262
,, 131, 255	. . ,, ,, 263
,, 131, 256	. . ,, ,, 264
,, 131, 257	. . ,, ,, 265

180
181
182
183
184
185
186
187
188
189
190
191
192
193
194
195
196
197
198
199
200
201
202
203
204
205
206
207
208
209
210
211
212
213
214
215
216
217
218
219
220
221
222
223
224
225
226
227
228
229
230
231
232
233
234
235
236
237
238
239
240
241
242
243
244
245
246
247
248
249
250
251
252
253
254
255
256
257

258
259
260
261
262
263
264
265
266
267
268
269
270
271
272
273
274
275
276
277
278
279
280
281
282
283
284
285
286
287
288
289
290
291
292
293
294
295
296
297
298
299
300
301
302
303
304
305
306
307
308
309
310
311
312
313
314
315
316
317
318
319
320
321

PLATE 132

INSCRIPTIONS

Stūpa 1 : Ground Railing—

Plate 132, 258	. . Inscription No.	266
„ 132, 259	. . „ „	267
„ 132, 260	. . „ „	268
„ 132, 261	. . „ „	269
„ 132, 262	. . „ „	270
„ 132, 263	. . „ „	271
„ 132, 264	. . „ „	272
„ 132, 265	. . „ „	273
„ 132, 266	. . „ „	274
„ 132, 267	. . „ „	275
„ 132, 268	. . „ „	276
„ 132, 269	. . Too much worn and illegible	
„ 132, 270	. . Inscription No.	277
„ 132, 271	. . „ „	278
„ 132, 272	. . „ „	279
„ 132, 273	. . „ „	280
„ 132, 274	. . „ „	281
„ 132, 275	. . „ „	282
„ 132, 276	. . „ „	283
„ 132, 277	. . „ „	284
„ 132, 278	. . „ „	285
„ 132, 279	. . „ „	286
„ 132, 280	. . „ „	287
„ 132, 281	. . „ „	288
„ 132, 282	. . „ „	289
„ 132, 283	. . „ „	290
„ 132, 284	. „ „	291
„ 132, 285	. . „ „	292
„ 132, 286	. . „ „	293
„ 132, 287	. . „ „	294
„ 132, 288	. . „ „	295
„ 132, 289	. . „ „	296

Stūpa 1 : Ground Railing—contd.

Plate 132, 290	. . Inscription No.	297
„ 132, 291	. . „ „	298
„ 132, 292	. . „ „	299
„ 132, 293	. . „ „	300
„ 132, 294	. . „ „	301
„ 132, 295	. . „ „	302
„ 132, 296	. . „ „	303
„ 132, 297	. . „ „	304
„ 132, 298	. . „ „	305
„ 132, 299	. . „ „	306
„ 132, 300	. . „ „	307
„ 132, 301	. . „ „	308
„ 132, 302	. . „ „	309
„ 132, 303	. . „ „	310
„ 132, 304	. . „ „	311
„ 132, 305	. . „ „	312
„ 132, 306	. . „ „	313
„ 132, 307	. . „ „	314
„ 132, 308	. . „ „	315
„ 132, 309	. . „ „	316
„ 132, 310	. . „ „	317
„ 132, 311	. . „ „	318
„ 132, 312	. . „ „	319
„ 132, 313	. . „ „	320
„ 132, 314	. . „ „	321
„ 132, 315	. . „ „	322
„ 132, 316	. . „ „	323
„ 132, 317	. . „ „	324
„ 132, 318	. . „ „	325
„ 132, 319	. . „ „	326
„ 132, 320	. . „ „	327
„ 132, 321	. . „ „	328

PLATE 133

INSCRIPTIONS

Stūpa 1 : Ground Railing—

Plate 133, 322	. .	Inscription No. 329
„ 133, 323	. .	„ „ 330
„ 133, 324	. .	„ „ 331
„ 133, 325	. .	„ „ 332
„ 133, 326	. .	„ „ 333
„ 133, 327	. .	„ „ 334
„ 133, 328	. .	„ „ 335
„ 133, 329	. .	„ „ 336
„ 133, 330	. .	„ „ 337
„ 133, 331	. .	„ „ 338
„ 133, 332	. .	„ „ 339
„ 133, 333	. .	„ „ 340
„ 133, 334	. .	„ „ 341
„ 133, 335	. .	„ „ 342
„ 133, 336	. .	„ „ 343
„ 133, 337	. .	„ „ 344
„ 133, 338	. .	„ „ 345
„ 133, 339	. .	„ „ 346
„ 133, 340	. .	„ „ 347
„ 133, 341	. .	„ „ 348
„ 133, 342	. .	„ „ 349
„ 133, 343	. .	„ „ 350
„ 133, 344	. .	„ „ 351
„ 133, 345	. .	„ „ 352
„ 133, 346	. .	„ „ 353
„ 133, 347	. .	„ „ 354
„ 133, 348	. .	„ „ 355
„ 133, 349	. .	„ „ 356
„ 133, 350	. .	„ „ 357
„ 133, 351	. .	„ „ 358
„ 133, 352	. .	„ „ 359
„ 133, 353	. .	„ „ 360
„ 133, 354	. .	„ „ 361
„ 133, 355	. .	„ „ 362
„ 133, 356	. .	„ „ 363

Stūpa 1 : Ground Railing (loose)—

Plate 133, 1	. . .	Worn and illegible
„ 133, 2	. . .	Inscription No. 364
„ 133, 3	. . .	„ „ 365
„ 133, 4	. . .	„ „ 366
„ 133, 5	. . .	„ „ 367
„ 133, 6	. . .	„ „ 368
„ 133, 7	. . .	„ „ 369
„ 133, 8	. . .	„ „ 370
„ 133, 9	. . .	„ „ 371
„ 133, 10	. . .	„ „ 372
„ 133, 11	. . .	„ „ 373
„ 133, 12	. . .	„ „ 374
„ 133, 13	. . .	„ „ 375
„ 133, 14	. . .	„ „ 376
„ 133, 15	. . .	„ „ 377
„ 133, 16	. . .	„ „ 378
„ 133, 17	. . .	„ „ 379
„ 133, 18	. . .	„ „ 380
„ 133, 19	. . .	„ „ 381
„ 133, 20	. . .	„ „ 382
„ 133, 21	. . .	„ „ 383
„ 133, 22	. . .	„ „ 384
„ 133, 23	. . .	„ „ 385
„ 133, 24	. . .	„ „ 386
„ 133, 25	. . .	„ „ 387
„ 133, 26	. . .	„ „ 388

Stūpa 1 : Northern Gateway—

Plate 133, 1	. . .	Inscription No. 389
„ 133, 2	. . .	„ „ 390
„ 133, 3	. . .	„ „ 391
„ 133, 4	. . .	„ „ 392
„ 133, 5	. . .	„ „ 393
„ 133, 6	. . .	„ „ 394

STUPA I: GROUND RAILING: LOOSE

STUPA I: NORTHERN GATEWAY

STUPA I: EASTERN GATEWAY

SOUTHERN GATEWAY

WESTERN GATEWAY

PAVEMENT SLABS

PAVEMENT SLABS: LOOSE

PLATE 134

INSCRIPTIONS

Stūpa I—

Plate 134, Eastern Gateway	1	.	Inscription No. 395
,, 134, ,, ,,	2	.	,, ,, 396
,, 134, ,, ,,	3	.	,, ,, 397
,, 134, Southern Gateway	1	.	,, ,, 398
,, 134, ,, ,,	2	.	,, ,, 399
,, 134, ,, ,,	3	.	,, ,, 400
,, 134, ,, ,,	4	.	,, ,, 401
,, 134, Western Gateway	1	.	,, ,, 402
,, 134, ,, ,,	2	.	,, ,, 403
,, 134, ,, ,,	3	.	,, ,, 404
,, 134, Pavement Slab	1	.	,, ,, 405
,, 134, ,, ,,	2	.	,, ,, 406
,, 134, ,, ,,	3	.	,, ,, 407
,, 134, ,, ,,	4	.	,, ,, 408
,, 134, ,, ,,	5	.	,, ,, 409
,, 134, ,, ,,	6	.	,, ,, 410
,, 134, ,, ,,	7	.	,, ,, 411
,, 134, ,, ,,	8	.	,, ,, 412
,, 134, ,, ,,	9	.	,, ,, 413
,, 134, ,, ,,	10	.	,, ,, 414
,, 134, ,, ,,	11	.	,, ,, 415
,, 134, ,, ,,	12	.	,, ,, 416
,, 134, ,, ,,	13	.	,, ,, 417
,, 134, ,, ,,	14	.	,, ,, 418
,, 134, ,, ,,	15	.	,, ,, 419
,, 134, ,, ,,	16	.	,, ,, 420
,, 134, ,, ,,	17	.	,, ,, 421
,, 134, ,, ,,	18	.	,, ,, 422
,, 134, ,, ,,	19	.	,, ,, 423
,, 134, ,, ,,	20	.	,, ,, 424
,, 134, ,, ,,	21	.	,, ,, 425
,, 134, ,, ,,	22	.	,, ,, 426
,, 134, ,, ,,	23	.	,, ,, 427
,, 134, ,, ,,	24	.	,, ,, 428
,, 134, ,, ,,	25	.	,, ,, 429
,, 134, ,, ,,	26	.	,, ,, 430
,, 134, ,, ,,	27	.	,, ,, 431
,, 134, ,, ,,	28	.	,, ,, 432
,, 134, ,, ,,	29	.	,, ,, 433
,, 134, ,, ,,	30	.	,, ,, 434
,, 134, ,, ,,	31	.	,, ,, 435
,, 134, ,, ,,	32	.	,, ,, 436
,, 134, ,, ,,	33	.	,, ,, 437
,, 134, ,, ,,	34	.	,, ,, 438
,, 134, ,, ,,	35	.	,, ,, 439
,, 134, ,, ,,	36	.	,, ,, 440
,, 134, ,, ,,	37	.	,, ,, 441
,, 134, ,, ,,	38	.	,, ,, 442

Stūpa I—contd.

Plate 134, Pavement Slab	39	.	Inscription No. 443
,, 134, ,, ,,	40	.	,, ,, 444
,, 134, ,, ,,	41	.	,, ,, 445
,, 134, ,, ,,	42	.	,, ,, 446
,, 134, ,, ,,	43	.	,, ,, 447
,, 134, ,, ,,	44	.	,, ,, 448
,, 134, ,, ,,	45	.	,, ,, 449
,, 134, ,, ,,	46	.	,, ,, 450
,, 134, ,, ,,	47	.	,, ,, 451
,, 134, ,, ,,	48	.	,, ,, 452
,, 134, ,, ,,	49	.	,, ,, 453
,, 134, Pavement Slab (loose)	1	.	,, ,, 736
,, 134, ,, ,,	2	.	,, ,, 737
,, 134, ,, ,,	3	.	,, ,, 738
,, 134, ,, ,,	4	.	,, ,, 739
,, 134, ,, ,,	5	.	,, ,, 740
,, 134, ,, ,,	6	.	,, ,, 741
,, 134, ,, ,,	7	.	,, ,, 742
,, 134, ,, ,,	8	.	,, ,, 743
,, 134, ,, ,,	9	.	,, ,, 744
,, 134, ,, ,,	10	.	Only upper portions of some letters; not restorable
,, 134, ,, ,,	11	.	Inscription No. 745
,, 134, ,, ,,	12	.	,, ,, 746
,, 134, ,, ,,	13	.	,, ,, 747
,, 134, ,, ,,	14	.	,, ,, 748
,, 134, ,, ,,	15	.	,, ,, 749
,, 134, ,, ,,	16	.	,, ,, 750
,, 134, ,, ,,	17	.	,, ,, 751
,, 134, ,, ,,	18	.	,, ,, 752
,, 134, ,, ,,	19	.	,, ,, 753
,, 134, ,, ,,	20	.	,, ,, 754
,, 134, ,, ,,	21	.	,, ,, 755
,, 134, ,, ,,	22	.	,, ,, 756
,, 134, ,, ,,	23	.	,, ,, 757
,, 134, ,, ,,	24	.	,, ,, 758
,, 134, ,, ,,	25	.	,, ,, 759
,, 134, ,, ,,	26	.	,, ,, 760
,, 134, ,, ,,	27	.	,, ,, 761
,, 134, ,, ,,	28	.	,, ,, 762
,, 134, ,, ,,	29	.	,, ,, 763
,, 134, ,, ,,	30	.	,, ,, 764
,, 134, ,, ,,	31	.	,, ,, 765
,, 134, ,, ,,	32	.	,, ,, 766
,, 134, ,, ,,	33	.	,, ,, 767
,, 134, ,, ,,	34	.	,, ,, 768
,, 134, ,, ,,	35	.	,, ,, 769

PLATE 135

INSCRIPTIONS

Stūpa 1 : Berm Railing—

Plate	135, 1	Inscription No.	463
,,	135, 2	,, ,,	464
,,	135, 3	,, ,,	465
,,	135, 4	,, ,,	466
,,	135, 5	,, ,,	467
,,	135, 6	,, ,,	468
,,	135, 7	,, ,,	469
,,	135, 8	,, ,,	470
,,	135, 9	,, ,,	471
,,	135, 10	,, ,,	472
,,	135, 11	,, ,,	473
,,	135, 12	,, ,,	474
,,	135, 13	,, ,,	475
,,	135, 14	,, ,,	476
,,	135, 15	,, ,,	477
,,	135, 16	,, ,,	478
,,	135, 17	,, ,,	479
,,	135, 18	,, ,,	480
,,	135, 19	,, ,,	481
,,	135, 20	,, ,,	482
,,	135, 21	,, ,,	483
,,	135, 22	,, ,,	484
,,	135, 23	,, ,,	485
,,	135, 24	,, ,,	486
,,	135, 25	,, ,,	487
,,	135, 26	,, ,,	488
,,	135, 27	,, ,,	489
,,	135, 28	,, ,,	490
,,	135, 29	,, ,,	491
,,	135, 30	,, ,,	492
,,	135, 31	,, ,,	493
,,	135, 32	,, ,,	494
,,	135, 33	,, ,,	495
,,	135, 34	,, ,,	496
,,	135, 35	,, ,,	497
,,	135, 36	,, ,,	498
,,	135, 37	,, ,,	499
,,	135, 38	,, ,,	500
,,	135, 39	,, ,,	501
,,	135, 40	,, ,,	502
,,	135, 41	,, ,,	503
,,	135, 42	,, ,,	504
,,	135, 43	,, ,,	505
,,	135, 44	,, ,,	506
,,	135, 45	,, ,,	507
,,	135, 46	,, ,,	508
,,	135, 47	,, ,,	509
,,	135, 48	,, ,,	510
,,	135, 49	,, ,,	511
,,	135, 50	,, ,,	512
,,	135, 51	,, ,,	513
,,	135, 52	,, ,,	514
,,	135, 53	,, ,,	515
,,	135, 54	,, ,,	516
,,	135, 55	,, ,,	517
,,	135, 56	Completely worn; illegible	
,,	135, 57	Completely worn; illegible	
,,	135, 58	Inscription No.	518
,,	135, 59	,, ,,	519
,,	135, 60	,, ,,	520
,,	135, 61	,, ,,	521
,,	135, 62	,, ,,	522
,,	135, 63	,, ,,	523
,,	135, 64	,, ,,	524
,,	135, 65	,, ,,	525
,,	135, 66	,, ,,	526
,,	135, 67	,, ,,	527
,,	135, 68	,, ,,	528
,,	135, 69	,, ,,	529

Stūpa 1 : Berm Railing—contd.

Plate	135, 70	Inscription No.	530
,,	135, 71	,, ,,	531
,,	135, 72	,, ,,	532
,,	135, 73	,, ,,	533
,,	135, 74	,, ,,	534
,,	135, 75	,, ,,	535
,,	135, 76	,, ,,	536
,,	135, 77	,, ,,	537
,,	135, 78	,, ,,	538
,,	135, 79	,, ,,	539
,,	135, 80	,, ,,	540
,,	135, 81	,, ,,	541
,,	135, 82	,, ,,	542
,,	135, 83	,, ,,	543
,,	135, 84	,, ,,	544
,,	135, 85	,, ,,	545
,,	135, 86	,, ,,	546
,,	135, 87	,, ,,	547
,,	135, 88	,, ,,	548
,,	135, 89	,, ,,	549
,,	135, 90	,, ,,	550
,,	135, 91	,, ,,	551
,,	135, 92	,, ,,	552
,,	135, 93	,, ,,	553
,,	135, 94	,, ,,	554
,,	135, 95	,, ,,	555
,,	135, 96	,, ,,	556
,,	135, 97	,, ,,	557
,,	135, 98	,, ,,	558
,,	135, 99	,, ,,	559
,,	135, 100	,, ,,	560
,,	135, 101	,, ,,	561
,,	135, 102	,, ,,	562
,,	135, 103	,, ,,	563
,,	135, 104	,, ,,	564
,,	135, 105	,, ,,	565
,,	135, 106	,, ,,	566
,,	135, 107	,, ,,	567
,,	135, 108	,, ,,	568
,,	135, 109	,, ,,	569
,,	135, 110	,, ,,	570
,,	135, 111	,, ,,	571
,,	135, 112	,, ,,	572
,,	135, 113	,, ,,	573
,,	135, 114	,, ,,	574
,,	135, 115	,, ,,	575
,,	135, 116	,, ,,	576
,,	135, 117	,, ,,	577
,,	135, 118	,, ,,	578
,,	135, 119	,, ,,	579
,,	135, 120	,, ,,	580
,,	135, 121	,, ,,	581
,,	135, 122	,, ,,	582
,,	135, 123	,, ,,	583
,,	135, 124	,, ,,	584
,,	135, 125	,, ,,	585
,,	135, 126	,, ,,	586
,,	135, 127	,, ,,	587
,,	135, 128	,, ,,	588
,,	135, 129	,, ,,	589
,,	135, 130	,, ,,	590
,,	135, 131	,, ,,	591
,,	135, 132	,, ,,	592
,,	135, 133	,, ,,	593
,,	135, 134	,, ,,	594
,,	135, 135	,, ,,	595
,,	135, 136	,, ,,	596
,,	135, 137	,, ,,	597
,,	135, 138	,, ,,	598

1 2 3 4 5 6 7 8 9 10 11 12 13 14 15 16 17 18 19 20 21 22 23 24 25 26 27 28 29 30 31 32 33 34 35 36 37 38 39 40 41 42 43 44 45 46 47 48 49 50 51 52 53 54 55 56 57 58 59 60 61 62 63 64 65 66 67 68 69 70 71 72
73 74 75 76 77 78 79 80 81 82 83 84 85 86 87 88 89 90 91 92 93 94 95 96 97 98 99 100 101 102 103 104 105 106 107 108 109 110 111 112 113 114 115 116 117 118 119 120 121 122 123 124 125 126 127 128 129 130 131 132 133 134 135 136 137 138

139 140 141 145 144 142 143 146

HARMIKA RAILING

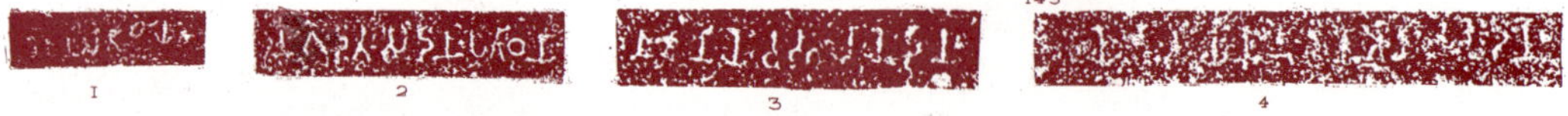

1 2 3 4

STAIRWAY RAILING

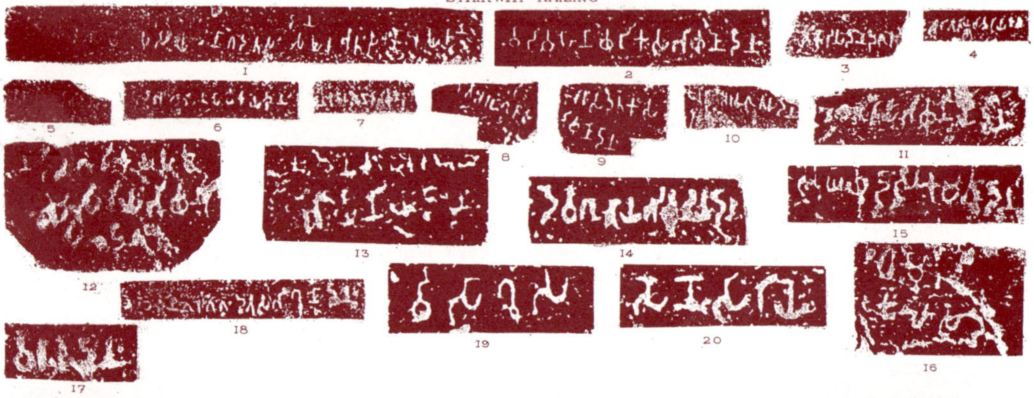

1 2 3 4 5 6 7 8 9 10 11 12 13 14 15 18 19 20 16 17 36 37

PAVEMENT SLABS: LOOSE.

38 39 40 41

STUPA II: GROUND RAILING

1 2 3 4 5 6 7 8 9 10 11 12 13 14 15 16 17 18 19 20 21 22 23 24 25 26 27 28 29 30 31 32 33 34 35 36 37 38 39 40 41 42 43 44 45 46 47 48 49 50 51 52

PLATE 136

INSCRIPTIONS

Stūpa 1—

Plate 136, Berm Railing (loose)	139	Inscription No. 599
,, 136, ,, ,, ,,	140	,, ,, 600
,, 136, ,, ,, ,,	141	,, ,, 601
,, 136, ,, ,, ,,	142	,, ,, 602
,, 136, ,, ,, ,,	143	,, ,, 603
,, 136, ,, ,, ,,	144	,, ,, 604
,, 136, ,, ,, ,,	145	,, ,, 605
,, 136, ,, ,, ,,	146	,, ,, 606
,, 136, Harmikā Railing	1	,, ,, 607
,, 136, ,, ,,	2	,, ,, 608
,, 136, ,, ,,	3	,, ,, 609
,, 136, ,, ,,	4	,, ,, 610
,, 136, Stairway Railing	1	,, ,, 611
,, 136, ,, ,,	2	,, ,, 612
,, 136, ,, ,,	3	,, ,, 613
,, 136, ,, ,,	4	,, ,, 614
,, 136, ,, ,,	5	,, ,, 615
,, 136, ,, ,,	6	,, ,, 616
,, 136, ,, ,,	7	,, ,, 617
,, 136, ,, ,,	8	,, ,, 618
,, 136, ,, ,,	9	,, ,, 619
,, 136, ,, ,,	10	,, ,, 620
,, 136, ,, ,,	11	,, ,, 621
,, 136, ,, ,,	12	,, ,, 622
,, 136, ,, ,,	13	,, ,, 623
,, 136, ,, ,,	14	,, ,, 624
,, 136, ,, ,,	15	,, ,, 625
,, 136, ,, ,,	16	,, ,, 626
,, 136, ,, ,,	17	,, ,, 627
,, 136, ,, ,,	18	,, ,, 628
,, 136, ,, ,,	19	,, ,, 629
,, 136, ,, ,,	20	,, ,, 630
,, 136, Pavement Slab	36	,, ,, 770
,, 136, ,, ,,	37	,, ,, 771
,, 136, ,, ,,	38	,, ,, 772
,, 136, ,, ,,	39	,, ,, 773
,, 136, ,, ,,	40	,, ,, 774
,, 136, ,, ,,	41	,, ,, 775

Stūpa 2 : Ground Railing—

Plate 136, 1	Inscription No. 631
,, 136, 2	,, ,, 632
,, 136, 3	,, ,, 633
,, 136, 4	,, ,, 634
,, 136, 5	,, ,, 635
,, 136, 6	,, ,, 636
,, 136, 7	,, ,, 637

Stūpa 2 : Ground Railing—contd.

Plate 136, 8	Inscription No. 638
,, 136, 9	,, ,, 639
,, 136, 10	,, ,, 640
,, 136, 11	,, ,, 641
,, 136, 12	,, ,, 642
,, 136, 13	,, ,, 643
,, 136, 14	,, ,, 644
,, 136, 15	,, ,, 645
,, 136, 16	,, ,, 646
,, 136, 17	,, ,, 647
,, 136, 18	,, ,, 648
,, 136, 19	,, ,, 649
,, 136, 20	,, ,, 650
,, 136, 21	,, ,, 651
,, 136, 22	,, ,, 652
,, 136, 23	Too much worn: first letter *sa*
,, 136, 24	Inscription No. 653
,, 136, 25	,, ,, 654
,, 136, 26	,, ,, 655
,, 136, 27	,, ,, 656
,, 136, 28	,, ,, 657
,, 136, 29	Only a single letter *si* can be read
,, 136, 30	Inscription No. 658
,, 136, 31	,, ,, 659
,, 136, 32	,, ,, 660
,, 136, 33	,, ,, 661
,, 136, 34	,, ,, 662
,, 136, 35	,, ,, 663
,, 136, 36	,, ,, 664
,, 136, 37	,, ,, 665
,, 136, 38	,, ,, 666
,, 136, 39	,, ,, 667
,, 136, 40	,, ,, 668
,, 136, 41	,, ,, 670
,, 136, 42	,, ,, 673
,, 136, 43	,, ,, 674
,, 136, 44	,, ,, 675
,, 136, 45	,, ,, 676
,, 136, 46	,, ,, 677
,, 136, 47	,, ,, 678
,, 136, 48	,, ,, 679
,, 136, 49	,, ,, 680
,, 136, 50	,, ,, 681
,, 136, 51	,, ,, 682
,, 136, 52	,, ,, 683

PLATE 137

INSCRIPTIONS

Stūpa 2: Ground Railing—

Plate 137, 53 . . . . Inscription No. 684
" 137, 54 . . . . . " " 685
" 137, 55 . . . . . " " 686
" 137, 56 . . . . . " " 687
" 137, 57 . . . . . " " 688
" 137, 58 . . . . . " " 689
" 137, 59 . . . . . " " 690
" 137, 60 . . . . . " " 691
" 137, 61 . . . . . " " 692
" 137, 62 . . . . . " " 693
" 137, 63 . . . . . " " 694
" 137, 64 . . . . . " " 671
" 137, 65 . . . . . " " 672
" 137, 66 . . . . . " " 669

Stūpa 2: Pavement Slabs—

Plate 137, 1 . . . . Inscription No. 696
" 137, 2 . . . . . " " 697
" 137, 3 . . . . . " " 698

Stūpa 2: Stairway Steps—

Plate 137, 1 . . . . Inscription No. 699
" 137, 2 . . . . . " " 700

Stūpa 2: Stairway Railing—

Plate 137, 1 . . . . Inscription No. 701

Stūpa 2: Berm Railing—

Plate 137, 1 . . . . Inscription No. 702
" 137, 2 . . . . . " " 703
" 137, 3 . . . . . " " 704
" 137, 4 . . . . . " " 705

Stūpa 2: Berm Railing—contd.

Plate 137, 5 . . . . Inscription No. 706
" 137, 6 . . . . . " " 707
" 137, 7 . . . . . " " 708
" 137, 8 . . . . . " " 709
" 137, 9 . . . . . " " 710
" 137, 10 . . . . . " " 711
" 137, 11 . . . . . " " 712
" 137, 12 . . . . . " " 713
" 137, 13 . . . . . " " 714
" 137, 14 . . . . . " " 715
" 137, 15 . . . . . " " 716
" 137, 16 . . . . . " " 717
" 137, 17 . . . . . " " 718

Stūpa 3—

Plate 137, 1 . . . . Inscription No. 13
" 137, 2 . . . . . " " 14
" 137, 3 . . . . . " " 720
" 137, 4 . . . . . " " 721
" 137, 5 . . . . . " " 722
" 137, 6 . . . . . " " 723
" 137, 7 . . . . . " " 724
" 137, 8 . . . . . " " 725
" 137, 9-10 . . . . . " " 726
" 137, 11 . . . . . " " 727
" 137, 12 . . . . . " " 728
" 137, 13 . . . . . " " 729
" 137, 14 . . . . . " " 730
" 137, 15 . . . . . " " 731
" 137, 16 . . . . . " " 732
" 137, 17 . . . . . " " 733

53 54 55 56 57 58 59 60 61 62 63 64 65 66

PAVEMENT SLABS

1 2 3

STAIRWAY STEPS

1 2

STAIRWAY RAILING: LOOSE

1

BERM RAILING: LOOSE

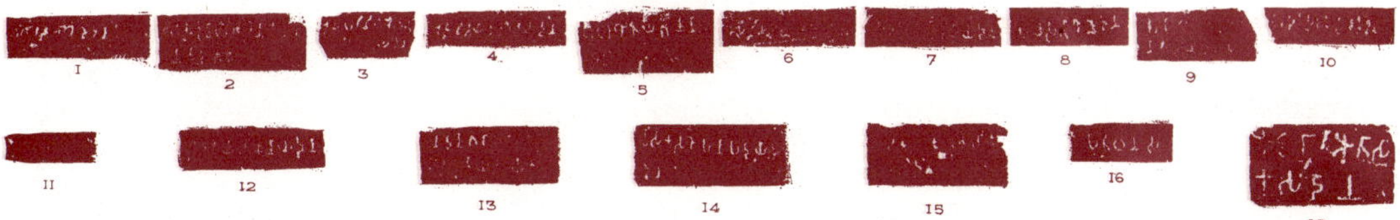

1 2 3 4 5 6 7 8 9 10 11 12 13 14 15 16 17

STUPA III.

1 2 3 6 11 4 5 7 12 13 9-10 8 14 15 16 17

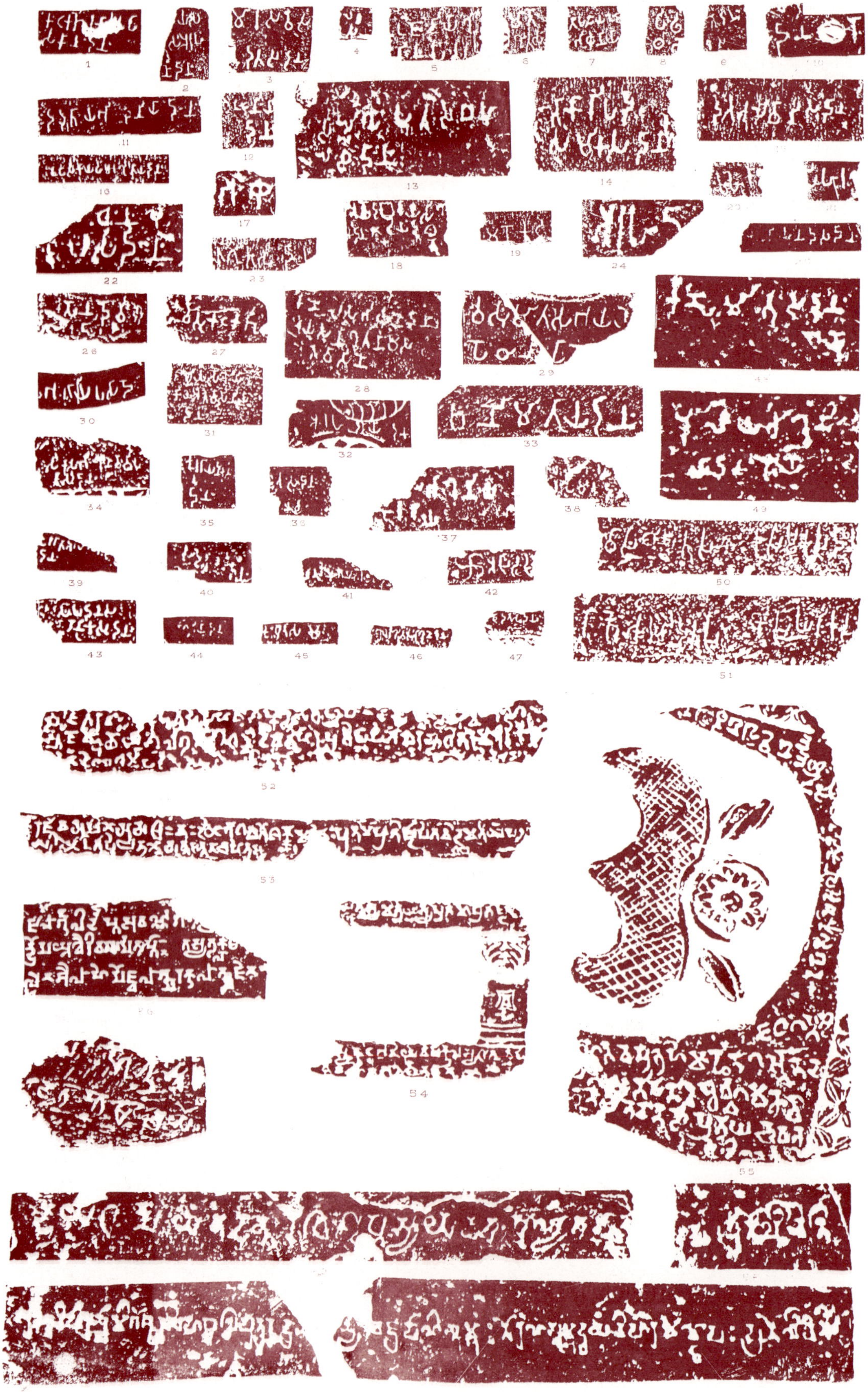

PLATE 138

INSCRIPTIONS

Miscellaneous—

Plate	138, 1	Inscription No. 776
,,	138, 2	,, ,, 777
,,	138, 3	,, ,, 778
,,	138, 4	,, ,, 779
,,	138, 5	,, ,, 780
,,	138, 6	,, ,, 781
,,	138, 7	,, ,, 782
,,	138, 8	,, ,, 783
,,	138, 9	,, ,, 784
,,	138, 10	,, ,, 785
,,	138, 11	,, ,, 786
,,	138, 12	,, ,, 787
,,	138, 13	,, ,, 788
,,	138, 14	,, ,, 789
,,	138, 15	,, ,, 790
,,	138, 16	,, ,, 791
,,	138, 17	,, ,, 792
,,	138, 18	,, ,, 793
,,	138, 19	,, ,, 794
,,	138, 20	,, ,, 795
,,	138, 21	,, ,, 796
,,	138, 22	,, ,, 797
,,	138, 23	,, ,, 798
,,	138, 24	,, ,, 799
,,	138, 25	,, ,, 800
,,	138, 26	,, ,, 801
,,	138, 27	,, ,, 802
,,	138, 28	,, ,, 803
,,	138, 29	,, ,, 804
,,	138, 30	,, ,, 805

Miscellaneous—contd.

Plate	138, 31	Inscription No. 806
,,	138, 32	,, ,, 807
,,	138, 33	,, ,, 808
,,	138, 34	,, ,, 809
,,	138, 35	,, ,, 810
,,	138, 36	,, ,, 811
,,	138, 37	,, ,, 812
,,	138, 38	,, ,, 813
,,	138, 39	,, ,, 814
,,	138, 40	,, ,, 815
,,	138, 41	Too much worn ; illegible
,,	138, 42	Inscription No. 816
,,	138, 43	,, ,, 817
,,	138, 44	,, ,, 818
,,	138, 45	,, ,, 819
,,	138, 46	,, ,, 820
,,	138, 47	,, ,, 821
,,	138, 48	,, ,, 822
,,	138, 49	,, ,, 823
,,	138, 50	,, ,, 824
,,	138, 51	,, ,, 825
,,	138, 52	,, ,, 828
,,	138, 53	,, ,, 829
,,	138, 54	,, ,, 830
,,	138, 55	,, ,, 831
,,	138, 56	,, ,, 832
,,	138, 57	,, ,, 835
,,	138, 58	,, ,, 836
,,	138, 59	,, ,, 837
,,	138, 60	,, ,, 838

PLATE 139

INSCRIPTIONS

Miscellaneou —

Plate 139, 61 . . . Inscription No. 839
„ 139, 62 . . . „ „ 840

Miscellaneous—contd.

Plate 139, 63 . . . Inscription No. 841
„ 139, 64 (*a-n*) . . „ „ 842

61

62

63

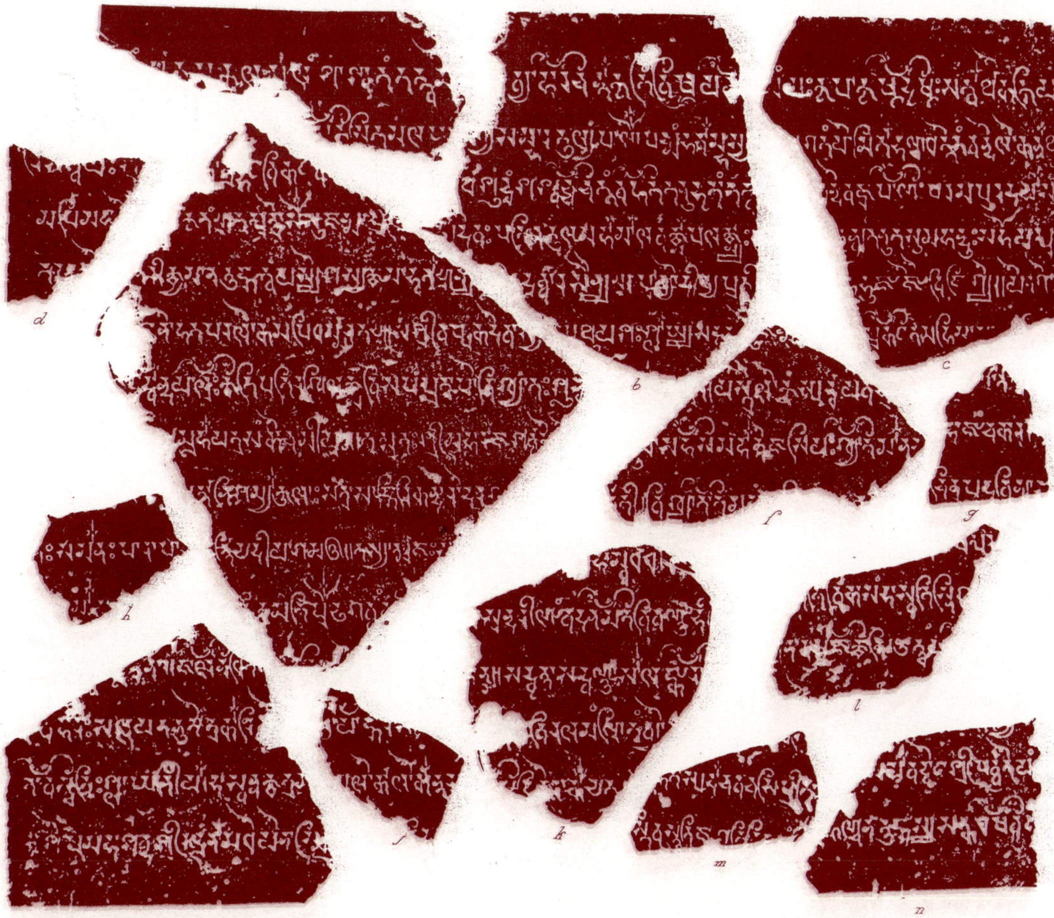

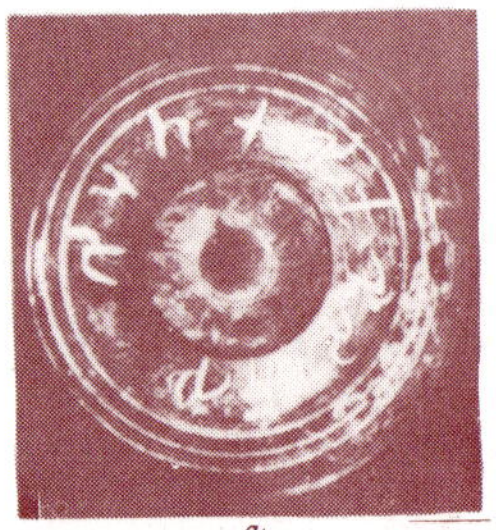

a

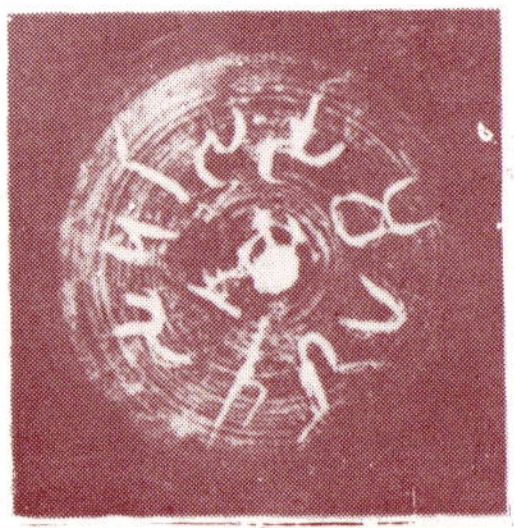

b

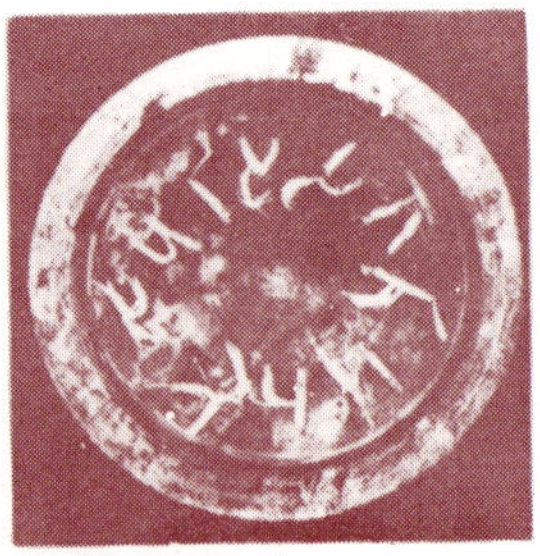

c

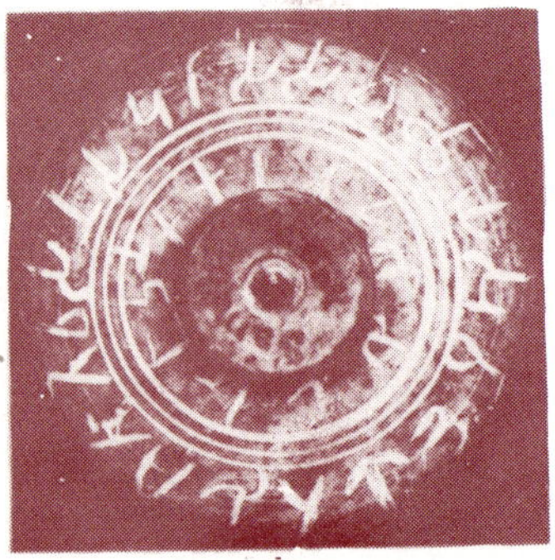

d

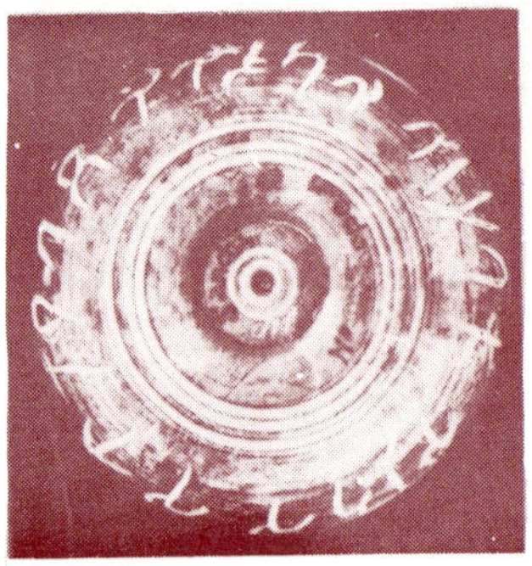

e

f

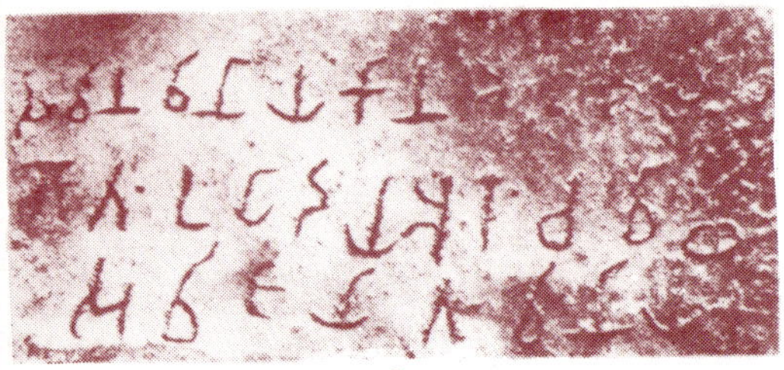

g

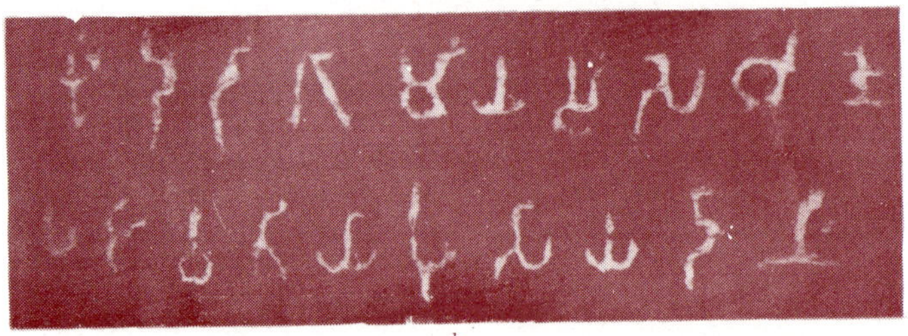

h

i

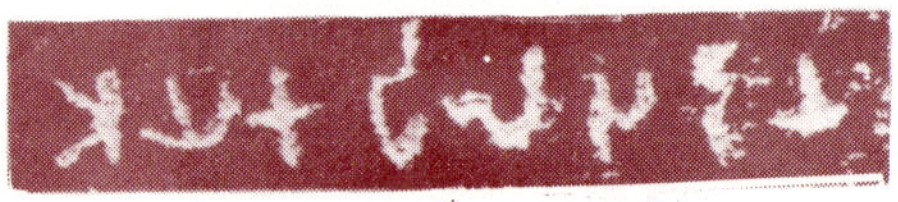

j

k

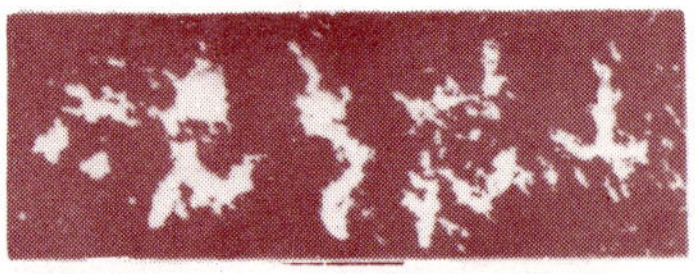

l

m

n

o

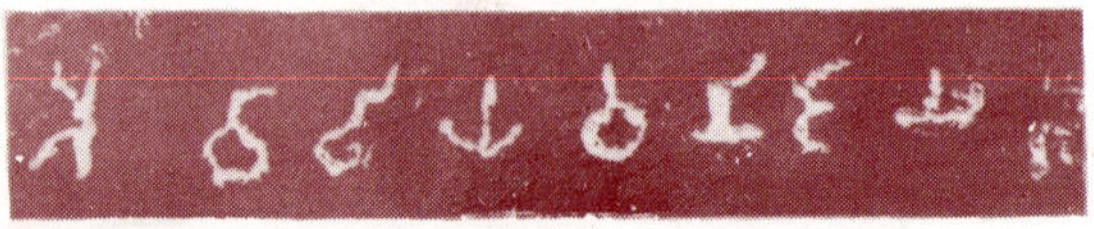

p

q

r

s

PLATE 140

INSCRIPTIONS

Miscellaneous—

Plate 140 *a*	. . . Inscription No.	10
„ 140 *b*	. . . . „ „	12
„ 140 c	. . . . „ „	11
„ 140 *d*	. . . . „ „	6-7
„ 140 *e*	. . . . „ „	8
„ 140 *f*	. . . . „ „	9
„ 140 *g*	. . . . „ „	2
„ 140 *h*	. . . . „ „	44
„ 140 *i*	. . . . „ „	457
„ 140 *j*	. . . . „ „	695

Miscellaneous—contd.

Plate 140 *k*	. . . Inscription No.	454
„ 140 *l*	. . . . „ „	459
„ 140 *m*	. . . . „ „	455
„ 140 *n*	. . . . „ „	456
„ 140 *o*	. . . . „ „	458
„ 140 *p*	. . . . „ „	462
„ 140 *q*	. . . . „ „	734
„ 140 *r*	. . . . „ „	460
„ 140 *s*	. . . . „ „	461

15*b*. At t
middle, an e
jets of the v
a half-rosace

16*a*. Fra
garlands.—I

16*b*. Pal
no. 17*b*).—(
passant to t
—Half-rosac

17*a*. Pal
of lotuses co

17*b*. Pal
shield (*cf*. n

A TABLE OF DISTINCTIVE BRĀHMĪ LETTERS

Cir. 3rd Century B.C. to 1st Century A.D.

Pl. CXLI

HELIO. S. I. O., CALCUTTA.